Eus in adiutorium me
um intende. Domine
ad adiuuandum me
festina. Gloria patri et filio
et spiritui sancto sicut erat
in principio et nunc et semper.
et in secula seculorum amen.
ynuus.

Frontispiece   A fifteenth-century schoolmaster and his pupils.

MEDIEVAL SCHOOLS

BY THE SAME AUTHOR

Education in the West of England
The Minor Clergy of Exeter Cathedral
Early British Swimming
From Childhood to Chivalry
Exeter Cathedral As It Was
Education and Society in Medieval and Renaissance England
John Lydgate: Table Manners for Children
Unity and Variety: A History of the Church in Devon and Cornwall
Nicholas Roscarrock's Lives of the Saints
English Church Dedications
Education in Early Tudor England
The Saints of Cornwall
Medieval Children

(*with John Chynoweth and Alexandra Walsham*)
Richard Carew: The Survey of Cornwall

(*with David Lepine*)
Death and Memory in Medieval Exeter

(*with Margaret Webster*)
The English Hospital: 1070 to 1570

(*Fiction*)
White Bird Flying

MEDIEVAL SCHOOLS

FROM ROMAN BRITAIN TO RENAISSANCE ENGLAND

Nicholas Orme

Yale University Press
New Haven and London

For information about this and other Yale University Press publications, please contact:
U.S. Office: sales.press@yale.edu   yalebooks.com
Europe Office: sales@yaleup.co.uk   www.yaleup.co.uk

Set in Baskerville by Northern Phototypesetting Co. Ltd, Bolton
Printed in China through Worldprint

Library of Congress Cataloging-in-Publication Data
Orme, Nicholas.
  Medieval schools : from Roman Britain to Renaissance England / Nicholas Orme.
     p. cm.
  Includes bibliographical references and index.
  ISBN 0-300-11102-9 (cl. : alk. paper)
  1. Schools—England—History—16th century. 2. Education, Medieval—England. I. Title.
  LA631.3.O753 2006
  370.942'09031—dc22

                                                                                 2006004516

A catalogue record for this book is available from the British Library.

10 9 8 7 6 5 4 3 2 1

To Bevis

Contents

Illustrations

The author and publishers are grateful for permission to reproduce illustrations, as follows: Bede's World, Jarrow, no. 7; The Bibliographical Society, no. 45; Bibliothèque d'Arras, no. 79; The Bodleian Library, Oxford, nos 3, 8, 9, 12, 16, 21, 22, 26, 30, 39, 50, 53, 67–70, 92; The British Library, London, nos 1, 5, 11, 19, 23, 31, 40, 52, 66, 71–3, 76, 91; Cambridge University Library, no. 78; Columbia University, New York, no. 17; The Master and Fellows of Emmanuel College, Cambridge, no. 85; The Rector and Fellows of Lincoln College, Oxford, no. 24; The President and Fellows of Magdalen College, Oxford, nos 35–7; The Warden and Fellows of Merton College, Oxford, no. 62; The Warden and Fellows of New College, Oxford, no. 58; The National Archives (Public Record Office), London, no. 51; The National Monuments Record, Swindon, nos 43, 54–5, 59, 61, 82, 84, 89–90; The National Portrait Gallery, London, nos 42, 83, 88; The Pierpont Morgan Library, New York, frontispiece; The Reece Winstone Archive, Wookey, Somerset, no. 13; Somerset Record Office, Taunton, and the Luttrell Collection, no. 25; The Dean and Chapter of Winchester Cathedral, no. 43

Preface

Medieval Schools is a sequel to *Medieval Children*, published in 2001. That book centres on children at home and how they grew up there. This one follows them to school. Not all of them, of course, because schools probably taught a minority of children in the middle ages, chiefly boys. Nevertheless, a substantial minority went to school, and far more evidence survives about children and adolescents in classrooms than it does about them in the home. Hundreds of schools are recorded as offering teaching. Much can be learnt about their pupils, the topics they studied, the teachers who taught them, and the impact made by schooling on those who received it. From all this we may gain a clearer understanding of the culture and society in which these schools existed.

I first wrote about medieval schools in a book called *English Schools in the Middle Ages*, published in 1973. Since then I have continued to work on their history, and other scholars have made valuable contributions towards it, to the extent that a fresh appraisal of the subject is now appropriate. *Medieval Schools* broadly follows the plan of my earlier book, but it is essentially a new work with additional information and more mature judgments. There are two major changes in the contents. I have removed my original first chapter, a survey of medieval literacy, which appeared before Michael Clanchy's ground-breaking work *From Memory to Written Record*. Now that his book is widely known and available, the issue of literacy no longer needs the exploration that it once did. Instead I have extended my book chronologically with a new chapter on Roman Britain and Anglo-Saxon England, knowledge of which is essential to appreciate what happened later. The rest of *Medieval Schools* includes much else that is new about school organisation, the curriculum, teachers, pupils, and historical changes and continuities. It also gives closer attention to visual evidence and spatial matters. Like its predecessor it ends with a list of schools in England from 1066 to 1530, other than those in religious houses, and this too has been updated and extended.

I have many debts to acknowledge. Four scholars gave me as good a start in academic research as anyone could wish for: K. B. McFarlane and J. R. L. Highfield who supervised my thesis and A. B. Emden and R. W. Hunt who took a kindly interest in my work. All were generous to a beginner to an extent that it is hard to praise enough, especially Emden, who gave me the notes he had made for a similar book. Those who provided information, advice, and encouragement towards *English Schools in the Middle Ages* included Dr J. Critchley, Prof. A. Gransden, Mr T. Hassall, Mr A. Jackson,

Prof. M. C. E. Jones, Dr P. Lock, Dr J. N. T. Miner (Brother Bonaventure), Mr W. Mitchell, Mr W. A. Pantin, the Revd D. Powell, Mr I. Rowlands, and Mr P. J. Wallis. Since then I have incurred many further obligations, notably to the Ven. Dr D. Thomson on medieval grammar, Dr R. Bowers on almonry boys and music, Dr J. G. Clark on monastic history, Dr J. Crick and Prof. B. Yorke on Anglo-Saxon history, Dr C. Fenwick on poll-tax records, and Mr P. Northeast and Dr J. Ridgard on East Anglian schools. Others who have kindly sent me information or answered queries include Miss C. Annesley, Mrs J. Barlow, Prof. C. Barron, Dr C. Bland, Dr P. Coulstock, Prof. C. Cross, Dr D. Dymond, Dr C. Fraser, Dr J. A. A. Goodall, Prof. S. Gwara, Dr H. Gwosdek, Dr M. W. C. Hassall, Dr M. Heale, Dr L. Hellinga, Mr J. Hillaby, Dom S. F. Hockey, Dr H. Jewell, Dr D. Lepine, Prof. J. A. Moran Cruz, Mr J. Munby, Mr A. E. B. Owen, Mr J. de Putter, Dr N. J. Richardson, Mr J. Rhodes, Dr M.-H. Rousseau, Prof. N. Saul, Dr H. Summerson, Dr S. Sweetinburgh, Dr C. Thornton, Dr S. Townley, Prof. J. B. Trapp, Dr J. J. Vickerstaff, and Prof T. P. Wiseman. To them should be added the librarians, archivists, and authors of all the institutions and books mentioned in the following pages. This book, indeed, sums up my working life, and the pleasure of researching it has been matched by the enjoyment of sharing the interest with so many other people, not least my patient family and one of my oldest friends, to whom it is dedicated.

It remains for me to thank the British Academy for a grant towards the cartography and illustration research, to Mr M. J. Rouillard for his admirable plans and maps, and to Yale University Press and my editors Robert Baldock, Candida Brazil, Laura Davey, and Stephen Kent for their care and support in bringing the project to publication.

Nicholas Orme
Brampford Speke

INTRODUCTION

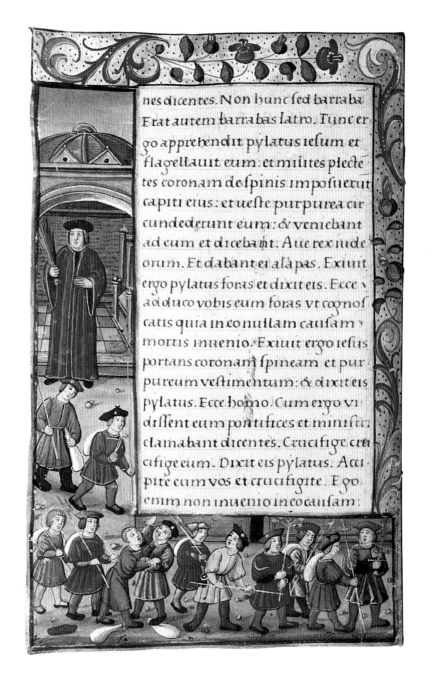

nes dicentes. Non hunc sed barraba
Erat autem barrabas latro. Tunc er
go apprehendit pylatus iesum et
flagellauit eum: et milites plecte
tes coronam de spinis imposuerut
capiti eius: et ueste purpurea cir
cundederunt eum: & veniebant
ad eum et dicebant: Aue rex iude
orum. Et dabant ei alapas. Exiuit
ergo pylatus foras et dixit eis. Ecce
adduco vobis eum foras vt cognos
catis quia in eo nullam causam
mortis inuenio. Exiuit ergo iesus
portans coronam spineam et pur
pureum vestimentum: & dixit eis
pylatus. Ecce homo. Cum ergo vi
dissent eum pontifices et ministri
clamabant dicentes. Crucifige cru
cifige eum. Dixit eis pylatus. Acci
pite eum vos et crucifigite. Ego
enim non inuenio in eo causam:

INTRODUCTION

The Study of Medieval Schools

Going to school is not usually associated with the middle ages, at least in the mind of the general public. Did anyone go, apart from trainee clergy? And when they went, was it to schools that we would recognise, or to primitive places without adequate teachers, well-designed lessons, or helpful equipment? This book sets out to show that there were indeed genuine schools, operating in creative and effective ways, and attended by many young people. It traces their history in England from Roman times, when education starts to be recorded, up to and including the Reformation, ending in the first year of the reign of Elizabeth I (1558–9). It argues that medieval education was not a precursor of modern education, but the same thing in different circumstances.

Medieval schools suffer from an absence of profile rather than a lack of substance. Although they were numbered in hundreds, they have received only modest attention even from scholars. Most textbooks on the middle ages say little about them, and they inspire few books of their own. A striking contrast can be made with monasteries. The first list of abbeys and priories in England was drawn up as early as about 1200, and many more such lists, histories, surveys, and collections of records were compiled and published during the sixteenth, seventeenth, and eighteenth centuries.[1] Monasteries caught people's interest because they vanished. Schools, although equally medieval, survived, prompting little awareness that they had a history, let alone that it might be recovered. In the late seventeenth century Anthony Wood, the Oxford antiquary (d. 1695), made a few notes about old schools,[2] and Christopher Wase, a school headmaster and later bedel of Oxford University (d. 1690), delved deeper into the subject. He was the first to attempt a general enquiry into their origins and resources and to make lists of their teachers.[3] His notes were not published, however, and a belief grew up that medieval schooling was mainly provided by monasteries. Monks, wrote Thomas Fuller in his *Church History of Britain* (1655), were 'tutors for the education of youth, there being a great penury of other grammar schools in that age'.[4] Wood's great friend John Aubrey thought the same. 'There were no free schools. The boys were educated at the monasteries.'[5]

1   Aristotle, imagined in the fifteenth century, teaching at the court of Philip of Macedon.

Little happened to dispel this belief for a long time. A few eighteenth-century local historians brought to light instances of free-standing schools in the counties and boroughs of medieval England, but their discoveries failed to impinge upon the accepted view of the past.[6]

This situation changed in the nineteenth century. After the end of the Napoleonic Wars, English public opinion began to embrace the reform of national institutions: Parliament, Church, local government, and education. People asked whether the endowments of schools were being used to best advantage, and this led to enquiries into their origins and purposes. In 1818 Nicholas Carlisle published a private survey in which he tried to list all the endowed grammar schools in existence and to describe their histories. During the course of the work he drew attention to records of medieval schools anterior to those with which he was dealing.[7] In the same year Lord Brougham opened a campaign for the reform of endowed schools, which led to the establishment of a parliamentary commission on the subject. After this there was a steady growth of interest, both public and private, in the history of schools. Charity commissions were appointed, which published thirty-two reports between 1819 and 1840, including material on schools, and in 1853 a permanent Charity Commission was established. In 1864 an Endowed School Commission conducted even more searching enquiries, and its evidence, which ran to twenty-one volumes, contained a good deal of historical material. At a local level the popular concern for education, and the reforms that this eventually produced, began to stimulate the production of individual school histories, although these were usually stronger on recent times than they were on the middle ages.

The work of the Charity Commission helped to bring about the first large piece of research into medieval schools. Arthur Francis Leach (1851–1915) was educated in medieval surroundings at Winchester and Oxford, where he gained a first-class degree in classics and a prize fellowship of All Souls College.[8] He did not follow an academic career at Oxford but turned to the study of law, was called to the bar, and became an assistant charity commissioner in 1884. Shortly afterwards he was assigned to investigate the history of the Prebendal School at Chichester and, a little later, that of the grammar school at Southwell. He found that both had originated in the middle ages, and came to realise that there had been many other schools of a similar kind. This, he recognised, was a major discovery. The general public and most historians still assumed that schooling in medieval England came from the monasteries. Free-standing schools of a modern kind were thought to have appeared with Winchester College in 1382 and Eton College in the 1440s, and to have become widespread only at the Reformation, when Henry VIII and Edward VI founded cathedral schools and free grammar schools. Leach became convinced that, long before these foundations, education had been chiefly supplied by schools independent of monasteries, staffed by non-monastic 'secular' clergy or laymen and open to the public. These schools, he concluded, had the essential features of schools in his own day. The belief that modern education began with the Renaissance and Reformation was very far from the truth.

To be fair to his contemporaries, Leach was not alone in this discovery. F. J. Furnivall, one of the inspirations for 'Toad of Toad Hall', had written an account of medieval English education in 1868 in an edition of poems on manners and meals published by the Early English Text Society.[9] Furnivall gave generous help to Leach in later years, but his own work on the subject is impressive. It was broader in scope than Leach's and included the study of education in homes and great households, in a way that was not developed until much later. In 1876 J. Grant brought out an excellent history of schools in Scotland, with an analysis of their constitutions, curricula, and teachers.[10] In 1894, two years before Leach produced his first important book, two other writers drew attention to schools in late medieval England: J. H. Wylie in his *History of England under Henry the Fourth* and Alice Stopford Green in her *Town Life in the Fifteenth Century*. Both authors collected references to education in the course of their research, and were able to demonstrate its existence outside the monasteries.[11] Leach exceeded these scholars not in quality but in scale and impact. He gave much of the rest of his life to his interest and wrote extensively about it. His achievement in doing so remains impressive, especially given that he had a full-time job and rose to the second most senior post in the Charity Commission. During the twenty-one years between 1894 and 1915, he published nine volumes on the history of education, including general works, collections of documents, and local histories, as well as more than fifteen lengthy articles in the *Victoria County History*, the project that aimed at writing a thorough history of each English county. He examined and brought to notice a huge range of material, not only from printed sources but from charters and manuscripts in the British Museum, the Public Record Office, and dozens of local archives and muniment rooms. He created the modern study of the subject and his writings are still indispensable.

Leach's best work lies in his editions of local records, *Early Yorkshire Schools* and *Early Education in Worcester*, together with his histories of Warwick School, Winchester College, and St Paul's School (London). These were concise and manageable subjects that he researched thoroughly and described on the whole judiciously. Much the same is true of his larger collection of original records, *Educational Charters and Documents, 598–1909*, except that allowance must be made for the more accurate dates and texts which have been established since he wrote. The articles he composed for the *Victoria County History* are more variable. Worcestershire, for example, where he had some good local assistance,[12] is superior to Gloucestershire, the treatment of which is often sketchy and unreliable. At times one detects a tension between the author's wish to contribute to the *VCH* and the demands of his paid work. The contributors to the *VCH* do not always seem to have pooled their discoveries, and Leach's own articles can sometimes be supplemented from elsewhere in the volumes, which are always worth checking with this in mind.[13] Much profit may still be gained from his *VCH* articles, but they can no longer be regarded as definitive, since the last eighty years have added much to what the author missed himself.

The most ambitious of Leach's works were two general studies, written to summarise his detailed research. *English Schools at the Reformation* (1896) and *The Schools of Medieval England* (1915) were both the fruit of a knowledge of educational sources unequalled in his day.[14] They are not lacking in shrewd comments and valuable pieces of information including, in the latter volume, some fieldwork that was never published elsewhere. At the same time these two works display more fully than his others their author's defects as an historian. Not only are they limited by his failure to discuss relevant topics which did not interest him, but they suffer from the extravagance with which he extolled his theories and denounced his opponents, to say nothing of his careless regard for accuracy about dates and facts. The best medieval historians of the day were shocked by these shortcomings. 'He gives the rashest judgment about the most disputable matters', complained F. W. Maitland of one of Leach's earlier works in 1900, and the reckless assertions which mar *The Schools of Medieval England* drew

2   The entrance to the oldest English abbey: St Augustine's (Canterbury). Far from ignoring learning, it supported teaching for its monks, a school for its almonry boys and external pupils, and a printing press.

strong rebuke in a review by A. G. Little, encouraged by R. L. Poole. Far from crowning his reputation, his general studies clouded it. They caused misgivings about the whole of his work and weakened his achievement.[15]

None of the deficiencies in Leach's major works is more serious than his treatment of the religious orders. Reacting too strongly against the opinion, once held by himself, that the monks were the schoolmasters of medieval England, he failed to do justice to their contributions to education. First, he misunderstood the teaching they provided for the lay children maintained in their almonries, overestimating its musical content and undervaluing its grammatical basis.[16] Secondly, he belittled the training of their novices and adult brethren in grammar and theology, relying too much on the shortcomings reported in visitations of monasteries, which, although relevant, form only part of the evidence. As for the friars, the orders most committed to the pursuit of learning, he ignored them altogether. His handling of non-monastic schools was also limited in that, with the exception of Winchester and Eton, he gave scant attention to what was taught. He lived, of course, at a time when academic historians were preoccupied with constitutional history, and his own employment led him in the same direction, but it is odd that he did so little to penetrate what he called 'the darkness of our ignorance of the curriculum'. By the time that he wrote there were scholarly editions of, and articles on, several of the grammarians and authors used in medieval schools, and he himself chanced more than once upon relevant information.

His limitations were compounded by exaggerations. One was an overestimation of the educational role of minsters and collegiate churches in the middle ages. Having found that schools existed at an early date in churches of this kind like Beverley and Hastings, Leach rashly concluded that all similar institutions had such schools, and the theory became an article of faith to be recited even without evidence. In truth no collegiate church should be credited with a school unless there is specific information to that effect.[17] He also overrated the role of the chantries. Much of the evidence about their part in education comes from the chantry surveys made by the crown in 1546–8, which he gathered and edited in *English Schools at the Reformation*. Leach tended to suppose that if a chantry was supporting a school at that time, it was founded to do so – a judgment wide of the mark. Most chantries never maintained a school, and chantry schools became numerous only in the second half of the fifteenth century. He was right to point out that the dissolution of the chantries in 1548 had adverse effects for education. Chantry reading schools were not continued, while many chantry grammar schools had the incomes from their endowments converted into fixed stipends – a disadvantage in an age of inflation. He was justified in criticising the educational achievements of Edward VI's regime (as did some of Edward's subjects), but his view of the regime was too negative. He gave the dissolution of the chantries too much importance in the history of Tudor education, a subject that he never explored as a whole.

Leach's death in 1915 left the study of medieval schools in a weak position. He had not inspired many to follow him, and his published work suffered from the reservations expressed about it by academic historians. Coincidentally the *Victoria County History*, which had been an active project up to 1914, became relatively inactive afterwards and remained so until the 1940s. For the next fifty years those who worked on education before 1500 (apart from university education) were individualists. They had no common task in mind, and education was often only one of a range of topics that concerned them. First on the scene were two women, Eileen Power, whose *Medieval English Nunneries* (1922) gave careful attention to the educational concerns of nuns, and Dorothy Gardiner, whose *English Girlhood at School* (1929) is still a clear and readable account of the subject from Anglo-Saxon times to 1800. Next monastic education began to be revalued by W. A. Pantin, with an important article in 1929 and three volumes of records in the early 1930s. After that it was the turn of medieval grammar and the cathedral schools, thanks to R. W. Hunt, who completed his thesis on Alexander Nequam in 1936 and published his first article on twelfth-century learning in the same year.[18] Other landmark writers were Kathleen Edwards, whose study of medieval English cathedrals (including their schools) was first published in 1949, and A. B. Emden, the university historian, whose biographical registers of men who had studied at Oxford and Cambridge came out between 1957 and 1974.

By the 1960s there was a quickening of interest in the history of English school education, marked by the appearance of books, articles, and (in 1972) a periodical, *Journal of the History of Education*. Meanwhile the *Victoria County History* had been revived, and histories of schools in six more counties were published in its volumes during the second half of the twentieth century. The interest of educational historians, however, was slow to penetrate to the middle ages. Their earliest focus in chronological terms was the Tudor period, which featured in W. K. Jordan's studies of English charities (1959–62), Kenneth Charlton's *Education in Renaissance England* (1965), and Joan Simon's *Education and Society in Tudor England* (1966). These authors were aware that they could not fully evaluate Tudor education without relating it to what had existed before, and there was some debate in print about Leach's work.[19] But the focus of their work did not allow for much research on the period before about the 1480s – catastrophically in the case of Jordan, who reached the egregious conclusion that Buckinghamshire, Norfolk, and Yorkshire contained only twelve public grammar schools *between them* in 1480, a total that he proceeded to show had increased dramatically in Tudor times![20]

The present author was the next after Leach to write a large-scale history of English schools from the twelfth to the mid sixteenth centuries. This was the first version of the present volume, published in 1973. It followed Leach in giving much of its attention to schools in terms of their numbers and continuity, because in the 1960s there was still much doubt about the reliability of Leach's work on these subjects. At the same time it tried to move beyond his work by exploring what schools taught and how they related to the world around them. A detailed study of *Education in the West of England 1066–1548* by the same author followed three years later, and further institutional studies by him have included a history of the early years of Magdalen College School (Oxford) and articles on Glastonbury Abbey, Herefordshire, and Worcestershire. Valuable research was also done by Jo Ann Moran (now Moran Cruz), whose pamphlet on schooling in the city of York was followed by a substantial book, *The Growth of English Schooling 1340–1548*, on literacy and education in a large area of the north of England. Apart from these writers, however, and a few historians of individual schools who have covered the middle ages, no substantial group of scholars has worked on numbers of schools, schools as institutions, or schools at the Reformation. Instead the most important advances have been made in aspects of education that lie beyond schools.

One initiative has explored the history of literacy in the middle ages. In 1979 Michael Clanchy published his magisterial survey *From Memory to Written Record* (revised 1993), which showed how society was affected by the growth of documentation during the twelfth and thirteenth centuries. It is not primarily about schools, but is illuminating about why they existed and what effects they had. Other historians have studied education in relation to

3   St Katherine, seated with a book. Women, although usually educated in homes rather than schools, acquired skills in reading, especially in French or English.

social groups rather than schools. *From Childhood to Chivalry* (1984) by the present author, examined the education of the English royal family and aristocracy, both girls and boys. *The Ties that Bound* by Barbara Hanawalt (1986) took peasants as its focus, and dealt with their education in terms of their upbringing and training for work. The theme of upbringing has also been pursued by the present author in *Medieval Children* (2001), which includes a chapter on 'Learning to Read'. A third sphere of activity has been research into the medieval school curriculum, and this has been especially fruitful. Our knowledge has been transformed for three periods: Anglo-Saxon England, the twelfth and thirteenth centuries, and the later middle ages. The first of these has been dominated by the work of Michael Lapidge and Vivien Law, who have revolutionised the understanding of school studies up to 1066, and in Law's case afterwards too. They have brought to light a vast amount of material, especially grammars, glossaries, and literary texts, presented, analysed, and explained to the highest standards.

The curriculum after the Norman Conquest was first investigated by R. W. Hunt, in a notable series of papers on grammar and learning published from 1936 to 1964. These were collected as *The History of Grammar in the Middle Ages* (1980) by G. L. Bursill-Hall, who produced his own *Census of Medieval Latin Grammatical Manuscripts* in 1981. Tony Hunt's *Teaching and Learning Latin in Thirteenth-Century England* (1991) has built on his namesake's work with discussions and editions of Latin school texts and glossaries of the twelfth and thirteenth centuries, with relationship to the history of the French and English languages. Two other first-rate contributions, centred on the fifteenth century, have been David Thomson's *Descriptive Catalogue of Middle English Grammatical Texts* (1979) and his *Edition of the Middle English Grammatical Texts* (1984). The works of Tony Hunt and Thomson reveal, more clearly than before, the texts that schoolmasters and their pupils used in the classroom, together with their methods of teaching and study. Further contributions in this area include an edition and detailed analysis of a fifteenth-century school manuscript by Cynthia Bland (1991) and editions of compositions in Latin and English from five different schools by the present author, together with a study of the Tudor grammarian John Holt. Hedwig Gwosdek has listed many of the early grammars printed in England, as well as editing some of those ascribed to Holt's contemporaries John Stanbridge and William Lily. Altogether the last thirty years have been a productive period, in which historians have entered new territories and done much to survey and map them.

All this makes it harder for a general history of the subject to do it justice than was the case thirty years ago. *Medieval Schools* is inevitably more of a survey and less of a monograph than *English Schools in the Middle Ages*. We benefit from our advancing knowledge, on the other hand, in that the subject is not a closed one, barren of opportunities. Much remains to be done in the complex field of the study of grammar, in the identification of school sites and buildings, and in reconstructing the careers of schoolmasters and their pupils. There is a vast scope for relating the history of schools in England to that of their counterparts in the rest of the British Isles and in continental Europe.[21] I hope that this book will encourage such work, and be helpful to those who undertake it.

ORIGINS

1

From the Romans to 1100

THE ROMAN FOUNDATION

The written word in Britain, like the coming of day, has its morning star, its first light, and its sunrise. The morning star is Pytheas, who sailed to Britain from Marseille in the fourth century BC and wrote or inspired a book about his voyage, making him the earliest person in the history of the island to leave a literary record.[1] The first light – the oldest surviving texts – appears on coins of the first century BC, issued by Commius, king of the Atrebates, a people centred in what is now Hampshire. He had these coins embellished with his name, and the practice was soon copied by other princes, who added their titles and the places they claimed to rule.[2] The Roman conquest of Britain, beginning in AD 43, marks the sunrise. It brought reading and writing to Britain on a large scale, so successfully that they have endured ever since.

Much remains of the literate culture of Roman Britain from 43 until the evaporation of Roman authority four hundred years later. There are laws and commands of the imperial government that would have been sent to Britain, and inscriptions on military and civic buildings, milestones, religious altars, and tombstones. Letters and inventories have been preserved on wooden tablets at *Vindolanda* near Hadrian's Wall. Prayers and curses survive on metal plates deposited at shrines, notably in the springs of Bath. Words are found stamped on pottery, tiles, and pigs of lead; scenes from Virgil's *Aeneid* decorate the walls or floors of some high-ranking houses.[3] We can infer from this evidence that literacy was not limited to the incoming Roman civil and military rulers. It spread to the British aristocracy, many of whom adopted Roman culture, and to some lesser people, Britons or incomers, who traded or followed crafts in the towns. While the Latin of public inscriptions is often carefully composed, that of the wooden tablets and metal plates is frequently poor in spelling and expression, suggesting writers who were basically literate but had not learnt the refinements of spelling and style.[4]

How did people learn to read and write in Roman Britain? It is a paradox that the acquisition of education leaves far fewer traces than the skills it

4   Latin literacy outlived the Romans in western Britain. Here it appears on sixth-century or later memorial stones from Cornwall.

produces. Virtually nothing is recorded about schooling in the island, which means that we can only conjecture its nature from what is known about the process in the rest of the empire. Literary culture was valued in the higher ranks of Roman society – the senatorial, equestrian, and decurial orders who qualified to hold public offices. Three levels of education were recognised: elementary learning (reading, writing, and arithmetic), grammar (correct composition and the study of literary texts), and rhetoric (the theory and practice of oratory).[5] In many western parts of the empire education was assisted by the fact that Latin, the literary language, was also the spoken tongue, although some students of grammar went on to learn Greek. The elementary subjects were learnt from a private tutor (usually a slave), or from fee-earning teachers who were widely available in cities. Even a girl, and one of modest rank, might go to an elementary school, if we can believe a story told by Livy about a centurion's daughter who attended such a school in the Forum of Rome.[6] The more advanced studies of grammar and rhetoric were patronised by those of the higher ranks who wished to read the literary classics, to write correctly, and to speak well in public. Typically such people studied grammar for about five years until their mid teens, and then graduated to rhetoric. These two subjects were not necessarily taught in every city, so that pupils might have had to leave their homes to study them. Most pupils at this level were probably boys, but it is possible that some of their sisters followed similar studies at home, since we know of one or two female Latin poets, Sulpicia and Proba.

The teaching of grammar and rhetoric had some prestige. Imperial decrees gave those who taught them exemption from public duties, and protected their right to enjoy their fees and salaries.[7] The Emperor Diocletian's 'Edict on Prices' of 301 laid down rates for school fees, although the edict was published only in the eastern half of the empire. Elementary teachers could charge their pupils 40–50 *denarii* per month, grammarians 200, and rhetoricians 250, at a time when craftsmen might receive 50–60 *denarii* per day as well as their keep.[8] Salaries appear to have been provided only in major towns, but as late as the year 376 the imperial government ordered the chief cities of Gaul to provide chairs of Latin grammar, Greek, and rhetoric from public funds – the rhetoricians receiving one and a half times as much as the others.[9] Tacitus tells us that Agricola, governor of Britain from 78 to 84, tried to assimilate the sons of British leaders by educating them in the liberal arts, making them eager (so Tacitus claimed) to learn Latin and to dress in Roman style.[10] A few words from the *Aeneid* on one of the *Vindolanda* tablets have been interpreted as part of a writing lesson.[11] More substantially there are three or four references to teachers of rhetoric in Britain between the first and the fifth centuries, and the writings of the sixth-century British author Gildas, who appears to have had a traditional Roman education, contain both echoes of Virgil and rhetorical devices like those of Cicero.[12]

All this suggests that Britain shared to some extent in the educational curriculum of the Roman Empire and in some of its institutions. There may have been private teachers in some aristocratic households and fee-earning teachers of grammar and rhetoric in certain towns. A further knowledge of letters may have been passed informally from one literate person to another. The written word, however, was available only in Latin, as far as we know, not in the native British language. This must have affected teaching, because Latin was less widely spoken in Britain than it was on the Continent. For many, learning to read must have involved learning Latin as a foreign language, making it difficult to pick up such knowledge informally. Even in schools teachers would have been more challenged to teach Latin to those who did not speak it naturally, as we know they were after the end of Roman rule. How they tackled the problem is not recorded.

EDUCATION IN ENGLAND TO AD 800

The Roman occupation of Britain coincided with the rise of Christianity, which was officially tolerated from 313.[13] A Church council held at Arles in the following year included three British bishops from London, York, and possibly Lincoln, pointing to organised communities of Christians in these towns and, by implication, elsewhere.[14] It is unlikely that Christians in Roman Britain organised their own system of education. Rather they would have continued to follow the traditional one that included the study of pagan Latin literature, using the knowledge it gave them to read the Bible and other religious works in Latin.[15] But Christianity had scarcely established itself as a public religion when Roman rule in Britain evaporated during the early fifth century. The imperial government disappeared, and urban life weakened along with the Latin culture that had been based in the towns. Anglo-Saxon migrants, who were German speakers and religious pagans, occupied the eastern and southern coastal regions and established small kingdoms. Christianity, too, experienced disruption as a result of these challenges, but it reacted dynamically. In the first place it spread geographically to Ireland in the fifth century and to western Scotland in the sixth, neither of which had ever been ruled by the Romans. Secondly, it established new bases for its survival in the form of monasteries, which had been developing in western Europe during the fourth century. Monasteries worked better than towns in the new conditions as centres of religion and education. They existed in western Britain and Ireland by the end of the fifth century,[16] and after a further hundred years they began to be founded in the parts of Britain ruled by the Anglo-Saxons, those parts that can now be called England.

Christianity revived in south-east England when Pope Gregory the Great sent a group of monks to evangelise Kent in 597, led by Augustine of Canterbury. It spread further west and north during the sixth century, meeting a second wave of missions from Ireland and western Scotland that entered northern England in the 630s. Augustine made his headquarters at Canterbury, where he founded two churches: each an important model for the future. One was a cathedral named Christ Church, intended to be the personal church of the archbishop of Canterbury and his household of clergy. The other, dedicated to SS Peter and Paul (but later known as St Augustine's), was a monastery.[17] Both churches were centres of literacy, since their members worshipped with books and studied religious texts, and each needed to recruit boys and men to sustain their activities in the future. The schooling of these recruits had to be organised internally because no other schools existed locally. As Christianity spread or reorganised itself over England, it reproduced both kinds of institution. The cathedrals formed a small group, one for each bishop and diocese, amounting to seventeen by the year 800. The monasteries were commoner since there was no restriction on their number, and they may have totalled two or three hundred by that year. Most of them were communities of men but at least fifty catered for women, usually in the form of a double house of women and men, ruled by an abbess.[18] Cathedrals and monasteries were not vastly different in this period. The clergy of both institutions lived a communal life, engaging in daily worship. Those of the cathedral were involved with the outside world by virtue of their closeness to the bishop, and some cathedral clergy might travel with him round his diocese. At the same time monasteries were not entirely secluded places, since they usually acted as centres of worship and pastoral care for the surrounding countryside. Another common factor was that bishops themselves were often monks. They might have individual monks in their households, and at least two of the cathedrals (Hexham and Lindisfarne) were also monasteries.

We know more about education in monasteries than in cathedrals during the seventh and eighth centuries, partly because our best source, Bede's *Ecclesiastical History*, completed in 731, was the work of a monk with other monastic informants. The need of monasteries to find and train young members gained early recognition in the Rule of St Benedict, drawn up in

5   St Benedict, imagined as presenting his Rule to the monks of Christ Church (Canterbury).

Italy in about 535. Benedict envisaged two kinds of monastic recruits: boys and young men. Parents, both noble and poor, could offer their sons as monks in childhood, with the assumption that the boys concerned would remain so for the rest of their lives. Such boys were to be placed in the charge of the cellarer of the monastery, under the abbot's supervision, until they reached fifteen, the age of adulthood. Appropriate food was to be given to them (overriding the rules of fasting imposed on adults), and they were to attend church and learn how to recite the material of the daily services: psalms, antiphons, responds, and lessons. Misdeeds were to be punished by whipping, but not with undue severity. Benedict also provided for the admission of novices, by implication outsiders in their teens or early twenties, who had been to school elsewhere (a process possible in Italy). They were to live in a special place within the monastery, under the supervision of a senior monk, while they learnt to take part in monastic life and worship. The Rule was to be read to them after two months, four months, and six months. If they were willing to embrace it after three readings, they were to be received into the community.[19]

Most early Anglo-Saxon monasteries did not follow the Rule of St Benedict closely, but the largest and most ambitious ones probably adopted similar practices. They too admitted inmates who were child 'oblates', offered for life by their parents. The age of seven was commonly regarded as the boundary between infancy and childhood, and may have been considered a suitable time for such an offering. Bede was that old when his family placed him in the monastery of Wearmouth in about 680.[20] Once we hear of a boy named Æsica, who died of the plague in Barking Abbey when he was three, but Barking was a double house whose nuns may have cared for little children merely in the sense of looking after them.[21] Other entrants came to monasteries on their own initiative in their teens, their adulthood, or even their old age. Wilfrid, the controversial bishop of York and other dioceses, entered Lindisfarne Abbey when he was fourteen as the companion of an elderly nobleman who had decided to adopt the monastic life.[22] Cathedrals probably resembled monasteries in taking both kinds of recruits, boys and adolescents, but they did not educate girls, who were brought up only in double houses. Education need not have been a permanent activity in religious communities, but may have started and stopped when new recruits arrived, which, in small establishments, would have happened only occasionally. Numbers of pupils are not recorded but are likely to have been modest in most places, ranging from one or two to a couple of dozen. Teachers, in the early days when churches, books, and pupils were comparatively few, might include bishops, abbots, and abbesses themselves on an occasional basis, but were most likely to be senior clergy, monks, or nuns of the community who specialised in teaching.[23]

The churches of Canterbury and of other early Christian centres like London and Rochester must have begun to train local boys or men within a

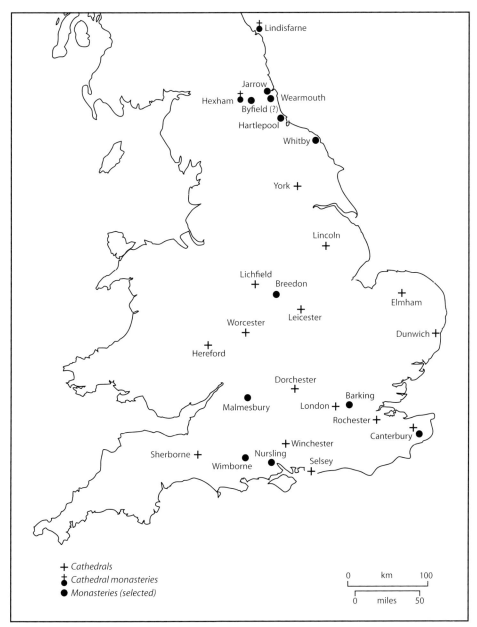

6   Education in England, 600–800.

few years of 597. Bede identifies five of the earliest Englishmen who rose to
be bishops, having changed their names to Christian ones: Ithamar at
Rochester in about 644, Thomas and Boniface in East Anglia by 653,
Deusdedit at Canterbury in 655, and Damian at Rochester a little later.[24]
Schooling appears to have been well established in Kent by the 630s, when
Sigeberht, king of the East Angles, who had become a Christian during an

exile in Gaul, 'established a school where boys could be taught letters'. He
did so, Bede informs us, 'with the help of Bishop Felix, whom he had
received from Kent, and they provided themselves with teachers and
masters following the Kentish manner'.[25] Education in Kent received a
further impetus with the arrival of Theodore as archbishop of Canterbury
in 669, followed shortly afterwards by that of Hadrian as abbot of SS Peter
and Paul. Both men came from the Mediterranean lands, both were fluent
in Latin and Greek, and both involved themselves in teaching, attracting a
crowd of students from as far away as Ireland.[26]

In the north of England the parallel movement of mission from western
Scotland and Ireland led to the foundation of the monastic cathedral of
Lindisfarne in 635, whose first bishop, Aidan, gathered English boys for
training as the Kentish missionaries had done.[27] Two other leading northern
centres of education were the monasteries of Wearmouth and Jarrow,
founded by Benedict Biscop in 674 and 682 respectively, and richly
endowed with books acquired by him on visits to Rome. Bede was educated
at both monasteries, and subsequently taught at Jarrow (Fig. 7).[28] A further
place of importance in the north was York, which had a cathedral school of
distinction during the eighth century. Ælberht, one of its teachers, became
bishop (later archbishop) there in 766–7, and was followed as teacher by his
pupil Alcuin, who left England in 781–2 to join the court of Charlemagne.[29]
Alcuin praised Ælberht for the breadth of the subjects he taught and the

7   A reconstruction of the monastery at Jarrow in the time of Bede.

8 A tenth-century portrait of
Aldhelm (d. 709), bishop of
Sherborne, grammarian, and
author.

books he collected as archbishop. The subjects included grammar, rhetoric,
natural science, the calendar, and the Bible, and the books were obtained on
journeys to the Continent.[30] When Alcuin's former pupil Eanbald II became
archbishop of York in 796, Alcuin wrote to urge him to take education
seriously, arranging separate classes for reading, singing, and writing, and
providing masters for each.[31]

There was good schooling in other places, at least intermittently. Aldhelm
(Fig. 8), abbot of Malmesbury and afterwards bishop of Sherborne during the
late seventh century, was the author of a treatise on poetic metre and
so skilled as a writer of Latin prose and verse that it is hard to imagine
him indifferent to the provision of teaching in these churches.[32] In the
early years of the eighth century, Boniface, later a leading missionary and
Church founder in Germany, taught at the monastery of Nursling, where
he composed one of the earliest Latin grammars to be written by an
Englishman.[33] At about the same time, Tatwine, a future archbishop of
Canterbury, created his own Latin textbook in the monastery of Breedon-on-
the-Hill.[34] Information about schooling in a third monastery, somewhere in
the north of England, appears in a history of its abbots written by a monk

named Æthelwulf in the early ninth century. He does not reveal its location, which may have been Bywell near Hexham, but he wrote proudly of its teaching tradition. Its founder, a nobleman named Eanmund in the early eighth century, had imported an instructor from Lindisfarne Abbey to teach the monks knowledge and the monastic rule. Later teachers included Hyglac and Eadfrith, who were both active later in the century and taught Æthelwulf himself. His own writings show that they had at least one competent pupil.[35]

Women also shared in education. Bede tells how, in about the 640s, before opportunities existed to become a nun in England, some Christian parents sent their daughters to the kingdom of the Franks (modern France) to be taught in nunneries there and to enter the religious life: notably at Faremoutiers-en-Brie and Andelys-sur-Seine. One of those who went was Eorcengota, daughter of a king of Kent.[36] Double houses of women and men were established in England during the later seventh century and afterwards. The earliest known is that of Hartlepool, founded by a woman named Heiu by about the 640s. One of its early abbesses was Hild, who later made her own foundation at Whitby in 657 which she ruled until her death in 680.[37] Girls, like boys, might be offered as nuns in childhood. In 654 King Oswiu of Northumbria celebrated a victory in battle by dedicating his one-year-old daughter Ælfflæd to a life of virginity, and she duly joined the Whitby community.[38] Others may have entered nunneries when they were older girls or women. An abbess might involve herself in teaching, like the head of a monastery. Hild is said to have supervised the studies even of the male clergy attached to her house.[39] More often instruction would be carried out by a senior nun. Ælfflæd probably rose from pupil to teacher at Whitby, before becoming its head,[40] and Leofgyth, another famous abbess, followed a similar track. She was taught by a sister named Eadburg at Wimborne Minster in the 730s, her studies including the writing of Latin verse.[41] In due course Leofgyth herself became a teacher at Wimborne, succeeding a woman who had been so harsh to the junior nuns that, when their mistress died, they climbed on the mound of her grave and stamped it down.[42] Leofgyth, in contrast, distinguished herself in her studies and life. She was asked by her kinsman Boniface to establish an abbey in Germany at Bischofsheim, where (known as Lioba) she died and was subsequently venerated.

The English cathedrals and monasteries achieved much in terms of education and learning during the seventh and eighth centuries (Fig. 6). The standards they reached were necessarily uneven, given that they were independent and self-governing bodies. In 734 Bede wrote a famous letter to Archbishop Egberht of York, complaining that noble men and women were founding monasteries in order to acquire or safeguard landed property, in which the religious life (and by implication learning) was taken less seriously. He pointed to the existence of clerics and monks who were ignorant of the Latin language, probably meaning that they could read and pronounce but not understand it.[43] A few years later, in 747, an English

Church council meeting at Clofesho concurred that not enough clergy were willing to work at their studies, and ordered bishops, abbots, and abbesses to improve the standard of learning in their churches, especially where children were concerned.[44] This problem was not new. Bede tells how, two generations earlier, John of Beverley, bishop of Hexham (687–706), asked a youth in his household if he had been baptised. When the youth said 'yes' and named the priest, John replied that the baptism could not have been perfect, because the man concerned was so slow-witted that he was unable to learn the service. John had ordered him not to baptise for that reason.[45] Even a well-run, well-provided monastery like Jarrow might include men challenged by study, and the provision of education in lesser houses may have been limited. Boniface started his career as a boy or youth in a monastery at Exeter, but his biographer believed that 'the lack of masterly teaching' there impelled him to move to Nursling.[46]

Most of what we hear about schooling in this period of English history relates to clergy, monks, and nuns, and this may reflect real conditions. But there were certainly some educated laymen by the end of the seventh century. One likely example is Sigeberht, who became king of the East Angles in 630–1 after an exile in the Frankish kingdom that had included baptism. The school he established on his return, together with his later abdication and entry into a monastery, show that he was closely in touch with Latin culture.[47] His contemporaries Oswald and Oswiu, later kings of Northumbria, underwent a similar exile among the Irish until about 633, receiving baptism and acquiring the Irish language. They too may have learnt to read.[48] A third Northumbrian king, Oswiu's son Aldfrith, lived with the Irish before his accession in 685–6 and is said to have engaged in reading and teaching.[49] Bede called him 'a man most learned in the scriptures', 'most learned in all respects', and told how Abbot Adamnan of Iona gave him a book on the holy places in Palestine.[50] Aldfrith is probably the person to whom the scholar Aldhelm addressed his treatise on metre.[51] Other kings of the early eighth century interested in learning included Ceolwulf of Northumbria, to whom Bede sent both a draft and final copy of his history, and Ælfwald of East Anglia, who asked Felix of Crowland to write the *Life of St Guthlac* and received the dedication of the work.[52]

Kings were special people, but it is clear that bishops and monasteries gave education to other laymen who did not become clerics or monks. Some of those concerned may have abandoned the religious life after failing to develop a vocation for it, or because they inherited property unexpectedly. Others may have wished to be educated in order to imitate the literate noblemen of the Roman Empire and its successor states in France, Italy, and Spain. Bede tells us that Bishop Aidan of Lindisfarne (635–51) had clerics and laymen in his household, all of whom he made to learn the psalms or read the scriptures.[53] A story about John of Beverley, while bishop of Hexham, tells how he was riding with young men, mostly laity, when one of them, Herebald, galloped his horse and had an accident. Since Herebald was learning to read and sing, it is possible that his lay companions were doing so too.[54] Noblemen entrusted their sons to Wilfrid, the aristocratic bishop of York (669–78), for teaching, without a definite idea of what their adult careers should be. He was seen as a suitable mentor for boys wishing either to serve God or to become warriors, and would commend the latter to the king for employment.[55] These bishops with their households of clergy and laity, their willingness to educate young men, and their ability to further their pupils' careers look forward to similar figures later in the middle ages, like William Longchamps, Robert Grosseteste, and Cardinal Wolsey.[56] By the early eighth century Bede could tell a story about a warrior in Mercia, who died between 704 and 709 after seeing a vision of angels and demons. They showed him books in which his good and bad deeds had been written, and in each case he was given the book 'to read' and did so. Bede mentions this fact without comment, implying that his readers might not have been surprised by a literate warrior.[57]

It is possible that education of a basic kind was available to lay people outside religious communities before 800. Royal and noble households were traditional places of education, in the sense of raising boys and girls in the skills and behaviour required for adult life. Guthlac, born in about 674 as the son of a Christian nobleman in Mercia and later a hermit and saint, is said to have learnt 'the noble discipline of ancient times' in his father's hall, and the epic poem *Beowulf* tells how its hero left his family at the age of seven to be brought up by his uncle, the king of the Geats in Sweden.[58] Might some noble boys and girls also have learnt letters in royal or noble households before the time of King Alfred, the first king mentioned as providing for such learning?[59] In about the 780s Alcuin wrote to King Offa of Mercia praising him for his attention to teaching, and sending him, at Offa's request, one of his, Alcuin's, scholars. He asked Offa to give the newcomer further pupils and to ensure that he taught properly – a request that may relate, of course, to a royal monastery. A second of Alcuin's letters encouraged Ecgfrith, Offa's son and heir, to learn virtue, and a third, addressed to Offa, sent greetings to Ecgfrith and urged that he be trained in the fear of God. A fourth, addressed to a nun named Hundrada, spoke of her living at Offa's court and of those growing up being taught by her moral example.[60] All four letters point to a close connection between the Mercian royal family and the world of learning, which may have been accompanied by literary studies within and alongside the family.

Lay people who learnt to read in the seventh century are likely to have done so in Latin, as clergy did.[61] Some of them must have shared the problem of the less able clergy in finding Latin difficult, and in due course a practice developed of producing writings in English that could be read more easily. This development may have begun early on. Æthelberht, the king of Kent who received Augustine's mission in 597, had a code of laws written down by the time he died in 616, the surviving text of which is in English. Later Anglo-Saxon kings issued similar laws in the language.[62] At least a few lines of the English poetry composed by Cædmon (d. 670–80) were recorded in writing, and Bede, when he died in 735, was engaged in translating the Gospel of John into English.[63] *Beowulf* was probably written later in the eighth century. It is hard to identify the readers of these texts; indeed they may have included the better educated, who read them aloud to the illiterate. Nevertheless a custom of writing in English began to emerge, whose products offered a simpler way for the less learned to gain information, whether they were clergy or laity. We shall see how this custom grew in status and extent during the ninth and tenth centuries.

THE SCHOOL CURRICULUM TO AD 800

The teaching of reading and writing in Anglo-Saxon England was based on Roman traditions. Roman grammarians recognised the elements of language and literature as being the voice, the letter, the syllable, and the word.[64] This shaped or mirrored how children learnt to read. A pupil in England would be taught to articulate sound by saying 'ah' and then to pronounce the names of the letters in order: 'a', 'be', 'ce', the letter names being the Roman ones. He or she would learn to link each letter with its written form, probably by using a tablet containing the letters and held in the hand, like those of the later middle ages.[65] There may have been other teaching aids: a Breton writer in about 700 imagined the Welsh saint Samson mastering reading in the early fifth century from tiles, apparently inscribed with letters.[66] Having learnt to recognise and pronounce the letters, the pupil would practise joining them into Latin syllables and then into Latin words. The Paternoster or Lord's Prayer was the first text learnt in later centuries, and it may have had this role from early times. Bede comes close to describing the process of learning to read when he tells us how John of Beverley enabled a dumb youth to speak. John first encouraged the boy to utter a sound, the word *gae* or 'yes'. Then he taught him to say the names of the letters, 'a', 'be', and so on. When the youth could articulate these the bishop showed him how to form syllables, words, and sentences.[67] John's speech therapy was identical with the method of learning to read.

Once pupils could read words and sentences, they could learn Latin texts from a book or from dictation. The favourite texts for this purpose were the psalms, the core of the daily worship (Fig. 11).[68] Psalms, however, were not read in church but chanted (meaning sung), and a pupil had to be able to do this too, so that learning to read soon led to learning to sing. Singing in church was largely learnt through oral tradition, since musical notation had not yet been developed. Boys were taught how to sing by their masters in school, or picked up the skill from the choral routine in church. Religious leaders were aware of the difference between good and bad chanting, and sought for expert help in making improvements. Bede tells us of three skilled chanters in the north of England: James the Deacon, who gave instruction in the manner of Rome and of Kent;[69] Æddi Stephen, whom Bishop Wilfrid brought from Kent to York;[70] and Abbot John, whom Benedict Biscop invited from Italy to Bede's monastery to teach the method of chanting used at St Peter's (Rome).[71] Most pupils probably began to read, sing, or memorise psalms without fully knowing their meaning. Only later, as they learnt Latin grammar, syntax, and vocabulary, would they come to understand what they read. Moreover learning Latin presented a problem that has already been postulated as existing in Roman Britain. Latin shared little in common with the languages of the British Isles. It had to be learnt as a foreign tongue, but at first the only available textbooks to help with this process were the grammars that the Romans had produced in the fourth and fifth centuries.

The most widely read Roman grammarian in post-Roman times was Donatus, who lived in the mid fourth century and taught Jerome, the translator of the Latin Vulgate Bible. Donatus wrote two famous works: the elementary *Ars Minor* and the longer, more advanced *Ars Grammatica* or *Ars Major*. The *Ars Minor* is in question-and-answer form, which lent itself to teaching and learning by heart. It begins, in translation,

> How many are the parts of speech? Eight. What are they? Noun, pronoun, verb, adverb, participle, conjunction, preposition, interjection. What is a noun? A part of speech that has a case, signifying a body or a thing that is proper or common. How many features has a noun? Six. What are they? Quality, comparison, gender, number, figure, and case.[72]

Even a short extract like this shows what the *Ars Minor* was for. It aimed itself at those who already spoke Latin and wished to improve their knowledge. It showed you how words fell into categories, how these words behaved, and how to use them properly. The *Ars Grammatica* made the same assumption, but had a wider compass. It began by discussing sound, letters, syllables, metre, and accent; covered the parts of speech in more detail; and ended by reviewing faults of style, faults of spelling, and elegant features of style with examples from poetry – chiefly that of Virgil.

Donatus's treatises were helpful in terms of what they set out to do: teaching pupils how to analyse the elements of language and to comprehend its relationships. The *Ars Minor* continued to be used throughout the middle ages in revised forms, and Donatus became the classical figure associated with elementary grammar, like Boethius for music and Ptolemy for astronomy. He was less helpful in meeting the needs of non-Latin speakers, because he did not have them in mind. Latin is a highly inflected language. Its words, especially nouns, verbs, and adjectives (included by Donatus under nouns), have many paradigms or variants, like *dominus*, *domine*, *domini*, and *domino* ('a master', 'O master', 'of a master', and 'to a master'). Donatus did not cover all these in his grammar. He listed the paradigms of only three of the five main types or 'declensions' of nouns and only one of the four main types or 'conjugations' of verbs. He also had shortcomings for Christians, since he did not deal with names and words from the Bible, such as Adam, Daniel, or *pascha* (Easter), and his literary citations came from pagan texts. From the fifth century onwards, at first on the Continent and later in the British Isles, these defects were remedied by revising Donatus to incorporate more material, often taken from other late Roman grammars. Biblical names were included, and some of the words used to illustrate the paradigms were changed: *musa* ('a Muse') to *ecclesia* ('the Church'), and *scamnum* ('a bench') to *ieiunium* ('fasting'). New elementary grammars were produced along the same lines. One, an anonymous work on *The Declensions of Nouns* that may have originated in England, listed the paradigms of all five declensions and gave lists of Latin nouns of each type. Two other texts that are certainly of English provenance were the *Ars Tatwini* written by Tatwine at Breedon-on-the-Hill and the *Ars Bonifatii* composed by Boniface at Nursling. Both followed the format of the *Ars Minor* but were original works, taking and synthesising material from other classical grammarians and doing more justice to paradigms. Manuscripts show that both works circulated on the Continent, although neither appears to have been widely employed.[73]

Anglo-Saxon students of Latin, therefore, were likely to use Donatus in an expanded or revised form. This taught them what was later known as 'accidence': the forms of Latin words. Along with their accidence they needed to acquire vocabulary and to be able to check spellings and meanings of words. These requirements were achieved by means of glossaries: lists of Latin words with Latin definitions, arranged alphabetically, by topic, or according to sources (difficult words from a particular text). Bede himself wrote a work of this kind, *On Orthography*, which listed words whose spellings, paradigms, meanings, or uses called for explanations.[74] By the eighth century such glossaries were sometimes provided with the equivalent words in English.[75] Once pupils had a reasonable command of grammar and vocabulary, they would be made to translate from Latin, compose in it, and read Latin texts. The psalms and Bible passages were probably the commonest texts for reading purposes. What else was read in schools in the seventh and eighth centuries is difficult to say, but the list is likely to have embraced late Roman works of Christian poetry that are known to have been popular in England. These included the *Four Books of the Gospels* by Juvencus and the *Easter Song* by Caelius Sedulius, which both retell the life of Christ, Arator's version of The Acts of the Apostles, and the *Epigrams* of Prosper of Aquitaine.[76]

The best-trained pupils might progress to more difficult authors. In terms of grammar the most authoritative was Priscian, who had taught at

Constantinople in about 500. His monumental study of grammar, *Institutiones Grammaticae*, was a prose work in eighteen books, the first sixteen of which became known as 'the greater' or Major Priscian and the last two, which formed a self-contained study on syntax, as 'the lesser' or Minor Priscian, or 'Priscian on construction'.[77] He also wrote an influential work called *Partitiones*: a minute examination of the words in the first line of each book of Virgil's *Aeneid*.[78] Priscian was known in England from the seventh century and became, from about 800, a widely respected authority to whom teachers and senior pupils turned for enlightenment. The *Aeneid* itself was read by scholars like Aldhelm and Bede, but was probably too difficult in its entirety for most schoolboys. Another advanced topic was the writing of verse: a challenging one because it involved an awareness of the value or 'quantity' of Latin syllables and the way they were accented. This knowledge could be given orally by fluent Latinists like Hadrian and Theodore, who are reported to have taught the art of metre, but such men were rare and the gap was eventually filled by books: Aldhelm's *On Metres* and *On the Rules of Feet*, and Bede's *On the Metrical Art*.[79] Both authors explained the different kinds of 'feet' or units of Latin verse, and both helped with the understanding of quantity and accent. Aldhelm provided lists of words with their metrical values, and Bede made an analysis of the characteristics of the first, medial, and final syllables of words. He arranged them according to the different parts of speech and illustrated them by quotations, chiefly from Virgil's *Eclogues* and *Aeneid*.

The fame of Hadrian and Theodore arose especially from their ability to teach a range of advanced subjects, hitherto little available: Holy Scripture, the art of metre, astronomy, ecclesiastical computation, Latin literature (both secular and divine), and Greek.[80] Bede records former pupils of theirs 'who knew Latin and Greek as well as their native language', particularly Albinus, abbot of SS Peter and Paul, and Tobias, bishop of Rochester.[81] He himself appears to have known a little Greek, since he claims to have corrected a piece of translation from Greek into Latin,[82] and the language held a fascination for some Englishmen throughout the middle ages. It was rarely studied in a full sense, however, from Bede's time until the Renaissance, probably through shortage of teachers and the competing claims of Latin. Instead its vocabulary was used as a source for coining Latin words. From the seventh century onwards there was a fashion among skilled Latinists for writing what is known as 'hermeneutic Latin' embellished with unusual words: some taken from ancient Latin, others newly invented, and yet others borrowed from Greek.[83] The other subjects taught by Hadrian and Theodore had more success in establishing themselves. Holy Scripture was obviously relevant in religious houses, and Bede wrote numerous commentaries on books of the Bible. The teaching of chronology may have been common, because it was needed to establish the calendar of the church year, and Bede produced two works on this subject as well. Other basic science could be learnt from Isidore of Seville's *De Natura Rerum* ('On the Nature of Things'): a short treatise on time, the heavens, meteorology, seas, and rivers.[84]

It is not easy to pass from the curriculum to the pupils and their surroundings. Grammars, histories, and literary sources have equally little to say about the organisation of early Anglo-Saxon schools. We do not know whether religious communities possessed schoolrooms, as they had places to worship, eat, or sleep, or whether teaching went on in spaces with other functions such as the church or cloister. The daily school timetable is likely to have been subordinate to the framework of worship in church. This framework probably allowed three principal times for teaching, each a couple of hours long: two in the morning and one in the afternoon.[85] The tools of the classroom may have included tablets containing the alphabet and the Paternoster, tablets for making notes, and styluses for writing on them. Seventh-century wooden tablets, covered with wax and inscribed with psalms, have been found in an Irish bog.[86] Books could have come from the church (such as psalters) or from the monastery's book collection (if it had one). Instruction must have been partly done in English until the pupils had progressed far enough to understand and speak Latin fluently. Bede's pupil Cuthbert, in his account of his master's last days, talks of Bede dictating to his pupils while they wrote. One of the texts he dictated was a selection from

9   King Alfred (d. 899), as he was visualised in the later middle ages.

Isidore's *De Natura Rerum*; another was a translation of part of the Gospel of St John. As well as these Bede recited verses in English on the subject of death and sang Latin antiphons.[87] Cuthbert gives a charming picture of a harmonious class, but it is unlikely that all teaching was so trouble-free. The beating of naughty children recommended in Benedict's Rule is also mentioned in Theodore's seventh-century treatise on penance, and was probably a regular punishment in schools of this period.[88]

That Cuthbert was moved to sketch Bede as a classroom teacher gives us an insight into perceptions of teaching and of those who did it. Teaching was not yet a full-time profession but a duty, carried out by someone who was primarily a cleric, monk, or nun. Nonetheless the duty was a recognised one, and there were accepted Latin words – *lector*, *magister*, *pedagogus*, and *praeceptor* – to describe its holders. Many teachers must have been ordinary clergy, undertaking the task (as Bede did) during a life spent in a single community. Equally teaching was not without status. In the early days of the English Church, when bishops, abbots, and abbesses had less to do by way of administration, it was both possible and gratifying for leaders like Theodore and Hadrian to teach, at least to supplement the work of the full-time masters. Church leaders sought the services of teachers from elsewhere. Sigeberht's masters came from Kent to East Anglia, Abbot John from Rome to Wearmouth, and clergy from Lindisfarne and Ireland to Æthelwulf's monastery. The death of a *lector* named Egric in 771 merited inclusion in a list of northern annals, alongside those of kings and bishops.[89] At least a few teachers went on to high office. Three rose to archbishoprics: Boniface at Mainz, Tatwine at Canterbury, and Ælberht at York. Lioba and Alcuin became important figures in continental Europe. Teaching in schools was to retain this relatively high status until the twelfth century.

EDUCATION FROM AD 800 TO 1100

In 793 Lindisfarne was sacked by Norse raiders. Jarrow suffered a year later. During the following century Viking raids and settlements, accompanied by political upheavals in the English kingdoms, disrupted the Church and therefore education. Four of the bishoprics in northern and eastern England disappeared and so did some of the religious houses, especially those for women. Those that survived turned imperceptibly into minsters – a word that was the English equivalent of 'monastery' but is often used by historians to indicate religious communities less tied to traditional monastic practices.[90] Their clergy might live separately in houses, own property individually, move more freely in the world, and even marry and have families. Minster communities resembled monasteries, however, in supporting daily worship and in needing to educate their members for that purpose. How that education was provided is unclear. We know little about either monasteries or minsters during the ninth century, and historians' assessments of their

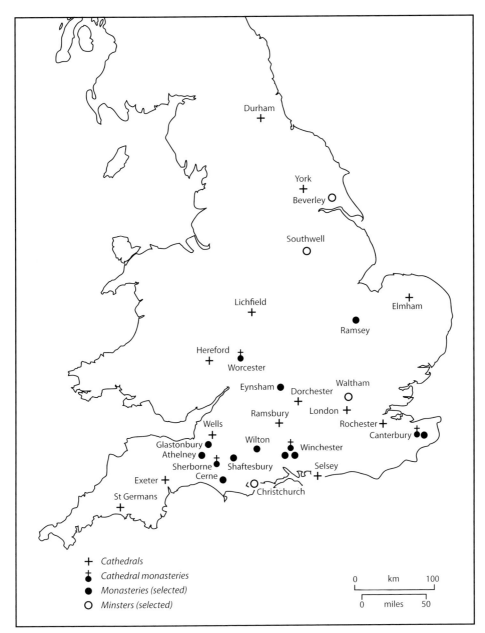

Durham
✝

York
✝
Beverley ○

Southwell
○

Lichfield
✝
Elmham
✝

●
Ramsey

Hereford
✝
Worcester

Eynsham ●
Dorchester
Waltham
○

Ramsbury
London ✝

Wells
Rochester ✝
Canterbury ✝ ●●

Glastonbury ●
Wilton ●
Winchester

Athelney ●
✝ ●●

Sherborne
Shaftesbury
Selsey

Exeter ✝
Cerne ●
✝

St Germans
✝
Christchurch ○

✝ Cathedrals
✝● Cathedral monasteries
● Monasteries (selected)
○ Minsters (selected)

0   km   100
0   miles   50

10   Education in England, 800–1066.

culture owe a good deal to the famous retrospective view of it outlined by Alfred, king of Wessex (southern England), in his translation of Pope Gregory's *Pastoral Care*, made in about 890.

Alfred prefaced this work with a gloomy account of learning in England in his own day. Once, he claimed, the country had enjoyed a golden age when kings obeyed God and kept the peace, and when the clergy were eager to teach, learn, and worship. People from abroad had come to it in search of wisdom and instruction. Since then learning had declined so much that in recent times few men to the south of the River Humber (midland and southern England) could understand the meaning of the Latin services or translate from Latin into English. Alfred thought that hardly more existed to the north of the Humber, and said that he could not remember there having been one to the south of the River Thames (in his own kingdom) when he became king in 871.[91] There is a little evidence to support these assertions.[92] It has been noted that the Latin charters produced at Christ Church (Canterbury) between the 860s and 880s exhibit falling standards in their calligraphy, spelling, and drafting.[93] Alfred himself grew up in a modestly learned environment. His biographer Asser tells a famous story of Alfred's mother promising a book of English poetry to whichever of her sons could 'learn' it first. Alfred did so, but his learning was evidently restricted, since Asser states that he was *illiteratus* until his twelfth year, due to the negligence of his parents and tutors. *Illiteratus* may mean illiterate altogether or unlearned in Latin, implying that the younger Alfred 'read' his mother's book by heart or, at most, in English. Whichever was the case, the episode hardly suggests that his father, King Æthelwulf of Wessex, maintained a household school of much significance.[94] But we know too little of contemporary learning to be able to test Alfred's remarks. Broad and sweeping, they are a sign of his desire to reform it rather than a trustworthy account of what it was like.

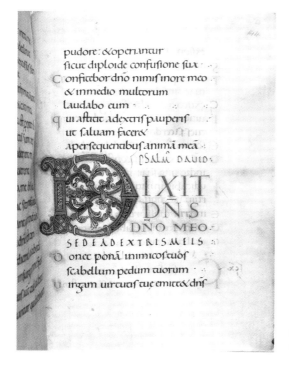

11   A tenth-century pslater, a popular text for teaching reading until well after the Reformation.

Alfred evolved three strategies to deal with the decline that he perceived. One was to revive monasticism. He established a monastery for men at Athelney, but encountered problems in staffing it. Noble and freeborn adults would not take up the monastic life, and he was obliged to draft in foreigners and children.[95] Athelney never became a religious community of the first rank, and no similar foundations were made for several decades. Alfred planned another religious house for men, the New Minster at Winchester, but this was instituted after his death as a minster, not as a monastery. He also founded an abbey for women at Shaftesbury, and his queen established one at Winchester, but here too the initiatives failed to stimulate others. His second strategy centred on developing education in the royal household. Alfred's sons Edward and Æthelweard went to school there, as did his daughter Ælfthryth, various boys gathered by the king from among his nobility, and others of lesser birth. The pupils in the household learnt skills that included the reading of texts in Latin and English and the ability to write. Tutors were employed, perhaps both male and female, and Alfred himself took part in teaching reading. He assigned one eighth of his revenues to the cost of this 'school' as Asser terms it, but its history after his death is elusive.[96]

The king's third strategy was to encourage writing and reading in English as well as, or instead of, Latin.[97] This happened in the royal household school, where Edward and Ælfthryth are said to have learnt books in English, especially poetry, and Asser claimed that the practice spread elsewhere through the king's command that the sons and servants of his illiterate nobility should read to them in English.[98] Alfred encouraged the making of translations from Latin, such as his own *Pastoral Care*, and the writing of history in English developed during his reign in the form of the famous *Anglo-Saxon Chronicle*. This linguistic strategy was the most effective of the three, because it built on tradition. The custom of writing in English appears to have been growing during the ninth century, the date of the earliest surviving charters and wills in the language.[99] Producing such records in English may point to a wider demand for literary texts than Latin could satisfy, and to a growth of literacy in English that needs to be weighed alongside the alleged decline of Latin. The impetus of the strategy to encourage English writings outlasted Alfred's death in 899. When a religious revival began in England some thirty years later, its leaders sought to establish better standards of Latin education, but some of them, such as Ælfric of Eynsham, Byrhtferth, and Wulfstan, also tried to reach a larger audience through composing and translating works in English.

The revival grew in part from the achievements of Alfred's successors as kings of Wessex in extending their control over the rest of England. By the middle of the century they had brought the country under a single ruler for the first time, and more peaceful conditions ensued until the 980s. A new generation of clergy rediscovered the appeal of monasticism.[100] One of the

pioneers in this respect was Dunstan, who adopted the monastic life at
Glastonbury in about the late 930s.[101] A second was Æthelwold, who joined
him as a monk there shortly afterwards.[102] Others were Oda, archbishop of
Canterbury, and his nephew Oswald, both of whom took monastic vows in
France at Fleury-sur-Loire, in about the early 940s and 950s respectively.[103]
These men were supported in reviving monasticism by the contemporary
kings of England: Eadred (946–55) and more notably Edgar (959–75).
Dunstan established it at Glastonbury during the 940s, and later, when he
became archbishop of Canterbury, at Christ Church (Canterbury).
Æthelwold introduced it at Abingdon in about 954, and in 963, as bishop of
Winchester, forcibly installed monks at his cathedral and the adjoining New
Minster, displacing the minster clergy who had served these houses
previously. Oswald, who rose to be bishop of Worcester, founded Ramsey
Abbey in about 969 and brought monasticism to Worcester Cathedral. By
the end of the tenth century the monastic life was observed in about forty
religious houses of men, mostly former minsters, and in about a dozen
houses of women – now made up of women alone, not double foundations.
The latter included the two abbeys that Alfred and his wife had founded at
the end of the ninth century.[104]

An important influence on the monastic revival came from the Rule of St
Benedict, and from this time onwards it is possible to talk of English
Benedictine monasteries (Fig. 5). The revival involved education, and its
leaders saw good teaching and book resources as essential elements of a
fervent spiritual life. Æthelwold invited monks from Corbie in France to
instruct the monks of Winchester to sing, and personally helped to teach
them literary subjects while he was bishop. Oswald sent to Fleury for a
schoolmaster for Ramsey, and was given Abbo, who had studied at Paris and
Reims.[105] Abbo stayed in England for two years (985–7), before returning to
Fleury where he rose to be abbot. The teacher best known nowadays, Ælfric
of Eynsham, named from the monastery that he later headed, was a pupil
of Æthelwold and spent his teaching career at the abbey of Cerne
(c.987–1005).[106] The monastic reformers did not produce an educational
guide for their followers, but in about 970 a Church council at Winchester
approved a code of religious observances for monasteries, called the
Regularis Concordia ('Harmonisation of the [Monastic] Rule'). This included
directions for the care and duties of monastic children. They were to be
looked after by a guardian (*custos*), and never to be alone with an adult
monk, even the guardian, presumably for fear of sexual temptation. In
church they were to form two groups, stationed on either side of the choir,
each group having a master whose duties would have encompassed teaching
them to chant psalms and read lessons. They are mentioned as attending at
least three of the eight daily monastic services – a sign that they were
envisaged as trainee monks. They went to bed, like the monks, in what to us
would be the early evening and had to rise at midnight, as the monks did,

for the service of matins or nocturns. When this was over they were allowed to leave, presumably to return to bed, while the adults said the service of lauds. They had special duties of reading and singing during Holy Week (the week leading up to Easter), and on Easter Day itself.[107]

Towards the end of the tenth century there was a renewal of Viking attacks, which lasted until 1016. The monastic revival slackened, and only a few monasteries were founded or converted during the period between 1000 and the Norman Conquest of 1066. Most religious houses in England continued to be minsters during this period, staffed by canons, priests, or clerks (Fig. 10). The seventeen cathedrals of the period fell into this category,[108] except for the four that had been monasticised: Christ Church (Canterbury), Sherborne, Winchester, and Worcester. There were at least a couple of hundred other minsters, enjoying a modest prosperity in the eleventh century that was marked by some rebuilding and re-endowment.[109] It is harder to define the educational role of the minsters, however, than it is that of the monasteries. Minsters were less uniform in their customs and we know little about their cultural life until the middle of the eleventh century, when they too began to be affected by a reform movement. One of the leaders of this reform was Leofric, bishop of Crediton, who moved his cathedral to Exeter in 1050. Another was Earl Harold, the future King Harold II, who founded an important new minster at Waltham in the 1060s.

Leofric wished the clergy of Exeter to make a fresh start in terms of their life and behaviour, and he turned for this purpose to a text now known as the 'Enlarged Rule of Chrodegang'. The rule originated with Chrodegang, bishop of Metz, who devised it for his cathedral clergy in the mid eighth century. Chrodegang was influenced by the Rule of St Benedict, and sought to make the clergy of Metz adopt a life approaching that of monks. They were to renounce personal property, dwell within an enclosed area, share a common life in dormitory, refectory, and cloister, and worship in church, all on monastic lines. The rule was expanded with legislation from a Church council held at Aachen in 817, and in this form, the 'Enlarged Rule', it was translated into English in the eleventh century.[110] Leofric's copy of the translation survives, and the early history of Exeter Cathedral confirms that he introduced it there. It seems likely to have come into use at some other major churches during the second half of the eleventh century, such as the cathedrals of Hereford, St Paul's (London), Wells, and York, the minsters at Beverley and Southwell in the north, and those of Christchurch and Waltham in the south.[111] The 'Enlarged Rule' had a chapter about the bringing up and care of children, which was not dissimilar to the monastic template except that it did not mention their participation in worship. It visualised each church as having a number of boys and adolescents, training to become its adult clerics. They were to share a chamber where they were locked in (presumably at night) to keep them from youthful escapades outside. An adult brother of good conduct was to supervise their life, but their teaching (meaning their schooling) could be deputed to somebody else. If the supervisor was negligent, or involved them with anything corrupt or unfitting, he was to be removed and replaced.[112]

Something is also known about minster schooling at Harold's foundation at Waltham, albeit from a much later source – a history of the house written soon after 1177 when it was converted into a monastery. The author of the history was one of the former minster clergy, who wished to place on record how they had been founded and what they had achieved. He tells us that Earl Harold increased the clergy of Waltham from two to thirteen: a dean and twelve canons. Hearing that churches in Germany were subject to carefully drawn up rules, Harold chose as one of the senior canons a certain Master Adelard, a native of Liège who had been a student at Utrecht. This was done so that Adelard could establish at Waltham the rules and customs of the churches in which he had been educated.[113] The chronicler does not say that Adelard acted as schoolmaster, a fact asserted only by a later writer who wrote a highly romantic 'Life of Harold' in about 1200.[114] The original teacher may have been Ailric 'Childmaster' [*Childemaister*], another senior canon, who went with a colleague to beg the body of Harold from William the Conqueror after the battle of Hastings, and brought it back to Waltham.[115] In the 1120s Adelard's son, Master Peter, acted as a teacher. By Peter's time there were a number of boys attached to Waltham, whom he taught 'in accordance with the methods of the Germans' to read, sing, and compose verse, implying that they reached a good standard of Latin. The boys took part in the daily services in church, reading lessons and chanting, and behaved with as much dignity as if they were in a monastery.[116] The chronicler describes them as if they were members of the church foundation, like the boys in the 'Enlarged Rule of Chrodegang', and we are left in doubt as to whether the schoolmaster of Waltham was available to teach boys from outside the church – a question to which we shall have to return.

During the tenth and eleventh centuries another kind of church spread widely across England: the small local church staffed by a single priest. Hitherto, from 600 to about 900, the ministry of the Church to lay people had been chiefly provided by the monks and clergy of monasteries and minsters. These churches served large areas, involving travel by the clergy to the people or by the latter to the church, although there were some subordinate churches or chapels. After about 900 this situation changed, as more and more small churches were built and gradually took over the pastoral duties of their bigger and older sisters. The process is referred to in a code of laws issued by King Edgar in 960–2, which talks not only of minsters but of churches with graveyards belonging to local lords, and similar churches without graveyards.[117] Several forces may have propelled this change, including the breaking up of large estates, the formation of more villages, and the growth of towns, but it was facilitated by the introduction of the tithe system. This required lay householders to pay a tenth of their agricultural produce to the cleric or clergy of their church, enabling the new small churches to be staffed by resident priests. Gradually these churches gained independent status, with their own parishes. The large parishes of the monasteries and minsters were subdivided, and many minsters declined into churches of one clergyman. The classic English parish system developed. In the countryside, except for the wilder upland regions, there was a church every few miles with a single priest in charge of a relatively small territory. In the towns there were often several such churches.[118]

This process had an educational outcome. It brought into existence a large body of clergy – several thousand of them by 1066, more than the number of clergy in minsters and monasteries. Nor was this all, since each parish priest required a clerk to help him. Church services were dialogues for at least two people, and because services were in Latin, an assistant was needed who could at least read and pronounce that language effectively. On the one hand parish clergy needed to be educated; on the other, once trained, they had the potential to act as teachers themselves. Their primary role in this respect was to instruct their parishioners in prayer and behaviour, which did not involve literacy, but as literate men they could, if appropriate, pass on this skill to others. English Church leaders seem to have become aware of this new larger class of parish clergy towards the end of the tenth century, and sought guidance in how to deal with them from France, where there had been such clergy for a long time. Theodulf, archbishop of Orléans (d. 821), had issued *Capitula* or rules for his clergy, which touched on education. No priest was to entice or receive the clerk belonging to another. If a priest wished to put his nephew or relative to school at a church under the bishop's control, he was free to do so. Priests, both in towns and the countryside, should hold schools, and if people wished their children to learn letters, the priests should not refuse to receive and teach them. They should decline any reward for doing so, except for what parents might voluntarily give them.[119]

Theodulf's legislation reached England, and although it was apparently not re-enacted formally by Church councils, it circulated in Latin and English versions.[120] Its most authoritative reissue was made by Wulfstan, archbishop of York and bishop of Worcester, in the first few years of the eleventh century. Two versions of this exist: a Latin 'Sermon to Priests' drafted for Wulfstan by Ælfric of Eynsham, and a code of practice for clergy written in English and subsequently known as the 'Canons of Edgar'. The 'Sermon' tells priests that they should teach boys and adolescents or young men, and receive help from them in ecclesiastical work. Priests ought to be masters and teach pupils: 'not carnal children but spiritual ones'.[121] The 'Canons' state that 'it is right that priests should readily teach the young and instruct them in skills, so that they may have help in church'. No priest should receive the scholar (*scolere*) of another priest without permission.[122] Neither text contains the word 'school', perhaps because the idea of a school outside a religious house was less familiar in England than in France, and the advice to priests to teach is not precisely linked with teaching letters. Yet the fact that the 'Canons' use the word 'scholar' and talk about help in church suggests that parish clergy were envisaged as teaching their clerks to read. There is a good deal of evidence in later centuries that parish clerks were trainees, en route to becoming priests themselves, and that they were expected to gain fluency in reading while working with their priests.[123] It is less likely that many parish clergy or clerks instructed classes of children. Recommendations or orders that they should do so were not made by English Church leaders in the eleventh or twelfth centuries, and although we encounter individual cases of boys being taught by priests after the Norman Conquest, it is not clear whether these priests were ordinary parish clergy or ones who specialised in teaching.[124]

THE SCHOOL CURRICULUM FROM AD 800 TO 1100

The early stages of learning in the last three Anglo-Saxon centuries probably continued along traditional lines. We still lack evidence of tablets or books for teaching the abc in this period, but a few alphabets survive in the margins of manuscripts from about the tenth century onwards.[125] These include, after 'z', the abbreviations for the Latin word *et* and its English equivalent 'and', together with the special letter forms for 'w', 'th', and 'ae' that were employed for writing in English. This suggests that the alphabet was now in common use for teaching reading in English as well as in Latin. One alphabet is followed by the opening words of the Lord's Prayer in Latin, probably reflecting the habit of making pupils learn that prayer in Latin as their first reading text.[126] Afterwards they would have practised reading the psalms like their forebears and as Alfred's children are mentioned as doing.[127] The study of Latin grammar, which came next, also accorded broadly with earlier procedures. You learnt the parts of speech and how to read, compose, write, and speak the language. You read approved works in Latin.

There are several clues as to the school texts used in late Anglo-Saxon England. The most helpful is a list of books written in the mid tenth century in a manuscript of Isidore's *De Natura Rerum* belonging to the monastery of SS Peter and Paul, alias St Augustine's (Canterbury).[128] It states 'These are the books that were Æthelstan's', and contains thirteen titles. The works look like a schoolmaster's collection which the monastery had acquired, one of them being the copy of *De Natura Rerum*. Others included Donatus's *Ars Minor* and *Ars Major* (the *Ars Grammatica*), an unnamed 'gloss on Donatus', and 'Alcuin', probably that author's work on grammar or on orthography. 'A

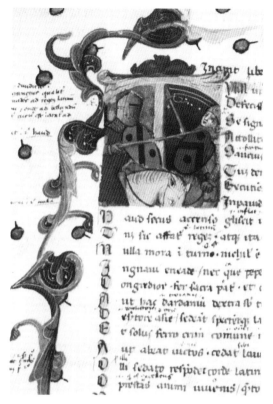

12 Virgil's *Aeneid* was a respected but advanced school text in Anglo-Saxon England. Here Aeneas fights Turnus, as imagined by a fourteenth-century artist.

little book of grammar that begins *Terra que pars?*' was a 'parsing grammar', a treatise in question-and-answer form, which made pupils take a Latin word, identify what part of speech it was, and describe its forms and characteristics.[129] 'Dialogues' may be colloquies: conversational exchanges in Latin, which we shall encounter presently. Two books dealt with the art of metre. Students who mastered works like these could go on to tackle more difficult grammatical issues. Abbo of Fleury, while teaching at Ramsey, wrote a short work entitled *Grammatical Questions* addressed to his 'English brothers', discussing Latin words with unusual formations and pronunciations.[130] Byrhtferth, who was probably his pupil and taught there in the 990s, tells us that Ramsey's young monks studied the grammarians Sergius and Priscian.[131] A text called *Excerptiones de Prisciano*, known in England during the tenth and eleventh centuries, supplied a good deal of Priscian in an abridged form, together with material from Donatus, Sergius, and Isidore of Seville.[132]

The Canterbury list includes four literary texts besides the grammars. They are Persius, a glossed text of Cato, the *Apocalypse* (the Biblical 'Book of Revelation'), and Sedulius. Byrhtferth mentions his students having studied Cato and the writings of Bede,[133] and a third schoolmaster, Ælfric Bata, who was active around the year 1000, talks of Cato, the Rule of St Benedict, and the Bible, especially the Book of Proverbs.[134] Other texts are grouped together in manuscripts and booklists from the late Anglo-Saxon period, in circumstances that suggest they were read in schools.[135] The texts in question were works of poetry, some by pagan authors and some by Christians. Here too we find Cato, in other words the wise couplets in verse known as the *Distichs of Cato*, the short *Satires* of Persius on human follies, the epic poems of Statius (*Thebais* and *Achilleis*), a Latin version of the *Iliad* (*Ilias Latina*), the *Fables* of Avianus, Virgil's *Eclogues* and *Georgics*, and (perhaps for senior pupils) his *Aeneid* (Fig. 12). In earlier centuries such pagan literature had seemed objectionable, but now that its religious threat was long dead it could be appreciated in terms of its matter and style. Moreover Christian ideas could be absorbed from poets like Sedulius, who have already been conjectured as popular in the times of Aldhelm and Bede, and from a tenth-century work, the *Eclogue of Theodulus*, which showed how the truths of Christianity surpassed the falsehoods of pagan mythology.[136] In the best centres of learning students would have proceeded to some of the higher studies that had been followed under Theodore and Hadrian. Byrhtferth trained his senior pupils in astronomy, the calendar, numbers, and rhetorical terms, the difference being that his *Manual* of the 990s expounds these topics in English for the benefit of those who could not cope with Latin.[137]

England produced an important grammarian of its own at the end of the tenth century. This was Ælfric of Eynsham, schoolmaster of Cerne in the 990s.[138] Twenty-four manuscripts or fragments of his *Grammar* are known, attesting to its popularity in England up to and after the Norman Conquest.[139] Ælfric began his work with a preface explaining that it was for children or 'little ones', not for older people. He said that it was based on Priscian (although in truth he used the *Excerptiones*), framed in the form of Donatus, and written in Latin and English so that pupils might learn to understand both languages together. In fact the *Grammar* is largely in English, Latin being used for some definitions (with English translations) and for most of the grammatical terminology. The format of the book blends those of Donatus's *Ars Minor* and *Ars Grammatica*. It briefly surveys the voice, the letters of the Latin alphabet, syllables, and diphthongs, before turning to the eight parts of speech, followed by sections on numbers and grammatical terms. As usual it adopts the improvements that had been made to Donatus by dealing with all five declensions of nouns, all four conjugations of verbs, and the many irregular ways in which nouns form their paradigms. The *Grammar* also presents a large number of Latin words as it goes along, with their English equivalents, including topical names like Dunstan, Æthelwold, and Edgar. It gives illustrative phrases in Latin and English like those that came to be known in the fifteenth century as 'latins' and 'vulgars'. 'Master, teach me something.' 'Where have I put my book?' 'The hen gathers her chicks beneathher wings.' Some of the phrases are drawn from the Bible. 'Unless the Lord keeps the city.' 'Are you he who is to come?' 'Even though he is dead, he shall live.'[140] The *Grammar* is followed in manuscripts by a glossary of nouns and adjectives in Latin and English arranged by topic: God and creation, the human body, social ranks and occupations, birds, fishes, animals, plants, trees, and objects such as buildings, tools, and utensils.[141]

Ælfric's *Grammar* was traditional in its form and content. Its originality lay in its use of English as the language of exposition – an originality of which he was aware. His preface anticipated criticism for writing a grammar in English, and he defended himself by saying that his book was meant only for little boys who knew nothing. Of course he cannot have been the first to use English as a classroom language. Schoolmasters must have used it since the seventh century until their pupils were fluent enough to be taught in Latin alone. Pupils must have turned pieces of English into Latin, or vice versa, and Latin words in glossaries were sometimes provided with English translations. Ælfric's importance lay in taking this process further by writing a grammar in English, which formalised the use of the language for teaching and provided a model for other teachers to follow. He was able to do this because of the greater stability of usage and meaning which the language had acquired since Alfred's time. The recent political unification of England and the production of so much literature in English, especially in the south of England, meant that standard forms of written English were spreading. It was more realistic to write an English grammar and to expect it to circulate than would have been the case in earlier centuries. Ælfric, to his credit, realised this possibility and exploited it.

His use of English is a topic in itself. He regarded English and Latin as markedly different languages, and drew attention to only a few similarities between them.[142] This reflected the fact that English was still highly Germanic, as yet untouched by French and lacking large numbers of words derived from Latin, particularly (it seems) the standard grammatical terms. Ælfric used only one or two anglicised forms of these terms, notably *declinung* ('declension'). Usually he employed the original Latin forms, or turned to an English word or phrase that meant roughly the same, such as *nama* ('name') for 'noun'. Thus in discussing the tenses of the verb, he did not write in English about 'the perfect tense' but used an illustrative phrase 'I loved completely', while he explained the pluperfect tense as 'I loved distantly' and the future tense as 'I love still tomorrow'. Here he may have been following a deliberate policy, as a result of teaching in a lesser monastery in the countryside. He may have felt that it would suit his pupils better to use purely English words and concepts than to give them anglicised versions of the Latin ones that would still require explanations. His approach in this respect contrasts with that of John Leland, the next pioneer of grammatical writing in English, in the years around 1400. By Leland's time English was closer to Latin, thanks to three hundred years of absorbing Latin words directly or through French, and the Latin grammatical terms in particular had been turned into English. Leland and his successors could use these terms with more confidence and draw more parallels between English and Latin than Ælfric felt able to do.[143]

Grammars were not the only school texts to undergo development in tenth- and eleventh-century England. Another was the colloquy: a series of dialogues about everyday subjects in Latin alone or Latin and English, which pupils could memorise, copy, study, translate, or even perform as a way of improving their reading and oral skills.[144] The inspiration for the colloquies of late Anglo-Saxon England came from a bilingual Greek and Latin schoolbook used in western Europe in the early middle ages, known today as *Hermeneumata Pseudo-Dositheana*, which contained passages 'Of Daily Conversation' about getting up in the morning, dressing, and going to school – material evidently aimed at schoolboys. These passages were imitated and developed in a Latin work, now called *De Raris Fabulis*, preserved in a tenth-century manuscript that may have come from St Germans, the seat of the bishops of Cornwall. This work too begins with rising and dressing:

> 'Get up, friend, from your bed; it is time, if you are going to get up today.'
> 'I will indeed get up. Give me my garment, and then I will rise.'
> 'Show me where is your garment.'
> 'It is on the stool which is at my feet (or, which I placed near you, or, which is nearby). Give me my shoes so that they may be on my feet when I walk. Give me my staff, which supports me on my journey, so that it may be in my hand.'[145]

There are twenty-three of these short dialogues, including references to a prince, a bishop, an abbot, a pilgrimage to Rome, and wars between Britons and Saxons. The same device was used by Ælfric of Eynsham in his more famous *Colloquy*, which also belongs to his time at Cerne. He starts with pupils asking their master to teach them to speak correctly, because they are unlearned and speak badly. The master asks what they wish to talk about, and they answer 'anything that is accurate and useful, not frivolous or filthy'. The *Colloquy* meets this request by introducing a number of characters, including a monk, a ploughman, a shepherd, and a merchant, who take turns in explaining the work they do. Their explanations lead to a debate about which occupation is best, concluding that we must all help one another and perform our duties conscientiously. A final discussion explores the daily life of the pupils.

 The most helpful colloquies for reconstructing the work of a late Anglo-Saxon school are those of Ælfric Bata. This Ælfric is described as a pupil of Ælfric of Eynsham, and taught in a monastery that seems to have lain near a city to which one might ride or travel by boat.[146] A hostile reference to him by a writer at Christ Church (Canterbury) implies that his monastery was either in that city or somewhere between it and London. His twenty-nine colloquies, with another fifteen that are categorised as 'more difficult', start with getting up in the morning, like *De Raris Fabulis*. They go on to feature church duties, taking a bath, meals, the monastery buildings and grounds, theft and punishment, and a sermon on what makes a good Christian. The focus of the colloquies, however, is school life, which they depict in a way that has no parallel until we reach the school notebooks of the fifteenth century.[147] The boys in Ælfric Bata's school were apparently in their teens, since he mentions the ages of twelve and sixteen.[148] Their numbers and status are not clarified, but they seem to have been a relatively small group of trainee monks involved in the daily round of services. Adding to Bata's evidence the information on the pupils' day given by Ælfric of Eynsham in his *Colloquy*, we gather that boys in monasteries at this time rose at midnight and joined the monks in church to say matins, probably returning to bed afterwards. They woke up again at about dawn and worked in school for a period. When the bell rang for the next service, prime, they visited the lavatory to wash (singing the seven penitential psalms as they did so), and went to church. A second period of school ensued, followed by the services of terce, mass, and sext, leading to dinner in the refectory where the boys sang grace before and afterwards. After this they probably joined in saying the service of none. In the afternoon there was a third period of school, followed by the service of vespers, then probably supper, and finally the evening service of compline, after which they went to bed for their first sleep.

This timetable was adhered to as much in church as in school and, by our standards, cut down the amount of time available for schooling. Contemporaries would have regarded both places as educational: the church giving practice in singing and saying the services, while the school imparted the skills to pronounce and understand what was said, together with a wider context of religious learning. No schoolroom is described as such, and it may be significant that a dialogue enumerating all the parts of the monastery includes no reference to one. Benches are the only classroom furniture to be mentioned. The school is run by a single monk-schoolmaster, who is once implied to have an assistant, but we are told little about the master, perhaps because he seemed little different from the rest of the monks in the community. There is a detailed account of writing materials, including wax tablets, styluses, penknives, rulers, ink, and parchment scraps, although some of these may relate to the work of the adult monks. Boys have individual copies of books from which they read; they also write. They are given assignments called *accepti*, which include learning the material to be read or sung in church. In due course they are made to repeat to the master what they have learnt.

Some of the pupils are characterised as lazy or negligent. They are punished by beatings with a whip or rods. A culprit is ordered to take off his cowl, presumably to strip, and two assistants are used to hold him down while he is thrashed. He is depicted as crying that he is about to die, only to be told 'You are not dead yet.' Beatings really took place; a story at Christ Church (Canterbury) told how the dead St Dunstan himself appeared and saved the boys from a whipping.[149] But the colloquies handle the subject with humour, and indicate that the master was sometimes lenient. On one occasion, possibly a feast day, he allowed the boys to play in the afternoon before vespers. Monastic boys were capable of being lively and getting into mischief. Tradition at Ramsey recalled how four of them had climbed the bell-tower and broken one of the bells.[150] Teachers tried to cope with this liveliness by choosing topics for schoolwork that would be appealing to boys. Both Ælfrics did so in their colloquies, and Ælfric Bata in particular entered into schoolboy culture. His fictional boys quarrel and hurl scatological insults: 'Goat shit!' 'Cow dung!' 'Pig turd!'[151] This material is presented without embarrassment alongside proverbs and exhortations to be wise, good, and faithful to Christ. Exactly the same happens in the schoolbooks of the later middle ages, showing that church schools did not confine themselves to what was pious.[152]

As so often, we have nothing like the colloquies with which to reconstruct the education of girls in the tenth and eleventh centuries. There were few abbeys for women in this period, but where they existed their girl recruits would have learnt at least to pronounce the Latin of the services. Ælfric of Eynsham's *Grammar* contains the phrase 'This nun is vigilant in teaching girls'.[153] Edith, daughter of Earl Godwine and wife of Edward the Confessor, who spent part of her childhood with the nuns of Wilton Abbey in the 1030s and 1040s, was later credited with having known music, grammar, and languages, presumably learnt in the abbey.[154] If such knowledge was unusual, an ability to read psalms, poems, and other works in English, as Alfred's daughter Ælfthryth is said to have had, may have been more widespread among both nuns and lay noblewomen. Women, like men, would have benefited from the growth of written material in their own language since Alfred's time. Literacy, which had begun in the seventh century as a fairly restricted and difficult skill, had become (at least in English) an easier and more widely achieved one for both sexes. There may have been informal teaching of the Latin alphabet and basic reading in Latin, leading to reading in English, about which we do not hear. Literate parents could have done such teaching, as could literate members of great households, or the clergy. The religious reformers of the tenth century, however, continued to place a value on Latin teachers in monasteries and minsters, and teaching continued to have status in the best religious circles. Æthelwold paralleled Theodore in teaching personally while he was a bishop, and Ælfric of Eynsham looked back with pride at having been Æthelwold's pupil.[155] He himself rose from the teacher's chair to the abbot's stall.

THE NORMAN CONQUEST: A NEW ERA?

The Norman conquest of England in 1066 resembled the coming of the Anglo-Saxons and the Viking attacks in being a political and social process that affected education. Broadly speaking it had two effects. The more obvious one was ethnic and linguistic. Norman kings, bishops, and lay magnates became involved in founding or reorganising cathedrals, minsters, and monasteries in England, with consequences for the teaching that went on in such places. Some schoolmasters from France made their way to England. We hear of Ebroin teaching at Canterbury in the time of Archbishop Lanfranc, and of Geoffrey de Gorron at Dunstable in the twelfth century.[156] French-speaking boys from Norman families in England needed to be taught in English schools, and brought their language into the classroom. English, in contrast, lost some of the status it had gained in schools as a supplementary language for teaching and as a medium of grammatical writing.[157]

The second effect of the Conquest on education was legal and documentary. Anglo-Saxon England had long known the charter, a grant of lands or privileges made by a king, bishop, or nobleman to clergy or laity. No charter survives from before 1066 that deals with education, but after the Conquest we begin to encounter ones that refer to schools as distinct activities or institutions. The first such charters claim to date from the late eleventh century, but their authenticity raises problems because they survive in later texts bearing signs of alteration. The oldest may be the foundation charter of the church of St Gregory (Canterbury), ostensibly issued by Lanfranc, archbishop of Canterbury, in 1085–7 but extant only in a version that appears to have been rewritten soon after 1200.[158] Another early

13   The ruins of St Oswald's Priory (Gloucester), which claimed that in about 1100 it was granted control of schooling in Gloucester.

example is a charter of Robert Malet, a Norman magnate, in favour of the priory of Benedictine monks at Eye in Suffolk, datable between 1086 and 1105 but possibly reworked later.[159] A third instance relates to Samson, bishop of Worcester (1096–1112), and concerns a charter granted by him to the church of St Oswald (Gloucester). This is known solely from a late fourteenth-century confirmation of it, which includes a proviso suspiciously late in character.[160] The evidence is therefore weaker than is desirable. It is favoured by the facts that the three charters appear to relate to much the same date, anticipate similar evidence by only a decade or two, and are plausible in what they say about schools. They seem unlikely to be wholly later inventions in this respect, although it is not impossible that one or more of them attributes practices to the late eleventh century that were more typical of the opening or middle of the twelfth.[161]

In the first of these grants Lanfranc established the church of St Gregory as a body of six canons to carry out daily worship. He also commissioned them to confess the inmates of a nearby hospital, perform baptisms and burials, and 'hold, within the enclosure of the church, schools of grammar and music for the city and its villages'.[162] Robert Malet's charter endowed the priory of Eye with a number of properties including 'the school of Dunwich', while Samson's document bestowed 'the school of Gloucester' on the church of St Oswald in the town – a church of canons like St Gregory's (Fig. 13).[163] Similar charters granting schools to churches at Colchester, Huntingdon, Thetford, and Warwick claim to originate from the early years of the twelfth century, and others survive from shortly afterwards, giving the evidence a critical mass that inspires respect.[164] These grants of schools cannot refer to the internal teaching given by religious houses to their junior members. Such teaching did not need official approval or regulation. They indicate a more public kind of education, as Lanfranc's charter suggests: 'schools of the city and its villages'. A parallel development was the formal creation of an office of schoolmaster in some of the English 'secular' cathedrals – those not staffed by monks. In 1091, Osmund, bishop of Salisbury, drew up a foundation ordinance for his cathedral, which provided for an *archiscola* or schoolmaster.[165] His contemporary Thomas of Bayeux, archbishop of York, made similar arrangements for a schoolmaster there between 1070 and 1100, and the office spread to most, if not all, of the remaining seven cathedrals of this type in the course of the twelfth century.[166] In terms of evidence, then, education moves in about 1100 from being part of the inner life of a monastery, minster, or great household to having, in some places, a more formal and public status regulated by legal documents. It is as if the modern school has emerged, because we can now talk of the schools of Canterbury, Dunwich, or Gloucester as being (at least to some extent) distinct activities.

To talk of such an emergence also calls for caution. It is based on a little evidence in a period when hardly anything is known about the organisation of education. The process by which schooling moved from being an internal process of churches and households to an external one in a public free-standing institution was probably slow and complicated. Its seeds were planted as early as the seventh century, when bishops' households taught not only their own core members but youths from outside who went on to careers elsewhere. Alfred's court fulfilled a similar role by taking in noble boys from his kingdom and sending them out again afterwards. It is likely that the education of outsiders went on in some large churches long before the Conquest, especially in minsters whose clergy had more ties with the everyday world. True, Ælfric Bata's exercises suggest that his school was wholly for trainee monks, and the Waltham evidence gives a similar impression of a school for the boys of that church. But Bata's church was a monastery and Waltham a reformed minster – neither of them typical of minsters in general. Many minsters lay in settlements and centres of administration or trade.[167] Their relatively open way of life made them suitable places for public education, supplied by a cleric of the minster or by someone else who was allowed to teach there. A public demand for schooling must have existed by the eleventh century from boys and youths who were not members of religious houses or great households but wished to be trained as parish clergy, parish clerks, and literate laity. Admitting outsiders to a minster school would have been a way of doing favours and of making money.

There is a further pointer in this direction. Although the Norman school charters had various contexts (some concerning old foundations and some new ones), they were united by their concern with cathedrals or minsters. Dunwich, Huntingdon, St Oswald's, Thetford, and Warwick were all minster churches, and Colchester may have been too.[168] Those who issued the charters evidently associated such churches with public teaching and thought the association one to encourage. This supports the view that some cathedrals and minsters had been in the habit of providing education for the public before 1066, either through an internal school or through a separate, external school. St Gregory's differed in being a new foundation, but it is possible that Lanfranc created it to carry out pastoral work (including education) that had formerly been done by Christ Church, the cathedral of Canterbury. He was engaged in restoring monastic life to the cathedral, after a period when this life had declined, and his restoration made it unsuitable to offer schooling to the public. The Gloucester evidence may reflect a similar change. There the chief local minster, St Peter's, was also monasticised in the 1090s, which may have led Samson to entrust education to St Oswald's, a smaller minster but one that remained as a body of canons. The likelihood that pre-Conquest minsters and cathedrals had schools open to public access was first realised by A. F. Leach, who argued the case robustly.[169] Sadly, the strength of the case in general cannot easily be confirmed in particular places. Pre-Conquest sources do not exist to prove it, and the Norman charter givers fail to tell us whether they are making new arrangements for schools or confirming old ones. Leach contended earnestly that a charter of Henry I, issued in 1123, showed that Warwick possessed a school before 1066. In fact the charter focussed on ratifying other rights of the local minster of All Saints, as they were held in the time of King Edward the Confessor (1042–66). Only at the end does it add that the minster might 'have a [or the] school in like manner', leaving it unclear whether the school was an ancient right or a new one.[170]

If the interpretation just outlined is accepted, the Normans continued a tradition in which cathedrals and some minsters provided schooling for the public – schooling that was gradually acquiring a separate institutional character. From this point of view the school charters may be seen as formalising practices that already existed, rather than starting them off. Much else that went on in Anglo-Saxon classrooms probably survived the Conquest without much attempt by the Normans to change it. The internal schools of the monasteries and minsters continued to provide education in England for centuries afterwards, alongside schools of a public kind. Even some public minster schools long remained close to their mother churches, spatially and constitutionally. Children were recruited and trained as monks until the twelfth century, and fundamental change to this practice took place in that century rather than the eleventh.[171] Similar kinds of school texts were used after 1066, often identical ones, and classroom procedures continued because they were so natural and effective. Schoolmasters in the later middle ages produced grammars like Ælfric of Eynsham's and exercises that resemble Ælfric Bata's.[172] Many teachers after 1066 were still clergy for whom teaching was only a part of their daily work.[173]

Equally it would be wrong to deny the Normans any credit for innovation. Osmund made new arrangements at Salisbury and Lanfranc may have done so at Canterbury. The use of charters to create posts for schoolmasters at cathedrals and to give religious houses control over education in towns brought greater regulation to schooling. Normans would have been used to the presence of schoolmasters as recognised officers in great churches, and to the control of free-standing urban schools by bishops and monasteries. Both customs were features of education in France, and it is quite probable that the Normans introduced them to some places in England or used them to strengthen what already existed.[174] Most definitely the Norman charters form a new series of educational records and to that extent open a fresh era, at least for historians. Once schools and teachers appear in their own right in documents, we can analyse their numbers, locations, features, and histories. These tasks will occupy the rest of this book.

FEATURES

prez quant il
fu maire le roy
phe lefist mert
u leroolle adopra

2

The Tower of Learning

VARIETIES OF SCHOOLS

A charming woodcut of the early sixteenth century shows Lady Grammar standing by a tower. She holds out an alphabet to a schoolboy. If he learns it, she will open the tower with her key. Inside are rooms on every storey teaching different subjects, through which he may climb to the top (Fig. 14). The world of learning in medieval England was like this tower, although it was a little more complicated than the woodcut suggests. Knowing the alphabet you could enter the building and pass through reading, song, and grammar. After grammar there was a choice of routes. One direction led you to business studies such as letter writing, accountancy, and common law (i.e. English secular law). Another took you to the liberal arts and philosophy, which eventually became the basic studies in universities. Having graduated in these, you could make further ascents to the postgraduate subjects of medicine, civil (i.e. Roman) law, canon (i.e. Church) law, or theology. No single school could teach you all these things after the Norman Conquest. There were different kinds of schools for the different stages of the tower, and different words and phrases to describe them.

All the three major languages of medieval England had a word for 'school', each taken from the classical Latin *sc(h)ola*, which was derived in turn from the Greek word for 'leisure'. In medieval English and French the word was *scole* and *escole* respectively, usually in the singular form as we use it today. In medieval Latin it was *scola*, but this is often found in the plural form *scolae* or *scole*, even when one school was meant, just as we talk of 'scissors' or 'trousers' although they are single objects. Each of the languages used 'school' in various senses.[1] Most frequently it meant a class of children or adolescents, but it could also refer to a place of higher education such as a university. It could denote the building where children were taught, or the lecture rooms for students at Oxford and Cambridge. It could describe a group of people learning or studying together, not necessarily in a school classroom. The Lollard followers of John Wycliffe in the fifteenth century

14   Lady Grammar invites a boy to climb the Tower of Learning. Donatus and Priscian are on the lowest levels, with Theology at the top.

were said to hold 'schools', which may have been meetings to discuss religious matters in the manner of a modern house-group.[2] A school could even be a style or manner of doing something. Chaucer's Prioress spoke French 'after the school of Stratford-at-Bow' and his parish clerk Absolon danced 'after the school of Oxford' where he lived.[3]

People defined schools further by what they taught. Medieval writers invented the terms 'song school', 'grammar school', 'school of logic', and 'school of theology'. Alternatively, they described schools in relation to how they were organised or how they operated. The phrases 'high school', 'general school', 'common school', and 'school of the city' are found in medieval and early modern times, denoting a large school open to the public as opposed to a small private school. 'Free school' also occurs, meaning a school providing education free of charge, unlike the usual kind of school where fees were paid. Modern historians have invented further terms such as 'almonry school', 'chantry school', 'cloister school', and 'endowed school'. Either method of classification, by schoolwork or organisation, is permissible as long as the two are not combined and confused. It would be logical to make a comparison between, say, a school for the public and a private school, or a song school and a grammar school, but not between a chantry school and a grammar school. Some chantry schools were grammar schools, while others were not.

The most widespread and best-attended medieval English schools, and the chief subject of this book, were the free-standing schools whose appearance in records after the Norman Conquest has just been described. As well as being free-standing, rather than activities in monasteries or households, they were public in nature. Anyone (at least any boy) could go to them. Their teachers and pupils were secular priests, clerks, or laity who lived in the world, not people who withdrew from the world like monks, nuns, or friars. From the twelfth century onwards these were the major schools of medieval England, embracing a larger proportion of the population than the private schools in the households of the nobility or the schools of the religious orders, both of which we shall also explore in due course.[4] The free-standing schools can be roughly divided into four kinds, according to what they taught. There were places for teaching reading and song, grammar, business studies, and higher education of the kind pursued in universities. The Jewish minority had a further system of teaching. Not every school fell neatly into one of these categories, but they provide us with a way of understanding the Tower of Learning and the institutions that guided the learner upwards.

READING AND SONG AFTER 1100

Literacy, as we have seen, was brought to England from Rome: first under the Roman Empire and later by clergy from Rome. It was literacy in Latin. The alphabet of letters learnt in Anglo-Saxon England was the Latin alphabet, and the names of the letters were the Latin names. This alphabet had twenty-three letters, lacking 'j' and 'w' and making no distinction between 'u' and 'v'. Children who learnt it in England from about AD 597, even if they learnt nothing else, were learning Latin. By the late Anglo-Saxon period, however, when the alphabet was written out for children to learn, the

Latin letters were sometimes augmented with other signs. These signs have already been mentioned: the letters called 'thorn' and 'eth' for 'th' and 'wyn' for 'w', which were used for writing English, as well as the abbreviations for Latin *et* and English 'and'. Their addition to the alphabet reflected the rising use of English as a written language. Those who learnt their letters needed to use them for reading and writing English as well as Latin.

The Normans differed in this respect. They were accustomed to read and write wholly in Latin, and the Conquest was followed by a greater emphasis on the use of Latin for written purposes, especially for official documents and religious writings. This gradually affected schools, and the English signs ceased to appear in school alphabets during the twelfth century, although they went on being used for writing English outside schools. They were replaced at the end of the alphabet by two more of the common abbreviation signs used in writing Latin, for *con-* and *est*. As a result the alphabet, as usually taught to children from the twelfth to the sixteenth centuries, was once again directed to learning Latin, rather than Latin and English together. It was laid out in a format that sometimes varies slightly from text to text, but is fairly uniform from Norman to Tudor times (Fig. 17). This is the format as it is usually found in later medieval England:

> + A a b c d e f g h i k l m n o p
> q r ʒ ſ s t v u x y z & ꝯ ꞉ est Amen.

The letters of the alphabet were always written in the same order, but not according to a standard grid. Writers arranged the letters in two or three lines, with as many letters to each line as they desired.[5]

Reading this alphabet aloud enables us to reconstruct the process by which it was learnt in class. The cross at the beginning was a prompt to make the sign of the cross with your right hand, from head to body and across the chest, and to say the words 'Christ's cross speed me', or something similar. Then you pronounced the name of each letter in turn, 'a', 'be', 'ce', sometimes adding the Latin phrase *per se* followed by the pronunciation: 'a *per se* ah', 'be *per se* buh', and so on. This meant that 'a by itself is sounded ah'. As you read through the letters you encountered variant forms for 'a', 'r', 's', and 'u', reflecting the fact that these letters could be written in different ways. It is not clear whether you said a name for the variant forms, or if so what you said. After 'z' you pronounced the names of the abbreviations *et*, *con-*, and *est* (represented by three dots or 'tittles'), and finally you said the word 'amen'. The alphabet, by the twelfth century, was no longer a mere list of letters. It had become Christianised. Saying it was a kind of devotion, beginning with the act of crossing yourself and ending, as all prayers did, with 'amen'.

There were probably several ways of presenting the alphabet to children. One was to display it on a board or a wall, like the musical notation preserved on a wall near St George's Chapel (Windsor) or the three Tudor abcs on the vestry wall of North Cadbury church in Somerset.[6] Another was to give a child the letters written on a small tablet. A piece of slate that may have been used in this way survives from Hastings, incised in the late twelfth century with an alphabet and the opening words of the Paternoster in Latin.[7] By the thirteenth century, however, literary references imply that alphabet tablets consisted of a wooden board with a sheet of parchment nailed to it, containing the letters. Later on, by the 1580s, the writing on the tablet was covered with a thin transparent sheet of horn to protect it, hence the term 'horn-book', but it is not certain if this refinement goes back to earlier times (Fig. 15). A third option was to provide the alphabet in the form of a book, and this became common after primers appeared in the late thirteenth century. The primer was a small-sized book of prayers designed for use by lay people rather than clergy. It contained the Paternoster, Ave Maria, Creed, confession, graces for mealtimes, and other material, usually in Latin but occasionally in English. Some surviving copies of the book start with an alphabet, suggesting that one of its functions was to teach children to read.

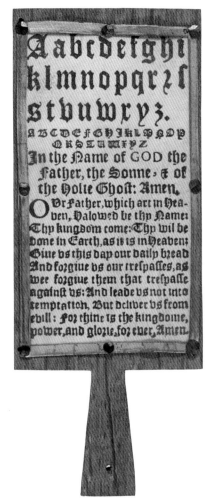

15   A replica of a seventeenth-century horn-book

The form in which children were given the alphabet would have reflected how they were taught. A wall alphabet would have been shown to a class together. A tablet or primer would have been used with a child on a one-to-one basis by a schoolteacher, parent, or other adult. William Caxton's version of *Reynard the Fox* (1481) tells how the fox pretended to teach the hare his Creed by sitting down and placing him between his legs, facing away from him.[8] An identical posture is shown in a picture of 1622, depicting a man instructing a boy with a horn-book (Fig. 18).[9] A girl might learn standing or kneeling beside a seated woman (Fig. 16). The person teaching would hold the tablet or primer in front of the child, point to the letters, and elicit answers. Alternatively the child could be given the text to study alone. How pupils learnt to read after 1066 probably differed little from Anglo-Saxon times.[10] After memorising the alphabet, they would practise how to put the letters together to make syllables and words. Some sixteenth-century horn-books and primers printed lists of syllables after the alphabet – 'ab eb ib ob ub', 'ba be bi bo bu', and so on – but we do not know whether medieval children were made to learn in this way. Many, after learning the alphabet, may have grappled with words directly. The most popular text for beginners continued to be the Latin Paternoster. This was usually placed below the alphabet on horn-books in the sixteenth century, and may have been so earlier; it was also one of the first texts in the primer. At this stage the child would be made to take a word of the Paternoster, identify and pronounce the letters in turn, join them into syllables, and finally join the syllables into words. There is a description of the process in John Rastell's play *The Four Elements*, written in about 1520, in which a comic character mocks another for his ignorance and offers to teach him:

> Lo, he hath forgotten, you may see,
> The first word of his abc.
> Hark, fool, hark! I will teach thee:
> P, a, pa; t, e, r, ter.[11]

'Pater' was the first word of the Paternoster, and may have been the first one that a pupil learnt to spell and pronounce.

A tablet had restricted space for texts, and sooner or later all readers were likely to encounter a book with pages. Up to the thirteenth century Latin church service-books were probably most commonly used for this purpose, as they had been in Anglo-Saxon times, especially the psalter, antiphonal, and hymnal. The antiphonal contained antiphons, short biblical texts sung by clergy in church before and after the psalms, while the hymnal comprised the church hymns, sung like the psalms by the clergy, not by the laity. Psalters, antiphonals, and hymnals had several advantages for reading purposes. They were relatively common, and worn or defective ones could have a second life in the classroom. They were often large in size with big clear letters, easy for children to recognise. They were texts used every day in church, knowledge of which was essential for anyone becoming a priest, monk, nun, or friar. They also facilitated another branch of learning: song, meaning plainsong. Psalms, antiphons, and hymns were sung to plainsong melodies, and these melodies needed to be learnt by pupils who aimed to enter the Church. But as in Alfred's time, psalms were also studied by children who were meant to grow up as laity.[12] We still possess the beautiful psalter made for Prince Alfonso, son of Edward I, in 1284, when he was eleven, which apparently passed to his younger sister Elizabeth after his death in that year.[13] Walter of Dinedor, a young noble ward of the bishop of Hereford, had a psalter bought for his use in 1290–1.[14]

In the thirteenth century there began to be alternative books from which a child could start to read. One was the primer already mentioned: the book of basic prayers. Another was the 'book of hours', 'hours of Our Lady', or 'hours of the Virgin': a simple Latin version of the daily services said by the clergy in church, with special devotions to the Virgin Mary. Confusingly this book was also known as the primer. There is a good deal of evidence that children, after about 1300, went from the alphabet to studying one or other of these books. Bishop Grandisson of Exeter wrote in 1357 of pupils learning to read and write the basic prayers and the hours of the Virgin before they studied Latin grammar.[15] Bishop Alcock of Ely made a similar reference in the 1490s to children in school learning graces and the hours.[16] Henry VI was given a richly illuminated book of hours in 1430, when he was nine.[17] Books that taught good manners advised young people to start the day by saying the basic prayers and the hours, implying that the texts containing them were widely available.[18]

Why did children learn their first texts in Latin rather than English, which would have been easier to understand? The answer is that the immediate goal of teaching the alphabet was to enable pupils to read prayers – a not inappropriate goal in a Christian society where prayer-books and service-books were the commonest kinds of books. After the Conquest it became normal to use Latin when praying formally, whether you were a cleric, a literate lay person, or an illiterate one. You might pray informally in English or French, but when you used structured prayers you generally said them in Latin. Everyone was supposed to know three of these prayers: the Paternoster, the Credo (Apostles' Creed), and after the twelfth century the Ave Maria (Hail Mary). In the late fourteenth century, Chaucer's time, there were some attempts to promote the saying of the three basic prayers in English, but these attempts subsided after the emergence of the Lollards in the 1380s. The Lollards combined an enthusiasm for the English language with views that were regarded as heretical. Praying in English came to seem dangerous, and most people in the fifteenth century went on saying the basic prayers in Latin. They continued to do so until the 1530s, when Church policy changed in favour of English as a result of the Reformation.[19]

The practice of making children do their earliest reading in Latin, rather than English, meant that learning to read was a different process from that of today in that it involved an unfamiliar language. Beginners at school learnt to recognise words and pronounce them, but they could not understand what they read unless they were told. Chaucer's picture of a school in 'The Prioress's Tale' depicts two pupils at this stage of learning. The hero of the story, a boy aged seven, sits in the school at his primer, learning the alphabet or the basic prayers. A slightly older boy is part of a more advanced group that is learning the antiphonal. Its members are singing the text in praise of the Virgin, *Alma Redemptoris Mater*, and the younger boy, through listening, learns the first verse by heart. He asks the older pupil what it means, but his friend is not sure. He only knows that it is a hymn to the Virgin, saluting her, and asking for her help. He explains the defect in his knowledge thus:

16   St Anne teaching the
Virgin Mary to read: a
popular image after the
thirteenth century.

I learn song; I know but little grammar.[20]

Such a boy was being taught to read, pronounce, and sing a text correctly at
sight. He would not know what it was about until he began to study Latin.
Some children who learnt to read may never have progressed to that stage.
Once they knew how to recognise words and pronounce them, it would not
be difficult for them to read a text in their own language, English or French,
because they would more easily understand the structure of the sentences
and the meanings of the words. It is very likely that, as in Anglo-Saxon times,
a large proportion of pupils took this path, especially girls who tended to be
taught informally at home. They would then read in their own language for
pleasure or information, although they would be able to read a Latin prayer-
book in the sense of pronouncing it properly, and might do so devoutly.

    The home must have been a common place for learning to read, perhaps
more common than schools. The only tools required were simple tablets and
prayer-books that wealthy adults would own or could acquire, and the role
of teacher could be undertaken by anyone who was literate: a parent, an

older sibling, and in a large household a chaplain, clerk, or governess. 'The wise man taught his child gladly to read books and well understand them.' So begins the register of Godstow Abbey, compiled in about 1450 to teach nuns to read their charters in English, and the sentence looks like a proverb.[21] There was an ancient tradition of fathers writing texts to instruct their sons.[22] The books of Proverbs, Ecclesiastes, and Ecclesiasticus in the Bible claim to be aimed at sons, and the Roman emperor Augustus was said to have taught his grandsons to read and write. A number of works were written by fathers for their sons in medieval England, which may owe something to these biblical and classical precedents. They include Walter of Henley's treatise on *Husbandry* in the thirteenth century, Chaucer's *Astrolabe* at the end of the fourteenth, and Peter Idley's *Instructions* in the fifteenth. A French knight, Geoffrey de La Tour Landry, began to compose *The Book of the Knight of the Tower* for his daughters in 1371, a book that subsequently made its way to England, and he wrote another for his sons.[23] By the early sixteenth century Sir Thomas Elyot could argue that it was 'no reproach to a nobleman to instruct his own children, or at least to examine them, by the way of dalliance or solace'. He pointed to Augustus as a precedent.[24]

Mothers, too, might take an interest in their children's education, as King Alfred's mother is said to have done.[25] One who did was Denise de Montchensey, an Essex lady of the thirteenth century. She wished her children to learn French, and a neighbouring knight, Sir Walter of Bibbesworth, obliged her by writing a treatise in verse for the purpose in about 1250 – a treatise that, significantly, later acquired the name *Femina*.[26] Small children usually spent more time with their mothers than with their fathers, and it is very likely that literate mothers used the opportunity for teaching. The evidence for this is not easy to find, but by about 1300 the linkage of women with children's reading was familiar enough for a poem comparing men and women to include the statement 'woman teacheth child on book'.[27] At about that date we also begin to encounter pictures in manuscripts, wall-paintings, and stained-glass windows showing the Virgin Mary being taught to read from a tablet, roll, or book by her mother St Anne (Fig. 16).[28] The scene is not based on any known literary source, but it was a popular topic in the art of late medieval England and Europe. It may have aimed to make a religious point – Mary preparing herself to bear the Word of God – but it may also reflect the fact that people exaggerated the social status of the Holy Family. Joseph and Mary were sometimes imagined as having noble ancestors, and depicted as living in the style of wealthy medieval families. Anne may have been envisaged teaching Mary because mothers in wealthy families taught their daughters. In turn the scene may have encouraged mothers to do so. If Mary learnt to read, modern girls may have been trained to follow her example.

Parents, of course, might not wish to teach their children, or might have insufficient time for the task. When that happened and some other suitable

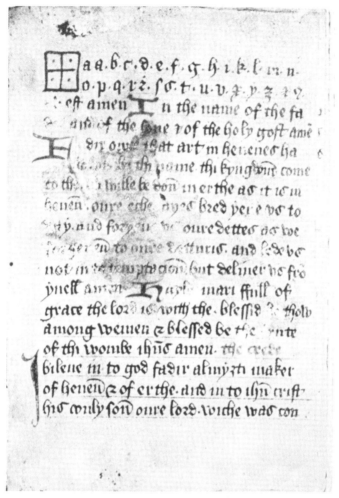

17   A manuscript primer of *c.* 1400, showing the alphabet as it was
usually presented to children in the later middle ages. Next come the
Paternoster, Ave Maria, and Creed – unusually here in English.

person had to be found, the clergy were an obvious choice, especially for boys.
We have seen how, by the eleventh century, priests were being encouraged to
teach clerks to help them with their liturgical duties.[29] Although this activity
never became compulsory and was probably never universal, a good many
parish clergy – rectors, vicars, curates, or chantry priests – taught one or more
boys alongside their other duties, without ever becoming full-time
schoolmasters. We tend to hear about such teaching by chance, when it
infringed the rights of local schools. In 1367 the archbishop of York
reprimanded chaplains and clerks in the city who were keeping song schools
in parish churches and private houses, thereby undermining the cathedral's
monopoly of such teaching.[30] In 1395 the chapter of Lincoln Cathedral
summoned a chaplain named John Austin to explain why he kept a number

of boys to teach them singing, without licence from the master of the cathedral song school. A few years later in 1408 one of the vicars-choral of Lincoln was accused of teaching three boys in the cathedral close, and was made to pay a fine for his offence.[31] Less is known about such teaching outside the places where it was restricted, but it probably went on. In about 1500 a Somerset chantry priest giving evidence in a tithe dispute recalled that, in about the 1460s, he had lodged in the vicarage of Bridgwater where the parish chaplain had taught him to 'learn read and sing' at the command of the vicar.[32]

As common as the parish priest was the parish clerk, who helped the priest in church by ringing the bell, dressing the altar, reading the epistle at mass, and saying the responses in the services (Fig. 53).[33] The medieval English parish clerk was usually a young unmarried man, often at school himself with the aim of becoming a priest when he reached his mid twenties.[34] By the fifteenth century, however, parish clerks tended to be older and we begin to hear of them teaching groups of boys. In 1442 Bishop Alnwick of Lincoln expressly conceded the right to do so to the parish clergy and clerks of Lincolnshire.[35] At the church of St Nicholas (Bristol) a rule of 1481 forbade the parish clerk to take books out of the choir for children to learn from, unless the churchwardens gave him permission – presumably in case the books were unavailable or damaged.[36] A little later some instructions for the parish clerks of Faversham, drawn up in 1506, directed that one of them should teach children to read and sing in the choir and to do service in the church, and allowed him to charge fees for doing so.[37] During the sixteenth century the teaching of reading by parish clerks seems to have become very common. In the early 1550s the English government even considered making it one of their statutory duties, and Francis Clement, in a book on elementary education in 1587, took it for granted that any child could learn to read from them.[38]

There were also officially recognised schools for teaching reading, open to the public. They were generally referred to as song schools because they taught plainsong, but it is likely that this included reading as well. One of the earliest may have been the music school of Canterbury mentioned in the charter ascribed to Lanfranc between 1085 and 1087.[39] Others came into existence by the twelfth century in connection with the nine English secular cathedrals: those staffed by canons like Lincoln, St Paul's, and York.[40] The responsibility for cathedral song schools belonged to the cathedral precentor, the dignitary in charge of the choir and music. He did not teach the school himself but gave the task to his deputy, the succentor, or to a special song schoolmaster. Song school buildings are mentioned at Exeter, St Paul's, and York, and probably existed elsewhere too; the school of St Paul's was held in the church of St Gregory, which adjoined the south-west side of the cathedral. Cathedral song schools catered for the cathedral choristers, but at first they seem to have been open to outsiders as well. At Hereford we are told that the choristers were chosen from among the boys who resorted to the song school, and the authorities at Lincoln and York who tried to restrict the teaching of song by other local clergy evidently did so because the cathedral song school was the sole authorised place for teaching song in those cities.[41]

Certain other towns and cities had song schools. Sometimes these schools resembled those of the cathedrals in having a local dignitary or institution in charge of them, and a monopoly of teaching in the neighbourhood. There was a song school at Huntingdon by the reign of Henry I (1100–35), when the historian Henry of Huntingdon, who was the local archdeacon, presented the control of the school to the canons of Huntingdon Priory.[42] At Bury St Edmunds the song school belonged by 1268 to a local religious guild, the Congregation of Twelve, and did so still in 1426.[43] At Warwick, where the chief local church was the college of St Mary, the master of the song school, there known as the music school, was appointed by the dean of the college and had to attend mass in its Lady chapel every day with two of his scholars.[44] In the Yorkshire towns of Howden and Northallerton, which belonged to Durham Cathedral, the prior of Durham is recorded as appointing schoolmasters of reading and song during the fourteenth and fifteenth centuries.[45]

The history of song schools in medieval England is not as straightforward as that of grammar schools. In the English cathedral cities, apart from Lincoln and York, we rarely hear of the song schools after about 1300. Instead cathedral records centre on the teaching of the choristers alone, without mentioning other boys. Elsewhere too the term 'song school' becomes less common by the end of the fourteenth century. This change seems to reflect two different developments. One of these was the growing use of documents in society and a probable growth in the number of literate people – the process that Michael Clanchy has called the change 'from memory to written record'.[46] The classic song school of the twelfth and thirteenth centuries may have reflected a society in which fewer children went to school and many of those who did were likely to follow careers as clergy. A single local school teaching the alphabet, prayers, liturgical texts, and plainsong corresponded well with these conditions. By 1300 literacy was a useful accomplishment for careers outside the Church – careers that did not involve plainsong. There were now many opportunities to learn reading from parents, clergy, parish clerks, and (as we shall see) in some grammar schools. Song schoolmasters probably found themselves losing potential pupils to these competitors – competitors who could not easily be suppressed because they were so common and acted for the most part in private. It may have become uneconomic for a public song schoolmaster to gain a living, even if he had a nominal monopoly of teaching, and a waste of time for the authority that controlled the song school to enforce its rights.

The other change was a musical one. Worship in medieval English churches was originally confined to the chancel or choir of the building,

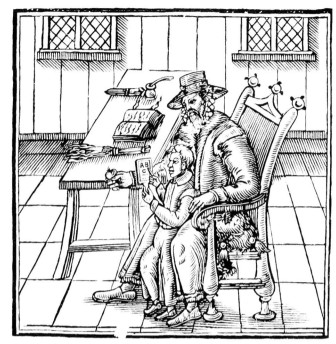

18   Teaching posture: a boy learns to read between his father's or master's legs.

where the clergy sang the psalms, antiphons, and hymns to plainsong melodies, sometimes with improvised descants. Large churches such as cathedrals employed boys as choristers, but the boys sang, for the most part, with the adults in the choir, and sang what the adults sang. Musically they were learning to be adults, and they came under the same authorities – the precentor and succentor – as the adults of the choir. During the thirteenth century large churches began to acquire Lady chapels in which they staged additional services in honour of the Virgin Mary. By the middle of the fourteenth century these services were embellished with polyphony: music in more than one part. At first this church polyphony was usually sung by a group of four men, taking three or four parts. Later, during the 1450s, the number of parts increased. Adult basses and boy trebles were added, and later still, boy altos. The number of singers rose from a small group to a large chorus of as many as two dozen. Boys, for the first time, made a distinctive and essential contribution to church music through singing separate parts, thereby acquiring the special role that they have had in English choirs down to the present day. Cathedrals diverted their choristers into this kind of singing, and sometimes increased the number of boys for the purpose. A new cathedral officer began to be employed to organise the performance of polyphony and to teach it to the boys, a person usually called the 'clerk of the chapel', meaning the Lady chapel. The teaching of the succentor and song master became less important, or ceased altogether.[47]

These practices spread to other large churches during the second half of the fifteenth century. We find them in the minsters and collegiate churches staffed by secular clergy, the household chapels of the king and the great magnates, and the greater monasteries. They also developed in the bigger and wealthier parish churches. Existing boys were redirected to polyphonic duties, or new groups of boys were established for the purpose. As a result the teaching of music became more complicated. The quality of a boy's voice came to matter more, and polyphonic singing required more rehearsal. The song schools linked with cathedrals and other large churches turned into smaller and more specialised institutions for choristers. They were no longer suitable to receive other boys to learn reading and plainsong, as had been the case in the older song schools. This is probably another reason why we hear less about such schools in the fifteenth and sixteenth centuries. There continued, of course, to be a demand for elementary instruction of a broader kind, including the alphabet, the basic prayers, the primer, the book of hours, and even plainsong. It was filled by priests and clerks teaching part-time, as mentioned above, and by some full-time teachers. A man teaching reading and song appears in Southwark in 1365, and another in Harnhill in 1386.[48] We encounter a few schoolmistresses in the fifteenth century, who are likely to have taught these subjects to girls and perhaps to small boys,[49] and an abc school is mentioned (or imagined) in Oxford in about 1500.[50] You could also learn to read and sing in some grammar schools, because the dividing line between elementary education and grammar was not a hard and fast one, as we shall now discover.

GRAMMAR AFTER 1100

Reading and song were often considered to be part of grammar, since they centred on two of its elements: the letter and the syllable. In practice, however, grammar meant the study of Latin words and phrases. In this narrower sense it had more status than reading or song, because it was more difficult and required more sophisticated teaching. It possessed a large body of works dealing with both its theoretical and its practical side, which scholars were continually developing. It was taught by full-time masters, more experienced and therefore more expensive than elementary teachers, and its schools attracted more support from patrons and benefactors. These topics – books, teachers, and patrons – will be examined later in the book, but for the present, in terms of the Tower of Learning, we must establish where the teaching of grammar fitted in. Was there a clear difference between schools that taught reading and song, and those that taught grammar? Did pupils move from one kind of school to the other, or were both levels of education available from the same teacher or in the same institution?

There were certainly places in medieval England where we hear of two authorised schools, one of reading, song, or music, and one of grammar, implying different locations or masters for the two levels of study. Bury St Edmunds and Hastings are examples in southern England, as are Chester, Howden, Northallerton, and Penrith in the north.[51] At Warwick in the early fourteenth century the master of the music school was restricted to the teaching of reading and song, while the study of Donatus's basic Latin textbook began only in the grammar school.[52] By the early Tudor period some of the more ambitious grammar schools expected boys to be able to read and write by the time they arrived. Parents bringing their children for admission to St Paul's school (London), refounded by John Colet in 1508–12, were told, 'If your child can read and write Latin and English sufficiently, so that he be able to read and write his own lessons, then he shall be admitted into the school for a scholar.'[53] This implies that such children had learnt the rudiments of learning under an elementary teacher, and shows a wish to keep such learning out of the grammar school. The statutes of Bruton grammar school, founded by Colet's bishop Richard FitzJames in 1519, take the same view. The schoolmaster 'shall not teach his scholars song nor other petty learning, [such] as the cross row [i.e. the alphabet], reading of the matins [i.e. the book of hours], or of the psalter, or such other small things, neither reading of English, but such [things] as shall concern learning of grammar'.[54] When Henry VIII and Edward VI reorganised the cathedral schools in the 1540s and 1550s, they too had a clear sense of children entering them at the ages of eight, nine, or more, having already mastered the skill of reading.[55]

Yet schooling was not always divided so neatly. Some schools taught reading, song, and grammar. At Canterbury the rector of St Martin's church was allowed to keep a school for any number of boys learning the alphabet, the psalter, and song, and for up to thirteen boys studying grammar. The fact is recorded because in 1321 he was sued for exceeding the statutory number by the master of the city grammar school.[56] In 1377 the vicar of Kingston-on-Thames was licensed to keep a school for boys learning reading, song, and Latin 'up to and including' Donatus.[57] The 1400 statutes of Winchester College, followed by those of Eton College of 1447, both grammar schools, expected their scholars to arrive already knowing Donatus.[58] They anticipated St Paul's in regarding elementary teaching as beneath their notice and in seeing such teaching as including basic Latin. One can envisage many fee-earning schoolmasters being happy to take pupils at any level. This is likely to have been especially true in small towns and villages, where there was a single teacher struggling to make a living.

When, in the fifteenth and early sixteenth centuries, wealthy benefactors began to endow grammar schools and to regulate them with statutes, they did not all exclude elementary teaching in the manner of Bruton and St Paul's. Endowed schools in the countryside seem particularly to have been designed to provide the whole range of teaching. The grammar school of

Newland, founded in 1446, admitted boys to learn the alphabet, matins book (i.e. the book of hours), and psalter, as well as those who came to study grammar.[59] A year or so later the grammar master of Ewelme was envisaged as teaching a reading class as well.[60] When Robert Sherborne, bishop of Chichester, founded Rolleston grammar school in 1524, he ordered the master to take special care over teaching his better pupils so that they might deputise in instructing boys who came to school ignorant of the alphabet and the first elements of learning.[61] A year later the statutes of Manchester grammar school required the master to appoint one of his scholars for a month at a time to teach the abc and the primer to the infants, who sat in the same schoolroom as the grammarians.[62]

These instances suggest that a strict demarcation of elementary and grammar schools was not universal in medieval England. There were places where it was enforced, but many where it was not. As so often, we are reminded that the system of education was not rigid or tidy. Numerous people offered their services as teachers, and many may have taught whatever their customers wanted. Children must have varied in their experience of education, both in where they learnt the different stages and in how far up these stages they progressed.

BUSINESS SKILLS

The grammar school curriculum was both liberal and practical. In the first respect it taught how Latin worked as a language, and speculated why this should be so. It introduced pupils to good literature and to the wisdom and morality enshrined therein. In the second it taught them to speak, read, and write Latin fluently and correctly – skills useful in everyday life. Most schoolmasters were probably broad rather than specialised teachers, catering for a wide range of needs, so it not surprising that a brand of practical teacher emerged by the fourteenth century (at latest), offering more focussed instruction for careers in trade and administration. Such instruction might include 'dictamen' (the art of writing letters), the methods of drafting deeds and charters, the composition of court rolls and other legal records, and the keeping of financial accounts. Since documents of these kinds were often written in French between about 1200 and 1400, the practical teachers came to teach French too, in ways to be outlined later in this chapter.

At least three groups of people needed to learn the arts of business. First there were those who followed careers as servants of the king, nobility, and gentry. Some were clerks who wrote letters and documents, and kept records (Fig. 19). Others were stewards, bailiffs, and auditors in charge of manors, manorial courts, and revenues of property.[63] The second group consisted of apprentices in trades or crafts that entailed letter writing, record keeping, and financial accounting. This was especially the case with the wealthier

trades of London. In 1402 a Yorkshire knight, Sir John Depeden, left £20 for
the education of a boy with the proviso that, when he could read or write, he
should be sent to London to train as a fishmonger, grocer, or mercer.[64]
Indentures, by which apprentices agreed to serve a master in return for
board, lodging, and training, sometimes laid down that the master should
provide the youth with schooling.[65] In 1450 an apprentice haberdasher,
Thomas Bodyn, asked the king's chancellor for redress because, when he had
signed his indentures eight years previously, he had been promised schooling

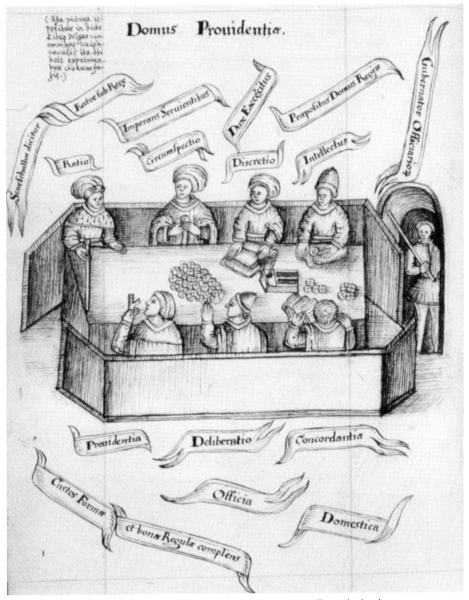

19   The arts of business: the royal counting house with money, rolls, and a book.

in grammar for eighteen months and in writing for half a year – obligations that his master had not fulfilled.[66]

The third group came from the aristocracy, especially those who came to be known in the fifteenth century as gentlemen. In their case practical studies developed a more exalted form based on 'common' or English law rather than on the arts of business.[67] These studies developed in London, or more specifically in the suburbs along the Strand where the common lawyers lived, near the royal courts of law at Westminster. By or soon after 1400 ten lesser 'inns of chancery' and four greater 'inns of court' developed in this district, the latter consisting then as now of Gray's Inn, Lincoln's Inn, the Inner Temple, and the Middle Temple. The inns housed some seven hundred to eight hundred practising lawyers and two hundred to three hundred students in the fifteenth century, the practitioners exercising supervision over the studies and behaviour of the students. 'Readings' or lectures on the common law were held in the halls, and students practised how to work in the king's law courts by pleading mock cases in 'moots', judged by their seniors. Students attended the real courts too, and observed the proceedings. Some of those who studied at the inns were gentlemen's sons who aimed to become professional lawyers. Others were eldest sons who would inherit family property. For them attendance at the inns was an acceptable way of leaving home, living under supervision, and acquiring useful knowledge for adult life. Sir John Fortescue, who wrote a laudatory account of the inns in the 1460s, praised them as being

> like a school of all the manners that nobles learn. There they [i.e. the students] learn to sing and to exercise themselves in every kind of harmony. They also practise dancing and all the games proper to noblemen, just as those in the king's household are accustomed to practise them.[68]

At this end of the social scale legal education came close to that of young noblemen and gentlemen in the king's household or in the households of the great aristocracy.

For most people who studied the arts of business the work was less pretentious and more practical. It ranked above grammar, because the study of dictamen could only properly come after learning the rudiments of Latin. Some of the pupils who attended business schools were, as today, youths and men older than schoolboys, and they were charged more for what they were taught. One of the chief centres of such studies in late medieval England was Oxford, where a succession of masters gave instruction in dictamen, accountancy, French, and the principles and procedures of the common law.[69] These subjects did not lead towards a university degree, and their availability in Oxford reflected the popularity of the city as a resort of scholars of all kinds. The origin of business studies in Oxford goes back to at least the time of King John, when a formulary was composed there for teaching the drafting of letters and documents, although in this case orientated towards the clergy rather than the laity. In about 1280 a certain John of Oxford, whose works show a familiarity with the town, wrote several tracts on the keeping of courts, conveyancing, accounting, and the writing of model deeds and letters. Similar treatises with an Oxford connection survive from the reign of Edward II (1307–27).

The leading exponent of commercial subjects in the city in the second half of the fourteenth century was Thomas Sampson, a married man whose career extended from about 1350 until about 1409. We know more than usual about his teaching and the kind of clientele at whom he aimed because of the survival of several formularies, or collections of his model letters and deeds, in which he alluded to his work, his pupils, and the city where he taught. He tells us that he was principally a teacher of dictamen in Latin and French, but that writing, accountancy, and conveyancing were also among his specialisms. His pupils were of varying ages. One model letter relates that Sampson 'has newly come to Oxford to teach boys dictamen and writing', and these boys may have followed something similar to a course in grammar, albeit with a more practical bias. Other pupils were older and needed teaching for some special purpose. We are told of an imaginary youth who has left the university arts course to learn writing and composition under Sampson, in order to go into service with an earl.[70] In another letter a man who has been appointed steward of a household asks his brother to learn to write and count, and then to come and help him with his job.[71] The older students were crammed more quickly than the grammar-school pupils, and one reference names six months as the period for becoming proficient in business studies.[72] Sums of £2 and £5 are reported as being sent to pay Sampson's fees – possibly to cover board and lodging as well.[73] He seems to have been a popular and successful master. His formularies for teaching letter writing circulated widely and were frequently copied or adapted by later instructors.

Business teaching continued at Oxford during the early fifteenth century. Formularies survive from the reign of Henry V (1413–22) belonging to a teacher who identifies himself only as Simon O., who taught conveyancing and letter writing as Sampson had done. In about 1420 William Kingsmill, a London scrivener, moved to Oxford where he too engaged in teaching business skills. There were still a number of practical teachers in 1432, when the university passed a statute designed to bring them and their students into closer touch with the arts course followed by most undergraduates. The statute provided that scholars who were learning the arts of writing and speaking French, composing deeds, writing, the holding of lay courts, and the English method of pleading, should all frequent the university lectures on Latin grammar and rhetoric. It also ordered that the teachers of business skills should come under the supervision of the university officers who were delegated to supervise the grammar schools of the city.[74] But by the second half of the fifteenth century the study of dictamen and its associated subjects was withering away. The city suffered from several bad outbreaks of plague at this time, deterring incomers, and the existence of business teachers in other towns made it less necessary to go to Oxford in any case.

For, by the fifteenth century and probably very much earlier, it is probable that legal drafting and accountancy were taught in other towns. Cambridge may have attracted such teachers for the reasons that Oxford did. A grammatical miscellany compiled at a Bristol grammar school in the 1420s contains two short tracts, one explaining the Latin words employed in deeds and charters, and the other describing the Arabic numerals and relating them to their Latin equivalents.[75] London most of all, the largest centre of commerce, law, and administration, must have had facilities for teaching those who wished to learn these arts. In 1459 Simon Eyre, citizen, draper, and sometime lord mayor, died leaving a vast fortune to establish a college and school at the Leadenhall for masters teaching song, grammar, and writing. His plans were never carried out, but his inclusion of writing probably referred to secretarial skills rather than the ordinary ones of the grammar course.[76] This likelihood is supported by comparing Eyre's foundation with two similar ones established in Yorkshire in about the 1480s. Robert Stillington, bishop of Bath and Wells, and Thomas Rotherham, archbishop of York, each founded a large endowed school in the place where he was born: Rotherham at Rotherham in 1483, and Stillington at Acaster Selby a few years previously.[77]

Both founders provided endowments for three masters to give free instruction to all comers in song, grammar, and writing. In Stillington's foundation writing was coupled with 'all such things as belonged to scrivener craft', and in Rotherham's with the teaching of accountancy. Rotherham said that he included tuition in writing so that the many able youths of the area who did not wish to enter the priesthood could be better fitted for the mechanical arts and other concerns of the world. The history of Acaster school is obscure, and when we next hear of it in 1546 the writing school has disappeared, but writing continued to be taught at Rotherham until the Reformation in 1548. Two other schools that offered to teach writing were Brough-under-Stainmore and Rolleston, endowed in 1506 and 1524 respectively. Brough provided lessons in writing, song, and grammar, like Rotherham on which it may have been modelled.[78] Rolleston's founder, Robert Sherborne, was primarily interested in promoting a grammar school, but he foresaw that dull or lazy boys might find their way to the classroom, and told the master to improve them as best he could by teaching them to read, write, and cast accounts.[79] These foundations were unusual in their concern with writing, but, as Sherborne's instructions suggest, they generally rated it lower than grammar or even song. In Rotherham's school each master received a graduated salary, in proportion to the status of his subject. The grammarian received £10, the teacher of song £6 13s. 4d., but the writing master only £5 6s. 8d.

There is a further likelihood that writing and the composing of letters and deeds were learnt from scriveners, the men in charge of copying such documents. William Kingsmill had been a scrivener himself. A man of Carlisle sued for unpaid fees 'for teaching writing' in 1436, and a boy of Nottingham learnt writing from a scrivener dwelling in the Long Row for five weeks in about 1532.[80] Nor should we forget how many people must have gained a knowledge of business techniques informally from their seniors in a merchant's house or great household. Although the kind of personal records that are likely to reveal such training rarely survive from medieval times, there is an illuminating example from the early sixteenth century. This is an application written by John Fairchild to his uncle, Cardinal Wolsey, in 1515, when he sought appointment as clerk of the works at Tournai in France. Fairchild claimed that he could file writs, enter pleas, engross legal records, act as an attorney, and conduct the business of a court. He had studied these things at Gray's Inn, London, and had practised them while working for his father. He could audit accounts and act as a household officer, secretary, comptroller, clerk of the kitchen, or clerk of the works, and this he had learnt with his father in the service of the duchess of Norfolk.[81] There must have been many young men like him who absorbed these skills 'on the job' rather than in a classroom.

FRENCH

The Norman Conquest gave the French language in England a dynamic that lasted for over three hundred years. French became one of the spoken languages of the king, his court and law courts, many senior clergy, the lay aristocracy, some monasteries and nunneries, some merchants and leading townspeople, administrators and clerks, some schools, and eventually the universities.[82] The Normans initially used Latin for writing, but by about the middle of the twelfth century French too began to be adopted in England for literary purposes: at first for story literature (chansons de geste and romances), saints' lives, and devotional treatises, and later for laws, documents, letters, and financial accounts. A good deal of French was spoken in England until the mid fourteenth century, and its reading and writing went on well into the fifteenth. Indeed, in one redoubt, the royal law courts, it was used by judges and barristers for a further three hundred years.

How French was learnt is a complicated matter. The Conqueror himself and those who came with him spoke it naturally and used it by preference, while those he conquered were natural speakers of English. This situation was followed, probably fairly soon, by a mixing process in which many people became bilingual. On the one hand Normans learnt English to communicate with those they ruled, and their children, growing up with

English-speaking servants, acquired it from childhood. On the other the wealthy and important English – the gentry (to use a later term), the higher clergy, and the ruling elites of the towns – learnt French to converse with their superiors and, in doing so, to acquire superior status. This situation was more favourable for English, the majority language, than it was for French. By 1100 or soon afterwards it is likely that the grandchildren of the Norman conquerors learnt English naturally from childhood and spoke it by preference. They now often had to learn French artificially, as English speakers did. During the twelfth century there were still many French speakers in England, including people who moved between England and France like the aristocracy, the higher clergy, and their servants. This made it possible to learn French in England by ear or by oral instruction, but since those who learnt it were already speakers of English, they tended to adopt English pronunciations and usages when speaking French. By the end of the twelfth century Gerald of Wales and Walter Map were poking fun at those who spoke uncouth French – 'Marlborough French' as it was known – and Gerald (who came of a baronial family) claimed that one of his nephews had not bothered to learn the language at all.[83]

After 1204, when the king of England lost his lands in northern France, links weakened between the two countries. French in England became even more of a language artificially learnt than a true vernacular. The anomaly developed by which French was widely used in the legal system and for writing, yet those who needed to read, write, or speak it had difficulty in learning it. This prompted the production of written treatises for teaching French. The oldest known text, which apparently dates from the early part of the thirteenth century, is a two-page treatise in Latin on the tenses of the verb *aimer*.[84] It shows how the tenses are formed and how they correspond to their Latin equivalents. Two other works, also in Latin and a few pages long, are the so-called 'Glasgow Glossary', a vocabulary with French equivalents,[85] and the *Tractatus Orthographiae*, a work on how to spell and pronounce French by a certain 'T. H.', student of Paris, who apparently aimed it at people in both France and England.[86] The Latin framework of these aids suggests that they were meant for schoolboys, clergy, or other Latinate people who needed to improve their skills in French. They were joined, in about the 1240s, by a treatise for teaching French that was itself in French. This was Walter of Bibbesworth's work for Denise de Montchensey and her children, and a most interesting one it is, the creation of a layman aware of how language was taught by the most sophisticated teachers of the day: the Latin grammarians.[87]

Walter's *Tretiz* ('treatise') bears a striking resemblance to some of the writings by these grammarians that we shall encounter in the following chapter. It is cast in verse, a popular format for Latin grammatical treatises, and is primarily a vocabulary, including a large number of French words with explanations of their meanings. Rather than compiling a mere vocabulary, however, Walter followed Latin writers like Adam of Balsham and Alexander Nequam in constructing his poem as a narrative based on scenes of everyday life. Aware that he needed to appeal to parents and children, he started with an account of how babies are born and reared before going on to describe the parts of the body, household tools and implements, and subjects such as hunting, beasts and birds, flowers, and trees. He also aimed at readers or listeners who were speakers of English, and English translations of words are written between the lines of the poem. The *Tretiz* further reflected contemporary Latin vocabularies by giving special attention to what the grammarians called *differentia* – words that are written or pronounced similarly but which have different meanings. Its account of the body, for example, starts, in translation:

La teste, le chef, both mean 'the head';
La greve's the crown, the topmost spread,
So wash la greve to keep it neat,
But have la grive ['fieldfare'] to eat . . .
Le toup's the forelock, or may mean
A tuft of flax for scraping clean,
Or toy for playing in the street.[88]

The popularity of the *Tretiz* is shown by the existence of sixteen surviving manuscripts, some of which contain additional material.[89]

At the beginning of the fourteenth century French was still widely used in England for spoken and written purposes. When Ranulf Higden, monk of Chester, composed his history of the world, the *Polychronicon*, in the 1320s, he claimed that the children of gentlemen learnt French from infancy, and that social climbers who wished to be reputed gentlemen spoke it assiduously.[90] It was used in schools for teaching Latin and (he could have added) as a conversational language in the universities. Sixty years later such a statement was quite out of date. In the interim, during the reigns of Edward III and Richard II, English developed at an enormous rate to rival French as a medium of documents and literature, and displaced French from most of the places where it had been spoken. When John Trevisa translated Higden's *Polychronicon* into English in 1385, he pointed out that since the year 1349 English had supplanted French as the language of teaching in schools, and claimed that in his time it was unfamiliar to schoolchildren.[91] In 1362 a parliamentary petition alleged that many difficulties were caused in the law courts because French was now 'too little known' in the realm, and tried, without success, to replace French by English for pleading and by Latin for the keeping of records.[92] In the following year the chancellor opened Parliament with a speech in English.[93] Throughout the second half of the fourteenth century a spate of literature in English testifies to the great revival of the language in every field of writing: devotional and religious treatises, poetry, letters, translations of the Bible, and works of scholarship.

Some contemporaries, far from approving the encroachments of English in areas where French had hitherto been used, viewed them with concern and tried to obstruct their progress. The statutes of the three Oxford colleges founded in the first half of the fourteenth century – Exeter (revised 1325), Oriel (1326), and Queen's (1341) – laid down that only Latin or French should be spoken by college members.[94] The university itself, in statutes compiled during the same century for the guidance of its grammar masters, ordered that they should use both French and English when they translated Latin words or explained their meanings, 'lest the French language be altogether lost'.[95] The French historian Froissart believed that in 1337 Edward III commanded noblemen, gentlemen, and burgesses of the good towns to teach their children French so that they would be more familiar with it in time of war.[96] These attempts did not succeed in reversing the decline of French, but the decline was long drawn out. The Hundred Years' War with France may have helped keep the language alive until 1453, when the war ended, and French continued to be used for some private letters and deeds until as late as the 1450s. It was needed in order to read many popular literary works in French – notably the main cycle of Arthurian stories – until Caxton produced a number of English translations in the 1470s and 1480s. In the chief courts of law it remained as a language of pleading, judgment, and record until the eighteenth century, and it never disappeared among those who had dealings with France and the French: the royal family, some of the aristocracy, and merchants and mariners.

Who then taught French in medieval England? In the earlier centuries after the Norman Conquest learners must often have made use of any person, teacher or not, who could already speak it. Gerald of Wales tells us of a young man he knew named John Blund who learnt it from his uncles, men who had lived in France.[97] Schoolmasters of Latin must often have taught it as well. This is shown by the presence of French glosses in many Latin school texts of the thirteenth century, by the similarity of the thirteenth-century tracts on French grammar and vocabulary to Latin ones, and by Higden's and Trevisa's assertions that French was used in grammar schools for teaching Latin up to the middle of the fourteenth century. It went on being taught to children in certain schools well into the fifteenth, notably by business teachers like Thomas Sampson and William Kingsmill. However, as its use in England grew rarer it needed more structured teaching. More ambitious treatises began to appear, which taught in more detail the different forms (morphology) of nouns and verbs, taking as their model the *Ars Minor* of Donatus. At least two such works circulated in England during the early fifteenth century, both claiming to teach the 'douce françois de Paris'. One, *Le Donait*, was the work of a certain R. Dove, while the other, the *Donait François*, claimed to have been compiled by certain clerks at the command and expense of John Barton.[98] Barton had been born and bred in Cheshire, had studied at Paris apparently in the early fifteenth century, and aimed his work chiefly at children.

New dialogues and conversations in prose were also produced at this time, some in French, some in French and English, replacing the older vocabularies in verse, like Bibbesworth's *Tretiz*. Three survive from between 1396 and 1415, one of which (dated 1399) calls itself 'a little book to teach children', while another (dated 1415), by William Kingsmill, adopts a similarly simple approach and may well have been meant for children too.[99] Notwithstanding Trevisa's remarks, French was still seen as something worth teaching to young people in Kingsmill's time. His treatise took pains to arouse their interest. Different kinds of greetings and salutations are followed by a conversation about the battle of Agincourt. Two travellers meet and ride from Tetsworth to Oxford, where they put up at 'The Mill on the Hoop' in Northgate Street. There they negotiate about board and accommodation, after which they question the innkeeper's son, aged twelve, about his knowledge and education. This gives Kingsmill the opportunity to advertise his services:

'My child, have you been to school?'
'Yes, sir, by your leave.'
'At what place?'
'Sir, at the house of William Kingsmill, scrivener.'
'Fair child, how long have you been dwelling with him?'
'Sir, for less than a quarter of a year.'
'That is only a short while, but what have you learnt there during that time?'
'Sir, my master has taught me how to write, to indite [i.e. compose in words], to count, and to speak French.'
'And what can you say in French?'
'Sir, I know my name and how to describe my body.'[100]

By the second half of the fifteenth century French had largely disappeared for administrative purposes, and its chief learners had probably shrunk to the nobility, gentry, and merchants. Members of the first two groups still learnt it as a cultural accomplishment in order to read French literature or to converse with French people, and those of the third group because of their business links with francophone regions. Henry VIII and his elder brother Arthur had a French tutor during the 1490s, Giles D'Ewes, who was a native of France,[101] and their sisters (and other aristocratic girls) appear to have studied the language in this period.[102] Lesser people are likely to have continued to acquire it from specialised teachers or by using treatises, now available in print. In 1480 William Caxton published a phrase book in parallel columns, French and English, which he adapted from one in French and Flemish, and seems to have envisaged it being used by any potential learner, adult or child, since the phrases cover subjects appropriate to both.[103] Another book, *A Good Boke to Lerne to Speke French*, was issued between 1497 and about 1500 by the printers Richard Pynson and Wynkyn de Worde. This too ranged widely, including basic vocabulary and phrases, a 'Book of Courtesy' aimed at children, and two model letters: one from an apprentice to his master and the other from a merchant to his friend.[104] By 1500 French was the language of a foreign country, rather than a language domiciled in England, but it remained the most obvious foreign language for English people to learn, and held on to a secure if limited base among the wealthy and commercial ranks of society.[105]

THE JEWS

In a niche of the Tower of Learning were the Jews, a distinct minority with its own racial, religious, and cultural integrity. They first entered England from France after the Norman Conquest, establishing a strong presence in London during the twelfth century. Gradually they spread to the other larger towns, and by the thirteenth century they were active in about twenty-seven of these – a fact recognised by the establishment of official *arche*, or chests, in such places for preserving deeds and contracts between Jews and Christians, money-lending being one of the Jews' chief functions in society. The towns concerned included the major provincial centres like Bristol, Exeter, Norwich, and York, several of the cathedral cities, Cambridge and Oxford, and some of the county towns. The Jewish population was not large, perhaps never more than six thousand or so, and during the later twelfth and thirteenth centuries its members experienced hostility from some Christian lords, clergy, and ordinary people. The crown repeatedly imposed taxation on them, and in 1290 Edward I expelled them totally, after a residence of about two hundred years.[106]

The Jews had a reputation for education and learning. A writer from France of the late twelfth century, whose work survives in England, compared them favourably with Christians. The latter, he argued, educated their sons in the hope of financial gain. Such men would become celibate clerics, and the wealth they gained from their careers would pass to the rest of their family.

> But the Jews, out of zeal for God and love of the law, put as many sons as they have to letters, that each may remember God's law. . . . A Jew, however poor, if he had ten sons would put them all to letters, not for gain, as the Christians do, but for the understanding of God's law, and not only his sons but his daughters.[107]

Our knowledge of Jewish life in medieval England does not allow us to reconstruct their education, although a Jew named Isaac, living in Essex in

1190–1, is mentioned as having a tutor or schoolmaster for his children.[108] Rather we have to focus on the outcome of that education. The large towns had synagogues, known in Latin as 'schools of the Jews' (*scole Iudeorum*), not schools in our sense but centres of worship and of the reading of scripture. Jews used books and documents like other people. Bonds and receipts issued by them to Christians survive from the 1180s. These are partly in Latin, partly in Hebrew, and occur in French and Hebrew by the 1260s. They indicate literacy in Hebrew among Jewish men, and probably an ability by some to read or write in Latin or French, unless they used Christians for this purpose. Jews' own written transactions were solely in Hebrew. Writings of this kind, from the second half of the thirteenth century, include an arrangement for the maintenance of two Jewish women in Norwich, correspondence to and from the leader of the Jews of Nottingham, and a betrothal contract made at Lincoln. In the last of these the prospective bride gives her husband a Massoretic Bible (i.e. the Hebrew scriptures with the traditional commentary). A rare surviving Hebrew prayer-book, of about 1200, contains a list of a man's English debtors, written in Arabic using the Hebrew alphabet.[109] All this shows that the Jews widened the range of knowledge and skills in England, but the difference and unpopularity of their culture meant that it had little positive impact outside their community.

HIGHER EDUCATION

Our final group of medieval schools provided higher education: the university arts course, academic medicine, canon and civil law, and theology.

20   The first university-level college in England for secular clergy: De Vaux College, Salisbury, founded in 1262.

Teachers of these subjects are recorded as gathering students around them in England from about the middle of the twelfth century. The earliest gatherings tended to happen in or near the secular cathedrals staffed by canons rather than monks, notably Exeter, Hereford, Lincoln, and St Paul's. Some leading scholars of the day were given posts as canons in such places, and they found an audience from the clerks and clergy who lived in the cathedral cities or gravitated to them.[110] Lincoln had two important teachers in the late twelfth century: the lawyer Robert Blund, who also studied and taught at Bologna, Oxford, and Paris, and the theologian William de Montibus, who wrote a number of widely copied works.[111] Two masters are known at Exeter: Thomas of Marlborough, a scholar of canon and civil law there in about the 1190s, and a certain Master John, a theologian, in about 1200.[112] At Hereford Simon de Fresne, one of the canons, wrote a poem in about 1195–7 urging his friend Gerald of Wales to visit the city, where he would find men of similar tastes and where the liberal arts were studied and taught more than anywhere in England. Simon went on to enumerate the arts and mentioned astronomy, astrology, and geomancy among them.[113]

In the long term higher education did not develop on a large scale in any English cathedral city. Scholars like the above were essentially individuals, whose work came to an end when they died or left. Locally the demand for their teaching was strongest in the areas of canon law and theology, which were of practical value to ordinary clergy. William de Montibus was particularly successful in simplifying theology for such consumers. During the late twelfth and early thirteenth centuries larger and more permanent communities of teachers and students grew up in certain non-cathedral towns of the east Midlands: Cambridge, Northampton, and Oxford. All three towns had the advantages of being relatively large, well supplied with food and lodgings, situated on major roads, and close to regions of higher population. They also lay in a part of England whose speech (the 'East Midland' dialect) was not too hard for speakers of other kinds of English to understand. At first the gatherings of students in these towns lacked permanence, and during the thirteenth century lawlessness in Oxford between the students and the townspeople, or among the students, caused some teachers and students to withdraw to other places, notably to Salisbury in 1238. There was another large secession from Oxford to Stamford in 1334.[114]

The students at Salisbury stayed sufficiently long to encourage the bishop, Giles of Bridport, to found an academic college there in 1262. It was called De Vaux (probably in imitation of one so named in Paris), and provided for a warden, two chaplains, and twenty poor scholars studying arts and theology (Fig. 20). But the embryonic university communities at Northampton and Salisbury wasted away during the thirteenth century, leaving only those at Oxford and Cambridge to flourish and develop institutional form.[115] A probable factor in this matter was that neither of the two latter towns was a cathedral city. The dynamic that created universities was a desire by teachers and scholars to organise their own affairs without interference from bishops or cathedrals. Cambridge fitted this requirement because it was sixteen miles from its bishop and cathedral at Ely, while Oxford lay 120 miles from its mother church at Lincoln, almost as far away as one could get in England. Stamford shared this feature too, but by 1334 Oxford was powerful enough to persuade the king to disperse the students who had gone there. After that Oxford and Cambridge ruled unchallenged until the nineteenth century.

The development of universities left the secular cathedral cities with a restricted role in higher education. It centred on the appointment of a member of the cathedral foundation to give regular lectures on canon law and theology without charging for the service. Lectures on these topics continued to be useful to local clergy, who did not have the time or resources to follow them at Cambridge or Oxford. In 1215 the Fourth Lateran Council of the Catholic Church, meeting at Rome, ordered every metropolitan cathedral, the seat of an archbishop, to provide a master to teach theology.[116] If this order had been implemented in England, only Canterbury and York would have maintained such teachers, but the English Church followed the spirit of the legislation rather than the letter. Virtually all of the nine English secular cathedrals came to support teachers of higher education, while the ten cathedrals staffed by monks (including Canterbury) made no formal provision.[117] Responsibility for the teaching at most of the secular cathedrals was given to the chancellor: the officer who acted as librarian, secretary to the cathedral chapter, and supervisor of the local grammar school.[118] This was the case at Lincoln by 1200, Salisbury by 1240, York by 1250, and Exeter and London by the end of the thirteenth century. Two cathedrals made different arrangements: Chichester, where a special office of theologian was created and endowed with the prebend of Wittering between 1224 and 1244, and Hereford, where the duty of lecturing was annexed by 1356 to the office of penitentiary.[119]

The chancellor or his counterpart was expected to deliver lectures personally or by deputy in theology or canon law, and something can be learnt of the circumstances in which the lectures were given. A special building for the purpose is mentioned more than once. At Salisbury the chapter built a new range over the west side of the cloister in 1454 for a lecture room and library,[120] while at St Paul's in 1465 the school of theology took place in a chamber under the chapter house.[121] At Exeter by the 1530s the lecturer used the charnel chapel in the cathedral cemetery.[122] Lecturing varied in frequency from place to place. Once a fortnight is mentioned at Salisbury in 1454, and three times a week at St Paul's in the early sixteenth century.[123] There were also terms and vacations. The chancellor of Wells was bound to lecture from 15 October until 3 July, while his colleague at St Paul's was told to teach from the autumn until Advent, from Epiphany to Quinquagesima, and from Whitsuntide to the beginning of August.[124] The audience for the lectures is rarely recorded, but the listeners seem to have included clergy of the cathedral, from the adjoining city, and sometimes from the rest of the diocese. Bishop Hugh of Lincoln (1209–35) told the vicar of Barton-on-Humber to study theology at Lincoln for two years, while Archbishop John Romeyn of York permitted the rectors of his diocese to reside away from their cures in 1293 to attend the theology lectures at York.[125] These lectures were still attracting a local audience in 1365 when Simon Langham, bishop of Ely, after visiting the hospital of St Leonard (York), prescribed that those of its brethren who were apt and wished to study should attend the theological school and be supplied with parchment for recording 'what might seem devout and notable'.[126]

The subjects prescribed for chancellors to teach were simply defined as theology or canon law, but sometimes we have more precise knowledge of the topics they covered. Robert Winchelsey, canon of St Paul's and later archbishop of Canterbury, lectured at London between 1283 and 1293 on the nature of the Trinity and the relations between its persons, questions that he had already discussed in the university of Oxford.[127] In 1355 two friars, a Franciscan and a Dominican, disputed in the chancellor's school at York about the conception of the Virgin by her mother St Anne, which the

21   A lecturer and students from fourteenth-century Italy, the latter sitting in two rows with books.

Franciscan held to be immaculate.[128] Some lectures on the Apocalypse
survive in manuscript form that were given at Wells by John Orum, doctor
of divinity and canon of the cathedral, in the early fifteenth century.[129] Once,
at least, the teaching in a chancellor's school engaged with a matter of
contemporary debate. In 1465 a controversy broke out in London between
the friars and the secular clergy about the poverty of Christ. William Ive,
master of Whittington College (London) and the person responsible for
giving the chancellor's lectures at St Paul's, joined in the debate. He lectured
on it in scholastic form, wearing cap and gown and attended by a verger
bearing a silver wand, reading, in the words of a contemporary witness,
'many full noble lessons to prove that Christ was lord of all and no
beggar'.[130]

Inevitably there were negligent lecturers and failures to lecture. At
Salisbury in 1349 an elderly chancellor, Elias of St Albans, tried to depute his
work to a Dominican friar who was not a graduate, but his colleagues forced
him to employ the archdeacon of Salisbury, a doctor of divinity. In 1357
another chancellor of Salisbury, Simon Sudbury, appointed a deputy from
Suffolk who had an appropriate degree, yet only after his colleagues
prompted him to do so.[131] At Wells the bishop found the chancellor negligent
in 1335 and ordered him to resume lecturing, but in 1348 the bishop and the
cathedral were obliged to seek a papal confirmation of the duty from Rome,
because it rested on custom not statute.[132] In 1365 the bishop of Chichester
complained to Pope Urban V that although the prebend of Wittering was
reserved for a lecturer in theology, former popes had appointed men to it who
were not theologians, so that the purpose of the foundation was frustrated.
The pope agreed that in future only theologians should hold the office.[133] In
the early sixteenth century Richard FitzJames, bishop of London (Fig. 62),
discovered that the chancellor of St Paul's had omitted to lecture, apparently
on the ludicrous grounds that he was required to do so 'continuously', which
was impossible! FitzJames was equal to the challenge and provided his
chancellor with an exposition of the word, declaring that it meant regular
lectures three times a week during certain seasons of the year, as specified
above.[134] These interventions show the weakness inherent in an institution so
dependent on one person, but they make clear that some bishops and
cathedral chapters took action to ensure that the duty continued.

The secular cathedrals were not the only churches to teach the higher
studies. During the thirteenth century the friars developed an elaborate and
effective system of schools of the liberal arts and theology for their members,
and they were imitated in this, albeit with less zeal, by the greater houses of
monks and regular canons. These schools, which will be mentioned in a
later chapter, were primarily intended for the members of the houses and
orders concerned, but the friars may have admitted outsiders at times.[135]
There were also schemes to improve the education of the parish clergy in
the fifteenth century, which led to the creation of a small group of new

institutions providing lectures, books, and scholarly advice for their benefit. The pioneering project was the Guildhall Library in London, founded by the executors of Sir Richard Whittington and William Bury, citizens and mercers of London who died in 1423. The leading executor was John Carpenter, the clerk to the corporation of the city, but it is impossible to say how far the library was his idea or that of Bury or Whittington.[136] Opened in or shortly before 1425, it was linked to the college of priests attached to the London Guildhall, the centre of city government. Two of the priests were paid to look after the library, a collection of chained volumes, chiefly Latin works of theology, which was open to all comers, most of whom were probably parish clergy. We are told that the place was a resort of students who wished to be educated in Holy Scripture. The foundation must have been popular since it received several gifts of money and books during the fifteenth century, and it functioned until the Guildhall College was dissolved at the Reformation in 1548. According to the historian of London, John Stow, the Lord Protector, Edward duke of Somerset, then sent for the library books, which were loaded onto three carts 'with promise to be restored shortly', but they were never returned.[137]

The Guildhall Library may have been the inspiration for some other library foundations of the same period. One was planned nearby at St Paul's Cathedral in 1457 as the result of a bequest by one of the cathedral canons, Walter Sherington (d. 1449). His executors founded a chantry of two graduate priests at the cathedral, and a library above the cloister known as Pardonchurch. The priests were required to open the library to the public from sunrise to 9 a.m. and from 1 p.m. to sunset, but we have no record of whether it functioned or what it contained.[138] Two further libraries were initiated at Bristol and Worcester by another John Carpenter, bishop of Worcester (1443–76), who had spent part of his early career in London.[139] He had been master of the hospital of St Anthony in the city and had been closely involved with his namesake the town clerk, who may have been his relative. A fifth foundation was in prospect at Norwich in 1462, when a local priest bequeathed it a volume if it should be established.[140] The then bishop of Norwich, Walter Lyhert, was an Oxford contemporary of Bishop Carpenter and succeeded him at St Anthony's, which suggests a link with the other schemes, but it is not known if this library came into being.

Bristol, Norwich, and Worcester were all suitable places for establishing institutions of higher education. Norwich and Worcester had monastic cathedrals, and therefore lacked chancellors to lecture on theology. Bristol offered challenges of another kind. It was the largest town in England without a cathedral or a resident bishop and lay on the edge of the diocese of Worcester, making supervision difficult. It supported nearly a hundred parish clergy, for whom some sort of instruction was desirable, and had a strong tradition of Lollardy, which made it an obvious target for orthodox teaching. Carpenter used two existing foundations as the basis for his schemes: the Carnary Chapel built over the charnel of Worcester Cathedral cemetery, and the guild of Kalendars based in a house next to the church of All Saints (Bristol), staffed by four chantry priests. In 1464, with the consent of the patrons of each foundation, he established a library in both places, consisting of chained volumes, apparently of theological works, open to public access on weekdays from 10 a.m. until 2 p.m. These times were the opposite of those at St Paul's, which specifically excluded the middle of the day.

Carpenter gave the care of his libraries to the chaplain of the Carnary Chapel and to the prior or master of the guild of Kalendars, both secular priests. Like Sherington, he laid down that each priest should be a university graduate, preferably a bachelor of theology, and he required them to supervise the library, expound obscure and difficult points of theology to readers, and deliver a theological lecture in the library once a week. The Carnary Library remained in being until the Reformation. It was served by a succession of graduate chaplains, and weekly lectures were still being given there in 1539 when the foundation came to an end with the dissolution of the monastic cathedral. The success of the Bristol scheme is harder to gauge. There was a distinguished series of graduate priors at the guild in the second half of the fifteenth century, and the library seems to have been in existence in 1480. Later the academic credentials of the priors were more varied, and evidence about their work is lacking. When information about the house was being collected in 1548, at the time that chantries and religious guilds were abolished by the government of Edward VI, no reference was made to either the library or the lectures.

It was still possible, therefore, for a secular clerk or priest in the fifteenth century to study theology at an elementary level without going to a university, in one of the dozen or so local centres which have been mentioned. The same applied to monks and friars, for whom the private schools of their orders were available. John Rous, the Warwick historian, writing in about 1486, believed that 'today, fruitful lectures and disputations are held in cathedral churches and some noble colleges, and in the friaries of the four mendicant orders'.[141] The teaching of theology on a local basis continued to find approbation during Tudor times. In the cathedral sector, Exeter, St Paul's, and Salisbury are all known to have continued or revived the provision of lectures in the early sixteenth century.[142] John Hooker, the post-Reformation Protestant historian of Exeter, praised the lectures given there in the 1530s by Canons Robert Tregonwell and Robert Weston as profitable and innovative. The Reformation was a catastrophe for lecturing in monasteries, friaries, and the fifteenth-century libraries, but the cathedral lectures escaped a similar fate. Henry VIII not only spared the nine secular foundations but transformed the eight former monastic ones and six other monasteries into similar bodies. During the reigns of his children, Edward VI, Mary I, and Elizabeth I, royal visitors to the cathedrals ordered that lectures should take place, in both the old foundations and the new.[143] The unobtrusiveness of cathedral lectures may mislead us about their importance. Many people, for a very long time, regarded them as useful and worth preserving.

3

The Teaching of Grammar

THE NORMAN CONQUEST

We must now retrace our steps down the Tower of Learning to grammar – the study of Latin, the one part of the building we have not explored. Not everyone who learnt to read learnt grammar. Many who mastered the alphabet in England after the Conquest may have been content to use it to access French or English, or to look at Latin words and say them without fully knowing their meaning. Yet grammar was very important. It was the chief concern of formal schooling, to which reading and song were only introductions. Most professional schoolmasters taught it, and thousands of schoolboys at any one time were learning it. It gave you the knowledge that you needed to be a credible king, nobleman, gentleman, cleric, merchant, lawyer, or administrative clerk. First we shall look at what grammar consisted of between the Conquest and the Reformation; then, in the following chapter, at how it was learnt in the classroom.

In one sense the teaching of Latin in England forms a continuous story from about the year 600 to the middle of the nineteenth century, when the leading English schools stopped teaching virtually nothing but Latin and Greek. Like all long-lasting traditions, however, this teaching changed with time, both in what it taught and in how it did so. The Norman Conquest itself helped bring about change. The teaching of grammar in Anglo-Saxon England had always had links with similar teaching in Europe. Latin textbooks from Donatus onwards had crossed the English Channel. Foreign teachers and students had done the same, and English ones had travelled the opposite way. But the Conquest greatly strengthened such links and kept them strong for the next two hundred years. Norman bishops and barons helped to organise or reorganise the English schools whose origins we have just traced. Some continental masters taught in these schools, and some French-speaking students studied in them. More widely, the Conquest helped bring England more closely within the common culture of western Europe. This culture, from 1066 to 1250, was a highly international one. The Church was growing more centralised under papal leadership. Crusades drew in knights from many countries, and new religious orders spread across national frontiers. Grammar shared in this process. Students travelled to study or teach it, especially to Paris, and new textbooks by French, Italian, German, and even English grammarians circulated widely over the Continent. Many of the key works used in western schools until the Renaissance date from this period.

At first, the Norman Conquest need not have involved much change in the way that grammar was taught in England, or in the kinds of authors read in schools. These were broadly similar in France and England, except that England was unusual in having a grammar like Ælfric's in its own language. Rather change came about in the relative status of the Latin and English languages, and through the presence of French. The Normans were more used than the English to reading and writing wholly in Latin. France lagged behind England in the extent to which the local speech was used for written purposes, although it caught up during the twelfth century. This difference may have caused schools in England after the Conquest to place more emphasis on making their pupils fully conversant with Latin rather than partially reliant on reading in English. Ælfric's grammar must have kept a place in some classrooms, since three surviving copies of it contain French glosses added during the twelfth century. This shows that the work was used by people who either spoke French or were engaged in learning it.[1] But the experiment of writing a Latin grammar in English was not repeated. After 1066 all the new texts that made their way into English grammar schools were wholly in Latin, and no others appeared in English until the end of the fourteenth century.[2]

Ranulf Higden's description of the status of the French language in England in the 1320s has already been mentioned.[3] Some of his words on the subject have become well known. 'Children in schools, since the coming of the Normans, are compelled to translate [Latin] into French, to the forsaking of their own common language, against the custom of the rest of the nations.' John Trevisa, who translated Higden into English in 1385, endorsed this view, saying that 'this manner [of teaching] was much used up to the [Black] Death', but adding that the tradition changed in the second half of the fourteenth century.[4] Higden's remarks almost certainly oversimplify the ways that French and English were used in schools after 1066. Speakers of French were dominant in England politically, but speakers of English were dominant numerically. There must have been some pupils in English grammar schools after the Conquest whose preferred language was French, yet the majority would have been natural speakers of English. Most teachers would have been obliged to go on explaining Latin in English, and pupils to translate Latin into English and vice versa, at least at the elementary stages of learning. It is hard to imagine that English ever stopped being spoken in grammar schools.

Rather than wholly replacing English in schools, French came to be used alongside it. This is shown by the existence of the copies of Ælfric's grammar with French glosses, and by manuscripts of Latin school texts, written or used in England during the twelfth and thirteenth centuries, containing glosses in

English and French.[5] Not only were a number of pupils French-speaking, but there were good reasons for English-speaking pupils to use French as well, or to try to learn it. Schoolboys who aimed to become clergy, gentry, or merchants would mix with the ruling orders among whom French was used. They would benefit from learning to speak French, and some may have come from families who spoke it already. As time went on French also became a written language in England. By the second half of the twelfth century there were religious works in French, and secular literature such as histories and romances. By 1200 it was growing in use for laws, letters, and records. This is likely to have reinforced the pressure on schoolmasters to teach or speak in French as well as Latin, so that their pupils gained literary skills in both. As a result three languages gained currency in grammar schools. A master in a twelfth- or early thirteenth-century school might have spoken English with the beginners and moved on to French as they improved. Younger pupils might have written notes on their writing tablets in English and older ones in French. Meanwhile they were all learning Latin. Higden's remarks, one suspects, are better suited to some of the schools of his own day than to the history of school education since the Conquest.

GRAMMAR DURING THE TWELFTH AND THIRTEENTH CENTURIES

The Conquest did not affect the status of the two most influential Latin grammarians. Donatus's *Ars Minor* went on being used as a standard elementary textbook, in the improved and expanded versions that had appeared since the end of the Roman Empire.[6] 'After [a pupil] has learnt the alphabet and has been imbued with the rest of the childish rudiments,' wrote a commentator of about 1200, 'he learns Donatus.'[7] Numerous other references in fourteenth- and fifteenth-century England testify to children possessing or studying copies of the *Ars Minor*, or texts like it.[8] Indeed, the word 'Donet' became a popular term for any elementary treatise or course of instruction.[9] Priscian's works continued to be highly rated too, and during the mid twelfth century Peter Helias, a French grammarian, wrote an exposition and commentary on them (*Summa super Priscianum*), which was widely used in its own right.[10] When English universities developed in the late twelfth century, grammar became one of the subjects of the university arts course, and Donatus and Priscian were chosen as texts for study. A number of statutes enacted at Oxford between 1268 and 1431 laid down that students reading for a degree in arts should spend a term on grammar, listening to lectures on Donatus's *Barbarism*, *Priscian Major* (the first sixteen books), or *Priscian Minor* (the last two).[11] Copies of Priscian are recorded in monastic libraries and occasionally as belonging to town schools and masters.[12]

Not all grammar after 1066, however, was learnt from Donatus and Priscian. A surge of new works on the subject appeared in the twelfth and thirteenth centuries. They included texts for every stage of learning Latin and for every aspect of it: grammar, vocabulary, pronunciation, composition, and linguistics. Some of these works reached England from the Continent, others were produced in England itself, and a few of the latter crossed the Channel in the other direction. Italy was the source of the three major Latin dictionaries used in late medieval England: those of Papias, Hugutio, and Giovanni Balbi. France was influential in terms of grammatical writing. During the twelfth and thirteenth centuries Paris attracted English students and teachers to its schools and university, and two French writers on grammar in this period, Alexander of Ville-Dieu and Evrard of Béthune, had a profound influence in England. Grammarians native to England included Adam of Balsham (d. *c*.1157–69), who came from Cambridgeshire and taught at Paris, and Serlo of Wilton and Osbern Pinnock of Gloucester, who were both active during the third quarter of the twelfth century.[13] A fourth scholar, Alexander Nequam (1157–1217), the son of the wet-nurse of Richard the Lionheart, studied at Paris and later taught grammar in England.[14] He was followed at Paris by John of Garland, who began his academic studies at Oxford in about 1210–13 but spent most of his life in France and died there in or after 1258. Other writers of the later thirteenth century were Nicholas of Breckendale (fl. *c*.1261) and Richard of Hambury (fl. 1288–93), teachers at Cambridge and Oxford respectively.

These writers differed from their Anglo-Saxon precursors in being mostly secular clerks or secular priests. 'Secular' means that they lived in the world, studying or teaching in schools or universities, not in religious houses, although Serlo, Osbern, and Nequam entered monasteries in later life and Alexander of Hales (d. 1245) became a friar. This secularity reflects the fact that, in the twelfth century, free-standing schools for the public overtook the monasteries as centres for the study and teaching of grammar. Their masters were more focussed on teaching than were monks, and their classes were probably larger. Osbern Pinnock and John of Garland were also the first English grammarians for a long time whose works reached the Continent, although they did not have the impact of the major French and Italian writers. John is a particularly important figure. He wrote extensively on grammatical and literary subjects, and he still lives as a personality since he was free in giving his opinions on the works of other people. Indeed he conveys a sense of belonging to a modern community of scholars engaged in a common task, rather than being the heir of a tradition like so many of the grammarians whom we met in earlier centuries.[15]

Many of the grammars produced after about 1100 were wholly or partly in verse. This practice seems strange to us, but it was widely followed by writers of works of instruction up to about 1500. Such works occur in Latin, French, and English on subjects as varied as religion, history, good manners, and sports, and the fashion extended to grammar as well, in a way that had hitherto been uncommon.[16] Grammarians tended to employ verse for conveying lists of words or summaries of rules. Sometimes they inserted passages of verse within prose grammars. Sometimes they wrote entirely in verse, like Serlo of Wilton, one of the first to do so, in his *De Generibus Nominum* ('on the genders of nouns') and *De Differentiis* ('on homonyms'). The technique reached its apotheosis in the works of Alexander of Ville-Dieu and Evrard of Béthune, who used it for large-scale grammars covering multiple topics, although their grammars contain much that is in list form. Contemporaries regarded verse as allowing information to be conveyed more succinctly and remembered more easily. An early commentator on Alexander's grammar asked rhetorically why it was written in such a medium, when Priscian had already covered the subject in prose. He answered his question as follows:

> A metrical discourse is more useful because of its easier accessibility, its graceful and lucid beauty, and its easier retention in the memory. . . . It is not therefore to be wondered that this book is read, since it makes compendious what was originally prolix and confused, renders orderly what was originally disorderly, and gives enlightenment to what was originally obscure, so that it is possible to grasp easily what many despaired of grasping.[17]

One also wonders if the use of verse arose from the proliferation of town and village schools. They would not have had the book resources of monasteries, and verse grammars could have helped to fill the gap by enabling matrial to be memorised. The writing of such grammars was at its most popular in the thirteenth century, and after 1300 there was a tendency in England to return to writing grammars in prose. In turn this may reflect a growing supply of books and writing materials in schools that reduced the need to learn information by heart. The popularity of Alexander and Evrard, however, caused grammatical verse to be read until the sixteenth century, and late medieval authors continued to use it for short vocabularies and, in grammars, to summarise what had been stated in prose.

The new grammatical works of the period from 1100 to 1300 can be divided into large-scale grammars, vocabularies, and dictionaries. In the first group the most important text was the *Doctrinale* ('teaching manual') of Alexander of Ville-Dieu (in Latin, *de Villa Dei*), a man who was born in the 1160s, studied at Paris, and entered the service of the bishop of Dol. He wrote it for the education of the bishop's nephews in about 1199. It consists of some 2,645 Latin hexameter lines, beginning with a prologue explaining that it is aimed at young clerklings or children. They are to read it after they have learnt the *Alphabetum Minus* and before they proceed to the *Alphabetum Maius*, terms that probably refer to Donatus and Priscian respectively. If they cannot understand the *Doctrinale* at first, their master should expound it to them in their own language.[18] The work was criticised by John of

Garland, the pre-eminent grammarian of the next generation, on the grounds that, 'closing the way to philosophy, it does not engender distinguished language but tautology'.[19] But his complaints were unusual. Most teachers found it so helpful that it became used almost universally, not just for clerklings but for students right through the curriculum. In 1366 it was even prescribed as a set book by the university of Paris.[20]

The *Doctrinale* is not a systematic guide to the whole of grammar. It concentrates on a number of topics that everyone needed to know and that lent themselves to being made into lists and put into verse. The work is divided into four sections. The first deals with accidence: the morphology or different forms of nouns, verbs, and adjectives. It does not present all the verb paradigms, but focusses on how verbs form their perfect tenses and supines – the processes where complications occur – with a further section on verbs that are otherwise irregular or defective. It also ignores the rest of the eight parts of speech, presumably because its readers were expected to have learnt these from Donatus. The second section covers syntax, including rules of agreement and construction, and the third is a thorough analysis of metrical quantity, taking every possible syllable in alphabetical order and showing its quantitive value. The final part deals with grammatical 'figures', or good and bad points of style, in a similar manner to Donatus's *Barbarism*. As the work became popular, it was revised by various editors, who improved, added, or excised particular passages. John of Garland was one of these, despite (or because of) his reservations, and his revision circulated together with other versions.[21]

The success of the work reflected the way in which it conveyed a large amount of information in a small compass, suitable for memorisation. Alexander's method can be illustrated from his opening lines, which lay out the paradigms of nouns of the first declension. These are, in Latin,

Rectis as es a dat declinatio prima,
atque per am propria quaedam ponuntur Hebraea,
dans ae diphthongon genetivis atque dativis.
am servat quartus; tamen en aut an reperimus,
cum rectus fit in es vel in as, vel cum dat a Graecus.
rectus in a Graeci facit an quarto breviari.
quintus in a dabitur, post es tamen e reperitur.
a sextus, tamen es quandoque per e dare debes.
am recti repetes quinto, sextum sociando.

This is the effect if we turn the Latin hexameters into English ones:

First declension nouns have -*as*, -*es*, -*a* for their endings,
As well as -*am* in some proper names taken from Hebrew.
Genitives, likewise datives, diphthongs carry in -*a-e*,
While the accusative gives us -*am*, although we discover

> That -*es* and -*as* produce -*en* and -*an*, while all Greek words
> Ending with -*a* become -*an* in a similar manner.
> -*a* is the vocative form, but -*es* has an -*e* termination;
> Ablatives also adopt -*a*, -*es* taking -*e* as beforehand,
> Saving that -*am* in the first case stays so in both of the latter.

In ten lines Alexander gives us the singular paradigms of every possible noun of the first declension, in each of the six cases. He lists the cases in the classical order, which remained in use down to the nineteenth century: first the nominative, then the genitive. With the information he gives, you can 'decline' or recite the forms not only of common Latin words like *mensa* ('a table') but of Greek names that occur in Latin, such as Aeneas and Atrides, and Biblical ones like Adam and Thomas.

The other outstandingly popular verse grammar of the middle ages, the *Grecismus* ('work about Greek') by Evrard or Eberhard of Béthune, had a similar history.[22] Little is known of the author except that he was probably a Fleming by origin, died in about 1212, and wrote it just before or just after the beginning of the thirteenth century. Notwithstanding its name it is a treatise on Latin grammar in Latin verse, some 4,545 lines long, which starts untypically with grammatical 'figures' and with metre, before running through the eight parts of speech and concluding with a short section on syntax. The *Grecismus* complemented the *Doctrinale* by focussing on the characteristics of words other than their morphology or paradigms. Thus, listing masculine nouns (mainly from the third declension), Evrard taught vocabulary, derivations, genders, and meanings at the same time:

> An *orátor* is pupil under a *rhetor*'s direction;
> *Rhetor* from *resis* is taken, *oro* gives us the other.
> *Aër* is air we breathe, *aether* that which is higher;
> He who plays host is a *hospes*, so is the guest whom he welcomes,
> Just as both carer and cared for merit the title *alumnus*;
> One who composes in metre, him we entitle *poëta*,
> One telling people their fortunes, him we refer to as *vates*,
> While a *propheta* utters (Latin *profatur*) what's godly.[23]

Evrard shared a technique that was used by Alexander: the listing of words of a particular type, which could be learnt by heart:

> Which of the monosyllabic nouns are of masculine gender?
> If you need help on this subject, soon you may note them completely:
> *As*, *dens*, *flos*, and *Dis*, *fons*, *mons*, *pes*, *mos* (giving *moris*),
> *Lar*, *mas*, *pons*, *pus*, *glis*, *rex*, *ros*, *nar*, *sol* (giving *solis*).[24]

Sometimes he went further and invented mnemonics:

Cre-, do-, se-, nex-, iu-, sto-, la-, mi-, ve-, to-, fri-, pli-, ne-, cu-, so-,
Turn in the perfect to *-ui* or *-i*, never to *-avi.*[25]

Here clues alone are given to the words. You have to remember that *cre-* is *crepo*, *do- domo*, *se- seco*, and so on. They are verbs of the first conjugation that form the perfect tense in an unusual way as *crepui*, *domui*, and *secui* rather than ending in *-avi* like most such verbs. Two other distinctive features of the work occur in chapters 7 and 8. The first collects names from mythology, such as the Muses, the gods, the signs of the zodiac, the Sirens, and the Eumenides. The second, 'Nouns Derived from Greek', lists Greek words and the Latin ones that they have generated. Thus *ares* is said to signify 'virtue' and to have produced *Areopagus*; *a-* means 'without' in words like *acephalus* ('headless'); while *amphi* denotes 'around' as in *amphitheatrum*. This knowledge of Greek was sufficiently unusual to gain the book its title and the author his nickname of 'the Grecist', but John of Garland thought the title unjustified. Poking fun at the word, he observed that 'The mendacious *Grecismus* is more *mus* ['a mouse'] than *Grecis* ['from the Greeks'].'[26] Nevertheless, like the *Doctrinale*, it was widely used down to the early sixteenth century.

Most of the grammars by English writers had a more limited circulation than those of Alexander and Evrard. They included a general work, *Compendium Grammatice* ('compendium of grammar'), by John of Garland, his guide to the *Art of Reading in Church* also known as *Accentarium*, and treatises on deponent verbs and syntax by Nicholas of Breckendale and Richard of Hambury.[27] The English had a wider impact through the collection and study of words. One popular genre that they helped to develop was the prose vocabulary. Adam of Balsham wrote a work called *De Utensilibus* ('of things in common use'), cast in narrative form. He describes how he visited a country estate and observed the landscape, a hunt in progress, a great house, a household, and an entertainment. The story is attractively told, and Adam managed to introduce a large number of Latin words into the narrative, as well as allusions to classical literature.[28] His treatise survives in at least fifteen manuscripts, but is exceeded in this respect by Alexander Nequam's *De Nominibus Utensilium* ('on the names of domestic utensils'), of which there are over thirty. This is less literary and more like an encyclopaedia. Nequam describes a series of places and activities, including the kitchen, travelling, a bedroom, food, castles, ships, jewellery, and ecclesiastical objects, all illustrated with appropriate words.[29] John of Garland wrote two similar works, of which the *Dictionary* is another short encyclopaedia in eighty-four short sections. It ranges from the human body through different human occupations and their equipment to lists of birds, fish, animals, ships, and finally Heaven.[30] The *Commentary* is longer and was dedicated to Aymer of Valence, half brother of Henry III. It resembles Adam's work in focussing on aristocratic life but is largely a list of words like Nequam's, covering social ranks, buildings, clothes, horses, hunting, hawking, clerical life, and health and recreations.[31]

Two further kinds of vocabulary call for attention. One, usually in verse, collected synonyms (different words with similar meanings) or homonyms (words spelt similarly but with different meanings). Serlo of Wilton's 200–line poem *De Differenciis* was a pioneering effort in this genre,[32] but the two most widely read were the *Synonyma* and *Equivoca* which date from the early thirteenth century. These poems (more truly halves of a single work) had a European circulation and are often ascribed to John of Garland, although the ascription is not absolutely certain.[33] In the prologue the author declares that he does not intend to carry water to the sea or sparks to a fireplace, but to provide milk for children, teaching the elements of Latin to those who know only their mother tongue. After explaining the difference between synonyms and homonyms, he undertakes to list them in alphabetical order, but he observes this order only as far as the first letter of each word. The *Synonyma* takes key words, beginning with *anima* ('soul' or 'being'), and gives their synonyms, often with indications of the specialised senses in which the latter are used:

> Several words encompass *anima*, one for each function:
> *Sensus*, meaning feeling; *ratio*, used of one's judgment;
> *Mens* is the term for remembrance; *animus* when we consider;
> *Cor* is employed for affection; while our desire is *voluntas*.[34]

In the *Equivoca* lists of homonyms are given and explained, beginning with *augustus*:

> *Augustus*, *-ti*, *-to*, stands for a month or a ruler;
> *Augustus*, *-tus*, *-tui* indicates telling the future;
> *Augustus* used adjectivally signifies 'noble'.
> *Augeo* gives the first, *avis* and *gustus* the second.
> *Aura* indicates favour, splendour, air, or a soft breeze;
> *Abacus* stands for a table, measure, or top of a column.[35]

The remaining type of vocabulary collected *exotica* – unusual words, generally of Greek origin, of the sort that had fascinated the Anglo-Saxons. At least three works of this kind were compiled in the thirteenth century, notably the *Exoticon* of Alexander of Hales, whose opening line introduces us to the words *Chere teoren quem gignos crucis andro phalando* ('Hail! O Lamb [of God], whom I see naked on the wood of the Cross').[36]

Vocabularies were useful tools in class, and the shorter ones could be committed to memory, but teachers and older scholars needed guides to the whole range of Latin words. It was in this field that medieval scholars made one of their chief contributions to knowledge by inventing the dictionary in its modern form.[37] An early work that could be used for this purpose was the *Liber Etymologiarum* ('book of etymologies') by Isidore of Seville (*c*. 560–636), an encyclopaedia in which the different branches of knowledge were described and the terminology of each one traced and explained.[38] Isidore began by discussing grammar and the other liberal arts before traversing such topics as law and chronology, God, the Church, geography, human beings, and the animal kingdom. He provided information on the words proper to each subject and discussed their etymologies. The next stage of development was represented by the *Elementarium* of Papias, a Lombard of Pavia, whose preface tells us that others had tried to compile a dictionary and that he had given ten years to the task, which he probably completed in about 1053.[39] The *Elementarium* is basically a word list in alphabetical order. 'Anyone,' says the author, 'who wishes to find anything quickly must also notice that this whole book is composed according to the alphabet, not only in the first letters of the words but in the second, third, and sometimes even the fourth determinative arrangement of the letters.' In other words Papias undertook to carry his alphabetical arrangement to at least the third letter of every word. He also promised to explain the genders and declensions of nouns, the conjugations of verbs, and the quantities of doubtful syllables, and to cite the books and authors he had consulted. The execution does not always match these intentions, but the *Elementarium* shines as a pioneer work, struggling to evolve the techniques of arrangement that we take for granted. It was widely used in medieval times and printed on several occasions during the late fifteenth century.

England contributed to lexicographical studies in the person of Osbern of Gloucester, whose *Liber Derivationum* ('book of derivations') listed words according to their stems or word families, with their origins and relationships to other words.[40] He began it when he was a schoolmaster and finished it years later, by which time he had become a monk of Gloucester Abbey. It circulated on the Continent and was one of the sources consulted by Hugutio of Pisa (d. 1210) in his *Derivationes*, a very popular dictionary during the later middle ages. Hugutio also took key words, discussed their etymologies and meanings, and provided lists of their compounds and derivatives.[41] The *Derivationes* was less easy to consult than the *Elementarium*, because the alphabetical arrangement took account of only the first letter of the word (it begins with *augeo*). Moreover, compound words were not arranged according to their own spelling but followed that of their parent word. For this reason manuscripts of the work often contain finding-lists of words in a more rigorous alphabetical order, with references to their places in the text. The modern kind of dictionary was most fully realised by Giovanni Balbi, John of Genoa, or *Januensis* as he was called in Latin. Balbi, a Dominican friar, completed his *Catholicon* (a word signifying totality) in about 1286. This work marked a great improvement on its predecessors. It follows an alphabetical order down to the last letter of every word, and the entries provide stems, principal paradigms, etymologies, and meanings. The *Catholicon* soon established itself in western Europe as *the* Latin dictionary, and seems to have reached England by the end of the thirteenth century. It was copied in many manuscripts and was one of the first books to be printed: by Gutenberg at Mainz in 1460.[42]

Most of the works described so far were written primarily for those who were teaching or learning Latin in school or in the lower stages of the university curriculum. But the twelfth and thirteenth centuries also saw the development of academic interest in how and why Latin worked as it did – in other words, the study of linguistics. The classical grammarians had not been uninterested in this topic. They had identified eight kinds of words (the parts of speech) and had tried to define the nature of each one. Their definitions, however, were found inadequate by the twelfth century, when the rise of logic as a discipline led scholars to wish to categorise and explain linguistic matters more rigorously. Peter Helias, writing his commentary on Priscian in the 1140s, reckoned that there were eight parts of speech because there were eight ways of expressing or signifying things. Signifying substance with quality was done through a noun, substance without quality by a pronoun, and activity or passivity by a verb.[43] Words, in this view, reflected understanding, and understanding reflected what existed and happened in the natural world. During the thirteenth and fourteenth centuries it became popular to examine grammar in this way, and to link it with the whole of created matter and human knowledge. The term *modus* (or *modi*) *significandi* ('the way (or ways) of signifying') came into common use, causing historians to call its scholars 'modists' and their studies 'modistic' or 'speculative' grammar.[44]

The leading writers of speculative grammar were based at the university of Paris in the second half of the thirteenth century and the first half of the fourteenth. One of the most popular of their works in England was the *Questiones de Modis Significandi* ('questions on the ways of signifying'), written in about 1285 and attributed to the famous German friar Albertus Magnus, although not actually by him. Several of the modists were Germans or Danes, like Martin of Dacia (d. 1304), who was active in the 1260s and 1270s. Martin argued that whatever exists has one or more properties, which constitute its mode of being. These properties are recognised by our minds, in the form of concepts that we signify to other people by words. Grammar, from this point of view, is not so much an historical or literary subject based on authors and texts as a scientific one related to the workings of nature. Approaching it in a scientific way enabled one not only to categorise and define its principles but apparently to solve specific problems. Martin asked why an inanimate object, which has no gender, should be expressed by a Latin noun with a gender. *Lapis* and *petra* both mean 'a stone', but they are respectively masculine and feminine. He answered the question partly from literary evidence in the form of etymology – the origin of words – and partly from physics. *Lapis*, he considered, was derived from *laedens pedem*, 'that which injures the foot', in other words from an active process that gave rise to the active masculine gender. *Petra*, on the other hand, signified *pede trita*, 'that which is rubbed by the foot', a passive process that produced the passive feminine gender.[45] Such an argument shows both the extent to which the modists were original as grammarians and how far they were not. They were so in their interest in linguistics and science, and in the logical arguments they used, but much of their knowledge was derivative. They accepted the classical notion of the eight parts of speech and, in the example mentioned, traditional notions of etymology. Speculative grammar was influential until the early sixteenth century, percolating downwards into schools. Some schoolmasters had studied it at university, and its reasoning and conclusions were regarded as authoritative even by those who had not.

LITERARY TEXTS

During the twelfth century, before the rise of the modists, there was a lively interest in classical Latin literature throughout western Europe, a phenomenon now known as 'the twelfth-century Renaissance'. The classics were not only read; they inspired new works of poetry, history, and romance in Latin, French, and English. This interest reinforced the practice of reading classical texts in schools, and a description of an ideal school curriculum written in France or England soon after 1200 recommends a wide range of authors. Once a child has mastered the alphabet and Donatus, he should start to learn

> the useful compendium of morality which the multitude supposes to be that of Cato, and let him pass from the *Eclogue of Theodulus* to the eclogues of the *Bucolics* [of Virgil]. . . . Then let him read satirists and historians, so that he may learn about the vices to avoid in the age of minority, and let him look for the noble deeds of those [who ought] to be imitated. From the joyful *Thebaid* [of Statius] let him pass to the divine *Aeneid*, nor let him neglect the poet [Lucan] whom Cordoba brought forth. . . . Let him reserve the moral sayings of Juvenal in the secrecy of his breast, and study hard how to avoid the shamefastness of nature. Let him read Horace's *Satires* and *Epistles* and *Art of Poetry* and *Odes* with the book of *Epodes*. Let him hear Ovid's *Elegies* and *Metamorphoses*, but especially let him be familiar with the little book [by Ovid] of *The Remedy of Love*. It has seemed right to men of authority, however, that the amatory songs and satires should be withdrawn from the hands of adolescents. . . . Statius's *Achilleid* is approved by men of much gravity. The *Bucolics* and *Georgics* of Virgil are of much usefulness.

The writer goes on to list authors of increasing rarity, making us feel that he has become more interested in showing off his knowledge of the classics than in describing the school curriculum. Still, he gives us the impression that many Latin works, all of them poems, were available and valued for educational purposes, although some people thought that erotic and satirical items should not be included.[46]

We can get a more truthful idea of what was studied from tracing the texts that occur in manuscripts likely to have been used in schools. This evidence points to the popularity of a collection of Latin poems, all but one of them classical: the *Sex Auctores* ('six authors'), as it has come to be called. The authors of the poems consisted of Cato, Theodulus, Avianus, Maximian, Claudian, and Statius, usually in this order.[47] The first of the texts, the *Distichs of Cato*, has already been noted as popular in Anglo-Saxon England. It is an anonymous third-century compilation of wise advice and reflections, allegedly written by a Roman Stoic philosopher who lived at an earlier date, and edited to make it Christian.[48] The work begins with a preface and fifty-eight short precepts in prose, such as 'Pray to God', 'Love your parents', 'Respect the magistrates', and 'Say little at banquets'. These were known as the 'Small Cato'. They are followed by the 'Great Cato': four books of hexameter couplets, making up some 306 lines of verse providing counsel and comfort, of which the first three couplets are typical:

Given that God is a spirit, which is what poetry tells us,
See that you offer him worship spiritually and purely.

Fix your devotion on keeping vigils rather than slumbers;
Resting during the daytime easily nourishes vices.

What is the first of the virtues? Guarding your tongue is the answer;
Those who pay honour to silence come very close to their Maker.

Cato's popularity can be seen from the manifold quotations and reproductions found in medieval literature. Three translations into French were made in England during the thirteenth century, and several into English during the fourteenth or fifteenth.[49] In these vernacular forms it may have been used to teach children in literate homes. Alone of the six authors' works it survived both the clear-out of school texts that took place in about 1300 and the similar purge of about 1500. It was still being studied by pupils in Tudor England.

The tenth-century *Eclogue of Theodulus* was the only medieval work among the six, and the most overtly Christian.[50] Also of unknown authorship, it is a debate between Pseustis ('falsehood'), an Athenian shepherd, and Alithea ('truth'), a Hebrew virgin of the line of David, judged by Fronesis ('prudence'). Each stage of the debate is initiated by Pseustis, who outlines a story from classical mythology in a four-line stanza. Alithea replies to this with a similar episode from the Bible. The contest starts with human origins. Pseustis claims that

> First in the world came Saturn, out of the shores of the Cretans,
> Sowing the human races over lands that were golden.
> No one is named as his parent; no one existed before him;
> All who are noble rejoice, having this god as their father.

Alithea provides the correct account:

> Man at his first creation lived in a paradise garden,
> Till, at his wife's persuasion, poisonous serpentine venom,
> Which he consented in sharing, brought humanity's downfall;
> Still their children suffer from their parents' transgression.[51]

Although Pseustis leads the debate, the order of topics follows the Bible because that is the truthful record. The order starts with Genesis, runs through the Old Testament to the stories of Judith and Esther, and ends with some references to Jesus and his significance. Each biblical story is

22   Cicero at his desk. Classical writers were not forgotten in the later middle ages, but played little part in school education.

linked with a classical contrast or parallel: the attack of the giants on
Olympus with the tower of Babel; Hercules and Deianeira with Samson and
Delilah. Eventually Pseustis admits defeat, because the fables of mythology
cannot compete with the historical truths and moral authority of the Bible,
and Alithea concludes the poem with a prayer to God to raise up his servants
and to cast down the proud. The *Eclogue*'s popularity, no doubt, reflected
both its usefulness as a little dictionary of mythological and biblical topics
and its reassuring messages about the rightfulness of Christianity.

The rest of the *Sex Auctores* introduced pupils to other genres of poetry.
Avianus, who flourished about the year 400, supplied the *Fabulae*: forty-two
short fables on human and animal subjects. Maximian's work was the *Elegies*,
dating from the sixth century: six poems about love by a disillusioned old
man and therefore acceptable in schools that catered for, among others,
future clergy. Claudian, a contemporary of Avianus, was represented by his
poem *On the Rape of Proserpine* – or rather, since Claudian was a Christian,
on her abduction, marriage, and the cheer that she brought to Hades.
Statius, who lived from about AD 45 to 96, contributed *Achilleis*, an
unfinished epic. It tells how the youthful Achilles was concealed as a girl
to avoid his involvement in the Trojan War, and how the stratagem failed.
He fathered a child on one of his female companions (the most risqué
episode in the *Sex Auctores*), and inadvertently revealed himself by handling
weapons laid in his way by the crafty Ulysses. Both Claudian and Statius are
replete with classical imagery and mythological references, supplementing
the *Eclogue of Theodulus* with information about the culture of the ancient
world.

These poets were not the only classical authors read in schools. Persius
appears to have retained a place, while Juvenal, Horace, and Ovid seem to
have had some popularity.[52] During the thirteenth century, however, tastes
in western Europe moved away from the classics towards poetry that was
more Christian and therefore more moral, more recent and therefore more
easily understood. This movement is already perceptible in Alexander of
Ville-Dieu's *Doctrinale*, which attacks Maximian's poems as 'follies'.[53] It was
well established by the fourteenth century, when the university of Oxford
warned local schoolmasters to teach only 'morals or metaphors or honest
poetry', and forbade the reading of works like Ovid's *Ars Amatoria* and the
twelfth-century Latin comedy *Pamphilus*, both of which centre on men
making love to women.[54] A new anthology of poets, the *Auctores Octo* ('eight
authors'), was compiled on the Continent to provide the kind of material
now desired in schools, and was widely used there down to the early
sixteenth century.[55] The *Auctores Octo* kept Cato and Theodulus as the first
and second constituents, but replaced the other classical works with poems
of the twelfth and thirteenth centuries: *Facetus* on moral behaviour; *Cartula*
on the vanity of the world; Matthew of Vendome's retelling of the biblical
story of *Tobias*; the *Liber Parabolarum* of Alain de Lille; a version of the *Fables*

of Aesop; and *Floretus*, a poem about faith, virtue, sin, and the sacraments. The English grammar schools followed a similar path, but not an identical one, reflecting the relative decline of their links with the Continent during the late thirteenth century. They adopted some of these works, including Cato, Theodulus, *Facetus*, *Cartula*, and *Liber Parabolarum*, but they added other titles popular in England, and the list of works they used was not as fixed in its titles or its order as the *Auctores Octo*.

The poems read in English schools after about 1300 dealt with worship, wisdom, morality, and behaviour. Children began their elementary studies, as we have seen, by learning basic prayers, psalms, and the hours of the Virgin Mary.[56] After this, in grammar schools, boys read the *Hymnal*, containing the Latin hymns sung during the daily services and a similar collection of the *Sequences* sung at mass. These texts were obvious ones for schools to use, because their pupils were so often choristers, parish clerks, or trainee clergy. Even boys intended for lay careers would benefit from knowing what the clergy sang in church. Some schools also prepared their pupils for going to church to make their confessions – a task required of everyone over the age of puberty, at least once a year during Lent. We still possess an English prose treatise on penance which John Drury, schoolmaster of Beccles, composed for his school in 1432,[57] and many schoolboys after 1300 would have read the *Liber Penitencialis* ('book of penance'), also known from its opening words as *Peniteas cito*:

Sinner, come soon to repentance. Know that the One who will judge you
Also is One who has pity. Five are the stages of penance:
Hope that your sin will be pardoned, showing contrition, confessing,
Making amends through a penance, fleeing thereafter from evil.[58]

The poem is almost certainly the work of William de Montibus, an English scholar of the early thirteenth century, whom we have already encountered as chancellor of Lincoln Cathedral and lecturer in theology there until his death in 1213.[59] It calls on the reader to confess and explains why this is necessary, how to make your confession, and how to expiate your sins when confession is over. The work was special to schools in England, where it occurs in many school manuscripts and must have been widely used in classrooms.

Peniteas cito was rather unusual in its concern with religious practice. Most late-medieval school poetry gave more attention to attitudes than to observances, by teaching wisdom and morality. One of the most popular texts was the *Liber Parabolarum* ('book of parallels'), also known as the *Parvum Doctrinale* ('small teaching manual') and nowadays usually ascribed to Alain de Lille, a Latin poet of France who died in 1203.[60] The title reflects the fact that each stanza evokes an image and draws an analogy from it, as can be seen from the poem's opening couplets:

Phoebe, the moon, acquires lustre from Phoebus the sun god;
So does a fool from a wise man, sparkling with light that is borrowed.

Etna, for all that she blazes, merely consumes her own substance,
Just as the fires of the jealous injure themselves but no others.

Even a pig on a dunghill rises in order to forage;
Why then do humans in contrast never forsake what is filthy?

The work is divided into six books, in which the stanzas grow from one couplet to six, the longer stanzas extending the comparisons and becoming more reflective. Moralising is also the theme of *Cartula* ('a little writing'), an anonymous work of the twelfth or thirteenth century named after its opening word.[61] Ornamentally written, with rhymes within each line, *Cartula* is sombre in content, reflecting on the vanity of human life and the transience of everything around us, whence the other title by which it was known, *De Contemptu Mundi* ('of contempt for the world'):

All that with beauty refreshes, every thing that is precious,
Closely resembles a flower, coloured by natural power;
Soon it is fated to wither, passing whoever knows whither,
Empty: the place it embellished, vanished: the fragrance we relished.
Royalty too and its story, pomp and terrestrial glory,
All of the goods that we treasure, lives of whatever their measure,
Steadily draw to an ending; death is for each of us pending;
Though its arrival is hidden, yet to its stroke we are bidden.

Have faith in Christ, exhorts the author; only this will bring us lasting rewards.[62]

Poems on the subject of behaviour became popular in the twelfth century, a pioneer work being *Urbanus Magnus* ('the courteous man') by the English writer Daniel of Beccles.[63] Boys in grammar schools read two such poems, the shorter and simpler being *Stans Puer ad Mensam* ('O boy standing at the table'), which dealt with table manners. This composition is usually ascribed to Robert Grosseteste, bishop of Lincoln from 1235 to 1253, a man renowned for his scholarship and his courteous behaviour (Fig. 23).[64] John Lydgate translated it into English during the fifteenth century, and in this form it probably circulated, like Cato, in homes as well as in schools.[65] Its forty-odd lines list the manners that boys should observe when they wait at table in noble households or eat there themselves. They are warned not to fidget on duty, not to take overlarge portions, and not to speak while food is in their mouths:

Never eat bread with abandon till they have set down the dishes;
People may think you are famished, else they may judge you a glutton.

23 Robert Grosseteste (d. 1253), bishop of Lincoln, a notable scholar, educator of noble boys, and the probably author of the school poem *Stans Puer ad Mensam*.

Tidy the nails of your fingers – dirt to your friends is offensive.
Eat what is served as your portion, send what is left to the needy.
Relish such talk as is peaceful; try not to chatter when speaking,
Nor let your laughter be raucous, lest other people condemn you.[66]

This practical advice was complemented by the longer and more ethical *Facetus* (also meaning 'the courteous man'), a twelfth-century work read widely in England and Europe, where it was one of the *Auctores Octo*. The English version begins *Est nihil utilius*.[67] 'I believe,' says the unknown author, 'that there is nothing more useful to the welfare of man than to know the rules of life and to practise good manners.' Rhyming in couplets he lays out our duty to God, our obligation to honour God's Church and clergy, and the importance of good behaviour in church. The rest of the work deals with such topics as respect for parents, self-discipline, good manners towards others, and etiquette at meals. Three of its passages give advice or make remarks about women:

If for a wife you are looking, be on your guard lest you marry
Daughters or widows of these, else all your plans will miscarry:

Celibate priests and canons, torturers, beadles malicious,
Actors, or those who lend money; any such woman is vicious.

Never speak lewdly concerning those of the feminine gender;
Honour to all you encounter, that is your duty to render.
If the wife you have married keeps all your interests before her,
Always be properly grateful; cherish, revere, and adore her.

Roofs that leak are a nuisance, smoke-filled rooms are a bother,
So is a worthless woman; each is as bad as another.[68]

The interest in marriage shown by *Facetus* brought a breath of the lay world to the schoolroom, just as *Stans Puer ad Mensam* did through its focus on life in a household.

By the end of the middle ages Latin commentaries had been written on each of the major school poems, which teachers could expound and pupils could eventually read by themselves, since the commentaries were printed with the texts by 1500. The commentators, like modern editors of classical works, explained the meanings of words, showed how each passage of the text fitted into the structure, and provided contextual knowledge. In the *Eclogue of Theodulus*, for example, the exposition of the stanza about Saturn explains why he is discussed at that point and summarises the mythology about him. He inaugurated the age of gold, the first of the four ages of the world. He married Ops and fathered Jupiter, Juno, Neptune, and Pluto, but eventually Jupiter dethroned and castrated him. He is depicted in art and literature as a sad and pallid old man holding a scythe and devouring a child, because he consumed all but four of his offspring. Then the myth is interpreted. Saturn may have been an historical king of Crete who was overthrown by his son. Alternatively the story may be an allegory about the overthrow of tyrants, or about the fate of anything born in time to be devoured by Time itself. The responsive stanza, about the Fall of Mankind, is treated similarly. It is placed within the Christian structure of the poem, and the story of the Fall is told in full from the book of Genesis. Readers are recommended to look at what biblical scholars have written on the subject. Metaphors and words are elucidated, and we are reminded that Christians believe the world to have had seven ages, not four. The commentator ends by praising the apt relationship between the two stories. One concerns the first god, and the other the first man. One portrays a king deprived of his kingdom, and the other a man expelled from his paradise.[69]

The late medieval school texts, when their commentaries are taken into account, contain a larger body of knowledge than might at first appear, including material on classical mythology. There is also anecdotal evidence that at least a few pupils continued to read some classical authors. The prohibition of Ovid's *Ars Amatoria* at Oxford must have been prompted by fears that it might be studied, and a book containing Horace was bought for boys at Merton College, Oxford, in 1347–8.[70] The fourteenth-century almonry boys of St Paul's Cathedral had access to a large collection of classical texts that, in principle, they could have read.[71] Nevertheless there was enough of a shift in the choice of texts by 1300 to make school reading different in character: more recent in origin and more Christian in tone. In turn this change was sufficient for the revival of interest in the classics during the late fifteenth century to confront masters and pupils with something fresh and unfamiliar.

GRAMMAR DURING THE FOURTEENTH AND FIFTEENTH CENTURIES

As society and learning underwent changes during the fourteenth and fifteenth centuries, so did the study and teaching of grammar. One cause of change was the rise of speculative grammar, and the consequent search for grammatical truths and explanations in reason and science. Another change arose from political events and their linguistic effects. During the thirteenth century England became less closely linked with France, due in part to the loss of the English king's possessions in Normandy and Anjou. English grammarians ceased to study or teach in Paris and continental grammarians to have an impact in England, apart from those already established like Alexander, Evrard, and the modists. A late example of an English teacher with French links is Thomas Hanney, who began to write a comprehensive grammar in prose called *Memoriale Juniorum* ('memoranda for the young') at Toulouse on 20 April 1313, and completed it at Lewes on 28 November of the same year, 'at the instance of Master John Chertsey, rector of the schools in that place'. The treatise, which discusses orthography, accidence, syntax, and metre in 160 pages, had some success. It survives in nine manuscripts and is mentioned in several medieval library catalogues, but its continental context was unusual for its time.[72] By the late thirteenth century Oxford had superseded Paris as the leading centre of grammatical writing as far as England was concerned, and it maintained this leadership until about 1500. The city attracted many young people to study grammar as schoolboys or as undergraduates, and a larger number of masters to teach them than in an ordinary town. Three or four of these masters have left identifiable treatises, including Richard of Hambury, John Cornwall (d. 1349), and John Leland (d. 1428), as well as those like Thomas Sampson who specialised in delivering business skills.[73]

The greater isolation of England from France gradually led to the replacement of French by English for many official and administrative purposes during the fourteenth century – the process described in the previous chapter.[74] While we must doubt Ranulf Higden's statement that only French was used in schools to teach Latin, it was presumably employed for that purpose in certain places and may have been particularly entrenched in the Oxford schools, in view of the university's determination to maintain the language.[75] When John Trevisa came to translate Higden's words in 1385, he pointed out that they were obsolete, because the use of French in teaching Latin had greatly declined since the Black Death of 1348–9. He attributed this decline to the Oxford schoolmaster John Cornwall, who is known to have taught there between 1344 and his death in 1349.[76] According to Trevisa, here modernised, Cornwall

> changed the lore in grammar schools and the [language of] translation from French to English, and Richard Pencrich [a schoolmaster active in Oxford during the 1360s] learnt that manner of teaching from him, and other men from Pencrich, so that now, the year of our Lord 1385, . . . in all the grammar schools of England children leave French and construe and learn in English.[77]

This statement has become famous, appearing to provide us with the kind of single invention or change that makes history dramatic and intelligible. Cornwall was indeed the author of a Latin prose treatise called *Speculum Grammatice* ('a mirror of grammar'), completed in 1346, which includes some English translations of verb paradigms and some pairs of illustrative sentences in Latin and English. There are also a few in Latin and French. The amount of vernacular material is small but it is larger than that of any other grammatical treatise since the time of Ælfric.[78] On the other hand Trevisa may have been influenced by personal knowledge and loyalty. He studied at Oxford University, and although he arrived there in about 1361, long after Cornwall's death, his stay overlapped with that of Pencrich who may have told him stories about Cornwall.[79] These would have interested Trevisa, because both he and Cornwall were Cornishmen and Oxonians, and he may have overrated the roles of his fellow countryman and their adopted city.[80] Schoolmasters in less important towns are more likely to have emphasised the English language before this happened at Oxford, than to have copied the practice from Oxford afterwards. Cornwall's originality may have been to introduce English to a grammatical text, and even this was limited to a few lines.

We can sense the vitality of English in grammar schools during the late fourteenth century from the appearance of English words for grammatical terms in contemporary literature. Words such as 'adjective', 'plural', 'positive', 'singular', and 'substantive' occur in works like the poem *Piers Plowman*, the Wycliffite translation of the Bible, and John Trevisa's writings: a sign that such words were current in schools and spreading more widely through society.[81] Then, in about 1400, the earliest grammars survive that are wholly written in English – the earliest, that is, since the time of Ælfric. Much, if not all, of the credit for producing them belongs to another Oxford schoolmaster, John Leland, who was teaching in the city by about 1401 and subsequently held his school at Peckwater Inn on the site of the modern college of Christ Church. He was a married man, who died in 1428 and was buried in the nearby church of St Frideswide, now the cathedral. His works were only short tracts on grammatical topics in Latin or English, but they became very popular and were widely copied. Indeed, Leland is a rare example of a medieval schoolmaster in England who can be shown to have had a wide reputation in and after his own day. Complimentary references to him survive from London, Bristol, and north Wales, calling him *flos grammaticorum*, 'the flower of grammarians'.[82] Manuscripts of his work reached places as far apart as Beccles and Bristol within a few years of his death.[83]

Four short treatises in English survive from the early fifteenth century, which are either by Leland or in his style. Their contemporary titles were *Accedence*, *Comparacio*, *Informacio*, and *Formula*. The *Accedence*, an English version of Donatus's *Ars Minor*, may have existed before Leland's time and been revised by him. It describes the characteristics of the eight parts of speech and provides some of the paradigms of nouns but not of verbs. *Comparacio* deals with the comparison of adjectives, and *Informacio* with understanding and writing Latin constructions. Both these texts are likely to be by Leland, but *Formula*, which is a reworking of *Informacio*, probably stems from one of his pupils or successors. All four works were widely used in English schools and the first three kept their popularity down to the early sixteenth century, as a result of which they underwent adaptation by other masters who improved and extended them. The surviving manuscripts and the printed versions that began to appear in the 1480s differ greatly in details, and it is now impossible to reconstruct the original texts. Their popularity no doubt reflected both their similarity to the Latin Donatus and their brevity, clarity, and awareness of the needs and problems of pupils. They also represent a change of approach, by which pupils were taught through a series of short treatises rather than a single long one like the *Doctrinale*. This may reflect the growing use of paper, which enabled pupils to have their own copies of texts to study instead of listening to the schoolmaster reading from his.[84]

The effectiveness of Leland's works as teaching aids can be illustrated from the *Informacio*, which seeks to help pupils understand the structure of English and Latin sentences. One of the earliest surviving versions of the work, written down in the mid fifteenth century, introduces the subject in the following words, here modernised:

What shall thou do when thou hast a matter to make Latin by? I shall look out my principal verb personal, and look whether it betokens 'to do' or 'to suffer'. And if it betokens 'to do', the doer shall be in the nominative case and the sufferer in such case as the verb will have after him. And if my

principal verb personal betokens 'to suffer', the sufferer shall be in the
nominative case and the doer in the ablative case with a preposition; and
if my principal verb be a verb impersonal, I shall begin with it to make my
Latin and to construe.[85]

'Do' and 'suffer' are simple ways of presenting the concepts of active and
passive verbs. By the end of the century the instructions had been further
refined and clarified:

> What shalt thou do when thou hast a piece of English to make in Latin? I
> shall rehearse my English once, twice, or thrice, and look out my principal
> verb and ask the question 'who?' or 'what?' And the word that answereth
> the question shall be the nominative case to the verb (except it be a verb
> impersonal), as in this example. 'The master teacheth scholars.'
> 'Teacheth' is the verb. Who teacheth? The master teacheth. This word
> 'master' answereth to the question here, and therefore it shall be the
> nominative case.[86]

Passages like these reflect three processes, not new in the fifteenth century
but easier to trace. One is pedagogy – making teaching as clear and effective
as possible. Another is adaptation – taking an older text and refining it to
improve it, reflecting the way that teachers' views and needs are constantly
changing. The third involves the impact of Latin teaching on the English
language. Although English was not formally taught in schools, its use in
teaching and translation meant that pupils studied its grammar to some
extent while they learnt Latin. The previous passages showed them that
English too had what we would now call subjects, verbs, and objects. Since
most pupils after about 1400 probably read a grammatical textbook in
English at some stage of their lives, the spellings, vocabulary, and prose style
of such textbooks must have had a significant effect on the way in which the
nation came to understand and write its own language.

   The rising status of English helped to bring about another educational
achievement: the creation of the first dictionaries of Latin words with English
equivalents.[87] The earliest large-scale work of this kind, *Medulla Grammatice*
('the marrow of grammar'), was probably compiled in the first third of the
fifteenth century. It is an alphabetical list of Latin words with English
meanings, and survives in a large number of manuscripts.[88] A successor to it,
called *Ortus* (or *Hortus*) *Vocabulorum* ('the origin (or garden) of words'), was
drawn from the *Medulla*, the *Catholicon*, and other collections, printed in
1500, and frequently reissued until the early 1530s.[89] Compiling a Latin-
to-English dictionary was a relatively easy task, since one had only to abridge
a Latin one and add the English words. The reverse process, an English-
to-Latin volume, was more difficult. It required drawing up an alphabetical
list of words in English, for which there was as yet no precedent, and involved

the challenge that English vocabulary and spelling were still not uniform, although they grew more so in the course of the fifteenth century. The task was first accomplished in 1440 by a man identified by Tudor bibliographers as Geoffrey.[90] He himself did not reveal his name, and tells us only that he had been brought up from infancy to speak the dialect of Norfolk and that, at the time of writing, he was a Dominican friar and recluse of King's Lynn in that county. He thus belonged to the same religious order as Giovanni Balbi.[91]

Geoffrey, if that was his name, stands out for his originality in the context of fifteenth-century England. Not only did he compile the earliest English-to-Latin dictionary but, in doing so, he effectively produced the first English dictionary too, albeit with definitions in Latin. He was unusual in aiming his dictionary at children (its title, *Promptorium Parvulorum*, means 'a prompter for little ones'), and in including several words and phrases special to them (Fig. 26). These included terms that are rarely encountered in other sources, such as names for dolls ('moppe' and 'popyn'), kinds of tops ('pryll', 'spylkok', and 'whirlgig'), and active games ('bace pley', 'buck hid', 'shuttlecock', and 'tennis'). The dictionary was arranged alphabetically in order of English words, except that verbs were listed separately under each letter. Every word was given at least one Latin equivalent with its principal grammatical parts, the Latin words being drawn from the works of Hugutio, Nequam, Garland, Balbi, and other vocabularies. The *Promptorium* was a success, since it survives in six manuscripts and was printed at least as many times between 1499 and 1528.[92] Nor was it the only effort made in this direction, since two manuscripts exist of a similar work, the *Catholicon Anglicum* ('the English *Catholicon*'), one of which is dated 1483. This work was never printed and contains fewer words than the *Promptorium*, but it is often more ambitious in providing Latin synonyms and sometimes includes illustrative quotations.[93]

LATINS AND VULGARIA

The sentence or short prose passage was a common unit of study in grammar schools. Masters used them in English, French, or Latin to illustrate Latin grammar, and pupils composed them in Latin or translated them from one language to another. Ælfric's grammar, as we have seen, included sentences to demonstrate how Latin worked. John of Garland did the same in his *Dictionary*, where he uses them to convey vocabulary. Here, for example, are his observations on various kinds of tradesmen found in towns:

> Shield makers prosper in the cities of the whole of France, selling shields to knights, depicted with lions and fleurs-de-lys.

> Buckle makers are wealthy through their buckles and straps and horse-bits, files and bridle-reins.

24   A school notebook. Latin and
English sentences from the
anthology compiled by Thomas
Schort at Newgate school (Bristol),
c. 1430.

William, our neighbour, has before him needles and needle-cases, soap
and mirrors and razors, whetstones and spindles to sell in this market.[94]

By the fourteenth century grammarians called an illustrative sentence of
this kind a *latinum* (plural *latina*) or a *latinitas* (plural *latinitates*).[95] John
Cornwall's *Speculum Grammatice* provides lists of them at the end of each
major section, as if inviting his schoolmaster-readers to use or imitate them
in class. Some are accompanied by English translations. Cornwall's
sentences are brief and simple, like those of Ælfric, and only rarely try to
portray daily life or current events:

I am at Oxford and at London, good towns.

If I go to the Carfax [i.e. the centre of Oxford], I may be met by misdoers.

The king of England shall be well helped by me, the stalwartest of
creatures.

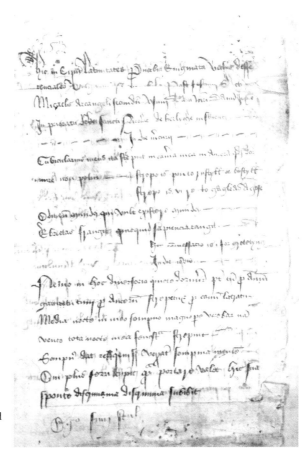

25 A notebook in diary form, made at Barlinch school (Somerset), *c*. 1500. The notes and compositions are headed by the days on which they were written.

> Would that no man in France were stronger than I, and if it be so, I know well that our king (whom God preserve) should have the upper hand (or, should acquit himself well) over Philip, who holds himself to be rightful king of France.

The references to France reflect the fact that Cornwall finished his book in the year of the battle of Crecy. [96]

In the fifteenth century this material is augmented by collections of sentences that appear to embody the work of masters and pupils in particular schools. They occur in school notebooks, the earliest of which survive from soon after 1400 and seem mostly to have been compiled by pupils rather than masters. Their survival appears to be another consequence of the development of paper as a cheap and accessible medium, which enabled pupils to keep notes of their work or to copy it for permanent use. At least fifteen such notebooks, compiled between about 1400 and 1520, can be attributed geographically, sometimes to identifiable schools and pupils (see Figs 24 and 25). The places concerned include London, six important provincial cities (Bristol, Exeter, Hereford, Lincoln or nearby, Oxford, and Winchester), a small town (Beccles), somewhere in Kent, and a couple of rural monasteries (Barlinch in Somerset and Basingwerk in north Wales).[97] Notebooks may encompass transcripts of grammatical works, literary texts, vocabularies, and sentences or short prose passages. Those books that have survived must have had some special value for their makers, and for other people after their makers discarded them or died. Most represent a fairly high standard of work, worth keeping and using. Two of the books, Thomas Schort's from Newgate school (Bristol) in the 1420s and John Hardgrave's from Beccles school in the following decade, were compiled by young men who may have aimed at becoming schoolmasters themselves.

The sentences or passages in school notebooks must have been exercises given out by the master or composed by the pupil. Some occur singly, while others are gathered into sequences. They may be in Latin alone, or in Latin accompanied by English translations, but French is not featured, having disappeared from Latin teaching by this date.[98] People called a sentence written as an exercise a *latinum* or *latinitas* like a sentence in a treatise, and by the 1420s there was an equivalent word in English: a 'latin'. 'A hard latin to make, my face waxeth black', as a pupil is imagined saying in one such exercise.[99] 'English' occurs at about the same time, meaning a sentence in that language, and later in the century *vulgus* in Latin (plural *vulgaria*) and 'vulgar' in English came into use to mean an English or a Latin sentence set as a school exercise. When notebook sentences are written in two languages, the Latin may appear first with an English translation after it, or the reverse order may be followed. The material probably reflects a variety of tasks that went on in a school. A pupil might be given an English sentence, or be told to invent one, for turning into Latin. Alternatively he might be assigned a Latin sentence and asked to translate it into English. In a third case, he might be ordered to compose a Latin sentence or passage on a theme, without being given a piece of English to start with; this would be a more advanced task. The resulting pieces of work were meant to develop a wide vocabulary and an understanding of syntax: agreements between words and the construction of phrases. Hardgrave's collection of English and Latin phrases from Beccles in the 1430s gives humorous examples of the way in which Latin is *not* to be translated:

I saw thee drunken while thou were sober.
Ego vidi ebrius dum fuisti sobrius.
[correctly: 'I, being drunk, saw you while you were sober.']

My primer lieth in my lap that knows Our Lady's matins.
Primarium meum iacet in gremio meo qui scio matutinas Sancte Marie.
[correctly: 'My primer lies in my lap, I that know Our Lady's matins.'][100]

Þe entil fire fait il qui tant maues chier
s us toute riens aues ame bon cheualier

26   Words for children's toys and games, including tops, are a feature of the first English-to-Latin school dictionary, *Promptorium Parvulorum* (1440).

The message is conveyed that Latin grammar does not depend on word order, like English, but on the paradigms of the subject, verb, and object.

Vulgaria, as we shall call them, have a value beyond what they tell us about the teaching of Latin. Schoolmasters used them like colloquies to introduce subjects that would edify the pupils or engage their interest by drawing on everyday life. English proverbs were favourite texts for this purpose. The Lincoln notebook of about 1425–50, for example, contains 'Better friend in court than penny in purse', 'As the cock crows, the chicken hears', 'Burnt hand fire dreads', and 'Was he never good swain that left his errand for the rain.'[101] At other times more obviously religious and moral material makes its appearance. The following passage comes from Bristol in the 1420s:

Cunning [i.e. knowledge] is a high tree, of which the root is full bitter but the fruit is full sweet. He that despiseth the bitterness of the root shall never taste the sweetness of the fruit.[102]

This is wisdom from Exeter, in about 1450:

One should not be too joyful and glad in prosperity and too sad in adversity, according to the counsel of the philosophers, for a poor spirit is to be avoided in favour of magnanimity, which endures and accepts adversity equally with prosperity.[103]

The goodness or effect of the prayer of a just man is more acceptable in the sight of God than any sacrifice, wherefore according to the exhortation of the great doctor of the Church we are to pray without interruption, wishing for the outcome of that for which we humbly pray.[104]

Material of this kind came close to the sentiments that pupils were reading in Cato and Alain de Lille. There are numerous references to the calendar of the Christian year and the familiar ceremonies of Church life. Baptism, confession, fasting, pilgrimage, and devotion to the Virgin all receive mention.

Other material in vulgaria collections is secular and humorous. School life is talked about: its early-morning start, its breaks for meals, the writing of exercises, the 'apposing' or examining of the class by the master, and the punishing of naughty boys by birching. Occasionally mention is made of rhymes, popular songs, and pieces of oral lore, such as would have circulated among the pupils. Thomas Schort's Bristol notebook, for example, includes a fragment of a popular lyric ('Light leaf of the lime-tree, lay the dew a-down'), a bit of ghost-lore ('Bloodless and boneless standeth behind the door'), and a riddle or counting-out rhyme ('One more than three and fewer than five, I plucked apples full ryve [i.e. plentifully]').[105] Food is a frequent topic: sometimes imaginary food that pupils might like to eat, and sometimes real food. 'Green [i.e. young] geese shall come hastily in season, with the garlic knuckle-deep.' 'In a short while we shall have beans, peas, strawberries, cherries, and wild pears for sale in the market.'[106] The writer from Bristol complains about the cost of meat before Lent, and takes pleasure in noting that the butchers must then close their shops until Easter.[107] His counterpart at Beccles grumbles at the high prices charged by innkeepers and cooks when fairs are held in the town. Let them weep, he warns ominously, 'for they are nearer to their death, perhaps, than they think'.[108]

Other social conflicts make their way into school compositions. A Winchester manuscript contains two rhymes in English, with Latin translations, one against shoemakers 'who stink like dogs' and another that takes in friars, haywards (those who impounded stray animals), and tapsters or ale-sellers:

A fox and a foumart [i.e. polecat], a friar and a hayward,
   Standing in a row,
A tapster standing thereby,
   The best of the company is an old shrew.[109]

The Lincoln notebook jeers at a Scot for a defeat inflicted on his nation, possibly at the battle of Verneuil in France in 1424, and imagines him thrown, as in a wrestling match, so that he breaks his neck.[110] Tensions of

another kind emerge in reports of epidemics: dangerous for schools since
they might not only affect the pupils but force the suspension of teaching. A
writer at Exeter notes that 'Scurfs or poxes and pustules have quite held
sway this year among children and youths which, so seers and magicians
assert, foretell that a pestilence will come rapidly.' In Oxford, he believes,
conditions are worse. 'We have heard . . . that a great pestilence is raging . . .
in the university. . . . The scholars are withdrawing and fleeing from it,
hurrying home each to his own birthplace.'[111]

News of the day, like this, was grist to the mill of the classroom.
Occasionally it was national news, like the mentions at Bristol of the arrest
of Lollards in various towns and of a judicial duel at Tothill near
Westminster. The Beccles notebook talks of the gathering of peers and
gentry in London for the opening of Parliament.[112] In the first half of the
fifteenth century, however, the topic of paramount interest was the war in
France, as it had been in Cornwall's time. The earliest known school
notebook, probably from Kent in the 1410s, is not quite early enough to
catch the battle of Agincourt in 1415, but its exercises refer to the visit of the
Emperor Sigismund to England and the attempt of the French to recapture
Harfleur, which both took place in the following year.[113] The Bristol
notebook talks of the king residing at Calais, probably in 1430,[114] and
during the next few years the problems of the war (now growing for the
English) were causing alarm at Beccles:

Because the king's military leaders are greatly troubled in heart by the
revolt of the common people of Normandy, retainers and men at arms
have incurred great expenses on saddles, bridles, horse-collars, and

27   A schoolmaster and
pupils, from a continental
woodcut also used in
early-Tudor English
schoolbooks.

halters, and they are ready to assault the defences of towns or to fight in the open fields, notwithstanding that men of peace at home . . . desire truces and good fortunes.

A later passage in the same manuscript prays 'that [if] the English and the French fight together, may the good will of our Saviour favour the English so that they may prevail against the French!'[115]

Vulgaria continued to be popular with schoolmasters well into the sixteenth century. They were one of the earliest kinds of grammatical literature to be printed in England, and four authors published collections of them in English and Latin up to the 1530s – authors whom we shall encounter in the following section. Two of these collections, by John Stanbridge and (probably) John Anwykyll, were traditional in format and centred on fairly short sentences. A third, by William Horman, was a huge compilation, arranged by topic like an encyclopaedia. A fourth, that of Robert Whittington, developed the genre by incorporating grammatical information, so that his *Vulgaria* contains a framework of rules illustrated by sentences that show the rules at work. Whittington also offered personal compliments, one to the king's father Henry VII and another to Thomas More, a phrase of which has grown famous:

> More is a man of an angel's wit and singular learning. He is a man of many excellent virtues (if I should say as it is); I know not his fellow. For where is the man in whom is so many goodly virtues, of that gentleness, lowliness, and affability? And, as time requireth, a man of marvellous mirth and pastimes, and sometimes of as sad gravity, as who [i.e. people] say 'a man for all seasons'.[116]

But not all Tudor exercises were so elegant. Others included oaths, insults, and sexual innuendoes. Stanbridge asked pupils to translate 'Thou stinkest', 'Thou art a false knave', 'Turd in thy teeth', 'He is a cuckold', and 'He is the veriest coward that ever pissed.'[117] Horman introduced boys to the thought that 'a common woman liveth by her body', and told of men who 'deflowered many women', 'keepeth other men's wives', 'gropeth uncleanly children and maidens', and consorted with a 'sister openly, as she had been his true wedded wife'.[118] Culture in school, like culture in society, was complex, enfolding both morality and vulgarity as we see in Tudor drama, and children were not shielded from sex even after the Reformation (Fig. 29).

Altogether vulgaria provide a rich source of evidence for educational, social, and cultural history between 1400 and 1520. Pedagogically they show that schoolmasters in the late middle ages took seriously the task of interesting and stimulating their pupils. Socially they demonstrate, as do *Facetus* and *Stans Puer ad Mensam*, that schools did not teach a culture that was narrowly religious. Classrooms opened their windows onto the secular

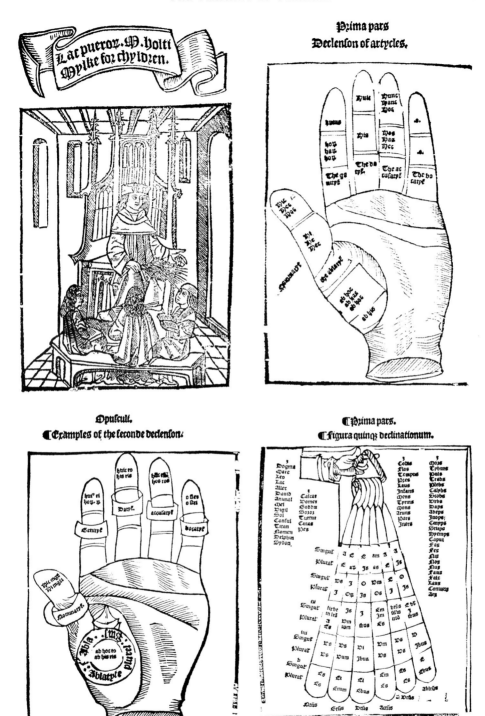

28   Illustrations from John Holt's *Lac Puerorum* of *c*. 1495: a rare example of pictures in a
schoolbook, here teaching the paradigms of nouns and pronouns.

world, reflecting the presence of pupils with varied career ambitions – ambitions that were not necessarily fixed. The boy whose parents meant him to be a cleric might not develop the vocation to become one, or might be thrust by family deaths into the inheritance and management of property. He too needed to be trained as a man for all seasons.

HUMANISM

During the fifteenth century a revival of interest in the pagan Latin authors spread from Italy through western Europe to England, especially during the last twenty years of the century. Once again education in England was affected by cultural changes beyond its borders, after two hundred years of relative insularity. The pagan authors had never been quite forgotten after 1300, but they had become marginalised. Now they returned to favour as treasuries of knowledge and models of Latin grammar, prosody, and literary style. The contemporary term for the study of secular Latin literature was 'humanity', as opposed to religious studies, 'divinity'. Subsequently 'humanity' came to be applied to the pagan Latin classics in particular, and this has led historians to call those who studied the classics 'humanists' and their studies 'humanism'. The humanists of this period, of course, were Christians, and the humanism that they practised had nothing to do with the word's modern meaning of a lack of belief in God.

Humanist Latin began to attract interest in England during the first half of the fifteenth century, and by the early 1480s it was receiving significant support and patronage. University scholars espoused it, and some were inspired to go and teach it in schools. Bishops encouraged their efforts, notably Waynflete of Winchester in the case of John Anwykyll, Morton of Canterbury with regard to John Holt, and Smith of Lincoln who patronised John Stanbridge. The first of the Tudor kings, Henry VII, was favourable to the new fashion, since he allowed his elder son Arthur, who died in 1502, to receive a thoroughly humanist education, based on grammatical works by recent Italian authors and on a wide range of pagan classical texts. Arthur's younger brother Henry VIII had humanist teachers too.[119] Humanism aroused enthusiasm for its own sake, as other cultural movements have done, but it offered the hope of practical gains as well. In the field of knowledge it appeared to provide fresh information from previously neglected authors. In terms of language it seemed better equipped to express matters clearly and elegantly. In the spheres of politics and society it promised to unite western Europe by rescuing Latin from the regional variations into which the language had fallen during the later middle ages. The nations of the Continent were adopting humanist Latin during the late fifteenth century in schools, universities, and the bureaucracies of rulers and the Church. Their English counterparts could not afford to fall behind in this process.

The first humanist grammarians to be influential in England were the Italians Lorenzo Valla (1407–57) and Niccolò Perotti (1429–80). Valla's work on grammar, *Elegantiae Linguae Latinae* ('elegances of the Latin language'), had reached Oxford by 1474, when Lincoln College is recorded as owning a copy donated by Robert Fleming, an English diplomat and traveller in Italy.[120] Perotti's *Rudimenta Grammaticae* ('rudiments of grammar') was printed at Louvain in 1486 with explanations in English, evidently for the English market.[121] The *Opus Grammaticum* ('grammatical work') of a third writer, Giovanni Sulpizio of Verona, was published in England several times between 1494 and 1514.[122] Later, in the early sixteenth century, some Dutch and German grammarians found English readers as well. One was Joannes de Spouter ('Despauterius') (d. 1520), the author of *Ninivitae* on accentuation; another was Peter Schede ('Mosellanus') (d. 1524), who wrote on *Figures of Speech*. The most popular was Erasmus of Rotterdam (d. 1536), whose schoolbooks included Latin *Colloquies*, *De Copia Rerum et Verborum* ('a store of matters and words') on composition, and a commentary on the *Distichs of Cato*.[123] Sulpizio and Erasmus came to be widely used in English schools, while Despauterius, Schede, and Valla, whose works were more advanced, tended to be read by senior pupils or teachers. But England did not depend for its humanist grammars on foreigners alone. Many of the texts that established the new Latin in English schools were produced by Englishmen, for the good reason that, after Leland's time, elementary grammars were normally written in English.

In 1480 William Waynflete, bishop of Winchester, founded Magdalen College School in Oxford, alongside the university college that he had already built there. Its first recorded schoolmaster, John Anwykyll, was appointed between 1480 and 1483.[124] Anwykyll was probably the author of a prose grammar entitled *Compendium totius Grammatice* ('a compendium of all grammar'), published at Oxford in 1483.[125] The work is anonymous, but it contains two poems that name the writer as John and praise Bishop Waynflete, which together with the date and the Oxford context make Anwykyll the most plausible author. This would distinguish him as the earliest English grammarian to have a textbook printed during his lifetime, as well as the earliest to incorporate humanist principles into such a book. The *Compendium* discusses all four parts of grammar, almost wholly in Latin, and was meant for pupils who had learnt the elements of the subject. Its layout was traditional, incorporating questions and answers, mnemonic verses, and illustrative latins, with quotations from medieval authorities such as Hugutio and the *Catholicon*. Equally it followed a new path in citing Valla and Perotti, the fourth-century Roman grammarian Servius, and classical authors like Cicero, Horace, Terence, and Virgil, who are mentioned more frequently than medieval writers. Another anonymous work printed at about the same time, a collection of *Vulgaria*, looks as if it was intended to be a companion to the *Compendium* and was therefore also by Anwykyll.[126] This too possesses an original feature, in that the sentences, although at first sight typical ones about everyday life, were based on material from the plays of Terence and therefore humanist in nature. Magdalen College showed its appreciation of Anwykyll's work by awarding him a fifteen-year contract in June 1487 to teach 'grammar, poetry, elegances of literature, and other humanities'. The document praised his labours 'concerning a new and most useful form of grammar, conceived and composed by him for the school' – a likely reference to the *Compendium*. Anwykyll died at the following Christmas, but the *Compendium* and *Vulgaria* were reprinted several times up to 1530, a sign of their value to teachers.

Anwykyll is the earliest known member of a group of humanist grammarians who studied or taught at Oxford at the end of the fifteenth century: the city's last period of dominance over English school education. They included Thomas Linacre of All Souls College, John Holt and William Lily of Magdalen College, William Horman and John Stanbridge of New College, and John Colet who had no college affiliation.[127] Thomas Wolsey was another member of Magdalen at this time and briefly taught in its school. He later took an important part in promoting humanist education as a patron and legislator.[128] The rest of these men went on to write grammars based in part on humanist Latin. Stanbridge was the most immediately successful. He was born in about 1463, served as Anwykyll's deputy at Magdalen College School, and succeeded him as headmaster in 1488, staying there until about 1493. His movements during the next few years are not clear, but may have taken him to teach at Lichfield. In 1501 he was appointed by the bishop of Lincoln to head a new grammar school at Banbury, where he remained until his death in 1510.[129]

Stanbridge resembled Leland in producing short elementary works in English. They included an *Accidence* on the eight parts of speech; *Sum es fui* on the forms of the common verbs *sum*, *fero*, and their compounds; *Gradus Comparationum* on the comparison of adjectives; *Parvula* on elementary syntax (a work like Leland's *Informacio*); *Vocabula* (a basic Latin vocabulary); and a collection of *Vulgaria*. Some of these works were directly attributed to Stanbridge on their printed title pages and others were described as 'of the Stanbridgian edition'.[130] The first four, in fact, are derived from versions of Leland's works current at the end of the fifteenth century, which Stanbridge modified, chiefly by revising the Latin usages to accord with those of humanism.[131] The *Parvula*, for example, cites authors such as Cicero, Ovid, Pliny, Sallust, Terence, and Virgil, as well as Valla. Stanbridge was therefore a traditionalist in the format of his treatises but an innovator in his Latinity. His books were highly popular, perhaps for those reasons. They were printed from about 1505 onwards, and went into many editions up to 1540, sometimes with further revisions. He was the first English grammarian whose works achieved a wide circulation in print, gaining use at four of the leading English schools: Eton, Magdalen, St Paul's (London), and Winchester.

Horman and Holt were less influential than Stanbridge, but both have much to commend them. Horman, who was headmaster of Eton College and later Winchester College, published an *Introduction to the Latin Language* in Latin in 1495 and *Vulgaria* in 1519 – the latter the largest collection ever published. Like the vocabularies of Nequam and Garland it covers all kinds of human activities and everyday objects, and is a valuable source for Tudor social history.[132] Neither of his books, however, achieved more than two editions. Holt worked at Lambeth Palace (London) between about 1496 and 1501, teaching the boys of the household of the archbishop of Canterbury, where he wrote an elementary grammar in English called *Lac Puerorum* ('milk for children').[133] This followed Leland in using simple phrases to explain the technical terms of grammar, such as 'the showing mood or indicative', 'the bidding mood or imperative', and 'the wishing mood or optative'. With more originality it featured three illustrations, an unprecedented device in an English grammar. Two of these portrayed the human hand, with information placed on the fingers and thumbs. Holt may have got this idea from the Continent, where hands were used as teaching devices in printed books on accounting, logic, and music during the 1490s.[134] One of the hands in *Lac Puerorum* displayed the paradigms of the pronoun *hic* ('this'), and another the paradigms of the second declension of nouns (Fig. 28). Holt went on to tutor Henry VIII, but his early death in 1504 helped to curtail his influence. Although his grammar was reprinted a few times, his pictures did not inspire imitations. Humanist teachers, like medieval ones, seem to have thought that school texts should be plain and committed to memory, rather than approached through visual images.

By 1510 the group of humanist grammarians based in Oxford had largely dispersed. London now became the leading centre of grammatical activity, a change that reflected the fact that most publishing, printing, and bookselling took place there. In about 1508 John Colet, who had risen to be dean of St Paul's Cathedral, began to reorganise its ancient cathedral school and busied himself in securing new grammars for use in its classes. He himself prepared an elementary treatise on accidence in English in 1509, the so-called *Aeditio*, and he asked Linacre to write an advanced grammar to follow it, although he rejected the completed work as too difficult.[135] For his first schoolmaster Colet chose William Lily, a Magdalen College pupil of the next generation who had been taught by Stanbridge. Lily was another outstanding grammarian, whose works included one on *The Genders of Nouns* and two on syntax: an elementary *Rudiments* and a more advanced *On Construction*, the latter of which received some revision by Colet's friend Erasmus.[136] At about this time, the 1510s, another pupil of Stanbridge came to London in the person of Robert Whittington, who hailed from Lichfield and saw himself as inheriting Stanbridge's mantle.[137] He formed links with the court of Henry VIII and eventually became schoolmaster to the king's henchmen – noble youths who lived in the royal household.

29 'Thou shalt not commit adultery.'
Thomas Cranmer's *Catechism* (1548),
although a work of the Reformation,
is late-medieval in the frankness with
which it discusses such matters with
children.

Whittington was not a university man, but went straight from school to become a working schoolmaster. Only later did he gain accreditation as a 'laureate' at Oxford: virtually an honorary degree, conferred for his skill in composing Latin verses. He was a productive writer, who revised the *Accidence* of Stanbridge and published a number of other grammars of his own in English or Latin during the 1510s and early 1520s, which had a wide circulation. Less happily, Whittington's laureateship and court connections led him to give himself airs and to criticise others. When Horman published his *Vulgaria* in 1520, containing commendatory poems by Lily, Whittington posted verses on the door of St Paul's school, ridiculing its size, its price, and Lily's judgment in praising it. This led to a 'grammarians' war', in which Lily and Horman published a two-part attack on Whittington entitled *Antibossicon* (1521), so named because it identified him with the bear-shaped water-tap in Billingsgate, London, built by his namesake Sir Richard Whittington. They satirised his abilities as a poet and grammarian, and mocked his descriptions of himself in his books as 'chief poet of England' – provoking a riposte from Whittington called *Antilycon* ('against the wolf'). The quarrel was largely a personal one. It did not relate to humanism in principle, which had the support of all the writers concerned.[138]

Several of the medieval grammars were printed in England after the 1480s, but during the 1510s the printers abandoned them in a tacit admission of changing fashions. The speculative grammar *De Modis Significandi* made the last of its three known appearances in 1515, and the *Doctrinale*, which achieved at least nine editions, did so in the following year.[139] The eleventh and final recorded printing of the *Ars Minor* of Donatus dates from 1517,[140] while the *Synonyma* and the *Equivoca* made their farewell bow in 1518, having been issued on several occasions since 1494.[141]

Even Priscian, who had been closely in touch with classical literature and its usages, fell out of favour. He was never published in England and rarely even on the Continent after 1530. His work was still prescribed reading in the arts course at Oxford in 1564–5, but students by that time were allowed to opt for Linacre's grammar if they wished.[142] The kinds of school texts used by 1520 can be gathered from the earliest record of bookshop sales, that of the Oxford bookseller John Dorne. In that year he sold quantities of the grammars of Stanbridge and Whittington, works by Sulpizio and Valla, and occasional copies of Perotti.[143] His counterpart at Cambridge, Garret Godfrey, retailed similar authors between about 1527 and 1533: Lily, Stanbridge, Whittington, and another new work in an old genre, the *Colloquies* of Erasmus.[144] The earliest school timetables to survive, from Eton, Ipswich, and Winchester between 1528 and 1530, confirm this evidence. Humanist grammars by Lily, Stanbridge, and Sulpizio had, by this time, completely replaced their predecessors.[145]

An equally large change overtook the literature read in schools during the first twenty-five years of the sixteenth century. Some of the poems popular in the later middle ages were still being printed in England in the years immediately after 1500. The *Eclogue of Theodulus* came out about seven times up to 1515, and *Peniteas cito* on three occasions between about 1514 and 1516.[146] Alain de Lille's *Liber Parabolarum* is known in five editions, the last of which appeared in 1525.[147] The *Hymnal* in its format as a school text survived for a little longer, but this too ceased to be published after 1530, nearly twenty years before the abolition of religious services in Latin.[148] Meanwhile, as these poems were disappearing, Colet put forward a new list of authors to replace them in the statutes of St Paul's, issued in 1518. He wished his pupils to begin by reading two works by his friend Erasmus, *The Institution of a Christian Man* and *Copia Verborum*, and to progress to a list of fourth- and fifth-century Christian poets, 'that wrote their wisdom with clean and chaste Latin': Juvencus, Lactantius, Proba, Prudentius, and Sedulius. To these Colet added one modern poet, Baptista Mantuanus, the Italian Carmelite friar and author of a popular set of Christian eclogues.[149] His scheme looks like an attempt to retain the Christian tone of the previous school readers while moving nearer to the type of classical literature now in fashion, but it seems to have had little or no influence. Hardly any of Colet's authors were published in England, and no later curricula include them.

Instead the pagan classical authors established themselves as the staple diet of Tudor schools. This process had probably begun in places like Magdalen College School by the late 1490s, where exercises were written that quote or allude to Cicero, Horace, Martial, Ovid, Sallust, Terence, and Virgil.[150] It was complete by the late 1520s, since the school timetables of that period include hardly anything of the late medieval reading list except at an elementary level. The basic prayers, of course, such as the Lord's Prayer and the Creed, remained in use: in Latin until the 1530s and afterwards in

30   Schools began to read Virgil's
Aeneid again in the late fifteenth
century, including scenes like the
death of Dido.

English. There continued to be poems on good manners, but the old *Stans Puer ad Mensam* gave way to newer works like *Quos Decet in Mensa* ('It is fitting at table . . .') by Sulpizio and *Carmen de Moribus* ('Song of manners') by Lily, the second of which gained wide currency.[151] The only reading text that survived from the medieval curriculum was the *Distichs of Cato*. Close enough in date and character to the great pagan classics, it remained acceptable in the new age as in the old, and was regularly prescribed for the junior forms of Tudor English schools.

   The list of other classical authors who dominated the curriculum by 1528 began, at the elementary end, with the *Fables* of Aesop and Lucian's *Dialogues* – Greek works in Latin translations. After this pupils encountered a variety of literary genres as opposed to the single form of poetry that had been favoured before. The comedies of Terence introduced them to conversation, and the letters of Cicero to literary prose. For history there were Caesar and Sallust, and for poetry Horace's *Epistles*, Ovid's *Metamorphoses*, and Virgil's *Eclogues* and *Aeneid* (Fig. 30). Cicero also figured as the author of *De Officiis*, which treats of ethical philosophy. Only a few modern works were admitted to join them, notably Mantuan's *Eclogues* and the *Colloquies* of Erasmus. Colet hoped to broaden the work of St Paul's with the language and literature of Greece, and he provided for the appointment of a 'high-' or head master with the appropriate knowledge, 'if such may be gotten'.[152] His first high-master, Lily, was indeed so qualified, having learnt the language on the island of Rhodes, and may have taught it to some pupils, but little is known about the teaching of Greek in English schools during the 1520s and 1530s.[153] It may have been available at Eton and Winchester as well as St Paul's, and it remained a goal for ambitious educationists. When King's School (Canterbury) was founded by Henry VIII in 1541, the headmaster was required to be knowledgeable in Latin and Greek, as opposed to his deputy who had to be proficient only in Latin.[154]

The diffusion of humanism coincided with the introduction of printing to England, raising the question what difference the new technology made in this respect. Printing can easily be overvalued as an agent of change. As we have seen, it was possible for manuscript grammars to circulate widely and fairly quickly, even from country to country. By 1400 handwritten copies of short texts were proliferating in classrooms, enabling some pupils to have their own. Printing brought about relative rather than absolute change, at least in its early decades, and although schools offered an obvious market for printing, printers in England took some time to exploit it effectively. This was partly because the first of them, William Caxton, concentrated on the production of literary works in English. Although some of his titles were educational and aimed at children, they were not schoolbooks, except for one Latin grammar that must have been a commissioned project. A press in Oxford during the early 1480s printed the *Doctrinale* and the *Long Parvula* (a version of Leland's *Informacio*), but the enterprise was short-lived.[155] It was not until the 1490s, when Caxton was dead and had been succeeded by two rival printers in London, Wynkyn de Worde and Richard Pynson, that serious attention was given to the printing of schoolbooks, and large numbers of titles and copies began to be printed.

Moreover the technology of printing was not the only factor in supplying the needs of schools.[156] The books produced had to be the ones that teachers wanted, and conveyed to their potential buyers in the English provinces. This caused problems for London printers, who had to rely on their wares being carried by merchants of other products. In principle there were openings for printers and publishers to set themselves up in the provinces to fill the gap, and there are at least three examples of this taking place. Hugo Goes printed an edition of *Ortus Vocabulorum* at York in 1506–9, and Jean Gachet published another at Hereford (printed in France) in 1517.[157] Martin Coeffin, a French bookseller in Exeter, arranged for two texts, the Latin vocabulary *Os Facies Mentum* and a tract on defective verbs, to be printed in Normandy and sold them himself, presumably to local schools.[158] None of these provincial ventures lasted for long, however, and in the end the London printers established a dominance over the national trade in schoolbooks that was virtually complete by the 1520s. A further problem was the achievement of consistency and quality. Schoolbooks had long been prone to variation, because schoolmasters were inclined to revise each others' works. A standard author like Alexander of Ville-Dieu might circulate in slightly different texts, and Leland's tracts, as we have seen, were altered later on. Printing did not change this situation but, if anything, increased it. By the end of the fifteenth century there was a *Short Accidence* and a *Long Accidence*, a *Parvula* and a *Long Parvula*. Later there was the choice of using grammars by Colet and Lily, Stanbridge, Sulpizio, and Whittington.

Even individual texts might vary when reprinted. Errors might creep in, particularly since some texts were printed in the Netherlands for sale in England. In the manuscript era variations in a classroom could be controlled to some extent by the master dictating from a single copy, but once printing made it possible for pupils to have their own copies, variations might arise in the texts that they used. They might have bought different editions, or be using older second-hand ones. Leonard Cox, a schoolmaster writing in 1526, suggested that a teacher should start the study of a new grammar by reading the text to his class. He should instruct the pupils 'to correct whatever mistakes they notice in their own copies, to fill in gaps, and rub out what does not appear in the teacher's text' – a cumbersome process.[159] By 1530 the convocation of the clergy of the province of Canterbury (southern England) was complaining of the difficulties experienced by pupils who moved from one school to another and had to cope with unfamiliar texts.[160] Printers could not resolve this problem by themselves because their horizons were limited to one book at a time, and because they were in competition with each other. It required the intervention of the English crown to settle the matter through the imposition of uniform grammars throughout the kingdom, but that did not happen until 1540.[161]

What did contemporaries feel about the advance of humanism in the schools? Our knowledge of the advance comes largely from editions of books, and not many writers seem to have commented on the process as it unfolded. One who did so, the writer of the first unpublished set of vulgaria from Magdalen College School in the 1490s, confessed to doubts about what was happening. 'These new authors do rebuke the noble deeds of them that were before them; therefore our minds are plucked hither and thither.' Change, he felt, might not be for the best. 'We be so variable and wandering of mind that we covet the newer things, although they be worse.'[162] Ten or fifteen years later, in 1508–9, the poet and schoolmaster Alexander Barclay translated Sebastian Brant's German satirical work *The Ship of Fools*, which contained a section on those who do not profit from learning. Brant made no mention of the medieval-humanist issue, but Barclay did. Those were fools, he thought, who clung to the ancient ways. They still relied on the *Doctrinale* and disdained to read Priscian or Sulpizio, with the result that they were as foolish after learning their grammar as they had been before they began.[163] A third observer, John Skelton, another schoolmaster-poet, shared the Magdalen writer's wistful view of the past as late as the 1520s. Noting that Donatus, Alexander, and Albertus Magnus had all been cast out, he painted the new order as one in which children read Plautus and Quintilian when they scarcely knew the tenses of their verbs, and could hardly construe a line of the prose introduction to *Cato*.[164] Change, for him, was by no means a self-evident improvement.

The forty years from 1480 to 1520, in which humanism percolated through the English schools, represented a tiny part of the era covered by this book but a long period for those who lived through it. Even in the middle of the sixteenth century there were still men alive who had been educated in the old curriculum. How easily change came from school to school is unknown. Very likely, as so often in education, masters did what they had always done and matters altered when they left or died. Moreover it would be misleading to regard this period as either self-contained or unique with respect to its impact on grammar. The early humanists used traditional formats, notably the English-language texts of the Leland tradition and the publication of vulgaria. Teaching through vulgaria petered out only in the middle of the sixteenth century. Nor was humanism uniform and unchanging: by the 1540s the works of Anwykyll, Stanbridge, and Whittington had been largely superseded by new ones authorised by the crown. The introduction of humanism has become one of the best-known periods of change in English educational history, because its principles dominated English school education down to the nineteenth century. Our survey of medieval grammar should have revealed that it was only one such period. We should be cautious about exalting it over the others.

4

The Schoolroom

THE FRAMEWORK OF SCHOOLING

Schooling takes place in a context. Schools are held in rooms laid out and organised in particular ways. Their pupils are of particular ages and come from particular places, sent by parents for particular reasons. Grammars tell us a little about these things, especially in dialogues and exercises of the vulgaria kind. A good deal more can be gathered from other sources. By the fourteenth and fifteenth centuries statutes were issued for schools, prescribing how they should be run. Letters and financial accounts refer to children at school. A handful of school buildings survive, as do pictures of masters and pupils in manuscripts and later in printed books. Imaginative literature, such as stories and songs, has a little to say on the subject, as we have seen in Chaucer's 'Prioress's Tale'. Most of this evidence refers to public grammar schools, and more of it exists as time goes on. The present chapter is inevitably weighted accordingly. While aiming to survey schools from 1100 to about 1530, it achieves its aim most fully in the second half of that period.

Who went to school in England? The question can be pursued with regard both to individual people and to social categories. Some schools recorded their pupils' names on arrival. This was the case by 1339 at St Albans and by the 1380s at Oxford, whose grammar masters were required to return lists of their pupils to the university.[1] Colet ordered that children entering St Paul's should pay 4d. to have their names enrolled.[2] The only extant records of this kind from before the Reformation, however, are the registers of Winchester College, beginning in 1393, which state the name of every holder of a scholarship, his place of origin, and the date of his entrance. After 1472 approximate ages are noted, and there are sometimes comments on deaths or departures.[3] Winchester's archives also identify some of the college's fee-paying pupils or 'commoners', but Eton College possesses no admission registers until 1661, although many names survive from before that date.[4] Some cathedral records preserve the names of choristers,[5] and a few other lists of schoolboys have come down to us for specific reasons. Thirty-four pupils from Wells (Fig. 51) and thirty-nine from Glastonbury are named paying poll-tax in 1377,[6] and thirty to forty boys at Basingwerk (north Wales) are identified in a grammatical miscellany of the mid fifteenth century.[7] Single names occur in connection with many other schools, which would total several hundreds if they were collected, but names by themselves are of limited value. We need to know their owners' places of origin, their status, their wealth, and preferably their adult careers in order to make sense of the information.

Pending such knowledge we have to be content with generalisations. Schools catered chiefly for boys. Girls were more likely to be taught informally at home, in a great household, or in a nunnery.[8] By the fifteenth century we hear of a few schoolmistresses who seem likely to have educated girls, and at least one man is mentioned as doing so, but nothing more is known about their work.[9] In principle any boy who was not a serf might go to school, and since most teachers taught for fees it was to their advantage to collect as many pupils as possible. The major factors limiting school attendance were social attitudes and economic constraints. Parents might have no interest in education or be reluctant to lose a son as a helper or money earner. They might not be able to afford the cost of attending a school, especially if it meant leaving home to do so. Age was a further issue in so far that pupils needed to be old enough to cope with schoolwork. Some people thought that seven was a suitable age to start school, since it was viewed as the point of transition from infancy to childhood. At this age boys were believed to become more fully male in gender, capable of looking after themselves, and eligible to be tonsured as clerks. It was an appropriate time for them to move from care by women to rule by men.[10] Aristotle, one of the major authorities on education, considered that boys should become observers of formal study when they were five and students when they reached seven.[11] Chaucer may have had this model in mind when he envisaged the boy-hero of 'The Prioress's Tale' as a schoolboy of seven who had just embarked on his studies.[12]

In practice schooling might start earlier, if circumstances were favourable. The chronicler Orderic Vitalis, who was born in 1075, tells us that he began to learn letters from a priest in Shrewsbury when he was five.[13] Hugh de la Tour, a gentleman's son, is said to have gone to school at Taunton at the same age in about 1293.[14] The writer John Hardyng observed in 1457 that lords' sons were set to school when they were four, and the 'Princes in the Tower' had a schoolmaster in May 1476 when the elder one, Edward, was five and a half, and his brother Richard two and three quarters.[15] The Roman educationist Quintilian, who became influential again in the early sixteenth century, suggested that children might learn letters as soon as they could speak, and Sir Thomas Elyot endorsed this view in his book *The Governor* in 1531.[16] All this relates to learning at home or at a nearby school. One did not normally send a child to school away from home until well after seven. Boys could board at Winchester College from the age of eight, but most of its scholars after 1472 were eleven or twelve, the latter being the closing point for entry.[17] The author of the Magdalen College School vulgaria, writing in the 1490s, appears to envisage a scholar leaving home when he was ten.[18]

There were other limits to how old you could be, or how long you could stay. The scholars of Winchester College were expected to leave at eighteen, or a year later if they were going to university. If they were relatives of the founder they could keep their places until they were twenty-five.[19] In 1389 William Tonge, a wealthy London citizen, provided for his two sons to receive support until they were twenty, observing that by that time they could be expected to know grammar and good manners.[20] Most boys probably left school by their late teens, but it is hard to imagine a schoolmaster excluding older youths or young adults who wished to learn, if they were prepared to pay for the privilege. Men could not become priests until they were twenty-four, and some may have lingered at school for that reason. A Suffolk clerk named John Melton went to Beccles school for six years until he was ordained as a priest in 1412, presumably having reached the appropriate age.[21] Bishops sometimes told ill-educated clergy to attend school. Bishop Bransford of Worcester (1339–49), for example, ordained several clerks as subdeacons and deacons on condition that they remained at school for one or two years before they were promoted to the priesthood.[22] These clerks must have been aged at least seventeen, and may have been in their early twenties.

How long one spent at school hinged on resources and ambitions. A couple of years of grammar might provide the basic skills required to follow a trade or business. For those who aimed to take holy orders, enter a religious order, go to university, or undertake a legal education in London, a longer period was needed. A boy named Henry Atkinson attended Ripon school for three years from 1408 to 1411, before going to Oxford.[23] Hugh Willoughby, the Arctic explorer of Elizabeth's reign and the son of a Warwickshire knight, spent about four years at Sutton Coldfield school after 1522, prior to entering one of the London inns of chancery.[24] The poor scholars of the almonry of St Albans Abbey were allowed to stay for up to five years in 1339, as 'this time is enough to become proficient in grammar'.[25] The scholars of Winchester and Eton usually arrived at the age of eleven or twelve and stayed for six, seven, or eight years until they left at eighteen or nineteen.[26] But schooling was not always the continuous process that it usually is today. It might be interrupted through poverty or lack of accessible teachers. William Green, the son of a 'husbandman' or peasant in Lincolnshire climbed the staircase of learning slowly and with difficulty. During the 1510s he spent two years in the free grammar school at Wainfleet, before leaving to work with his father for five or six years as a farmer and sawyer. Later he managed two more years at Boston school by lodging with his aunt and doing part-time work. Finally he got to Cambridge University, but found it almost impossible to survive on a combination of study, work, and poor relief. In the end he was tempted to forge the papers needed for ordination as a priest.[27]

SCHOOLBOYS

The pupils mentioned thus far show that the social ranking of those who went to school varied widely. At the topmost level we hear of one or two sons of the nobility. John de Balliol, later king of Scotland, studied at Durham school in the 1260s.[28] Alexander de la Pole, a younger son of the earl of Suffolk, boarded with the schoolmaster of Ipswich in 1416–17.[29] Boys of this status were probably rare in classrooms, however, because most of them grew up in great households and had their schooling there in private surroundings. Schools catered more fully for sons of the gentry, merchants, substantial townsmen, and rural yeomen, all of whom are well attested there in the later middle ages.[30]

Lower in status were the children of serfs (or villeins, as serfs were known in England). These were the only pupils who faced a legal bar to their schooling, since lords of manors insisted that their villeins' children could not be educated without their permission.[31] Manorial records show that requests for this were made and approved on many occasions, in return for paying a fee. The monks of St Albans in the fourteenth century charged

31   Aristotle, shown as a teacher of noble boys in the fifteenth century, each boy richly dressed and holding a book.

small amounts of 6d. or 1s. for the privilege, sums that have been described as little more than registration fees, enabling the abbey to keep track of its villeins' affairs.[32] Some lords asked for more. The Turvill family of Warwickshire levied sums of 3s. 4d., 5s., and 13s. 4d. on their manor of Wolston between 1361 and 1371, but it is possible that such payments included permanent freedom from villein status, so that the boys concerned could take up careers as clergy or townsmen.[33] The clientele of a town school might therefore include a variety of ranks, chiefly omitting the greatest in society and the humblest. This does not mean that every boy would have been treated in the same way, irrespective of status. Seniority would have ruled over juniority. Wells cathedral school in 1377 referred to boys with the same surname as *primus* or *secundus* (Fig. 51), while Eton College in the sixteenth century used *major* or *minor*.[34] Those of higher rank would have had privileges, and the lowly may well have been made to remember their place. The Eton statutes of 1447 provide a rare insight into the hierarchy of a school through their rules about seating at meals. The sons of noblemen dined at an upper table; the rank and file scholars (who were meant to be relatively poor) at a lower one. The poorest scholars of all, who acted as servitors, ate with the servants when the others had finished.[35]

A further factor determining who went to school was geography. Most schoolboys were likely to live in the vicinity, because it was cheaper and easier to study while living at home. The cost of schooling by itself was not vastly expensive. Merton College (Oxford) paid 4d. a term for boys in the college to attend a grammar school in Oxford in 1277, which was probably a typical sum for that date.[36] There might be three or four terms in a year. After the Black Death, when prices and wages rose, the Oxford grammar masters increased their charges, until, in about the 1380s, the university forbade them to take more than 8d. a term.[37] By the fifteenth century learning to read was likely to cost about 4d. a quarter, while 8d. remained a common sum for grammar, although there are a few references to 10d., 1s., and even 2s. and 3s. 4d. The latter two charges may have included other services, such as accommodation for boarders. There seems to have been no great divergence in fees from region to region or from town to countryside. Newland in the Forest of Dean charged half-fees of 8d. per quarter, and the schoolmaster at Basingwerk asked for 1d. per week, which would have added up to 1s. 1d. per quarter.[38] Furthermore, by the middle of the fifteenth century some schools were free of fees, increasing their attraction to families who lived within walking distance.

Not every schoolboy came from the neighbourhood. Some travelled from rural areas or small towns without schools of their own, or from larger towns to attend a school with a better reputation. Regional centres of local government and trade like Exeter, Lincoln, Norwich, and York were probably centres of education too. One fifteenth-century schoolbook imagines a squire from Devonshire at school in Bristol; another, apparently from the school of St Albans, mentions a pupil from Ely.[39] Oxford seems to have drawn boys and youths from all over England, because of the reputation of its schoolmasters or because attending school there was a convenient way of preparing for university studies. Winchester College recruited from much of the south of the country by giving scholarships to boys from places where the college had property and from certain named counties.[40] Eton awarded scholarships in a similar way, but offered free lessons to all.[41] St Paul's, after its refoundation in 1508–12, also attracted boys from far afield, no doubt because wealthy parents (particularly fathers) were used to visiting London and had contacts there. Between the 1510s and the 1530s we hear of pupils from Cheshire, Derbyshire, Devon, Hertfordshire, and Lancashire, as well as from London itself.[42]

Schooling away from home was expensive because it involved board and lodging. It therefore favoured the rich, or the less rich with rich patrons. In 1277 the young scholars of Merton College who were studying grammar cost the college 8d. a week in board, and the same sum was allowed for the scholars of Winchester College in 1400.[43] Commoners at Winchester paid anything from 8d. to 16d. a week in the fifteenth century, and sums of up to 1s. a week appear in accounts relating to other schools up to the Reformation.[44] Large-scale boarding schools of a modern kind scarcely existed, apart from Eton and Winchester. More often the schoolmaster took small numbers of pupils into his house to boost his income. Edmund Stonor, a gentleman's son from Stonor in the Chiltern hills, lived with a married master at Oxford in about 1380, as Alexander de la Pole did with his teacher at Ipswich.[45] Alternatively schoolboys stayed in private houses, with landlords of an appropriate status. John Hopton, son of a Suffolk esquire, lodged with the vicar of Covehithe, and Peter Carew, whose father was a knight of Devon, with an Exeter alderman.[46] The people of Ledbury claimed in 1548 that their economy benefited from the scholars who came there, requiring food and accommodation.[47]

There were other expenses involved in going to school. Clothes that are good enough for the backyard will not do in the public and formal surroundings of the classroom. Most medieval parents would have wished their offspring to demonstrate their status at school by dressing appropriately. Schoolboys usually wore a long gown over underclothes, belted at the waist and stretching to the ankles (Fig. 32). This resembled the dress worn by wealthy leisured adults, and indicated that you were not a manual worker. When Henry III sent Raulin the son of Master Stephen of Portsmouth to school at Bury St Edmunds in 1255, he ordered him to be given a robe of russet lined with lambskin, a tabard, stockings, a pair of shoes, and two sets of underwear.[48] Materials were needed for lessons, even at free schools. Books were one such item by 1400, as we shall see; writing materials were another. Tablets of wood had been in use since Anglo-Saxon times: polished or waxed for writing on or etching, and capable of being rubbed and reused.[49] An author of the early thirteenth century describes a scholar carrying diptychs (double tablets that folded shut like a book), 'on which are written things worth knowing'.[50] The grammar boys of Merton College had white tablets bought for their use in 1347 'for reporting arguments', as well as parchment and ink.[51] Slates also seem to have been used, perhaps in humbler schools.[52] After 1400 paper was relatively cheap and widely available, transforming schoolwork by enabling pupils to keep notes permanently yet compactly.[53] Paper, pens, ink, and books were staple items in early Tudor schools. 'Methinkest thou lackest many things that is need[ful] for a good scholar to have,' observes an Oxford master to his pupil in the 1490s, 'first a penner and an inkhorn, and then books.' A scholar of the same period describes his equipment thus:

> [At] the last fair, my uncle on my father's side gave me a penner and an inkhorn, and my uncle of my mother's side gave me a penknife. Now, and [i.e. if] I had a pair of tables [i.e. tablets], I lacked nothing.[54]

The penner was a little sheath in which pens were carried, often worn like the inkhorn at the belt. Hugh Willoughby had a penner and inkhorn bought for his use in 1526 for 4d.[55] The cost of maintaining a boy named Edward Querton at Ewelme school in 1464–5 included ½d. for ink, ½d. towards laying straw on the schoolroom floor, 1½d. for a pound of candles, and 4d. apparently for wood for the schoolroom fire.[56] Alexander de la Pole's school expenses mention candles, and Colet ordered his pupils to bring candles of wax, not tallow, for use at St Paul's.[57]

Starting school is one of life's passages or transitions. Small children may initially have gone with their parents. An early fourteenth-century English manuscript depicts Joseph entrusting Jesus to a teacher (Fig. 50), and the Virgin Mary is shown taking Jesus to school in German and Danish illustrations.[58] Older boys leaving home for a distant place would have needed a guardian or escort. Alexander de la Pole went from his home at Wingfield to Ipswich school accompanied by men of his family's household.[59] As a nobleman's son he was expected to travel in an appropriate style. Some medieval boys attended a series of schools. They might move from a teacher of reading or song to one of grammar, ascend from a local establishment to a national one like Winchester, leave a school that closed, or abandon one whose teaching seemed inadequate. Peter Carew was taken away from Exeter high school, where he had refused to knuckle down to his studies, and went to St Paul's but did no better there.[60] Another Devonian, John Jewel, bishop of Salisbury and apologist for the Church of England, learnt the elements of reading from the vicar of Heanton Punchardon in 1529, when he was seven, studied under masters at Braunton and South Molton, and concluded his school days at Barnstaple.[61]

The passage from home to school was sometimes accompanied by a religious ceremony. This was the cutting of a tonsure or shaved portion on the top of the head, often with the blessing of a bishop (Fig. 52). It could be conferred at any age from seven upwards, and bestowed ecclesiastical status – hence the frequent references to medieval schoolboys as clerks or clerklings. Not all pupils may have undergone this rite but it was probably common for choristers and 'almonry boys' who were boarded and taught in cathedrals, colleges, and monasteries in return for helping in church. Statutes issued for the almonry boys of St Albans Abbey in 1339 required them to be tonsured when admitted, and to cut short the rest of their hair.[62] Eton demanded much the same of its choristers.[63] The ordination registers of English bishops in the fourteenth and fifteenth centuries contain long lists of boys and youths on whom the bishop bestowed the tonsure, and although nothing is recorded about them except their names, it is likely that many were receiving education. In 1345 the bishop of Hereford confirmed the tonsure that a priest named John Pine had received when he was a boy at Gloucester school.[64]

The tonsure made you visibly a clerk. Invisibly it gave you the status of a member of the clergy and brought you under the jurisdiction of the Church, rather than that of the lay authorities of the place where you were living. The Oxford grammar schools were controlled by the university, and their scholars shared the privileges of undergraduates. They were judged by the university, not by the mayor of the city, for crimes and for civil disputes with Oxford citizens. The pupils of Glastonbury and Wells who paid the poll-tax in 1377 did so as clerics, not as laymen.[65] All over England scholars could claim 'benefit of clergy' if convicted of a crime in a lay court.[66] This caused them to be handed over to the Church authorities for punishment – a punishment usually lighter than secular ones. Originally you established your clerical status in court by displaying your tonsure, but in the mid fourteenth century this procedure was replaced by a reading test in Latin (eventually standardised as the first verse of Psalm 51). The lists of tonsured clerks tend to vanish from bishops' registers after about 1500, and it may be that this badge of distinction fell into disuse at that time, except in cathedrals and monasteries. But if the badge disappeared, the status it had symbolised did not. Benefit of clergy survived the Reformation, although the occasions on which it could be claimed were restricted. It remained a privilege of anyone who could read out a piece of Latin in court – a useful pay-off for having attended a school.

SCHOOL BUILDINGS

Buildings tell us a good deal about the status and functions of those who use them. Much can be learnt about medieval schools from studying where they were sited, what kinds of structures they occupied, and how these were arranged internally. Some institutions of the period, like castles, markets, and many parish churches, were located in prominent places. Others were thrust to the edges of settlements, as were brothels and leper hospitals. Schools are less easy to categorise. In towns they rarely occupied sites in the principal streets, alongside the houses and shops of merchants and prosperous tradesmen. Equally they were not confined to poor districts. A common location in towns was a street on the edge of the commercial centre. Exeter high school first lay peripherally in Preston ('priests'') Street, an old ecclesiastical district, and later moved to a more central site in an alley off the High Street. Salisbury's was in Exeter Street, a major route not far from the cathedral but on the fringe of the city.[67] Gloucester's was in Longsmith Street, off the chief southern thoroughfare, and Hereford's was at one time in Old School Street, north-east of the cathedral close and also away from the city centre.[68] Oxford had five schools in the High Street itself during the early fifteenth century, but these were some way from the focus of the city at Carfax. Two others lay down side streets (Fig. 64). School sites might or might not relate to ecclesiastical buildings. St Paul's and Winchester high school both stood close to cathedrals, and in smaller settlements like Long Melford and Newland the same was true with respect to the parish church, because such sites were easier to obtain.[69] In other towns, even cathedral cities like Exeter and Salisbury, the school might lie away from the principal church.

School buildings varied in their shape and history. Churches were used for teaching as far back as the twelfth century, when ones in Durham and Norham are mentioned as hosting schools.[70] In 1373 the bishop of Norwich forbade the practice in the churches of King's Lynn, on the grounds that the cries of beaten pupils interrupted services and distracted worshippers.[71] This prohibition may have been untypical: two hundred years later Shakespeare expected his listeners to recognise an allusion to the 'pedant that keeps a school i' th' church'.[72] Most schools in churches were probably elementary ones, teaching reading and song. A former pupil of such a school at Kirkham recalled that it was taught by a priest near the font, in other words inside the west door, and confessed that he used to aim stones at the top of the tall wooden steeple that covered the font.[73] Grammar schools normally had their own premises. Some of these were adapted from other uses. Between 1161 and 1185 Walkelin of Derby and his wife Goda gave their own house to accommodate Derby school. The hall of the house was designated for the schoolroom and the chambers for the master and clerks.[74] At Bury St Edmunds Abbot Samson bought some stone buildings in the town before 1193 and gave them for the use of the schoolmaster.[75] Gloucester school covered a double tenement site formerly held by private tenants, and Long Melford occupied one end of a wealthy merchant's house.[76] The latter was built of timber, a material that could look as magnificent as stone. Warwick school, by the fifteenth century, occupied the redundant church of St John in the market place.[77] Two schools at Bristol

32   A fifteenth-century schoolboy: John Kent, scholar of
Winchester College, who died in
1435 aged about fifteen.

operated in chambers over city gates (Fig. 33),[78] and the late medieval
schools of Banbury and Lichfield were refounded in the premises of former
hospitals, whose functions of care had declined.[79] Temporary use might be
made of almost any building. When it became fashionable in the late
fifteenth and sixteenth centuries to move out of cities in time of plague,
Magdalen College School (Oxford) and its scholars decamped to stay on
rural manors belonging to the college. A school exercise of about the 1510s
observed ruefully that 'when we last [went] forth from the university for
sickness, we had a foul slutty kitchen for our school, but now we be provided
of a place a little more honest, [although] it is but a stable'.[80]

   In the late fourteenth century wealthy people began to endow schools to
teach without charge. This often involved the creation of a special building
containing the schoolroom and sometimes the master's lodging. Money
might be spent to make the exterior proclaim the importance of the patron
and his or her benefaction. Winchester College occupied a spacious
collection of structures, including a gatehouse, quadrangle, hall, and chapel
(Fig. 57). Eton College was similar. Ewelme school, founded soon after Eton
in about 1448–50, had a two-storey building of brick embellished with
freestone window dressings, carvings of angels holding shields, and two

imposing chimneys (Figs 60 and 61). It formed part of a complex that
included a church and an almshouse near the palace of the founders, the
duke and duchess of Suffolk, all of which demonstrated their power and
piety. Brick was also chosen by William Waynflete, bishop of Winchester, for
his school foundation at Wainfleet in about 1464. He was born in this
Lincolnshire village, endowed it with free education, and commissioned
another impressive building in two storeys, with a classroom and lodging
beneath and a chapel above. Grandeur was projected through a pair of
towers at the west end (Fig. 38). Evesham and Taunton had single-storey
structures, but both displayed inscriptions commemorating the abbot and
the bishop who had erected them. Endowed schools in small towns or
villages could make a greater visual impact than their counterparts in cities,
because they had less to compete with. The perimeter wall at Week St Mary
still survives with battlements. When the Tudor traveller John Leland visited
Crewkerne in 1542, he observed that 'the church standeth on the hill, and
by it is a grammar school'. The school was one of only four buildings that he
noted in the town.[81]

Since schools made use of such a range of premises, there could be no
such thing as a typical schoolroom. We can gain an inkling of what
educationists considered to be an ideal shape and size, however, from those
that were purpose-built and survive in either extant or recorded form (Fig.
34). The earliest of these, the schoolroom of Winchester College, built in the
late fourteenth century, was an oblong chamber, 45'6" long and 28'10" wide
(13.8 by 8.8 metres).[82] Its counterpart at Eton, 'Lower School', dates from
1441–4 and was larger: 75' long and 25' wide (22.8 by 7.6 metres). The Eton
dimensions are repeated elsewhere, without revealing whether they formed
or followed fashion in this respect.[83] Bishop Waynflete's schoolroom at
Wainfleet was about 70' long and 20' wide (21.3 by 6.1 metres), and that of
his other foundation, Magdalen College School, 72' long and 24'9" wide
(21.9 by 7.5 metres).[84] Berkhamsted school, founded in the 1540s, was 70'
long and 27' feet wide (21.3 by 8.2 metres).[85] Such schoolrooms were lit by
several small windows, sometimes placed fairly high, perhaps to avoid
external distractions. There was usually at least one door to the outside, and
sometimes a second to the master's accommodation. The orientation of the
schoolroom, when deliberately designed, might follow an east–west axis like
a church, as happened at Winchester, Eton, and Wainfleet – the latter
having a chapel above. Alternatively a north–south line was chosen, as was
the case at Ewelme and Magdalen. Orientation seems to have been a matter
of choice and convenience.

The layout and furnishings of schools are difficult topics, requiring to be
pieced together from scraps of evidence in documents, pictures, and school
notebooks. There are paintings of schoolrooms in fifteenth-century French
and Flemish illuminated manuscripts, and woodcuts of a similar kind were
popular as illustrations in printed schoolbooks over most of western Europe

during the 1490s.[86] Visual sources like these must be read with care, however, because their scale involved simplification and because they may embody conventional views of what schools were like. Throughout the twentieth century, British cartoons and comics showed schoolmasters in caps and gowns with canes, even in state schools where few such masters wore such articles and the cane was sparingly used. All the early pictures of schools depict the master dominating the room from a large chair, often with a wooden back and canopy, which seems to reflect real practices. At Magdalen, and probably at Eton and Winchester, the master's seat was at the centre of the focal inner schoolroom wall (Fig. 36).[87] This left the outer entrance to the care of the assistant master or 'usher', a word that comes from the Latin *hostiarius*, 'door keeper'. Placing the master's assistant by the door ensured that someone could intercept boys who came in late or who wanted to leave (Fig. 37).

The pictorial sources usually show the pupils sitting around the master on simple forms (meaning benches), holding books on their laps (Figs 31 and 44). Forms appear to have been standard fittings in schools, and are mentioned in records relating to the building of schoolrooms.[88] In the second half of the sixteenth century, when documentary evidence first survives about their location, they seem normally to have been placed alongside the walls, sometimes backed by wooden boarding to give insulation from cold and dirt. The boys would therefore have lined the room, looking inwards, often (as the pictures show) without desks in front of them on which to rest books or writing materials.[89] In about 1625 the statutes of Bury school (Lancashire) state that 'when they have to write, let them use their knees for a table'.[90] Nor was this unusual; pupils at some leading English schools (Eton, Harrow, Rugby, and St Paul's) sat on benches or steps without desks as late as the early nineteenth century (Fig. 91).[91] There may have been variations on sitting one deep around the room. At Winchester by 1550 the eighteen prefects sat on the window ledges at the rear of and above the boys in front of them.[92] Some continental pictures show pupils sitting in rows and facing the teacher, and it is possible that certain English classrooms were arranged in this way, as in a modern school or lecture room.[93]

The earliest schoolroom of which we have detailed evidence is St Paul's, thanks to Colet's school statutes of 1518 and a description by Erasmus who went there on a visit in 1521.[94] He states that the building consisted of three sections: an anteroom in which the youngest boys learnt the catechism, a large rectangular classroom, and a chapel beyond it. These units were apparently open to one another architecturally, but could be closed by curtains. The pupils sat on nine forms, in a prescribed school order, with seventeen boys on each form, the senior boy of each form occupying a special seat. There were some visual aids in the main classroom: a 'table' or board containing the prayers that were said in school each day, and an image (statue or painting) of the child Jesus teaching in the Temple, placed

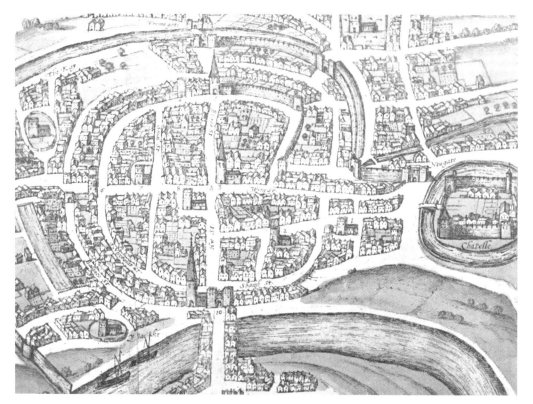

33   School sites and premises. One Bristol school was housed above Newgate (left of the castle) in the
1420s, and another above Fromegate (top) in the 1530s.

above the master's chair. Higher still was an image of God the Father
speaking the words *Ipsum audite*, 'hear him'. It is unlikely that Colet
introduced visual aids to schoolrooms. Earlier schools may have had images
or texts written up, as was the case in churches, secular halls, and even
private houses. The kind of text can be guessed from a Latin one in the hall
of Launceston Priory, where local scholars came each day to be fed. They
were advised that

> It is good, while you are young, Learning's house to fare to.
> They are foolish people who neither know nor care to.[95]

Pupils may have added their own embellishments to the walls and furniture
in the form of graffiti. Some schools in later centuries were liberally
decorated with the names of pupils, often inscribed in a large and
conspicuous way.[96]

What kind of room, then, was a schoolroom, and on what was it
modelled? An oblong shape was common in medieval buildings, both
religious and secular. The choir of a church was designed in this way, and
likewise had its seating along its sides. Seats in a large choir were arranged

in tiers called the first, second, and third forms, which may have suggested the system of numbering forms in schools, to be mentioned presently. The chapter house of a cathedral or monastery had some resemblance to a school as well, with the chief officer sitting in a central position and his subordinates round the walls. Perhaps the strongest influence was simply the hall of a lay building, given that some schools occupied former domestic houses. A hall was usually oblong. Its principal seat, that of the head of the household, was in the centre of the inner short side, like the master's chair. The outer door of the hall in a nobleman's dwelling had an usher to control ingress and egress, as in a school; indeed the title and function are likely to have passed from lay households to schools.[97] All the structures just mentioned may have helped shape school architecture and furnishings; at the same time the interior of a school, if not the exterior, would have been distinctive and recognisable.

THE MANAGEMENT OF THE SCHOOLROOM

The schoolmaster ruled the school, except when (as today) governing powers, local worthies, or parents tried to influence what he did. In the sixteenth century such people were apparently prone to ask for 'remedies' or holidays, a practice forbidden by Colet at St Paul's.[98] Many masters ruled alone, and most had no more than the usher to help them, even in large town schools. Only a very few establishments appear to have had a third member of staff. Ipswich, refounded by Cardinal Wolsey in 1528 on the scale of Eton and Winchester, was envisaged as having a master and two ushers, but the foundation lasted for only two years.[99] The Yorkshire schools of Acaster Selby and Rotherham each supported masters of grammar, song, and writing,[100] and St Paul's similarly had three staff: master, usher, and chaplain. The last of these taught boys the elements of the Christian faith, but such provision was unusual.[101] More commonly senior pupils were probably used to assist in the classroom. A clever boy is mentioned as helping the master and usher to examine boys at Beccles school in the 1430s, and similar practices in early Tudor times were noted in a previous chapter.[102]

Numbers of pupils in schools must have varied greatly. A private school in a noble household or a domestic house may have included no more than half a dozen, and an almonry school for boys in a larger monastery only a dozen or two. Some small country schools may not have been much bigger. The founders of Ewelme school in 1448–50 envisaged that there might be only four boys studying grammar, apart from 'petties' or little children and those who were learning to read.[103] In 1473 the master of Wollaton school agreed to restrict his teaching to twenty-six pupils so as not to encroach on the school of Nottingham nearby.[104] At Wotton-under-Edge an elderly inhabitant remembered in 1616 that there had usually been twenty to thirty boys in the school in about the 1540s.[105] When the crown enquired into the state of chantry schools in 1548, on the other hand, local people claimed that there were usually 60 to 80 scholars in the grammar school of Chipping Campden, 100 at Worcester in the school of the Trinity Guild, 120 at King's Norton, and between 120 and 140 at Crewkerne and Taunton.[106] These were round numbers and may have been inflated through anxiety to save the schools and their endowments, but there is evidence to suggest that schools in towns often reached 80 or more. In 1369 Richard Beckingham, an ecclesiastical lawyer, bequeathed 2d. each to 60 poor clerks of the grammar school of York, 'not being bad boys', to pray for his soul.[107] The school was therefore at least that large, and possibly bigger. The 34 scholars of Wells and the 39 of Glastonbury who paid poll-tax in 1377 were the older boys of fourteen or more, so that we may need to double these totals to allow for their junior colleagues.[108]

Some schools gathered over 100 pupils. The master and usher of Winchester College presided not only over the 70 scholars supported by the foundation, but over the commoners who paid for themselves. The college statutes of 1400 fixed the number of commoners at ten, but the institution was so popular that by 1412 the bishop of Winchester, Henry Beaufort, complained that between 80 and 100 outsiders were being accommodated as well as the scholars, which he considered too many for teaching.[109] Beaufort commanded that the statutes be respected and the number seems to have fallen, but commoners continued to augment the school throughout the fifteenth and sixteenth centuries. Eton resembled Winchester in this respect. It catered for 70 scholars, 16 choristers, and 20 commoners of noble birth, as well as offering free education to all. Since this was coupled with a prohibition against rival schools within ten miles, it looks as though Eton served at first as a local grammar school and that some boys attended the school on a daily basis.[110] St Paul's was another large foundation with 153 pupils, and Magdalen College School may have been a fourth. It took in students from all over the university who needed to improve their Latin, as well as the sons of Oxford citizens and boys from outside the city. A translation exercise from the school in the 1490s observes that it is easier to teach a hundred well-disposed scholars than twenty who are evilly disposed.[111]

Numbers were not always accidental. Medieval benefactors often fixed the membership of their foundations at precise and significant figures, and this was the case in some schools. We hear of twelve or thirteen scholarships, like Jesus and the apostles.[112] The 70 scholars of Winchester and Eton matched the size of the group of disciples whom Jesus sent out to assist the apostles.[113] Colet's choice of number at St Paul's, 153, followed this tradition. He based it on the gospel of his namesake, St John, which describes how the risen Jesus appeared to his disciples while they were fishing. Jesus told them to draw up their net on the right-hand side, and they caught 153 large fish without breaking the net.[114] St Augustine of Hippo explained this number as follows. It embodies the Trinity, since 153 is made up of three fifties plus three and contains the sum of the numbers from one to seventeen. (If these numbers were represented by bricks of appropriate lengths, they would form an equilateral triangle.) It signifies the true Church, unsullied by heretics, since the fish were caught in an unbroken net dropped on the right-hand side, the side where God will place his chosen people at the Last Judgment. Finally it stands for human perfection, since seventeen combines seven, the number of purification, and ten, that of reward.[115] So the scholarships and schools that have just been mentioned were designed not simply as secular bodies but as images of spiritual ones: the Godhead, the Church, the apostles, or perfect human beings. Their scholars were expected to model themselves on these exemplars, and to prepare to serve God as the apostles had done.

The ratio of pupils to masters was generally a high one. This was probably due to the economics of teaching. School fees had to be kept low to encourage business, making them insufficient to support more than one or two staff. This would help to explain the layout of schoolrooms and the ways in which they worked. Seating the pupils around the walls, with nothing to hinder the view, helped the master and usher to manage them. A crowd of boys of various ages and stages of learning would, of necessity, have called for varied teaching, the master perhaps dealing chiefly with the older boys and the usher with the younger ones. We do not hear about the division of schools into permanent classes, however, until the 1520s, when units known as 'forms' are mentioned in four of the largest foundations. At this time there was no standard number of forms. St Paul's had nine, eight were planned at Ipswich, Winchester had seven, and Eton six or seven.[116] Six eventually became the favourite number and this has influenced the numbering of classes in England down to modern times, but in Tudor schools a form was simply a bench within the single classroom. The forms all shared the same surroundings and teachers.

Work in school followed a daily routine framed in time. As we have seen, teaching in Anglo-Saxon monasteries probably adhered to a timetable, inserted between the daily services, but the details of the school day in free-standing institutions are not defined until the mid fifteenth century, when the statutes of endowed schools began to lay down how the day should function. This was a period when clocks were proliferating in society. People were learning to measure the day by the clock, and clock time found its way into some of the statutes.[117] At this end of the middle ages and up to the Reformation, the school day approached that of the adult working day in length and made full use of daylight, a custom that was probably very old. Most boarding schools and day schools alike opened at 6 a.m., even in winter. Colet postponed the hour until 7 at St Paul's and his example was followed at Manchester in 1525, where allowance was also made for the late

arrival of those who came from a distance. Schools worked from these
starting times until 8 or 9 a.m., when there was an intermission for
breakfast. Studies were resumed at 10 and continued until about noon when
all went out for dinner. They returned after an hour or two for four hours
of afternoon school, from 1 till 5 p.m. or from 2 till 6 p.m. A day of this kind
lasted for up to eight hours, as at Lancaster, or nine and a half in the case of
Newark. In summer the longer hours of daylight sometimes meant an even
earlier start: 6 a.m. at Manchester, 5 at Chichester. The school day at
Cuckfield, founded in 1528, seems to have lasted a full two hours longer in
summer than in winter.

Religion continued to influence the shape of the day, as it had done in
Anglo-Saxon times. There was an expectation that schoolmasters would
teach boys piety as well as grammar, and founders and benefactors of
schools often stipulated that their gifts should be remembered in prayer.
This was generally done soon after arrival or before pausing for breakfast,
and again after lessons finished for the day. The arrangements at Newland
school, founded in 1446, were fairly typical. At 9 a.m. the scholars said Psalm
67, 'God be merciful to us', with the Paternoster and Ave Maria. At 5 p.m.
they offered an intercession to the Virgin followed by Psalm 130, 'Out of the
depths' (the psalm traditionally said for the dead). The Paternoster and Ave
were repeated, and the rite concluded with the prayer 'Incline your ear, O
Lord'. All these prayers were said kneeling and in Latin, the almost
universal language of formal prayer until the 1530s. In Newland's case they
were said for the souls of Robert and Joan Greyndour, who had founded the
school, so that they acted like the prayers of a chantry priest.[118] Endowed
schools generally went to church once a year for a solemn 'obit' or requiem
mass to commemorate their founders, and scholars were occasionally
engaged to say prayers for other well-wishers, like the Bristol merchant
John Gaywood, who arranged in 1471 for a local schoolmaster and his
pupils to attend his funeral and left 8d. to buy them wine for their
refreshment afterwards.[119]

Pictures of schools at work show the master in his chair, never walking
about. He sits grasping the birch – a bundle of twigs – that formed his badge
of office, and once or twice a boy is shown standing before him to be
examined. Boys came to him, not he to them, just as the lord of a household
sat and was approached by his retainers. The master gave a lesson or issued
commands from his chair, and periodically called out boys to be questioned
or examined, the process known as 'apposing'. The birch was used to
punish indiscipline and inability to answer. It was the favoured tool of
English schoolmasters, and appears in the principal woodcut produced in
England to illustrate a school scene, commissioned by the printer Richard
Pynson in the 1490s (Fig. 44).[120] We also hear of the ferule, a wooden rod
employed for hitting the hand; its striking end was pierced with a hole that
raised a blister. This appears to have been used for minor offences, and

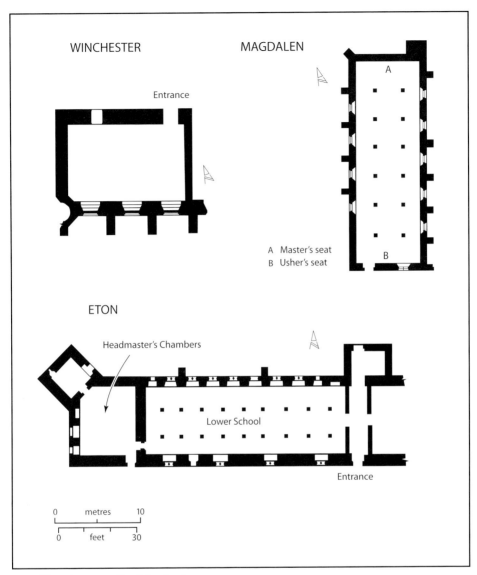

34   Fifteenth-century English schoolrooms.

references to it are rarer than those to the birch.[121] Some masters tried to
control indiscipline on the benches by appointing one or more boys to the
post of *custos*. They had the duty of reporting their colleagues for speaking
English or other misdemeanours.[122]

How often the birch was applied is hard to say, but it was probably a
common penalty (Fig. 40). After the body of an Oxford schoolmaster, John
Neushom, was found in the River Cherwell by the Petty Pont (now
Magdalen Bridge) in December 1301, the coroner's jury reported that he
had fallen out of a willow tree and drowned while cutting rods to beat his

pupils.[123] A man accused of assaulting a boy in Kent in 1390 pleaded that he was the boy's schoolmaster and was exonerated.[124] When the degree of 'master of grammar' was conferred in sixteenth-century Cambridge, the new graduate demonstrated his prowess by ceremonially flogging a 'shrewd' (i.e. naughty) boy, who received 4d. 'for his labour'![125] But corporal punishment in schools needs to be placed in context. Masters who birched their pupils were doing nothing unusual by contemporary standards. Parents beat their children, husbands their wives, and employers their servants, while officers of the law did so to beggars and criminals. In the fourteenth-century poem *Piers Plowman* Reason is depicted as a cleric delivering a sermon in which such practices were warmly encouraged.[126] The poem went through two revisions in which much was changed, but a similar passage appears in every version.

Some educationists called for leniency in beating. A French or English writer of the early thirteenth century observed that although the birch might be used for suitable offences, whips and scorpions – in other words excessive punishment – should be avoided.[127] Vincent of Beauvais, writing about fifty years later for the French royal family, discussed harshness and gentleness of discipline, and concluded in favour of the latter.[128] In England the statutes of Winchester College, issued by the founder, William Wykeham, in 1400, instructed the schoolmaster to punish his pupils in moderation – advice repeated in the statutes of Eton.[129] Thomas Beckington, bishop of Bath and Wells, who was an alumnus of Winchester College, went further in his statutes for the choristers of Wells Cathedral in 1460. He advised that boys who refuse to learn their lessons ought 'first to be warned kindly, secondly, if they neglect these warnings, sharply to be rebuked'. Only for third offences should they be flogged.[130] This tolerant approach was inherited by the humanist educationists who were influential in sixteenth-century England. Erasmus and Vives, like Beckington, believed that advice and then warnings should precede the use of physical punishment, which they considered only as a last resort. Vives thought that it could not be dispensed with entirely, but Erasmus, although he sanctioned it, admitted in his heart that he disliked its use, and would rather had dull or worthless boys removed from school altogether.[131]

Considered as one, the literary sources suggest a culture of beating, with some cautionary voices. So much is said in favour of the punishment, however, that the question arises why so many writers bothered to argue in its favour. Presumably they felt that teachers and parents were too easy-going. Boys had their own ways of avoiding the pains of the rod and the tedium of the benches. 'As soon as I am come into the school,' grumbles an Oxford schoolmaster of the 1490s,

this fellow goeth to make water and he goeth out to the common draught [i.e. privy]. Soon after another asketh licence that he may go drink.

Another calleth upon me that he may have licence to go home. These and
such other layeth my scholars for excuse often times, that they may be out
of the way.[132]

It was through going outside to relieve himself that the young Edmund of
Abingdon, at school in Oxford towards the end of the twelfth century,
miraculously escaped the impact of a large stone that fell from the wall onto
his place. He survived to become archbishop of Canterbury and to die in an
odour of sanctity.[133] Privies are mentioned at the London school of St
Martin-le-Grand in 1360 as being in need of repair,[134] and at St Paul's
nearby in 1518, when Colet, whose sharp eyes missed little, arranged that
the boys should go to an appointed place to urinate into a tank or cesspit. A
poor child of the school was given the job of arranging for the urine to be
removed from time to time (it was used by dyers and tanners for making
ammonia), in return for receiving the profits. 'For other causes if need be,'
added Colet curtly, 'they shall go to the water side', meaning that they were
to defecate on the banks of the River Thames – some hundreds of yards
from the school.[135]

SCHOOLWORK

What went on in the schoolroom, and how was schoolwork organised? We
can learn a good deal about this from studying grammars. Admittedly, like
other kinds of prescriptive literature such as laws and prayer-books, they tell
us what should be done rather than what was done. Nevertheless, they
provide many hints about classroom procedures – hints that can be
supplemented by material such as vulgaria. Grammars used two principal
means of conveying their information, which were probably reproduced in
schools. One was through memorisation, particularly in the case of the texts
that were written in verse, which could be dictated by the master or read by
the pupils from texts and learnt by heart. The other involved the use of
questions and answers, the format used by Donatus and his imitators, which
suggests that masters would have asked a question in class and trained the
pupils to make the appropriate response. This kind of catechism might be
done with the class as a whole or individually. Masters called out pupils who
had been given a task to do or a text to learn, and examined them on the
subject. Bishop Grandisson of Exeter in 1357 talks of boys 'replying as to
the parts of speech' as a necessary part of their education.[136] Parsing was
a common exercise. The master chose a word in a text, and asked the
pupil to identify it as noun, verb, and so on, to name the paradigm that it
was displaying, and to give the other principal paradigms of the word.
There were short parsing texts to explain this procedure, like *Dominus que
pars?* ('*Dominus*, which part of speech?'), as there had been in the tenth
century.[137]

35   Magdalen College
School (Oxford) before its
demolition in 1828. The
schoolroom on the ground
floor was built in *c*. 1480;
the upper storeys were later
remodelled.

    Classroom work therefore involved plenty of oral interchange, and this
was not merely a means but an end of teaching. Pupils were trained to speak
Latin, not simply to read and write it, and although the subject would be
taught in the pupils' own language at an elementary level, classes at a later
stage would be conducted entirely in Latin. Even in the fifteenth century,
when English had become a textbook language, this was primarily in
introductory treatises like Leland's. Advanced works of grammar, such as
the *Doctrinale*, remained wholly in Latin, and there is anecdotal evidence
that, in the best schools, pupils who had passed beyond the elementary
stages were required to speak Latin alone on school premises, whether they
were in a lesson or not. Beckington's statutes for the choristers of Wells
Cathedral laid down that, when at dinner or supper, they should 'ask for
anything they want in Latin, not in English'.[138] In 1484 the grammar master
of Southwell Minster was charged with letting his boys speak English, not
Latin, in school,[139] and Magdalen College School insisted on Latin speaking
in the 1490s. Exercises written in the school at that time feature an
imaginary schoolboy confessing his linguistic shortcomings. 'If I had not
used my English tongue so greatly, for which the master hath rebuked me
oft times, I should have been far more cunning in grammar. Wise men say

that nothing may be more profitable to them that learn grammar than to speak Latin.'[140]

At the higher levels of study pupils might be made to take part in Latin disputations on grammatical rules and questions. These are reflected in the textbooks of writers like John Cornwall, who debates whether the noun *leopardus* is to be declined as one word or two and marshals the theories and authorities on either side.[141] Such discussions could easily have been reproduced in class. The statutes of Eton College ordered a solemn disputation to be held between two of the scholars every summer, with the whole school looking on.[142] In London there were enough schools for their scholars to hold competitive disputations. William FitzStephen, who wrote his description of the city of London between 1170 and 1183, tells how masters and pupils met together on feast days in the church whose festival it was:

> The scholars dispute, some in demonstrative rhetoric, others in dialectic. Some 'hurtle enthymemes', others with greater skill employ perfect syllogisms. Boys of different schools strive against one another in verse or contend concerning the principles of the art of grammar, or the rules governing the use of past and future. There are others who employ the old art of the crossroads in epigrams, rhymes, and metre.[143]

This tradition still went on at one London church in the 1530s, according to the Elizabethan antiquary John Stow. 'I myself in my youth,' he later recalled,

> have yearly seen on the eve of St Bartholomew [23 August] the scholars of divers grammar schools repair to the churchyard of St Bartholomew's Priory in Smithfield, where upon a bank boarded about under a tree some one scholar hath stepped up, and there hath apposed and answered, till he were by some better scholar overcome and put down, and then the overcomer taking the place, did like as the first, and in the end the best apposers and answerers had rewards, which I observed not but it made both good schoolmasters, and also good scholars, diligently against such times to prepare themselves for the obtaining of this garland.[144]

Colet disliked these disputations, calling them 'foolish babbling and loss of time', and forbade his scholars to attend them, but his prohibition seems to have been relaxed after his death. Stow remembered that in the 1530s boys came to the ceremony from St Paul's as well as from schools at Westminster, St Thomas Acon, and St Anthony's, 'whereof the last named commonly presented the best scholars and had the prize in those days'.[145]

Back in their classrooms boys were also learning literary skills: the ability to read Latin, to translate and compose it, and to write it down. We know very little about how writing was taught, in the sense of letter formation. It

36

37   Top picture: Inside Magdalen College School, looking north to the master's seat. The seat
and other furnishings are later than the original ones. Bottom picture: Magdalen College School
as the master would have viewed it, looking south towards the usher's seat beside the entrance.

probably began with copying the letters of the alphabet and the basic prayers from the tablets used for learning to read. Later, having learnt to form individual letters, pupils would write out texts in which the letters were joined together. A grammatical miscellany of Edward IV's reign (1461–83), which may have originated in Lincolnshire and which later came into the hands of a monk of Christ Church (Canterbury), includes several folios on which somebody has been copying texts. They include a couplet from the *Distichs of Cato*, portions of English and Latin charters and petitions, and a Latin epitaph on Scogan, the famous jester of the period.[146] Composition, as distinct from handwriting, would begin with short sentences like those in Ælfric's *Grammar*, and proceed to longer ones with more complex constructions and wider vocabulary like the vulgaria mentioned in the previous chapter. The final stage of prose composition would involve learning how to write letters in the sense of correspondence, following the rhetorical conventions by which letters were constructed. Statutes for the Oxford grammar schools in the fourteenth century recommend masters to give out verses and literary compositions every fortnight, 'containing words apt and not prolix or overlong, but full of succinct and beautiful clauses and plain metaphors'. The pupils should write out these assignments on the next holiday, if not before, and on their return show their transcriptions and render the pieces by heart.[147]

A higher accomplishment still was the writing of verse, its difficulty arising from the requirement not merely to construct Latin sentences but to fit them into metrical forms. The ability to do so seems to have been regarded as setting the seal upon one's school career. In 1312 Nicholas Picot, alderman of London, directed that his sons should be put to school until they could compose letters and versify properly.[148] At Bredgar (Kent) the statutes of a chantry that maintained two scholars learning grammar laid down, in 1393, that when they could 'read, sing, construe, and compose twenty-four verses on one subject in a single day', they could join the chantry priest in saying the daily liturgy – having evidently qualified to be ordained as adult clergy.[149] William Paston, one of the well-known family of Norfolk gentry, was still a pupil at Eton in 1479 when he was nineteen, having stayed on to master versifying, 'which,' he wrote to his brother John, 'I trust to have with a little continuance'. He quoted in his letter an epigram he had composed, perhaps to show how well he was repaying the cost of his schooling. The theme set for the epigram was *Quomodo non valet hora, valet mora?* ('Why is delay worth something, when time is worth nothing?'). William produced an elegiac couplet (a hexameter followed by a pentameter):

Arbore jam videas exemplum. Non die possunt
Omnia supleri; set tamen illa mora.

('You see the example in a tree. All things cannot be supplied in a day, but all [is supplied] by delay.') 'And these two verses aforesaid,' he wrote proudly, 'be of mine own making.'[150] The epigram is neat but there is a mistake in the versification. Paston had not remembered his *Doctrinale*:

> Nouns of the fifth declension, ablative case, have a long *e*.[151]

This should have reminded him that *die* is correctly pronounced *diē*, a short syllable followed by a long one, whereas Paston's line required a word with two short syllables.

The Bredgar statutes imply the existence of a point at which pupils were recognised as having learnt the essential skills of grammar, and might assume a higher status in school or leave school altogether. In the early fourteenth century we hear of a grade of senior scholars known as 'bachelors'. They are mentioned at St Albans in 1309, Canterbury in 1314, and Beverley in 1338, which suggests that they existed widely in England, at least in the larger schools.[152] The statutes of St Albans school laid out the requirements for anyone wishing to rise to this grade. He had to take a proverb from the master and compose verses, model letters, and a *rithmus* (species of verse) on the subject, as well as carrying on a disputation in the school. If he was successful, he offered sixpence to St Nicholas and his achievement was celebrated with drinking and other customs.[153] At Beverley, where bachelors were also formally inaugurated, they presented gloves to the officers of the minster to which the school belonged. The ceremony was not necessarily one of leaving school, since the Canterbury bachelors are mentioned as being there when a discussion was held about punishing a violent scholar. Rather it was an endorsement of one's abilities, like a modern public examination, but its history after 1350 is elusive, as are its reputation and value outside schools.[154] Only in universities did grades of achievement develop public status in the shape of degrees.

BOOKS

Although much of the work of a medieval school was carried out aloud, books had a major role from at least the fourteenth century.[155] Long before the invention of printing, we find them in the hands of masters and pupils individually or belonging to schools as institutions. John Burdon, schoolmaster of Carlisle in 1371, and John Seward, master of a grammar school in Cornhill, London, in 1435, both bequeathed books to their friends.[156] Neither man identified the titles, but we can guess what they were: single large grammatical works or miscellanies of shorter ones, possibly written by the master himself. Occasionally masters' books are named. Thomas Romsey, schoolmaster of Winchester College until 1418, gave the college *Ferrum*, apparently some kind of vocabulary, while his successor Richard Darcy donated a *Grecismus*.[157] John Hamundson, schoolmaster of York who died in 1472, owned Papias's dictionary.[158] These are individual records and give us no clues about the size of masters' collections, but in one (probably untypical) case we can gain a clearer idea. John Bracebridge, schoolmaster of Boston in 1390 and of Lincoln in 1406, gave up teaching in about 1420 and entered Syon Abbey as a chaplain to the nuns. In due course his books passed to the convent library: over a hundred volumes, including five of philosophy, ten of medicine, forty-six of theology, liturgy, and canon law, and five of grammar. The latter included a miscellany of tracts and extracts, three important standard works (*Priscian Major*, Papias, and the *Catholicon*), and a work by Bracebridge himself, also called *Catholicon*, which seems to have been a survey of the four parts of grammar. Some of these books may have come to him after he entered the abbey, but they attest to his studious interests and the grammars may date back to his days as a teacher.[159]

Pictures of classrooms after about 1400 usually show boys holding books individually. This may have been the case among wealthier pupils, or ones with wealthy patrons, by the early fourteenth century, when copies of Donatus, Cato, and Horace were bought by Merton College (Oxford) for the use of the boys attached to the college.[160] Edmund Stonor had a Donatus valuable enough to cause worry in case it was lost, and another was purchased for a boy in Norfolk in 1466–7.[161] The usher of Winchester high school was accused of stealing three books from a fellow lodger (presumably a scholar) in 1407: Cato, *Facetus*, and 'Rules of the *Equivocus*', very likely the *Equivoca*.[162] Robert Hunter, a scholar of York in 1446 who was probably in his late teens or early twenties, willed 'all my books' to another young man.[163] The Merton Cato cost 2d. and the Donatus 3d., but by the fifteenth century schoolbook prices had risen like prices generally. Edward Querton's guardian paid 8d. for unspecified books at Ewelme in 1464–5,[164] and the Norfolk Donatus of 1466–7 cost 12d. Another manuscript that came into the hands of schoolboys during the fifteenth century survives in Nottingham University Library.[165] It is an anthology of works by Alexander, Evrard, John of Garland, and the *Sex Auctores*, some of which were out of date by the end of the middle ages, but enough remained useful for the book to be used by one or more pupils of that period, and a price of 12d. is recorded inside it. Several names of boys are inscribed on the pages: 'Johannis Wapplode', 'Johannes Cole de Wodyl', and (ungrammatically) *iste liber constat Radulfe Savage* ('this book belongs to Ralph Savage'). Master Savage, who describes himself as *bonus puer* ('a good boy'), was apparently the author of various other scribbles in the book, including the observation *Willelmus Cayso est pravus puer* ('a bad boy').

Books were also acquired by schools as institutions. One of the earliest known is a *Priscian Major* given to St Albans school by John Haule, apparently before 1310. It was entrusted to the master, but could be used by the boys.[166] Later references indicate the percolation of books not only to major schools like St Albans but to smaller and less institutional ones in market towns. In

1371 the subdean of Wells Cathedral bequeathed a copy of Hugutio to the parish church of Wellington for the use of the schoolmaster there, 'that he and his boys may especially pray for me'.[167] A similar bequest by a chaplain of Hedon in 1465 gave all his grammar books to the parochial chapel of the town 'for the teaching and reformation of the children learning in the grammar school there'.[168] A third example is forthcoming from Bridport. Here an inventory of books belonging to the parish church in 1476 refers to copies of Hugutio, Thomas of Hanney, 'an alphabet of Latin words', and a book of logic, whose presence is best explained as donations for use by a nearby school. The choice of parish churches to hold such volumes probably implies that the schools involved were not fully organised bodies. A volume given to a schoolmaster might not reach his successor unless it was kept in an independent place.

The larger schools, on the other hand, acquired and held books themselves, like St Albans and Winchester College.[169] Monastic schools can be added here, since their teachers and scholars could call on the resources of the monastic book collection, which often contained school grammars and literary texts, sometimes in more than one copy.[170] There was an outstanding collection of books in the almonry of St Paul's Cathedral – the building that housed the eight cathedral choristers and the almoner, a priest who looked after them. During the fourteenth century two almoners made generous bequests of books to further the boys' education. In 1329 William Tolleshunt left them all his volumes of grammar to use in school, including Hugutio, Isidore, and Priscian, as well as books on logic, law, and medicine which they could borrow when they left the almonry, presumably to go to university or some other form of higher education.[171] In 1358 William Ravenstone added a further collection, resulting in an inventory (probably embracing Tolleshunt's gifts) that listed eighty-two texts in forty-one volumes. The topics ranged from song to grammar and poetry, both classical and medieval, and copies of Alexander, Evrard, and Hugutio are mentioned.[172] When we reach the era of endowed schools, in the late fourteenth century, it is clear that books were often provided as part of the foundation. Indeed this practice was foreshadowed at Merton College in 1270, which arranged for a supply of books to teach its boys and other members.[173] The fine grammatical miscellany is still extant that was apparently written for Battlefield College when it opened in 1410.[174] Newland in 1454 and Whitkirk in 1521 are other schools whose founders are known to have furnished books.[175] Endowed schools also had the institutional continuity to encourage people to give them books directly, like the gifts already noted to Winchester College.

The impact of printing on late medieval English culture, as has been argued, should not be overestimated, but the new technology eventually made it easier to produce copies more cheaply than scribes could do. The earliest grammars to be printed in England were produced at Oxford between about 1482 and 1485,[176] and by the 1490s the rival London presses of Wynkyn de Worde and Richard Pynson were both busy issuing small and low-priced texts: versions of the *Accidence* and *Parvula*, the *Synonyma* and *Equivoca*, the *Hymnal*, and Theodulus.[177] Similar works were exported to England from the Continent. The earliest school recorded as owning printed schoolbooks is Wells in 1498,[178] and by the 1520s the Oxford bookseller Dorne was selling copies of the elementary grammars of Stanbridge and Whittington for 1d. or 2d. each, a good deal less than the prices for manuscripts mentioned above.[179] These printed copies often included a woodcut on the title page, showing a master directing an orderly school or a learned man in his study (Figs 27 and 44). Buy our books, these woodcuts seem to say, and your school will work well. Your pupils will imbibe the wisdom of the past and become the scholars of the future.

HOLIDAYS AND RECREATIONS

Late medieval school statutes are less forthcoming about the structure of the year than that of the day. This probably reflected the fact that schools observed a common calendar, which did not require definition. The English had a long-standing practice of dividing the year into terms or quarters, beginning at Michaelmas (29 September), Christmas (25 December), Easter (equated with 25 March), and Midsummer (24 June). Schools and universities adopted these terms for their teaching, with the proviso that the Midsummer term tended to be abridged or lost through the custom of taking a long vacation during the harvest season.[180] In the thirteenth century the schoolmaster of Bury St Edmunds is reported as beginning to lecture at Michaelmas, Christmas, and Easter, giving a three-term year.[181] The fact that Michaelmas is placed first in the sequence suggests that there was already a tradition of opening the school year at that point, and indeed the almonry boys of Durham Cathedral were required to start and finish their education at this date in 1417.[182] Equally pupils might commence or complete their studies at other times of the year. We hear of boys entering schools on St Gregory's Day (12 March) and after Lady Day (25 March), and leaving around Midsummer Day (24 June) and at the end of November.[183]

Modern English schools separate the terms with blocks of holidays, lasting at least two weeks. This procedure was adopted at Wotton-under-Edge, founded in 1384, and copied at Newland nearby in 1446.[184] Their statutes fixed the holidays to last for two weeks at Christmas, two at Easter, one at Pentecost or Whitsuntide, and six beginning on 1 August and ending on 14 September. Other schools may have done the same, or have had shorter holidays at Christmas and Easter. Major religious festivals that fell within the terms were often observed as well, with whole- or half-day holidays, and Newland and Wotton may have kept these too. John Colet estimated that the number of holidays throughout the school year amounted to 153, the

38   The grand school built by Bishop Waynflete at his birthplace, Wainfleet (Lincs.) constructed of brick with two imposing towers.

same as the number of the boys in his school.[185] Day-school pupils could stay at home on holidays, but those who boarded well away from home had to remain at school or in their lodgings. This could also apply during longer vacations. Alexander de la Pole went to Ipswich school in September 1416, and did not return to Wingfield until the following July.[186] Edward Querton stayed at Ewelme from 23 October 1464 to 16 April 1465.[187]

When many boys boarded on the premises or nearby, schools may have remained in session for most of the time. It has been said of Winchester College that 'the school never closed as a whole in the first few years', although it was possible for the scholars to go home at Christmas, Easter, or Whitsuntide.[188] Sixteenth-century records show that Eton almost always had pupils in residence. The college observed a series of feast-days, some commemorating major saints and others local benefactors. Each of these days involved a measure of change from the normal routine. Some were whole holidays, while lessons were given on others, or exercises done. There were longer holidays at Eton too, some fifteen days at Christmas and twelve at Easter, but most of the boys did not leave school and even pursued some studies. Eton's chief vacation began on Ascension Day (a moveable feast, usually in May) and lasted until Corpus Christi, three weeks later, during which boys could go home to their parents. This was the chief time of the year for holidays in lay society, because it preceded the arduous weeks of harvest.[189]

Twice in the year schoolboys had festivals of their own, all over England, with celebrations rooted in ancient custom. During December a boy-bishop was selected in large churches to preside over the religious festivities of St Nicholas Day (6 December) and Childermas – the feast of the Holy Innocents (28 December).[190] These days, or one of them, involved 'role reversal' in church. The adult clergy took the lower seats in the choir, and the boys replaced them in the upper ones. The boy-bishop led the services, blessed the congregation, and sometimes preached a sermon. After their duties in church the boys toured the neighbourhood begging for money, some of which was used for feasting. These ceremonies reached their most elaborate form at the cathedrals, where they centred on the choristers. At St Paul's the boy-bishop and his companions rode round the city on horses; at York they made long journeys through the nearby countryside, being entertained and collecting money. Other schools and schoolboys copied these celebrations. At Worcester towards the end of the thirteenth century the master and his scholars celebrated the first of the two feasts by carrying tapers into the parish church of St Nicholas.[191] Wykeham gave Winchester College a mitre of cloth of gold for the boy-bishop to wear, and during the fifteenth century the services in the college chapel concluded with merrymaking in hall, the 'bishop' presenting 20d. in 1406 to a party of mummers who danced before him.[192] Even Colet, a critic of foolish customs, endorsed the church-based part of Innocents Day. He ordered the pupils of St Paul's to attend the cathedral when the boy-bishop preached his sermon, after which they had to hear mass and offer the bishop a penny.[193]

The other great school festival was Shrove Tuesday, already well established when William FitzStephen was writing at the end of the twelfth century. On that day, he says,

> boys from the schools bring fighting-cocks to their master, and the whole forenoon is given up to boyish sport; for they have a holiday in the schools that they may watch their cocks do battle. After dinner all the youth of the city goes out into the fields to a much-frequented game of ball. The scholars of each school have their own ball, and almost all the workers of each trade have theirs also in their hands. Elder men, and fathers, and rich citizens come on horseback to watch the contests of their juniors, and after their fashion are young again with the young.[194]

Cockfighting was widespread in medieval schools on Shrove Tuesday. At Gloucester in 1400, the birds, apparently a perquisite of the schoolmaster after the fighting, were divided between the two priories that claimed to control the school.[195] Two school notebooks, one from Devon and another apparently from St Albans, contain Latin poems about the sport.[196] Colet forbade it at St Paul's and his example was followed by Manchester school in 1525,[197] anticipating the more severe attitudes towards recreation that surfaced during the Reformation period. Despite this Shrove Tuesday long remained a popular holiday, with cockfighting in remoter and more robust school communities.

Festivals and holidays give us a rosy picture of the past that is incomplete. Pupils at boarding school could be homesick, and any boys could be bullied by their peers or their masters. Robert Barbour accidentally gave Robert Fayred a mortal wound at Aylsham in about 1460, as a result of 'their negligent japing and disport in the said school', and was promptly removed to the county gaol since he was fourteen and on the cusp of adulthood.[198] Some Oxford school exercises of the early sixteenth century talk of a pupil beaten black and blue by a bully, and of another who was robbed in the street by three thieves posing as scholars.[199] Schoolboys stood out through their dress and, if they came from a distance, their accents, offering tempting targets for criminals. There were regular conflicts between scholars and townspeople in Cambridge and Oxford, and although schoolboys in other towns were normally younger and fewer, they too might get involved in local disorders. A brawl at Dunstable in 1274 between the scholars and the townsfolk left many people wounded. One of the townsmen was killed, and an accusation by the dead man's wife led to the flight of Robert the clerk of Sherrington before he could be arrested.[200] A certain Nyweton, one of the clerks of Exeter school in 1288, attacked Henna the Jewess in South Street as the clerks were going home, by throwing stones at her. One of the stones drew blood and caused her to raise the hue and cry.[201] In 1327 all the scholars of Newark were excommunicated by the archbishop of York on account of their violence, although he later allowed the parish priest of the town to absolve them.[202]

ONWARDS AND OUTWARDS

We started this chapter by asking where pupils came from. It remains to explore what became of them when they left school. A few never lived to do so, carried off by death before their schooling was over. Town schools lay in communities notoriously subject to epidemics. Fear of fatal diseases caused both schools and universities to be closed for periods during the fifteenth and sixteenth centuries. Scholars went home, or were sent in a body to the countryside like the boys of Magdalen College School. 'I was from school a great part of this last year,' says an imaginary boy at the school in about the 1510s, 'by the reason of the sickness that continued here in the town. God give grace that it begin not again here, for and if it do I shall shortly go hence.'[203] How well founded the fear was can be seen from the records of Winchester College. Although it was a relatively well fed and well provided community, contagion spread through its buildings from time to time with devastating effects. At least twelve scholars died in 1401, nine in 1430, twenty in 1431, eleven in 1434, and four in 1436.[204] The memorial brass survives of another, John Kent, who died in 1435 (Fig. 32).[205]

Most went out apparently improved, otherwise schools would not have attracted pupils. Schooling was considered to deliver two main qualities: virtue and learning. Virtue meant religious knowledge, pious observances, and moral values. Schools taught you basic prayers, psalms and hymns, and the ability to follow and understand worship in Latin. They trained you in religious observances – saying grace at meals, keeping saints' days, and making your confession. They introduced you to moral and religious literature like Cato and Theodulus. The discipline of school conveyed you from childhood and its playfulness to the self-control and hard work needed in adulthood. Grammar schools were flexible about pursuing these goals; they had to be, if masters were to gather enough pupils. Schoolwork was not unduly spiritual in character, and school exercises gave plenty of attention to things of the world such as news, marriage, money, and status. Learning Latin, with the bonus that you also learnt to spell and write French or English, equipped you for a wide range of careers. You could live or work as a gentleman, a cleric, a lawyer, a merchant or tradesman, a yeoman farmer, or a secretarial clerk. Nor did you need to commit yourself to any of these choices during childhood. The education you gained in school was suitable for any change in your circumstances, and if necessary could be supplemented by some business studies or by learning at work.

It gave you a Latin culture too, conferring knowledge that you could use as an outward badge or inward token to distinguish yourself from others. Latinate men, as we have seen, were clerics of a sort; they were described as 'lered' or learned, as opposed to 'lewed' or unlearned – a contrast of words and concepts often found in the later middle ages.[206] How people used their knowledge of Latin in later life is too large a question to examine here, but some certainly remembered what they had learnt in school and used it as occasion demanded. John Shillingford, mayor of Exeter, wrote to his fellow councillors in 1447 complaining that they had not sent a present of fish that he wanted to give the king's chancellor. Teasing them in English for their failure, he introduced phrases in Latin that he and they would have known from the classroom. He compared the two men responsible to 'one thief talking to another' (*ait latro ad latronem*) and likened their incompetence to 'an arse falling between two stools' (*inter scabella duo anus labitur humo*), a proverb straight out of the vulgaria collections.[207] A generation later one or more of the clergy of Exeter Cathedral began jotting down items of news in Latin in a calendar kept in the choir. Two or three of the descriptions of comets and tempests are remarkably like school latins in length and style, and suggest that those who wrote them reproduced what they had learnt in class in younger days.[208] William Worcester, the antiquary, amused himself in 1477 writing comic verses in Latin about a stay with the monks of

St Benet Hulme near Norwich ('linen – rubbish; saltless cabbage; bed and stable – execrable; mattress – dingy, welcome – stingy').[209] John Paston III of Norfolk, some time after 1485, composed or copied a set of facetious Latin verses about the earl of Oxford, meaning to send them to a knight of his acquaintance.[210] Evidently not all former schoolboys thought of their Latin as a purely practical tool; some went on relishing the cultural skills to which they had been introduced.

Signs of schooling being remembered or utilised in later life could doubtless be multiplied, and the point is an important one because schools and schoolboys do not have a high profile in the writings of medieval England. Some lives of saints and romantic stories dwell on the childhoods of their heroes and heroines and describe what they learnt or how they behaved, but this is usually in the context of a family or a great household. It is rare to find a romance like *Floris and Blancheflur*, which exists in French versions of the twelfth century and English ones of the thirteenth, where the boy and girl of the title go to school together, and even here that aspect of the story plays a fleeting part.[211] Chaucer's picture of the little scholar at school is equally uncommon: a testimony to its author's sharp-sightedness and originality, rather than to an interest by writers in school matters. The chief literary genre that goes into detail about schools and schoolboys is that of vulgaria, a genre of schools themselves. A small group of songs about the woes of being a schoolboy exists from the end of the middle ages, but they too seem to come from a school environment or, at most, to have been sung by boys at public entertainments.[212] The scarcity of literary references to schools may partly reflect the relatively poor survival of medieval literature, but not wholly. There seems to be a quickening of interest in schools and schoolboys during the sixteenth century, so that by the time of Shakespeare and his contemporaries they are depicted more often and even in stereotyped ways, a sure sign of greater profile.[213]

We hear remarkably little too in terms of literary reminiscences by medieval adults about their schooldays. There was a brief flowering of autobiography in the twelfth century, most notably in the memoirs of the French monk Guibert of Nogent (d. 1124), which talk of his schooldays in about 1070.[214] A few writers from England and Wales in this period recall incidents of their schooling. Orderic's memories of his teacher at Shrewsbury are complemented by those of John of Salisbury (d. 1180), who remembers the priest who taught him the psalter and tried to make him join in crystal gazing.[215] Gerald of Wales informs us about his schoolmaster at Gloucester Abbey (Master Hamo), Alexander Nequam about his schooling at St Albans, and Jocelin of Brakelond about the gratitude of Abbot Samson of Bury St Edmunds towards his (Samson's) schoolmaster, William of Diss.[216] The vein looks promising, but it peters out soon after 1200 and scarcely reappears before the fifteenth century. Adam of Usk (d. 1430) wrote an autobiographical chronicle in which he refers to two events in his life as a

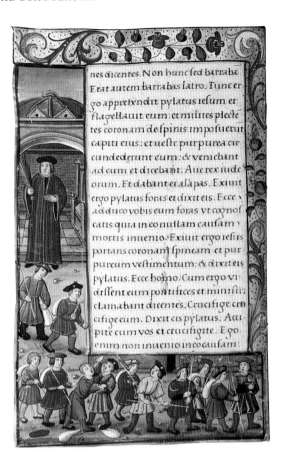

nes dicentes. Non hunc sed barraba
Erat autem barrabas latro. Tunc er
go apprehendit pylatus iesum et
flagellauit eum: et milites plecte
tes coronam despinis imposuerut
capiti eius: et ueste purpurea cir
cundederunt eum: & veniebant
ad eum et dicebant: Aue rex iude
orum. Et dabant ei alapas. Exiuit
ergo pylatus foras et dixit eis. Ecce
adduco vobis eum foras vt cognos
catis quia in eo nullam causam
mortis inuenio. Exiuit ergo iesus
portans coronam spineam et pur
pureum vestimentum: & dixit eis
pylatus. Ecce homo. Cum ergo vi
dissent eum pontifices et ministri
clamabant dicentes. Crucifige cru
cifige eum. Dixit eis pylatus. Acci
pite eum vos et crucifigite. Ego
enim non inuenio in eo causam

39   An early sixteenth-century
schoolmaster watching pupils leaving
his school.

student at Oxford, but not to his schooldays.[217] William Worcester visited
Bristol in 1480 where he had grown up sixty years earlier, and noted the site
of the school over the Newgate together with the name of its former
schoolmaster, Robert Londe. He may have made his note because he had
studied there, but he does not actually say so.[218]

One of the first literary references to a person's own schooling after the
early thirteenth century is that of Thomas Rotherham, archbishop of York,
in the foundation charter of the college he established at Rotherham in
1483. Here he was moved to tell how he passed his early years in the town
without knowledge of letters, until 'by God's grace' a teacher of grammar
arrived there from whom he received his first instruction.[219] A few years
earlier, in about 1478, the tomb of Edward Audley in Eton College chapel,
a young nobleman who had died aged about twenty, was given an
inscription which mentions that he studied grammar at Eton.[220] An epitaph
on the tomb of Thomas Howard, duke of Norfolk (d. 1524), contains a
similar reference, stating that he went to a grammar school.[221] Gradually,
during the sixteenth century, such references grow in number. Some occur
in the reviving genre of autobiography, like that of the musician Thomas

Whythorne written in about 1576, which describes his childhood of forty years earlier; others appear in biographies and yet others on tombs.[222]

It is misleading to argue too much from literary genres, which never reflect the whole of human interest and understanding. If we turn to legal records it is clear that people did remember their schooling and were capable of recalling it when required. One such strand of evidence comes from 'proofs of age' of the fourteenth and fifteenth centuries, in which feudal heirs sought to show that they had reached the age of majority and might therefore reclaim their lands from their guardians. A number of the witnesses brought by the heirs attested to the dates of the heirs' births on the grounds that the witnesses had been at school or had sent a child to school on that date.[223] Depositions in church courts during the sixteenth century contain similar evidence. One elderly man remembered his schooldays at Tywardreath Priory, guarding fish as it dried in the sun. Another had helped the schoolmaster of Wotton-under-Edge to say mass, wearing a surplice and kneeling on a cushion. A third had seen the tithe cheese brought into Wrington church when he went to school there.[224] In 1440 a Dorset rector wrote a letter to an English merchant at Rouen in Normandy reminding him that they had been at school together at Ilminster, and passing on greetings from the man with whom the merchant had lodged.[225]

The claim of fellowship at school is an unusual one to find in a letter, but we possess relatively little private correspondence before the sixteenth century. It can hardly be doubted that medieval people met former school friends, recalled their experiences, or traded on the link they had in common. In 1457 Robert Terry, a clerk in Leicestershire, needed to establish his credentials as a respectable Englishman. Fifteen people came forward to attest that they had been at school with him at Leicester or Melton Mowbray, including the masters of two hospitals, a prior and a subprior, seven parish clergy, and four merchants and shopkeepers of Leicester.[226] For a brief moment we glimpse a medieval group of alumni, bound together by the memories of their schooldays.

5

The Schoolmaster

DEFINITION AND NUMBERS

At the principal end of the schoolroom sat the schoolmaster in his chair of authority. By the end of the middle ages he was a familiar figure in western Europe. There were special words to describe him and ways of portraying him in pictures (Figs 31 and 40). Artists showed him with his fingers raised in a teaching gesture, or with his hand on his birch – the symbol of his office, like the king's sceptre or the bishop's staff. Teaching had been an identifiable occupation in English society for centuries and sometimes an esteemed one, as we have seen in relation to Theodore, Boniface, and Bede. These men, however, were primarily monks or bishops. Their work in school was only one of their daily activities, not a full-time profession. Late-medieval schoolmasters were different. They can be called modern: spending the working day in their classrooms, or much of the day if they were priests as well. When and how did such teachers emerge – professional teachers such as we have today?

Just as schools before the Norman Conquest are recorded as departments of religious houses or of the royal household, so references to teachers up to 1066 are usually to members of such bodies. Even after the Conquest, when schools begin to appear in charters as distinct activities or institutions, their teachers often seem to have been clergy – especially minster clergy.[1] Lanfranc was believed to have given the schools of Canterbury to the canons of St Gregory's. The first known schoolmasters of Salisbury and York were canons of those cathedrals. At Hastings in the early twelfth century the keeping of the song school belonged to one of the canons of the church in the castle, and that of the grammar school to another.[2] The likelihood is that such clergy did their teaching alongside their duties of saying daily worship, just as Anglo-Saxon clergy had done, even where the school was open to outsiders. This linkage loosened during the twelfth century as the claims of worship and teaching grew less compatible. On the one hand the demand for education produced larger classes that needed a teacher's full-time attention. On the other, the religious life became more exacting. Minsters

40   A fourteenth-century lay schoolmaster birching a boy, who is held by an usher or senior pupil.

became caught up in the contemporary enthusiasm for monasticism. Many adopted, or were made to adopt, the Augustinian rule and became abbeys or priories of regular canons. These canons followed a more religious, communal, and secluded life. They could supervise a local school for the public by choosing its teacher and providing its building, but they could no longer teach it themselves. A dedicated schoolmaster was needed.[3]

Other forces were working in the same direction. Ecclesiastical administration was growing in weight. Bishops were acquiring time-consuming duties in royal government and in running their dioceses. They were wealthier, grander, and more often away from their cathedrals than in the days when Æthelwold had taught in Winchester. Lanfranc was a former teacher and was afterwards said to have helped poor scholars at Canterbury take part in disputations.[4] Later bishops, in contrast, are unlikely to have had much involvement with public education, although they continued to accept boys into their households and no doubt oversaw the education of such boys by their household clergy and servants.[5] The schoolmasters of the secular cathedrals also acquired new tasks. They acted as secretaries to their churches, writing letters and keeping records, and took the new title of 'chancellor' to reflect this work. They kept a link with education but of a superior and less toilsome kind, based on the lectures in theology or canon law discussed in an earlier chapter.[6] Their original name of schoolmaster and its duty of teaching the cathedral school for boys passed to a deputy teacher, lower in status.[7] This may have happened in minster schools as well. Nicholas, canon of the minster of St Paul in Bedford and the local archdeacon, 'held' Bedford school in the 1170s, but he can hardly have spent much time in the classroom.[8] He must have appointed a substitute in his place.

By 1200, at the latest, there was a definite class of specialised teachers. At the same time, shreds of the previous order remained. Many schoolmasters were 'clerks' with minor ecclesiastical status. Some, although they were principally teachers, continued to have links with churches, notably in cathedral schools like Salisbury and Wells, where they were expected to join the cathedral choir for one or two of the daily services.[9] It was still possible to combine the work of a schoolmaster and that of a priest – indeed, it has never ceased to be possible, meaning that part of one's day would be given to prayer. Throughout the middle ages there were full-time clergy who taught. Monks, friars, and nuns instructed novices, and some parish clergy took in private pupils. During the fourteenth and fifteenth centuries there was even a resurgence of the priest who acted as a schoolmaster for the public, due to the foundation of collegiate churches and chantry schools in which the teaching was entrusted to clerics.[10] The emergence of the professional teacher in the twelfth century was therefore not complete. For a long time he (or she) existed alongside other purveyors of learning, part-time, clerical, or semi-clerical. As a result the general public did not necessarily view a teacher as distinctly as we do. The fact that a man was a cleric might overshadow his profile as a schoolmaster. Taxation records are especially prone to list such men as priests rather than teachers.[11] In the previous chapter we noted William Worcester's reference to Robert Londe, the master of a prominent grammar school in Bristol. When Londe died in 1462 a monumental brass was placed above his grave, depicting him as a priest in mass vestments holding a host and chalice, and describing him as a chaplain (Fig. 41). No reference was made on the brass to the teaching for which we now remember him.[12]

Medieval people used a variety of words to describe those who taught – a variety that was stylistic rather than based on differences between one teacher and another. A Latin writer after 1100 might call a male teacher an *archiscola*, *didascalus* and its compound *archididascalus*, *grammaticus*, *informator*, *magister scolarum*, *monitor*, *pedagogus*, *rector scolarum*, or *scolasticus*. There were fashions in the use of these words. *Archiscola* and *scolasticus* are words of the period immediately after the Conquest. *Rector scolarum* occurs from the twelfth century to the fourteenth, but then disappears. *Informator* was popular from the fifteenth century onwards, and *archididascalus* (meaning a headmaster where there were at least two teachers) emerged at the Reformation. *Didascalus*, *grammaticus*, *monitor*, and *pedagogus* are rather rare in any period. The commonest term, with the greatest staying power

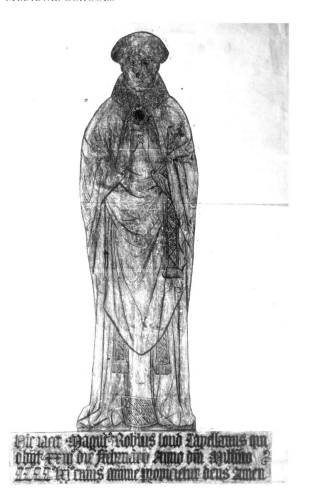

41   The memorial brass of Robert
Londe (d. 1462), master of
Newgate school (Bristol).

from the twelfth century to the sixteenth, was *magister scolarum*, no doubt
because it came closest to 'schoolmaster', which was the standard word in
English from at least about 1200. An assistant teacher was called a *submagister*
or *submonitor* in Latin, 'submaster' or 'undermaster' in English, up to about
1400, and subsequently a (*h*)*ostiarius* or its English equivalent 'usher', with
hypodidascalus coming into use in the sixteenth century.[13]

    Because most teachers were male, the vernacular word for women who
taught may at first have been the same as it was for men. The instructions
for anchoresses, known as the *Ancrene Rule* (*c*.1225), advise such ladies
against operating as a school*master*.[14] We occasionally encounter medieval
women with the surname 'Schoolmaster', but it is impossible to know from
that if they were practising teachers or the wives, widows, or daughters of
schoolmasters. A more promising surname is 'Schoolmistress', since this is
more likely to indicate what its owner did herself. The earliest woman with
this name so far discovered is Margaret Skolmaystres, who is mentioned in
Oxford in 1335.[15] A second, Matilda Maresflete, occurs in Boston in 1404

with her occupation in its Latin form, *magistra scolarum*, and two others, E. Scolemaysteresse and Elizabeth Scolemaystres, turn up in London in 1408 and 1441 respectively.[16] A fifth woman with a similar title, Agnes 'teacher of girls' (*doctrix puellarum*), is recorded in London before 1449.[17] This shows how easy it is to be misled by lack of evidence. No documents survive about the schools taught by these women, which were probably informal and unlikely to leave traces in records. Yet their surnames and titles show that they taught (or had taught) schools, and that people had a concept of them as schoolmistresses, implying a familiarity with such teachers. There may have been many women instructors in towns, ministering to girls, small boys, or both. Very likely they concentrated on the lower end of the curriculum: the abc, the reading of Latin prayers and primers, and perhaps the reading of works in French or English.

Male teachers have left more records about themselves, but even so the most basic piece of information about them – their numbers – is almost equally hard to establish. We do not know how many schools there were, and the total must have varied between 1100 and 1548. As a working hypothesis, let us assume that the average English county during this period contained about ten grammar schools with professional schoolmasters. Multiplied nationally, this would produce a total of about 400 schools and masters, excluding Wales. We need to add to this, in the later middle ages, about another 200 professional masters working in monasteries and great households, giving us a total of about 600, possibly more. Such a rough estimate is not presented as a reliable statistic but as a broad indication of how small the profession was as a proportion of the population, even of the clergy. Taken together the schoolmasters of medieval England were vastly outnumbered by the 4,500 monks and regular canons, the 2,200 friars, the 1,500 nuns, and the several thousands of parish clergy who made up the clerical estate, even when the English population reached a low ebb of two or three million in the late fourteenth century. Locally too they were thin on the ground. A typical small English town had one, with perhaps an assistant. Larger cities like Bristol, Exeter, Norwich, Winchester, and York may have supported up to about half a dozen professional or semi-professional teachers. Oxford would have contained as many as a dozen, and London perhaps two dozen or more, but the teacher was a relatively unusual figure in most communities. The consequences of this fact will become clear later in this chapter.

We have seen that teaching was a well-regarded activity in Anglo-Saxon England. Archbishop Theodore, King Alfred, and Bishop Æthelwold did not think it beneath themselves to give an occasional lecture or lesson, and some long-term teachers rose to be bishops and abbots. This relatively high status continued for some time after the Norman Conquest, notably in the emergence of schoolmasters at the cathedrals who were not only canons but senior officers of the church. When Bishop Osmund of Salisbury drew up the so-called 'Institution' or founding statute for his new cathedral in 1091, he made the schoolmaster (*archiscola*) one of the four chief dignitaries, and this arrangement was adopted in at least three other English cathedrals – St Paul's (London), Wells, and York – during the twelfth century. Usually the schoolmaster ranked third in order, after the dean of the cathedral and the precentor but before the treasurer and the rest of the canons.[18] There is a parallel within the royal family to these high-status cathedral schoolmasters. Matthew, the tutor who taught the future Henry II to read Latin at Bristol in the 1140s, was important enough to witness some of Henry's charters as 'teacher of the duke' (*doctor ducis*), and may have become the chancellor of Queen Eleanor of Aquitaine.[19] Several other schoolteachers of this period are known to have risen to important posts in the Church. Among bishops with English connections, Guy of Etampes, bishop of Le Mans, John of Salisbury, bishop of Chartres, Robert of Béthune, bishop of Hereford, and William of Corbeil, archbishop of Canterbury, had all been teachers privately or in a school for the public. In the monasteries, Geoffrey de Gorron, schoolmaster of Dunstable, became abbot of St Albans; Guy, an Italian schoolmaster, prior of Taunton and Bodmin; while Alexander Nequam, who taught at both Dunstable and St Albans, ended his career as abbot of Cirencester.[20]

The career successes of such men reflected the width of their knowledge, which in that pre-university era meant that they often taught not simply elementary Latin but the liberal arts and other advanced studies. A twelfth-century schoolteacher might be as learned as anyone, and consequently well qualified for appointment to high office. By the end of the century, however, school teaching was falling in status. The process by which bishops, cathedral chancellors, and minster clergy became dissociated from teaching caused schools to fall into the hands of men of lower standing and lesser earnings. In the royal family, too, an office of schoolmaster failed to develop. Although the king's sons after 1200 routinely learnt some Latin, the subject seems to have been regarded as only moderately important and suitable to entrust to chaplains and clerks who were not professional teachers. Only after the 1420s do we regularly hear again of schoolmasters teaching the royal princes.[21] The rise of the universities in the thirteenth century had a further adverse effect on the status of schools and schoolmasters. Universities took over the higher and more prestigious levels of learning, and schools became chiefly confined to the lowlier ones of reading, plainsong, and Latin grammar. For the next three hundred years knowledge of university studies – arts, canon and civil law, and theology – or of the common law of the king's courts was the qualification for high office in both the king's service and the Church. Schools became more humble institutions, schoolteachers more lowly and peripheral figures, and their best students university men with university loyalties. A period ensued of lower status and prominence for teachers, and it is this period, up to the early sixteenth century, that we shall now explore.

QUALIFICATIONS

How did you become a schoolmaster after 1200? As with most occupations there were two requirements. You had to possess certain general qualifications and to gain employment at a particular school. The qualifications varied from place to place, depending on the nature and importance of the school, and related to two standards: scholarship and ecclesiastical status. In the thirteenth century, after universities first developed, some of the best schools required their teachers to be graduate masters of arts (MAs) who had completed the arts course at university. This was the case at Hereford, Lincoln, St Paul's (London), and York among the English cathedrals.[22] At Oxford too the university statutes of the early fourteenth century assumed that the masters of the grammar schools in the city (controlled by the university) would usually be MAs. All newly graduated MAs in Oxford were required to be 'regents' or active teachers, and it appears that they found teaching grammar so lucrative that the statutes had to restrict them from running grammar schools for more than three years, lest the number of regents available for university teaching should be endangered.[23] The MA requirement was a high one, since the arts course lasted for seven years with a further two years of regency, so that a graduate schoolmaster in the thirteenth and fourteenth centuries was both learned and likely to be in his mid twenties or older.

By the middle of the fourteenth century there are signs of a shortage of graduates willing to become schoolmasters. The Black Death of 1348–9 and the subsequent decline of the population probably reduced the number of pupils and therefore the fees to be earned from teaching them. It certainly opened up more opportunities to gain a benefice as rector or vicar of a parish, with the better tenure, status, and income that went with such posts. In 1351 the chapter of Lincoln Cathedral granted the grammar school of Lincoln to a clerk named John Muscham who evidently lacked a master's degree because the condition was made that 'if a master of arts should come and ask for the school he should be admitted, since by custom the teaching of the school belongs to an MA'.[24] Similarly at York the cathedral chancellor noted in 1368 that since the last great plague, probably that of 1362, no master of arts had cared to teach in the cathedral on account of the scarcity of such men and the shortness of the term of office. He therefore appointed Master John of York, who was so qualified, not for the customary period of three or five years but until John obtained another benefice.[25] Oxford experienced similar changes. University statutes of the late fourteenth century provided for the admission of schoolmasters who were not MAs but who had the support of a grammar master who was one. If no such MA could be found, the support of two other good men of the university would suffice.[26]

The decline in the number of graduate schoolmasters after the Black Death does not mean that links between universities and schools were broken.

School patrons and teachers continued to value university study as a means of increasing knowledge and status, and qualifications came into existence that were easier to achieve than the MA. One resulted from the practice of regarding students as graduates when they had completed the first four years of the arts course, such students being known as bachelors of arts (BAs). Another was the introduction of degrees solely in grammar, which took even less time to achieve than a BA. A degree of 'master of grammar' (MGram) may have been conferred at Oxford by the mid fourteenth century and was awarded at Cambridge by about 1385.[27] Candidates for the Cambridge degree were expected to take part in three public disputations and to deliver thirteen lectures on Priscian's *Constructions*. After being admitted to the degree, they had to spend a year of regency during which they gave more lectures on the Major part of Priscian and on poetry in the manner of Priscian on Virgil.[28] Later, by the early sixteenth century, both Cambridge and Oxford took a more lenient attitude to the degree, allowing candidates credit for having studied or taught grammar outside the university and requiring them merely to lecture in public on a literary author or to compose Latin verses in praise of the university. By that time the public demand for such degrees was not large. About fifty-three were granted at Oxford between 1509 and 1568, and about fifty at Cambridge between 1500 and 1548, so that only three or four such people graduated in grammar from the English universities in a normal year. Still, their presence increased the number of 'graduate' masters in schools, and one Oxford candidate in 1514 claimed that he needed the degree to take up a post for which that status was required.[29]

What scholastic qualifications were usual among the schoolmasters of late-medieval England? Some of those at the cathedral schools continued to be MAs after the mid fourteenth century, but others were admitted with a BA, MGram, or no degree at all. The masters who taught for fees in the other towns are so shadowy that it is impossible even to guess at the proportions of graduates and non-graduates among them. In any case, the question is obscured by the custom of calling schoolmasters, particularly the well established, 'Master so-and-so', perhaps only because they were school*masters*. We can get a better idea of expectations and realities in grammar schools once we enter the era when schools were endowed and given statutes, beginning in the 1380s. Very few school founders explicitly stated that their masters should be graduates before about 1500. Even William Wykeham's statutes for Winchester College (1400) asked merely that the headmaster should have teaching experience, a request repeated by Henry VI in the statutes of Eton (1447), although Henry added that the master should be an MA and the usher a BA 'if possible'.[30] In the six counties of the west of England only nine of the eighty schoolmasters recorded between 1200 and 1500 were certainly graduates. Another twenty-six were sometimes styled 'master', but they may have been accorded the title out of courtesy. The remaining forty-five, over half, appear to have been non-graduates.[31]

42 Henry VI (d. 1471), a rare patron of schooling and schoolmasters such as John Chedworth, John Somerset, and William Waynflete.

Matters began to change in this respect during the fifteenth century, and more perceptibly in the early sixteenth. In practice, after about 1450 Winchester and Eton were normally staffed by graduate masters and sometimes by graduate ushers. Some other leading schools, while not stipulating the service of graduates, routinely employed them, notably Magdalen College School in Oxford (1480) and St Paul's, London (1508–12). A few smaller grammar schools founded in the English provinces, like Sevenoaks (1432) and Wye (1447), specified that their masters should hold degrees.[32] In other endowed schools, where there was no such requirement, the incidence of graduate masters appears to have increased in the early sixteenth century, with the proviso that graduate status tends to be better recorded as time goes by. Thus in our west-of-England counties, out of seventy known schoolmasters teaching between

1500 and 1548, twenty-two were graduates, five 'masters' of uncertain status, and forty-three apparently non-graduates. In Gloucestershire the endowed grammar school at Wotton-under-Edge had apparently only one or two graduate masters out of thirteen up to 1487, but after that date they were always graduates until the Reformation. At Newland in the same county the first graduate schoolmaster was the ninth to hold office, in 1536. His successors all seem to have had this status up to the 1550s.[33]

It is also worth remembering that schoolmasters who lacked university qualifications when they started to teach might acquire them while in service. Some had no resources or incentive to undertake higher study until they had gained a paid post, after which they might seek to remedy the deficiency. When the canons of Lanthony Priory granted the schoolmastership of Gloucester to John Hamelyn in 1396, the contract provided for him to leave the school for a year to go to university.[34] Maurice Plank, appointed master of Wisbech grammar school in 1407, was granted permission to study at Cambridge for two years, as long as he appointed an usher to teach in his absence.[35] The records of both universities in the early sixteenth century supply examples of schoolmasters who were taking time off from their charges to read for a degree. Sometimes they merely asked to be admitted to the grammar degree as a formality. Occasionally they supplicated for the BA or MA, and their teaching experience or their responsibilities in their schools earned them exemption from parts of the degree course. In 1505, for instance, Richard Church, BA, was permitted to count the three years he had spent as a schoolmaster in Canterbury towards the requirements of the MA at Oxford, and in 1510 Thomas Stanbridge, a candidate for the BA, received a dispensation in respect of his duties at Banbury school.[36]

The other kind of qualification relevant to teaching was being a cleric. This is a complicated matter, because there were grades of clergy. Those who held minor orders (tonsured clerks and acolytes) were free to do secular work and to marry, while those in major orders (subdeacons, deacons, and priests) were fully committed to a religious life and could do neither. It was never a general rule that schoolmasters should be in major or even minor orders, and the extent to which this was required varied from place to place. Schools that expected their masters to attend worship, like the cathedral schools of Salisbury and Wells, obliged them to be tonsured and to that extent to be clergy, but there was no bar to such men resigning, marrying, and resuming lay status. At York three masters in the later fifteenth century were married men, and masters who were not in major orders appear to have been acceptable at St Paul's.[37] Equally a post in a cathedral school was attractive to priests, who could augment their salaries by working at the cathedral as a vicar-choral or chantry priest, and we find examples of men who followed this path.[38] In town schools up to 1400, where the masters had no duties outside their schools, they were probably a mixture of priests, clerks in minor holy orders, and laymen. A cleric had the advantage of being able to supplement his wages by undertaking ecclesiastical duties, while a layman could acquire a wife to look after the boys who boarded in his house. Teaching, one suspects, became the destination of some young men who had aimed at the priesthood but lost their vocations through falling in love.

Oddly enough it was only in the fifteenth century that a requirement to be a priest became common. This reflected the foundation of endowed schools, beginning in the 1380s and increasing in number in the 1440s. Some of these were attached to colleges of secular priests while others doubled as chantries, providing intercessions for the founder as well as education. In the first case the master was sometimes a priest of the college, and in the second he was expected to celebrate a daily mass in addition to teaching his pupils. Over one hundred schools in these categories were founded up to about 1530, and in other cases chantry priests began to be given teaching as an additional duty, so that there came to be two hundred or more posts in England for schoolmaster-priests. The larger endowed schools were more relaxed about whether they employed priests or laymen. Winchester College's statutes made no ruling on the subject, and Eton's laid down merely that the master and usher should not be married; indeed the latter was forbidden to be in holy orders.[39] Archbishop Rotherham, who founded Rotherham college and grammar school in 1483, only gave preference to priests, and his first teacher, John Bocking, was married.[40] So was John Anwykyll, the first known master of Magdalen College School in the 1480s.[41] Colet's indifference as to whether the master of St Paul's was married, single, or in orders, provided he was a good Latinist, was therefore not new; it followed an older tradition.[42]

The acceptance of lay masters by the smaller endowed grammar schools took longer to achieve. Their founders had less money to spend, and wished to get a priest as well as a teacher in return for a single salary. There is an often quoted exception in the case of the grammar school at Sevenoaks, founded by William Sevenoaks in 1432, where the master was required 'by no means' to be in holy orders.[43] But this was unusual. It was not until about the 1510s that founders of schools such as Nottingham (1512), Winchcombe (1521), and Manchester (1525) opened the post of master to priests or to laymen.[44] Even then some priests held office in these schools. The first master of Nottingham had previously been a parish priest, and the master of Winchcombe in 1535 held a local chantry in tandem with the school. Clerical schoolmasters were to be familiar figures for centuries, but a significant change took place in 1548 when the crown dissolved the chantries. The grammar schools attached to them were preserved but their teaching posts were secularised and opened to all applicants. This restored the status quo of 1400, when few schools had insisted that their masters should be clergy.

CAREERS AND CONDUCT

There were other respects in which schoolteachers differed from one another, including age, experience, and commitment to teaching. Many were young men, particularly ushers who might recently have been senior pupils or have returned to teaching after graduation. The office of schoolmaster itself might be restricted to a period of three or five years. We have seen that the graduate masters of Oxford could not teach grammar there for more than three, while at York the term of office of the schoolmaster was three or five. Northallerton school appointed for terms of three and five years in the 1370s and 1380s, and Wells cathedral school appears to have done so for three in the early sixteenth century.[45] Sometimes short terms of appointment may have been intended to prevent an unsuitable master from acquiring permanent tenure, but it is also likely that the job of teaching was seen as an 'internship' suitable for a young man who would go on to some other kind of work, notably that of a priest. This was particularly the case up to the mid fourteenth century, before it became more difficult to find good teachers.

Not everybody shared this view of teaching. School patrons charged with finding schoolmasters, and parents who needed access to schooling, must often have been happy for a competent teacher to hold office indefinitely. There are many examples of men who spent a lifetime in the classroom, like the Oxford masters John Leland and Thomas Sampson. The endowed schools of the fifteenth and early sixteenth centuries improved the security of their masters' tenure by providing regular salaries as opposed to the uncertainty of fees, and some who worked in these schools settled down to teach for long periods. In the grammar school of Wotton-under-Edge, John Paradise held office for nearly thirty years between 1427 and 1456, and one of his successors, Robert Coldwell, resigned in about 1552 after more than forty.[46] Some men laboured on well into old age. Thomas Guyldesburgh had been a schoolmaster in Chichester for more than thirty years when he got himself imprisoned for debt during the 1460s, causing him to plead for his release on the grounds that he was over eighty, 'right corpulent, and hath a malady in his leg that he may neither well ride nor go'.[47] Another octogenarian schoolmaster was John Ree, who was still teaching the grammar school at Rock in Worcestershire in 1561, after a career that stretched back for at least a quarter of a century.[48]

Alongside these men there were others, more restless or more ambitious, who moved from place to place. Ushers did so to acquire schools of their own. Richard Darcy, usher of Gloucester in the 1410s, went to Winchester College as headmaster in 1418, while Thomas Stanbridge, usher of Banbury in 1511, moved to the senior post at Magdalen College School in 1517.[49] Occasionally they were promoted within their own schools, like John Stanbridge, who was elevated from usher to schoolmaster at Magdalen after the death of his colleague John Anwykyll in 1488.[50] Masters might also leave surroundings they disliked to rule a more prestigious or lucrative school, or be enticed to fill a vacancy. Thomas Romsey went to Winchester College in 1394 having previously taught at Chichester, and when the college needed another headmaster in 1424 it invited applications from the schoolmasters of Maidstone and Salisbury, before appointing Thomas Alwyn, who had apparently been teaching in Buckinghamshire.[51] John Stanbridge himself changed places more than once, first to a benefice in Gloucestershire (perhaps concurrently with teaching work at Winchcombe Abbey), then apparently to Lichfield, and finally to open a new grammar school at Banbury.[52]

Naturally, as in any profession or occupation, one can find examples of neglect of duty and criminality. The dean and chapter of Salisbury had problems with Henry Nugges, accused in 1350 of failing to teach the grammar school or fulfil his duties in the choir; two years later he was dismissed.[53] At Wells an unnamed master was docked of his commons (a daily allowance of food) and half his salary in 1409, 'because he did not wear his habit in the choir, nor did anything therein'.[54] Even at Magdalen College School a visitation of 1520 ordered Thomas Stanbridge to be more diligent about instructing his scholars.[55] The teaching profession also had its due share of the violent and lawless. There was Master Henry, schoolmaster of Huntingdon in 1255, whose under-master Robert was an overt doer of evil with greyhounds to the venison of the forest of Huntingdon, with Henry's connivance, or so it was said. Both men were arrested when the foresters discovered a buck, a haunch of venison, and a greyhound in their house.[56] There was Reginald, schoolmaster of Norham, who joined in an affray at the parish church of Auckland in 1302 in which a monk of Durham, who had come to deliver a legal judgment, was beaten up and dragged from the church by his feet.[57] There was John Oxford, usher of Clare school in 1381, indicted for taking part in the Peasants' Revolt, or rather in the riots and robberies that accompanied its course in Suffolk.[58] And there was the aggressive John Martyn, schoolmaster of the parish of St Michael-at-the-North-Gate in Oxford, who gathered a crowd of his scholars in St Michael's church on Sunday 9 August 1450 at the time of high mass, so that if the priest were to read a sentence of excommunication against him, the assembled scholars could snatch the sentence from the priest's hands and drag him out of the pulpit. When Martyn was committed to prison for a breach of the peace, some of his scholars tried to break in to rescue him during the night, but this insurrection, says the record thankfully, was peaceably put down by divine will. Martyn was obliged to make satisfaction to those he had wronged and to enter into a bond of £5 to observe good behaviour. Did he forfeit it, we wonder, when less than three years later he was in trouble for helping two chaplains to attack the house of an Oxford citizen, breaking open his doors, beating him up, and doing other damage against the peace of the king and the university?[59]

EARNINGS AND PROMOTIONS

Most teachers earned moderate sums rather than handsome ones. It is hard to be sure about those who worked for fees in the towns, but the scale of their charges suggests that a master with a class of seventy or eighty pupils could make about £10 a year. This may have been increased by gratuities and the profits of receiving scholars to board. Not all of this was clear profit, for the master had often to hire a building for his teaching and pay his usher. At Coventry the monks of the cathedral priory rented out the schoolhouse for 20s. a year, while at Exeter and Gloucester the sum was 14s.[60] The masters of the cathedral schools resembled their urban colleagues in being largely self-supporting. While some received small salaries (at Wells the rate was only £1 6s. 8d. a year), they got most of their living from fees like teachers in other towns. Indeed, they were sometimes expected to make financial contributions to the chapter. At York the cathedral vice-chancellor claimed 20s. a year from the grammar school, and at Salisbury the school furnished 13s. 4d. towards the anniversary mass or obit of a former chancellor, but by 1448 Salisbury Cathedral agreed to suspend the payment as long as the school was satisfactorily conducted.[61] With a few exceptions masters in cathedral cities depended mainly on fees until the 1540s.[62]

The endowed schools of the fifteenth and sixteenth centuries differed in providing regular salaries in return for teaching all or some of their pupils for nothing. Wykeham set a good standard in 1400 by providing the headmaster of Winchester with £10 per annum, commons worth 1s. a week, a chamber shared with the usher and one of the chaplains, and an annual allowance of cloth worth about 17s., totalling more than £13.[63] Henry VI's plans for Eton were more ambitious. In line with his hope that the master would be a graduate, he offered a salary of £16 with commons, cloth for a gown, and a chamber for the master's sole use, although the losses suffered by the college after Henry's deposition reduced the salary to £10.[64] Magdalen College School resembled Winchester in giving £10 and commons of 1s. a week, but improved the deal with a room for the master himself.[65] All these rewards were dwarfed by Colet's arrangements for St Paul's in 1518. He allocated his 'high-master' 13s. 4d. a week, amounting to more than £34 a year, over twice as much as his counterparts at Magdalen and Winchester. Indeed, their pay was exceeded by that of Colet's assistant teacher or 'sur-master', whose allowance was exactly half his superior's. The high-master did not receive commons, but he was assigned a house of very ample proportions and an allowance of cloth, while his deputy also received a lodging.[66]

Salaries like these were rather rare. The standard remuneration in the endowed foundations of the fifteenth and early sixteenth centuries came to be a simple annual sum of £10, without commons or cloth. A house or chamber was usually provided, often beside or above the schoolroom. Some small endowed schools did not offer even this much. Sevenoaks paid only £6 13s.

4d., and some rural chantry schools (especially those where teaching was added to the duties of an existing chantry) gave as little as £5 or £6.[67] Normally the patron or trustees of the school endowments delivered the salary in quarterly instalments, but a few schools were effectively benefices like parish churches. In this case the master was trusted to administer the lands and tenements of the endowment, lease them out, collect the rents, and maintain the property. The master of Wotton-under-Edge is recorded as holding a court for his tenants.[68] Not all income was profit, because masters had to pay dues to the Church and the king like everyone else. Church dues included small sums paid each year as personal tithes and offerings, and periodically there might be royal taxation, especially if the school was a chantry and therefore counted as an ecclesiastical benefice.[69] Taking in boys to board would raise one's income, but would involve keeping a wife or servants.

Schoolmasters employed in religious houses or private households received much the same as their colleagues in the free grammar schools. When the larger abbeys retained a layman or a secular priest to teach the younger monks or the boys of the almonry, they generally gave him board and lodging, fuel, a gown, and further wages of anything between £2 and £6.[70] Lay noblemen and gentlemen who employed their own teachers kept to similar levels. The master in the household of Edward IV was given food, fuel, light, clothing, and either 4½d. per day when he was present at court or a lump sum of £3 6s. 8d.[71] His colleague in the earl of Northumberland's household in 1511 had bread, beer, fuel, and £5 per annum (Fig. 46).[72] Some Tudor educational writers were scornful of the salaries offered in private households. In 1531 Sir Thomas Elyot complained that when gentlemen 'hire a schoolmaster to teach in their houses, they chiefly enquire with how small a salary he will be contented, and never do ensearch [i.e. investigate] how much good learning he hath, and how among well learned men he is therein esteemed, using therein less diligence than in taking servants'.[73] Roger Ascham agreed with this view in the 1560s, declaring that the gentry took more care to discover a good groom than a learned man to teach their children, gladly giving the groom a stipend of £50 a year while loth to offer the schoolmaster £10.[74]

These criticisms reflected conditions in the mid sixteenth century, when, as Bishop Hugh Latimer pointed out in a sermon, £10 a year was hardly enough to allow a clergyman to buy himself books or give drink to his neighbours.[75] That period saw a rise in prices and made the old £10 standard seem inadequate. 'There be in this realm many well learned,' declared Elyot, 'which if the name of a schoolmaster were not so much had in contempt, and also if their labours with abundant salaries might be requited, were right sufficient and able to induce their hearers to excellent learning.'[76] A year or two after Elyot was writing, Thomas Starkey put into the mouth of the future cardinal, Reginald Pole, the statement that it would not be amiss to unite two or three of the small £10 schools to make one good one, supporting an excellent master.[77] When the government of Edward VI ordered all cathedrals to maintain free schools in 1547, it fixed the master's salary at £13 6s. 8d. with a house, while the usher was awarded half as much and a chamber. In the new school foundations of Edward's reign (1547–53) there was a tendency for salaries to rise, but no uniform standard was adopted, and while £20 was offered in some places, the old £10 was considered sufficient in others.

If teaching paid so moderately, was it better to move to a different occupation? Many masters, as we have noted, left their schools for other work, but those whose careers are easiest to trace – the clergy – appear to have done only slightly better as a result. This can be illustrated by two representative biographies of men who went on from school work to careers in the Church: one from the fourteenth and one from the fifteenth century. The first is that of William Wheatley, who was born in about the 1280s, somewhere in the upper Thames valley.[78] He seems to have studied at Paris, and he got his first known benefice, Sulham in Berkshire, in 1305. It was not very wealthy, having been valued at only £4 in 1291, but it probably gave him enough money to continue his studies at Oxford, for which he was given three years' leave of absence in 1306. Three years later he resigned Sulham to become master of Stamford school, which ought to have paid him better, and from there he went to Lincoln – one of the major English schools – where he appears as master in 1316. He must have been a good candidate for appointment, since he was a scholar and author whose works we shall encounter later. Yet when he returned to parochial life in 1317 as rector of Yatesbury in Wiltshire, he got a benefice that was valued at only £10 and as far as we know he held it until his death, perhaps in 1331. This was a modest achievement for a talented and travelled man, but it was not capable of much improvement in the lifetime of Edward Janyns, born in the 1430s or thereabouts, probably near Monmouth in the Welsh Marches.[79] His first post after his ordination in 1459 was as chantry priest and grammar master of Newland, four miles from Monmouth and worth about £10. He left it after four years for a succession of benefices as a parish priest, each of which lifted his income a little until he emerged as vicar of Newland in 1476, with a stipend of about £18. Holding a benefice enabled him to support himself at university, where he studied canon law and eventually graduated as a bachelor in that faculty. He ended his life as a respected member of the local clergy, taking his turn as rural dean and dying in about the 1490s. Like Wheatley he did not rise very high, but he seems to have done as well as most ex-teachers could.

A few masters achieved more than this, but not until the fifteenth century. The interest in grammar that marked the court of Henry VI (Fig. 42) benefited a small group of men in the 1430s and 1440s. John Somerset, schoolmaster of Bury St Edmunds and subsequently tutor of the king, rose to be chancellor of the exchequer.[80] William Waynflete, headmaster of Winchester College when Henry went there while he was planning Eton College, was recruited by the king as provost of Eton and later promoted to be bishop of Winchester (Fig. 43).[81] John Chedworth, an Oxford don who tutored Robert Lord Hungerford at Oxford, acquired the patronage of the Hungerford family, was introduced to the court, and eventually became bishop of Lincoln.[82] Favours like these disappeared after 1450, however, to reappear only in about the 1490s and then at a lowlier level. The tutors of Henry VII's sons Arthur and Henry VIII – John Holt, John Rede, and John Skelton – were rewarded with parish benefices, but none was given a bishopric.[83] Bishop Smith of Lincoln, the patron of John Stanbridge, enabled him to combine the mastership of Banbury school with a rectory in Northamptonshire and a modest canonry of Lincoln Cathedral, bringing his total income to about £25 per annum.[84] Stanbridge's pupil Robert Whittington was more successful still. In the 1530s he taught the henchmen (young noble scholars) in the royal household for £20 a year while holding

43   William Waynflete (d. 1486), chancellor of England and bishop of Winchester, the most highly promoted schoolmaster of the fifteenth century.

the rectory of Stoke-on-Trent, a benefice in the king's gift worth £40, a total of £60 gross. But these were rare achievements, not typical of the schoolmastering profession even in the early sixteenth century.

The majority of teachers remained modestly paid and played equally modest roles in the world beyond their schools. We find a few of those who were laymen being admitted as burgesses or as members of religious guilds, and very occasionally they might hold municipal offices. Robert Simon was elected town clerk of Henley-on-Thames in 1419.[85] William Hardynge became one of the twelve governors of Beverley in 1446,[86] and John Squire was chosen to be treasurer of Ipswich in 1483.[87] Clerical schoolmasters are also found discharging minor administrative duties. One acts as a papal judge-delegate,[88] another proves a will in the absence of executors,[89] while a third enquires into the vacancy of a parochial benefice.[90] The schoolmaster of Canterbury in the early fourteenth century claimed rights of jurisdiction over not only his scholars but outsiders who assaulted them. He excommunicated offenders and called them before him for punishment, as if in a church court.[91] Authority like this, however, seems to have been unusual, and most of the evidence about schoolmasters does not suggest that they ranked any higher in their communities by virtue of their office than other clergy or literate laymen. This probably gives us a clue to a further, obscure topic: the social origins of those who taught. They must have come from modest burgess families, from the yeomanry of the countryside, or from lower orders still. Only for men of this kind did teaching offer rewards that were equal to or better than those to which they were accustomed.

LEARNING AND CULTURE

It is, of course, insufficient to judge a profession solely on economic grounds. A just assessment of medieval schoolmasters ought to include their contributions to learning and culture. They were, in the first place, collectors and owners of books, not limited to those they used in school but covering a range of titles and subjects. When Richard of Bury completed his *Philobiblon* in 1345, a survey of books and their owners, he did not omit 'the masters of country schools and the instructors of rude boys'. He even acknowledged that he had perused their collections with profit. 'When we had an opportunity, we entered their little plots and gardens, and gathered sweet-smelling flowers from the surface and dug up their roots, obsolete indeed but still useful to the student.'[92] We do not know what books of theirs he found, but a number of titles survive which belonged to their successors in the fifteenth century. A fine volume of Latin chronicles owned by John Pyke of St Martin-le-Grand (London) is still preserved in the British Library, with what appear to be his own grammatical notes.[93] William Fellows of Evesham bequeathed St Gregory's *Pastoral Care*, the *Sermons* of St Bernard, and Hugh of St Victor on *Ecclesiastes* to various Oxford libraries.[94] John

Hamundson of York had a book of chronicles in English.[95] Candidates for the degree of master of grammar at Cambridge, most of whom were previous or future schoolmasters, deposited nine books as pledges between 1480 and 1501. These included a breviary, a Latin dictionary, the guide for parish clergy known as *Pupilla Oculi*, two books of philosophy, the Bible, an exposition of the Holy Fathers, and *De Veritate* by Thomas Aquinas.[96]

Next to their reading we have a good deal of writing by schoolmasters. This falls into two groups: grammatical texts related to their work in class, and contributions to literature of a more general kind. The latter form the smaller group, but this reflects the fact that so many medieval literary works are anonymous. We may owe more of them to teachers than we realise. There are certainly examples of such men writing on general topics, both of a scholarly and of a popular nature. In Latin Walter of Wimborne, schoolmaster of Wimborne Minster in about 1260, wrote poetry encompassing satires and works of devotion to the Virgin Mary.[97] William Wheatley produced a commentary on *De Consolatione Philosophiae* by Boethius, another on the apocryphal *De Disciplina Scholasticorum* ascribed to him, a handful of letters, and two hymns inspired by the life of St Hugh of Lincoln.[98] John Seward, a schoolmaster in London between 1404 and 1435, belonged to a local group of literary men who exchanged Latin poems and epigrams. He also wrote *Arpyilogus* – a commentary on the story of the Harpies in Virgil's *Aeneid*, *Antelopologia* – a poem on the properties of the antelope addressed to Henry V whose emblem it was, and other such works.[99] In English John Lelamour of Hereford translated a Latin herbal treatise in 1373,[100] and the late fifteenth and early sixteenth centuries generated three notable writers of vernacular literature. One was Robert Henryson of Dunfermline in Scotland (d. *c*.1490–1500), who wrote the delightful animal *Fables* and the serious *Testament of Cresseid*.[101] Another was Alexander Barclay, who made his version of Sebastian Brant's *Ship of Fools* while teaching at Ottery St Mary in 1508–9. He went on to build a career as a poet and translator, although he did so by leaving the classroom for the monastery (Fig. 45).[102]

The third schoolmaster of this group affected literature as a publisher rather than an author. He was that anonymous and enigmatical figure, the schoolmaster-printer of St Albans. Nothing is known of his life beyond the information that he operated a printing and publishing business in the town from about 1479 to 1486 and that he was dead by 1497, when his fellow printer, Wynkyn de Worde, described him as a schoolmaster and asked God's mercy on his soul.[103] Eight of the books he published have survived. The first six, which appeared between 1479 and 1483, were Latin university texts on various aspects of the arts course, aimed no doubt at purchasers in Cambridge where no press had yet been established. They do not seem to have been very profitable, and the master changed his tactics. He next attempted to reach the market for popular works of instruction. Two such volumes ultimately appeared from his press, both of which he edited

44   An English woodcut of a
school in the 1490s, showing the
master in his chair holding a birch
and apposing a pupil, while others
study their books.

personally from earlier writings: *The Chronicles of England* in 1483 and the
famous *Book of St Albans* on hunting, hawking, and heraldry in 1486. They
were his last productions. Whether he ceased through failure or through
death we do not know, but he certainly died too soon to reap his rewards,
which went to others instead. In 1497 Wynkyn de Worde republished the
Chronicles with greater resources and wider connections. The work had a
great success; it was reissued every few years until 1528 and, through a
shortage of rival volumes, must have been the major work on English
history read by the literate public in England during that period.[104] *The Book
of St Albans* fared still better. Also reissued by de Worde, in 1496, it outlived
even the *Chronicles* to pass through more than twenty new editions, well into
the seventeenth century.[105]

   It is easier to judge the achievement of schoolmasters in the sphere of
their work: the writing of tracts, textbooks, and glossaries relating to the
teaching of Latin. This writing was virtually monopolised by them, for
although grammatical theory and analysis percolated into schools from
academic writers like the speculative grammarians, most of the practical
texts written in England after 1300 were the work of classroom teachers.
Oxford's place as the principal centre of grammatical study in medieval
England was established through a series of textbooks by its schoolmasters
from the late thirteenth century onwards, notably those of John Cornwall
and John Leland.[106] Teachers elsewhere exercised less influence, but a

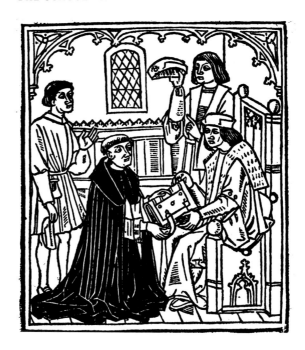

45   A schoolmaster-author:
Alexander Barclay (by then a
Benedictine monk), presenting
his work to a patron.

Bristol master (probably Robert Londe), John Borington of Exeter, and
John Drury of Beccles all produced or revised materials on grammar in the
early fifteenth century that were copied by pupils and circulated locally.[107]
When humanism reached the English schools in the 1480s, through the
works of continental grammarians like Sulpizio and Valla, a new generation
of English schoolmasters provided the necessary texts in English and Latin
to instil it at an elementary level, beginning with Anwykyll and Stanbridge.
It was again largely schoolmasters like Lily and Whittington who produced
the most popular grammars of the early sixteenth century.[108]

   The primary purpose of such writing was the teaching of Latin. But, as
we have argued in an earlier chapter, it had wider effects.[109] Because
schoolmasters, by the fifteenth century, taught partly in English and made
their pupils write in that language, they influenced the development of
English at a time when the regional dialects were giving way to a more
uniform national standard. Schoolmasters drew their pupils' attention to
English grammar and syntax and, through schoolwork, helped to regulate
spellings and grammatical forms and to form English prose style. Through
the use of latins and vulgars they introduced pupils to proverbs and wise
observations, and by encouraging the writing of exercises on everyday topics
they engaged with the world of childhood: its vocabulary, speech, games,
interests, and prejudices. Schoolmasters were the first to collect the lore and
language of schoolchildren, and were pioneers in writing about childhood.
The lengths to which this writing had developed by the end of the fifteenth
century can be seen from the famous description of a boy's life that occurs
in exercises from Magdalen College School, written probably in the 1490s:

The world waxeth worse every day, and all is turned upside down, contrary to th'old guise, for all that was to me a pleasure when I was a child, from three year[s] old to ten (for now I go upon the twelfth year), while I was under my father and mother's keeping, be turned now to torments and pain. For then I was wont to lie still a-bed till it was forth days [i.e. daytime], delighting myself in sleep and ease. The sun sent in his beams at the windows that gave me light instead of a candle. O what a sport it was every morning when the sun was up to take my lusty pleasure betwixt the sheets, to behold the roof, the beams, and the rafters of my chamber, and look on the clothes that the chamber was hanged with. There durst no man, but he were mad, awake me out of my sleep, upon his own head, while me list to sleep. At my will I arose with entreaties, and when th'appetite of rest went his way by his own accord, than I awoke and called whom me list to lay my gear ready to me. My breakfast was brought to my bedside as oft as me list to call therefore, and so many times I was first fed ere I were clad. So I had many pleasures more besides these, whereof some be forgotten, some I do remember well, but I have no leisure to rehearse them now.

But now the world runneth upon another wheel. For now at five of the clock by the moonlight I must go to my book and let sleep and sloth alone, and if our master hap[pen] to awake us he bringeth a rod, 'stead of a candle. Now I leave pleasures that I had sometime; here is nought else preferred but [ad]monishing and stripes. Breakfasts that were sometime brought at my bidding is driven out of country and never shall come again. I would tell more of my misfortunes, but though I have leisure to say, yet I have no pleasure, for the rehears[al] of them maketh my mind more heavy. I seek all the ways I can to live once at mine ease, that I might rise and go to bed when me list out of the fear of beating.[110]

This passage, like other vulgaria, combined at least three strategies. It introduced pupils to a good English style and challenged them to form an equivalent one in Latin. It tried to enlist their interest with humour and imagination, and to instil in them the virtues required for life as an adult. It exhibits a breadth and skill in teaching far wider than the mere inculcation of knowledge.

STATUS AND IMPACT

Contemporaries took such strategies for granted. Compared with government, war, religion, or trade, teaching had little impact on the public imagination, and the public at all its levels thought little of teachers. As we shall see, neither the Church nor the crown paid much attention to schools until the Reformation.[111] Society appears to have taken the same view. It knew what a schoolmaster was, and sometimes called him 'Master', a term of respect. People had dealings with their local teacher. They gave him

46   Some of the nobility employed private schoolmasters by about 1500, including the Percy
earls of Northumberland at Wressle Castle (Yorks.).

children to instruct and encountered him in the petty disputes and
transactions of everyday life. But they too had little consciousness of
schoolmasters as a group or of the schoolmaster as a type. Only once do we
hear of a confrontation between the laity and schoolmasters in general. This
is said to have taken place during the Peasants' Revolt of 1381, when the
rebels (intent on attacking tax collectors, lawyers, and manorial records) are
said to have warned schoolmasters not to teach children grammar. The
incident, however, is recorded by a single writer (Thomas Walsingham of St
Albans), and, if it did take place, was probably a minor feature of the
rising.[112] The more famous words of Jack Cade in Shakespeare's *Henry VI
Part II*, 'thou hast most traitorously corrupted the youth of the realm in
erecting a grammar school', are in the same tradition as Walsingham's
anecdote, from which they may have been derived through Raphael
Holinshed, the Tudor historian.[113] But the historical Cade (d. 1450) is not
known to have held such a view, and the man whom Shakespeare depicts
him addressing, Lord Saye and Sele, never founded a school.

Medieval English writers ignored schoolmasters too. William Langland,
the presumed author of *Piers Plowman*, mentioned them only once and then
merely as an example of men being paid for their work.[114] A bishop of Exeter
in 1382 referred to them sarcastically; berating some of his canons for
reducing the size of their households, he compared them to a schoolmaster
attended merely by a couple of boys.[115] The only teacher to be included in
the *Canterbury Tales* was Nero's tutor Seneca; Chaucer gave no attention to

contemporary schoolmasters.[116] One might have expected them to feature in satires or plays, but there is little sign of this except for the handful of fifteenth-century lyrics in which schoolboys lament being beaten.[117] It is not until we reach the second half of the sixteenth century, when more literature survives and when education had a higher profile, that a stereotype of a schoolmaster emerges – pedantic and irascible – as we see in Shakespeare's portraits of Holofernes and Sir Hugh Evans. Indeed, nine men of this kind appear in his plays.[118] There is little comment about teachers even from the groups with which they were most involved: their pupils and their pupils' parents. Autobiography, as we have seen, was not a strong literary genre in medieval England, and only became so in about the second half of the sixteenth century. In consequence people rarely set down memories or thoughts about childhood in which schoolmasters might have appeared.[119] Instead our knowledge of relationships between teachers and pupils in the later middle ages is largely confined to documentary references. We know that a few of the masters who tutored the great and famous were rewarded for their services. John Paynel, the instructor of Edward III, was raised to be chamberlain of Chester.[120] John Chedworth was given a rectory in Dorset for teaching Robert Hungerford.[121] John Rede was made a canon of Newark College, Leicester, after tutoring Prince Arthur.[122] Largesse of this kind implies a gratitude or sense of obligation that has not survived in words. Contrariwise we hear of some dissatisfied customers. Robert Buck claimed to have left school at Clitheroe in 1283 because he was so badly beaten.[123] Robert Eliot of Harnhill sued his master in 1390 for beating him, alleging damages of £20,[124] and Walter Skidmore, a London goldsmith, actually had the teacher of his son imprisoned in the 1460s on a similar charge.[125] But cases like these must be expected in any age, and they do not tell us about the feelings that most masters and scholars had for one another.

The period from 1200 to 1500 and even later, then, was one of relative obscurity for English schoolmasters. We can see why this was so. Their limited numbers, their geographical isolation, and their modest economic importance all told against them. Their work meant that they stayed secluded in their schools, rather than moving visibly in the world, and they ministered to children (the least powerful group in society) and to parents mainly interested in securing their services as cheaply as possible. Still, this obscurity was not their fault or due to their own shortcomings. Like the teachers of any age they taught what society required with the resources that it provided. They also had some solid achievements. They helped to supply the Church with priests and monks, the universities with scholars, and lay administration with clerks and lawyers. The literacy of the laity was in part the result of their efforts. They were inventive as educationists and they exercised an unseen influence on the development of the English language. The schoolmaster was an important agent upon the body politic, however low and undervalued the end that he touched with his birch.

HISTORY

Eus in adiutorium me
um intende. Domine
ad adiuuandum me
festina. Gloria patri et filio
et spiritui sancto. Sicut erat
in principio et nunc et semper.
et in secula seculorum amen.
ymnus.

6

Schools from 1100 to 1350

THE DISTRIBUTION OF SCHOOLS

Imagine that you are studying a town in medieval England. You will wish to know about its layout, population, trade, and government. How many parish churches did it have, and were there any monasteries, friaries, or hospitals? Much of this is not too hard to discover. Layout can be deduced from later maps, and population from taxation records. Charters exist granting towns self-government and economic rights, and there are medieval and modern lists of parish churches and religious houses. But ask, 'Was there a school?' and problems arise. No authority, religious or secular, kept systematic records of schools at any time within the coverage of this book. Hardly any school archives exist.[1] Our knowledge of medieval schools is accidental, due to the chance survival of their charters or through casual allusions in other sources. We do not know their numbers at any one time, or when most of them began, or whether they existed permanently. Often we cannot say if a particular town had one or not. Yet town schools are the best recorded schools; we are even less informed about those in the countryside.

Fortunately much can be done, despite these difficulties. After 1100 it is possible to compile lists of schools, and although these cannot be complete, they indicate the kinds of places where education was available and its geographical distribution. The features of schools can be studied and traced chronologically, so as to reveal their constitutional history. And because schools were animated by people – patrons, teachers, and scholars – we can construct their social history: the links they formed with men and women in medieval England. As early as the twelfth century educational provision was a complex matter. There were schools of reading, song, grammar, and higher studies. There were the internal schools of the religious houses, and the free-standing schools for the public, ranging from well-organised bodies in towns to small, private, and temporary operations in villages and parish churches. This chapter and the next will examine the schools that catered for the public from 1100 until the Reformation. A further chapter will

47   English schools, 1100–1200.

explore the history of education in the religious houses during the same
period.

The schools about which we know most in the twelfth century are those in
the cathedral cities. There were nineteen English cathedrals by the middle
of the twelfth century: nine 'secular' foundations staffed by secular (non-
monastic) canons, nine monastic cathedrals of Benedictine monks, and one

quasi-monastic cathedral (Carlisle) served by Augustinian canons. The cathedral cities, as we have observed, were fertile ground for schools. They were seats of bishops who came (at least occasionally) to reside with their households, homes of Church courts and diocesan administrators, and abodes of parish clergy and parish clerks. Most cathedral cities were also significant in their lay activities. Over half were centres of county administration and nearly all were places of some size, trade, and manufacture. On the one hand schools were needed to serve these people and their activities and functions; on the other their absence was more noticeable. No bishops or cathedral clergy were likely to have long tolerated a situation in which schooling was unavailable locally.

Schools are mentioned or implied in at least fourteen cathedral cities between the Conquest and the end of the twelfth century, and it is likely that most of the others possessed them too.[2] The nature of these schools depended upon whether the local cathedral was secular or monastic, Carlisle belonging to the second category. The first group of cathedrals usually supported two schools from early times. One was the song school for the boys of the cathedral choir, and possibly for outsiders. It was supervised by the cathedral precentor but usually taught by his deputy, the succentor. The other was the grammar school, referred to simply as 'the school', open to the general public and taught by a master who was often a member of the cathedral foundation. Salisbury and York, as we have seen, acquired such masters at the end of the eleventh century.[3] At St Paul's (London) Master Durand the *scholasticus* appears in 1102, and his successor Master Hugh was instituted as *magister scolarum* between 1111 and 1127.[4] Similar masters were probably added to the chapters of nearly all the remaining secular cathedrals during the twelfth century. We have already outlined the development by which, towards the end of the century, these masters turned into chancellors. They centred their teaching on theology or canon law, and assigned their grammar-school work to a deputy who took their earlier title of 'schoolmaster'.[5] These deputies were more loosely attached to the cathedral. Sometimes they had duties there, sometimes not, and their schools were usually sited in the city rather than close to the mother foundation.

Where the cathedral was staffed by monks, as at Canterbury or Winchester, the early schoolmasters did not evolve into chancellors or undertake higher education. Here they remained primarily grammar masters who were secular priests, clerks, or laymen. It was impossible for such men to be members of the cathedral body, and it was apparently thought inappropriate even for the cathedral to supervise the school, necessitating other arrangements. Lanfranc's solution at Canterbury (if his charter may be believed) was to give the charge of the school to a different body of clergy, the canons of St Gregory's Priory.[6] Such canons could have more contact with the world than monks were allowed. But this precedent was not followed elsewhere and lapsed even at Canterbury. There and in most of the other monastic cathedral cities by the thirteenth century, the schoolmaster came to be appointed and supervised by the bishop. He was essentially the teacher of a city school rather than a cathedral school. His school lay outside the precincts of the monastic cathedral, although it might have links with the monks. They might send him the boys whom they maintained in their almonry: boys who were not monks but acted as servers in church, as was the case at Durham and Worcester. They might offer assistance to poor scholars of the school. At Worcester the master was allowed to send a scholar to be fed in the cathedral almonry on every day of the week during term, and three scholars during Lent.[7]

London, besides being a cathedral city, was the capital of England by the twelfth century. For the rest of the middle ages it outstripped all other towns in population, wealth, and activities. The demand for education was consequently greater than elsewhere, and more teachers emerged to supply it. This situation led to friction with St Paul's Cathedral, whose schoolmaster (later known as chancellor) claimed the right to regulate teaching in the city. Between 1134 and 1139, when the see of London was vacant, the cathedral procured a letter from Henry of Blois, bishop of Winchester, ordering the Church authorities in the city to act against anyone teaching without the licence of the cathedral schoolmaster.[8] An exception was made for the schools attached to St Martin-le-Grand and St Mary Arches, churches that belonged to the king and the archbishop of Canterbury respectively. These were privileged places outside the jurisdiction of the bishop of London and the cathedral of St Paul's, which left them free to exploit the demand for schooling. Henry's letter therefore recognised three authorised schools in London, and this remained the official number until the middle of the fifteenth century. In practice the chancellor of St Paul's appears to have licensed other teachers. The London historian William FitzStephen, writing in the late twelfth century, tells us that additional schools were sometimes allowed as a personal favour by the authorities.[9] Later, in 1394, the clergy in charge of the three authorised schools claimed that they too were willing to grant licences, but (as in the 1130s) they complained about the activities of masters who had not been licensed. On this occasion the unlicensed masters retaliated by bringing a case in the lord mayor's court against the authorised schools, forcing the latter to turn to the king for help.[10] The unlicensed masters did not succeed in destroying the licensing system, but there continued to be several more schools besides the original three, either of a licensed or unlicensed nature, and it remained difficult for the authorities to enforce their rights of control.[11]

Next to the cathedral cities there were a number of other important places: the seats of county administration, the major ports, and the larger centres of commerce. Some towns of this kind, like Colchester, Dunwich, and Warwick, possess records of schools in the first half of the twelfth century, and they are joined in the second half by Derby, Northampton, and Oxford (Fig. 47).[12] The first half of the thirteenth century adds King's Lynn, Leicester, Lewes, Ludlow, and Shrewsbury, and the second half Cambridge, Dover, Guildford, Lancaster, Nottingham, Stamford, and Taunton (Fig. 48). It is impossible to track the diffusion of schools chronologically from this list of places. The appearance of more schools as time goes on is primarily a matter of better surviving evidence. There is no reason why towns such as Cambridge and Nottingham should not have had schools much earlier, since they were comparable in size and importance to places like Gloucester and Warwick. A provisional judgment might well be made that most major towns in England had a school for the public by the first half of the twelfth century, and that all did so by the opening of the thirteenth.

The evidence for schools in smaller market towns and lesser ports is not so plentiful in the twelfth century, although there are examples. Reginald of Durham's collection of the miracles of St Cuthbert, made after 1170, casually mentions two examples from the north of England, in what we might think of as wilder parts: a reading school at Yarm in the 1130s and a school kept by a secular priest in the parish church of Norham on the border with Scotland.[13] The Norham school was the scene of an amusing story. One of the pupils, fearful of being beaten, locked the church and threw the key into the river, whence it was miraculously recovered. A reference to a school at Brecon in 1160 shows that organised education had spread just as far to the west into Wales. But it is in the thirteenth century that the presence of schools in the smaller towns can be seen most clearly. In Yorkshire, for example, there is evidence of seven besides the cathedral school at York: Beverley, Guisborough, Hedon, Helmsley, Malton, Pontefract, and Wakefield. In the west of England schools appear at Bridgwater, Bridport, Cirencester, Malmesbury, Marlborough, Plympton, Shaftesbury, Wilton, and Wotton-under-Edge. Adding these instances to those of schools in the larger towns, it is possible to collect over seventy urban locations during the thirteenth century (Fig. 48). Their distribution, as the map suggests, is remarkably even across the country, and is not limited to the more populous and wealthy lowland areas.

It is very likely then that many lesser towns had a school by the thirteenth century. The situation in the countryside is less clear, but education was not altogether absent even there, since we hear of schools or masters in such places as Rudham (1240), Awre (c.1287), Taverham (1288), and Kinoulton (1289), all of which were villages although the first adjoined a priory. Some masters may have opened rural schools to escape the controls that often restrained them in towns. In other cases parish clergy may have sought to supplement their incomes by taking in pupils. Rural schooling, at least at the level of grammar, may have been patchily distributed and unpredictable in its duration. But there appears to be no reason why schools, public or private, should not have existed anywhere in England by the twelfth

48   English schools, 1200–1300.

century, and we need not be surprised by any that come to light in future. It is also unsafe to infer that towns where schools are not mentioned lacked the educational resources possessed by others of similar size, wealth, and character. Evidence of schools, let us repeat, is too incomplete to base arguments on silence.

The question of continuity is vexed by the same problem. It is rare, even in the case of the cathedral cities, to be able to show that schools, once recorded, had unbroken histories. We are as ill advised to imagine too much education from the scattering of records as to assume too little. The stability of a school depended on a succession of qualified masters being willing to work in a place where the demand for education was sufficient to give them a competent livelihood. It is possible to envisage many factors that might imperil the existence of such schools: bad masters, public indifference, poverty, plague, or unrest. Even at Oxford, one of the largest centres of education, we know that local disturbances sent scholars fleeing elsewhere on several occasions: to Cambridge and Reading in 1209, to Northampton and Salisbury in 1238, and again to Northampton in 1263.[14] This suggests that schools in lesser places might also suffer closures and suspensions. Equally there were forces working in favour of continuity, even in small communities. The schools of Hedon, Hexham, Mildenhall, Plympton, and Rudham first appear in records because the local authorities in these places intervened to regulate them. Benefactors came forward to provide buildings and scholarships, and there was some public demand for schooling. We are told that in the middle of the fourteenth century, when Kingston-on-Thames lacked a teacher, the people of the parish took the initiative to find one. They invited Hugh of Kingston, apparently a local man, to come from Canterbury where he had been teaching, and their invitation was accepted.[15]

PATRONAGE

No sooner do we hear of free-standing schools in charters than we encounter patrons claiming the right to control them. Control meant appointing their masters, protecting them from rival teachers in the vicinity, and (at first) taking some of their profits. Patronage over schools grew up haphazardly and was not uniform. The earliest recorded examples, as we have seen, relate to churches in Canterbury, Eye, and Gloucester,[16] and many other bodies or individuals held or asserted rights over schools in particular places during the rest of the middle ages. In the twelfth century patronage was sometimes disputed or seized. In about 1114 Herbert Losinga, bishop of Norwich, restored Thetford school to Bund, dean of Thetford, who had held it previously, and at about the same time Henry of Huntingdon handed back the song school at Huntingdon to the canons of the priory there.[17] In 1203–4 the archbishop of Canterbury heard a dispute between the rector and vicar of Ludlow over the control of the local school, and ruled in the vicar's favour.[18] Later there was a greater consensus about who owned the patronage of schools, although there were also attempts to ignore and defy those who did. Some people, who wished to teach unhindered or who favoured a competitive market in teaching, resented the

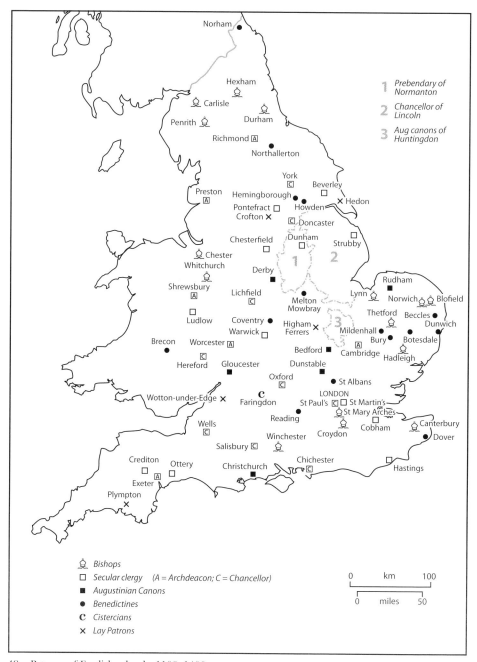

claim of one patron and school to have a monopoly of teaching in a particular town. We shall see illustrations of this in the following pages. At the same time patronage had the potential to ensure that schools remained in being. Without its support and restrictions the provision of education, especially in small towns, might have been a good deal less secure.

The study of school patronage helps to establish which categories of people exercised it and therefore had links with education. Most of the information on the subject, prior to the fifteenth century, occurs in ecclesiastical records and therefore gives the impression (probably true but over-emphatically so) that most school patrons were clerics. The highest ranking of these were the bishops, who held such patronage in at least eight of the seventeen English dioceses.[19] No English bishop seems to have claimed the right to appoint all the schoolmasters within his area of jurisdiction. The only such claim comes from Wales, where Bishop Pavy of St David's, when instituting a schoolmaster to Haverfordwest in 1488, asserted that the sole power of conferring the grammar schools of the cathedral city and the diocese belonged to him both by right and by custom.[20] Even this claim would have been contestable, since the diocese included Brecon, whose school was recognised by charter as belonging to Brecon Priory. In England the nearest example to a system of episcopal patronage over all local schools comes from Norfolk. There in the fourteenth and fifteenth centuries we find the bishops of Norwich appointing masters not only in Norwich and Thetford, where they had lordship, but in some country towns and villages with which they had little or no connection.[21] Nevertheless, at least one school in Norfolk lay under different patronage, as we shall see, and the bishops' activities do not seem to have extended to Suffolk, which also lay in their diocese. Most English bishops claimed and exercised the right of nominating schoolmasters in a restricted number of places, notably in cities with monastic cathedrals like Canterbury, Durham, and Ely.[22] Otherwise we find them making appointments only in places where they had special territorial rights, such as the archbishop of Canterbury possessed at Hadleigh or the bishop of Durham at Hexham.[23]

If bishops themselves did not claim a general right of appointing masters, did they pass on the duty to their assistants: the chancellors of their cathedrals or the archdeacons of their dioceses? The chancellors of eight of the nine secular cathedrals (all except Exeter) certainly appointed the schoolmasters of their respective cathedral cities from at least the thirteenth century onwards. But in only two or three places do they appear to have claimed and won a wider jurisdiction. At Lincoln it was recognised by 1236 that the chancellor had the right to appoint to all the schools in Lincolnshire, except for those upon the prebends (i.e. estates) belonging to his fellow cathedral canons.[24] Likewise the chancellor of York possessed by 1307, and probably long before, a power over every grammar school within the territorial jurisdiction of the cathedral, which included places as far away as Doncaster and Guisborough.[25] Similar control was exercised at Southwell Minster, which was one of the three lesser seats of the archbishop of York and resembled a cathedral in form. Here the canon who held the prebend of Normanton and acted as chancellor claimed by 1238 the right to appoint schoolmasters throughout Nottinghamshire, including towns as important as Newark and Nottingham. This canon's authority may also have excluded the prebends of his colleagues, one of whom, the prebendary of Dunham, appears to have allowed a master to teach on his estate.[26] Apart from these three examples there is no sign that other cathedral chancellors claimed, let alone exercised, the power of appointing schoolmasters outside their cathedral cities.

Archdeacons were patrons of schools in a handful of places. Those of Exeter, Shrewsbury, and Worcester nominated masters in the towns concerned, but not, it appears, more widely.[27] At Cambridge the archdeacon of Ely claimed jurisdiction over the grammar schools of the city, despite the development of the university. In 1276 his right was recognised of

50   Schooling not only entailed fees; it meant losing a boy's working power. Above, the child Jesus, sent to fill a water pot, hangs it on a sunbeam. Below, Joseph takes him to school.

appointing a deputy, called the master of glomery (i.e. of grammar), who was generally a university graduate in charge of supervising the Cambridge grammar schools. This deputy also had the power to judge legal cases affecting schoolboys in Cambridge, except for cases that involved the scholars of the university itself.[28] At Oxford, where the university shook off the power of local ecclesiastics earlier than Cambridge, the archdeacon appears not to have possessed such rights, and the Oxford grammar masters were appointed and supervised by the university's chancellor.[29] The remaining examples of archidiaconal control of schools and their masters relate to 'peculiar' jurisdictions outside the normal diocesan structures. In 1309 the archdeacon of St Albans (who was a monk of the abbey there) gave various privileges to the local grammar school, although it is not certain if he appointed its masters.[30] Further north the archdeacon of Richmond, who ruled with almost episcopal authority over a huge western swathe of the diocese of York, is found appointing schoolmasters in Preston and Richmond towards the end of the fourteenth century.[31] Once again these examples seem to be individual ones, and there is no evidence that archdeacons were involved in appointments more widely.

It seems from this that, while the English ecclesiastical authorities possessed a good deal of educational patronage, they did not control it completely. In most places the right to appoint schoolmasters lay locally and individually. Sometimes it belonged to the lord of the manor or borough where the school was held, who might be a lay man or woman. Baldwin, earl of Devon, who died in 1262, possessed the township of Plympton 'with the advowson of the schools'.[32] John of Gaunt and Henry IV, in 1372 and 1400, appointed schoolmasters at Higham Ferrers on the lands of their duchy of Lancaster.[33] The monks of Bury St Edmunds claimed the nomination of schoolmasters not only in their town of Bury but in Beccles, Botesdale, and Mildenhall, which belonged to their abbey.[34] Other religious houses gained the patronage of schools not through land ownership but through a grant from a king, bishop, or lay magnate, who considered a community of clergy best suited to govern a neighbouring school. Canons seem to have been preferred to monks for this purpose, perhaps because they had provided schools before the Norman Conquest, and certainly because they were less cloistered and better able to undertake a public responsibility.[35] The earliest houses of canons alleged to have been involved in this way, St Gregory's and St Oswald's, did not belong to a religious order, but after 1100 both houses adopted the Rule of St Augustine, and school patronage was given to some other Augustinian houses, including Bedford, Derby, Huntingdon, Lanthony (Gloucester), and possibly Keynsham.[36] The canons of Huntingdon even claimed patronage throughout the county of Huntingdonshire, as was done in Lincolnshire and Nottinghamshire. A few other clergy held patronage rights, as has been mentioned, including some cathedral prebendaries and the parish clergy of St Martin (Canterbury), Kingston-on-Thames, and Ludlow.[37] That seems to have been as far down the social hierarchy as patronage extended before the beginning of the fifteenth century (Fig. 49).

The right to appoint or license schoolmasters in a particular place resembled the right to nominate the rector or vicar of a parish church, known as an 'advowson', which was attached to every such church in England. Canon law, as we shall see, forbade patrons to charge for permission to teach, but the right to control education had other attractions. The local schoolmaster was a useful figure to have in one's sphere of influence; moreover, he taught for fees, which gave his office a monetary value worth seeking and worth bestowing. We find some patrons of schools taking care to preserve and enforce their rights. As early as the reign of Henry I the canons of Huntingdon were calling on their superior, the bishop of Lincoln, for help against 'adulterine' or illegal schools that threatened their rights of appointment.[38] In the early fourteenth century the chancellor of Beverley Minster strove to prevent unauthorised teaching in Beverley, Kelk, and South Dalton, which lay under his jurisdiction.[39] The Cistercian monks of Beaulieu went to law in 1343 to defend their rights over the school of Faringdon in Berkshire,[40] and in Gloucester St Oswald's fought legal battles with another local house of Augustinian canons, Lanthony Priory, for the privilege of controlling education in the town. Both the rival priories claimed to have charters supporting their case, and appeals were made to the bishop and to the king for support at different times. In the early fifteenth century the two houses came to an agreement in favour of Lanthony, which apparently held the patronage thereafter. It was still defending its rights in 1513.[41]

Patrons like these may have imposed their will on certain localities, but they did not create a national system of educational patronage like the patronage of parish churches. Schools after all were rarer and might be less permanent. Only in the counties of Huntingdon, Lincoln, and Nottingham did control become centralised in the hands of a single dignitary or body. Elsewhere this tendency does not seem to have been effective. When in 1240 the master of Norwich cathedral school tried to prove his authority over the grammar school of Rudham, some twenty-five miles to the west, he failed. The Augustinian canons of Coxford Priory, who were lords of the manor of Rudham, resisted his claim and won their case in the bishop's court.[42] Some towns produce no evidence of a patron, which may indicate that nobody claimed the right. Even when the right existed it was not always easy to enforce. London is a case in point, where the patrons of the three official schools waged a long and never wholly successful campaign against unauthorised masters, a campaign hampered by public demand for teaching.[43] Cathedrals and monasteries could usually rely on the local bishop to back up their rights over schools, but the king's courts were not always so amenable. In the Faringdon dispute of 1343 the crown insisted that it had the charge of deciding questions of school patronage, as was the

case with the patronage of a parish church. But when Lanthony Priory
approached the royal court of common pleas in 1410 to stop the teaching of
its rival's schoolmaster, Thomas More, the outcome was different. Two of the
judges who heard the case gave their opinion that competition and choice
in education were good things, and a third took the view that the dispute
was a matter for the Church courts, not the king's. The case was dismissed.[44]

The judges of 1410 may have been reflecting a change of feeling in
society, as judges sometimes do. As literacy grew, which appears to have
been the case after the twelfth century, there would have been more pupils
in major towns than a single school could handle, and less need to channel
such pupils in one direction. Most of the evidence about school patronage
comes from between about 1100 and 1400, suggesting that this was the
era when the issue was most contentious. After 1400 we hear less and less
about it.

CHURCH, CROWN, AND SCHOOLS

The complexities and limitations of patronage reflected the relationship of
schools with the authorities in England: Church and crown. This
relationship was local rather than national. It is often assumed that the
Church exercised a general control of school education during the middle
ages, but that is true only if we regard the Church as a large-scale movement
rather than a modern kind of organisation. Most people might have agreed
with the judge in the Lanthony case who observed that 'the teaching and
instruction of children is an ecclesiastical matter'.[45] Yet the Church in an
organised sense, the authorities, took little interest in schools as a whole, in
comparision with the attention given to religious houses, parish churches, or
the religious obligations of lay people.

The interest was greatest in the twelfth century: a time of Church reform
in many areas of life. It is first manifested in England by a Church council
at Westminster in 1138, which forbade schoolmasters to sublet their schools
to others for money, on pain of ecclesiastical punishment.[46] This practice,
the exaction of cash in return for permission to teach, seems to have been
widely perceived as a problem at the time. Between 1159 and 1181, Pope
Alexander III, apparently writing to the bishop of Winchester, prohibited it
and laid down that if anyone failed to appoint a schoolmaster because of the
prohibition, the bishop should do so instead.[47] In 1179 the Third Lateran
Council of the western Church, meeting at Rome, enacted a law on similar
lines. No one must demand money for a licence to teach, or take anything
from teachers on the basis that this was the custom, or forbid a teacher to
operate if he was suitable and had sought a licence.[48] This law was repeated
in England by a council at London in 1200, in the form of a simple
statement forbidding money to be taken from masters for teaching.[49] The
pronouncements of Alexander III and the Lateran Council were included

in the *Decretals* published by Pope Gregory IX in 1234, and became part of the corpus of canon law for the rest of the middle ages. But laws are evidence of policy rather than practice, and we do not know how effective they were in this case. Some masters in later times were certainly made to pay rent for their schoolrooms.[50]

The policy of freeing masters from exploitation was complemented, in the twelfth and early thirteenth centuries, by another aimed at setting up a network of major schools across Catholic Europe. The Lateran Council of 1179 laid down that every cathedral should provide a master with a 'proper benefice' so that he might teach the clerks of that church and poor scholars for nothing.[51] This did not quite specify that the teaching should be free to all, and it may be that those who could afford to pay fees were expected to do so. When the next general council of the Church took place in Rome in 1215, the Fourth Lateran Council, its members noted that the decree of 1179 was 'very little observed in many churches'. The council therefore repeated what had been ordered and amplified it. Each cathedral chapter, that is to say the ruling body of canons, was to nominate a master and the bishop was to appoint him. He was to teach grammar to the clerks of the cathedral and those of other churches, and to receive the income of a prebend, meaning an endowment like that of a cathedral canon. Each metropolitan cathedral, or seat of an archbishop, was to provide a prebend for a grammar master and one for a theologian teaching the Bible to priests and others. Neither kind of master was required to be a canon; they were merely to receive a canon's income while they taught. The amount of the income was not specified, but a stronger impression was given than in 1179 that it should be the equivalent of a complete salary and that the masters' teaching should be free in consequence.[52]

In England the Lateran decrees were implemented in spirit rather than by the letter. This was partly because half of the English cathedrals were staffed by monks, not by canons as was the case on the Continent and as envisaged by the councils. The decree of 1215 required the provision of lecturers in theology at Canterbury (a monastic cathedral) and York. In fact, as we have seen, arrangements in England were shaped by whether the cathedral was secular or monastic, not whether it was metropolitan or not. All the nine secular cathedrals came to establish theological lectures, generally given by the cathedral chancellor who was a canon with a prebend. None of the monastic cathedrals, on the other hand, made similar structured arrangements.[53] It could therefore be argued that the English did better than the Lateran decrees required with regard to theological teaching, with nine outlets rather than two, whereas they did worse in supporting grammar schools. Although every cathedral city probably possessed such a school by 1215, their grammar masters never secured the 'proper benefice' or prebend which the Lateran councils prescribed, and therefore went on charging fees. This continued to be the case down to the Reformation, with the exception of five places where cathedral schools, after 1400, were endowed to teach freely as a result of local initiatives.[54]

Little else can be said about official Church interest in English schools after 1215. The papal archives of the fourteenth and fifteenth centuries include hardly any examples of intervention by the pope in English school affairs, and then only in response to requests from particular masters or schools for licences to teach.[55] If we look at the two large volumes of *Councils and Synods* that gather together the statutes issued by bishops and their diocesan clergy between 1205 and 1313, it is remarkable how rarely schools are mentioned in comparison with other matters raised in the Lateran councils, such as worship, churches, clergy, and moral issues. The only educational topic to turn up several times is the use of the office of parish clerk to support scholars, which will be mentioned presently. Alexander Stavensby, bishop of Coventry and Lichfield from 1224 to 1238, was unusual in bothering to remind those in authority to appoint learned and virtuous men to the schools of the diocese.[56] His contemporaries did not see education as needing their attention.

Nor did most of their successors. John Grandisson, bishop of Exeter, felt moved to say in 1357 that boys in his diocese should be made to construe and understand the basic elements of the faith before going on to read Latin poetry.[57] In 1384 William Courtenay, archbishop of Canterbury, arranged for a question to be asked during his visitation of Exeter diocese 'concerning the holding of adulterine schools'.[58] In 1477 we encounter the borough authorities of Ipswich establishing a scale of fees to be charged by the local schoolmaster 'according to the assessment of the lord bishop of Norwich'.[59] Perhaps other such cases might be found, but they seem to have been uncommon. This was very different from the way the Church treated parish clergy. Rectors and vicars of parish churches were required to appear before the bishop to be vetted as satisfactory, to swear an oath of obedience, and to be formally admitted to office. From the late thirteenth century these admissions were recorded in registers kept by the bishop's staff. Periodically the bishop or his officials made visitations of his diocese, and the parish clergy had to appear before them. In contrast schoolmasters were not usually examined or approved before they practised. They are mentioned in bishops' registers only when the bishop himself was appointing them to a school in his gift, and they appear at visitations by virtue of being clergy rather than teachers. Church leaders felt a brief alarm about schools in 1408, when Lollard heresy was flourishing, which led to a piece of legislation that we shall examine in the next chapter.[60] But this was the exception that proves the rule, and it was not followed up for over a hundred years.

The crown and its agents were equally distant from schools. Interventions by the crown as in the Faringdon case, or legal pronouncements by judges as in the Lanthony dispute, were rare. During the late fourteenth and fifteenth centuries the king and Parliament received a few petitions that touched on schooling, but they did not see a need to devise policies for it or to give it regular attention.[61] The parliament of Scotland, called the Estates, passed a decree in 1496 requiring all barons and freeholders to send their sons to school at the age of eight or nine, but this decree has no parallel in England, and even in Scotland it is not known to have been enforced or repeated.[62] That does not mean that monarchs, the nobility, and other important lay people were indifferent to school education. They subsidised scholars and eventually they endowed schools, but they did so in private rather than public ways. For them schooling was a charity, to which people gave help on a personal basis. It was a trade, which (especially in the later middle ages) teachers were left alone to practise and parents to patronise. It was an everyday thing that was taken for granted. These attitudes persisted until well into the sixteenth century. Only with the coming of the Reformation was the role of schools in England reassessed as something crucial to the good of Church and state. Then indeed the crown and the bishops began to take effective action to supervise teachers and what they taught,[63] but attempts to exert control in such a general way were not a characteristic of the middle ages.

ENDOWMENTS FOR SCHOLARS

From their earliest days the English schools acquired privileges and possessions, which eased their work and helped their continuity. In this respect the appearance of patrons claiming the right to appoint schoolmasters was important. It may have seemed irksome when some religious house or local lord attempted to exercise control over the masters who wished to teach in a particular place. But provided that patrons respected the Church's rule against taking fees from teachers, their presence could be an advantage. Here was an authority capable of ensuring that a master was always in post, and of dealing with rivals who threatened his livelihood by drawing away his pupils. We do not know how diligently patrons exerted themselves in appointing and supervising teachers, but it is likely that kings and lay lords had this in mind when they granted control of schools to local religious houses. In one well-documented case, that of the abbey of St Albans, the patron's involvement seems to have been conscientious. When the school of the town became vacant in the time of Abbot Richard (1097–1119), he invited a clerk named Geoffrey de Gorron from Maine in France to come and teach it. Geoffrey was late in arriving and found when he came that the abbot had entrusted the school to another master, but he was promised the next vacancy and filled the time by teaching in the neighbouring town of Dunstable.[64] Later in the century the famous grammarian Alexander Nequam taught the school at Dunstable until he was able to negotiate appointment at St Albans with Abbot Warren (1183–95). The story was afterwards told that the abbot sent a witty message to Nequam, containing a pun on his name. '*Si bonus es, venias* [if you are good, you may come]; *si nequam, nequaquam* [but if not, by no means]!'[65]

Second in importance to the possession of a patron was the acquisition of resources. Already by the twelfth century schools were beginning to attract benefactions, the sequence of which forms one of the most interesting strands of educational history. It relates to social history too, since the benefactors who helped to make schools more stable and effective demonstrated the concern of society with the work that masters and pupils were doing. In the twelfth and thirteenth centuries recorded donations are few. Even allowing for what has not survived, gifts and endowments to schools were probably tiny compared with the resources granted to houses of monks, canons, and friars. One kind of benefaction was the provision of accommodation, like Walkelin's gift of the schoolhouse at Derby and Abbot Samson's purchase of buildings for Bury St Edmunds school.[66] Another consisted of books, the earliest known of which is the copy of Priscian's grammar presented to the school of St Albans before 1310.[67] From the very beginning there was also a need to subsidise the expenses of scholars. How were students to maintain themselves if their means were modest or poor? How were they to be fed and housed, often away from home, during the years they had to spend at school?

The twelfth century provides little evidence about this matter. It may be that charity to scholars at that time came individually and informally from wealthy people or, perhaps, from religious houses. By the thirteenth century, however, any such charity was augmented by the practice of appointing scholars as clerks in parish churches. These were the parish clerks whose origins we traced in the tenth century, and who had a continuous history down to about the nineteenth. In the middle ages they were often known as *aquebaiuli* or holy-water bearers, and were generally adolescent youths or young adults chosen, usually by the parish priest, to assist in performing worship, especially mass (Fig. 53). They rang the church bells for services or to mark deaths, served at the altar, and dispensed the holy water used in rites involving lay people. They received small payments and offerings for their work, which gave them a modest stipend while leaving much of their time free for other activities, such as attending school. Such clerkships seem to have been a common way of training a would-be cleric and of supporting him until the age of twenty-four, at which he could be ordained as a priest. There were a large number of such clerks. England had some 9,500 or more parish churches in the later middle ages plus chapels-of-ease, nearly all of which maintained a clerk, while some churches had more than one.[68]

The first reference to the office of parish clerk in connection with scholars occurs in statutes issued by William of Blois, bishop of Worcester, in 1229. It consists of a single sen-tence, 'that [the benefice of] holy water be conferred only upon poor scholars', an observation so brief that it suggests an

51   A list of the scholars of Wells Cathedral School, aged fourteen and over, in 1377. Boys with the same surname were styled primus or secundus (ij').

established custom rather than a new initiative, a custom that may go back to before 1200.[69] Similar pronouncements occur in seven other sets of episcopal statutes published during the thirteenth century.[70] One, from Lichfield diocese in the 1220s, talks of the clerkly office being given to scholars in rural settlements, but four others from the dioceses of Exeter, Wells, Winchester, and Worcester specify 'the churches that are near the schools of the city or of the castles'. 'City' meant the cathedral city and 'castles' probably referred to the larger towns possessing castles or walls, where schools would be likely to exist. In the Exeter example 'near' is defined as 'not further than ten miles', suggesting that clerks might travel some distance to local schools while remaining available to serve their churches, at least on Sundays and festival days. There are also instances where bishops ordered the practice to be enforced in particular churches. In 1280 Archbishop Pecham of Canterbury arranged for the two parish clerks of Bakewell in Derbyshire to attend school on weekdays, and Bishop Hazleshaw of Bath and Wells made the same provision for the clerk of Kingsbury Episcopi in Somerset in 1302.[71] We are left guessing where they studied.

Hazelshaw's successor, John Droxford, even ordered the removal of the clerk of Chedzoy in 1318 because he was not literate or tonsured, and installed a man who fulfilled these conditions.[72]

Less is heard of clerks engaging in learning after the early fourteenth century, but they undoubtedly did so in some places. At Torksey in Lincolnshire the borough customs of about 1345 relate that the parishioners shall choose the clerk and maintain him at school with their alms.[73] In 1369 William Wykeham, bishop of Winchester, who had noticed that married men and men who were unschooled held the office of clerk in the churches

52   A bishop administering the first tonsure to a youth, a rite often performed on schoolboys.

once reserved for scholars, ordered the restoration of the traditional rule.[74] In 1394 the parish clerk of Winterslow near Salisbury was told by the local bishop to attend school during the week – presumably in Salisbury, to which he could have walked.[75] His counterpart at Eton College in 1447 was meant to be a pupil of the school, if possible,[76] and some Latin school exercises from Exeter of about the same date contain a sentence in which three parish clerks of the city complain of receiving three halfpence and a farthing's worth of thin ale for bell ringing.[77] The fact that this information is given in an educational document suggests that such clerks were still attending school in Exeter. By this time, however, the nature of their office was

53   A parish clerk assisting his priest at mass.

evolving. It was tending to become a long-term post, whose holders kept it for its own sake and sometimes married instead of becoming priests. They gradually mutated, as we have seen, from scholars to teachers, at least teachers of reading to little children.[78]

In at least a few towns there were other schemes to provide food or accommodation for scholars. Hospitals were sometimes chosen for this purpose because they were already engaged in supporting needy members of the public. At Pontefract we hear in 1267 that the hospital of St Nicholas was bound to distribute forty loaves each week to the scholars of Pontefract school.[79] In 1298 Bridgwater hospital undertook to feed seven pupils from the town school every day from its kitchen, and St Cross Hospital (Winchester) fed thirteen every day (Fig. 54).[80] Similar help was given by some monasteries. As well as the meals at Worcester already mentioned, certain abbots of St Albans were said in about 1310 to have granted twenty-eight loaves a week for distribution by the schoolmaster to his poor scholars.[81] In 1342 Bishop Grandisson of Exeter, when carrying out reforms at Launceston Priory in Cornwall, ordered the monks to invite poor scholars apt for learning to partake of a daily meal. The Latin inscription in the priory guest hall, referred to in an earlier chapter, suggests that this command was carried out.[82]

An improvement on doles of food was the provision of permanent places for scholars in religious houses. Monasteries, as we shall see, began to support poor 'almonry boys' in the early thirteenth century, who carried out duties in church in return for board, lodging, and schooling.[83] After 1300 this custom spread widely among the larger Benedictine houses, supplying a valuable resource throughout the kingdom. Similar help was provided by some of the more important hospitals. At Norwich, Bishop Walter Suffield, who founded the 'Great Hospital' of St Giles for the relief of the poor and sick, arranged in about 1249 that the master of Norwich school should choose seven poor scholars to receive board at the hospital during school terms, and replace them with others when they had finished their studies.[84] A plan for the hospital of St Mark (Bristol) in 1259 allowed for twelve poor scholars to live in the house and sing in the choir.[85] This does not seem to have been implemented, but a scheme at St Katherine's Hospital by the Tower of London in 1273 provided for six scholars to be maintained, and another was established at Bridgwater. In 1298 arrangements were made to support twelve scholars there, as well as the seven who came for meals.[86]

Some other scholarship foundations of the thirteenth and fourteenth centuries are worth mentioning as evidence of the interest of important people – mostly clergy – in patronising education. In the north of England Simon of Farlington, archdeacon of Durham during the reign of King John (1199–1216), purchased the manor of Kyo near Durham and gave it to the cathedral there to support three scholars of Durham school. They were to be

54   The outer courtyard of St Cross Hospital (Winchester). Here poor scholars were given daily meals with other needy folk, in buildings on the right-hand side.

chosen by the schoolmaster each day and sent to the cathedral almoner, who was to provide them with food, drink, and beds in the almonry house. Unfortunately the archdeacon died before the conveyance had been completed, and his brother Henry granted the property to the hospital of the Trinity at Gateshead. Eventually a compromise was arranged by Bishop Poore of Durham (1228–37), so that the hospital retained the manor in return for paying half the income (40s. a year) to the almonry scholars.[87] At Carlisle exhibitions for poor scholars were provided by Bishop Irton (1280–92) out of the wealthy rectory of Dalston which lay near his palace, Rose Castle, four and a half miles south of the cathedral city. In 1285 he divided the rectory into three portions: one for a parish vicar, one for the archdeacon, and one to maintain twelve poor scholars chosen by the bishop and studying in the city of Carlisle. The new arrangements came into effect and in 1291 the scholars were receiving £16 a year out of the rectory, but when the bishop died in March 1292, the king, who had the right of filling benefices while the see was unoccupied, made an appointment to Dalston rectory. It then became clear that a division of the benefice had been made without royal approval, and the king overruled it. He ordered his nominee to be given possession, the scholars lost their rights, and the scheme collapsed.[88]

A more successful project in the south was carried out by another bishop, Grandisson of Exeter. This was the fulfilment of a plan by his predecessor, Walter Stapledon (d. 1326), who is best remembered as the founder of Exeter College (Oxford) in 1314 for thirteen scholars from Devon and Cornwall.[89] Grandisson tells us that after Stapledon had founded his Oxford college,

> he diligently fixed the affection of his heart towards the support of boys studying grammar and being educated in life and morals, and therefore he acquired three acres of glebe in the village of Yarnscombe in our diocese and the advowson of the church, and obtained a special licence to appropriate the same to the master and brethren of the hospital of St John the Baptist within the east gate of the city of Exeter for the support of boys studying and being instructed as aforesaid.

Stapledon's plans were interrupted when he lost his life at the hands of a London mob in 1326, during the disturbances which followed the overthrow of Edward II, but Grandisson, his successor-but-one as bishop, decided to complete it.

As arranged by Grandisson in 1332 there were to be not more than twelve scholars. The master of the city grammar school of Exeter was to choose up to two candidates from each of the four archdeaconries of the diocese, of whom one or two were to come if possible from Yarnscombe where the endowment lay. Three were to be nominated by the dean and chapter of Exeter from among the choristers whose voices had broken, and one by the Columbers family, lords of Yarnscombe. The scholars were to live in the

55   Bredgar church (Kent), the site of Robert Bredgar's curious educational foundation of 1392.

hospital of St John for up to five years and to have lodging, straw for their beds, pottage, and 5d. a week apiece to buy extra food. They had a tutor to watch over them, who was to be a priest if one could be found, but although he taught them manners and helped with their grammar, their formal education took place at the city grammar school. Economic changes after the Black Death reduced the scholars to eight and later disposed of the tutor, but there were still nine scholars in the 1530s.[90] The project has an additional interest because Stapledon planned both a school benefaction and a university college, anticipating the dual foundations of Winchester and New College, Eton and King's College, later on. The difference in his schemes (at least as they were realised) was the absence of a plan for the scholars of St John's to proceed to Exeter College; indeed the college did not admit any undergraduates until they had studied for two years.[91] Stapledon's two foundations were separate enterprises, not linked in the way that William Wykeham's were to be two generations later.

Moving eastwards brings us to Lincoln Cathedral. There in 1347 Sir Bartholomew Burghersh, an important local knight, endowed a chantry in the chapel of St Katherine for five priests to pray by the tombs of his father and brother. Finding that the generous endowment produced a surplus of £10 beyond what was needed to support the priests, the dean and chapter decided in 1349 to add six boys to the foundation. They were to be admitted at the age of eight or thereabouts, knowing Donatus, and able to sing. It was envisaged that they should stay for eight years, be removed at sixteen, and proceed in due course to the priesthood. They received board, lodging, clothing, and lessons at the cathedral grammar school in return for assisting in the services of the chantry and reading to the chaplains at meals. The success of the Burghersh scholarships led John Buckingham, bishop of Lincoln, to institute a similar scheme of his own in 1388. He founded the Buckingham chantry in the cathedral for two priests and two clerks, the latter being boys between the ages of seven and sixteen whose life and duties copied those of the Burghersh scholars. The Buckingham funds diminished as time went on, reducing the clerks to one in 1489, but in other respects the two foundations continued to support their scholars until the Reformation. Indeed the scholarships survived it, despite the abolition of the chantries which the boys had served.[92]

The last of the scholarship foundations requiring attention comes from Kent. It dates from after 1350, but qualifies for discussion here because it looks backwards as much as forwards. The project was also one of the strangest. In 1392 Robert Bredgar, a clerk of Canterbury diocese, founded with other local people what he called a 'college or chantry' at Bredgar church (Fig. 55). His interest lay in educating young men to be clergy, but he found difficulty in reconciling this aim with his desire to benefit Bredgar (a rural parish), and his foundation statutes, issued in 1393, were revised in 1398 and again in 1409.[93] The institution supported three staff: a chaplain in charge, saying mass and daily services, and two scholars. Originally Robert wanted the scholars to be local boys, one chosen from his family and the other from three local parishes. They were to be aged at least seven and able to read and sing, and could hold their posts until they were twenty-four (the age for ordination as priests). During this time they were to study grammar, and when they knew how to sing well, construe Latin, and compose Latin verses, they could help the chaplain to say daily services. One (but not both) could go to university. An odd point is that none of the statutes makes it clear where the boys were to study. Bredgar parish was not near a town, and since the chaplain was merely a chantry priest, the boys would have had to learn by themselves or go away to school.

In 1398 Robert arranged with the monks of Canterbury Cathedral that they should maintain a further two poor clerks in their almonry, evidently also to study. These clerks were to remain there until their twentieth year unless they were ordained as subdeacons, in which case they could stay longer, presumably until they were twenty-four. It is not clear how long this arrangement lasted, and his requirements for recruiting scholars at Bredgar proved impossible to satisfy. His statutes of 1398 allowed them to come from anywhere in Canterbury diocese and dropped the mention of university study. In the statutes of 1409 one of the scholars became a priest, presumably a young man studying to improve his knowledge, while the other remained a boy who was eligible to stay until he was twenty-four. Both scholars were now told to keep permanent residence, implying that they were envisaged as learning at Bredgar itself. These final statutes, like the others, contain some whimsical details. The boy scholar (if twenty or more) had to do harvest work for nine weeks of the year (presumably on the college lands), and each member of the foundation had to plant an apple tree every year and receive so many bushels of fruit. Robert Bredgar may have drawn some of his inspiration from the tradition of scholarly holy-water clerks, but his statutes suggest that he was either an eccentric or someone who suffered from a lack of models. They give the impression of a man trying to invent a wheel by himself.

ENDOWMENTS OF SCHOOLS

All the foundations mentioned so far did something to subsidise the costs of education. How far they benefited the poor and deserving is less certain. Medieval charity was not as impartial as modern welfare, and scholarships may have been awarded to those with influence and connections. They also invite the question why most charitable schemes of the thirteenth and fourteenth centuries aimed to fund scholars rather than schoolmasters: the expenses of food and lodging rather than schooling. This contrasts with what happened after about 1380, when founders began to switch their attention to supporting teachers and teaching. There are at least two possible reasons for the concentration on food and lodging up to that date, rather than on the costs of the classroom. One was that many scholars sought their education away from home, and therefore had to bear the additional expenses of food and accommodation. Bed and board costing 8d. or so per week required more help than the comparatively small fees charged by most schoolmasters. The other may have been that the economy of teaching did not seem to require assistance. In an age of high population, which was the case up to 1349, there may have been enough fee-paying scholars to keep masters at work, even in fairly small towns, and consequently no perception of need in this respect.

Certainly the endowment of teaching was slow to develop compared with that of the maintenance of scholars. One of the few places where we hear of it is Bury St Edmunds. There Abbot Samson, who had already provided the town with a schoolhouse, arranged in 1193 for an annual pension of £2 to be paid to the schoolmaster of Bury out of his abbey's church of Wetherden. This was not enough for a full-time stipend but resembled the arrangements at some of the cathedrals, where the master was given a modest sum to teach members of the cathedral staff. At Bury in later times he seems to have been expected to teach forty poor clerks without charge.[94] There was a similar but smaller scheme at St Albans, where a cleric named Master Richard of Naundes provided a schoolhouse in the 1280s on condition that the master taught sixteen of the poorest scholars for nothing in lieu of rent.[95] But the provision of a salary for a schoolmaster to teach wholly without fees was first achieved in a different kind of institution: the college or collegiate church.

Colleges were an updated version of minsters, those ubiquitous churches of the late Anglo-Saxon period whose clergy lived close to the everyday world.[96] During the twelfth century the interest of Church leaders and wealthy laity turned away from minsters to founding monasteries, and a number of minsters were converted into monastic houses of Augustinian canons. Later, as the thirteenth century wore on, the impetus for establishing houses of monks, friars, and nuns began to decline in its turn, and after 1300 it practically ceased. Vocations to be monks or friars levelled off and more recruits entered the Church as secular priests, remaining in the world as chaplains, chantry priests, and parish clergy. Minster-like foundations returned to favour in the form of colleges staffed by secular priests and clerks, and dozens of such colleges were founded from the thirteenth to the sixteenth centuries in what became the last great expansion of religious communities before the Reformation. Colleges were attractive to founders because they were easier to establish than monasteries. They could function with modest buildings, sometimes using existing church sites, and required less strict vocations from their members. Some foundations were university colleges, providing facilities for academic study, and these are familiar to us today because they have survived at Oxford and Cambridge. Most medieval colleges were not academic, however, and lay in other towns or in the countryside. The priests and clerks who operated them spent their lives saying daily services and celebrating masses for the souls of their founders and benefactors. Many colleges, both the academic and the non-academic, maintained boys and youths out of charity or to assist in worship, raising the issue of their training and schooling.[97]

Some of the Anglo-Saxon minsters survived the twelfth century without being monasticised, and a few of these employed schoolmasters in the manner of the secular cathedrals to teach the choristers and clerks of the foundation and the general public. This was so at the three great minsters of the diocese of York: Beverley, where the school existed by about 1100, Southwell, where it probably did by 1238, and Ripon where it is mentioned in 1348.[98] Other late Anglo-Saxon or Norman foundations with schools include the royal collegiate chapel in Hastings and the college of St Mary (Warwick).[99] When Leach traced the history of education, he emphasised the likelihood of schools in connection with both the old minsters and the new colleges of the later middle ages: schools for outsiders too. Not every college included a grammar school during this period, however, and we should resist the temptation to make the inference without explicit evidence. In some of these churches the chief clergy (canons or prebendaries) were not often resident, and the lesser clergy merely engaged in worship. Any boys who were present may have received no more than a

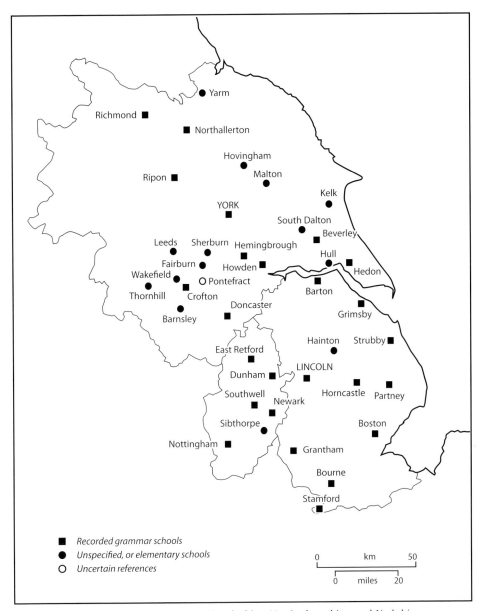

56   Some fourteenth-century schools in Lincolnshire, Nottinghamshire, and Yorkshire.

practical training in how to read and sing in church. Where there was a school for the public, the master appears to have taught for fees, receiving at best a small stipend (as at the secular cathedrals) for teaching members of the college foundation.

The first new college to include boy scholars and a master paid to teach them appears to have been Merton College (Oxford), founded by Walter of Merton, chancellor of England, in 1264. His college was chiefly intended as

an academic community of university scholars who had reached the
equivalent of the later BA degree and wished to study for the MA or for the
degrees in law or theology. At the same time the founder's statutes of 1270
provided for the education of up to thirteen of his relatives, envisaged as boys
studying grammar with a status lower than undergraduates. The college was
to include a grammar master to teach them, to whom any of its members was
urged to go 'without a blush' to improve his knowledge. By about 1270 an
additional group of twelve poor 'secondary scholars' appears, a benefaction
apparently intended by Richard earl of Cornwall and king of the Romans,
but put into effect by Merton himself. They too appear to have been boys
learning grammar rather than undergraduates. But the grammatical side of
the college did not flourish. The secondaries vanished after the middle of the
fourteenth century, and the boys of the founder's family were soon sent out
to a professional master in the town rather than having one of their own.
They themselves disappear from the records after 1460.[100]

The provision for grammar boys at Merton was imitated at some other
early university colleges. Plans were made for them at Peterhouse and Clare
College (Cambridge), although apparently without full-time masters to
teach them, and more ambitiously at the Queen's College (Oxford), founded
in 1341 by Robert of Eglesfield, chaplain to the queen of Edward III. He
designed his college to include not only an academic body of a provost and
twelve fellows, but a large group of poor boys, defined in one place as
numbering fewer than twenty-four and in another as not more than
seventy-two. They were to be chosen at the age of fourteen or younger from
the places where the college had property. Their instruction was to start
with plainsong and grammar, and proceed to logic and the rest of the
university arts course. Two clerks were to teach them song, and other tutors
grammar and the liberal arts, so that they would begin as schoolboys and
end as undergraduates. Yet the study of grammar in these early university
colleges did not develop to a significant extent. It remained a project rather
than a reality, an aspiration stillborn through inadequate resources. At
Queen's, for example, the number of scholars never got anywhere near
twenty-four – there were only four in 1415 – and they went outside the
college to be taught, their schoolmaster in the early fifteenth century being
John Leland. These pioneering schemes are interesting, but they had not
achieved much by the middle of the fourteenth century.[101]

Nor was this so outside the universities. Although many colleges were
founded elsewhere in England up to 1350, including boys to help with the
worship, very few seem to have taken seriously the education of these boys
in grammar, or that of outsiders. One that did was Ottery St Mary in Devon,
founded by Bishop Grandisson of Exeter in 1338, but Grandisson was
unusual in his educational interests. We have already seen three of these: his
implementation of Stapledon's scholarships at Exeter, his arrangement for
feeding poor scholars at Launceston, and his instructions for schoolmasters.

It accorded with these that his college at Ottery supported not only canons, chaplains, twelve clerks, and eight choristers, but a grammar master to teach the choristers at a salary of £1 6s. 8d. 'besides the emoluments of the school'.[102] This arrangement shows that Grandisson was following the cathedral and minster model. His schoolmaster was paid only for instructing the college members and was expected to get most of his living by teaching the public in return for fees. Another college with a school attached appears to have been Cobham in Kent, established by John Lord Cobham in 1362 for a master and five chaplains, clerks and choristers being added later. Whether one of the chaplains was meant to teach grammar is not certain, but in 1383 work was carried out on 'the college and schoolhouse of Cobham' and in 1389 the bishop of Rochester sanctioned the addition of two clerks to the foundation with the order that they should study letters 'in the school with the other scholars in so far as they are able'.[103] The nature of the school, private or public, is not revealed.

There may have been other new college foundations with schools, either for inmates or incomers, but such facilities do not seem to have been common or significant up to the mid fourteenth century. Indeed schools as a whole, in the first two hundred and fifty years of their recorded history, did not advance very far in providing free education. Yet they developed in other ways. They established 'critical mass' with a wide distribution in England (Fig. 56). Many, especially in cities and towns, acquired long-term stability, although others were probably private ventures and did not achieve permanence. Schools gained resources, including authorities responsible for appointing and overseeing their masters, school buildings, and scholarships in the form of money, food, and accommodation. Even so, they were still a relatively unobtrusive part of English culture in 1350 compared with religious houses, parish churches, or hospitals. No school yet existed as a legally self-governing body or a fully endowed one. All depended on patrons, formed parts of larger institutions, or were private ventures, and received supervision, revenues, or charitable assistance from outside. The achievement of full independence was to be the next stage of development.

7

Schools from 1350 to 1530

CHANGES AND CRISES

The second half of the fourteenth century is well known for its changes and crises. In 1348–9 the Black Death aggravated an earlier decline in the size of the population, which dropped to two or three million by about 1400 and remained at that level for the next hundred years or more. There was a tangible growth of insularity, reflected in the decreasing use of the French language, a revival of English for literary purposes, and the development of a native 'Perpendicular' style in architecture. The last thirty years of the century were also marked by political troubles and social unrest. John Wycliffe emerged as a challenge to the Church in the 1370s, the Peasants' Revolt broke out in 1381, and Wycliffe's followers founded a dissident movement, the Lollards, during the 1380s and 1390s.

These changes impinged on schooling, although it is not always easy to say how. Contemporaries were silent about the effects on schools of the Black Death and population decline, except for noting that the second major visitation of the plague in 1360–2 was particularly fatal to children.[1] A falling population may have reduced the number of pupils available to be taught, jeopardising the ability of teachers to live from their fees and lessening their number, especially in smaller towns. But we cannot measure this number in the fourteenth century or compare pre- and post-plague statistics, and the demand for education may not have reflected the size of the population. Schooling was a resource of the more prosperous. It may have benefited from the higher standard of living enjoyed by many after 1349, including peasants and labourers, thanks to the fact that fewer people were sharing the nation's resources. More definitely we can say that schools after about 1350 reflected, and helped to generate, the Englishness of English culture. From the mid fourteenth century grammatical textbooks began to use the English language and by the early fifteenth century some were written entirely in English. Dictionaries relating Latin to English and vice versa also made their appearance after 1400.[2]

57   A fifteenth-century picture of Winchester College, fronted by the founder William Wykeham
(d. 1404) amid the clergy and scholars of his foundation.

Education was an issue, albeit a minor one, in the social and religious disputes of the era. We have already encountered the claim of Thomas Walsingham, monk of St Albans, that participants in the Peasants' Revolt forced schoolmasters to swear to stop teaching children grammar.[3] There were attacks by the protesters on the written records of lords of manors and lawyers. At Cambridge, where local people pillaged the university archives that stored the evidence of the university's privileges against the town, a bonfire of documents was made in the market square. An old woman named Margery Starre is said to have tossed the ashes to the winds, crying, 'Away with the learning of the clerks, away with it!'[4] Yet it would be inadequate to characterise most of those who joined the revolt as unfriendly to learning as such. Indeed William Grindcob, who headed the rising at St Albans, had been educated in the abbey against which he led his supporters.[5] Rather the protesters' hostility was focussed on writings that disadvantaged them: records of serfdom, taxation, and legal processes. They circulated letters to gather support, some of which were preserved by contemporaries.[6] When they briefly held the upper hand over Richard II and his government, on Friday 14 June 1381, they demanded written charters to free them from serfdom and letters of pardon to absolve them from crime. 'All that day', we are told, various clerks were assigned 'to write the charters and patents and protections granted to them'.[7] The protesters were thoroughly supportive of writing and record keeping when such things were to their benefit.

It was as much the defenders of the established order who showed themselves hostile to education, on the grounds that it allowed the children of serfs and other lowly people to rise to wealth and power above their station. There was a long-established custom on the English manors that a serf's child could not be sent to school or apprenticed without the permission of his lord. Schooling and apprenticeship implied that the child would become a priest or townsman, robbing the lord of a pair of hands and threatening that a serf's holding might be claimed by an heir who was a freeman. In practice, as we have seen, lords often permitted such children to be educated or apprenticed in return for a payment, but in 1391 a petition was put forward in the House of Commons, an assembly of gentry and prosperous burgesses, asking the king to forbid 'neifs' (meaning serfs) from putting their children to school 'to advance them by clergy [i.e. learning], and this in maintenance and saving of the honour of all freemen of the realm'. The petition was effectively a request for a statutory prohibition, but the king returned a non-committal answer and nothing was done.[8]

Prejudice of this kind was not confined to Parliament. It occurs among Church reformers of the period, who complained about breaches in the traditional social order. William Langland, writing in about the 1380s, claimed that children who were serfs or illegitimate were becoming clergy, so that

... bondmen's bairns have been made bishops,
And bastard children have been archdeacons.[9]

The unknown author who copied him in *Piers the Ploughman's Creed*, a piece of anticlerical writing composed in the 1390s, fulminated that

Now may each cobbler his son set to school,
And each beggar's brat on the book learn,
And rank as a writer and with a lord dwell,
Or falsely a friar, the fiend for to serve!
So of that beggar's brat a bishop shall come,
Pressing to sit among peers of the land,
And lords' sons lowly to those wastrels bow down,
Knights bend to them and crouch full low.[10]

Even in the fifteenth century it was possible for a family to be disparaged for rising to wealth and rank by means of education. Enemies of the Pastons of Norfolk, newly established in the gentry, claimed that their ancestor Clement Paston 'rode to mill on the bare horseback with his corn under him', married a serf woman, and borrowed money to send his son to school: the son who became a judge and established the family's fortunes.[11]

It followed that there was no relaxation at this time of the manorial custom controlling the schooling of serfs. The belief that there was owes much to Leach, who argued that the Statute of Apprentices, passed by Parliament in 1406, permitted all (including serfs) to have their children educated as they wished, an argument that has been (and still is) repeated.[12] In fact the statute was not primarily about education or liberal in its intentions. Its chief concern was to control the movement of labour from the countryside by re-enacting earlier legislation forbidding people to apprentice their children in towns unless they owned land to the value of at least 20s. a year. It did indeed add a clause to the effect 'that any man or woman, of whatever estate or condition, be free to put his son or daughter to learn letters at any school in the kingdom', but this was evidently meant to apply to the matter in hand. The restrictions on apprenticeship were not to affect those who might lawfully send their children to school.[13] It is highly unlikely that the governing orders meant to surrender their control over the education of their serfs by this clause, and evidence shows that this control continued to be seen as legal and applicable. Boys were reported for having been sent to school without permission at Barton (Beds.) in 1410, Great Badminton (Gloucs.) in 1436–7, and Methley (Yorks.) in 1465, with consequent fines and penalties.[14] As late as the sixteenth century, treatises on how to hold manorial courts reminded their readers to ask 'if there be any bondman of blood that putteth his son unto the school to make him a priest or a prentice'. The last such treatise was published as late as 1552, when serfdom itself was all but dead.[15] There was no 'emancipation of the serfs' in terms of education; the restriction died only when serfdom died, itself never formally ended.

The antithesis between ordinary people valuing literacy and authorities anxious to control education is again apparent when we turn to the Lollards. They too were advocates of reading and writing: emphasising Bible reading in English, producing controversial works in English, and using leaflets for propaganda purposes.[16] The authorities even accused them of holding 'schools', although the word appears to refer to meetings of adults for religious study rather than classes for children.[17] In fact the Lollards seem not to have developed policies about schools in the latter sense. They probably took them for granted, like most people, and when in the 1390s they produced a plan to finance education and welfare from the property of bishops and monasteries, their proposals focussed on the foundation of universities and almshouses, not schools.[18] The Church authorities, on the other hand, came to view Lollardy as a threat not only to religion but to education. In 1408 Thomas Arundel, archbishop of Canterbury, issued constitutions for his province, the two-thirds of England that lay south of the River Trent, which included the only general legislation about schools made by the English Church in the fourteenth and fifteenth centuries. He ordered schoolmasters not to teach their pupils anything about the faith or the sacraments that was against the determination of the Church, and not to allow their pupils to hold disputations concerning matters of faith.[19] The order was duly reproduced in William Lyndwood's influential collection of English canon law, the *Provinciale*, in 1430,[20] and although the extent of its enforcement is unclear, the fact of its production is significant. Just as the Lollards anticipated the Reformation in some respects, so they stimulated the Church authorities to address the teaching of children in a way that presaged what would happen in the sixteenth century.

Those who viewed schooling from social and religious standpoints were complemented by one contemporary witness who saw it from a vocational one. In 1439 William Bingham, rector of the church of St John Zachary in London, addressed a petition to Henry VI on the subject of schools, a petition that was quite original. Little is known of Bingham except that he was probably born in the late fourteenth century and briefly held a benefice in Leicestershire before exchanging it for his church in London.[21] More certain is his interest in education and his perceptiveness in seeking the ear of the king to promote it. Henry, a young man in his late teens, was revealing a distinctive and unprecedented concern with schooling through his plans to found Eton College. Bingham wanted to gain his support for a project to establish a college at Cambridge for training grammar masters – a kind of training for which, he asserted, there was no provision in the existing colleges. His objective – or at least the one he judged likely to appeal to the king – was to strengthen 'the clergy of this your realm' which was 'like to be impaired and enfeebled by the defect and lack of schoolmasters of grammar'. Here he ventured on statistics,

> in so much that as your said poor beseecher hath found of late, over the east part of the way leading from Hampton to Coventry and so forth, no further north than Ripon, 70 schools void or more that were occupied all at once within 50 years past, because that there is so great scarcity of masters of grammar, whereof as now be almost none nor none may be had in your universities over those that needs must be occupied still there.

Bingham was apparently visualising the map of England, with Hampton (Southampton, not Hampton-on-Thames as Leach thought) at the middle of the bottom, Coventry at the centre, and Ripon towards the north. Focussing on the half of the kingdom that lay to the east of this, he claimed that seventy schools or more had disappeared over the last fifty years. Bingham did not attribute their disappearance to demographic or economic decline, leading to a shortage of pupils or of parents willing to fund them. He argued rather that the problem was lack of masters: by implication it was too expensive to train as a teacher, so that few were doing so.[22]

His petition concluded with proposals to found a house in the university of Cambridge to support twenty-four scholars of grammar with a priest to govern them, for which he sought the king's support and resources. The response was favourable. Royal permission was granted to proceed with the foundation, and some modest properties belonging to extinct religious houses were made available to provide an endowment. In 1448 the king's charter founding the college was issued, naming Henry as founder and Bingham as second founder. The college, called Godshouse, was governed by a proctor or master, and its statutes provided for twenty-five undergraduate scholars who were to read sophistry and logic and 'the subtler and deeper parts of grammar' such as Priscian, Virgil, and other poets, as well as the science of metre. When in due course they qualified to take the university degree of master of grammar, they had to be prepared to teach grammar at any grammar school built during the last forty years where there was a suitable salary or livelihood for the master. Unfortunately Godshouse did not develop as Bingham desired. It seems unlikely to have supported more than a master, a lecturer, and four scholars at any one time, and while some of the latter certainly took degrees in grammar, none has yet been traced to a school elsewhere. In 1505 the college was refounded by Lady Margaret Beaufort, who gave it new endowments and renamed it Christ's College. Most of the fellows and scholars of the new foundation were intended to follow the usual arts course, but Lady Margaret retained places for six scholars who were to study grammar, graduate in grammar, and teach wherever they were asked to go, provided that they were offered a stipend of £10.[23]

Bingham's petition warns us not to assume that the history of schooling in England was one of continuous growth. Equally it calls for caution; how much weight can we give to one man's opinion when we have so few others with which to compare it? Bingham's views were indeed repeated in one other document: a petition of 1447, to be discussed presently, by four London rectors for more schools in the capital. Two of these men were Bingham's friends, however, so it is not surprising that their petition also refers to 'the great number of grammar schools that sometime were in diverse parts of this realm, besides those that were in London, and how few be in these days'.[24] There may have been a shortage of graduates to teach after the Black Death; we have encountered signs of this at Lincoln and York in the 1350s and 1360s.[25] Thomas Rotherham's story points in the same direction: to the effect that his home town of Rotherham lacked teachers in his youth, in about the 1430s, until one chanced to arrive.[26] Bingham's assertions may find further support in the pattern of school endowments, to which we shall turn next. From the 1380s onwards benefactors of schools turned their attention to subsidising masters rather than pupils and to assisting schools in smaller rather than larger towns. This, perhaps, indicates a view that masters could no longer easily function in such places without charitable support.

Medieval assertions of decline must always be handled with care, however. Those who made them believed that the world had been flawless at its creation. They tended to view all change as change for the worse, and to ascribe it to human defects rather than to economic or environmental factors. Similar allegations were made about the declining numbers and quality of clergy, knights, and common people, and there were even one or two laments about school education after Bingham's time. The university of Oxford, writing to the bishop of Lincoln in 1466, concurred with his sadness that grammar, 'which stands as the root of the other sciences, has departed from the kingdom as if sent into exile'.[27] This statement was made when a movement to endow grammar schools had been in existence for two decades. In 1509–10 Henry VII's councillor Edmund Dudley gave a gloomy account of the state of education in his day in *The Tree of the Commonwealth*, the treatise on government that he wrote in the Tower of London shortly before his execution by Henry VIII. Perhaps being 'in worldly vexation and troubled with the sorrowful and bitter remembrance of death' helped to colour his view of affairs:

Look well upon your two universities, how famous they have been and in what condition they be now. Where be your famous men that were wont to read divinity in every cathedral church and in other great monasteries? Where be the good and substantial scholars of grammar that have been kept in this realm before this time; not only in every good town and city and in other places, but also in all abbeys, priories, and colleges, in prelates' houses, and often times in houses of men of honour of the temporality?[28]

The answer is that there were plenty of scholars of grammar in religious houses and in the great households of prelates and lay magnates, and that divinity lectures were still being read in cathedrals.[29] Dudley, one feels, was appealing to his readers' emotions rather than to real evidence, and it would not have been easy for him to prove that the past was so perfect or the present so marred.

WINCHESTER AND WOTTON

The endowment of school education took a fresh turn in the late fourteenth century with two foundations, one important in terms of its scale and the other as a precedent or model. The first was Winchester College, founded by William Wykeham, who was born in 1328 and died in 1404, rising from comparatively humble origins to become bishop of Winchester and chancellor of England.[30] His lifetime of service to the crown and his enjoyment of high preferment enabled him to amass a considerable fortune, much of which he used for his two educational foundations at Winchester and New College (Oxford). His projects were conceived and endowed on a grand scale. Winchester enjoyed an annual income of £628 net by 1535 and New College £877 net, equal to those of major monasteries.[31] The first was being planned by 1373, when Wykeham hired a grammar master to teach poor scholars in Winchester to whom the bishop was giving support. Foundation charters were issued for New College in 1379 and for Winchester College three years later.[32] In the latter Wykeham reserved the right to make statutes for its governance, and the final substantive version of these was drawn up in 1400. They provide a detailed guide to how the founder intended Winchester to work.[33]

Like earlier colleges it was primarily a religious house. It supported a warden, ten priest fellows, three chaplains, three clerks, and sixteen choristers maintaining daily services in the college chapel (Fig. 57). The school within the college, on the other hand, was much larger than in previous foundations, both inside and outside the universities. There were two fully paid staff (headmaster and usher) and scholarships for seventy pupils including free board, lodging, and education. The bishop's intention in endowing these scholarships was to train boys of modest means to a high standard for careers in the Church as secular clergy. His scholars were to be 'poor and needy', poverty being defined as not having an income greater than five marks a year (£3 6s. 8d.). They were to be aged between eight and twelve on admission, to be already competent in reading, song, and Donatus, and to study grammar in the college until they qualified to go to university or reached the age of eighteen. The warden and fellows of New College were required to visit Winchester once a year and to choose suitable scholars to proceed to Oxford. New College too had seventy scholars, who were maintained for the whole seven years of the arts course up to the MA degree, and (if appropriate) to study for further degrees in civil law, canon law, or theology.

The Winchester scholarships were confined to specified classes of people. Preference was given to the founder's relatives and their descendants, and then to the inhabitants of the places where the colleges had their estates. Next in eligibility were candidates from the diocese of Winchester followed by eleven counties in a given order, which were chiefly those containing the estates, and last of all, if any spaces were left, came the inhabitants of the rest of England. We have already encountered similar restrictions in the scholarships at Bredgar, St John's hospital (Exeter), and the Queen's College (Oxford), and far from being quaint or eccentric they reflect the bonds of family and lordship so important in the society of the day. Founders had a duty to their families, the more so because they had diverted to their foundations the wealth that the family might have inherited. Foundations had responsibilities to protect and patronise the tenants who paid them rents and services. Winchester, then, was not envisaged as a school for the general public in the modern sense, but its statutes provided that ten sons of noble and powerful persons who were friends of the college might be admitted to learn grammar.[34] This allowed the entry of outsiders who paid their own way, outsiders later known as commoners.

Winchester College is the first English school whose workings can be studied in detail, not with respect to its teaching (of which little is known until the late fifteenth century) but in relation to its pupils. Registers naming its scholars survive from 1393, and although there is no equivalent for the commoners, some of their names can be deduced from college records.[35] The registers show that the college developed largely but not wholly as Wykeham intended. It did indeed bring many boys through school and university to benefices and dignities in the Church. By 1500 the college had produced seven men who were or would be diocesan bishops and three archbishops: Henry Chichele and William Warham (Canterbury), and Hugh Ing (Dublin).[36] Equally the school diverged from its founder's plans in certain ways. First, a number of scholars came from prosperous families of gentry and were not poor in any real sense. Secondly, the college took in far more commoners than originally intended. In 1412 there were said to be eighty or a hundred, and although a reduction was ordered, the principle of admitting them continued on a large scale, so that by the early sixteenth century the college was virtually an endowed grammar school for the city of Winchester.[37] Finally, not all boys entered New College and became clergy. The very first scholar in the register, Andrew Goolde (admitted in 1393), is noted as having departed 'for secular work', and of the seventy scholars in his cohort four died at Winchester and thirty-three left the college without proceeding to Oxford. Similar patterns can be seen in subsequent years, although some of those who did not go to university entered the Church as non-graduate clergy.

As a project Winchester College both drew on the past and advanced from it. It was a college and therefore belonged to a well-established genre of foundation. Earlier educational schemes had centred on the support of scholars rather than teachers, and Wykeham's plans followed these in that most of the educational resources at Winchester were applied in the same direction. Some elements of his plans can be traced in earlier foundations. Merton, Grandisson, and Eglesfield had made provision for grammar masters. Eglesfield had envisaged a body of seventy-two scholars passing from school to university, albeit on the same site. King's Hall (Cambridge), founded by Edward II in 1317, catered especially for choristers of the chapel royal, and can likewise be seen as part of a double foundation: school and college.[38] Winchester's claim to originality lies rather in its size and success. The seventy boy scholars vastly exceeded the handful or dozen in earlier foundations, and the commoners increased the total further. No previous founder had given a school and its boy scholars such a large proportion of the revenues. Earlier college schools had been small or peripheral, not central to the buildings and life of the community as was the case at Winchester. No college had yet paid two masters fully to teach for

58   The tomb of Lady Katherine Berkeley, foundress of the first small chantry grammar school at Wotton-under-Edge (Gloucs.) in 1384.

nothing, and no educational scheme had enabled so many schoolboys to pass so seamlessly into university studies.

The grandeur of Winchester made imitation difficult. Only one king and one cardinal attempted to match its scale before the Reformation: Henry VI at Eton in 1440 and Thomas Wolsey at Ipswich in 1528, of which Eton alone succeeded. Winchester's linkage of school and university was also slow to spread. It is true that in 1381, when Wykeham was planning his colleges, Bishop Thomas Hatfield of Durham refounded Durham College (Oxford) as a college for eight monks from Durham Cathedral and eight secular scholars. Four of the scholars were to come from Durham, and two from Howdenshire and Allertonshire in Yorkshire. The fact that Durham, Howden, and Northallerton all had schools under the patronage of Durham Cathedral suggests that the Oxford places were meant to enable pupils from these schools to go on to university.[39] Connections of this kind between schools and colleges, however, are not common in the fifteenth century, apart from Eton. Only in the sixteenth did Wykeham's ideas come into their own, with the foundation of a number of large boarding schools like Henry VIII's cathedral schools, and the introduction of more closed scholarships from local grammar schools to Oxford and Cambridge colleges. Until then Winchester may have been an outstanding foundation, but it was a lonely one.

The immediate future of school endowment, then, was not determined by Wykeham's ambitious design. Instead the future was foreshadowed by a humbler plan that crystallised a mere two years after his charter for Winchester. This was the 'house of scholars' at Wotton-under-Edge in Gloucestershire, an endowed free grammar school founded by Lady Katherine Berkeley in October 1384 (Fig. 58).[40] The foundress, the daughter of a Worcestershire knight, had married twice, her second husband being a baron, Thomas Lord Berkeley. He died in 1361 and she withdrew to a dower house in Wotton. We rarely know why school benefactors favoured education over other charities, and Katherine is no exception in this respect. Was the endowment of the school her own idea, or one suggested to her by others? There had been a grammar school at Wotton in the late thirteenth century and an attempt had been made by the Berkeley family to endow it in 1349 – an attempt that was apparently unsuccessful. The needs of the school may therefore have presented themselves to the widow who lived nearby. Katherine's family by marriage was closely in touch with learning. A few years later, her stepson, Thomas Lord Berkeley, employed John Trevisa and other men to translate into English the standard Latin works on history, science, war, and philosophy. In short there were probably local influences on Katherine's plans, and although they crystallised soon after Wykeham's foundation, it is not clear how far they were inspired from that direction.

Like Wykeham Katherine issued not only a charter but a code of statutes, which do a good deal to illuminate her plans.[41] She endowed the school with land and rent in the neighbourhood, which produced a revenue of about £17 a year by the sixteenth century. This money supported a schoolmaster and two poor scholars receiving free board, lodging, and education. The master, who was to be in priest's orders, had two duties. He was to sing daily masses in Wotton parish church for the souls of the foundress and her relatives, and to teach grammar gratis to the two scholars and to anyone else who wished it. The patronage of the school, including the appointment of the master, was reserved for the Berkeley family, but the master was empowered to administer the endowments by leasing them and collecting rents, although he could not sell them without the patron's permission. He had to maintain the buildings and look after the scholars, and the residue of the income was available for his stipend (which was not specified).

Wotton resembled Winchester both in drawing on tradition and in moving away from it. Chantries had long been founded in England, but although some chantry priests may have taught on their own initiative, Katherine was original in making such teaching a duty.[42] Wotton followed other educational schemes of the fourteenth century in supporting scholars, but it only had two of these, and most of its income went to the chantry priest-schoolmaster to teach all comers for nothing. This was a policy that even Wykeham had not adopted, and one that at last tipped the balance of endowment from scholarships to teaching. Wotton was also notable for the practicality of its scale and objectives. Its cost was affordable by a larger group of founders, and it anticipated most of the basic features of the smaller endowed schools that were founded in England over the next couple of centuries. These included legal independence, free education to outsiders, and a linkage with the immediate locality rather than with large areas of the country as at Winchester.

THE ENDOWED SCHOOLS: A HISTORY

Winchester and Wotton strike us as significant milestones in the history of education. They would have struck their contemporaries less forcibly. Their teaching would have followed common practice: practice led, if anywhere, from Oxford. All the headmasters of Winchester were imported from outside until 1454, when John Barnard became the first college alumnus to hold the office. In 1424 the college even had some difficulty in filling the post.[43] Nor does either school seem to have inspired imitations for many years. The period from the 1380s to the 1430s resembles the early and mid fourteenth century in generating a modest number of educational projects with few traits in common. Even Wotton, which so much resembles the small school foundations of the mid fifteenth century and later, has few such counterparts before the 1440s. The scholarships at Bredgar, for example, date from the same period (1392), but did not include the teaching element provided at Wotton and Winchester.[44]

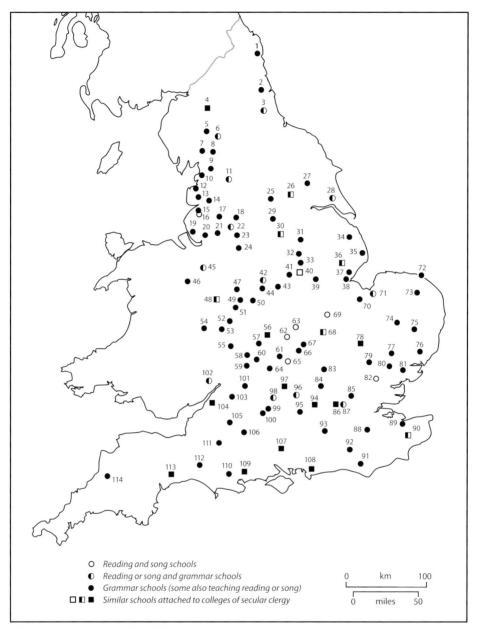

59   Endowed schools, 1380–1530.

Few college foundations of the early fifteenth century laid a strong emphasis on public education. Battlefield, founded on the site of the battle of Shrewsbury in 1410, commissioned a large grammatical miscellany at its foundation and there is a much later reference to a boy being educated there, but no evidence survives that public teaching was offered.[45] Tong, set up in the same year and the same county, included a chaplain who was to teach

1 Alnwick	39 Grantham	77 Sudbury
2 Newcastle	40 Sibthorpe	78 Cambridge
3 Durham	41 Nottingham	79 Saffron Walden
4 Kirkoswald	42 Rolleston	80 Earls Colne
5 Appleby	43 Castle Donington	81 Colchester
6 Brough	44 Burton upon Trent	82 Pleshey
7 Kirkby Kendal	45 Malpas	83 Houghton
8 Sedbergh	46 Oswestry	84 Berkhamstead
9 Hornby	47 Stafford	85 Walthamstow
10 Lancaster	48 Tong	86 London (St Paul)
11 Long Preston	49 Cannock	87 London (St Anthony)
12 St Michael-on-Wyre	50 Lichfield	88 Sevenoaks
13 Broughton	51 Wolverhampton	89 Faversham
14 Blackburn	52 Kinver	90 Wye
15 Leyland	53 Ludlow	91 Lewes
16 Rufford	54 Rock	92 Cuckfield
17 Bolton	55 Worcester	93 Guildford
18 Middleton	56 Warwick	94 Eton
19 Liverpool	57 Stratford	95 Reading
20 Farnworth	58 Evesham	96 Ewelme
21 Warrington	59 Winchcombe	97 Oxford
22 Manchester	60 Chipping Campden	98 Childrey
23 Stockport	61 Banbury	99 Lambourn
24 Macclesfield	62 Fawsley	100 Ramsbury
25 Whitkirk	63 Brington	101 Cirencester
26 Acaster	64 Chipping Norton	102 Newland
27 Pocklington	65 Farthinghoe	103 Wotton-under-Edge
28 Hull	66 Towcester	104 Westbury-on-Trym
29 Royston	67 Blisworth	105 Bradford-on-Avon
30 Rotherham	68 Higham Ferrers	106 Heytesbury
31 East Retford	69 Aldwinkle	107 Winchester
32 Kneesall	70 Wisbech	108 Chichester
33 Newark	71 King's Lynn	109 Wimborne
34 Louth	72 Cromer	110 Milton Abbas
35 Wainfleet	73 Aylsham	111 Bruton
36 Tattershall	74 Rushworth	112 Crewkerne
37 Boston	75 Eye	113 Ottery St Mary
38 Kirton-in-Holland	76 Ipswich	114 Week St Mary

grammar to the ministers of the college and to other poor youths of the place or from the neighbouring villages.[46] This looks more promising, but the subsequent history of the school is unclear. Fotheringhay (c.1415), founded by Henry IV's cousin Edward duke of York, provided for thirteen choristers, a chaplain to teach them grammar, and a chaplain or clerk to train them in song. The grammar master was required to act as a chantry priest for the founder (a possible echo of Wotton), but evidence that he and his colleague taught outsiders is elusive.[47] A free public grammar school is mentioned at Fotheringhay by 1548, but if this was in the college it may have been a recent development.[48] Higham Ferrers (1422), for which Henry Chichele, archbishop of Canterbury, was responsible, included a priest or clerk to teach grammar and another to rule the choir, and here the teaching of grammar was certainly public in later times.[49] Most colleges of this period, however, seem to have aimed primarily to teach their own staff. They did not develop large-scale schools or (in most cases) successful public teaching.

Small endowed grammar schools like Wotton are also rare before the 1440s. One was founded at Durham by Bishop Langley in 1414 for two chantry priests, teaching song and grammar respectively.[50] Another was set up at Oswestry for a single master, possibly by David Holbach, a Welsh lawyer and gentleman, during the first two decades of the fifteenth century. It is traceable, however, only from a conveyance by his widow Gwenhywfar in about 1423.[51] Neither foundation closely resembled Wotton except in scale. At Durham the masters received small salaries of £2 in the early days, although these later rose, and they were required to give free teaching only to the poor, taking moderate fees from others. The early history of Oswestry is obscure since it scarcely appears in records until the mid sixteenth century. By then it was described as a free school and did not require its master to be a priest, but how far back these features go is unknown. Its most original characteristic was the management of the endowment by a group of feoffees (trustees), who paid the master a stipend – an arrangement which became more common than Wotton's practice of giving the management to the schoolmaster. Neither Durham nor Oswestry is easy to fit into a line of development. Each seems shaped by local considerations as much as by models elsewhere.

It is not until about 1440 that a movement for endowing grammar schools is discernible, as opposed to a series of individual projects. An important influence in shaping this movement was undoubtedly Henry VI (Fig. 42). He was not quite the first English monarch to interest himself in education, for Edward II had endowed the King's Hall in Cambridge and Henry V had dreamt of a college at Oxford, but none of his predecessors had founded a grammar school. Henry was still only eighteen in the summer of 1440 when he began the creation of what we know as Eton College, but which he thought of as the Royal College of the Blessed Mary of Eton. Its site was half a mile from Windsor, his birthplace and residence, whence he could watch the buildings rise and visit them once they were occupied. As conceived in the foundation charter of 11 October 1440, the Royal College of Eton was to be staffed by a body of eleven clergy, four clerks, and six choristers undertaking daily worship and masses. It also included an almshouse for twenty-five poor men, and a school of one master and twenty-five poor scholars receiving board, lodging, and teaching. The master was to be paid a stipend to teach grammar not only to the scholars but to anyone else in England, without charge.[52] It should be noted that Eton was not yet a close copy of Winchester College. The scheme was smaller and included public teaching, lacking at Winchester. At the same time its provision for schooling was a good deal grander than that of any other college or school foundation since the 1380s.

In the following February, 1441, the king issued a foundation charter for a university college to be called the Royal College of the Blessed Mary and St

Nicholas of Cambridge, for a rector and twelve scholars, no explicit connection with Eton being specified.[53] Here too the scale fell short of Wykeham's plans, but this was remedied in the years that followed. In July 1441 Henry visited Winchester College, presumably to observe it at work, and was so impressed by its headmaster, William Waynflete, that he immediately recruited him to be provost or chief officer of Eton. Subsequently the king revised his plans to equal those of Wykeham and even surpass them. In 1443 he issued statutes for Eton, but the text that survives is a later version of 1447. It shows a considerable augmentation of both the liturgical and the educational sides of the college. Ten chaplains were added to the staff of the chapel, the clerks were raised from four to ten, and the choristers from six to sixteen.[54] The school was increased to the size of Winchester, with seventy scholars and an usher to help the master. As at Winchester the scholars were to be chosen first from natives of the parishes in which the two royal colleges held property, secondly from natives of particular counties (in this case Buckinghamshire and Cambridgeshire), and thirdly from the rest of the kingdom.[55] In addition the school was to be open without charge to all comers.[56] Up to twenty sons of the nobility or sons of friends of the college could board in the college at their own expense, and a further thirteen poor pupils were offered food and clothing in return for acting as servants.[57] The Cambridge college, which came to be known as King's, was also remodelled on the lines of New College. In 1443 Henry stated that he had long since

60   Ewelme school (Oxon.), founded c.1448–50. Its building reflects the wealth and power of its founders, the duke and duchess of Suffolk.

determined that the scholars of Eton should proceed to King's when sufficiently instructed in grammar. In 1445 he secured papal approval to make it an establishment of a provost and seventy scholars, and in the following year he refounded it by letters patent and an act of Parliament.[58]

This promising start had a troubled sequel. While Henry was king Eton flourished. It was lavishly endowed with lands and privileges, and the full complement of scholars was reached as early as 1447. After Henry was deposed in 1461, Parliament nullified the grants he had made and the college's hold on its estates became uncertain. The new Yorkist king, Edward IV, did not look kindly on his enemy's foundation and granted much of its property to the nearby college of St George in Windsor Castle. In 1463 he secured a papal bull annexing Eton to St George's, and although this never became effective, the college revenues fell sharply. The number of scholars had to be reduced and the stipends of the teaching staff were cut by one third. Only gradually did the college's own efforts and those of its influential friends win favours from the king and the restoration of some of its old endowments. With the accession of Henry VII in 1485 the continuity

61   The impressively decorated windows of Ewelme school (Oxon.). The leopards' heads stand for the duke of Suffolk, William de la Pole, and the wheels for his wife Alice, Chaucer's granddaughter.

of the college was no longer in doubt, but the damage of the previous twenty-four years was felt for some time afterwards. The masters' salaries remained less than the founder had intended, and it has been doubted whether there was a full complement of scholars even in the early sixteenth century. Still Eton remains an impressive foundation, standing supreme with Winchester in wealth and resources above all other grammar schools of the fourteenth and fifteenth centuries.

To whom should the credit be given? Much of it must belong to Henry, since a royal project of this kind was so original. The fact that it was put in hand as he emerged from his minority suggests that it was an interest that had fired him during his teens. At the same time some of this interest may have stemmed from leading figures at his court in the 1430s. Archbishop Chichele had founded the grammar school at Higham Ferrers in the 1420s. Walter Lord Hungerford had taken the unusual step of sending his son and heir Robert to study at Oxford in 1437, probably as a prelude to a lay career. Later Walter planned an almshouse and school at Heytesbury, a scheme carried out by others after his death in 1449. William de la Pole, earl (later duke) of Suffolk, established Ewelme Hospital as an almshouse in 1437, and by 1450 one of its chaplains was charged with teaching grammar to the public (Figs 60 and 61). Sir Ralph Cromwell's college of Tattershall was begun in 1437, and similarly came to include a schoolmaster for the public by about 1460. The latter three schools cannot be dated for certain before the foundation of Eton, and may represent responses to it rather than anticipations of it. Chichele and Hungerford, on the other hand, both had an interest in schooling that predated Eton, and could well have helped to form the tastes of the king.[59]

Certainly the early years of Henry's adult reign, the 1440s, saw school education in fashion at court: one of the few occasions in English history when that has been the case. Of the three lay founders just mentioned, one (Cromwell) founded a school attached to a college and the other two almshouses with schools. At a lower social level, but still within the circle of the court, John Ferriby, controller of the royal household, founded the grammar school at Chipping Campden in about 1441, while Thomas Gloucester, cofferer of the household, planned one in Gloucester in 1447 that was never established.[60] Then there were Henry's bishops. John Carpenter, another of Henry's Eton agents and afterwards bishop of Worcester, had a hand in four educational projects. As master of St Anthony's Hospital (London), he instituted a free grammar school there in 1441. As bishop, in the early 1460s, he set up theological lectureships and libraries at Worcester and Bristol, together with a grammar school at Westbury-on-Trym in 1463.[61] William Alnwick, bishop of Lincoln when Eton was being planned (it lay in his diocese), was a co-founder of the grammar school of Alnwick in 1448,[62] while John Chedworth, provost of King's and Alnwick's successor-but-one at Lincoln, established the grammar school at

Cirencester in about 1457.[63] Thomas Beckington, the king's secretary, later bishop of Bath and Wells, published statutes for the education of his cathedral choristers in 1459, and built them a new schoolroom above the cloisters.[64] William Waynflete, promoted by Henry as bishop of Winchester, was responsible for grammar schools at Wainfleet in about 1464 and Magdalen College (Oxford) in 1480 (Figs 35–8 and 43).[65] The activities of the king's circle spread widely, if slowly, through England.

At least ten school foundations were established during the decade 1441–50, most of them of the small chantry grammar school type. Establishing statistics, however, is difficult. Although endowed schools have left more records than their un-endowed counterparts, their numbers have been inflated by Leach and others through the inclusion of chantry and guild schools that first appear as such at the Reformation.[66] Leach supposed that many of these schools had been maintained since the origin of the chantries and guilds concerned, whereas the duty of teaching is often likely to date from as late as the 1530s and 1540s. Restricting ourselves to schools whose origins can be dated for certain, it appears that the number of foundations fell from the ten of 1441–50 to three or so per decade from 1451 to 1480. That is not surprising, given the shadows that fell over Henry VI's reign from 1450 onwards, and the removal of a champion of schools from public influence. The outbreaks of the Wars of the Roses between 1459 and 1485 may well have distracted or deterred some other potential founders. Interest in founding schools revived between 1481 and 1500, with at least seven foundations per decade, and then climbed steeply to at least twelve in 1501–10, at least sixteen in 1511–20, and at least twenty-six in 1521–30. By that time over a hundred projects had reached fruition since Winchester and Wotton (Fig. 59), and more may need to be added. They reached from Cornwall to Northumberland, and from Kent to Cumberland. There were analogous foundations in Scotland by the late fifteenth century, and during the sixteenth they spread first to Ireland and later to Wales.[67]

THE ENDOWED SCHOOLS: AN ANALYSIS

The English foundations were not only numerous but consistent. Founders had models to follow by the 1440s, and their plans had a good many common features after this date. The first matter to settle was where to place one's benefaction. Some founders preferred to strengthen an existing fee-paying school, a number of which became free as a result. Gloucester, Ipswich, Lewes, Nottingham, and Warwick were places where an existing school was augmented or replaced by a new endowed institution. Other people sought to bring education to remoter areas like Newland, Rock, and Week St Mary, where schools were probably thinner on the ground. The choice of place seems to have been dictated by at least two considerations. One, which may be termed personal, was the desire of wealthy people to set their foundations in places with which they were connected. This perpetuated their family name, impressed their neighbours, and did good to their tenants and the poor. William Sevenoaks and William Waynflete both founded schools in the towns from which they came and took their names. The other motive may be labelled practical: the wish to strengthen schooling where it was struggling. Many school foundations, including some of the earliest, were in small country towns: Alnwick, Chipping Campden, Chipping Norton, Oswestry, Wotton, and so on. These may well have been the kind of places identified by William Bingham as having lost their schoolmasters. Providing more attractive salaries for teachers would have helped to reverse that loss.

The foundations of the period 1450–1530 continued to encompass colleges, of which a school formed part, and self-contained schools. College foundations with schools included Acaster Selby and Rotherham (both *c*.1483), Kirkoswald (*c*.1523), Wolsey's college at Ipswich (1528), and examples in both Oxford and Cambridge. The last such schools were founded by Henry VIII at Burton upon Trent and Thornton as late as the 1530s. But only a minority of schools were founded in colleges after 1450, for the good reason that only the very rich had the resources to endow such institutions. Most school founders chose the cheaper option of the small endowed school staffed by a single master. This involved purchasing or setting aside enough land, rent, or cash to provide an annual sum of between £6 and £10, the usual range of masters' salaries. Adding a small amount for building repairs, and reckoning income at about 5 per cent of capital, meant that such an endowment cost between about £140 and £220. Legal expenses were an additional charge, notably the fee for securing the king's licence to amortise the property – that is, to grant it for a religious purpose. This cost £10 at Wotton and £35 at Newland.[68] Lastly, the site and building of the schoolroom and master's dwelling would add another £20 or £30. Rising prices and wages after 1350 made any kind of endowed foundation more expensive than would have been the case in earlier times, but a school of this kind was not beyond the means of gentry or merchants individually. As we shall see, even the less wealthy acted as founders by pooling their resources.

Most of the small endowed schools founded up to the 1510s were chantries like Wotton, their employee acting as both priest and teacher. This marriage of functions deserves to be examined. The benefactors of education belonged to a society most of whose members had a high regard for the spiritual value of masses, both for the living who witnessed them and for the dead who could be prayed for at them. Chantries without schools were still being founded during the fifteenth and early sixteenth centuries, and those who founded chantry schools stood, at the cost of a larger endowment, to gain spiritual benefits from both chantry and school. So strong was the interest in chantries in the fifteenth century that the vast majority of school foundations in that century were of the chantry kind. Even guilds and monasteries that maintained full-time schoolmasters during this period tended to expect them to be priests, and gave them priestly duties such as saying masses. Few thought of founding a school whose master would be simply a schoolmaster. The Holbachs at Oswestry may have been one such example, William Sevenoaks was another, and John Ferriby was possibly a third. Sevenoaks, as we have seen, when planning the endowment of Sevenoaks school, even stipulated that the master should not be in holy orders.[69]

These were exceptions. In general the chantry school model remained the favoured one throughout the century, reflecting a relatively good supply of clergy and making teachers a more priestly caste than before. It was not until the early years of Henry VIII's reign that the association of schools and chantries began to go out of fashion. When Colet refounded St Paul's (1508–12) he followed earlier cathedral schools in leaving the mastership open to both priests and laymen, whereas parallel refoundations at Chichester and Worcester restricted the post to priests. The founders of Nottingham (1513), Bruton (1520), Winchcombe (1521), and Manchester (1525) followed the open policy.[70] A movement now began away from the chantry school towards the school alone, perhaps as a portent of the coming Reformation, perhaps as a practical solution to problems that arose when a priest-schoolmaster had to spend two or three hours each day saying mass and the daily services. Nevertheless the large constituency of chantry schools that had already been founded remained in being, and continued to grow in the 1530s as some pure chantries began to give teaching as well. It was not until 1548 that the association of schools and chantries was broken with the forcible dissolution of the latter by the Protestant government of Edward VI.[71]

The organisation and economy of the endowed schools varied in details. All were provided with patrons or governors to supervise them and appoint masters; these we shall examine presently. Some founders left the schoolmaster to administer the endowment; others gave this task to a monastery or a group of lay feoffees with responsibility for paying the master a salary in cash in quarterly instalments. Salaries, as already noted, tended to range between about £6 and £10, the latter sum being exceeded at only a few leading schools such as Magdalen College and St Paul's.[72] Most school resources were directed wholly to this salary, and the maintenance of scholars became rare. It was common to require masters to teach all comers freely, but not universal. The chantry schoolmaster of Newland was allowed to take fees at the rate of 4d. a quarter from those learning the abc and psalter, and 8d. from the grammarians.[73] Ewelme school was free only to people who lived in Ewelme or on the lands of the school's endowment.[74] Other founders restricted free schooling to the poor. Richard Felaw, merchant of Ipswich, who endowed its school in 1483, envisaged pupils paying fees except for the children of those with lands and tenements worth less than 20s. a year, or

62   Richard FitzJames (d. 1522), bishop of
London. He reorganised the theology
lectures at St Paul's Cathedral and
co-founded Bruton grammar school
(Somerset).

whose goods were under the value of
£20.[75] John Crosse, a prosperous
London rector who gave lands in
1515 to support a chantry school at
Liverpool, allowed the priest-schoolmaster to 'take his advantage from all
the children except those whose
names be Crosse, and poor children
that have no succour'.[76]

Foundations like Felaw's and
Crosse's demonstrate a wish to help
the poor to be educated. We should
nevertheless be cautious in assuming
that the endowment of schools gave
them benefit or was primarily meant
to do so. Several factors hindered the
access of the poor to schooling. Free
schools had not reached all the major
towns by the Reformation, and were
slower still to penetrate the countryside. Once a free school was beyond
walking distance, it was not free. Nor
was free education all that it seems.
Even today, in a state school, education can involve a surprising range
of costs: uniform, sports kit, classroom materials, and subventions for
this or that good cause. The guardian
of Edward Querton, who received free
schooling at Ewelme in 1464–5, paid
1s. 3½d. for such extras over about six
months, almost exactly the same as the
cost of teaching during that period.[77]
It is a moot point how far school
founders even meant to help the poor.
Eton College did in part, with its
group of poor scholars doing duties in
return for benefits. The 1518 statutes
of St Paul's, on the other hand, which ordered boys to bring books and candles
of wax and to pay 4d. each for enrolment, hardly suggest that Colet was
seeking to widen social access. Rather, his school became a popular place for
sons of gentry and merchants, as we have seen.[78] The statutes mention only
one poor scholar, who had to sweep the school and supervise the sale of the
urine. It is easy to imagine the low esteem of such tasks![79]

63   The gate of Cardinal College, Ipswich, Thomas Wolsey's abortive college and school foundation (1528–30).

The tendency for endowed schools to attract the respectable and comfortably off was probably common. Then, as now, such people realised the value of education and eagerly exploited what the schools offered. Winchester College was meant for children with incomes of less than five marks, but soon became dominated by the sons of gentlemen, merchants, yeoman farmers, or shopkeepers. Ewelme school was free only to certain boys, yet Querton was taught for nothing because he had a personal link with the cleric who managed it. Week St Mary may have been based in the remote countryside of north Cornwall, but it was frequented in the sixteenth century, we are told, by the gentry of Cornwall and Devon. In consequence the school turned into a boarding school, an unusual development, and maintained a manciple and a laundress to look after the boarding pupils.[80] The really poor were not ineligible for free education, but they needed a good deal of encouragement or ambition to use it. It took determination to buy school clothes and materials, give up a boy's lost wages, and cope with the social tensions that might arise when he mixed with his betters.

THE ENDOWED SCHOOLS: FOUNDERS AND PATRONS

The endowed schools have a social history. They embody an interest in education on the part of their founders and those who later supervised or supported them. The founders of schools, by the 1530s, included all the higher ranks of society down to parish clergy, urban burgesses, and rural yeomen. We have already seen how a group of noble founders operated at the court of Henry VI. There was another cluster in the early sixteenth century, centred on the Stafford earls of Derby. The first earl, Thomas, married Henry VII's mother, Lady Margaret Beaufort, who played a role in education comparable to that of Henry VI. As well as founding two Cambridge colleges (Christ's and St John's) and instituting the Lady Margaret chairs of divinity in both universities, she planned the grammar school at Wimborne Minster which was completed in 1511 after her death.[81] Thomas's grandson and heir by his first wife, Thomas the second earl, contributed to the endowment of a school at Blackburn in 1514, and reserved the nomination of the master to himself and his heirs.[82] His uncle Edward Stanley, Lord Monteagle, stepson to the Lady Margaret, planned a grammar school at Hornby near Lancaster, and although this was never endowed his son and heir maintained a teacher there.[83] A fourth member of the Stanley circle, Thomas Lord Darcy, founded the grammar school of Whitkirk.[84]

Bishops also took a lead as founders. William Smith of Lichfield and later of Lincoln endowed the grammar schools of Lichfield in 1495 and Banbury in 1501.[85] Richard FitzJames of London (Fig. 62), despite some bad relations with his dean, John Colet, shared Colet's educational interests to the extent of founding a grammar school at Bruton, and even laid down that its teaching should follow the 'good new form' of Magdalen College or St Paul's.[86] Richard Fox of Winchester (a co-founder of Grantham) and Hugh Oldham of Exeter (Manchester) are other examples.[87] Most of these men chose the modest template of the small endowed school, but Thomas Wolsey aimed higher in this respect as in so many others. Born at Ipswich and educated at Magdalen, Wolsey was briefly in charge of the latter's school and retained an interest in grammar in later life (Figs 79 and 80).[88] When he reached the summit of his power in the 1520s as a cardinal, papal legate, archbishop of York, bishop of Durham, and chancellor of England, with enormous wealth and power, he turned his mind to educational schemes of a grandeur appropriate to his dignity. His chief project was a great Cardinal College at Oxford, begun in 1525, but – like Wykeham and Henry VI before him – he also wished to endow a grammar school, following the tradition that rich ambitious founders should work in both sectors of learning.

Wolsey considered founding his school at Tonbridge,[89] but he eventually settled on his birthplace, Ipswich, whose school (already endowed) could be enlarged on a more magnificent scale. There, in the summer of 1528, he began the foundation of a second Cardinal College on the scale of Winchester and Eton (Fig. 63). The college was to support divine worship and (like other late medieval colleges) an almshouse and a school. Worship was entrusted to a dean, twelve fellows, eight clerks, and eight choristers, while the school was provided with a master, two ushers, and a body of scholars receiving board and lodging. Fifty scholars are mentioned, but this number may have been provisional. As at Eton free instruction was extended to outsiders. On 1 September Wolsey drew up a detailed curriculum for the school, based on the humanist grammars of Colet and Lily and on the reading of classical Latin authors. By the following January the headmaster could write that the school was proceeding well, the boys of good intelligence, and the numbers rapidly increasing. Eight months later, in September, Wolsey was sacked as chancellor and began to fall from power. His Ipswich college was seized and closed by the king a year later. The school survived, since it had pre-existing endowments, but Wolsey's scheme collapsed. He had not yet drawn up statutes, and it is not clear whether he planned that suitable pupils from Ipswich would go on to study at his Oxford college, as at Eton and Winchester, but such a plan seems likely.[90]

Almost every region of the country experienced foundations of schools by lay men or women and by clergy of lesser rank. They include members of well-established county families, like Joan Greyndour, foundress of Newland, and Sir Thomas Boteler, who willed the grammar school of Warrington in 1520.[91] There are landowners who had made their way as lawyers, such as Sir Thomas Lovell and Humphrey Coningsby, founders of Nottingham and Rock.[92] London merchants are well represented too. Besides the grocer William Sevenoaks we find the mercer John Abbot (Farthinghoe, 1443), the goldsmith Edmund Shaw (Stockport, 1487), the merchant taylor John Percival (Macclesfield, 1503), and his wife Thomasine (Week St Mary, 1506).[93] Outside London Richard Felaw, the Ipswich founder (1483), was a merchant, bailiff, and parliamentary burgess of the town, while Vincent Tehy, merchant and mayor of Southampton, joined in a scheme to found schools on the island of Jersey in 1496.[94] From the middle-ranking secular clergy come William Sponne, archdeacon of Norfolk (Towcester, 1448), John Combe, canon of Exeter (Crewkerne, 1499), and John Edmunds, chancellor of St Paul's (co-founder of Bruton, 1520).[95] Even heads of monasteries have a place: Robert Kirton, abbot of Peterborough (Kirton, by 1518), Richard Kidderminster, abbot of Winchcombe (Winchcombe, 1521), and Clement Wich, abbot of Evesham (Evesham, by 1536).[96]

Involvement in endowing schools was not limited to wealthy individuals. The fifteenth century also provides several examples of educational patronage by urban communities. Town corporations begin to be recorded defending or improving their local schools. In 1407 the mayor and citizens of Lincoln took an interest in the threat of a new choristers' grammar school to the livelihood of the city schoolmaster. They appeared as parties to the treaty between the dignitaries of the cathedral that settled the dispute, and the treaty, with its definition of the rights of the city master, was copied into the civic records.[97] At Coventry the corporation took the initiative in inviting a schoolmaster to their city in 1425, and in 1439 its members sent a deputation to remonstrate with the prior of the cathedral against imposing a monopoly of education, urging the right of any citizen to put his child to school where he pleased.[98] In contrast one or two other town councils placed their own restrictions on teaching, with the idea of creating an attractive post for an official schoolmaster. At Ipswich it was laid down in 1477 that the grammar master should have jurisdiction over all scholars, and in 1482 the council specified the fees he could charge.[99] At Bridgnorth in 1503 the council of the twenty-four burgesses ordered that no priests should teach children on their own account once the schoolmaster had come, but that every child should resort to the common school.[100] There is also at least one example of a town council arranging a school endowment. In 1478 the mayor and burgesses of Appleby granted three chantries in their patronage to a single chaplain who covenanted, while he held them, to keep a grammar school, taking fees according to ancient custom. By 1548 this school was free.[101]

Sometimes the maintenance of the town schoolmaster was borne by a religious guild or brotherhood representing local people, clergy and laity. Such guilds had long existed in towns to pay chantry priests or carry out works of charity, although few seem to have concerned themselves with education before the early fifteenth century. One of the first guilds known to have supported a school was St John the Baptist and the Holy Cross at Stratford-on-Avon, where the schoolmaster was teaching in a house belonging to the guild by 1413. In 1426–7 the guild paid nearly £10 to build a new schoolhouse, and by 1482 Master Thomas Joliffe, a wealthy local priest, gave an endowment to make the school free. The master was henceforth to be one of the five priests on the guild establishment, inhabiting a chamber in the guildhall and celebrating mass in its chapel.[102] At Chipping Norton a grammar school appears as one of the primary objects of the guild of the Holy Trinity, which the vicar and four of his parishioners were licensed to found in 1450.[103] In 1506 there are references to the maintenance of schoolmasters by the guilds of St Mary at Boston and the Holy Trinity at Wisbech.[104] Guilds existed in the countryside too, led by gentlemen and yeomen, and the dissolution of the chantries in 1546–8 brought to light many cases in which the guild priest ran a school, either on his own initiative or on that of his employers. The guild of Brailes is a good example. Founded in the mid fifteenth century under the patronage of Warwick the Kingmaker, it maintained two priests, one of whom was assigned in 1537 to teach a grammar school.[105] In this way even guild members, middling or modest in rank, might contribute resources or steer their application to the purpose of schooling.

The same kinds of people who founded schools became involved in supervising them. Establishing a school entailed appointing a patron who would oversee its management and appoint its masters. Sometimes patronage remained with the founder's family. The Beverstone branch of the Berkeley family chose the schoolmasters of Wotton, while the Greyndour family and their heirs the Baynhams did so at Newland. Alternatively the responsibility was given to a group of local feoffees, as at Chipping Campden and Oswestry. London merchants tended to place their foundations in the care of London guilds: thus John Abbot's school at Farthinghoe was entrusted to the mercers, and Edmund Shaw's at Stockport to the goldsmiths. By the early sixteenth century borough corporations were also becoming involved. Agnes Mellers chose the corporation of Nottingham to supervise the free school which she co-founded there in 1512, and Joan Cook did the same at Gloucester in 1540; each lady's husband had been a burgess and mayor of the town.[106] A third solution was to give the patronage to a religious house. The Augustinian canons of Bruton carried out this function at Bruton, the Benedictine monks of Winchcombe at Winchcombe, and the Benedictine abbot of Faversham at the school established there in 1527.[107] As university colleges grew larger, stronger, and more familiar to outsiders, they too began to be seen as suitable patrons. Childrey, founded in 1526, was put under the government of the Queen's College (Oxford), while St John's College (Cambridge) acquired responsibilities at Pocklington (1525) and Sedburgh (1528).[108] Colleges became more popular for this purpose once monasteries disappeared at the Reformation.

The endowed schools were the largest but not the only benefactions to education. Many humbler gifts like buildings, books, and bursaries were made to schools during this period. In 1484 Robert Harset, clothmaker of Long Melford, bequeathed part of his large house there to be used as a school, while Isabel Hyet, a lady of the forest of Dean, left land worth about 10s. a year in about 1490 to support poor scholars of Newland.[109] Wills, which begin to survive in large numbers after the end of the fourteenth century, provide many examples of bequests to support 'scholars', either of schools or of universities, and many of those who made such bequests are likely to have dispensed educational charity earlier in their lives. The needs of poor scholars were urged by Langland in the late fourteenth century and Edmund Dudley in the early sixteenth century. 'Let not to depart [i.e. give away] with some of your silver,' urged Dudley, 'to comfort and relieve poor scholars, and especially such as be willing and apt to learn which lack exhibition. Let them have what is necessary . . . for a better chantry shall ye never found.'[110] Casual alms to scholars are rarely recorded, but the household accounts of Sir Henry Willoughby of Middleton in the 1520s show the knight dealing out pennies to poor scholars as well as making larger gifts to his neighbours' sons when they went to school or university.[111]

THE PROVISION OF SCHOOLING, 1350–1530

The provision of schooling in England during the twelfth and early thirteenth centuries had owed much to the cathedral schools, in terms of their resources and status. There continued to be grammar schools in virtually every cathedral city after 1350, together with song schools for choristers and lectures in theology in association with the secular cathedrals.[112] The shape of these grammar schools remained broadly traditional. Masters received small stipends or none, and most of their pupils were local fee-paying boys. Development came chiefly in modest forms such as the acquisition of buildings and books, and only five of the twenty-one English cathedral cities (and none of the four Welsh ones) came to possess an endowed grammar school where teaching was wholly or partly supplied without charge. The five exceptions were Durham (1414), Lichfield (1495), Chichester (1498), St Paul's (1508–12), and Worcester (between 1504 and 1532).[113] In the first three cases the initiative was due to the bishop, at St Paul's to the dean, and at Worcester to a guild of citizens. Much the largest and most successful of these endowed schools was St Paul's, which achieved national prominence, but Chichester also prospered in the first years after its re-endowment. One of its earliest masters was the grammarian John Holt, and both he and his successor William Hone left the school to become the tutors of Henry VIII.[114]

Most cathedral schools by the later middle ages, however, were probably of provincial rather than national importance. The rise of the universities in the thirteenth century caused Oxford and Cambridge, especially the former, to become the leading national centres of school education as they were of academic studies. Both towns attracted grammar masters offering teaching to schoolboys, to youths learning business skills, and to university undergraduates. Parents who wished their sons to follow non-graduate careers as gentry, in the Church, or in administration might as well send them to board and be taught in a university town as anywhere else, especially Oxford, where there were masters of repute such as John Cornwall, John Leland, and Thomas Sampson.[115] Students of grammar could lodge privately or live in one of the university halls that catered for such people, the names of which appear in a list of halls and their specialities compiled by the Warwickshire antiquary John Rous in the 1440s.[116] By this time the house where Leland had taught, called Peckwater Inn, was a community of lawyers, but five other halls are mentioned by Rous as places where grammar was still studied: Tackley Inn, Ing Hall, Lyon Hall, White Hall, and Cuthbert Hall, and there is independent evidence that the first three were rented by grammar masters during the middle years of the century. A further hall, St Hugh's, housed a grammar school in 1458 (Fig. 64).[117]

In the second half of the century the number of teachers at Oxford appears to have declined. This may have been the result of general problems, such as the epidemics which racked the university at that time, or it may have reflected the competition of the new endowed schools. Their appearance in so many localities, often teaching for nothing, must have attracted some families who might formerly have sent boys to study grammar in Oxford. The grammar halls disappear from the records one by one, and in 1492 the two masters of arts deputed by the university to oversee the schools were said to have no function.[118] This decline was briefly arrested by William Waynflete's foundation of Magdalen College School in 1480, which gave Oxford a free grammar school for the first time, with its opening series of distinguished masters: Anwykyll, Stanbridge, and Holt.[119] Magdalen School continued to flourish during the sixteenth century, but after 1500 it was hardly of national importance. Banbury, Eton, St Paul's, and Winchester had equally good and influential teachers, and drew in students as widely as Magdalen, or more so. Sixteenth-century Oxford was merely one place, not *the* place, to go for school education.

Events at Cambridge seem to have paralleled those at Oxford. Until the middle of the fifteenth century there was more than one fee-paying grammar school in the town and the 'master of glomery', appointed by the archdeacon of Ely, had the duty of supervising them. After 1500, on the other hand, he is hardly ever mentioned, and the office and its duties must have largely ceased to exist.[120] Here too the decline of older schools was offset by the endowment of a new foundation. In 1496 John Alcock, bishop of Ely, was licensed to found Jesus College for a master, six fellows, and 'a certain number of scholars being educated in grammar'. Alcock built a schoolhouse in the college, but he died in 1500 and his work was completed by his successor as bishop, James Stanley. In 1506 Stanley appropriated the rectory of Great Shelford to the college to support a schoolmaster, 'a good man, learned in grammar and rhetoric'. Assisted by an usher, he was to teach four choristers maintained by the college and to give free instruction to boys from outside. The school continued until the Reformation, and (like Magdalen) was spared in 1549 when royal visitors to both Cambridge and Oxford forbade the teaching of grammar in the university and its colleges.[121] It disappeared only in 1567, apparently through a decision within Jesus College, and Cambridge did not get another free grammar school until the seventeenth century.

Outside the university towns the schools of London were the most numerous and important. At the beginning of the fifteenth century the three ancient foundations of St Paul's, St Martin's, and St Mary Arches were still the only fully recognised places of teaching, but other masters were active. We hear of one based near the house of Crutched Friars in 1392, when the friars were accused of tricking one of his pupils into signing an agreement to join them.[122] Another, slightly later in date, was John Seward of Cornhill, whose teaching career goes back to at least 1404 and who died in 1435. His writings, as we have noticed, included Latin poems, epigrams, and grammatical treatises, shared with a circle of friends that included William Relyk, who kept a school at 'The Cardinal's Hat' in Lombard Street and was himself an author of Latin verse.[123] Several more masters appear in London records in the fifteenth century, probably working in private; it is not clear with how

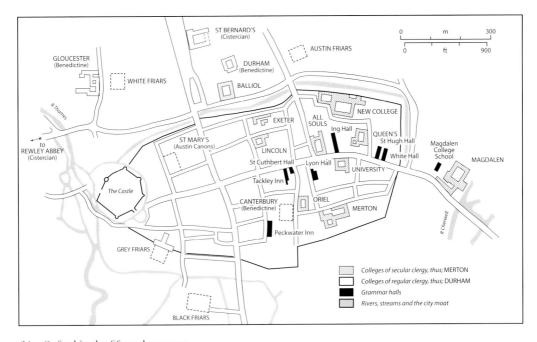

64   Oxford in the fifteenth century.

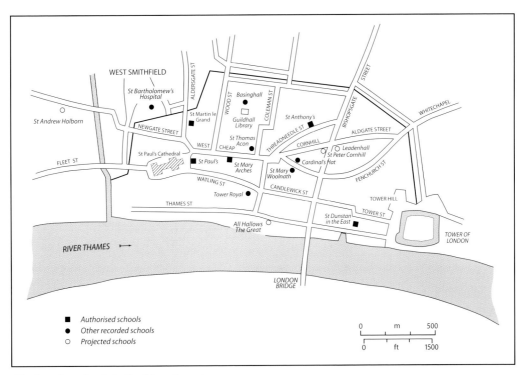

65   London schools in the fifteenth century.

much permission.[124] The authorities seem to have wavered about how many more schools there should be. In 1441 the bishop of London agreed to the request of John Carpenter, the master of St Anthony's Hospital and future bishop of Worcester, for permission to appropriate the revenues of the city church of St Benedict Fink to maintain a free grammar school in the hospital for the public.[125] This made London one of the earliest large English towns to possess such a school, and for the next hundred years St Anthony's enjoyed a high reputation. Its opening may have encouraged John Stafford, a layman who had taken holy orders late in life, to bequeath lands in 1444 to endow a chantry in the hospital of St Bartholomew, Smithfield, whose priest was to receive an enlarged stipend for teaching boys in grammar and song. Poor children and the founder's kin were to be taught for nothing.[126] There is no record that the scheme secured official approval, but it was probably effective, at least for a time, since schoolmasters are mentioned teaching grammar in the hospital in 1459 and 1476.[127]

Then a change of policy occurred. In 1446 the ecclesiastical authorities – the archbishop of Canterbury and the bishop of London – attempted to enforce the rights of the official schools, with the king's support. They claimed that this was necessary because unqualified masters presumed to hold schools 'in great deceit both of their scholars and of the friends that find [i.e. pay for] them'. The authorities made a concession by increasing the number of approved grammar schools to five: the traditional three, St Anthony's, and a school otherwise unknown in the church of St Dunstan in the East.[128] This brought a protest from four city rectors: William Lichfield of All Hallows the Great, Gilbert Worthington of St Andrew Holborn, John Coote of St Peter Cornhill, and John Neel of St Mary Colechurch and master of the hospital of St Thomas of Acon. In a petition to the king, submitted through the House of Commons in 1447, they drew attention to the superfluity of young people in London needing education, not only those born in the city but incomers from elsewhere, 'some for lack of schoolmasters in their own country . . . and some for the great alms-giving of lords, merchants, and others, the which is in London more plenteously done than in many other places of this realm'. This, the rectors argued, required an appropriate number of schools and masters in London, and not a monopoly 'for the singular avail of two or three persons . . . . For where there is a great number of learners and few teachers, and all the learners be compelled to go to the same few teachers and to none others, the masters wax rich in money and the learners poor in cunning [i.e. knowledge], as experience only showeth.' Lichfield and his colleagues asked permission to appoint a grammar master in each of their parishes, removable and reappointable by them and their successors: in other words to establish four more grammar schools in the capital. The king's response to this was not unfavourable: let it be done as it is desired, provided it be done with the advice of the bishop of London or the archbishop of Canterbury.[129] This advice may have been obstructive. None of the projected schools has yet been traced in later times except for one in the hospital of St Thomas of Acon, mentioned in 1535, which may have originated from the petition.[130]

The probability is that the ordinance of 1446, while not greatly increasing the number of authorised schools, failed to prevent a number of smaller operations continuing in private (Fig. 65). We saw in an earlier chapter how Simon Eyre, a merchant, draper, and former lord mayor, bequeathed £1,000 in 1459 to establish a college of priests at Leadenhall in Cornhill, including a school of grammar, song, and writing open to the public.[131] Eyre must have thought his plans compatible with the regulation of schooling in London, but in the event they were not effective and fifty years elapsed before the city gained another major endowed school in the form of Colet's refoundation of St Paul's between 1508 and 1512.[132] This refoundation was possible because Colet (Fig. 78) was dean of St Paul's, the school was an authorised one, and Colet was rich and able to endow it on a generous scale. We have already noticed the liberal salaries he provided for the headmaster and his deputy, the spacious layout of his schoolroom and chapel, the writing of new grammars for the lessons, and the large enrolment of 153 boys from London and beyond.[133] St Paul's was an outstanding foundation, but it was not as original or exceptional as is sometimes supposed. Some of Colet's arrangements followed tradition, like the opening of the mastership to laymen and the choosing of a scriptural number of pupils. Moreover other English schools of the period had their innovations and successes; indeed in 1598, when John Stow looked back at Tudor education in London, he gave the palm to St Anthony's.[134]

The evidence for schools in the larger towns that did not have cathedrals resembles that of previous centuries in being impressive in general but often elusive in detail. In some of them, such as Boston, Bristol, Coventry, Gloucester, and Nottingham, there are fairly frequent allusions to schools and their masters during the late fourteenth and fifteenth centuries, but in others, of which Newcastle, Plymouth, and Southampton are examples, few or no references have yet been found. Once more this is primarily due to the shortcomings of source material or to lack of research. The likelihood is that all the larger towns had fee-paying schools in this period, and sufficient custom to keep them in existence. This judgment is made, as before, on the grounds that records of schools in towns imply their presence in places of similar size and wealth where schools are not recorded. The point has already been made that the larger towns were relatively slow to acquire endowed schools, as if local people were felt to be able to afford education without the need for subsidy through endowment. Lancaster's free school began to be founded in 1469 but was not completed until 1500. Hull got one in 1479, and Ipswich in 1483. During the early sixteenth century other such schools were founded at Guildford, Lewes, Nottingham, and some other places, but they were still not the norm when the Reformation began.

66   A king at table with youthful attendants. By the fifteenth century boys and youths were often educated in royal and noble households.

Several important towns like Bristol and Gloucester, and even certain large cathedral cities (Canterbury, Exeter, Norwich, Salisbury, and York), did not get free schools until the 1530s or later.

The presence of schools in smaller towns and villages is also more perceptible after 1350, although once again this does not necessarily indicate an expansion of numbers. As well as the market towns and some villages that benefited from the endowment of schools, there are numerous records of schools that were not endowed, even in some small towns and villages, especially in counties where not many free schools had been founded. Norfolk, for example, provides evidence for seventeen schools in small towns and villages between 1350 and 1530, nearly all of them unendowed. In Yorkshire the list stretches to over thirty, and there may have been many more. Prof. Moran Cruz has listed dozens of references to 'scholars', often in rural parishes, who may have learnt reading at home or song in a parish church, but who reinforce the sense of a region in touch with education of one kind or another.[135] Similar references could be collected elsewhere in England. Even when we make allowances for some of these schools being of poor quality or short-lived, and for the likelihood that not all existed at the same time, the picture is an impressive one.

PRIVATE SCHOOLING

Medieval education should not be thought of simply in terms of officially recognised schools and endowed foundations. A great deal of teaching took place in less formal private surroundings, even in towns with well-established schools.[136] London, as we have seen, had many teachers besides the official ones, and although the capital was far larger than even the largest provincial cities it was not unique in this respect The principal schools of Exeter and Winchester were both called the 'high school' by about 1400, meaning 'chief school' and implying the presence of others. Bristol had more than one grammar school, and Canterbury, Gloucester, Norwich, and York each had at least one school other than the authorised foundation, with limited public access. Private elementary teaching was probably widely available in towns, without any regulation. There were two other important categories of private school, both ancient in origin. The first comprised the schools of the religious houses: principally for members of these houses, but often taking in members of the public. These will be examined in the following chapter. The second was to be found in the great households of the king, the bishops, and the lay magnates.[137] These had been centres of education since Anglo-Saxon times, and their role in this respect not only continued during the later middle ages but becomes easier to trace. This is partly the result of more plentiful records and partly because household schooling tended to become more formally constituted, especially during the fifteenth century.

The pioneering household in terms of developing educational institutions appears to have been the king's, as one would expect in view of its larger size and more sophisticated organisation. By the early fourteenth century it contained two groups of teachable boys: the children of the royal chapel, who assisted in singing the daily services there, and the 'henchmen' who were noble youths with ceremonial duties (Fig. 66).[138] The children of the chapel, numbering between eight and ten, received a musical education in the first instance, but they were not merely choristers, nor were they turned away when their voices had broken. They had the opportunity to learn grammar (their grammar teacher is first mentioned in 1401) and to proceed, if they were able and willing, to higher study at the king's expense. In 1317 Edward II founded the first royal university college, the King's Hall (Cambridge), its original nucleus consisting of a royal clerk to act as master and twelve former children of the chapel studying the arts course. Throughout the fourteenth and fifteenth centuries a proportion of the children proceeded either to the King's Hall or to other royal foundations in the two universities.[139]

The henchmen numbered eight by the 1440s, six of the king and two of the queen. They received education from the master of the henchmen, who acted as their general tutor, and from the grammar master who taught the boys of the chapel. The master of the henchmen was responsible for ensuring that they attended worship each day and for training them to joust, wear their armour properly, and understand rules of precedence. He supervised their training in 'languages' (probably French), as well as in harping, piping, singing, and dancing.[140] The grammar master was a priest or layman experienced in poetry and grammatical rules, and therefore evidently a career teacher. His services were also available to certain poor clerks of the king's almonry (probably boys maintained to do duties in the chapel) and to other men and children of the court desirous of learning his skills. The earliest grammar master known by name is Francis Philip, who probably held the post by 1521. He is recorded solely because, in December 1523, he was the ringleader in a plot with other members of the royal household to seize a consignment of taxation on its way to London in order to raise men and to capture Kenilworth Castle, or so it was said. His career came to a premature end on the scaffold at Tyburn.[141] The household got a more distinguished master with his successor, Robert Whittington, one of the leading grammarians of the day.[142]

The royal interest in education was reflected in other great households. Here too late medieval records throw more light than before on specific arrangements for teaching. Archbishop Morton of Canterbury had boys at Lambeth Palace in the 1490s under the teaching of Holt, whose grammar *Lac Puerorum* was made for their use.[143] Thomas More received part of his education in Morton's household. Another contemporary bishop, Thomas Langton of Winchester (1493–1501), kept a similar school. The humanist writer Richard Pace, who was one of the pupils, has recorded the delight with which the bishop heard his scholars repeat in the evening what their teacher had told them during the day.[144] Thomas Wolsey, grand in this respect as in everything else, gathered nine or ten young lords with an instructor to teach them, their parents doubtless glad of the chance to gain their children such favour. One of the boys was the earl of Derby, then in his teens, and another the son and heir of the earl of Northumberland.[145]

Some lay magnates took in boys as well. A previous earl of Derby, the future Henry IV, had henchmen in his household by 1388, and they occur in connection with several other noblemen in the fifteenth and early sixteenth centuries.[146] George duke of Clarence maintained five in 1468, together with a squire to teach them as in the royal household, and Henry Percy, earl of Northumberland, kept three, along with two young gentlemen whose families paid for their board and lodging (Fig. 46). The earl employed a grammar master too.[147] A third magnate, Edward Stafford, duke of Buckingham, had henchmen and a grammar master in 1521, the latter an Oxford BA who had studied for his degree at the duke's expense.[148] Even a knight might attract pupils if he was as important and influential as Sir Thomas Lovell, knight of the garter and treasurer of the royal household. When Lovell died at Enfield near London in 1524 his household included two henchmen who rode in the hearse with his body, while nine young gentlemen attended in funeral clothes with their yeoman 'keeper' and their writing master.[149]

A further kind of private education was provided in parishes by clergy and parish clerks.[150] Teaching children was not their duty, other than helping them to learn their basic prayers, but it is easy to imagine reasons why it might be done: the wish to train an assistant, a favour to other people, or a means of earning money. Sometimes the teaching may have been elementary, like that of a clerk teaching children to read, or practical, when a priest trained his clerk in church tasks. At other times the lessons were more ambitious and reached the level of a grammar school. The vicar of Cockayne Hatley, or someone employed by him, was teaching music and grammar in the vicarage in 1359 when a pupil brought a legal action for having been improperly beaten.[151] A second example emerges from a plea for debt, in which the rector of Bilborough claimed an unpaid bill in 1506 for boarding and schooling a boy for twelve weeks, probably in grammar because the rector afterwards became schoolmaster of Nottingham.[152] A third piece of evidence gives us a glimpse of a small private school in a rectory. In 1508 Richard Alkborough, rector of Burrough, witnessed a conveyance of property with ten young gentlemen who were living with him as scholars: boys from leading families in the county of Leicestershire, such as Ashby, Skeffington, and Villiers. Alkborough had a strong teaching vocation, and also moved to work as a professional grammar master in later years.[153]

DEVELOPMENTS, 1350–1530

How far did schooling change in its organisation and distribution between 1350 and 1530? This is not an easy question to answer, because the information we possess is so limited. Much, perhaps most, of the teaching that went on took place in homes or elementary schools and has left little trace. The majority of the surviving evidence relates to the better-established schools that taught grammar, and there is more of this evidence by 1530 than there is in 1350. In part this reflects the foundation of endowed schools, which generated more records than unendowed enterprises, but it is also because the survival rate of documents increases with time. The two years cannot really be compared.

As we observed early on in this chapter, it is important not to be seduced by the growth of evidence alone into assuming an expansion of education at particular times. Even in the twelfth century William FitzStephen talked about the presence of private teachers in London. There may have been more provision in major towns during the thirteenth and early fourteenth centuries than we know of. In 1439 William Bingham certainly saw things in terms of decline. Caution is also needed when identifying a process of 'laicisation', a process by which the control and funding of school education

is said to have moved from the hands of the clergy into those of the laity.[154]
The most certain index of development is that of the endowment of schools.
Even here we must be careful, in that the principal financial support for
education was probably always the funding of individual scholars by parents
and benefactors, to which systematic endowment formed only an extension.
Nevertheless, so many schools were endowed from the 1440s onwards that,
as we have argued, it is possible to talk of a movement of endowment from
that date, with common features in the schools endowed. The result was the
placing of many schools on a firmer footing than before, which did not, of
course, prevent them being badly run. By the 1530s the way one planned
and endowed a school was well established and known, both the college
school and the small independent foundation.

Late medieval schooling helped establish the context for the Reformation.
It spread a taste for texts that could be read, complementing images that
could be seen. Paradoxically, some of the schools that contributed to this
process were to suffer from the Reformation, particularly those linked with
religious houses and chantries. Nevertheless, the educational interest built
up in England over the previous centuries proved strong enough to survive.
The organisational structures of Wykeham, Lady Berkeley, and their
successors were so effective that they went on being copied and reproduced,
long after the world for which they were meant had changed.

8

The Religious Orders and Education

THE TWELFTH CENTURY

By about 1100 the English monasteries were no longer the chief or only providers of teaching. Schools were spreading to minsters, towns, and eventually villages, their teachers educating many pupils and taking the lead in studying grammar and writing textbooks. These schools supplemented monastic education, but they did not supplant it. On the contrary; education in monasteries also grew in volume and value during the twelfth, thirteenth, and fourteenth centuries. Quantitatively the religious orders of monks, nuns, and eventually friars increased from a few dozen houses at the time of the Norman Conquest to as many as a thousand by about 1300, containing over 17,000 clergy.[1] Qualitatively many of these houses extended their ambitions and activities. They tried to keep abreast of developments in the study of the liberal arts, philosophy, canon law, and theology. When university education developed they embraced it, founding friaries, priories, and colleges in the university towns to house scholars. Locally they admitted new groups of pupils, lay boys and girls whom they provided with board, lodging, and teaching in reading, grammar, or music. Some houses even became involved in public education, supplying governance and help for local schools. Altogether the involvement of the religious orders with education was an important one down to their dissolution in the 1530s, whose story deserves to be told.

This does not mean that education in religious houses was unaffected by changes in schooling elsewhere, particularly by the proliferation of free-standing schools for the public. Up to 1100, when such schools were rare, monasteries and nunneries had been obliged to teach their recruits themselves. Many of these recruits entered the houses as 'oblate' children, given by their parents to be brought up and trained until they reached adolescence or adulthood and could be professed as monks or nuns.[2] This system was still envisaged in the guide for monasteries issued by Archbishop Lanfranc, known as the 'Monastic Constitutions', in the 1070s or 1080s. He ordered that when boys were offered as oblates, their parents should bring them already tonsured into the monastery church at the time of mass. After the gospel, the oblate was to carry the bread and wine for the eucharist and offer it to the celebrant priest. Then the parents went with their son to the altar and wrapped his hands in the altar cloth, as a token that he too was a gift to the church. They had to promise the abbot that they would not remove the boy from the monastery, and their promise was written down and witnessed. The abbot was directed to undo the boy's cloak and say to him, in Latin, 'May the Lord strip you of the old man.' Then he was to give the boy a monk's cowl, with the words 'May the Lord clothe you with the new man.' After this the boy would be taken away to be fully shaven and clad in monastic dress.[3]

Some other details of the life of the oblates can be gathered from Lanfranc's constitutions. They were supervised by the 'master of the children', a trustworthy monk, assisted by other masters. They lived in the monastery and had their own chapter meetings as the monks did, for the punishment of misdemeanours. They attended many of the divine offices in the monastery church and sang antiphons when necessary. They learnt reading and practised chant. When they reached adolescence they made their profession as monks. By the twelfth century, however, the practice of child oblation in England was dying. It seems to have died for reasons of both need and opinion. Need was changing, due to the growing number of free-standing schools. Boys could be educated in such schools and join a religious order, if they developed the vocation to do so, when they grew up. This reduced the problem of discontented or unsuitable monks who had to stay in the monastery because they had been offered to it. Opinion was changing too. The twelfth century was an age of ecclesiastical law-making, aimed at both clergy and laity. Those who made these laws based them more emphatically than before on human psychology: what people could be expected to know or imagine about good or evil. Children, it was thought, gained mature understanding only when they gained physical maturity at puberty. Until then they were not capable mentally of committing deadly sins, and need not therefore go to confession or receive anointing when in danger of death. Equally they were not sufficiently adult to partake of communion (the bread and wine of the mass), to marry, or to take monastic vows, because they could not fully know what these rites involved.[4]

Accordingly the monasteries gradually stopped receiving children as oblates. The last recorded cases in the English Benedictine houses belong to the mid twelfth century. Meanwhile the new reformed order of monks, the Cistercians, had already decided in 1134 not to receive boys under the age of fifteen, and this threshold was raised to eighteen in 1175.[5] In 1168 the Benedictines of St Augustine's (Canterbury) procured a papal decree that no one should be received as a novice there until he was eighteen.[6] These initiatives set the minimum age somewhat higher than was observed later on, when novices were often received and even professed as monks in their mid

67   The monk-scholar Hugh of St Victor
(d. 1141), teaching other monks.

teens. The offering of prepubescent children, however, became relatively
uncommon except in certain nunneries and (as we shall see) some friaries.
Young girls were still regarded as suitable for oblation in the thirteenth and
fourteenth centuries. In 1282 the archbishop of Canterbury urged the nuns
of Stratford-at-Bow near London to veil such a girl as a nun, on the grounds
that she would be better able to learn their rule 'by reason of her minority'.[7]
Mary, the ninth child of Edward I, was given to Amesbury Priory in 1285
when she was seven,[8] and Katherine, the daughter of Sir Guy de
Beauchamp, entered Shouldham Priory at about the age of six in 1359.[9]
Edward III's granddaughter Isabel, whose father was Thomas of Woodstock,
duke of Gloucester, joined the Minoresses of Aldgate (London) as a child in
about the 1380s. After her father's death in 1397 she was offered the chance
to leave, but stayed and rose to be abbess.[10]

   The twelfth-century monasteries sometimes gave education to boys who
did not become monks. In 1149 Geoffrey of Quarrington, a Lincolnshire
landowner, gave his son Ralph to be brought up in Ramsey Abbey for a
seven-year period.[11] This was at about the same time that Gerald of Wales
went to school in Gloucester Abbey under Master Hamo,[12] before going on
to study at Paris and to a career as a secular cleric. These boys may have
resembled the noble youths whom we shall encounter later, boarding in
outer monastic precincts and being taught by men who were not monks.
There were probably also some poor boys in twelfth-century monasteries,

68   A Franciscan friar
preaching, one of the activities
that required friars to learn
philosophy and theology.

who were being maintained with a view to their either becoming monks or
following other careers. In the 1170s Queen Eleanor of Aquitaine sent a
child whom she had found abandoned on the highway to be brought up at
Abingdon Abbey, where we are told that he studied letters.[13] Even as they
shed their oblates, monks kept a door open for boys from the outside world
to stay and study in their houses.

THE FRIARS

The religious scene changed dramatically with the appearance of the friars
under their first founders, Francis and Dominic, at the beginning of the
thirteenth century. Friars followed a new form of the monastic life. They
lived in a religious community and said daily prayers, like monks, but in
other respects they differed markedly. They did not stay inside their
cloisters but went out to do pastoral work among the laity: preaching, giving
spiritual advice, and hearing confessions (Figs 68 and 69). They were more
strictly bound than monks to a life of poverty, having no endowments to
support them and living almost entirely from voluntary donations – hence
their name of 'mendicants' or beggars. Furthermore, they became zealous
pursuers of learning. Preaching and hearing confessions demanded more

69   A friar hearing a nun's confession, another activity underpinned by study.

knowledge than monks or canons needed, and more than most of the parish clergy possessed. The friars developed centralised systems of education to enable their members to gain the training they required for pastoral work. Humbert of Romans, master general of the Dominican Order who died in 1277, explained it thus: 'Study is not the end of the order, but it is exceedingly necessary to secure its ends, namely preaching and the salvation of souls, for without study we can do neither.'[14] The emphasis on study was a particular characteristic of Dominic and his followers, but all the mendicant orders came to realise the benefits of learning and to develop ways to promote it.

Four great orders of friars organised themselves in the first half of the thirteenth century. The Dominicans or Black Friars were the earliest to reach England in 1221, followed by the Franciscans, also known as the Friars Minor or Grey Friars, three years later. They were the two larger orders, the Dominicans having some fifty-three houses by the fourteenth century and the Franciscans fifty-seven. The first Carmelites, or White Friars, came in about 1240 and the Augustinians in 1249; these orders were smaller in size. There were usually thirty-seven Carmelite houses in the later middle ages, and thirty-three Augustinian. The total number of friars reached a peak of about 5,000 in the early fourteenth century, but this fell by as much as a half immediately after the Black Death, rising slowly again to 3,000 in the fifteenth and early sixteenth centuries. Very roughly the friars formed a

70   Bartholomew the
Englishman (d. 1272),
Franciscan friar, scholar, and
author of the widely read
encyclopaedia *On the
Properties of Things.*

quarter of the population of the religious orders at most periods during the
later middle ages.[15]

At first the friars adopted the new monastic policy of recruiting young
men in their late teens or older. Most of the mendicant orders, however,
came to modify this requirement in favour of admitting younger entrants.
The Dominicans held most firmly to the adult rule. In 1228 they laid down
that novices must be aged eighteen when admitted, and although this
threshold could be reduced to fifteen after 1265, special permission to do so
was needed from the order's leaders.[16] The Franciscans too decided on
eighteen in constitutions of their order drawn up in 1280, but they were
more sympathetic to younger entry. Not only did they allow boys to be
received from the age of fifteen in exceptional cases, but in 1316 they
lowered the age of entry to the minimum of fourteen permitted by canon
law. Nine years later they allowed even younger children to join the order if
their parents offered them, although such entrants could not be fully
professed until they were fifteen.[17] The Augustinians set their entry at
fourteen in 1290, but sixty years later they reduced it to eleven, and after
1385 allowed boys to come in below that age.[18] Such youthful admissions
prompted disapproval from outside the orders. In 1357 Richard FitzRalph,
archbishop of Armagh, a critic of the friars, accused them of enticing boys to
join them when they would never have been able to attract grown men. He
claimed to have met a man whose son had been 'abducted' by friars before
he was thirteen.[19] Shortly after this the university authorities at Oxford
passed a statute prohibiting friars from receiving converts who were less
than eighteen, but the friars appealed to Parliament, which rescinded the
statute in 1366.[20] In 1402 another attempt was made to restrict the reception

71 A novice being admitted as a
monk in the late thirteenth century.

of boys, this time by a petition from the House of Commons to the king
requesting that the age of entry should be raised to twenty-one. The king's
response was cautious. He reaffirmed that the minimum age of entry should
be fourteen, but allowed younger children to join the friars if their parents
so wished.[21] Boys continued to enter the mendicant orders, and the fifteenth
century provides more than one example of entry at ten or eleven.[22]

The early Dominicans envisaged that their recruits, being young adults,
would be basically literate in Latin when they arrived.[23] These entrants
would spend their first year learning the rule of the order and the daily
round of prayer, under the supervision of a master of the novices. Later they
would study practical theology to fit them for preaching and hearing
confessions. Each friary was to have one or more lectors giving daily lectures
on the Bible and on Peter Lombard's Bible commentary, known as the
Sentences. Attendance at these lectures was a requirement of friars
throughout their lives, so that education was seen as a continual process, not
a finite and qualifying one. As time went on, however, it is likely that some
houses also provided teaching in grammar. This became necessary as the
pool of recruits was extended to include younger and, it appears, less

educated people. Roger Bacon, the Franciscan philosopher, claimed in 1271 that 'many thousands' entered his order and that of the Dominicans who could read neither the psalter nor Donatus.[24] Grammar teaching also became desirable as the friars laid more emphasis on higher, academic education, for which a firm grounding in Latin was necessary. In 1328 the Dominican general chapter ordered that no one should be permitted to study logic until he was proficient in grammar.[25] Two references to Dominicans learning grammar survive from the early sixteenth century. In 1520 Clement Guadel was allowed to go to grammar school while living in the friary of Yarm,[26] and in 1538 the London friary of the order had a grammar master maintained at the expense of the Goldsmiths' Company.[27]

The foundation of the Dominicans coincided with the rise of the English universities in the early thirteenth century.[28] University study centred on the arts course, taken by most students, which included the seven liberal arts (grammar, rhetoric, logic, arithmetic, music, geometry, and astronomy) and the three philosophies (natural, moral, and metaphysical). There were also four higher studies: medicine, civil law, canon law, and theology. At first the Dominicans regarded the arts and philosophies as worldly subjects, incompatible with the study of theology which they wished to pursue. The order's constitutions of 1228 declared that students should not study the books of the 'Gentiles' and philosophers, without a special dispensation from the order's leaders.[29] But it gradually became apparent that theology could not be studied at more than an elementary level without at least a mastery of logic. Accordingly in 1259 the Dominican general chapter ordered each of its provinces to have a centre for the study of the liberal arts, meaning principally logic.[30] Later still, around the end of the century, philosophy was also embraced, including Aristotle's works on metaphysics, physics, and astronomy. Gradually an educational staircase evolved by which members of the order could climb from grammar through logic and philosophy to theology of an academic kind. The general chapter of 1297 laid down that recruits to the order should spend two years of instruction in song and the divine office before going on to the study of the liberal arts.[31] Finally, at a meeting at Genoa in 1305, it set out the order of studies as follows. No one was to study logic unless he had passed two years in the order. After three years of logic he could progress to natural philosophy (science, in our terms), and after a further two years he could listen to lectures on the *Sentences*. A student who had made progress in logic and philosophy and had heard the *Sentences* for two years could proceed to a *studium generale* – a centre of advanced study open to friars from throughout the order, which might or might not be in a university town.[32] In 1309 it was stipulated that a year should be passed in hearing lectures on the Bible before entering the *studium generale*.[33]

Instruction in logic, philosophy, and theology was not provided at every Dominican friary, but at a smaller number of centres in each province of the order. In 1335 the general chapter commanded each province (of which England was one) to maintain two centres for the study of arts, two for natural philosophy, and two for theology.[34] This minimum was probably exceeded in England, but the situation is not very clear. The study of logic and the arts is mentioned at Glasgow in 1476 and at Oxford in 1505, while philosophy was apparently learnt at King's Lynn in 1397. Towards the end of the fourteenth century there are indications that the higher study of theology was pursued at several English friaries: Guildford, Ipswich, Lincoln, Newcastle-on-Tyne, Norwich, and Thetford, as well as London in 1475.[35] Lastly there were the *studia generalia* at Paris, Oxford, and later Cambridge, where the Dominicans established houses for their students. At this level study meshed with that of the universities, the friars attending public lectures, taking part in disputations, and sometimes graduating as bachelors or doctors of theology. Such study was also international. Dominicans from overseas were received at English houses, and some of their English counterparts crossed the Channel to read theology at Paris and elsewhere.[36]

The organisation of studies among the early Franciscans is badly obscured by lack of records, but it was well developed by the middle of the thirteenth century.[37] The first historian of the order in England, Thomas of Eccleston, tells us that by 1254 there were thirty lecturers solemnly disputing in the English houses, and three or four who lectured without disputation. He added that the minister in charge of the English province, William of Nottingham, had assigned students in the universities to succeed these lecturers on their death or removal.[38] At first the Franciscans shared the Dominicans' distrust of learning that was not theological. Their ideal was to have lectors in their friaries lecturing on practical theology, and to provide such lectors by sending their better students to university, so that they could return well instructed for the purpose. Eccleston mentions lecturers who had studied at Oxford going on to teach in friaries at Bristol, Canterbury, Hereford, Leicester, and London.[39] There are also references to theology schools at Gloucester, Northampton, and Norwich in the middle of the thirteenth century.[40]

Then, like the Dominicans, the Franciscans came to realise that theology could only be effectively studied after a grounding in logic and philosophy, preceded if necessary by basic training in grammar. During the thirteenth century schools of grammar, logic, philosophy, and theology developed – not in every house but in at least one friary within each district or 'custody', of which there were seven in England. In 1292 the general chapter of the order commanded centres to be set up for the study of the liberal arts, where young members might be instructed.[41] In 1421 a decree prescribed that friars must lecture on arts and philosophy for seven years and on the *Sentences* for at least one year before they could graduate as a doctor of divinity in a university.[42] Almost nothing is known of the siting of the

Franciscan schools of grammar, logic, or philosophy, but they may have been quite widespread. Dorchester is mentioned as teaching boys in 1485, presumably partly in grammar.[43] Six major centres of the study of theology were mentioned in England in 1337: Coventry, Exeter, London, Norwich, Stamford, and York.[44] These friaries belonged to different custodies, and it is probable that each served the other houses in its district. The teaching of theology in some of these schools approached that of a university, and we know of some leading friar-theologians who lectured in them, including William of Ockham and William Woodford.[45] Most Franciscans probably remained at this level of study; only a minority went on to learn theology at a *studium generale* such as Paris or Oxford. Like the Dominicans, the Franciscans drafted their members from one country to another for purposes of higher education.

The educational arrangements of the Augustinians followed much the same pattern.[46] The young friars of the order spent a year as novices during which they learnt the daily services and became eligible to study grammar. A decree of the general chapter in 1315 directed each province (England being one) to set aside two houses for the teaching of grammar. In reality there were probably more, since we hear of fourteen boys at Thetford in 1424 and sixteen at King's Lynn in 1446, both in East Anglia, while the friary at York is known to have owned a good collection of grammar books.[47] Next the students could pass to schools of logic and philosophy, which were ordered to be established in each province in 1326, either in one or in two places. In England three of these schools are mentioned, corresponding to three of the four districts or 'limits' into which the province was divided. Friars from the limit of Cambridge would have attended Norwich for this purpose, those from Lincoln, Leicester, and those from Oxford, Bristol. After at least three years in such a school one could attend a *studium generale*, of which there were three kinds in the order. The English province possessed its own *studia generalia* for its own friars, and once again these corresponded to the limits: King's Lynn for Cambridge, Stamford for Lincoln, and London for Oxford. Two other advanced schools at York and Lincoln were called *studia concursoria*, but their exact nature is unknown. Lastly the schools at Oxford and Cambridge ranked as *studia generalia* of the whole order, to which friars from all over Europe might be sent to study after they had passed three years in the *studia generalia* of their provinces. All three grades of *studia generalia* were concerned with the study of theology, but logic and philosophy could also be pursued there.

The Carmelite constitutions issued in 1324 ordered that places should be provided in each province for the education of the friars in grammar, logic, philosophy, and theology.[48] Traces of these study centres can be found in England, where Hitchin and Maldon are known to have had schools of grammar and logic, while philosophy was studied at Winchester and theology at Coventry, London, and Stamford.[49] Higher than these schools were the *studia generalia* where theology and philosophy could be studied, and to which all the provinces in the order might send their friars. Curiously enough the constitutions of 1324 mention London as the English *studium generale*, but subsequently Oxford and Cambridge seem to have taken its place. In 1396 we hear that England was divided into four districts centred on London, Norwich, Oxford, and York, each of which sent an equal number of friars to the universities. A year later Pope Boniface IX ordered that the study of arts in the order should last for seven years, with another seven for theology, after which three years must be spent lecturing upon the *Sentences* and one upon the Bible before taking the doctorate of divinity.[50]

Monasteries, as we shall see, involved themselves in education beyond their own members. They often came to accommodate almonry boys and choristers on their premises – boys who were not monks – providing them with schooling which was sometimes extended to other children from the neighbourhood. Friaries differed from monks in not maintaining boys in this way, but there are signs that some outsiders may have benefited from friary education nevertheless. There must have been leakage from the friars' own recruitment systems, as some boys failed to develop vocations and passed out into the world again, having had teaching at the friars' expense. 'Secular' students who were not friars may have had been admitted to the friars' lecture rooms. The Dominican constitutions of 1228 made a distinction between public and private lectures, and although the general chapter of the Franciscans in 1292 forbade seculars to be admitted to lectures on law and 'physic' (natural science), the prohibition suggests that they may have been allowed to attend those on theology. Secular clerks are mentioned in the classrooms of the mendicant orders on the Continent.[51]

By the end of the middle ages there are bits of evidence that friars taught younger boys who either came from the outside world or ended up following careers there. In 1492 Henry Lord Grey of Codnor bequeathed an endowment of £3 6s. 8d. per annum to the Carmelite Friars of Nottingham to maintain a friar teaching children the alphabet and further studies without charge, until they were able to become priests.[52] The use of the term 'priests' suggests that he envisaged the children as becoming parish clergy as well as priest-friars, and his requirement that the friar should say masses for the founder made the endowment similar to the foundation of a chantry school. It is not known if Grey's bequest became effective, but the education of outsiders was also an issue in the Augustinian Order in 1497, when its general chapter forbade the entry of seculars to the friary schools of grammar and song.[53] Nevertheless, a man named John Gaunte of Tickhill gave evidence during a tithe dispute in 1568 that in about 1502–13, between the ages of four and fifteen, he had 'learned in the schools in the friars of Tickhill' (an Augustinian house) before leaving to take up a career in agriculture.[54] A similar case is that of Henry Triplett, who told an Oxford church court in 1579 that sixty years earlier, when he was fourteen, he went to school for a year at the Dominican priory in the city. He later became a glover.[55]

Two other pieces of early Tudor evidence mention the teaching of children by friars, although they do not specify whether this was done 'in house' or by friars visiting private households. One is a story in the humorous anthology *A Hundred Merry Tales*, published in 1526, which tells how a friar taught Latin to a gentleman's son, inadvertently causing the boy to write a sentence containing a rude remark about friars.[56] The other occurs in a letter of 1533 written by John Coppledyke, a Lincolnshire gentleman, on behalf of an Augustinian friar who was being transferred to London from one of the local houses of the order. Coppledyke praised the friar's diligence in teaching his children and added, 'such another, to my mind, of his conversation and kindness and good disposition in my house, shall be very hard for me to get'.[57] Friars may have had more influence on public education than has been realised.

MONKS AND REGULAR CANONS AFTER 1200

The influence of the friars spread beyond their own organisations to the older religious orders: monks and the similar kinds of clergy known as regular canons. There were two great orders of monks in England after the twelfth century: the Benedictines or black monks, and the Cistercians or white monks. The black monks, the more numerous, had about 250 houses and 4,200 members (including Cluniac houses) in the peak period between 1216 and 1350, while the Cistercians owned about seventy-five houses with some 2,100 members.[58] After the disappearance of child oblation in the twelfth century, recruits to the monastic life were often admitted aged about fourteen to sixteen, not vastly older than those who joined the friars.[59] Entry began, as it had done in previous centuries, with the ceremony of being 'clothed' in the monastic habit (Fig. 71). This was followed in due course by 'profession', the taking of the religious vows. Clothing could lead to profession within months or even weeks, so that it was possible – and apparently quite common – to make a full commitment as a monk in one's mid teens. After admission and clothing, an entrant was known as a novice and spent at least one year, and sometimes more, under the care of the master of the novices, a senior monk. The novice master taught practical rather than intellectual matters: the rule of the order, the behaviour and duties required in church and cloister, and the traditions of the house. Most demanding of all was the process of learning (often by heart) the material of the daily services – prayers, hymns, and psalms.[60] A novice's status did not change when he made his profession or even when, a year or so later, he became ordained as a priest. It probably ceased only when he was recognised as having learnt the rule and the services, and as being capable of following the religious life without supervision.[61]

Those who became monks in this way after the twelfth century had probably undergone some form of schooling, either as almonry boys in the same monastery (a topic to be treated presently) or at a school in the outside world. In principle they were expected to be literate before they were admitted. Bishop Walpole's injunctions for Ely Cathedral in 1300 declared that scholars or clerks seeking entry as monks were to be received 'if literate and otherwise fit'.[62] Archbishop Winchelsey, visiting Gloucester Abbey in the following year, ordered that candidates should be tested for their knowledge of letters and song.[63] The monks of Christ Church (Canterbury) refused admission to an inexperienced clerk named Edmund Basing in 1324, and advised him to learn reading, song, and grammar before presenting himself again.[64] These qualifications were meant to ensure that monks could fulfil the basic literary tasks of the monastic life: performing the liturgy correctly and doing a modicum of private study. However the Rule of St Benedict, the basic inspiration of monastic life, was not very exacting with regard to study, since it laid down only that each monk should receive a book at the beginning of Lent and read it for a short space every day.[65] This fell far short of the standards set by the friars, and a realisation of the shortfall dawned on both the black and the white monks by the middle of the thirteenth century. In 1245 the Cistercian general chapter (i.e. synod), meeting at Cîteaux in France, urged that every abbey should have facilities for study if possible, and that there should be at least one place in each of the order's provinces (of which England was one) where monks could study theology all the year round.[66] Two years later a general chapter of the English Benedictine houses of southern England made a similar pronouncement. A lecture in theology or canon law was to be established in each abbey or priory where resources permitted, to be read by either a religious or a secular person.[67] The effect of these orders is not certain. It cannot have been easy to persuade monks to embrace the higher standards of the friars, particularly in the case of the Benedictines, a congregation of independent houses, hard to mould to common purposes.

Still, the impulse towards improvement did not die away. On the contrary, it grew, as the importance of university study, and the benefits it gave to friars and ordinary non-monastic scholars, became ever more apparent. In 1275 Christ Church (Canterbury) instituted a lecturer in theology, William Everal, who was a friar in the absence of suitable monks – a point that caused misgiving. 'This,' grumbled the chronicler of the priory, 'was unheard of in former times, and what will be the result of this lecture and school the future will show, since novelties produce quarrels.'[68] Two years later the Benedictine chapter of Canterbury province decided that the time had come to establish a centre at Oxford University for brethren of the order, 'so that study may cause our religion to flourish again'.[69] A rate was levied on each Benedictine house to pay for the scheme, but this caused disagreements that held up the project and enabled the white monks to overtake the black. In 1280 Edmund earl of Cornwall, a leading patron and supporter of the Cistercians, came to an agreement with their general chapter to found a place of study at Oxford for white monks. The foundation, Rewley Abbey, opened in the western suburbs of the city in 1282 – the first attempt to found a monastic college at an English university. But Rewley disappointed expectations. Poorly endowed and apparently lacking in scholars, it turned within a century into an ordinary Cistercian monastery.[70]

The Benedictines did better than this in the end, although their progress was slow. In 1283 Sir John Giffard of Brimpsfield provided them with a site for a college, also in the west of Oxford, but nothing had been done with the site by 1288 when the leaders of the order called their colleagues' attention to the 'reproach we have borne in the past for not erecting a house at Oxford for the students of our order, while the Cistercians . . . have built their place of study like prudent and honest men whom the Lord has blessed'.[71] By 1291, however, the first Benedictine scholars appear to have arrived at Oxford, and in 1298 the study centre of the black monks, Gloucester College, was formally established on Giffard's land.[72] It reflected the disparate nature of the Benedictine Order, since although there was a prior in charge and a common hall and chapel, the chambers were built and maintained by different monasteries, which housed their own monks there or rented them out to others. The coats of arms of some of these monasteries can still be seen attached to the former monastic buildings, now part of Worcester College. Two of the largest Benedictine houses held aloof from the Gloucester scheme in favour of their own arrangements. In 1286, before Gloucester College was properly open, the monks of Durham Cathedral began to buy land in Oxford for a house for their own students, duly established as Durham College.[73] In 1331 Christ Church (Canterbury) opened a hall for four monks, subsequently endowed as Canterbury College in 1361–3.[74] A third Benedictine house carried out a similar but smaller project at Cambridge. Here the prior of Ely Cathedral, John Crowden (1321–41), founded a house (later known as Borden's Hostel) for a few of his brethren who wished to study in the university. This may have accommodated one or two monks from other monasteries of the order.[75]

William Broc of Gloucester Abbey, the first Benedictine monk to gain a doctorate of divinity at Oxford, took his degree in 1298 to the great rejoicing of his order. Five abbots and many priors, monks, clerks, and gentlemen attended the festivities held to mark the occasion.[76] Others followed him, both white and black monks, making it possible for monasteries to employ monks to lecture who had studied or graduated at university. Christ Church (Canterbury), which had been obliged to introduce a friar-lecturer in 1275, remained dependent on friars for the purpose until 1314, but after that it was able to utilise monks.[77] Worcester Cathedral boasted two of its own graduate monks as lecturers in the early fourteenth century: Richard

Bromwich and Ranulf Calthrop, both doctors of divinity. It also lent its graduates to other Benedictine houses. One of them, John of St Germans, lectured at St Augustine's (Canterbury) from 1308 to 1310, while Calthrop did so at Ramsey until 1318, when, despite the pleading of its monks, he was recalled to Worcester to take the place of Bromwich.[78]

The Benedictines and Cistercians were complemented by a large number of religious houses in England belonging to the three orders of regular canons – the Augustinians or black canons, the Premonstratensians or white canons, and the Gilbertines. These orders, founded in the twelfth century, resembled the monastic orders as communities engaged in daily prayer but often had closer links with the outside world, supervising parish churches, hospitals, and schools. The Augustinians, the largest of the three, with about 208 houses and about 2,700 canons in the early fourteenth century, were second in numbers only to the Benedictines and equally widespread over the kingdom. All three orders resembled the monks in expecting their novices to be literate in Latin and to study, and in providing teaching by senior canons to achieve this. All three came to espouse the cause of higher education, as the monks did, but less is known of this process among the canons. Not until 1325 do we know of an ordinance of the Augustinian general chapter requiring scholars from the order to be sent to the 'schools', signifying the universities. In 1334 the requirement was repeated, and a rider was added that heads of houses should provide teachers (*lectores*) in their monasteries and assign them times and places to teach.[79] The Premonstratensians are not recorded as making any general arrangements for education in England, but twenty-five of their canons from England are recorded as studying at universities between 1382 and 1532.[80] Since the Augustinians had no university college until the end of the middle ages and the Premonstratensians never had one, they had to rent rooms for their canons in other colleges or private houses in the university towns.[81]

Curiously it was the smallest of these orders, the Gilbertines, with only twenty-four houses and about 250 inmates, which achieved most during the late thirteenth century, probably because it was more compact and so more easily organised. In 1290 its chief house, the priory of Sempringham, received a papal licence to appoint a doctor of theology to teach the brethren in that subject.[82] At the same time it acquired a site in Cambridge for a house of study, which opened in 1291 as the priory of St Edmund. The students there, according to one local observer, were assiduous in attending lectures and disputations.[83] St Edmund remained a small institution, however, and may have ceased to take scholars by the mid fifteenth century. In 1301 Sempringham was given a site in Stamford by a Lincolnshire rector, Master Robert Luttrell. According to the bishop of Lincoln, who confirmed the grant in 1303, this was intended to provide a place for scholars of the order to study philosophy and theology, but nothing more is heard of this scheme.[84] In later times any Gilbertine houses that sent members to university are likely to have made individual arrangements for their accommodation, like the other orders of canons.

The eighty years from 1245 to 1325 saw nearly all the great orders of monks and canons develop an interest in improving their members' education. The main objective was the study of theology, which would enhance the religious life of their houses and enable them to keep up with the friars. At first the impulse for improvement came from within the orders themselves, but during the first half of the fourteenth century the popes began to encourage the process. The first papal intervention was the decree *Ne in Agro* issued by Pope Clement V at the general council of Vienne in 1311. It laid down that every monastery whose resources sufficed for the purpose should maintain a master to instruct the brethren in the elementary branches of learning.[85] Elementary learning meant grammar and logic, and the decree probably aimed to improve the basic education of monks as well as ensuring that they went through the usual progression of studies before moving on to theology. Clement's decree was carried further by his successor but one, Benedict XII, a Cistercian monk who reigned at Avignon from 1334 until 1342 and earned a reputation as a reformer of the clergy. During his pontificate Benedict issued three reforming constitutions for the three largest religious orders: *Fulgens sicut Stella* for the Cistercians in 1335, *Summi Magistri* for the Benedictines in 1336, and *Ad Decorem Ecclesie* for the Augustinian canons in 1339. The question of education is prominent in each of them.[86]

Benedict's educational policies centred on two points. Basic teaching was to be given to all monks in their monasteries, and the best monastic students were to receive university training in theology or canon law. The Benedictine and Augustinian constitutions required each monastery to maintain a schoolmaster to instruct the monks in the 'primitive sciences', meaning grammar, logic, and philosophy. This master could be a member of the order concerned, a member of another order, or a secular (priest or layman). If a secular, he was to receive board, clothing, and a salary of not more than 20 *livres tournois*, equalling about £3 6s. 8d. in the English currency of the day. If a member of the order, he was entitled to only 10 *livres tournois* together with his food and clothing. Secular students were not to be admitted to these monastic schools. There was no corresponding provision for schoolmasters in the Cistercian constitutions of 1335, presumably because the white monks had recently made laws on the subject. Four years earlier the general chapter of their order had laid down that communities of forty monks or more should maintain a lecturer to instruct the younger brethren in grammar and logic, and that smaller houses should either do the same or send their monks to larger ones for the purpose.[87]

The pope's legislation went on to provide that monks and canons who had passed through the elementary branches of learning should study theology or canon law or, in the case of the Cistercians, theology alone. His arrangements for the Cistercians reflected their strongly centralised organisation, which transcended national frontiers. There were to be five local centres of higher study in western Europe and an international one at Paris. Every monastery of over forty monks was to choose two of them to study theology at Paris, while monaseries over thirty monks were to choose one. Houses of between eighteen and thirty monks were to send one of them to the local centre of higher study, which in the case of the British Isles was to be Oxford. The constitutions for the Benedictines and Augustinians did not provide for an international study centre, because these orders were not organised internationally. It was thought sufficient in their case that each monastery with twenty inmates or more should send one of them to university, the place being unspecified. As the focus of this chapter is the local facilities for education in monasteries, we need only summarise the remaining history of monks and canons at the universities. There were three major developments after 1350, each of them centred on the early years of Henry VI's reign (1422–38) and partly the result of discussions about monastic reform that took place under his father, Henry V, especially at the so-called Council of Westminster in 1421. In 1428 the Benedictines acquired land to build a hostel for their students at Cambridge, which came to be known as Buckingham College.[88] In 1438 the Cistercians replaced Rewley with a new house at Oxford called St Bernard's College, on the site of the modern St John's. Its buildings and corporate life developed slowly, and it became a significant body only in the early sixteenth century.[89] An Augustinian college at Oxford, St Mary's, had a similar long gestation. The order acquired the site in 1435, but the buildings were not completed until the 1520s, and in the meantime monasteries sending canons to Oxford went on making their own arrangements for lodgings.[90]

Let us now return to the provision of schooling for monks in their own religious houses. The cloister was a traditional place for teaching novices, in terms of learning the rule and the daily services. Westminster Abbey had seats for its novices and their master in the west cloister walk by the late thirteenth century,[91] and Durham had similar arrangements on the eve of the Reformation. In 1593 an anonymous author set down his memories of Durham as it had been in about the 1530s, memories now known as *The Rites of Durham*:

> In the west side of the cloister, on the south side of the cloister door, a little distant from the said door, there is a strong house called the treasure-house. . . . Over against the said treasure-house door there was a fair great stall of wainscot where the novices did sit and learn, and also the master of the novices had a pretty stall or seat of wainscot on the south side of the treasure-house door over against the stall where the novices did sit and look on their books, and there did sit and teach the novices both forenoon and afternoon. And also there were no strangers nor any

other persons suffered to molest or trouble any of the said novices or monks in their 'carols' [i.e. cubicles], they being studying on their books within the cloister, for there was a porter appointed to keep the cloister door for the same use and purpose.[92]

The cloister was one of the focuses of monastic life out of church, so it was an appropriate place for a school, but we should allow for the possibility that some monasteries used other locations instead or as well. We hear of schools or *studia* at St Augustine's (Canterbury), Gloucester, and St Albans; these may have been places for student monks to learn grammar, logic, or philosophy.[93]

The number of novices in a monastic school can rarely have been large. Nine are mentioned at Winchester in 1460, but in 1496 there were only four, and in 1533 just one. At times there were none at all. At Durham there are said to have been usually six. Durham and Winchester were large houses, with forty monks or so, but the majority of houses had fewer inmates and are likely to have taken in a small group of novices only every few years, training them as a cohort. New arrivals were put under the general care of the master of the novices, a senior monk or canon, who would have taught the rule and the liturgy. Another suitably learned brother of the monastery might deal with grammar, logic, and the other subjects required by the papal legislation. William Trent, who fulfilled this duty at St Albans in about 1400 was later described as 'another Donatus', 'a profound grammarian and a distinguished instructor of the monks'.[94] Robert Walton, monastic teacher at West Dereham in 1503, and Robert Joseph, who held the post at Evesham in about 1530, were both former university scholars, capable of teaching to a high standard.[95] Monks with such qualifications were not always available, however, and monasteries often found it easier to hire a secular priest or layman for the purpose. Winchester Cathedral employed a succession of such men from 1495 until the dissolution. In 1495 Peter Druett, MA, was appointed to teach grammar at a salary of £4, and in 1510 William Parkhouse, MA, BMed, agreed to teach logic for £6 as well as acting as medical adviser to the monastery. John Pottinger, the last of these masters, who took up office in 1538, was not a graduate, but he had studied at New College (Oxford) before marrying and taking the post of usher at Winchester College.[96]

The papal legislation laid down that monastic schoolmasters, whether monks or seculars, should be paid by the house. Most of the evidence about payments relates to seculars, as in the case of Winchester, and we hear little of the practice in relation to monks. A rare example is one at Bath Cathedral in 1532 in which the prior appointed John Pitt, one of the senior monks, to the office of schoolmaster at an annual stipend of £4.[97] Sometimes an external benefactor helped with the costs. In 1519 the earl of Northumberland was paying £6 13s. 4d. for the wages of the schoolmaster of

Alnwick Priory, a house of white canons.[98] In 1527 John Cole, warden of All Souls College (Oxford), endowed a schoolmaster to teach grammar to the novices of Faversham Abbey and to secular boys from the town outside.[99] During the later middle ages the use of money grew in monasteries, and the custom developed that monks should receive a *peculium*, or allowance in cash, to buy clothes and other necessary gear, instead of having such things supplied by the monastery. In some houses the novices and junior monks were expected to pay the schoolmaster from this allowance, like boys in a fee-paying school. Bishop Alnwick of Lincoln, for example, visiting Newnham Priory in 1442, an Augustinian house, and finding the canons 'unlettered and almost witless', ordered the provision of a schoolmaster supported partly by the house and partly by his pupils.[100] A similar arrangement is mentioned at Glastonbury Abbey, a Benedictine monastery, in 1538: there the house is said to have paid the master £2 13s. 4d. and the monastic students as much as 20s. a quarter.[101] This pay-as-you-go system did not always work; in 1440 another Augustinian priory, Kyme, had only two student canons, and the senior brother who taught them refused to discharge his office fully because they could only afford to pay him 20d. a quarter.[102]

After the 1330s, then, the best cloister schools extended their teaching well beyond the monastic rule and the daily services. In the Benedictine Order the schooling of novices increased to several years to allow for all that had to be learnt.[103] Large monasteries often possessed substantial collections of books, some of which were suitable for teaching purposes.[104] Sometimes these books included the basic grammars and poems studied by boys in free-standing schools, and appear to have catered for novices in their mid teens who were still at that level.[105] Two grammatical miscellanies that seem to have been written or used by monks of Canterbury and Winchester replicate, in their contents, the miscellanies produced in schools in the outside world.[106] In the larger houses, especially Benedictine ones, basic grammar might be followed by more advanced work in Latin language or by higher studies. The books of the Durham novices in 1395 included Latin dictionaries, Guillaume Brito's guide to difficult words in the Bible, Priscian, and a treatise on logic.[107] In the early sixteenth century these novices were said to have been kept at their books until they could understand the services and the Scriptures.[108] After about 1500 monastic schools, like public grammar schools, moved to teaching humanist Latin. The library catalogue of Syon Abbey, drawn up between 1504 and 1526, lists works by grammarians such as Perotti, Sulpizio, and Valla alongside those of medieval authors.[109] Robert Joseph of Evesham studied at Oxford in the 1520s where he met monks from Bury St Edmunds, Glastonbury, and elsewhere, who read Erasmus and were critical of medieval scholasticism. When he was recalled to Evesham to teach the novices in 1530, he introduced them to typical humanist texts. We still possess his inaugural lecture, on Terence's play *The Eunuch*, as well as another on a poem by Baptista Mantuanus in praise of St Katherine.[110]

University study also continued to be an ideal for monks and canons in the fourteenth, fifteenth, and early sixteenth centuries. Our Durham witness believed that novices judged apt for learning were picked out and sent to Durham College (Oxford) to study theology.[111] Indeed the monasteries bred more university graduates between 1500 and 1540 than in any earlier period. At the same time there was much variation from house to house. Glastonbury, a large abbey, boasted only four graduate monks between 1505 and 1539, all bachelors of theology or canon law. None of the four gained a doctorate.[112] Many medium-sized and smaller monasteries rarely sent members to university, because they had none suitable or because it was too expensive. The most practical way of educating monks beyond the 'primitive sciences' was to do so at home, and the most conscientious foundations provided lectures, chiefly on theology but occasionally on canon law. William Gillingham, doctor of theology, lectured at Christ Church (Canterbury) in the 1380s, as did Richard Godmersham, doctor of canon law, in the early fifteenth century.[113] Thornton Abbey had a lecturer in canon law in the latter period.[114] Richard Kidderminster, abbot of Winchcombe from 1488 to 1525, tried to make his abbey a model of study and learning. He claimed that in his time two bachelors of theology lectured daily, one on the Old Testament and the other on the New, while he expounded the *Sentences* twice weekly.[115] The last burst of monastic lecturing came in 1535, when Henry VIII required all monasteries to provide a daily lesson of Holy Scripture lasting one hour, to be attended by all the monks or canons.[116]

The underlying weakness of monastic education seems to have been its disparate nature. Communities were often smaller after the Black Death, and it was hard for them to keep their senior members up to the mark in terms of learning, let alone deal adequately with the entry of a cohort of novices. Time and again bishops who visited monasteries in the fifteenth and sixteenth centuries found that teaching was inadequate or lacking, both of novices and of the older brethren.[117] Some houses were persistent offenders. The Augustinian priory of Canons Ashby housed a dozen canons in the fifteenth century. When Bishop Gray of Lincoln visited it in about 1432 he ordered that someone should be assigned to teach the novices and younger canons in the elementary branches of learning. At the next visitation ten years later, one of the brethren protested about the lack of a grammar master, and a third visitation in 1520 found the house again without a teacher.[118] Even the greater abbeys and priories were not always satisfactory. Defective teaching arrangements were noted at Tewkesbury in 1378, Winchester in 1387, Durham in the same period, Peterborough in 1432, and even Christ Church (Canterbury) in 1511, to name but a few.[119] At Glastonbury in 1538 two junior monks actually complained that they had no access to books or to the library.[120] Still, the ideals of monastic education continued to be remembered by the authorities, and visitations did something to maintain them. On the very eve of the Reformation the convocation of Canterbury (representing the clergy of southern England) ordered the re-enforcement of Clement V's decree *Ne in Agro*, and Henry VIII's monastic visitors inquired whether novices had a master to teach them grammar and good letters as late as 1535.[121]

NUNS

Nuns were a smaller presence in medieval England than monks, regular canons, or friars. There were only about 146 nunneries, containing some 3,350 nuns at the peak of their numbers in about 1300. Many of the houses were poor, and nuns lacked the public roles as teachers and nurses that they acquired in later times. Over half of the houses followed the Benedictine rule and the rest were female counterparts of other male orders such as the Augustinian canons, Cistercians, Dominicans, Franciscans, and Gilbertines.[122] In principle, a nun, like a monk, was expected to be literate, and there are records of Church authorities requiring such women to be able to read and to sing (Fig. 72).[123] In practice, the education of nuns resembled that of women generally. It took place at home or in a nunnery, might be given by a parent or nun who was not a professional teacher, and was less formal than the schooling of boys. It involved learning the abc, the basic prayers, and the psalter, but did not venture far into the grammar of Latin. As a result most nuns could read Latin in the sense of recognising and pronouncing words, but their ability to understand and study it would have been limited. Only in French or English would they have read with full comprehension.

Nunneries followed monasteries in their system of training novices, or at least in the system that prevailed in the male orders up to the early fourteenth century (Fig. 73). There was (or should have been) a mistress of the novices, whose duty was to train them in the rule of their order and in the daily services.[124] Sometimes it may have been necessary to teach them reading and song, as it was at Ankerwyke Priory in 1441.[125] Like monks, however, nuns did not always carry out their duty to educate, and bishops sometimes had to correct this fault at their visitations. Only a few of the nunneries belonged to national or international organisations which could coordinate and develop their work. Most were either Benedictine or Augustinian – independent houses whose heads did not even meet and agree laws together to the extent done by their male counterparts. Unlike monks and canons they failed to improve their educational provision in the thirteenth and fourteenth centuries, and the Church authorities did not encourage them to do so. The attainments of most nuns remained low and old-fashioned in consequence. They probably varied little from those of wealthy lay women; indeed, it was one of the weaknesses of nunneries that they failed to develop a religious life that was more dynamic than that of a noble or gentle household.

The literary skills of nuns can be deduced from a number of contemporary records. When bishops preached at nunneries, or sent injunctions after

72   Dominican nuns in choir. Nuns said the daily services, like monks, but their education failed to match that of the male religious houses.

visitations, they envisaged the nuns as being unable to understand Latin. French and later English were used instead, and if Latin needed to be employed, arrangements were made for it to be interpreted in one of the other languages.[126] In 1319 Bishop Stapledon of Exeter told the sisters of Polsloe Priory to keep the times of silence enjoined by their rule, and if they needed a candle, book, or missal in an emergency to ask for it in simple ungrammatical Latin: *candela*, *liber*, and *missale*.[127] In the early fifteenth century a guide in English to the daily services was written for the nuns of Syon Abbey because, the author tells us, they could sing and read (Latin is implied) but could not 'see what the meaning thereof is'.[128] In the middle of the century, Alice Henley, abbess of Godstow, commissioned an English translation of her abbey's Latin charters, because she and her nuns could not consult them without expert help. The male translator observed in his preface to the work that most of the nuns of Godstow were well learned in English, but that 'women of religion, in reading books of Latin, are excused of great understanding where it is not their mother tongue'.[129] Books known to have been owned by medieval nunneries, or used by nuns individually, tell a similar story. Those in Latin are chiefly liturgical works, and it is rare to find examples of scholarly works in the language, like the small collection recorded at the Yorkshire priory of Swine.[130] Far more common are works in

73   A novice nun having her hair cut as part of her entry to the religious life.

French or English, and the majority of volumes bequeathed to nuns in wills or bearing their names fall into this category.[131]

A culture existed therefore in which girls became nuns with only basic skills in reading Latin. It followed that most of the nuns who taught or supervised them could take them no further. There may have been exceptions. Two early Tudor sisters of Syon Abbey, the sole English house of Bridgettine nuns, are recorded as having owned a couple of Latin books, one a printed edition of the works of Thomas Aquinas.[132] Dartford Priory, another unique house, belonged to the Dominican Order. One of its fifteenth-century sisters, Emma Wynter, wrote her name in a manuscript of the *Distichs of Cato* which contains both the Latin text and an English verse translation.[133] Another, Jane Fisher, was permitted to have a master to instruct her in grammar and the Latin tongue in 1431. He was allowed to visit her in the priory parlour, a public place, and to teach other gentlewomen – perhaps meaning other nuns. The arrangement, however, required the consent of the head of the order in

Europe and was granted partly on the grounds of her 'noble birth' – raising the question how often such permission was sought or given.[134]

ALMONRY BOYS

The educational concerns of the English monasteries did not stop at their own monks and canons. Many of them came to support groups of boys and youths, called in contemporary records the 'clerks' or 'boys' of the almonry, and termed by modern historians 'almonry boys'.[135] The almonry was the monastic building from which food left over from meals was distributed to the poor, and it lay on the outer edge of the monastic precinct. The almonry boys lived in this building, reflecting the fact that they were not junior monks but secular boys, free to leave the community when they wished. Originally they appear to have been destitute children taken into monasteries for reasons of charity, like the foundling boy at Abingdon mentioned above, and not only fed but accommodated. The maintenance of such boys is first recorded in the early thirteenth century. At Bury St Edmunds, by about the 1230s, the abbey allowed the master of the town school to nominate two of his scholars to board in the almonry, evidently because they were poor and needed support.[136] There was a similar arrangement at Durham Cathedral for three boys by the same date.[137]

74   Durham Cathedral, typical of large monasteries in providing education for novice monks and schooling for almonry boys in song and grammar.

The best early evidence comes from Norwich Cathedral, where a set of statutes for the almonry school was drawn up in about 1288–9, apparently when the school was instituted.[138] It was to consist of a master and thirteen 'clerks' (meaning boys), appointed and removed by the subprior and the almoner – both monks, who had general responsibility for the institution. The master (an outsider, not a monk) was to teach the boys literature (signifying Latin) and behaviour. The boys were to be poor but 'of elegant stature' (without physical defects). They were to live in the almonry, receive a daily ration of bread, and have first call on the food left over from meals in the monastery before it was given to the poor at the priory gate. A servant was to be kept to look after them. On Sundays and festivals they were to attend worship, not in the monastery but in the parish church of St Mary-in-the-Marsh nearby. There they were to contribute to the services 'according to the capability that God has given them'. One group (who could sing, or be taught to do so) was to help with the plainsong of the services, while the other (less able to sing) read lessons and chanted psalms. The boys therefore did little or nothing for the benefit of the monastery, and their presence there was primarily dictated by charity.

Almonry boys, and sometimes schools for them, were established in other monasteries during the second half of the thirteenth century. Augustinian canons were particularly tolerant of such links with the outside world. Guisborough Priory, one of their houses, maintained poor boys out of charity by 1266–8 and kept a master to teach them.[139] Another, Barnwell Priory near Cambridge, had a school by 1296.[140] Two Benedictine cathedrals other than Norwich are known to have maintained boys and schools by the end of the century: Christ Church (Canterbury) by 1292 and Rochester by 1299.[141] The practice developed in two respects after 1300. One was social. It is not surprising that the generous arrangements at Norwich – free board, lodging, and education – attracted interest from families that were very far from poor. Monks of the priory begged places for their relations, and influential people from outside intervened on behalf of their children or protégés. At Ely Cathedral in 1314 it was laid down that the monks should choose the boys, no individual choosing more than once every four years, so that all might share in doing so.[142] This became the common arrangement elsewhere, although at Durham the prior was allowed to override the system 'at the instance of lords and magnates whom we may not offend'.[143] As a result the almonry came to be filled by boys who might be technically poor but had patrons and friends. It became envisaged that some of the boys might become monks or monastic servants, so that what began as charity grew into a system that benefited the monastery, its members, and its friends.

This development paralleled another, by which the almonry boys came to be given tasks to do in the monastery. During the thirteenth century it was increasingly common for monks to be ordained as priests and to celebrate masses in the monastic church for the souls of the church's founders and

benefactors. Celebrating mass required an assistant to serve at the altar and
say the responses, and at first monks helped each other in this respect.
Later, as more and more monks became priests and said masses each day, it
grew difficult to organise such help and there was a need to find
alternatives. In 1278 the Benedictine monasteries of southern England
enacted a law that no monk should celebrate mass without the aid of a fellow
monk or at least an honest clerk – a term that would include an almonry
boy.[144] At first the employment of clerks was probably regarded as a last
resort, because it involved bringing outsiders into the monastic area. In
1287 the Benedictine monasteries in the north of England actually forbade
the use of 'secular clerks', although the rule was withdrawn six years later.[145]
Norwich in 1288–9 clearly had no intention of using its boys in this way, and
the archbishop of Canterbury talked of monks serving monks at Worcester
Cathedral as late as 1301.[146] But practicality triumphed. In 1343 the general
chapter of the Benedictine Order in England told its constituent houses to
maintain clerks from their alms – in other words almonry boys – to be
available to serve at mass, a requirement that may have been in force in the
southern houses of the order as early as 1309.[147] By the middle of the
fourteenth century almonry boys were widely used for this purpose. After
the Black Death of 1348–9, when the number of monks fell sharply, the
assistance of boys at masses became indispensable.

Between this date and the Reformation it is likely that they came to be
widely employed in the larger Benedictine and Augustinian houses, and in
some smaller ones. Dr Roger Bowers has made a list of seventy-seven
monasteries for which there is evidence of almonry boys. Most relate to the
two orders already mentioned, but at least a few Cistercian houses, such as
Forde and Furness, adopted the practice by the early sixteenth century.[148]
Numbers of boys varied from place to place and time to time. Some large
monasteries, such as Norwich and Gloucester, fixed a complement of twelve
or thirteen and tried to keep to it. Others had grander schemes – Durham
provided for thirty – but did not always manage to sustain them. Reading's
total fluctuated between ten and fifteen, while Westminster's dropped to
nine in 1369–70 before rising again to twenty-two by the 1380s. Ely had
twenty-three boys and two masters in 1378–9, but only five boys in 1448.[149]

The daily life of the almonry boys of Durham was remembered after the
Reformation by the witness who told us of the school in the cloisters:

> There were certain poor children, called the children of the almonry, who
> only were maintained with learning and relieved with the alms and
> benefactions of the whole house, having their meat and drink in a loft on
> the north side of the abbey gates. . . . The which loft had a long porch
> over the stairhead, slated over, and at either side of the said porch or
> entry there was a stair to go up to it, and a stable underneath the said
> almonry or loft, having a door and an entry in under the stairhead to go
> into the stable. . . . And also the meat and drink that the aforesaid poor

children had was the meat that the master of the novices and the novices left and reserved, and was carried in at a door adjoining to the great kitchen window into a little vault in the west end of the frater house like unto a pantry, called the covey, which had a man that kept it called the clerk of the covey, and had a window within it, where one or two of the children did receive their meat and drink of the said clerk, out of the covey or pantry window so called, and the said children did carry it to the almonry or loft. Which clerk did wait upon them every meal and to see that they kept good order.[150]

Such boys were probably recruited when they were ten, twelve, or so, and left in their mid or later teens. Christ Church (Canterbury) required them to be at least ten when they came, and able to read and sing.[151] Ely allowed them to stay for up to four years in 1314, and St Albans for up to five in 1339.[152]

Sometimes, as at Norwich, the monastery employed its own grammar master to teach the boys. Occasionally this man combined such teaching with instructing the novices or lecturing to the monks, an arrangement found at Bristol, Forde, and St Peter's (Gloucester).[153] At other times the boys were sent to a school outside the abbey, as was the practice at Worcester in 1294, St Albans in the 1330s, and St Oswald's (Gloucester) in 1400.[154] Leach consistently underrated the educational importance of almonry schools in terms of size and quality, but his view is not supported by the qualifications of the masters, especially in the early sixteenth century when they were sometimes university graduates. In Norwich, John Hancock, master of the city school, preferred to move to the almonry school in 1424 and lease the city school to a deputy.[155] Some almonry schools admitted pupils from outside, despite the provocation that this caused to neighbouring schools. Hancock, as almonry master, reserved the power to teach twelve boys from the city or the countryside, and in 1453 the monks of Durham insisted on their right to receive boys into their school from inside and outside the city.[156] A little earlier, in 1431, the monks of St Augustine's (Canterbury) decided to set up a school for their own and other boys, and took the precaution of gaining the pope's permission to do so (Fig. 2). This was probably meant to forestall opposition from the schoolmaster of Canterbury or from his patron, the archbishop, to whom he might turn for help.[157]

There was another major development in the life and work of the almonry boys: a musical one. By the end of the fourteenth century it was common in the secular cathedrals and larger collegiate churches to stage a daily 'Lady mass' in the Lady chapel in honour of the Virgin Mary.[158] An antiphon in her honour would also be sung towards the end of the day. This music consisted of plainsong, performed by adult men with a small group of choristers, and its popularity spread to the larger monasteries. We hear of boys helping the monks to celebrate the Lady mass at Westminster by 1373, Norwich by 1378, and Ely by 1383. Just as monasteries hired a schoolmaster to teach the boys grammar, so they brought in a cantor to teach them song, and there are references to such teachers from the 1380s onwards, training a group of almonry boys: four, six, or eight in number. Bowers has pointed out that the musical involvement of the boys at this stage was fairly limited. Monasteries used only four settings of the Lady mass, with a relatively small repertoire of chant. The cantor may have taught the boys to improvise descant to plainsong, but the time needed to rehearse them would have occupied less than an hour each day, leaving the boys free to join their colleagues in the grammar school for the rest of the time. This commitment did not compare with what was required of a chorister in a secular church. Choristers sang the daily services with the adult clergy, while monastic singing boys did duty only in the Lady chapel, not with the monks in the choir. Indeed the word 'chorister' was not normally used in monasteries, where the equivalent term was 'the children' or 'the boys'.

Around the middle of the fifteenth century the larger English secular churches began to enhance the Lady mass and votive antiphons with elaborate polyphony, and this fashion duly spread to the monasteries in about the 1480s. Christ Church (Canterbury), Durham, Ely, Winchester, and Worcester adopted it early among the monastic cathedrals, and Bristol and Westminster among the abbeys. Polyphony, as we have seen, involved the singing of highly demanding music in several parts, two of which – the treble and alto – required the help of boys.[159] The adult parts were undertaken either by monks or by adult clerks who were professional singers retained for the purpose. Teaching this music required a 'master of the children' or 'master of the boys' with appropriate skills, and the boys had to spend more time learning singing techniques and mastering a wide and developing repertoire of music. They continued to live in the almonry but became somewhat detached from the other boys there. The monastery, doubtless with the advice of the singing master, was prompted to select a proportion of almonry boys on the basis of vocal ability – a consideration that had hitherto mattered little. Song schools begin to be mentioned where the boys were trained. As before the arrangements are best recorded in the Tudor account of Durham:

> There was in the centory garth in under the south end of the church . . . betwixt two pillars adjoining to the nine-altar door, a song school builded to teach six children to sing for the maintenance of God's divine service in the abbey church, which children had their meat and their drink of the house's cost among the children of the almonry. Which said school . . . was very finely boarded within round about a man's height about the walls, and a long desk from one end of the school to the other to lay their books upon, and all the floor boarded in underfoot for warmness, and long forms set fast in the ground for the children to sit on. And the place where the master did sit and teach was all close-boarded both behind and of either side, for warmness.[160]

The number of boys maintained to sing in monasteries varied from about six to ten. At Winchester they were promoted from eating the leftovers in the almonry hall to having meals in the hall of the prior's household. Even so, monastic polyphony remained limited to the Lady mass and antiphon, with an additional Jesus mass and antiphon on Fridays, and training and performances still took up only a third of the working day. It remained possible for the singing boys to go on learning grammar, and it is likely that they did. In 1515 the monks of Gloucester appointed the learned Tudor musician John Tucke, BA, to teach grammar to all thirteen boys of the 'clerks' chamber' or almonry, as well as plainsong and descant to the five or six who specialised in singing. At Winchester Cathedral the singing boys learnt grammar in 1538, and the canons of Cirencester, appointing a 'master of the children' in the same year, told him to teach them 'pricksong' (polyphony) and then, once they were sufficiently instructed, Latin grammar.[161]

The resources that the monasteries put into supporting and educating almonry boys were a significant addition to the resources of education in England as a whole. Individually the numbers of boys were often small but nationally they added up to a thousand or two. In effect the religious houses provided scholarships that delivered knowledge of grammar or advanced musical skills. The boys passed out of the almonry to various destinations. Some became monks of the house that had maintained them, an outcome of which we hear particularly in the fifteenth century. In 1431–2 the bishop of Lincoln ordered the monks of Bradwell Priory to maintain teachable children who in the course of time might be admitted as brethren of the house.[162] Durham in 1449 looked for boys who might grow to be monks, and at least one, William Ebchester, rose to be prior.[163] In 1468 the chronicler of Christ Church (Canterbury) recorded the admission of four new monks from the almonry school.[164] At Furness after the Reformation local people believed that the boys had been either chosen as monks or promoted as lay servants of the abbey, and we hear of such promotions elsewhere: an officer of the stables at Canterbury and a groom of the chamber at St Osyth's.[165] Alternatively the boys left the monastery for the world. Some became secular priests, a destination approved by the canon lawyer William Lyndwood in the fifteenth century, because it justified the giving of monastic alms to scholars rather than to the poor.[166] Others went on to lead lives as husbandmen (peasant farmers) or yeomen (wealthier farmers).[167] In short the system proved highly popular, both with monasteries and with the families of almonry boys. There was apparently no shortage of candidates for the places until the Reformation suppressed them.

EDUCATION FOR OUTSIDERS

Monasteries and nunneries left such a strong imprint on people's imagination after their dissolution that they came to be thought of as the chief providers

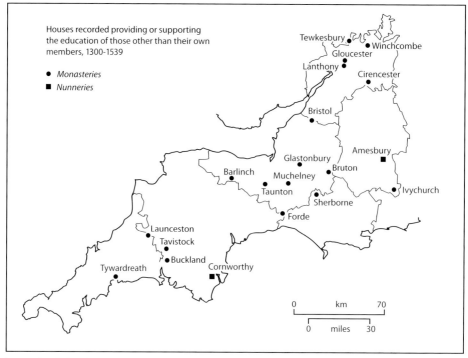

75   Schools in religious houses in the west of England.

of schooling in the middle ages, not only for their inmates but for the general public.[168] This belief, as we have seen, fails to do justice to the work of the free-standing schools, but it contains some truth. Many monasteries did not confine their involvement with education to their own precincts. Their possessions and privileges inexorably forced their attention away from a secluded life to the concerns of the world, and this included schooling. As soon as schools for the public appear in documents in the late eleventh century, monasteries claimed rights of patronage over those that lay in the towns or rural manors under their lordship. The Benedictines of Bury St Edmunds, Durham, and St Albans all did so, as did the Cistercians of Beaulieu at Faringdon.[169] In other places kings and bishops granted rights of educational patronage to monasteries, particularly those of the canons of the Augustinian Order and notably at Bedford, Darley (for Derby), and Gloucester.[170] The instances in which religious houses went to law to protect these rights confirm the value they attached to them.[171] Some monasteries came to subsidise the schools for the public over which they held rights. Abbot Samson of Bury set an example in this respect, with his gift of a schoolhouse to the town school at the end of the twelfth century and his endowment of the schoolmaster with a partial salary.[172] Battle, Darley, and Lanthony (Gloucester) provided or maintained other school buildings,[173] while Launceston and Worcester gave meals to local schoolboys in their almonries.[174]

A second custom in the larger monasteries was the admission of lay pupils to be taught on their premises, albeit in the outer precincts. Some were allowed into almonry schools, as we have seen. Others lived in the household of the abbot or prior. These were the sons of wealthy parents who sent them to live with the head of the monastery as an alternative to growing up in a nobleman's household. They learnt letters, religion, and good manners as a preparation for life as a gentleman or as a cleric. John of Hertford, abbot of St Albans (d. 1263), became renowned for his courtesy and generosity, and a historian of the abbey writing two centuries later believed that 'many noblemen of the kingdom commended their children to his care to be educated'.[175] Glastonbury Abbey is said to have trained noble boys before its fall, and we know that one of its abbots, Richard Beere, gave his nephew a gentleman's education there in the 1510s as a prelude to study at Oxford and the inns of court.[176] Sometimes such boys may have had access to the schoolmaster of the almonry. In 1266–8 John Blaby, a landowner in the North Riding of Yorkshire, was permitted to send his two sons to Guisborough Priory to study under the master who taught the poor boys there.[177] Sometimes they may have brought their own private tutor, like the three young gentlemen at Woburn and the four at Lilleshall mentioned for 1538.[178] The admission of outsiders extended to the monasteries attached to the universities. Canterbury College (Oxford) maintained five poor secular scholars after 1384, as well as occasional boarders who paid for their lodgings.[179] At St Bernard's College in the same city we hear by chance of a Yorkshireman named Thomas Grey, who served as a Bible clerk and butler in the 1520s before going on to become a secular priest.[180]

The reception and teaching of outsiders also took place in nunneries, for here nuns rivalled monks and canons in their willingness to take in children to board and be taught.[181] Such children were mainly girls and small boys from the nobility, gentry, and sometimes wealthy burgess families, the latter especially in houses near towns. The poor, it seems, were not usually provided for. Nunneries must have appealed to wealthy adults who wished to place a small boy to be cared for, which was hardly possible in a school, monastery, or great household, where the environment was that of older males. Girls too were barred from such places, and there was nowhere else suitable for them to live (if home was not a possibility) until they reached puberty and could be sent to board in a noble household. Childcare was the one social act that nuns could offer without compromising their life of seclusion and worship. It also offered a means of making money. In some houses the sisters developed the practice of taking pupils individually and pocketing the fees, but this was frowned on by the Church authorities as a breach of the rule of personal poverty. The nuns of Romsey were forbidden to take private pupils in 1387, and those of St Helen's Bishopsgate (London) in 1439 could do so only if the profits were paid to the house.[182]

Children are widely recorded as boarding and being taught in late
medieval nunneries. Eileen Power, who investigated the subject in detail,
found examples in forty-nine houses in twenty-one counties.[183] At first their
presence met with some disfavour. In 1223 Pope Honorius III forbade the
nuns of the Gilbertine Order to bring up girls except to become nuns, and
we have seen how the guide for women recluses, *Ancrene Rule*, warned them
not to turn their cells into schools.[184] Subsequently prohibition gave way to
regulation, and bishops, who were responsible for supervising most of the
nunneries, allowed them to take in boys up to ages that varied from five to
twelve, and girls until they were ten, twelve, or sometimes fourteen. Board
and teaching were charged at 6d. a week, rising on one occasion to 10d.
Little is said about the children's studies, but the likelihood can be
established from what we know of the culture of nunneries and of the noble
families for whom they catered. Boys and girls would have learnt the abc
and to read at sight the basic Latin prayers and the hours of the Virgin
Mary. They would have been schooled in good manners at the table and in
church: quiet deportment, crossing oneself, saying prayers, and venerating
images. It is noteworthy that Chaucer, when depicting nuns and nunneries,
seems to envisage them as people and places of education. His Prioress
possesses teachable skills: good table manners and French of the decaying
Anglo-Norman variety. His 'Reeve's Tale' tells of a priest's daughter who was
brought up in a nunnery and learned 'nortelrie', a deliberately distorted
form of the word 'nurture', meaning education.[185]

In the second half of the fifteenth century, when the fashion developed for
endowing free public grammar schools, some monasteries came to be
involved in this process. A few were chosen by founders to act as trustees,
with the responsibility for administering the endowments or appointing the
schoolmasters. The earliest known example comes from Gloucestershire,
where Winchcombe Abbey was paying the master's salary at Cirencester
school by 1483.[186] Other religious houses involved in one or other of these
roles were Bruton, Faversham, Hinton, Launde, and Lewes.[187] In a few cases
monasteries or their leaders took the initiative in founding free schools for
the public, especially after 1500. One monastic head, Robert Drax, prior of
Monk Bretton, is said to have been involved in setting up the grammar
school of Royston in 1503.[188] Another, Robert Kirton, abbot of Peterborough,
established a free grammar school at Kirton-in-Holland by 1518, apparently
as a benefaction to the place from which he or his family had come. He used
resources from his abbey for the purpose, but the project foundered after his
resignation in 1528 and petered out in the 1530s.[189] A third foundation, at
Winchcombe, came about through a bequest of money to endow an
almshouse, which was diverted by the abbot, Richard Kidderminster, to
support a grammar school in 1521.[190] Three other places where abbeys set
up free schools were Evesham (probably between 1513 and 1524), Burton
upon Trent (in about 1530), and Reading (by 1532).[191] At least two of these

schools were of good quality. The monks of Evesham appointed a succession of masters up to the Reformation, two of them graduates and a third a competent Latinist, and paid them salaries of £10. Reading recruited a good scholar in the person of Leonard Cox, a graduate of both universities, a wide traveller in Europe, and the author of several educational and religious works. His *Art or Craft of Rhetoric*, published in 1532, was dedicated to Abbot Faringdon of Reading and states that the abbot was paying him a stipend – probably the £10 a year that he is mentioned receiving in 1539.[192] A few more monastic foundations of this kind may come to light in the future.

Altogether the importance of the schools of the religious orders in medieval England cannot be doubted. They were responsible for the further education of large numbers of monks, canons, and friars in grammar, arts, and theology, and they enabled many thousands of lay boys and girls to be educated (Fig. 75). At university level they established some nine or ten communities at Oxford and half a dozen at Cambridge. This achievement was partly driven from outside the orders, by popes and bishops, but it was also due very much to their own spontaneous efforts. The range of studies was wide, from reading and song through grammar to philosophy and theology, and if the quality often sank low in some smaller monastic communities it also rose to the high levels recorded in certain of the greater monasteries and friaries. Unfortunately these achievements did not impress contemporaries sufficiently to save the religious houses from the fate that was to befall them in the 1530s.

9

The Reign of Henry VIII

THE EARLY YEARS OF THE REIGN

When Henry VIII became king in 1509, aged seventeen, no one could have foreseen the violent changes that would engulf the English Church and its daughter, education, twenty-five years later. Changes in schooling during the early sixteenth century were of an evolutionary rather than a revolutionary kind. There was the practice of endowing grammar schools, which continued to inspire wealthy benefactors throughout the century. There was the process by which schools were embracing humanist Latin. Late medieval Latin had not quite disappeared in 1509. Medieval poems like *Peniteas cito* and *Theodulus* were still being printed for school use during the 1510s, but by the 1520s the outcome had been settled in favour of humanist grammars and reading texts. And there was the technical change by which schools used such books in printed copies. This was probably the case in most classrooms by about 1500, or soon afterwards.

None of these changes called for action by the new king or his government. Henry inherited a kingdom in which neither the Church nor the crown gave formal attention to schooling. Founding schools was a matter for individual patrons and schoolmasters. The teaching of humanist Latin was encouraged rather than enforced by those in authority, and the publication of schoolbooks was largely left to the printers. The sole occasion in Henry's early reign on which his regime addressed the teaching of children related to war not learning. In 1512 Parliament enacted a statute aimed at training the male population in archery. Many such statutes had been passed in previous decades but this one broke new ground by extending its concern to young people. It laid down that anyone whose household included boys aged between seven and seventeen should provide each one with a bow and two arrows 'to induce and learn them and bring them up in shooting'.[1] The order was not necessarily effective, but it was a straw in the wind, involving the authorities in children's physical training some twenty-eight years before such involvement extended to children in classrooms.

76   Henry VIII (d. 1547) reading, the first English monarch to be educated in
humanist Latin.

There was another sign for the future in Henry VIII's own education
(Fig. 76). He studied under a series of teachers: John Skelton (Fig. 77), John
Holt, and William Hone. All three taught him Latin and the latter two were
professional schoolmasters, Holt the author of an inventive school grammar
(Fig. 28).[2] We know little about Henry's studies, but there can be no doubt
that they included humanist Latin. His elder brother Arthur was credited
with having read a large number of humanist authors, and Holt's grammar
drew on such authors and their usages. Henry's education was therefore
modern. His Latin was the Latin of the Renaissance, and he was probably
more fluent in the language than previous kings of England. He certainly
had confidence in his Latinity. In 1518 he wrote a Latin reply to Luther's
attack on the papacy and on indulgences, a work that lay unfinished for a
time until it was extended and printed in 1521 as *An Assertion of the Seven
Sacraments*.[3] Even if he had help with the writing, it was unprecedented for

Eterno maniura die dumlideɾafulgent
Equoɾadumq;tument heclaurea noſtra virebit.
Hinc noſtrumceɫebɾe etɾoméreferetuɾad aſtra.
Vndiq;Skeltonismemoɾabituɾalteɾadonis

77   John Skelton (d. 1529), the first of
Henry VIII's three boyhood tutors,
depicted as a poet laureate.

an English ruler to claim the authorship of a religious treatise in Latin, and
when in 1534 he became head of the English Church, Henry showed
himself willing to make religious pronouncements and decisions. In 1540 he
helped draft the parliamentary Act of Six Articles, which defined six major
topics of belief and practice, and he visited Parliament to expound them in
person. Three years later he supplied the preface to *The King's Book*, a work
intended as a broader statement of English Church doctrine. Without the
education he received in his youth it would have been far harder for him to
pose as a religious leader, capable of doing what had hitherto been done
only by clergy.

   Equally it took the Reformation to unlock the potential power of Henry's
schooling. Until that event he displayed no marked concern with schools or
their work. English kings had not traditionally done so – Henry VI was
exceptional here – and royal duties did not require that they should. School
and university education came to Henry's attention only once before the
Reformation began in England. In 1529 Thomas Wolsey fell from power as
the king's chief minister while in the process of founding his Cardinal
Colleges at Oxford and Ipswich. Henry must have been asked to decide
their fates. The Oxford college was allowed to continue under a new name,

King Henry VIII College, but it became largely a centre of worship, its educational functions reduced to teaching song and grammar to a group of choristers.[4] The Ipswich foundation was less attractive for Henry to rescue because its site at Wolsey's birthplace linked it so firmly with the fallen cardinal. The college disappeared but the school was allowed to continue. It was rechristened 'the King's School' and received a generous royal annuity to pay the master and usher.[5] How much of all this was due to Henry and how much to the intervention of Wolsey's former protégé Thomas Cromwell is not certain. The treatment of Wolsey's foundations enabled the king to appear benevolent to colleges and schools, but it need not suggest that he had developed much interest in either kind of body.

THE REFORMATION

The ideas of the Reformation began to reach England in the 1520s, and to transform it during the 1530s. In due course education too was changed. Many ancient schools were destroyed and new ones were founded. Alterations were made to the school curriculum, to the lifestyle of some teachers, and to the career prospects of their pupils. At the same time many aspects of education did not alter during the Reformation, just as much stayed the same in the Church, and the historian of education during the Reformation, like the historian of the Reformation itself, must do justice to both change and continuity. The Reformation has long been regarded as a movement that promoted education. In the nineteenth century, when little was known about schooling in medieval England, the cathedral schools created by Henry VIII and the grammar schools established under Edward VI appeared to introduce a new and better era of provision. Leach convincingly reduced the claims of both monarchs in this respect, but the Reformation has retained a reputation for being favourable to schooling. Its emphasis on the written word – the Bible in English, the sermon, and the printed book – rather than on the ceremony or the image has seemed to embody a culture in which lay people would learn and practise reading.

This reputation does not altogether benefit from closer study. Reform, as a process, is inseparable from Christianity and has manifested itself throughout Church history, not simply in the sixteenth century. Reformers in other periods have had educational policies. The Church councils of the twelfth and early thirteenth centuries issued legislation to free schools from financial charges and to provide them at cathedrals.[6] Papal reformers of the fourteenth century gave their attention to monastic education, and Lollard reformers in England during the 1390s and 1410s dreamed of founding new universities.[7] The interest of sixteenth-century reformers in education reduplicated that of their predecessors; it was not original to them. Nor, at first, did it engage them much more than it had done before. Medieval Church authorities had given more attention to education in a Christian sense than in a classroom one. Lay people were to learn to say basic prayers in Latin, and the clergy were to teach them what to believe and how to behave. The laity were not required to be literate for these purposes, and the clergy often had little more education than the educated laity. Sixteenth-century reformers inherited some of this thinking. They too stressed the learning of basic prayers (now in English), while adding an emphasis on learning through services (also in the vernacular). They encouraged Bible reading but, at first, in restricted ways. The frontispiece of Henry VIII's 'Great Bible' of 1539 reminds us that personal Bible reading was originally associated with the upper orders of society. The lower orders were expected to hear the Bible read or expounded to them (Fig. 81). No English government of the sixteenth century tried to institute universal schooling and literacy, and none before that of Mary Tudor made changes to the traditional system by which the clergy were trained. Until her reign their training remained a matter of going to school and (in a minority of cases) to university, at the initiative and expense of the person concerned.

The Reformation had a more original and effective impact upon schools through its emphasis on uniformity. Uniformity – the requirement that everyone should believe and do the same – had been a principle of the medieval Church, but it was stressed more firmly by the reformers of the sixteenth century, both Protestant and Catholic. This arose from the confidence with which both sides approached religion. Most of their members believed that they understood God's word more fully and correctly than people had done before, and they were correspondingly more anxious to put what they thought into practice. New rigid formulations of belief and behaviour were made and enforced through measures such as the Act of Six Articles of 1539, the Forty-Two (later Thirty-Nine) Articles of 1553, and the Acts of Uniformity in worship of 1549, 1552, and 1559. These attitudes affected education; indeed, as we shall see, Latin grammar was a target of uniformity before religious beliefs or practices. Positively there was a realisation that school was an effective place for teaching children religion as well as letters, and thereby an important means of establishing reformist beliefs and habits among the rising generation. Negatively there was a fear that the opponents of reform might, through controlling schools, be able to frustrate it and to promote their own heterodoxy. These considerations grew during the 1530s, 1540s, and 1550s, but their growth was slow, reflecting the fact that the early reformers had grown up in a world that took schooling for granted. The brief concern with schools in 1408, when Archbishop Arundel had legislated on the matter, had not been sustained for the rest of the fifteenth century.[8] People's attitudes took time to adjust to the new conditions.

The Reformation in Europe is conventionally reckoned to start in 1517, with Luther's attack on indulgences. His writings were reaching England by 1519, and the Church authorities in England were taking action against

them by 1521, when a solemn burning of Lutheran books was held at St
Paul's (London) in the presence of Cardinal Wolsey.[9] By 1525 the authorities
were also turning their attention to schools – a concern so unusual that one
is bound to ask if it was linked with the Reformation. This may have been so
in that the Reformation generated a new sense of vigilance about defending
the Church, and therefore a greater stress on uniformity of belief and
behaviour. The initial concern of the authorities with schooling, however,
was not ostensibly about the entry of unwelcome religious views into
classrooms. It claimed as its primary motive the sorting out of the confusion
caused by the diversity of Latin grammars: a diversity which we have seen
emerging as a problem during the 1520s.[10]

The first sign of an interest by the Church in this matter occurs in the
revised statutes of Manchester grammar school in 1525, which prescribed

78   Right, John Colet (d. 1519), the refounder of St Paul's School
(London). Though often regarded as a Renaissance figure, some of his
ideas (like this depiction) were rooted in the later middle ages.

79   Thomas Wolsey
(d. 1530), who tried but
failed to authorise a uniform
grammar and to found a
grammar school to rival
Winchester and Eton.

the use of the grammar of Stanbridge, or any other form which 'in time to come shall be ordained universally throughout all the province of Canterbury'.[11] This phrase suggests a project to impose a uniform grammar on schools, a project that probably originated with (or was espoused by) Cardinal Wolsey: ex-teacher, school founder, papal legate, and therefore the highest Church authority in England. In 1529 the Southwark printer Peter Treveris issued what he claimed to be an authorised grammar, although it was actually the treatise of John Colet and William Lily used at St Paul's School, with revisions by Wolsey for his Ipswich foundation (Fig. 80). The Latin title of Treveris's edition may be translated as 'The rudiments of grammar and the method of teaching, not merely of the school of Ipswich, happily established by the most reverend Lord Thomas, Cardinal of York, but also prescribed for all the other schools of all England'.[12] Wolsey may have been on the point of approving the book for general use when he lost his authority in September 1529. The initiative then passed to other people.

   In the following month a convocation of the province of Canterbury met at St Paul's to consider ecclesiastical reform and take action against heresy. Its decrees, approved on 22 March 1530, included three that aimed at improving and regulating education in the province.[13] First, with regard to the regular clergy, Convocation laid down that each religious house should have an instructor in grammar, and that those of the religious who proved apt in letters should be sent to study at university. This was essentially a

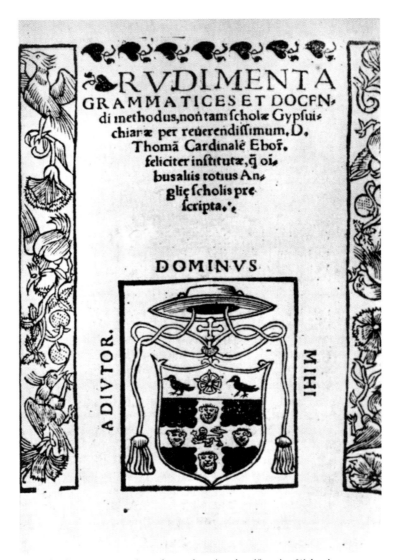

80 The first attempt to introduce educational uniformity. Wolsey's grammar
for Ipswich school in 1529, prescribed, as it claims, for other schools as well.

traditional measure, going back to the fourteenth-century decrees of
Clement V and Benedict XII.[14] Secondly, the parish clergy – rectors, vicars,
and chantry priests – were ordered, when they were not engaged in divine
service, to study, pray, preach, or instruct boys in the alphabet, reading,
song, or grammar. This policy too was not entirely novel. Some parish clergy
had taught children in previous centuries and the legislators of 1529–30
may have been influenced by the linkage of chantries and schooling through
the foundation of chantry schools. By 1532–3 some chantry founders were
already endorsing Convocation's decree by asking that the priest who

prayed for their soul should perform other tasks, such as teaching children.[15] Later in the 1530s certain English bishops threw their weight individually in the same direction. Some, like Lee of Lichfield and Veysey of Exeter, told their parish clergy merely to teach the Lord's Prayer, Hail Mary, Creed, and Ten Commandments – something that did not necessarily involve literacy. Others, including Latimer of Worcester in 1537, Shaxton of Salisbury in 1538, and Bonner of London in 1542, specified the teaching of reading too, and the latter two bishops sanctioned the charging of moderate fees for the purpose.[16]

Finally, Convocation turned to schoolmasters. It ordered them to teach boys simple summaries of the faith and of what to do and to avoid, and to refrain from giving them books that might corrupt their minds or their faith. This harked back to Arundel's decree of 1408. The assembly then engaged with the problem of diversity in the teaching of Latin, a problem that it claimed was causing difficulties when children had to move school because of plague or the death of a schoolmaster. As a result of this

> it happens many times that someone who has begun to learn grammar for a year or two under one teacher, having left him is obliged to go to a new teacher by whom another method of teaching is used, so that he is almost laughed at by all; and so it comes about that those who are still inexperienced in grammar suffer great harm as a result in the progress of their learning.

A decision was taken to establish a uniform method of teaching grammar throughout the province within a year. During that time the archbishop of Canterbury, four bishops, four abbots, and four archdeacons were to choose a suitable text and prescribe it for general use.[17] We do not know if this committee was formed, and, if so, who its members were. If it met it may have run into difficulties, as no outcome of its work is known. Soon afterwards the issue of grammar was eclipsed by other events. In December 1530 the crown began to attack the Church for breaching *praemunire*: the law restricting papal authority. In the following months the archbishop of Canterbury, the elderly William Warham, was preoccupied with grave political matters.

The next three years saw a steady worsening of relations between the crown and the papacy, culminating in the Act of Supremacy of 1534 by which Henry replaced the pope as head of the Church of England. Henry's first act in his new role was to order the publication of his headship by parish priests to their congregations and by schoolmasters to their pupils, but for the moment this was all that he and his government required of schools and their members.[18] As head of the Church Henry was soon obliged to take educational measures, but their initial focus was on higher and adult learning. In 1535 the king sent visitors to the universities of Oxford and

81   Henry VIII's authorised English Bible of 1539. The king dispenses the book to clergy and
nobility for reading; the lower orders hear it being read.

Cambridge, who established new lectureships and forbade the study of
canon law and parts of the theology degree course.[19] Other visitors went to
the monasteries, with questions to put and injunctions to deliver. Houses
were asked if their novices had a master to teach them grammar and good
letters and senior monks to train them in the monastic rule. The age at
which monks could be professed was raised to twenty-four. Every monastery
was required to organise a daily 'lesson' or lecture of Holy Scripture, lasting
one hour and attended by the whole community. Heads of houses were told
to arrange for one or two of their brethren to study at a university, so that
they might return to instruct their fellows and to preach. These orders were
largely traditional ones, which bishops and other monastic visitors had made
in the past, albeit with greater emphasis in 1535 on the collective study of
Scripture. The originality of the process lay more in the crown's
involvement than in the policies adopted. Moreover, the visitation took no
interest in the maintenance and education of almonry boys, except that it
limited their contact with the monks to serving them at mass.[20]

The king's first ventures into educational policy centred on law and
theology because these studies were crucial in making the Church of
England independent of Rome. Reading and grammar mattered less at this
point, and schools received correspondingly little attention. They first
experienced the force of the king's headship of the Church through
financial rather than educational measures, and through oversight rather
than design. In 1534 Parliament subjected the clergy to new royal taxation,
and empowered the king to make a valuation of clergy revenues for the
purpose.[21] The valuation, now known as the *Valor Ecclesiasticus*, was carried
out by royal commissioners in 1535. It included the religious houses, the
beneficed parish clergy, and some of the chantries, as a result of which it
affected a number of schools supported by these bodies. This effect was not
foreseen by Parliament, and when the commissioners began to record
clerical incomes and expenditures they had no special brief with regard to
education. At the religious houses they were allowed to take into account
only regular almsgiving 'by reason of any foundation or ordinance', which
meant that they could exempt for taxation purposes money spent on
maintaining almonry boys or poor scholars but not on teaching them.[22] No
exemption was made for monks or other clergy who taught, and their
revenues or salaries were taxed like those of non-teachers. Similarly the
Valor did not discriminate between chantries with and without schools. Both
were valued and their incumbents subjected to tax: a serious burden. Under
the royal taxation a clergyman appointed to a benefice of any kind had to
pay the crown his whole income for the first year (first fruits) and 10 per
cent each year thereafter (tenths). This meant that a new chantry priest-
schoolmaster, whose salary was £10 a year, had to pay £10 in respect of his
first year of tenure and £1 per annum thereafter, which if he stayed for ten
years would amount to £20: an average of a fifth of his income during that
time. If he moved to a similar school, the process was repeated.

This problem soon attracted attention. In October 1536 John and William Dinham, Cornish gentry involved with the government of the chantry grammar school of Week St Mary, wrote to Thomas Cromwell, the king's minister, to intercede on behalf of their schoolmaster. They claimed that he was having difficulty paying his tenths because certain people were wrongfully occupying some of the school property, and asked that he should not be pressed for immediate payment by the bishop of Exeter, the local collector of the tenths.[23] They seem to have done more than this, since a draft of a petition made at about this time survives among the state papers, endorsed 'for the school of Week and others like'. It observed that first fruits and tenths diminished the salaries of masters in chantry schools and discouraged good men from taking up posts in such schools, which ought therefore to be exempted from taxation.[24] There is no evidence that the proposal even got as far as discussion within the government and it did not result in legislation. Chantry schools went on bearing the burden of first fruits and tenths until the two taxes were abandoned by Mary Tudor in 1555. Only when they were re-established in 1559, in the first Parliament of Elizabeth I, were schoolmasters at last officially excused from them.[25] However, because those who compiled the *Valor* were so busy dealing with religious houses and parish clergy, they failed to track down many chantries and religious guilds, particularly the smaller and poorer ones run by groups of parishioners. These were not discovered by the crown until the chantries and guilds were abolished in 1546–8, and their incumbents (some of whom were also acting as teachers) escaped the taxation up to that date.

THE DISSOLUTION OF THE MONASTERIES

The first involvement of the crown with the monasteries, between about 1535 and 1538, was marked, at least in part, by a plan of reform. Abbeys and priories were to be made to follow a more regulated life as part of the new Church of England, hence the commands to maintain schoolmasters and lecturers. Visitations of monasteries by bishops in the late 1530s continued to enquire about education as they had done in previous centuries.[26] But the reform of the monasteries, from the start, involved dissolution, beginning with the closure of the smaller houses in 1536. This turned into a creeping process of suppression. In 1538 the friaries were all closed and at about the same time a decision or assumption was made that all the monasteries and nunneries would share the same fate. It took another year or so to achieve this object, which was reached with the surrender of Waltham, the last of the abbeys, on 23 March 1540.[27]

The dissolution of the monasteries had immense implications for education, given the wide range of teaching with which the religious houses were involved. Schooling was still common for the religious themselves, for children of gentry in nunneries and abbots' households, for almonry boys and choristers, and sometimes for outsiders admitted to almonry schools. Certain houses were running public grammar schools. Most of this was of small concern to Henry VIII's regime. Those who aimed first to reduce and then to abolish the religious life had no interest in perpetuating the internal schools for the monks, friars, and nuns who were being disbanded. Almonry boys, almonry schools, and song schools probably had more credit, but nearly the whole of this provision was abolished between 1536 and 1540 and was replaced (as we shall see) at only a few new cathedral schools. There were about 840 monasteries, friaries, and nunneries in England in the mid 1530s, and if we assume an average of only six children in each house, the Dissolution caused the disappearance of 5,000 assisted places in education. The number may well have been higher.

What of the teachers and children maintained in these schools, whom the Dissolution left stranded? Children do not seem to have been eligible for compensation, but the crown was prepared to pay pensions to the adult officers and servants of religious houses, including teachers. People of this kind were required to make an application to the Court of Augmentations at Westminster, the body set up by the crown to administer monastic property.[28] They had to bring written evidence of the salaries they had enjoyed (in the form of the contract made between them and the monastery at the time of their appointment), and were then awarded pensions for life in recompense. The award and often the original contract were subsequently recorded in the registers of the court.[29] An example is that of William Tyler, a secular priest and MA, who had been retained by the abbey of Forde in 1537 to teach grammar to the almonry boys and to give the daily lecture on theology. His stipend had included board, lodging, a gown once a year, and an annual salary of £3 6s. 8d. For this he received a pension of £3: hardly enough to live on but leaving him free to work in some other school or post while he held it.[30] Even monks who had taught novices were eligible for an extra pension, although there are fewer examples of this, presumably because it was rare for such teachers to be formally appointed with salaries. John Pitt, referred to in the previous chapter as schoolmaster of Bath Abbey, secured a pension of £4, equal to his former salary, as well as the £9 that he received as an ex-monk.[31]

The Dissolution affected some schooling outside religious houses. A number of monasteries had been involved in providing or running grammar schools for members of the public, taught by professional masters. These schools were of two kinds. First there were those that had grown up in towns like Burton upon Trent, Bury St Edmunds, Evesham, Reading, and St Albans, where a powerful abbey exercised local government and gave the school patronage and support. The monks appointed the schoolmaster, owned and maintained the schoolhouse, and in at least the first four places paid the master a stipend to teach for nothing. Secondly, the founders of some endowed schools had entrusted them to the care of monasteries, with the responsibility for appointing masters and administering the endowments. Schools of this kind included Bruton, Cirencester, Farnworth, Faversham, and Winchcombe, as well as Lewes where the local prior merely appointed the master. The machinery for dissolving monasteries did not provide for saving either kind of school, and their fates varied widely, depending on individual factors rather than on crown policy. Two of the ancient abbey schools continued without difficulty. At Reading the schoolmaster, Leonard Cox, was a well-known grammarian and in 1541 the king confirmed him in office. He was granted tenure of the schoolhouse and his annual stipend of £10 was restored with arrears from Michaelmas 1539, when he had last been paid by the abbey.[32] At Evesham the master did not even suffer a temporary withdrawal of his wages. The new receiver appointed to administer the abbey lands went on paying him until the master's rights were confirmed by the Court of Augmentations in 1542.[33] At Burton upon Trent the school survived for a time, as part of a new collegiate church established by Henry VIII, but got into trouble later, as we shall see.[34] At Bury and St Albans the fate of the schools is obscure and local education may or may not have been disrupted until the re-establishment of St Albans school by a private benefactor in 1549 and of Bury by the king in 1550.[35]

The schools in the second group suffered various fates. At Cirencester the grammar school came to an end soon after the disappearance of its trustees, the monks of Winchcombe, and nothing officially was done to save it. In the end the people of the town were driven to fill the gap in 1545 by assigning one of the chantry priests in the parish church to teach a school with a salary of £7, £3 less than his predecessors.[36] At Faversham too the free school came to an end with the abbey, although, if the last schoolmaster is to be believed, this was the result of dishonesty on the abbot's part.[37] At Bruton the schoolmaster sued for his rights before the Court of Augmentations, which ought to have respected the separate foundation of which he was incumbent and sent him back to his old duties with his old stipend. Instead of this the court chose to regard him as an officer of the abbey and not only awarded him a pension but exonerated him from teaching the free school in future. To the great indignation of the people of Bruton, the free school came to an end, and by 1549 the pensioned master seems to have given up teaching altogether, for he was accused of turning the schoolroom into a malthouse.

Bruton school was eventually re-established, but only after the local inhabitants had twice petitioned the crown to bring this about. In 1550 the government of Edward VI belatedly restored the old endowments and made a new foundation, after an interregnum of ten years.[38] At Winchcombe things almost went the same way. The Court of Augmentations treated its master similarly as an employee of the abbey, giving him a pension and allowing him to cease from teaching free of charge. But for reasons now obscure this decree was never put into effect. The local receiver of the abbey lands paid the schoolmaster his regular salary of £10 in 1542 with arrears from 1539, and the school continued its existence with the loss of only its schoolhouse.[39] Farnworth school was even more fortunate; the court respected the endowment which had been in the keeping of Launde Priory and the annual income went on being paid.[40] At Lewes, where the prior had only nominated the master, the school endowments were administered by lay feoffees and did not fall within the scope of the dissolution, but when the mastership fell vacant in 1548 there was a little delay in getting a new incumbent appointed.[41]

The fate of the monasteries was shared by the larger hospitals staffed by religious brethren or sisters. Despite their charitable work, these houses were regarded primarily as monasteries and many were closed between 1536 and 1540. A few were spared for a little longer, but fell victim to a further attack on religious property in 1544, and by the end of Henry VIII's reign in 1547 virtually all had been dissolved.[42] Their educational facilities perished with them: the relatively small number of hospital schools like that of St Leonard's (York), and the larger number of scholars maintained in hospitals such as Bridgwater, Durham, and Exeter, who went to schools outside. This tale of woe had certain exceptions, as was the case with the schools attached to monasteries. Some hospitals had largely lost their medical functions in the later middle ages and had been turned into almshouses and schools, as at Banbury, Lichfield, and St Anthony's (London). These were spared dissolution and survived, although the latter lost its equilibrium and was despoiled (it was said) by the venality of its master, falling into decay in the reign of Elizabeth I.[43] Another London hospital, St Thomas of Acon, was seized by the crown in 1538, but when the premises and possessions were sold off to the London Company of Mercers in 1541, the condition was made that they should keep a free grammar school in perpetuity, staffed by a master paid £10 a year and teaching twenty-five children.[44] Almshouses, where the clergy were confined to one or two priests, were generally spared as well. The grammar school at Ewelme survived and its sister foundation at Heytesbury should have done so, had not another unscrupulous hospital master suppressed it until he was evicted in the reign of Mary I.[45] Examples like Heytesbury and St Anthony's remind us that the Reformation was an unsettling time even for religious foundations that were eligible to survive. Some of the disruption in this sector was due less to the crown than to local people seeking their own advantage.

CATHEDRAL AND OTHER SCHOOLS

What we have seen so far of the Reformation of Henry VIII has not conveyed much sense of concern for schools. Many perished in the wreck of the religious houses, and those that survived did so by luck as much as by goodwill. Yet although the crown can be justly accused of failing to take schools into account between 1535 and 1538, there was a strand of reform in its policies, and as the dissolution of the monasteries drew towards its close this crystallised in feelings that the process ought to include some positive schemes of charity that would benefit children and the poor. During the early and mid 1530s Thomas Starkey, humanist scholar and royal chaplain, had suggested that monasteries might be turned into schools for the sons of the nobility, or alternatively for youths as a whole, 'out of the which you may pick men apt to be ordained bishops and prelates'.[46] By the autumn of 1538 rumours were in the air that some abbeys were to be converted into colleges of secular priests engaged in preaching, teaching, and hospitality. The monks of Evesham wrote to Thomas Cromwell to beg that their house might be altered in this way, and Bishop Latimer of Worcester put in a plea on behalf of Great Malvern asking, 'Shall we not see two or three in each shire changed to such a remedy?'[47]

In the end none of the houses for which intercession was made gained respite from dissolution, and it was not until the spring of 1539 that the crown committed itself to doing something to assist religion, education, and charity. On 23 May 1539 a bill passed hurriedly through Parliament in a single day, authorising the king to establish a number of new bishoprics, cathedrals, and collegiate churches. The preamble to the bill, drafted by the king himself, declared an intention of diverting resources that had hitherto sustained 'the slothful and ungodly life' of those 'which have borne the name of religious folk' to the support of institutions 'whereby God's word might be the better set forth, children brought up in learning, clerks nourished in the universities, old servants decayed to have livings, almshouses for poor folk to be sustained in, readers of Greek, Hebrew, and Latin to have good stipend, daily alms to be administered, mending of highways, [and] exhibitions [i.e. scholarships] for ministers of the church'.[48] The king and his ministers now planned to utilise the buildings of some of the great monasteries to house these new cathedrals and colleges, and to give them charitable functions including the maintenance of grammar schools.

At first the royal plans were generous ones. Seven cathedrals had to be dealt with because they had been staffed by monks and needed to be re-established as non-monastic foundations of canons.[49] Henry also considered creating further dioceses, cathedrals, and schools – more than were forthcoming in the end. A memorandum in the king's own handwriting, which probably belongs to the spring or summer of 1539, proposed thirteen new cathedrals, all on the sites of former abbeys and priories, and as many as eighteen schemes were considered at one time or another.[50] In the autumn of the same year detailed lists were drafted of the deans, prebendaries (meaning canons), and other ministers needed in each foundation, together with the cost involved. Generous provision was to be made for education. Each cathedral was to have between six and ten boy choristers with a master to teach them, and a grammar school for the study of Latin, Greek, and in some cases Hebrew. Every school was to include a number of foundation scholars, varying from twenty to sixty, all of whom would receive free board, lodging, and clothing. Teaching was to be done by a master and usher, with generous salaries of £20 and £10 respectively, and it is probable that they were envisaged as teaching outsiders free of charge. Lastly there was to be provision for higher education. Most of the new cathedrals were to have between four and twenty exhibitions for scholars to attend the universities, as well as a reader in divinity to give lectures locally. But the three most important foundations in the scheme – Canterbury, Durham, and Westminster – were to engage in work of university level themselves, with readers in Greek, Hebrew, Latin, civil law, and physic.[51]

On 27 November 1539 Thomas Cromwell sent a copy of the draft scheme for Canterbury to Archbishop Cranmer for his comments. Cranmer's reply was only moderately favourable. He conceded that the plan would produce 'a very substantial and godly foundation', but he raised several objections to it. He thought the prebendaries unnecessary, observing ironically that 'commonly a prebendary is neither a learner nor teacher but a good viander [i.e. food lover]'. The five readers, he thought would not have any audience, 'for as for your prebendaries, they cannot attend to apply [themselves to] lectures, for making of good cheer. And as for your sixty children in grammar, their master and their usher be daily otherwise occupied in the rudiments of grammar.' Far better, he suggested, to do away with the prebendaries and establish in their stead 'twenty divines at £10 apiece, like as it is appointed to be at Oxford and Cambridge; and forty students in the tongues, and sciences, and French, to have ten marks apiece; for if such a number be not there resident, to what intent should so many readers be there? And surely it were great pity that so many good lectures should be read in vain.'[52]

In the end such criticisms or the financial costs caused the cathedral projects to be much abridged. A second scheme was produced which proposed to concentrate the readerships at the two universities, where they were later established as regius chairs, leaving a single reader in divinity at each cathedral like the chancellor of medieval times. The university exhibitions were severely reduced in number, and some cathedrals lost them altogether. This left the grammar schools as the main educational feature of the plans, and even here economies were made in some places.[53] The next step seems to have been to reduce the number of new foundations from the twenty proposed in the second scheme. This may have been due to Cromwell, whose papers include a note in the summer of 1539 'to diminish some of the bishoprics'.[54] The final outcome was the refoundation of seven old monastic cathedrals – Canterbury, Carlisle, Durham, Ely, Rochester, Winchester, and Worcester – and a sextet of new foundations on the sites of former abbeys. The six consisted of Bristol, Chester, Gloucester, Oxford, Peterborough, and Westminster.

Foundation charters were issued for the new cathedrals between 1540 and 1542, but it was not until 1544 that a commission was appointed to draw up

82   The Reformation and education. The monastic refectory of Worcester Cathedral, with its shattered image of Christ in majesty, became the schoolroom of Henry VIII's new King's School in the 1540s, seen here in a nineteenth-century photograph.

statutes for their government. Its members included Nicholas Heath, bishop of Worcester, George Day, bishop of Hereford, and Richard Cox, archdeacon of Ely, the first two of whom were to suffer in the cause of Catholicism and the third in that of Protestantism. The statutes they drafted were sent out to most of the cathedrals in the summer of 1544, but the contents were not closely related to the earlier schemes of 1539, nor were they uniform among themselves.[55] They ranged from the still comparatively lavish arrangements at Canterbury and Westminster down to the very modest ones thought good enough for Bristol and Carlisle. In most cases provision was made for a schoolmaster 'learned in Greek and Latin', with a stipend of between £13 and £20, and an usher 'learned in Latin'. These men were to give free instruction to all comers according to a prescribed curriculum. Most cathedral schools were given a number of endowed scholarships, varying from fifty at Canterbury to eighteen at Durham. Their holders, who were normally expected to stay at school for four or five years, received board and lodging worth £2 13s. 4d. or £3 6s. 8d. a year, as well as free education. At first provision was made for exhibitions from some of the cathedrals to the universities, these again ranging from twenty-six at Canterbury to four at

Rochester. But the exhibitions did not last for long, and by the end of the reign they had been abolished, the cathedral chapters being obliged to return the endowments to the crown.[56]

There were several anomalies in the schemes that were implemented. The three smallest foundations, Bristol, Carlisle, and Gloucester, were treated poorly and did not receive endowed scholarships or university exhibitions. At Durham the king incorporated into his cathedral the older grammar school endowed by Bishop Langley in the early fifteenth century.[57] At Oxford the cathedral school had only a brief existence. As first founded in 1542, the cathedral of Oxford was established in the abbey of Osney beyond the western edge of the city, and at this time it included a schoolhouse and schoolmaster's lodging.[58] Later, in 1546, the king began turning King Henry VIII College (his reshaping of Wolsey's foundation) into a new university college of Christ Church, and transferred to it the cathedral staff from Osney. The plans for the joint foundation drawn up in October 1546 included a grammar school with a master, usher, and forty scholars, but were never put into effect. When the college opened in January 1547, shortly before the king's death, the resources intended for the school were diverted to support forty undergraduate scholars. Apart from maintaining and teaching some choristers, the cathedral-college became restricted to university studies.[59]

Two other cathedrals experienced different treatment. Winchester was not awarded a school, presumably because Henry's regime, which allowed Wykeham's college to remain intact, thought another foundation superfluous. The seventy scholars of the college approximated to those of the other Henrician cathedrals, for which they were one of the models, and although Wykeham's college had not been planned as a school for the public of the neighbourhood, there are signs that it functioned as such in the sixteenth century, admitting local boys as commoners.[60] Norwich was another special case. This old monastic cathedral surrendered to the crown before the rest, in April 1538, and was immediately re-established with a dean and a chapter of prebendaries. The plans for Norwich appear to have included a schoolmaster, usher, twenty endowed scholarships, and free public education, and the cathedral was paying two teachers by 1545. But it was not until May 1547, just after Henry's death and in accordance with his intentions, that the crown implemented its plans, and it did so by negotiating with the city not the cathedral. The city corporation was made responsible for maintaining the chief local centre of charity, the Great Hospital, including the duty of supporting a master and usher. Norwich thus emerged with an endowed city grammar school, not a cathedral school.[61]

In one or two cases there was some continuity between the new Henrician cathedral school and the monastic town school that preceded it. This was so at Canterbury and Durham, where the old schoolmasters were reappointed to the new foundations.[62] But Henry's schemes for cathedrals and schools did not copy the constitutions of the medieval secular cathedrals like Lincoln and

Salisbury, which had grown up organically and, by the 1530s, were complex and individualistic bodies. Instead the king's foundations took inspiration from the collegiate churches and university colleges of the later middle ages, especially the royal foundation of St George's Chapel (Windsor).[63] Like these colleges the new cathedrals were given a comprehensive code of statutes, a chief officer (the dean) who was a ruler rather than a chairman, a free school, and an almshouse. The schools also conformed to recent collegiate models. Unlike the rather semi-detached cathedral schools of the middle ages, the Henrician schools formed part of the site and society of the cathedral. They usually occupied premises adjacent to the church, their masters were appointed by the dean and chapter collectively rather than by a chancellor individually, and the masters had dwellings and dining rights alongside the other lesser clergy of the church. Finally they provided free teaching, like most fifteenth- and early sixteenth-century school foundations, but unlike the majority of the old cathedral schools in the 1530s.

At the time that Henry's regime was planning new cathedrals, it contemplated founding some additional collegiate churches on monastic sites. Two of these were established at Burton upon Trent in 1541 and Thornton in the following year, and both included free grammar schools. Neither college lasted for more than a few years. The king suppressed Burton in 1545, pensioning the schoolmaster and putting the school (which had existed under the abbey) into jeopardy, although it appears to have survived, possibly as a fee-paying enterprise.[64] Thornton was dissolved by the government of Edward VI in 1548, but in this case the crown continued to pay the master's salary and the school was safeguarded.[65] The last of Henry's college schools was at Cambridge. Here in 1546 he embarked on a magnificent new foundation at Trinity College by amalgamating the two older colleges of the King's Hall and Michaelhouse. As at Christ Church (Oxford) the initial plans included not merely a university college but a grammar school consisting of a master, usher, and forty children given board and lodging. The college's foundation charter issued on 19 December 1546 mentioned the 'boys or pupils in the grammar school of the college'; the school appears to have opened in 1547 with six boys, and the complement of forty was reached the following year. This scheme fell foul not of Henry VIII but of changes after his death. In 1549 commissioners of Edward VI held a visitation of Cambridge University, in which they ordered the colleges to cease from teaching grammar in order to concentrate on higher education. An exception was made for the school at Jesus College because it served the city, but the Trinity grammar school was closed and its endowments were diverted to support undergraduates.[66] Neither university city secured a Henrician grammar school in the end.

Henry VIII had a hand in at least two other new schools of the 1540s. In 1541 he allowed the bishop of St David's, William Barlow, to convert some of the endowments of the collegiate church of Abergwili in his diocese towards founding Christ's College (Brecon) for the maintenance of a master, usher, and twenty foundation scholars.[67] This was one of the first endowed schools in Wales, which had lagged behind England in such amenities. Four years later the king sold to John Hales, a Coventry man and one of the officials of the chancery, the site and lands of the hospital of St John the Baptist, Coventry, at a very advantageous price, on condition that Hales founded a free grammar school there to be called King Henry VIII's School.[68] The favour of cheap land for endowments was not extended to all such founders of schools. Joan Cook of Gloucester, who bought some of the lands of a local priory to endow the Crypt School at Gloucester in 1539, received a grant after Bishop Latimer intervened in her favour, but she paid the typical purchase price of twenty times the annual value.[69]

THE UNIFORM GRAMMAR

The growth of a royal policy towards schools in about 1538–40, which is palpable in relation to the cathedrals, is also apparent more widely. It appears briefly in the second set of royal injunctions to the clergy, issued in 1538. These are best known for their attack on images and their order that churches be provided with English Bibles, but they also contain an educational directive that wealthy clergy should give charity to poor scholars, 'to the intent that learned men may hereafter spring the more'. Clergy with incomes of £100 or above were ordered to support one scholar at university or at a grammar school for every £100 of their stipends, 'which [scholars], after they have profited in good learning, may be partners of their patrons' cure and charge . . . or may, when need shall be, otherwise profit the commonwealth with their counsel and wisdom'.[70] It was not new for the clergy to raise up scholars to succeed them. The Oxford theologian Thomas Gascoigne claimed to have known a rector in the middle of the fifteenth century who had supported twenty youths at school from the profits of a single church, all of whom became priests, and clergy wills of the later middle ages often include bequests to pay for education.[71] Giving such charity was traditional, and although it now received official sanction, no arrangements were made for enforcing it.[72]

More significantly than this, towards the end of the 1530s the king took up the project of the uniform Latin grammar, which had languished since the convocation of 1530. Two textbooks were produced for use in schools, the first to be published, in 1540, consisting of an advanced-level work in Latin called *Institutio Compendiaria totius Grammaticae* ('a concise arrangement of all grammar'), published in 1540 by Thomas Berthelet, the king's official printer in London.[73] Its preface explained that the king had noticed the diversity with which grammar was taught in different schools, and had appointed learned men to compile a clear short grammar based on the best authors. The names of these men are not known, but they drew up a treatise taken in part from William Lily's works with additions and modifications from other writers of the early sixteenth century. It provided a detailed treatment of grammatical rules, syntax, and prosody. Two years later the *Institutio* was supplemented by an elementary grammar in English entitled *An Introduction of the Eyght Partes of Speche*, based partly on Lily's works, with material from further sources.[74] This gave a brief account of the basic Latin accidence and the simpler constructions, in the traditional manner. Both works carried the king's authority and expressly forbade the use of any other grammar in school, as a result of which the works of Stanbridge and Whittington virtually ceased to be printed. After 1542 the two royal grammars were usually published together, but they retained the character of separate works.[75]

The authorised grammars proved to be very successful. As usually printed in the sixteenth century, beginning with the alphabet, moving on to a catechism in Latin and English, and finally giving the texts in turn of the *Introduction* and *Institutio*, they provided a textbook for every stage of the school curriculum. They continued to be prescribed and enforced by Edward VI, Mary I, and Elizabeth I, and went on being used in revised versions for three centuries, the very last edition appearing in 1858. In 1545 the king supplemented the grammar with a uniform primer of prayers for use in school. The primer was in English, but when pupils had gained sufficient knowledge of Latin they had the option of using a Latin version. Its larger religious content meant that it was more affected by the religious vacillations of the following reigns than the grammar, and by 1549 alterations to it were already being made.[76]

THE LAST YEARS: COLLEGES AND THEIR SCHOOLS

The last years of Henry VIII's reign, from the fall of Thomas Cromwell in 1540 to the death of the king in January 1547, continued the mixture of positive and negative policies towards education that had marked the 1530s. Once the monasteries had fallen, it was not long before the crown began to cast covetous eyes upon the collegiate churches, despite the favour with which they had been regarded while the monasteries still stood. During the early 1540s they were called on, one by one, to surrender themselves and their property into the king's hands. The process was not finished when Henry died, but it was completed soon afterwards. Towards the end of 1547 the first Parliament of Edward VI passed the second Chantry Act, which authorised the suppression of those that remained, and they were wound up in the spring and summer of 1548. All that survived of the array of collegiate churches that had existed in the later middle ages were the university colleges, their associated institutions at Eton and Winchester, and the royal college of Windsor. It will be convenient here to consider the passing of these churches as a whole, and to ask what effect it had upon English education.

Not all the collegiate churches had possessed schools, but many had come to do so during the previous two centuries. Their schools were of two kinds. Some were internal operations for the ministers of the college, especially choristers and adolescent clerks. Such students needed training in plainsong and polyphony, and in some colleges this extended to grammar. The 1415 statutes of Fotheringhay, as we have seen, had provided for thirteen choristers and masters to teach them song and grammar,[77] while Rushworth had an endowed grammar school to teach five children from inside the college and seven from outside.[78] Some college schools were open to outsiders. This was so at some ancient minsters such as Beverley, Ripon, and Southwell in the diocese of York, and at a number of fourteenth- and fifteenth-century foundations like Acaster Selby, Higham Ferrers, Ottery St Mary, Rotherham, Tattershall, Westbury-on-Trym, and Wye. None of the schools meant only for college inmates survived the surrender of their houses, either under Henry VIII or Edward VI. They simply disappeared like the almonry schools of the monasteries.

The public grammar schools maintained by colleges fared better. Most of them were treated with more care by the crown than had been the case in the previous decade. At Higham Ferrers, where Archbishop Chichele's college surrendered itself to the king in 1542, the buildings and estates were granted to Robert Dacres, one of the king's councillors, on condition that he maintained two chaplains, thirteen almsmen, and a competent schoolmaster in Higham, the latter to be nominated by the crown and to receive £10 a year.[79] Exactly the same happened at Wye, the foundation of another archbishop, John Kemp, which came to an end in 1545. When the college and its possessions were awarded later that year to the queen's secretary, Walter Buckler, the condition was made that he must maintain a sufficient schoolmaster to teach a free grammar school, with a salary of £13 6s. 8d.[80] Tattershall grammar school also outlived the dissolution of its college in 1545, for it is mentioned as existing at the beginning of Elizabeth's reign,[81] and the survival of Thornton in 1548 has already been noted. It was untypical therefore that the surrender of the college at Westbury-on-Trym in 1544 included the closure of its public grammar school, founded by John Carpenter in 1463. Westbury college had been an unofficial cathedral for Bristol, three miles away, but Bristol now possessed its own cathedral and school. Presumably Westbury was seen as redundant.[82]

In two or three places Henry himself erected foundations to replace collegiate schools. In May 1545 he granted the college of St Mary (Warwick) to the burgesses of the town and gave them the duty of maintaining a free grammar school called 'the king's new school of Warwick', the master to be appointed by the crown and to receive a house and the usual £10 a year.[83] Later that year at Ottery St Mary, where the college had just been surrendered, the king conveyed the site to a corporation of four local men and re-established the college school as 'the king's new grammar school of Ottery St Mary', with a £10 master teaching grammar to all comers.[84] A third probable case, also in Devon, was that of the ancient minster at Crediton, where the bishops of the county had been based before they moved to

Exeter. It is not certain that this church maintained a public grammar school before its surrender in 1545, but it is highly suggestive that in April 1547, just after Henry's death and probably at his initiative, a corporation of governors of the church was established at Crediton on the Ottery model, charged with supporting a similar grammar school. It looks as though this too was the continuation of an older school, rather than a new benefaction.[85]

How should we sum up the relationship of crown and schools under Henry VIII? It was one that evolved. The king and his ministers were scarcely aware of schools for most of the reign and had no policy towards them, because schools had never been a responsibility of government. It followed that the first royal actions that affected schooling – the taxation of the clergy and the dissolution of the monasteries – took place with little or no thought of what the effects might be. By the late 1530s this lack of awareness was changing and the crown was developing educational policies: the foundation of cathedral schools, the imposition of the authorised grammar, and greater care about saving schools when the colleges were dissolved in the 1540s. The result was that school education both suffered and benefited under Henry's regime. On the negative side the dissolutions of monasteries, friaries, nunneries, and a great many colleges and hospitals meant the disappearance of all the education that they had provided for their own members and dependants. Individually such schools were small, but collectively they benefited thousands of people and made an important contribution to English life. The effect of the dissolutions on schools that catered for the public is less easily summarised, because it is so hard to know how many such schools were associated with the religious houses before their fall. Our own survey has mentioned nineteen schools for the public, dependent to some extent upon the houses seized by Henry VIII. Twelve of these survived his reign without much difficulty.[86] One (Bruton) was temporarily extinguished, and three came to an end altogether.[87] The history of the other three is obscure.[88]

So much for the debit account. Against this we can credit Henry and his ministers with the endowment of twelve permanent grammar schools in the cathedral cities and at Thornton, as well as a share in at least two other foundations. They also created more than 250 scholarships and over 100 places for choristers. This caused the educational effects of the dissolutions to resemble the religious ones, in that destruction in one area led to improvements in another, but on a smaller scale. Beyond what Henry did, for good or ill, a large sector of education lay untouched by his actions, larger than that which he touched. The schools of the old secular cathedrals continued their work through Henry's reign, little affected by change. So did the majority of the endowed schools, all the still numerous masters who worked for fees, and the clergy and others who taught small numbers of pupils. Mighty though Henry was, most of what went on England was beyond his interest or power to affect, and the same was true of schools.

10

From Edward VI to Elizabeth I

THE FIRST CHANTRY ACT, 1545

In 1545, Henry VIII, having dissolved the monasteries and many of the colleges, turned his attention to the chantries and religious guilds. Once again a process aimed at religious foundations had an effect on education. Most of the small endowed schools established in England up to the 1510s were linked with a chantry or guild, and their schoolmasters still had the duty of saying mass each day (Fig. 84). Even in the 1510s, when some school founders began to omit this requirement, others stayed faithful to the chantry model, and this continued to be the case until at least the late 1520s.[1] A great many chantry schools therefore existed by 1545, and few of these appear to have abandoned their chantry functions during the turmoils of the Reformation. On the contrary, other chantries and religious guilds, founded without educational purposes, came to maintain schools during the 1530s and 1540s because their governors or clergy decided they should do so. There was a spur in this direction from the convocation of Canterbury in 1530, with its order that parish clergy (including chantry priests) should teach children – an order which, as we have seen, had consequences.[2] The reform of chantries was bound to involve many schools.

At the same time the educational importance of chantries and guilds should not be exaggerated. Leach's enthusiasm on this subject has led many people to assume that they provided most of the schooling of late medieval and early Tudor England, but this cannot be true. The total number of chantries and religious guilds at the Reformation is still unclear, but when the crown tried to count and describe them in the so-called chantry certificates of 1546–8, there were probably about 4,000 of them supporting one or more priests.[3] The proportion of these that kept a school was small, whether as a requirement of their foundation or through subsequent adaptation by their patrons or governors. When Leach combed the certificates for references to chantry and guild schools, he found only about 184. His sources omitted four English counties completely and probably some others in part, so that this figure ought to be raised above 200, but even if we put it somewhat higher, it cannot have gone far beyond 5 per cent of the total: one in twenty. [4] The average number of chantry schools per county works out at about five or six, although a few had more: Lancashire nine, Essex seventeen, and Yorkshire (England's largest county) at least thirty. Herefordshire had fourteen, the highest total in terms of its size, mostly at the northern end and possibly due to some unusual local influence or initiative (Fig. 86). In Devon, on the other hand, the third largest county in size with some 110 functioning chantries and guilds with priests, only three were mentioned as running schools.[5]

Chantry schools were not only maintained by a minority of chantries; they represented a minority of schools, as they always had done. Even in the fifteenth century a few grammar schools had been endowed without the addition of a chantry: Sevenoaks, Magdalen College School (Oxford), and possibly Oswestry. In the 1510s this arrangement became the fashion, so that by the 1530s schools were founded purely as schools and their masterships were open to priests or laymen. Most of the schools of recent foundation, as well as those that Henry VIII had established in the cathedrals, were therefore unaffected by the suppression of the chantries. So were the very large number of private and fee-paying schools, which in many places provided the only education available. In the six counties of the

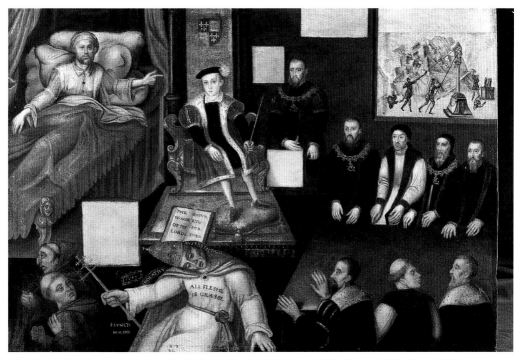

83   Some of the leaders of educational change in the 1540s and 1550s; Henry VIII, Edward VI, Edward duke of Somerset (standing), and Thomas Cranmer, archbishop of Canterbury

west of England, for example, about twenty-three chantry and guild schools were reported as existing in the late 1540s. We know of about twenty schools of other kinds at around that date, and that figure, based on casual records, points to a total that was very much bigger.[6] There is, however, one oddity about the statistics. At least 138 of the 184 chantry schools recorded in the certificates were grammar schools, which leaves a curiously low residue of priests who were teaching only reading or singing. One would expect such teaching to have been common, because it was a way for poorly paid clergy to improve their earnings and had been encouraged by the Church authorities since 1530. So either the encouragement had little effect or people did not bother to report the teaching of reading and song. In 1548, at least, the authorities made it clear that such teaching would not be preserved for the future.

The interest of Henry VIII and his government in chantries and religious guilds first became manifest on 15 December 1545, when a 'bill for the dissolution of chantries, colleges, and free chapels' was read for the first time in the House of Lords, which passed it two days later. It stayed a little longer in the Commons, but there too it went through all its stages within a week, and was ready for the royal assent on 23 December.[7] The crown's ostensible purpose in securing this first Chantry Act was to prevent unauthorised seizures and alienations of chantry and guild lands and endowments. In its preamble the act claimed that many founders and incumbents of chantries had already entered upon the lands or made alienations of the endowments. There is evidence to support that view.[8] At least four unauthorised dissolutions were subsequently discovered in Essex, four in Sussex, and thirteen in Somerset.[9] Accordingly the act provided that all colleges, chantries, hospitals, and guilds illegally dissolved within the last ten years should revert to the crown.

The measure also posed as one of reform. It claimed that in many places where chantries and guilds had been founded to give alms to the poor and to perform other charitable deeds, the governors and incumbents did not rule their properties or employ the revenues according to the virtuous intentions of the founders. Accordingly, 'for that the king's highness . . . intendeth to have the premises used and exercised to a more godly and virtuous purpose', Henry was empowered during his lifetime to appoint commissioners under the great seal to enter upon chantries, hospitals, guilds, and their possessions, and vest them in the king. The Chantry Act did not commit the king to any particular actions thereafter or safeguard any of the chantries' existing functions, but Henry was careful to convey the impression that the act would achieve a positive good for the realm, not just for his purse. On Christmas Eve 1545, he came to Parliament in person and delivered a speech – the last time, as it happened, that he addressed the assembly:

84   A school chantry chapel in Rock church (Worcs.), with modern furnishings. The chantry
priest said mass here every day, as well as teaching in a school nearby.

I cannot a little rejoice when I consider the perfect trust and sure
confidence with which you, without my desire or request [*sic*], have
committed to my order and disposition all chantries, colleges, and
hospitals. Surely if I, contrary to your expectation, should suffer the
ministers of the Church to decay, or learning (which is so great a jewel) to
be diminished, or poor and miserable people to be unrelieved, you might
say that I were no lover of the public wealth nor yet one that feared God.

He sought to give reassurance. 'Doubt not, I pray you, but your expectation
shall be served more godly and goodly than you will wish or desire, as
hereafter you shall plainly perceive.'[10]

The king appointed commissioners to make a survey of the chantries on
14 February 1546. They were organised in twenty-four panels, one for each
county or for a pair of adjoining counties. Each panel was headed by the
diocesan bishop and comprised between four and fourteen other members.
The latter were generally men of knightly or gentry rank who were officers
of the Court of Augmentations or of other departments of government. This
enabled the commissions to achieve maximum effect by combining social

status with administrative experience.[11] Much of the work probably fell on the king's local receivers and stewards of crown lands, many of whom were included on the panels for the sake of their intimate knowledge of local affairs. The commissioners began by sending injunctions to the clergy and churchwardens of each parish. They asked how many chantries, hospitals, free chapels, religious guilds, and stipendiary priests were maintained there, the names of the founders, the purpose of the foundations, and how the endowments were being employed. The clergy and wardens were to ascertain the annual revenues of the endowments and the value of the plate, jewels, ornaments, and other goods belonging to each foundation. They were to make a certificate of all these things and bring it before the commissioners at an appointed time and place, together with any documents relevant to the enquiry. This process put the onus of collecting information upon the parishes, while enabling the crown to vet the information and ensure that it was complete and accurate.

The work of producing certificates and reporting them to the commissioners appears to have been carried out, all over England, in the spring of 1546. Copies were then made of the certificates, county by county, and these copies form the first, or Henrician, series of chantry certificates.[12] The enquiries uncovered most of the extant chantries and guilds, but not all. In Devon, for example, about ninety such foundations were reported, whereas later events were to show that this was at least twenty short of the total.[13] Once the crown had received the information, there were a few suppressions of chantries and seizures of their property, but not many.[14] The sole chantry school in England thought to have been a casualty was a foundation at Aldwinkle for teaching six children to sing. It was seized by the crown in December 1546, and granted to one of the king's chief justices.[15] No definite royal policy about the chantries appears to have developed during the summer or autumn of 1546, and by the winter the king was sick. He died on 28 January 1547, and the first Chantry Act, valid only for his lifetime, died with him. The chantries and guilds received a short respite.

THE DISSOLUTION OF THE CHANTRIES, 1547–1548

Henry was succeeded by Edward VI, or rather by a government headed by the new king's uncle, Edward Seymour, duke of Somerset (Fig. 83). This government soon made clear its intention of continuing the Reformation of the Church on Protestant lines. One of its earliest actions was to send out royal commissioners to each diocese during the summer of 1547, with a new set of injunctions to the clergy, which carried further Henry's religious policies. All lights in churches were suppressed, except for two lights on the high altar. Religious processions were forbidden; and the epistle, gospel, and Bible lessons were ordered to be read in English. The injunctions included some educational clauses, but these largely repeated the policies of the 1530s. Clergy were to tell parents to put their children and servants to learning or to some honest occupation, so that they grew up to be responsible adults, not criminals or beggars. Every wealthy clergyman with benefices worth £100 was to continue to support one scholar at grammar school or university for each £100 of his income. Finally, those who taught were reminded of their duty to use only Henry VIII's primer and grammar, and chantry priests were urged once more to teach children reading, writing, good manners, 'and other virtuous exercises'.[16]

The commissioners also visited the cathedrals. There they took with them a further set of injunctions, to which they added commands appropriate to each place. These injunctions were mainly concerned with matters of government and religion, but they touched on education in two respects.[17] Every cathedral without a free grammar school in its precinct or nearby was ordered to provide one out of its common funds, staffed by a master with a salary of £13 6s. 8d. and a rent-free house, and an usher receiving £6 13s. 4d. and a rent-free chamber. This order was aimed at the 'old foundation' cathedrals, the non-monastic bodies that had not been refounded under Henry VIII and had hitherto been spared educational reform by the crown. Only three of them ran or were connected with free schools in 1547, these being Chichester, Lichfield, and St Paul's. The other six (Exeter, Hereford, Lincoln, Salisbury, Wells, and York) still had traditional grammar schools charging fees. These six schools now became free of charge and their cathedrals were required to bear their costs. In addition the cathedral commissioners gave their attention to choristers. Nothing was done to stop cathedrals maintaining such boys or teaching them song, although it was presumably envisaged that their repertoire would no longer include superstitious anthems to the Virgin Mary and would accord with the changes in worship that were being planned. However, orders were made in at least two places that choristers should no longer have tonsures shaved on their heads,[18] and the commissioners emphasised more firmly than before that they should emerge from their employment with a good knowledge of Latin. When their voices had broken and they were no longer eligible to stay in the choristers' school, the cathedral was to give them each an annual sum of £3 6s. 8d. for five years, to support them while they studied at grammar school.

The reforming policies of Edward's government became clearer towards the end of the year, when the first Parliament of the reign met on 4 November 1547. This saw the first steps towards the creation of a Protestant religious settlement. Statutes were passed modifying the mass and repealing the medieval heresy laws, and a new bill was introduced to deal with the chantries and religious guilds. Unlike its predecessor, which had mentioned only the abuses in these bodies, the new bill took a thoroughly Protestant line, attacking the idea of the chantry itself and castigating those who trusted in 'vain opinions of purgatory and masses satisfactory [i.e. masses of intercession]' rather than in 'their very true and perfect salvation through the death of Jesus Christ'. Protestant reformers regarded chantries as not only useless but pernicious, and ripe to be extinguished altogether. The new bill therefore proposed to convert all the endowments of prayers for the dead to 'good and godly uses, as in erecting of grammar schools . . , the further augmenting of the universities, and better provision for the poor and needy'. All colleges, chantries, and chapels that had maintained a priest in perpetuity within the last five years were to be vested in the crown, as were religious (but not craft) guilds and their possessions. The king was to appoint new commissioners to make another survey of all colleges, chantries, and guilds. Where such institutions had maintained a grammar school or a preacher by the terms of the foundation since the previous Michaelmas, an appropriate part of their endowments was to be assigned to maintain the amenity in future. Where the foundation was also a parish church, a vicar was to be endowed to care for the parishioners. The commissioners were to carry out their survey within a year, and the legislation was to take effect from the following Easter (1 April 1548). An exemption was made for the universities and the chantries within them, the colleges of Windsor, Eton, and Winchester, and the cathedrals (but not their chantries).[19]

The impression given by the second chantry bill was one of suppressing obsolete religious institutions while preserving and improving their charitable work. In addition new resources would be made available for other grammar schools, universities, and the poor. Public opinion was not convinced of these good intentions, however, and the bill encountered resistance in Parliament. In the House of Lords it was at first opposed not only by the more conservative bishops but by Archbishop Cranmer himself. When it went to the House of Commons on 15 December it aroused opposition on account of its threat to the properties of religious guilds, which had supported parish churches or public works in certain towns. Such activities were not included among the charities safeguarded by the bill. The opposition was led by the members of Parliament for King's Lynn and Coventry, with such success that the privy councillors who sat in the Commons feared that not only might the clause on the guilds be lost but the whole bill be put in jeopardy, since the parliamentary session was nearing its end. A compromise was reached with the representatives of the two towns. They were promised that, if they withdrew their objections, the king would make them a special grant of the guild endowments at issue. This promise was duly kept. After this it was possible to present the bill again, and it was passed by the House of Commons on 22 December.[20]

On 14 February 1548 new panels of commissioners were appointed to survey the chantries. A fresh survey was required because of the different circumstances of the second or Edwardian Chantry Act. All chantries were now to be confiscated, grammar schools and preachers to be safeguarded, and dispossessed chantry priests to be pensioned. The government also took the opportunity to identify and seize the endowments of church lights, but it ignored the hospitals which had been included in 1546. Again there were twenty-four panels, consisting of between five and thirteen members, eight or nine being the commonest numbers. Each panel dealt with one or two counties; in the latter case the members divided to carry out the survey, so that each county received separate treatment. Only a few of the commissioners of 1546 were reappointed, and the bishops were almost entirely absent, but as before most of the new members were officers of the Court of Augmentations or other departments of central government.[21] In 1547, just before Henry died, the court had been reconstituted. The crown lands in each county were put under the supervision of a 'particular surveyor', and these men were included on the commissions as being best informed about local conditions. They seem to have borne the brunt of the work as well. It would be wrong to regard them as servile or narrow-minded officials more concerned to seize lands for the crown than to discover and preserve useful charities. They were gentlemen of local standing, often justices of the peace, who applied themselves to compiling accurate information. The crown took the final decisions about confiscation or preservation.[22]

The arrangements for the new survey were probably similar to those of 1546, involving the sending of questionnaires to each parish, whose representatives brought their answers to the panels at central points. In Devon the commissioners are mentioned at such places as Exeter, Paignton, and Tiverton.[23] The information required was more extensive than before. Each parish's certificate began with an estimate of the number of communicants at church, in case the crown should feel disposed to appoint an extra priest to work in the parish. After the name of each chantry came details of the original founders and the date and purpose of the foundation. Then followed the incumbent's name, his age, his stipend, and any other benefices or pensions he held. Sometimes there were observations about his morals and learning. The revenues of the foundation were given, along with the value of the goods and ornaments. Occasionally the parishioners added a memorandum, recommending the usefulness of a chantry in supporting a grammar school or of a guild in maintaining public works. In certain cases they took the initiative in asking for a free school to be founded in their locality, evidently in view of the promise to convert chantry lands to 'good and godly uses'. Some commissioners themselves suggested where teachers or extra parish clergy might be provided. In Gloucestershire they named four places for schools, and in Staffordshire six. The parish certificates and the commissioners' observations were eventually copied into sets, county by county, which form the second, or Edwardian, series of chantry certificates.[24]

The chantry certificates have long been used as a source for the history of schools and charities, as well as of chantries and guilds, and rightly so. Yet they have shortcomings in this respect. They were first compiled in the parishes, not by the commissioners, and the temptation to conceal information from the crown was strong. At Powick, for example, the parishioners appear to have dismissed the chantry priest, and they certainly failed to make a certificate about the chantry, whose existence only came to light two years later.[25] At Wotton-under-Edge the oldest of all chantry grammar schools was deliberately misrepresented as a mere grammar school, and as the commissioners never discovered the truth, it escaped the act.[26] Other schools at Chipping Campden and Crewkerne, which had probably started as chantries, were similarly camouflaged and spared.[27] In Staffordshire so many foundations were withheld that new commissioners were appointed in 1549 to make a fresh survey.[28] For the next fifty years concealed chantry lands were a hunting ground for informers, attracted by the share of the proceeds they could receive when the crown recovered the property.

Even without the deliberate frauds, the information returned was sometimes vague or inaccurate. The figures for church communicants in certain parishes were generally given only in round numbers, and the two sets of figures that appear for Oxfordshire are often wildly incompatible. Its parishes sometimes failed to give correct information about the founders of chantries or returned them vaguely as 'diverse persons' even though, as at Burford, the original deeds and muniments should have been accessible. Nor were the priests of the chantries always who they claimed, for it was not unknown for the deputy of some absent cleric to represent himself as the true incumbent, and in Oxfordshire it has been noticed that the ages of clergy were given in round numbers. Still the commissioners were not entirely the passive recipients of tall stories, and the particular surveyors and their deputies did their best to verify the certificates. John Maynard, deputy surveyor of Oxfordshire, discovered the grammar school at Banbury, which had not been presented, as well as two cases of deputies pretending to be incumbents.[29]

Once the commissioners had completed their work it was up to the crown to carry out the promises made in the act. But even before the surveys were finished, the pressing demands of government had made it unlikely that the crown would be as generous as it had promised. War with Scotland had broken out in August 1547, French intervention was imminent, and there was a threat of rebellion in Ireland. Money was desperately needed, and the properties of the chantries offered a ready resource. On 17 April 1548 the king's privy council decided that chantry lands worth £5,000 a year should be sold, and appointed two officials to supervise the sales. The task was given to Sir Walter Mildmay, one of the general surveyors of the Court of Augmentations (Fig. 85), and Robert Kellway, surveyor of liveries in the Court of Wards.[30] To be fair to the crown, it did not altogether forget its obligations to education and charity, nor to the chantry priests who would be deprived by the confiscations. On 20 June a second commission was issued to Mildmay and Kellway in which the young King Edward recalled his intention 'to erect diverse and sundry grammar schools in every county in England and Wales, for the education and bringing up of youth in virtue

85 Sir Walter Mildmay
(d. 1589), the man charged
with reorganising the chantry
schools in 1548. The portrait
shows him in later life as
founder of Emmanuel
College (Cambridge).

and learning and godliness, and to make provision for the relief of the poor'. He stated, however, that this promise could not be fulfilled immediately. In the meantime Mildmay and Kellway were ordered to pension the incumbents of chantries who had been merely chantry priests. Those who had also been masters of grammar schools and preachers were to stay at their posts and to receive stipends from the crown equal to those they had enjoyed before 1548, 'until such time as other order and direction should be taken therein'.[31]

The reforms and improvements of schools promised by the act were thus put off, and the way was opened for the wholesale confiscation and sale of chantry and guild property. A third set of chantry certificates was now drawn up, abstracted from the fuller returns sent in by the commissioners. Notes were made against each chantry or guild and its incumbent, either awarding a pension or, in the case of grammar schools and preachers, writing the words *continuatur quo-usque*, meaning that the incumbents should continue in office and receive their previous stipends until the crown took a further decision. Chantry and guild lands were then sold off indiscriminately, whether or not they had supported schools. On 20 July 1548 Mildmay and Kellway signed a number of warrants, authorising the continuance of the grammar schools and other charities and ordering the receivers of the Court of Augmentations in each county to pay the schoolmasters their old stipends as from the previous 1 April. For the present therefore the crown took over the responsibility of financing the ex-chantry schools – the first time that an English government had financed school education on a national scale.[32] It did not necessarily appoint the masters of these schools as their posts became vacant; this power often remained with local patrons. Such patrons were now free to appoint laymen or priests to the posts, because these no longer carried priestly duties.

How many schools survived this crisis and secured a warrant for their continuance? The second Chantry Act had proposed to save grammar schools maintained by chantries and guilds as part of the original foundation, and these were accordingly respited. The classic chantry grammar schools of the fifteenth century – Alnwick, Newland, and Towcester – came into this class. Equally there were chantries and guilds which, while not having been founded to maintain schools, had since come to do so. Places of this kind included Bromsgrove, King's Norton, and Stourbridge, where priests employed by the parishioners to say masses and help with parish work had been given the further task of teaching grammar.[33] Some of these arrangements may not have been of long standing, and if the act was strictly interpreted they failed to qualify for continuance, not being part of an original foundation. Nevertheless, the commission to Mildmay and Kellway of 20 June empowered them to continue the stipends of any grammar masters, and in most cases they did so. Very few grammar schools, whatever their origin, seem to have been callously ignored; nearly all survived the dissolution of the chantries, at least to begin with. Two exceptions were the grammar school of the Trinity guild at Worcester, which had recently been revived after a period of lapse, and the famous school at Banbury, which had been concealed from the commissioners. Even these two schools were re-established by the crown within the next few years.[34]

The teaching of reading, writing, and song was treated differently. No provision was made in the act or in the instructions to Mildmay and Kellway for the continuance of such teaching, and those who had supplied it were pensioned like mere priests. This is aptly illustrated at Rotherham, where Archbishop Rotherham's college founded in 1483 to give free instruction in grammar, song, and writing was still in full working order in 1548. The chantry commissioners continued the grammar school, but the masters of writing and song got only pensions, reducing the value of a school originally intended to benefit the community in the widest possible sense.[35] Instruction in reading and writing, it seems, was regarded as so easily available as to need no support, while song would have been associated with Catholic Latin worship. Barely a year after the Chantry Act, in 1549, Latin worship itself was abolished, which dealt a further blow to the teaching of song. During

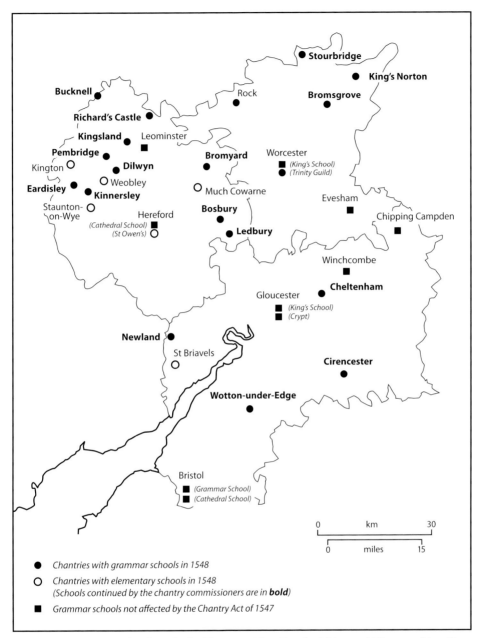

86   The dissolution of the chantries in Gloucestershire, Herefordshire, and Worcestershire. Note the unusual concentration of chantry grammar schools in north Herefordshire.

the fifteenth and early sixteenth centuries many of the larger and wealthier English parish churches had come to maintain small groups of singing boys to perform anthems or Lady masses, in the manner of the cathedrals and monasteries. This work involved learning or practising the reading of Latin words and musical notation with the help of a chaplain or clerk of the church. Recalling Hatfield church in Yorkshire before the Reformation, a local writer described 'the singing boys, some on one side of the church, and some on the other, with their books on their stands before them, who made most sweet and pleasant music'.[36]

There must have been dozens of such choirs up and down the kingdom until the 1540s, involving hundreds of boys. In the west of England alone they are recorded at Ashburton, Cirencester, Lyme Regis, and in at least two churches in Bristol.[37] Some had endowments that fell within the Chantry Act and failed for that reason, like the song school and boys of Cirencester. Others were maintained from parish income and lay outside the act, but when the Latin services were replaced by the new English ones of the *Book of Common Prayer* in 1549, there was no role in church for singing of this kind. The schoolboy choirs then disappeared in most places.

THE GRAMMAR SCHOOL FOUNDATIONS OF EDWARD VI

The care of the commissioners in arranging for the continuance of chantry grammar school stipends could not disguise the fact that the crown had gone back on its promises. It had undertaken to provide more schools and to save the lands of those that already existed, but it was slow to do the first and failed to do the second. In 1547 only three new schools were created: two, Crediton and Norwich, originating in the previous reign, and a third, Grimsby, with a minimal endowment.[38] In 1548 no foundations were made, and when the parishioners of Long Melford (on the advice of the local chantry commissioners) sent a deputation to London to ask for a grant of their chantry school's endowments, they had no success. A local knight secured the lands instead.[39] In 1549 the crown made three foundations, but only one of these, at Saffron Walden, involved the return of the school's property. In the other two cases, at Maidstone and Wisbech, local people paid £205 and £260 respectively for chantry property, receiving permission to found grammar schools as part of the transaction.[40] This added up to scarcely any benefit to school education from Edward VI's government up to 1550. Meanwhile the lands of the chantry schools were fast being sold off, and the temporary arrangement by which the crown paid the masters had the appearance of becoming permanent. No wonder that there was disappointment at the outcome, and not a little indignation. In January 1549 an attempt was made to force the government's hand by introducing a bill in the House of Commons 'for making of schools and giving lands thereto'. It was read three times and approved, but was shelved when it reached the Lords. A second attempt in December of the same year did not get beyond its first reading in the Commons.[41]

In 1550 discontent was voiced in the pulpit. Thomas Lever, master of St John's College (Cambridge), was one of the leading Protestant divines. The college had held the patronage of the chantry grammar school at Sedbergh, and had made valiant but unsuccessful attempts to prevent the endowment from being seized and sold. Preaching at St Paul's (London) on 2 February, Lever launched an attack on the wry results of the recent appropriations of religious property. He was careful to say that the purpose of Henry VIII and Edward VI in suppressing abbeys, colleges, and chantries was 'very godly'. But he complained that

> covetous officers have so used this matter that even those goods which did serve to the relief of the poor, the maintenance of learning, and to comfortable necessary hospitality in the commonwealth be turned to maintain worldly, wicked, covetous ambition.[42]

Harsh words, which he repeated in a sermon before the king himself on 16 March. This time he particularised, referring to Sedbergh (though not by name), and again adroitly avoided attack on the crown by placing the blame on dishonest people:

> There was in the north country . . . a grammar school founded, having in the university of Cambridge of the same foundation eight scholarships, ever replenished with the scholars of that school, which school is now sold, decayed, and lost. More there be of like sort handled. But I recite this only because I know that the sale of it was once stayed of charity, and yet afterwards brought to pass by bribery, as I heard say, and believe it because that it is only bribery that customably overcometh charity.

'If you that be now in authority do not look upon such things to redress them,' he concluded, 'God will look upon you to revenge them.'[43] Lever made a further protest in December, again at St Paul's. Once more he attacked the damage recently done to the universities and reiterated the case of the schools:

> Yea, and in the country many grammar schools founded of a godly intent to bring up poor men's sons in learning and virtue, now be taken away by the greedy covetousness of you that were put in trust by God and the king to erect and make grammar schools in many places. . . . Take heed unto the king's statutes, the acts of Parliament: there ye shall find that the nobles and commons do give . . . abbeys, colleges, and chantries for erecting of grammar schools, the godly bringing up of youth, the further augmenting of the universities, and better provision for the poor. This shall ye find in the acts of Parliament, in the king's statutes, but what shall be found in your practice and your deeds? Surely the pulling down of grammar schools, the devilish drowning of youth in ignorance, the utter decay of the universities, and most uncharitable spoil of provision that was made for the poor.[44]

How far this moved the government is hard to say. Nevertheless, the year 1550 saw the first of a number of royal foundations, usually called the 'free grammar schools of King Edward VI', by which the crown re-established chantry schools with new endowments or created wholly new schools. Five schemes were authorised in 1550, four in 1551 (including Sedbergh), nine in 1552, and six in 1553 – omitting minor grants. Some of the places chosen for this purpose had been recommended in the chantry certificates of 1548, but in the end vigorous petitioning or influential backing were also important factors. Most of the letters patent founding the new schools state at whose request the foundation was made, and these tell us that Sir John Mason forwarded the case of his home town of Abingdon, while Chelmsford owed its good fortune to Sir William Petre and Sir Walter Mildmay, both of whom lived in the neighbourhood. The foundation at Bath seems to have been due to the exertions of the town authorities there.[45] Altogether there were twenty-six major royal benefactions to schools under Edward VI, if we count Grimsby and Saffron Walden along with the post-1550 foundations. Thirteen of these related to pre-existing chantry and guild schools. The arrangements varied in their scale, and at Saffron Walden and Ludlow the crown merely returned the endowment of the earlier school.[46] In most cases greater generosity was shown, and schools whose endowments had produced £10 or less before 1548 were re-established with incomes of around £20. Lever ought to have been pleased to see Sedbergh's former lands worth £11 per annum replaced with new ones worth £20, and at Giggleswick nearby the endowment went up even more, from £6 to £23.[47]

The second group of benefactions gave rise to thirteen foundations that were either entirely new ones or replaced earlier schools that had not been affected by the second Chantry Act. Here again cases differed. There were Bruton, where the school endowments had come into the hands of the crown in 1539 after the dissolution of the abbey, and Bury St Edmunds and Sherborne, whose schools may well have been disrupted in the same process. There were Guildford and Nuneaton, apparently non-chantry schools endowed before the Reformation, now re-established and augmented. Lastly there were some places where no endowed schools appear to have existed before, such as Bath, Birmingham, Shrewsbury, and Spilsby.[48] These schools complete the list of the more obvious Edwardian foundations, but there were a few instances in which the crown made small grants to schools or empowered private benefactors to found schools and to acquire endowments without paying fees for permission.[49] One or two other chantry schools were privately refounded during the reign. Stamford was re-established in 1549 by a private act of Parliament through the efforts of William Cecil, afterwards Lord Burghley.[50] Pocklington was revived by its founder's nephew, Thomas Dowman, in a similar way in 1552.[51] At Towcester some of the parishioners bought back the chantry house between 1550 and 1552, after it had been confiscated and sold, and conveyed it to feoffees for the perpetual use of the schoolmaster.[52]

THE SCHOOLS FROM EDWARD VI TO ELIZABETH I

When Edward died in 1553 the new foundations of his reign, private and royal, still fell short of the expectations of 1547–9. Most of the places noted by the chantry commissioners as suitable for endowed schools had not received them, and a hundred or so of the old chantry grammar schools were probably dependent on the temporary payments from the crown. Still, it would be unfair to dismiss his regime as uninterested in school education, and in fact it is possible to trace a slow but upward trend in this respect. Henry's government had imposed the primer and grammar on schools in general, but it had not given much attention to supervising the work of individual masters and schools, beyond setting up cathedral schools in 1540–2. Interest in this matter grew a little in the 1540s. Nicholas Heath issued injunctions for Rochester Cathedral in 1543, which touched on the cathedral school, and Edward VI's visitors did likewise for Canterbury Cathedral and Winchester College in 1547.[53] At Canterbury the dean was ordered to visit the grammar school at least once a quarter and examine the diligence of the masters as well as the learning of the pupils. At Winchester there were more stringent requirements. The master, when handling 'profane' or pagan authors, was to use the Bible to refute any material that contradicted the Christian religion. The scholars were to be instructed not only in the king's primer but in Erasmus's *Catechism*, and the warden of the college was told to read them a part of the *Catechism* every Sunday and to prove it from Holy Scripture.

There are some other signs of governmental interest in children and education under Edward VI. One is the English *Catechismus* published in 1548 'for the singular commodity and profit of children and young people' by authority of Archbishop Cranmer. This book, expounding the Ten Commandments and the Lord's Prayer, was translated from German and made attractive with pictures. Most of these show episodes from the Bible, but once or twice the Reformation creeps in. In the retelling of Christ's parable of the Pharisee and the poor man praying in the Temple, the Pharisee is dressed as a monk (Fig. 87). Elsewhere Christ casts out a devil, watched by monk-like figures.[54] Another royal initiative appears in the foundation charters of the new Edwardian schools, in the form of a clause requiring that they should have statutes drawn up with the advice of the local bishop. This requirement first appeared in the instrument setting up Wisbech school in 1549, and became common during the rest of the king's reign.[55] The notion that bishops should supervise how schools were run was in essence traditional, but had been honoured in the breach not the observance. Its revival under Edward reflects the beliefs of the Reformation that bishops should be pastors rather than prelates, and that school education should be more firmly under the control of the authorities. In Edward's reign this supervision was restricted to individual schools; it did not become a general policy. Nor was it necessarily effective wherever it was

applied. The headmaster of Wells cathedral school from 1549 to 1551 was
Richard Edon, a former Cistercian monk who returned to the monastic life
in Mary's reign. His usher, Rowland Mynever, was sufficiently Catholic to act
as Edon's successor in Mary's first year of power.[56] It is unlikely that the
spirit of the Edwardian Reformation made much progress in their school,
although its outward rules were probably followed.

The educational policies of Edward's reign were most fully and finally
expounded in the *Reformation of Ecclesiastical Laws*, a new draft code of
Church law in Latin produced by Archbishop Cranmer and a committee of
divines and lawyers between 1551 and 1553. The code was presented to the
House of Lords in March 1553, but it encountered criticisms and did not
receive official approval before the king's death in July of that year. It dealt
with the education of children in three respects. First it required each parish
clergyman to spend an hour on Sunday afternoons teaching and explaining
the catechism to children and young adults 'so that they may be taught the
main points of religion'.[57] The catechism was a short text in English, capable
of being committed to memory, which taught the Apostles' Creed, the Ten
Commandments, and the Lord's Prayer, with explanations of their
meaning. The duty of teaching the catechism had been laid on the parish
clergy by Edward's government in the *Book of Common Prayer* in 1549,
initially for half an hour on an occasional basis. This duty was now to be
increased and regularised.[58] Secondly, every parish clerk was to instruct the
children of the parish in the catechism and the alphabet, 'so that children
may begin to understand both what to believe and how to pray and how to
live well and blessedly'.[59] This proposal was the nearest that the Edwardian
regime came to adopting a policy in favour of universal primary education.
Indeed the words it used for child and childhood, *puer* and *pueritia*, were

87   Religious controversy affects
education. Cranmer's *Catechism* for
children (1548) depicts Christ's parable
of the Pharisee and the poor man, with
a monk as the Pharisee.

ANNO DNI   1544

LADI MARI   DOVGHTER TO
THE MOST   VERTVOVS PRINCE
KING HENRI   THE EIGHT

THE AGE OF   XXVIII YERES

88 Queen Mary Tudor (d. 1558), during whose reign the supervision of schools became a
regular part of state policy and procedure.

gender inclusive, so that girls were not specifically excluded from the
provision. The wages of clerks were to be paid by their parishioners, as they
had been traditionally, and Cranmer's committee proposed that clerks who
refused to teach should be removed from office. Bishops were ordered to
supervise their wages and to increase those that were inadequate.

At the same time the novelty of the policy should not overemphasised. The words 'all the childhood of their parish' were qualified by the phrase 'offered to them', meaning that parish clerks were merely required to teach those who asked for the favour. No arrangements were made for training them to teach, and no resources (rooms or books) were provided to help them do so. Presumably they were envisaged as teaching in the church or in the church house used for parish social events, and parents as providing their children with alphabet books. Similar limitations are visible in the Cranmer committee's third engagement with education: policy towards schools. Although their law code contains a section entitled 'Of schools and schoolmasters', this was concerned with cathedral schools, not schools in general, a respect in which it followed in the footsteps of the Fourth Lateran Council.[60] Deans and chapters were ordered, as they had been in 1547, to pay a schoolmaster £20, but nothing was said of an usher. Masters were to be appointed in future by the bishop, instead of other local authorities (in other words cathedral chapters or chancellors). The boys of the school were to be aged between eight and fourteen on their admission, and were to be examined twice a year, leading to the removal of those who were unfitted for instruction. School was to start and finish each day with recitation of the Creed, Ten Commandments, and Lord's Prayer. Unsuitable books were not to be taught, and only the authorised grammar was to be used. On Sundays and feast-days the schoolmaster was to bring the boys to worship in the cathedral, both morning and afternoon.[61]

These regulations developed the regime's involvement with cathedral schools, but the involvement was not extended to schools in general. Moreover, Edward VI died in July 1553, Mary I succeeded, and the draft code of law was never implemented. Mary (Fig. 88) and her regime have acquired a reputation for 'reaction' and for putting back the religious clock to the 1530s, but this view does insufficient justice either to her reign or to its interest in education. On the contrary, the concern of Edward's government with certain schools was enlarged to include schools and their teachers in general. This process probably owed something to Mary's advisors such as Cardinal Pole, who were in touch with the Continent where school education was taken more seriously. It also reflected the current state of the Reformation in England. The incremental changes which had swept people along under Henry VIII and Edward VI were being reversed. There were now two clear religious alternatives, Catholic and Protestant, and control of education was recognised as an essential tool in the struggle to re-establish one and repress the other. Accordingly in March 1554, less than a year after her accession, Mary sent a series of instructions to all the bishops, one of which ordered them to

> examine all schoolmasters and teachers of children, and finding them
> suspect in any wise to remove them, and place Catholic men in their

rooms, with a special commandment to instruct their children so as they may be able to answer the priest at the mass, and so help the priest to mass as hath been accustomed.[62]

Nothing so searching had been required by previous monarchs. Just as Mary in 1554 embarked on an unprecedented attack on unreliable clergy, depriving those who had married under Edward VI, so she sought to weed out unreliable schoolmasters. A month later an act of Parliament empowered the queen to make new statutes for the cathedrals reorganised by Henry VIII and for such grammar schools as had been established under Henry and Edward VI.[63]

By the autumn of 1554 educational policy was being enforced by at least one bishop: Mary's stout supporter, Bonner of London. He drew up articles and injunctions for a thorough visitation of his diocese that included two whole sections 'concerning schoolmasters and teachers of children'. Masters were to be examined before they were allowed to teach, and were to be honest, diligent, Catholic, and effective in teaching Catholicism to their charges.[64] The concern of Mary and Bonner may be due in part to the fact that some clergy who had married under Edward VI, like William Alley the future bishop of Exeter, lost their parishes at this time and took to teaching, a role in which they would have been regarded as unreliable if not dangerous.[65] Indeed in December 1554 there were attempts in the House of Commons to promote a bill to prevent married or seditious priests from becoming schoolmasters, but the attempts seem to have lacked official support and nothing came of them.[66]

Mary inherited the problem of the ex-chantry schools. One of the complaints of the convocation of the province of Canterbury, which met at the end of 1554, was that although the second Chantry Act had provided for the foundation of schools, hospitals, and other works of charity, this had not been carried out in accordance with the meaning of the act, and the bishops were asked to petition the queen to amend the matter.[67] If they did, they had little success, for Mary's reign marked no improvement on her brother's in this respect. Three former chantry schools seem to have been re-endowed by her regime at Basingstoke, Boston, and Bromsgrove, and three new endowments were made at Clitheroe, Leominster, and Walsall.[68] Some further royal encouragement was given to private founders of schools by waiving fees for foundation charters and the acquisition of endowments.[69] Against this the arrangements for paying the schoolmasters in receipt of salaries from the crown were not always as satisfactory under Mary as they had been under Edward. The payments ceased in Cornwall in 1556, and in Northamptonshire at about the same time. Only after 1559, when Mary had been succeeded by Elizabeth, was it possible for aggrieved masters to sue for their salaries from the Court of the Exchequer (which had now taken over the functions of the Court of Augmentations). Orders were then issued that the payments should be resumed, and in some cases arrears were awarded for the unpaid years.[70]

In the winter of 1555–6 a further attempt to reform the Church in the interests of Catholicism was made by Reginald Pole: cardinal, papal legate, and archbishop of Canterbury. On 2 December 1555 he opened a national synod of the clergy, which enacted twelve decrees including one devoted to schooling. This ordered each cathedral church to maintain a certain number of boys, 'or rather a seminary', according to the wealth and size of the diocese. The boys chosen were to be aged eleven or more, able to read and write, and the children of poor rather than rich parents. They were to attend a school organised in two classes, and to learn grammar and ecclesiastical discipline. In the junior class the boys would receive food and clothes, and in the upper one a sum of money as well. All were to be tonsured and to wear ecclesiastical dress, and the upper class (probably those over fourteen) were to be ordained as acolytes. When they had reached the legitimate age to do so, they were to take higher orders and be sent to minister in a church under the bishop's supervision. Other boys could also be admitted, as long as they conformed to this order. The expenses of these schools were to be borne by the clergy's payments of first fruits and by a new tax of 6d. in the pound on the income of bishops and holders of benefices worth more than £20 a year. This was to make more general the obligation to support scholars which Henry and Edward had already imposed on all benefices worth more than £100 a year. As a pendant to this legislation the synod repeated the prohibition against people undertaking the office of teaching until they had been examined and approved by the bishop, on pain of excommunication and a ban on teaching for three years.[71]

The decree of 1555–6 made a bold attempt to restore a Catholic ethos to cathedral education in terms of dress, training (the boys were to assist in religious services), and the production of future priests. The scheme was put into effect in at least two places. At Lincoln Bishop White founded the 'College of Thirty Poor Clerks' in 1556, into which he gathered the adolescent secondaries and altarists who had always been maintained in the cathedral, and added to their number.[72] At York St Mary's Hospital was taken over by the dean and chapter to house fifty boys learning grammar with a view to their becoming priests.[73] At Wells, where no seminary seems to have been established, a new schoolmaster and usher were appointed in about 1556, both university men from Corpus Christi College (Oxford) – a strong centre of Catholicism. Each was given a canonry of the cathedral – an unusual dignity for schoolmasters – and the master was allowed to hold a parochial benefice too.[74] The effectiveness with which the Marian regime stiffened the Catholicism of the cathedral schools can be measured in part by what happened after Mary died and Protestantism was restored in 1559. Several cathedral schoolmasters then preferred to lose their posts rather than conform to the new order. They included both masters of Winchester College, and the headmasters of Durham, St Paul's, Salisbury, and Wells.[75]

The accession of Elizabeth I in November 1558, following the deaths of Mary and Pole, soon led to the re-establishment of Protestantism, but policies towards schools remained essentially those that had developed under Henry, Edward, and Mary. Elizabeth's first Parliament (January to May 1559) enacted similar legislation to that of Mary in 1554, empowering the queen to make new statutes for cathedrals and schools established under the previous three Tudor monarchs.[76] In the summer a fresh set of royal injunctions to the clergy was issued. Beneficed men with incomes of over £100 were once more commanded to support scholars, and the licensing of teachers was retained. 'No man,' declared the injunctions, 'shall take upon him to teach but such as shall be allowed by the ordinary [i.e. the bishop], and found meet as well for his learning and dexterity in teaching, as for sober and honest conversation, and also for right understanding of God's true religion.'[77] The licensing of schoolmasters by the diocesan bishops was now an important part of state control of society. It was widely implemented

89   Benefits of the Reformation. The grammar school of Higham Ferrers (Northants.) moved into this handsome fifteenth-century chapel.

down to the eighteenth century and did not finally disappear until 1869.
Meanwhile the foundation of schools by the crown continued on the rather
modest scale of Mary's reign. Although a number of 'free grammar schools
of Queen Elizabeth' were established after 1559, most were endowed by
private benefactors, the queen's contribution being to grant the charter
setting up a body of governors and give permission to acquire lands without
further fees. The crown itself made only a few additions to what Edward and
Mary had done in re-endowing the old chantry schools. Two were
refounded at Worcester (1561) and Penrith (1564), with annuities equal in
value to the stipends that the incumbents had formerly enjoyed.[78] At
Darlington (1563) and Middleton (1572) two more chantry schools whose
masters had been receiving their stipends out of the crown lands were
granted endowments of land.[79] There were some other less obvious
manifestations of royal patronage where, on the foundation of new schools
or on the refoundation of old ones, buildings were made over and lands
assigned: if not as a gift, at least on favourable terms.

CONCLUSION

The debate about the Reformation and school education, opened by Leach
in 1896 and intermittently pursued by scholars thereafter, has chiefly
centred on the economy of schooling. How far was it damaged by royal
policies and actions? In our present state of knowledge it appears that Leach
underrated the injury caused to schools under Henry VIII, because of his
poor regard for the education provided by monasteries. In turn he
overestimated the adverse effects of the dissolution of chantries and guilds
under Edward VI. He was right to modify the older view of Edward's
government as providing schools where none had been before. He was
justified in expressing disappointment – shared by people in Tudor
England – at the treatment of the existing chantry schools and the small
amount of property transferred to endow new ones. Nevertheless, although
some schools and localities suffered from royal policies, it is unlikely that
there was any great recession of school education in mid sixteenth-century
England. The crown's involvement with schooling touched only a minority
of its outlets. Most Tudor schools (and there were many of them) flourished
or died not because of what the crown did to them, but through the efforts
or failings of wealthy benefactors, private-venture schoolmasters, and fee-
paying parents.

Much of the crown's engagement with schools between 1534 and 1560
arose not so much from a concern with education but because schools got
caught up in its religious and financial policies. Henry's government
founded cathedral schools because it had to fill the gap left by the
dissolution of the monastic cathedrals. Edward's took over the payment of
chantry schoolmasters because it wanted to sell school property and the

payments cost less in the short term. Neither government wished to set up a system of state education. Still, the Tudor regimes were not altogether lacking in proactive educational policies, at least from about 1540. Henry VIII imposed the authorised grammar. The government of Edward VI made visitations of cathedral schools, gave bishops supervision of school statutes, and planned to involve parish clerks in teaching children. Under Mary teachers began to be licensed and seminaries were envisaged at the cathedrals. These initiatives marked a departure from the later middle ages, when neither the Church nor the crown had involved itself with schools on a national scale. At the same time the development of policies for schools was slow and often limited, and teaching received far less attention from the authorities than other social issues of the day. If we add up all the Tudor statutes and proclamations relating to schools, the total is small compared with those about poverty, law and order, wages and prices, and even recreations. During the sixteenth century the crown turned the parishes of England – originally units of the Church – into agencies of royal government. Parishes became responsible for poor relief, roads and bridges, and military defence, but (save for the canon law of 1553, which was never implemented) schooling was excluded. The Reformation, which laid such emphasis upon the written word, did not provide for everyone to read it.

School education certainly underwent changes between 1520 and 1560. Negatively, the links between schooling and monasteries, chantries, and church choirs were broken. Positively, teachers were licensed, given more direction in what they taught, and in some cases paid by the central government. Yet periodising education into 'pre-Reformation' and 'post-Reformation', as into 'medieval' and 'Renaissance', can be misleading. Much about the schools of Elizabethan England, when Shakespeare was growing up in the 1560s and 1570s, was still medieval. Many of them pre-dated the Reformation and commemorated founders who were Catholics. Their buildings often survived from earlier times, and even new foundations might be housed in former monastic halls or chantry chapels (Figs 82 and 89). What was taught owed much to ancient practices. The master still apposed his pupils, made them engage in disputations, had them perform plays, and administered corporal punishment in traditional ways. Education was still inextricably linked with religious teaching, and formal schooling still catered chiefly for boys. Whenever we terminate a history of medieval schools, as we are doing now, must be an arbitrary decision, for there is no definitive stopping point. No moment occurred at which schooling passed from one era into another. To repeat the assertion with which we began our journey, medieval education was not a precursor of modern education. It was the same thing in different circumstances.

REFLECTIONS

ℭ The Byble in
Englyshe, that is to saye the content of all the holy scrypture, bothe
of þ olde and newe testament, truly
translated after the veryte of the
Hebrue and Greke textes, by þ dy-
lygent studye of dyuerse excellent
learned men, expert in the forsayde
tonges.

℃ Prynted by Rychard Grafton &
Edward Whitchurch.

Cum priuilegio ad imprimen-
dum solum.
1539.

11

Reflections

A history of schools is different from a history of childhood. Children and parents are human beings. Although they share in historical change, many aspects of being a child and bringing one up remain the same today as they were in the past. Schools are human inventions. They centre on human beings and broadly follow similar tasks, but they are more subject to variation and change. Their teaching differs and alters, depending on the careers for which they give training, the strategies of teachers, the wishes of parents, and the intervention of exterior bodies like governments and churches. Only a minority of modern schools are ancient institutions. None of those that exist today can be truthfully traced back before 1100, and not many before 1400. There has been education in Canterbury, for instance, since about 597, but it has been provided by a series of different schools, not a single one. School buildings and resources change more rapidly than institutions. How many buildings are still in use after two centuries; how many schoolbooks after fifty years? The history of schools is therefore highly complex, and a book about them must be complex too. It must not only describe their features but trace how those features developed chronologically.

'Medieval schools' is a useful phrase to put on the front of a book about education from the Romans to the Renaissance. But 'medieval' is no more than convenient shorthand. It is a word coined after the time to which it refers, misleadingly suggestive that the centuries from 400 to 1500 were uniform and changeless, whereas each year, generation, and century was distinctive in certain ways. Education underwent changes throughout this epoch: the countless small ones caused by the comings and goings of masters and pupils, and the larger ones produced by educational fashions or external events. Schools changed partly from within, through the work of teachers and pupils, and partly through the impact of the world outside the classroom. Schooling was not detached from its surroundings, any more than it is today. Every major political and social process of the middle ages had an effect on schools. These processes included the fall of the Roman Empire, the re-establishment of Christianity, the Viking invasions, the unification of England in the tenth century, the Norman Conquest, the Black Death, the Hundred Years' War, and the Reformation – to name the most obvious ones. Their effects can be traced to individual schools. A fifteenth-century schoolroom, for example, had analogies with the hall of a large house of the day. Its schoolmaster had a modest rank in society, reflecting the decline in the status of schools since their proliferation in the twelfth century and the rise of universities in the thirteenth. He might be endowed to teach, because he needed support in an age of smaller population. His pupils used textbooks in English as a result of greater English insularity and the decline of the French language in England. They worked with little outside supervision because, until the Reformation, the rulers of Church and state took education for granted.

The reverse process, the effect of education on politics, society, and culture, is a more speculative one. Although there are often parallels between developments inside and outside schools, it is usually difficult to judge how far schools were causing changes beyond their walls and how far responding to changes. The developments to which schools are likely to have contributed were large ones that involved other factors. One was the integration of England as a nation and its integration into western Europe.

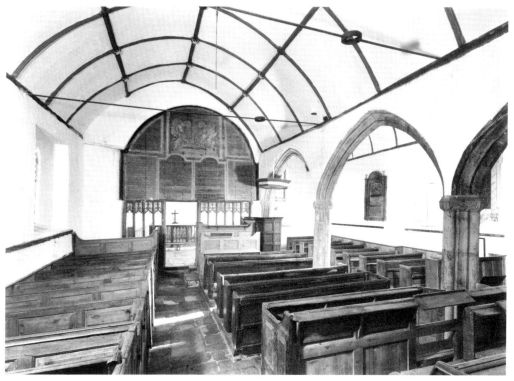

90   Education and change. After the Reformation, written texts replaced images of Christ and the saints in churches like St Petroc's church in Parracombe (Devon), a change made possible by education and literacy.

Schools must have helped in both respects, through teaching in similar ways across local and national frontiers, and through teachers and pupils moving from place to place. Another was the growth of literacy and literature, in particular the well-known transition 'from memory to written record', marked by the proliferation of documents during the twelfth and thirteenth centuries.[1] Without education there could not have been a literary culture like that of the later middle ages, when even private individuals kept financial accounts, communicated through letters, and read for recreation. A third effect of schooling was to help to shape the details of different cultural epochs. The 'twelfth-century Renaissance' was underpinned by the reading of classical literature in schools, the didactic literature popularised from 1200 to 1500 by the school texts of that period, and the humanist revival of interest in the classics by teachers like Anwykyll, Stanbridge, and Lily. Nor, without schooling and literacy, could popular religion have become based not simply on ceremony and imagery but on reading – a shift that made possible the English Reformation.

There has been a tendency to see the history of education as incremental, particularly by scholars in America. W. K. Jordan's ponderous works sought to show a large expansion from 1480 to 1660. Jo Ann Moran in *The Growth of English Schooling* and Michael Alexander in *The Growth of English Education* saw growth as the principal feature of schooling in the later middle ages and early-modern period respectively.[2] Growth has been perceived as both quantitative and qualitative. Writers have drawn attention to the apparent increase in numbers of schools from century to century, and to their acquisition of resources. Printing has been credited with developing education by making schoolbooks cheaper and easier to procure, and with raising the demand for education through the mass-production of other kinds of written material. None of these assertions is inaccurate. Doubtless there were more schools, teachers, and literate people in 1500 than there had been in 800 or 900. Yet the incremental view is also imperfect. It partakes of the distortions caused by the growth of evidence as time goes on. More schools are recorded in 1500 than in 1400, and in 1400 than in 1300, because more sources exist that mention them. This increase is a result not only of more sources having been created but of more having survived. The further back in time, the greater the losses. Education is an economy, and economies undergo fluctuations. We need to allow for decline as well as advance. The first person who tried to estimate numbers of schools in England, William Bingham in 1439, believed that seventy had closed in half of the country during the previous fifty years. He lived in a world that saw history in terms of fall and salvation, but it is quite possible that the reduction in the size of the population after 1300 led to a drop in the number of schools.

Another theory about medieval school history is that it witnessed a process of laicisation. This argues that education evolved from being largely

91   Education and subversion. The protesters of the Peasants' Revolt of 1381 communicated by letters and demanded written charters and pardons.

managed by clergy for clergy to having lay governors and teachers, and to catering for pupils who aimed at lay careers. A. F. Leach was a pioneer of this view in 1916, linking it with the Renaissance and, by implication, the Reformation.[3] More recently Moran discerned it as a major feature of the later middle ages. In truth laicisation was an inconsistent process, as Leach himself admitted.[4] Lay people were a force in education from the beginning. Anglo-Saxon kings and noblemen established the cathedrals and monasteries where teaching was given. Parents put their children into monasteries and later into schools. The fifteenth century certainly provides more examples of lay founders of schools and of an interest in schools by town authorities. Yet there were also trends that ran counter to this. One was the growing involvement of monasteries in training secular boys, another the fashion for founding chantry and college schools whose masters were bound to be priests. A third was the growth of boy choirs and song schools in religious houses, great households, and the larger parish churches. As late as the middle of the sixteenth century the Tudor monarchs (Protestant and Catholic) decided to make bishops, not secular officers, responsible for monitoring schoolmasters, schools, and their teaching. As a result the senior clergy of the Protestant Church of England came to have more power over education than their Catholic predecessors had done.

A similar caution is needed in tracing other '-isations'. At first sight school teaching seems to have become more professionalised between the Conquest and the Reformation. The monks and minster clergy of the eleventh century, who combined teaching with the religious life, eventually gave way to teachers who spent most of their time in the classroom and came to be known as 'schoolmasters'. By the end of the fourteenth century there was a university degree of 'master of grammar' for which such men could apply, and by the fifteenth century teachers who were salaried usually received nationally accepted wages of between £6 and £10 a year. Yet even in the sixteenth century some teaching was still done by parish clergy, parish clerks, and scriveners – people with other interests and duties – and schoolmasters were rarely identified as a group by the crown, the Church, or public opinion. Medieval and early-modern teachers did not form themselves into professional bodies like guildsmen, lawyers, and eventually doctors. The organisation of schools improved during the middle ages, in so far that many acquired governors, buildings, and endowments. But even in the middle of the sixteenth century most of them were small-scale institutions, run by one or two masters who might be effective or ineffective. When human capability mattered so much, organisation did not necessarily dictate the quality of teaching.

In short, progress and development in education were often complex and contradictory, as they were in other areas of life. Education had (and still has) a way of being old and new together. The history of schooling in the middle ages is distinguished by innovations. Teachers constantly revised the standard texts or produced new versions. They struggled to keep up with developments such as the need to teach Latin to non-Latinists, the rise of scholasticism, and the coming of humanism. In other matters they could be conservative. The alphabet in early-Tudor England still carried luggage that it had picked up long before in terms of the cross, the capital 'a', the three dots, the 'est', and the 'amen'. Some of this was superfluous and even, perhaps, unclear, yet the alphabet went on being taught in that form. The use of the Paternoster and psalter as reading texts, of elementary treatises modelled on Donatus, and of mnemonic verses continued from century to century, well after the Reformation. Anthony Wood, the historian of Oxford, 'was put to school to learn to read the psalter' in 1637, when he was five, in time-honoured fashion.[5] As late as 1816 the pupils of Eton College still studied in ways that went back to their fifteenth-century foundation. They worked in a large oblong schoolroom, facing inwards on benches without desks, several classes in the same room, with their masters in high seats above them – features that Henry VI would have recognised (Fig. 92).[6] Even today the school year follows a three-term structure, starting in the autumn, on virtually the same lines that are first recorded in the thirteenth century.

Simple judgments about medieval education are hindered by its diversity. It took different forms for the very young, for those who wished only to learn English, for moderate Latinists, and for future undergraduates and scholars. There was teaching at home, and there was schooling – private and public. There were schools for reading, song, grammar, and business skills, and for specialised groups such as noblemen, parish clergy, and members of the religious orders. So varied was education that it is hard to summarise what it involved, or what kind of person it formed. It certainly taught skills: the ability to read, write, and speak in English, French, or Latin. It imparted knowledge, but not always knowledge that was needed or useful. How many pupils utilised their acquaintance with linguistics, classical literature, or mythology once they left school? It conferred, or confirmed, social status. Most schooling cost money and therefore required the backing of relatively prosperous parents or patrons. Schoolboys were often clerks: members of the clergy and participants in clerical privileges. They became eligible for careers in the Church, law, trade, and administration, although wealth or patronage was important for this as well. Going to school had a further significance in terms of gender, because most pupils were boys and men. Schools were places where they bonded together, and where (if they learnt Latin grammar) they absorbed something special to men rather than to women.

92   Education and tradition. The schoolroom of Eton College in 1816, still observing late-medieval practices such as masters in high seats and pupils sitting around the room on forms without desks.

Education, then, supported wealth, hierarchy, and masculinity. It also undermined them. Lords of manors viewed the schooling of their villeins' sons with misgivings. They envisaged such boys growing up to be clergy or townsmen with free status, robbing lords of their services and (if they inherited villein property) subverting manorial lordship. Some social commentators from the late fourteenth century onwards saw unworthy people rising to status and power through schooling. The rebels of the Peasants' Revolt in 1381 were sufficiently educated to gather recruits with letters (Fig. 91). They may have presented their demands in writing, and certainly demanded written charters. The Lollards used literacy to translate the Bible and to write polemical works in English, threatening the power of the Church. They posted bills and placards to circulate their ideas, as did other dissident people – notably William Collingbourn in his famous rhyme on a handbill ridiculing Richard III and Richard's courtiers Catesby, Ratcliffe, and Lovell.[7] The humanist education of Henry VIII and his servants is likely to have helped give them the confidence to assert their authority over the clergy during the Reformation. It added credibility to the king's claim to be head of the Church. As for the education of women, although it cannot be shown by itself to have improved their status, wives and daughters of the upper orders must have profited from it devotionally by reading prayer-books and saints' lives, practically by reading letters, and recreationally by reading romances.

'Medieval' is an opprobrious term. Few worse insults can be hurled at a modern policy or practice. Yet medieval schools achieved a lot. In England they established themselves as free-standing bodies and eventually as legal and self-contained institutions. They taught skills and knowledge to hundreds of thousands of pupils, and developed sophisticated procedures and structures for doing so. They reinvented the full-time professional schoolmaster and, in a shyer, more unobtrusive way, the schoolmistress. They were meticulous in their analysis of Latin and inventive in teaching it to children. They devised the foreign-language textbook as we understand it, first for Latin and later for French. They helped create modern English, in its spelling and style, through using it for teaching Latin. They laid the foundations of the structure of schooling in England today: the custom of going to school between about five and eighteen, the hierarchy of primary and secondary schools, the three-term year, and the six-form organisation. Even the philosophy of education was being studied by the thirteenth and fourteenth centuries, from the works of continental scholars like Hugh of St Victor, Vincent of Beauvais, and Giles of Rome.[8] Apart from schooling for all, which did not become a national policy until the late nineteenth century, there is hardly a concept, institution, or practice of modern education that cannot be traced, somewhere or other, in medieval England.

A List of Schools in England and Wales, 1066–1530

It would take a large volume to present all the evidence for schools and schooling in medieval England and Wales. The following list centres on schools that existed as independent or semi-independent bodies open to the public, and on private schools held in minsters and collegiate churches or run by parish clergy or laity. For reasons of space it excludes schools in monasteries, friaries, and nunneries. The reader is referred to the standard guide by D. Knowles and R. N. Hadcock, *Medieval Religious Houses: England and Wales*, for an inventory of religious houses, and to chapter 8 of this book for a survey of the kinds of school likely to have been maintained by them. Two other categories of school are generally absent on account of their numbers or their elusiveness. Parish churches, by the early sixteenth century, often retained small groups of boys who were taught to sing, examples of which are cited on pp. 322–4 of this book. Household schools are difficult to identify and may have moved from place to place; evidence about them is provided in Nicholas Orme, *From Childhood to Chivalry*, pp. 16–28, 48–60.

The entries in the list are based on references to a school, schoolhouse, or schoolteacher. Mentions of scholars alone are not normally included because such mentions are primarily evidence about literacy and, while they imply schooling, are not reliable guides as to where it happened. Places are attributed to their historic counties and their schools are credited, as far as possible, with what they taught (reading, song, grammar, or higher education), the dates at which they are recorded, the existence of endowments to support a schoolmaster, and the appropriate references. No systematic lists of schools were kept in medieval England, and the information presented here is illustrative, not complete. There must have been many more schools than we have evidence of, and schools for which we possess only one or two references may have existed for long periods. The earliest date recorded in the following list is simply the earliest so far encountered, and is not a date of foundation unless specifically stated. Nor are these medieval schools necessarily the ancestors of those that claim descent from them today.

Help in compiling this list has been kindly given by, among others, Miss C. Annesley, Mrs J. Barlow, Prof. C. Barron, Dr P. Coulstock, Prof. C. Cross, Dr D. Dymond, Dr C. Fenwick, Dr C. Fraser, Dr J. A. A. Goodall, Prof. A. Gransden, Mr J. Hillaby, Dom S. F. Hockey, Dr H. Jewell, Prof. M. C. E. Jones, Dr D. Lepine, Dr I. Luxton, Prof. J. A. Moran Cruz, Mr J. Munby, Mr P. Northeast, Mr A. E. B. Owen, Mr J. Rhodes, Dr J. Ridgard, Dr M.-H. Rousseau, Mr I. Rowlands, Prof. N. Saul, Dr H. Summerson, Dr S. Sweetinburgh, Dr C. Thornton, Dr S. Townley, and Dr J. J. Vickerstaff.

ABBREVIATIONS

Abbreviations are listed on pp. 373–4 and references, where not given in full, relate to the bibliography. The following abbreviations are also used in this section:

c.   *circa*

×   a single, unknown point of time between two dates, e.g. 1066 × 1087

–   the whole period of time between two dates, e.g. 1250–1350

→   the continuity of a school from a particular date until after the year 1530

The traditional abbreviations of county names are used.

ABINGDON, Berks.
School, 1100 × 1117, 1388–1415 (*Chronicon Monasterii de Abingdon*, ed. J. Stevenson, vol. ii (RS, 1858), 123; *VCH Berks.*, ii, 259–62).

ACASTER SELBY, Yorks. W.R.
COLLEGIATE CHURCH. Endowed writing, song, and grammar school, founded *c.*1483; grammar school → (*EYS*, ii, pp. xxi–xxii, 89–96; Moran, 1985, 237–8).

ALDWINKLE, Northants.
Endowed reading school, founded 1489 →; apparently dissolved *c.*1546 (BL, Harley MS 604, f. 48r; *ECD*, 434–5; *VCH Northants.*, ii, 281–2).

ALFORD, Lincs.
School, probably of grammar, 1511 (Owen, 69, 73).

ALNWICK, Northumberland
Endowed grammar and possible song school, founded 1448 → (*CPR 1446–52*, 170; *ESR*, part ii, 156–7).

APPLEBY, Westmorland
Grammar school, 1478, endowed by 1518 → (Leach, 1916, 268–9; Nicolson and Burn, i, 329; Storey, 153).

ARUNDEL, Sussex
School, 1269 (*VCH Sussex*, ii, 398; v part i, 99).
COLLEGIATE CHURCH. Song school for the choristers, possibly from 1387 → ; 1419–59 (M. T. Elvins, *Arundel Priory* (Chichester, 1981), 15, 24–6).

ASHBY-DE-LA-ZOUCH, Leics.
Probable school, 1379 (Fenwick, ii, 544).

ASHWELL, Herts.
Grammar and song school, 1529 × 1532 (PRO, C 1/603/50).

AVELEY, Essex
School, 1340 (*VCH Essex*, viii, 15).

AWRE, Gloucs.
School, *c.*1287 (*EWE*, 93).

AYLSHAM, Norfolk

Grammar school, 1460×1465; endowed grammar school, founded 1530 → (PRO, C 1/27/343; *The Paston Letters*, ed. J. Gairdner, 5 vols (London, 1904), iv, 242; Jordan, 1961a, 153).

BANBURY, Oxon.

School, 1345, 1400, 1430×1432; endowed grammar school, founded 1501 → (*VCH Oxon.*, i, 461–2; x, 120).

BARLINCH, Somerset

Grammar school in the priory, possibly open to the public, *c*.1500 (Orme, 1989a, 113–21; Orme, 1990b).

BARNACK, Northants.

Reading, song, and grammar school, 1359 (*VCH Northants.*, ii, 280).

BARNSLEY, Yorks. W.R.

School, 1370 (E. Hoyle, *History of Barnsley and the Surrounding District* (Barnsley, 1924), chapter 36, section 12).

BARNSTAPLE, Devon

School, probably of grammar, by 1528×1535 (*EWE*, 112–13).

BARTON-ON-HUMBER, Lincs.

Grammar school, 1329–34 (*ECD*, 280–3; *VCH Lincs.*, ii, 449–50).

BASINGWERK, Flint (Wales)

Grammar school in the abbey, probably open to the public, *c*.1460 (Thomson, 1979, 114–31, especially 124–5; Thomson, 1982).

BATH, Somerset

Grammar school, *c*.1113 (*EWE*, 93–4).

BATTLE, Sussex

School, by 1240, 1253, and other occasions (E. Searle, 118, 426).

BATTLEFIELD, Shropshire

COLLEGIATE CHURCH. Grammar school, possibly public, *c*.1410, *c*.1526 (Thomson, 1979, 158–68; *VCH Shropshire*, ii, 128–31).

BECCLES, Suffolk

School, 1198×1216, *c*.1235, 1396–1404; grammar school, 1432 (*The Letters of Pope Innocent III*, ed. C. R. and M. G. Cheney (Oxford, 1967), 187; Gransden, 1973, 4; *VCH Suffolk*, ii, 337; Meech, 1934).

BEDFORD, Beds.

School, *c*.1160, *c*.1170×*c*.1180 (*ECD*, 116–17; *VCH Beds.*, ii, 152–7; *Twelfth-Century Archidiaconal and Vice-Archidiaconal Acta*, ed. B. R. Kemp, C&Y, 92 (2001), 39–40).

BERKHAMSTED, Herts.

School, early 13th century; endowed grammar school, founded *c*.1523 → (charter in the possession of Prof. A. Gransden; *VCH Herts.*, ii, 71–5; B. G. G. Williams).

BEVERLEY, Yorks. E.R.

MINSTER. Song school, 1423–4, and probably permanently for the choristers; grammar school, *c*.1100, *c*.1150, 1251, 1276, 1304–66, 1436–57 (*EYS*, i, pp. xxxix–li, 80c-109; Moran, 1985, 241).

BICESTER, Oxon.

Schoolmaster in the priory, possibly for the public, 1445 (A. H. Thompson, 1915–27, ii, 35).

BILBOROUGH, Notts.

Tuition in the rectory, probably in grammar, 1505 (*VCH Notts.*, ii, 221–2).

BILLINGSHURST, Sussex

Endowed school, projected 1521 (*Transcripts of Sussex Wills*, ed. R. G. Rice, vol. i, Sussex Record Soc., 41 (1935), 145; *VCH Sussex*, ii, 398).

BISHOP AUCKLAND, Co. Durham

Probable grammar school, 1499 (Vickerstaff, 7–8).

BLACKBURN, Lancs.

Endowed grammar school, founded 1514 → (Preston, Lancashire Record Office, DDBK 1; Stocks, i, 1–8; Jordan, 1962, 35–6; *VCH Lancs.*, ii, 590).

BLISWORTH, Northants.

Endowed grammar school, probably founded 1505 → (*CPR 1494–1509*, 461; *ESR*, part ii, 147, 151–2; *VCH Northants.*, ii, 229–30).

BLOFIELD, Norfolk

Grammar school, 1350 (Norwich, Norfolk Record Office, Reg/2 Book 4, f. 118v).

BODMIN, Cornwall

Probable school, 1469 × 1472; school, 1523–4 (*Camden Miscellarny VII*, Camden Soc., n.s. 14 (1875), 47; Truro, Cornwall Record Office, B/Bod/314/3/42d).

BOLTON-LE-MOORS, Lancs.

Endowed grammar school, founded 1524 → (Jordan, 1962, 65; *VCH Lancs.*, ii, 596).

BOSTON, Lincs.

Grammar school, 1329 →, endowed by 1514 (*ECD*, 280–3; *VCH Lincs.*, ii, 450–3). SCHOOLMISTRESS. 1404 (*VCH Lincs.*, ii, 451).

BOTESDALE, Suffolk

Grammar school, 1389 (Sylvia L. Thrupp, 'The Problem of Replacement Rates in Late Medieval English Population', *Economic History Review*, 2nd series, 18 (1965), 113).

BOUGHTON, Kent

School, 1301 (*Reg. Winchelsey, Canterbury*, ed. R. Graham, vol. ii, C&Y, 52 (1956), 953).

BOURNE, Lincs.

Grammar school, 1330 (Leach, 1916, 199; *VCH Lincs.*, ii, 450).

BRADFORD-ON-AVON, Wilts.

Endowed grammar school, probably founded 1524 → (*EWE*, 114–17).

BRAUGHING, Herts.

Tuition in grammar by the parish chaplain, 1460s (Heath, 208).

BRECON, Brecknock (Wales)

School, 1165 (*Cartularium Prioratus Sancti Johannis Evangelistae de Brecon*, ed. R. W. Banks (London, 1884), 82–3, dated in D. G. Walker, 'Charters of the Earldom of Hereford, 1095–1201', *Camden Miscellany XXII*, Royal Hist. Soc., Camden 4th series (1964), 51).

BREDGAR, Kent

Grammar scholarships for two clerks, founded 1392 →; dissolved *c*.1542 (Sheppard, iii, 15–25; *VCH Kent*, ii, 230).

BRENTWOOD, Essex

School, *c*.1514–19 (*VCH Essex*, viii, 105).

BRIDEKIRK, Cumberland

School, 1511 (PRO, E 101/691/41, f. 21v).

BRIDGNORTH, Shropshire

School, 1503 (*HMC, Tenth Report*, part iv, 425).

BRIDGWATER, Somerset

School, 1298, 1379; possible school 1535 (*EWE*, 94–5).

Tuition, in reading and song, in the vicarage, *c*.1450 × 1474 (ibid.; reference now Taunton, Somerset Record Office, D\B\bw/115).

BRIDPORT, Dorset

School, 1240; grammar school, 15th century (*EWE*, 95–6).

BRINGTON, Northants.

Endowed song school, founded 1522 (R. M. Serjeantson and H. I. Longden, 'The Parish Churches and Religious Houses of Northants.', *Arch. Journal*, 70 (1913), 287).

BRISTOL, Gloucs. and Somerset

School, *c*.1166×1183, 1243; two schools, 1379 (*EWE*, 35–38).

NEWGATE. Grammar school, 1426–62 (ibid., 38–40).

SOUTH BRISTOL (i.e. south of the Avon). Grammar schools, 1463–1480×1483 (ibid., 40–1).

GUILD OF KALENDARS. Endowed theology lecture, founded 1464 (Orme, 1989a, 209–19).

FROME GATE. Grammar school, 1513–36 (*EWE*, 41)

BROUGH-UNDER-STAINMORE, Westmorland

Endowed writing, song, and grammar school, founded 1506 → (Nicolson and Burn, i, 573–5; *Valor Ecclesiasticus*, v, 297; *ESR*, part ii, 251–2; Storey, 146–7).

BROUGHTON (near Preston), Lancs.

Endowed grammar school, founded 1527 → (Jordan, 1962, 39).

BRUTON, Somerset

Endowed grammar school, founded 1520 → (*EWE*, 117–23).

BUCKINGHAM, Bucks.

School, 1423 (*VCH Bucks.*, ii, 145).

BURFORD, Oxon.

School, 1518×1521 (Foxe, iv, 237).

BURROUGH, Leics.

Tuition, probably in grammar, in the rectory, 1508 (Oxford, Brasenose College, Principal Yate's Book (1668), 97–8).

BURTON UPON TRENT, Staffs.

School, 1453; endowed grammar school, founded *c*.1530 → (*VCH Staffs.*, vi, 154).

BURY ST EDMUNDS, Suffolk

School, *c*.1100 (*Anglo-Normannische Geschichtsquellen*, ed. F. Liebermann (Strasbourg, 1879), 270). Song school, 1268–1426; grammar school, late 12th century, with partial endowment →; illegal song and grammar schools, late 13th century (*VCH Suffolk*, ii, 306–13; *EEA*, vi, 139–40; Jocelin of Brakelond, 45; Gransden, 1963, 32, 38–9, 67–9, 84; Gransden, 1973, 4, 38–9).

BUSHMEAD, Beds.

Grammar school, projected 1332 (*VCH Beds.*, ii, 149–50).

CAERNARVON, Caern. (Wales)

Grammar school, mid-15th century (J. Wynn, *The History of the Gwydir Family*, ed. J. Ballinger (Cardiff, 1927), 50).

CAMBRIDGE, Cambs.

UNIVERSITY. Higher Studies, 1209 → (Rashdall, iii, 274–324; *VCH Cambs.*, iii, 150–66; Leader, 1983, 1988; Cobban, 1988).

GRAMMAR SCHOOLS. 1261–1470 (*BRUC*, 90; Feltoe and Minns, 20–3; Stokes, 43–57).

GODSHOUSE. Endowed college for grammarians, founded 1439, refounded as Christ's College, 1505 → (Lloyd; statutes in Rackham).

KING'S COLLEGE. Song school for the choristers, by 1453 → (*VCH Cambs.*, iii, 382).

JESUS COLLEGE. Endowed grammar school, founded 1496×1506 → (Gray, 31–3, 61; Gray and Brittain, 30–2, 49).

CANNOCK, Staffs.

Endowed grammar school, allegedly founded *c*.1518; occurs 1548 (*ESR*, part ii, 202).

CANTERBURY, Kent

ST GREGORY. Music school, allegedly 1085×1087; grammar school, allegedly 1085×1087 (*EEA*, xxviii, 1–3).

CITY (BISHOP'S) SCHOOL. Grammar school, 1219, 1259 → (Woodruff and Cape, 16–44; CCA, DCc, ChAnt/X/4/1, /5; ChChLet/I/18, /II/20).

ST ALPHEGE. School taught by rector, *c*.1490 (CCA, DCc, CC/B/C/A/13).

ST AUGUSTINE'S ABBEY. Grammar school for the boys of the almonry and for members of the public, licensed by the pope 1431 (*CPL 1427–47*, 348–9).

ST MARTIN. Reading, song, and grammar school, 1321 (*ECD*, 260–267).

CARLISLE, Cumberland

CITY (BISHOP'S) SCHOOL. School, probably usually of grammar, 1188, 1264–1371, 1425–*c*.1436, 1510, 1515×1518 (Prescott, 1–4; J. Wilson; Summerson, i, 166–8, 363–5, 686; PRO, C 1/438/31).

Teaching of writing, 1436 (Summerson, 365).

CASTLE DONINGTON, Leics.

Endowed grammar school, founded *c*.1511 → (*LPFD*, i, no. 784 (3); *ESR*, part ii, 126–7).

CHELMSFORD, Essex

School, 1292, 1327, 1373–1403; grammar school, 1532 (H. Grieve, *The Sleepers and the Shadows*, 2 vols (Chelmsford, 1988–94), i, 19, 25, 46, 51, 58, 65, 98).

CHELTENHAM, Gloucs.

Possible school, 1422 (PRO, SC 2/175/26, m. 6).

CHESTER, Cheshire

Grammar and music schools, 1353 (Lichfield Record Office, B/A/1/3, f. 133v); grammar school, 1368 (*Reg. Stretton, Lichfield*, ed. R. A. Wilson, William Salt Arch. Soc., n.s., 8 (1905), 20).

CHESTERFIELD, Derbs.

School, 13th century, 1323–37, 1465 (Nottingham, Nottinghamshire Record Office, DD/FJ/1/64/40, /1/107/15, /5/2/2, /10/3/3; *VCH Derbs.*, ii, 223).

CHICHESTER, Sussex

CATHEDRAL SCHOOLS. Song school for the choristers, probably from the 12th century → (*Chichester Cathedral: an historical survey*, ed. M. Hobbs (Chichester, 1994), 247–9. Grammar school, 1232–47, 1384–1479, endowed 1497 → (statutes, etc., in *VCH Sussex*, ii, 399–406; C 1/27/371; E 328/425). Higher Studies, theological lectureship founded 1224×1244, 1373 (Edwards, 197; *CPL 1362–1404*, 189–90).

CHILDREY, Berks.

Endowed reading, song, and grammar school, founded 1526 → (*VCH Berks.*, ii, 275–6).

CHIPPENHAM, Wilts.

Possible grammar school, *c*.1430×1450 (Orme, 1989a, 93).

CHIPPING CAMPDEN, Gloucs.

Endowed grammar school, founded *c*.1441 → (*EWE*, 124–8).

CHIPPING NORTON, Oxon.

Endowed grammar school, founded 1450 → (*CPR 1446–52*, 402; Salter, 1909, 264; *ESR*, part ii, 173–4; *VCH Oxon.*, i, 467).

CHRISTCHURCH, Hants.

School, 12th century (*ECD*, 74–5); grammar school maintained by the priory, possibly public, by 1538 (*LPFD*, xiii part ii, no. 1117).

CIRENCESTER, Gloucs.

School, 1242, 1340, 1433 (*EWE*, 96–7); endowed grammar school, founded *c.*1457 → (ibid., 128–31).

CLARE, Suffolk

School, 1381 (E. Powell, *The Rising in East Anglia in 1381* (Cambridge, 1896), 62).

CLITHEROE, Lancs.

School, *c.*1283 (*CIPM*, iv, 171–2).

COBHAM, Kent

COLLEGIATE CHURCH. Endowed song and grammar school, apparently for the clerks and choristers but possibly also public, perhaps founded 1362, 1383–8 (BL, Harley Charter, 48 E 46; Leach, 1916, 203; Tester, 119).

COCKAYNE HATLEY, Beds.

Music and grammar school in the vicarage, 1359 (PRO, CP 40/440, m. 94).

COCKERMOUTH, Cumberland

School, *c.*1250 × 1300; endowed grammar school by 1526 × 1527–1548 (*Register of the Priory of St Bees*, ed. J. Wilson, Surtees Soc., 126 (1915), 560–1; 'Letters of the Cliffords', ed. R. W. Hoyle, *Camden Miscellany XXXI*, Royal Hist. Soc., Camden 4th series, 44 (1992), 94–5; *ESR*, part ii, 44; Moran, 1985, 244–5).

CODSALL, Staffs.

School, 1480s (*VCH Staffs.*, xx, 89).

COLCHESTER, Essex

School, 1108 × 1127, 1163 × 1187, 1206, 1353–7, 1377–1464, 1512; endowed grammar school, founded 1520 → (*EEA*, xv, 9–10, 89; *Curia Regis Rolls, 1205–6* (1929), 74–5; *Court Rolls of the Borough of Colchester*, ed. I. H. Jeayes, vol. ii (Colchester, 1938), 9, 57; Fenwick, i, 194; *VCH Essex*, ii, 502; ix, 352).

COOMBE BISSETT, Wilts.

Apparently teaching of at least one boy by the vicar, 1354 (PRO, CP 40/405, m. 71d).

COUGHTON, Warws.

Endowed grammar school, projected 1518 (*VCH Warws.*, iii, 86).

COVEHITHE (alias Northales), Suffolk

School, 1463–9 (Richmond, 52, 133–4).

COVENTRY, Warws.

School and also private tuition, 1318; grammar school, 1357, 1410–39, 1548 (*The Liber Albus of Worcester Priory*, ed. J. M. Wilson, Worcestershire Hist. Soc., 35 (1919), 65 no. 801; *Reg. Norbury, Lichfield*, ed. E. Hobhouse, William Salt Arch. Soc., 1 (1880), 284; *VCH Warws.*, ii, 318–24).

CREDITON, Devon

COLLEGIATE CHURCH. Song school for the choristers, 1334 → ; grammar school, 1377 and possibly later, endowed 1547 (*EWE*, 97–9)

CREWKERNE, Somerset

Endowed grammar school, founded 1499 → (*EWE*, 131–2).

CROFTON, Yorks. W.R.

Grammar school, 1372 (Armitage-Smith, i, 111; Moran, 1985, 245).

CROMER, Norfolk

Endowed grammar school, founded 1505 → (Jordan, 1961a, 152; PRO, C 1/845/38–9). See also Shipden.

CROYDON, Surrey

Grammar school, 1393–5 (London, Lambeth Palace Library, Reg. Morton, ii, ff. 182v, 183v; Rickert, 1926–7, 251–2; *VCH Surrey*, ii, 189).

CROYLAND, Lincs.

Grammar school, perhaps public, 1526–35 (Salter, 1909, 92; *LPFD*, ix, no. 1107).

CUCKFIELD, Sussex

Endowed grammar school, founded *c*.1521 → (*VCH Sussex*, ii, 416–19).

DARLINGTON, Co. Durham

School, 1417 (*Account Rolls of the Abbey of Durham*, ed. J. T. Fowler, vol. i, Surtees Soc., 99 (1898), 226; Vickerstaff, 8–9).

DARTMOUTH, Devon

School, 1490 (*EWE*, 99).

DERBY, Derbs.

School, 1154 × 1159, 1176 × 1182, 1379, 1406, 15th century; grammar school, 1481–3 (Darlington, i, pp. xl–xliii, 80–1; ii, 596, 599; *EEA*, xiv, 50–3; xvi, 27–9; Fenwick, i, 98; PRO, C 1/16/336; J. C. Cox, *Churchwardens' Accounts* (London, 1913), 163–4; *VCH Derbs.*, ii, 208–16).

DEVIZES, Wilts.

School, 1322; grammar school, 1463 (*Reg. Martival, Salisbury*, ed. D. M. Owen, vol. iv, C&Y, 68 (1975), 73; *EWE*, 99).

DONCASTER, Yorks. W.R.

Grammar school, 1351; school 1436 (*EYS*, i, 22; Moran, 1985, 246).

DOVER, Kent

School, 1284 (C. R. Haines, *Dover Priory* (Cambridge 1930), 350).

DROITWICH, Worcs.

School, 14th century; probable grammar school, 1530 (*VCH Worcs.*, iii, 76; Aveling and Pantin, 79–81, 286; Orme, 1989a, 35, 47–8).

DUNHAM, Notts.

Grammar school, before 1351 (*VCH Notts.*, ii, 179).

DUNSTABLE, Beds.

School, 1097 × 1119, 1131 × 1133, 1183 × 1195, 1244–37 (*ECD*, 78–81, 92–5, 132–5; *Regesta*, ii, no. 1827; *VCH Beds.*, ii, 178–9; *Cartulary of Oseney Abbey*, ed. H. E. Salter, vol. iv, Oxford Hist. Soc., 97 (1934), 461–2).

DUNSTER, Somerset

Possible school, 1355, 1410, 1424 (*EWE*, 99–100).

DUNWICH, Suffolk

School, *c*.1086 × 1105, 1109 × 1131 (*Eye Priory Cartulary and Charters*, ed. V. Brown, 2 vols, Suffolk Records Soc., Suffolk Charters, 12–13 (1992–4), i, 12, 14; ii, 88–9; *Liber Eliensis*, ed. E. O. Blake, Royal Hist. Soc., Camden 3rd series, 92 (1962), 270–4; *VCH Suffolk*, ii, 303).

DURHAM, Co. Durham

CITY (BISHOP'S) SCHOOL. School, *c*.1170s, 1229– *c*.1260, 1377 × 1381; endowed song and grammar schools, founded 1414 → (Reginald of Durham, 1847, 59–60, 366–8; *Historiae Dunelmensis Scriptores Tres*, ed. J. Raine, Surtees Soc., 9 (1839), 74; *EEA*, xxv, 271, 275–6; *Bishop Hatfield's Survey*, ed. W. Greenwell, Surtees Soc., 32 (1857), 163; *VCH Durham*, i, 371–5; Vickerstaff, 9–11).

CATHEDRAL. Grammar school in the almonry, mentioned in 1453 as open to the public from time immemorial (Bowers, 1999, 201).

ST MARY (-LE-BOW?). Reading and song school, *c*.1110 (Reginald of Durham, 1847, 59–60).

EARL'S COLNE, Essex

Endowed grammar school, founded *c*.1519 → (*VCH Essex*, ii, 526).

EAST RETFORD, Notts.

School, before 1318; grammar school, 1393, endowed *c*.1518 (Nottingham, Nottinghamshire Record Office, DDA/10/20; *CCR 1392–6*, 135; A. D. Grounds, *A History of King Edward VI Grammar School, Retford* (Worksop, 1970), 13–18).

ELY, Cambs.

CITY (BISHOP'S) SCHOOL. Grammar school, 1403–6, 1527 (Cambridge University Library, Ely Diocesan Records, G/1/3, ff. 149r, 196r; Crosby, *Ely Diocesan Remembrancer* (1899–1900), 158, 198; Owen and Thurley, 26–7).

ETON, Bucks.

COLLEGIATE CHURCH. Song school for the choristers and endowed public grammar school, founded 1440 → (Maxwell-Lyte; *VCH Bucks.*, ii, 147–86).

EVESHAM, Worcs.

School, 1379; endowed grammar school, possibly founded 1462, refounded 1513×1524 → (Orme, 1989a, 36, 40–2, 47).

EWELME, Oxon.

Endowed reading and grammar school, founded *c*.1448×1450 → (*HMC, Ninth Report* (1883), i, 216–22; *VCH Oxon.*, vol. i, 470; Goodall).

EXETER, Devon

CATHEDRAL SCHOOLS. Song school for the choristers, 11th century → (*EWE*, 43–6; Orme, 1983, 85–96). Grammar school (in the city, called the High School) 12th century, 1288, 1329 → (*EWE*, 46–56; Orme, 1978b, 23–4). Higher studies, 12th century; lectures in theology, *c*.1230, in theology or canon law, 1337 → (*EWE*, 52–5; Orme, 1978b, 23).

ST JOHN'S HOSPITAL. Grammar school for thirteen boys (linked with the High School), 1332 (*EWE*, 49).

GODSHOUSE. Reading school, projected 1436 (ibid., 46).

BUTCHER ROW. School, 1525–30 (ibid., 46).

EYE, Suffolk

Possible school, *c*.1170s; school, 1452×1459; endowed grammar school, 1495 → (J. C. Robertson, i, 341; C. Paine, *The History of Eye* (Diss, 1993), 36).

FAIRBURN, Yorks. W.R.

School, 1348 (*Select Cases from the Coroners' Rolls, 1265–1413*, ed. C. Gross, Selden Soc., 9 (1896), 111; Moran, 1985, 249).

FARINGDON, Berks.

Grammar school, 1343 (*Registrum Brevium*, 4th edn (London, 1687), f. 35r).

FARNWORTH, Lancs.

Endowed grammar school, founded 1507 → (Jordan, 1962, 33–4).

FARTHINGHOE, Northants.

Endowed school, founded 1443 → (*ECD*, 414–17; *ESR*, part ii, 146–7; *VCH Northants.*, ii, 280–1).

FAVERSHAM, Kent

Reading and song school, 1506; grammar school, *c*.1420, endowed 1526 → (F. F. Giraud, 'On the Parish Clerks and Sextons of Faversham, 1506–1593', *Archaeologia Cantiana*, 20 (1893), 205; PRO, E 36/196, p. 45; Hasted, vi, 355–6; Jordan, 1961b, 72).

FAWSLEY, Northants.

Endowed song school, founded 1528 (*VCH Northants.*, ii, 282).

FINCHAM, Norfolk

Grammar school, 1432 (Norwich, Norfolk Record Office, Reg/5 Book 9, f. 59r).

FOTHERINGHAY, Northants.

COLLEGIATE CHURCH. Endowed song and grammar school for the clerks and choristers, founded 1415 → (A. H. Thompson, 1918, 272–3). Endowed public grammar school, either the same or another foundation, by 1548 (*VCH Northants.*, ii, 223–4).

FRAMLINGHAM, Suffolk
Grammar school, 1327×1377; school, 1378, 1414, 1465 (Bodleian, MS Charters, Suffolk, a.1, no. 1303; Cambridge, Pembroke College, Framlingham B.1, D.1, F.).

GIGGLESWICK, Yorks. W.R.
Grammar school, 1507 →, endowed by 1546 (*EYS*, ii, 232–40; Moran, 1985, 251).

GLASTONBURY, Somerset
The abbey educated novices, almonry boys, and choristers, but the presence of thirty-nine 'clerks of the school' in 1377 indicates either an unusually large school of this kind or one open to the public (PRO, E 179/4/1, m. 3; Orme, 1991, 292–4).

GLOUCESTER, Gloucs.
SCHOOL SUPERVISED BY ST OSWALD'S PRIORY. School allegedly 1096×1112, possibly 1286–9; grammar school 1380–1410 (*EWE*, 57–63).

SCHOOL SUPERVISED BY LANTHONY PRIORY. School 1154×1179, 1286–9; grammar school, 1392–1535 (ibid., 58–65).

LANTHONY PRIORY. Internal grammar school in the priory, open to outsiders, 1502 (*A Calendar of the Registers of the Priory of Llanthony by Gloucester*, ed. J. Rhodes, Bristol and Gloucestershire Arch. Soc., Record Series, 15 (2002), 59–61).

ST NICHOLAS. Endowed grammar school, projected 1447 (*EWE*, 133–7).

ST MARY CRYPT. Endowed grammar school, founded 1528–40 → (ibid., 137–41).

GRANTHAM, Lincs.
Grammar school, 1329–34, endowed *c.*1478–94 → (*ECD*, 280–3; *VCH Lincs.*, ii, 479–80; Foster and Thompson, 55–6).

GREAT TORRINGTON, Devon
School, 1486, 1524 (*EWE*, 100).

GRIMSBY (GREAT), Lincs.
Grammar school, 1329–34, 1390 (*ECD*, 280–3; *VCH Lincs.*, ii, 480).

GUILDFORD, Surrey
School, 1299; endowed grammar school, founded 1509–12 → (*Reg. J. de Pontissara, Winchester*, ed. C. Deedes, vol. ii, C&Y, 30 (1924), 577; *VCH Surrey*, ii, 164–5).

GUISBOROUGH, Yorks. N.R.
School, 1266×1268, 1280 (Cheney, 629, 633; *Cartularium Prioratus de Gyseburne*, ed. W. Brown, Surtees Soc., 89 (1891), 360–2; Moran, 1985, 252).

HADDENHAM, Cambs.
Grammar school, 1463 (Cambridge University Library, Ely Diocesan Records, G/1/5, ff. 51v-52r).

HADLEIGH, Suffolk
School 1299×1300; grammar school, 1376–7, 1382 (CCA, DCc, U15/16/8, BR/Hadleigh/25; *VCH Suffolk*, ii, 325).

HAINTON, Lincs.
School, 1345 (Poos, 189)

HALIFAX, Yorks. W.R.
Endowed school, projected *c.*1497; grammar school, 1516×1517 (M. W. Garside, 'Halifax Schools Prior to 1700', *Halifax Antiquarian Soc. Papers* (1924), 186–7; Moran, 1985, 253).

HAREWOOD, Yorks. W.R.
School, *c.*1505 (J. S. Purvis, *Select XVIth-Century Causes in Tithe*, Yorkshire Arch. Soc., Record Series, 114 (1949), 68; Moran, 1985, 253).

HARLESTON, Norfolk

Grammar school, 1433–6 (Norwich, Norfolk Record Office, Reg/5 Book 9, f. 65r; PRO, E 179/45/111).

HARNHILL, Kent

Reading and song school, 1386 (PRO, CP 40/517, m. 340; Rickert, 1948, 118).

HASTINGS, Sussex

Song and grammar schools, *c*.1095×1140 (*ECD*, 68–9; *VCH Sussex*, ii, 409–10; Whittick).

HAVERFORDWEST, Pemb. (Wales)

School, 1325; grammar school, 1488 (McFarlane, 1973, 246; *Episcopal Registers of the Diocese of St David's, 1397–1518*, ed. R. F. Isaacson, vol. ii, Cymmrodorion Soc., Record Series, 6 (1917), 524–5).

HEDON, Yorks. E.R.

Grammar school, 1271–1465, 1530×1531 (N. Denholm-Young, 'The Yorks. Estates of Isabella de Fortibus', *Yorkshire Arch. Journal*, 31 (1934) 392; J. R. Boyle, *The Early History of Hedon* (Hull, 1895), pp. cxii, cxxiii–cxxix, clxxxv, cxc–cxciii, 92, 162, 169–70; *Testamenta Eboracensia*, ii, 270; Moran, 1985, 254).

HELMSLEY, Yorks. N.R.

School, 13th century (*HMC, MSS of the Duke of Rutland*, vol. iv (1905), 91; Moran, 1985, 254).

HEMINGBROUGH, Yorks. E.R.

Grammar school, 1394 (BL, Cotton MS Faustina A. VI, f. 71v; Moran, 1985, 254).

HENLEY-ON-THAMES, Oxon.

School, 1419–20; possible school, *c*.1483 (*Henley Borough Records*, ed. P. M. Briers, Oxfordshire Record Soc., 41 (1960), 28; *DNB*, s.n. 'John Longland').

HEREFORD, Herefs.

CATHEDRAL SCHOOLS. Song school for the choristers and others, 1246×1264 → (Orme, 2000, 567–8, 570–4). Possible grammar school, 1232; grammar school, 1246×1264, 1373–96, 1492, 1536 (ibid., 565, 568–9, 574–8). Higher Studies, possibly taught 1178–1201×1219, 1208×1213; lectures in theology or canon law, 1356 (ibid., 566–7, 570, 578).

HEXHAM, Northumberland

Grammar school, 1294 (J. Raine, *The Priory of Hexham*, vol. i, Surtees Soc., 44 (1863), p. lxxix).

HEYTESBURY, Wilts.

Grammar school by 1449, endowed 1472 → ; closed 1544–57 (*EWE*, 141–8).

HIGHAM FERRERS, Northants.

Grammar school, 1372–1400 (Armitage-Smith, i, 103–4; Fenwick, ii, 242; *VCH Northants.*, ii, 217–18).

COLLEGIATE CHURCH. Song school for the choristers and endowed public grammar school, founded 1422 → (*CPR 1416–22*, 441; *VCH Northants.*, ii, 218–21).

HORNBY, Lancs.

Endowed grammar school, projected 1523, founded by 1548 (Jordan, 1962, 37–8; Moran, 1985, 255).

HORNCASTLE, Lincs.

Grammar school, 1329–54 (*ECD*, 280–3; *VCH Lincs.*, ii, 449–50, 482).

HOUGHTON REGIS, Beds.

Endowed grammar school, probably founded 1515 → (*VCH Beds.*, ii, 150–1; *ESR*, part ii, 1–5).

HOVINGHAM, Yorks. N.R.

School, *c*.1310 (*CIPM*, vii, 192; Moran, 1985, 256).

HOWDEN, Yorks. E.R.

School 1378 × 1379; reading, song, and grammar school, 1393–1456 (Fenwick, iii; *EYS*, ii, 84–7; Moran, 1985, 256).

HULL, Yorks. E.R.

School, by 1347, 1437; reading and grammar school, by 1454; endowed song and grammar school, founded 1479 → (Lawson, 12–42; *VCH Yorkshire East Riding*, i, 348; Moran, 1985, 256–7).

HUNTINGDON, Hunts.

Song school, *c*.1109 or later; school, *c*.1094 × 1123, *c*.1130, 1148 × 1166, 1255, 1392 (Bateson; *Regesta*, ii, 241; *EEA*, vi, 312; *Select Pleas of the Forest*, ed. G. J. Turner, Selden Soc., 13 (1901), 21; *VCH Hunts.*, ii, 107–9).

ILMINSTER, Somerset

School, early 15th century (*EWE*, 100).

IPSWICH, Suffolk

Grammar school, 1412, 1416–17; reading, song, and grammar school, 1477, endowed *c*.1483 → (Gray and Potter, 1–30; Blatchly, 1–49; BL, Egerton Roll 8776; *VCH Suffolk*, ii, 325–32).

CARDINAL'S COLLEGE. Song school for the choristers and endowed public grammar school, founded 1528, dissolved 1530 (Gray and Potter, 16–30; Blatchly, 27–42).

JERSEY, Channel Islands

Grammar school, projected 1496 (*CPR 1494–1509*, 83).

ST ANASTASE (in St Peter parish). School, 1532 × 1538 (PRO, C 1/835/146, 1/867/18).

KELK, Yorks. E.R.

School, 1305 (*EYS*, i, 81; Moran, 1985, 258).

KING'S LYNN, Norfolk

School, probably of grammar, 1205, 1383; grammar school, 1461; endowed song and grammar school, founded *c*.1510 → (*The Charters of Norwich Cathedral Priory*, ed. B. Dodwell, Publications of the Pipe Roll Soc., 78 (n.s. 40) (1974), 101–2, dated in *EEA*, vi, *Norwich, 1070–1214*, 310–13; Toulmin Smith, *English Guilds*, EETS, os, 40 (1870), 51–3; Norwich, Norfolk Record Office, Norfolk Consistory Court Wills, 223 Brosyard: will of John Buntyng; Jordan, 1961a, 152–3).

OTHER SCHOOLS. Probable reading or song schools, 1373 (Norwich, Norfolk Record Office, DCN 43/79; Shinners and Dohar, 106).

KINGSTON-ON-THAMES, Surrey

Reading, song, and elementary grammar school, 1377; school, probably of grammar, 1364; endowed school, projected 1528 (*VCH Surrey*, ii, 155–9).

KINOULTON, Notts.

School, 1289 (*Reg. Romeyn, York*, ed. W. Brown, vol. i, Surtees Soc., 123 (1913), 285–6; Moran, 1985, 258).

KINVER, Staffs.

Grammar school, 1511; endowed 1515 × 1548 → (*VCH Staffs.*, xx, 157; *ESR*, part ii, 200–1).

KIRKBY KENDAL, Westmorland

Endowed grammar school, founded 1526 → (*ESR*, part ii, 251; Storey, 169–70; Moran, 1985, 259).

KIRKHAM, Yorks. E.R.

Teaching in the church, probably elementary, *c*.1465 (Burton, 338).

KIRKOSWALD, Cumberland

COLLEGIATE CHURCH. Endowed school, perhaps founded *c.*1523; dissolved 1548 (*VCH Cumberland*, ii, 208–11; *ESR*, part ii, 43–4).

KIRTON-IN-HOLLAND, Lincs.

Endowed grammar school, founded by 1518, apparently defunct by 1535 (A. H. Thompson, 1940–7, iii, 79; *LPFD*, ix, no. 1107).

KNEESALL, Notts.

Endowed school, founded *c.*1528–32 → (*VCH Notts.*, ii, 179–80).

LAMBOURN, Berks.

Endowed grammar school, founded 1501–7 → (*CPR 1464–1509*, 233; Reading, Berkshire Record Office, D/Q1 Q3; *ESR*, part ii, 7–8, 13).

LANCASTER, Lancs.

School 1284; endowed grammar school, founded 1469–1500 → (*VCH Lancs.*, ii, 561–4, including statutes; Jordan, 1962, 30–1; Moran, 1985, 260).

LANGPORT, Somerset

Teaching here or in the vicinity, *c.*1504×1515 (PRO, C 1/337/12).

LAUNCESTON, Cornwall

Grammar school, 1342; possible grammar school, 1462 (*EWE*, 100–1).

LAVENHAM, Suffolk

Grammar school, *c.*1400 (PRO, SC 6/1297/22).

LEEDS, Yorks. W.R.

School, 1341–1400 (J. Le Patourel, *Documents Relating to the Manor and Borough of Leeds, 1066–1400*, Thoresby Soc., 45 (1956), 41, 44, 74; Moran, 1985, 261).

LEICESTER, Leics.

School, 1229, 1270, late 13th century, 1367; grammar school, 1440 (Cross, 5; CCA, DCc, ESRoll/8; *Calendar of Miscellaneous Inquisitions 1422–85*, 152–3).

LEIGHTON BROMSWOLD, Hunts.

Endowed school, by *c.*1540, perhaps by 1535 (Leland, i, 3; *Valor Ecclesiasticus*, iv, 258, 315).

LEIGHTON BUZZARD, Beds.

Probable grammar school, 1441 (*BRUO*, i, 29, s.n. 'Thomas Alwyn').

LEOMINSTER, Herefs.

School, probably of grammar, early 14th century; grammar school, long-standing in 1548 (Hereford, Herefordshire Record Office, M 31/8, f. 72r; *ESR*, part ii, 102).

LEWES, Sussex

School, 1248, 1285, 1307–10; grammar school, 1313; school, 1405; endowed grammar school, founded 1512 → (Hunt, 1964, 175 note 3; Lewes, Sussex Record Office, GLY 996; *VCH Sussex*, ii, 411–14).

LEYLAND, Lancs.

Endowed grammar school, founded 1524 → (*VCH Lancs.*, ii, 600; Jordan, 1962, 38).

LICHFIELD, Staffs.

CATHEDRAL SCHOOLS. Song school for the choristers, *c.*1190 (Bradshaw and Wordsworth, ii, 23), 1490×1520 (*VCH Staffs.*, iii, 164–5). Grammar school, *c.*1190, 1272, 1312×1313, 1335, 1440–66, endowed 1495 → (Bradshaw and Wordsworth, ii, 23; *Magnum Registrum Album*, ed. H. E. Savage, William Salt Arch. Soc., 48 (1924), 360–1; *VCH Staffs.*, iii, 280–2; vi, 159; xiv, 170).

LILLESHALL, Shropshire

Possible school, 1408×1409 (*VCH Shropshire*, xi, 174).

LINCOLN, Lincs.

CATHEDRAL SCHOOLS. Song school for the choristers and others, 1147×1148,

1236–1440 (*The Registrum Antiquissimum of Lincoln*, ed. C. W. Foster, vol. i, Lincoln Record Soc., 27 (1931), 262–3; *VCH Lincs.*, ii, 422–4; Bradshaw and Wordsworth, ii, 157; iii, 299). Grammar school, 12th century, 1174×1182, 1236 → (Edwards, 185; *EEA*, i, 203; *VCH Lincs.*, ii, 421–40). Cathedral choristers, separate tuition in song and grammar, 1308, 1389–1407, 1524–6 (*VCH Lincs.*, ii, 424–6; R. E. G. Cole, i, 52, 210). Higher Studies, *c.*1158×1160–*c.*1176; lectures in theology, *c.*1190–1213, 1209×1235, 1236, *c.*1300, 1390, 1440 (Edwards, 185–6; *Rotuli Hugonis de Welles*, ed. F. N. Davis, vol. iii, Lincoln Record Soc., 20 (1914), 101–2; Bradshaw and Wordsworth, i, 284; ii, 158; iii, 300–1; *VCH Lincs.*, ii, 421–4).

LIVERPOOL, Lancs.

Endowed grammar school, founded *c.*1517 → (*VCH Lancs.*, ii, 593–4; Jordan, 1962, 37).

LONDON, Middx.

ST PAUL'S CATHEDRAL. Song and grammar school for the choristers, 1296×1300 → (W. S. Simpson, 22, 49–50, 226; Rickert, 1931–2). Public grammar school, *c.*1102 →, endowed 1508–12 (Le Neve, 1968–, St Paul's, 25; *EEA*, viii, 55; xv, 17–19, 31; Gibbs, 215–20; Leach, 1910). Higher Studies, 12th century; lectures in theology, 1281–1308, *c.*1465, 1505×1523 (Edwards, 188–9, 199–200; W. S. Simpson, 413–15).

ST MARTIN-LE-GRAND. Possible song school for the choristers, 1304–1503 (*VCH London*, i, 562); grammar school, 1134×1139–1446 (*EEA*, viii, 55; xv, 31; Gibbs, 251–9; Leach, 1910; *ECD*, 90–2, 416–18; Leach, 1916, 142–3).

ST MARY ARCHES. Grammar school, 1134×1139–1446 (references as for St Martin-le-Grand grammar school).

CRUTCHED FRIARS, NEAR. Grammar school, 1392 (*Calendar of Plea and Memoranda Rolls of London, 1381–1412*, ed. A. H. Thomas (London, 1932), 182).

THE STOKKES (near St Mary Woolchurch). School, 1404 (C. Barron, *London in the Later Middle Ages* (Oxford, 2004), 52).

CORNHILL. Grammar school or schools, 1404–1439×1441 (Galbraith, 1941–3, 85–104; *ECD*, 396–7; Thrupp, 156).

CARDINAL'S HAT. Grammar school, *c.*1410 (Galbraith, 1941–3, 89–91, 104).

WHITTINGTON COLLEGE. Possible song school for the choristers, 1424–1548 (*VCH London*, i, 579).

GUILDHALL LIBRARY. Endowed for the study of theology, founded *c.*1425; dissolved *c.*1549 (Brewer; *Calendar of Plea and Memoranda Rolls of the City of London, 1458–1482*, ed. P. E. Jones (London, 1961), pp. ix–xiii; Smith, 1952, 1956; Borrajo).

ST THOMAS ACON. Possible song school for the choristers, from *c.*1432; grammar school, projected 1447, occurs 1535 → (Watney, 1906, 14, 41, 51, 60, 94, 132; C. L. Kingsford, 'Two London Chronicles', *Camden Miscellany XII*, Royal Hist. Soc., Camden 3rd series, 18 (1910), 11).

BASINGHALL. Grammar school, 1438 (London, Guildhall Library, MS 9171/4, f. 1r-v).

ST ANTHONY. Endowed grammar school, founded 1441 →; endowed song school, founded 1449 (London, Guildhall Library, MS 9531/6 (Reg. Gilbert, London), f. 183r; *CPR 1436–41*, 238; R. R. Sharpe, ii, 524–5).

ST DUNSTAN-IN-THE-EAST. Grammar school, 1446 (*ECD*, 416–18; *CPR 1441–6*, 482).

ALL HALLOWS THE GREAT, ST ANDREW HOLBORN, ST MARY COLECHURCH, ST PETER CORNHILL, parishes of. Grammar schools, projected 1447 (*Rotuli Parliamentorum*, v, 137; *ECD*, 418–20).

LEADENHALL. Endowed writing, song, and grammar school, projected 1459 (Stow, i, 74).

ST BARTHOLOMEW'S HOSPITAL. Grammar and song school, projected 1444; grammar school, 1459–76 (R. R. Sharpe, ii, 508; London, Guildhall Library, MS 9171/5, ff. 270v-271r; *CCR 1476–85*, 28).

TOWER ROYAL, NEAR. School, 1465 (*CPR 1452–61*, 285).

GUILDHALL COLLEGE. Tuition of four choristers, 1477 or earlier → (A. E. Douglas-Smith, *The City of London School* (Oxford, 1965), 22–8, 511–14).

ST MARY WOOLNOTH. Endowed song school, founded 1492–4 (R. R. Sharpe, ii, 600–1; *ESR*, part ii, 145).

ST MARY-AT-HILL. School, 1523 → (H. Littlehales, *The Medieval Records of a London City Church*, 2 parts, EETS, o.s., 125, 128 (1904–5), pp. xx, xxxiv, 321; *ESR*, part ii, 145).

OTHER SCHOOLS. c.1394, 1445, 1504×1515, 1518 (PRO, SC 8/22/1051; London, Guildhall Library, MS 9171/4, f. 172v; PRO, C 1/290/78; London, Guildhall Library, MS 9171/9, f. 96r).

SCHOOLMISTRESSES. 1408, 1441, by 1449 (see above, p. 167).

LONG MELFORD, Suffolk
School, 1484, 1535–48 (Bury St Edmunds, Suffolk Record Office, IC 500/2/11/365; *VCH Suffolk*, ii, 340).

LONG PRESTON, Yorks. W.R.
Endowed song and grammar school, allegedly founded 1468 → (*ESR*, part ii, 296).

LOUGHBOROUGH, Leics.
Possible school, c.1480; endowed school, projected 1514, founded by 1553 (Nicolas, 543; N. Watson, *Five Hundred Years Enduring* (Loughborough, 2000), 7–10).

LOUTH, Lincs.
School, 1276; grammar school, 1433, possibly 1472, endowed 1533 → (*VCH Lincs.*, ii, 460–2; Owen, 57).

LUDLOW, Shropshire
School, probably of grammar, 1203×1204, 1349–50, c.1431; endowed by 1521 → (*EEA*, iii, 193–6; *Reg. Trillek, Hereford*, ed. J. H. Parry, C&Y, 8 (1912), 500, 508, 519; *VCH Shropshire*, ii, 147).

MACCLESFIELD, Cheshire
Endowed grammar school, founded 1503 → (Wilmot, 10–11, appendix pp. xli-li).

MAIDSTONE, Kent
School, 1293, 1343–6; grammar school, 1393–1418 (CCA, DCc, ChAnt/M/390; F. R. H. Du Boulay, *The Lordship of Canterbury* (London, 1966), 259; *Reg. Edington, Winchester*, ed. S. F. Hockey, 2 vols, Hampshire Record Series, 7–8 (1986–7), ii, 625; London, Lambeth Palace Library, Reg. Morton, ii, f. 182; Kirby, 1892, 188).

MALDEN, Surrey
COLLEGIATE CHURCH. School for the boys of the college, projected 1264 (*ECD*, 174–5).

MALDON, Essex
Grammar school, 1408–35 (*VCH Essex*, ii, 516).

MALLING, Kent
School, 1348 (*Reg. Hethe, Rochester*, ed. C. Johnson, vol. ii, C&Y, 49 (1948), 985).

MALMESBURY, Wilts.
School, c.1260s (*EWE*, 101).

MALPAS, Cheshire
Endowed reading and grammar school, founded 1528 → (Chester, Cheshire Archives, DCH/C/446, /448; statutes, etc., in 'Malpas Grammar School').

MALTON (OLD), Yorks. N.R.
School, 1245, 1391 (Bodleian, MS Laud Misc. 642, ff. 4v–6r; *Testamenta Eboracensia*, i, 164; Moran, 1985, 261).

MANCHESTER, Lancs.
Endowed reading and grammar school, founded 1510–15 → (*VCH Lancs.*, ii, 578–84; Jordan, 1962, 34–5).
COLLEGIATE CHURCH. Possible song school for the choristers, 1421 → (*VCH Lancs.*, ii, 167).

MARKET HARBOROUGH, Leics.
Probable school, 1379 (Fenwick, ii, 516).

MARLBOROUGH, Wilts.
School, 1232, 1301 (*EWE*, 101–2).

MELBOURNE, Derbs.
Endowed school, projected 1514 (*VCH Derbs.*, ii, 207; Nicolas, 542).

MELLS, Somerset
Grammar school, 1524 (*EWE*, 102)

MELTON MOWBRAY, Leics.
School, 1347; school, probably of grammar, *c.*1440 (*CPR 1345–8*, 361; *Calendar of Miscellaneous Inquisitions 1422–85*, 152–3).

METTINGHAM, Suffolk
COLLEGIATE CHURCH. Song school for the boys, 1452 (PRO, PROB 11/5 (2 Godyn: will of Robert Willoughby)); grammar school for the same boys, also attended by some outsiders, 1479–1535 (Norwich, Norfolk Record Office, Norfolk Consistory Court Wills 168 (A. Caston), will of George Fen; ibid., 90 (Spyltymber), will of Geoffrey Markant; PRO, PROB 11/26 (7 Crumwell, will of John Brend)).

MIDDLEHAM, Co. Durham
School, 1261 (*EEA*, xxv, 136).

MIDDLEHAM, Yorks. N.R.
COLLEGIATE CHURCH. Song school for the choristers, projected 1478 (J. Raine, 'The Statutes for the College of Middleham', *Arch. Journal*, 14 (1857), 163; Moran, 1985, 262).

MIDDLETON, Lancs.
Endowed grammar school, founded 1440 → (*CPR 1436–41*, 399; *VCH Lancs.*, ii, 574–5; v, 159–60).

MILDENHALL, Suffolk
School, *c.*1235 (Gransden, 1973, 4).

MILTON ABBAS, Dorset
Endowed grammar school, founded 1521 → (*EWE*, 151–2).

MONTGOMERY, Mont. (Wales)
Endowed elementary school, allegedly founded *c.*1518, 1548 (*ESR*, part ii, 219).

MUCH WENLOCK, Shropshire
School, 1404 (*VCH Shropshire*, x, 444).

NEWARK, Notts.
Grammar school, 1238, 1327–1499, endowment projected 1512; endowed reading, song, and grammar school, 1531 → (*VCH Notts.*, ii, 199–208; C. Brown, ii, 175–94; Moran, 1985, 263; *Reg. Melton, York*, ed. R. Brocklesby, vol. iv, C&Y, 85 (1997), 81).

NEWCASTLE-ON-TYNE, Northumberland
Grammar school, *c.*1518 (Foxe, vii, 407); endowed grammar school, founded 1525–45 → (R. F. Tuck, 'The Origins of the Royal Grammar School Newcastle upon Tyne', *Archaeologia Aeliana*, 4th series, 46 (1968), 230–1).

NEWLAND, Gloucs.
Endowed reading, song, and grammar school, founded 1445 → (*EWE*, 153–65).

NEWMARKET, Suffolk

Probable school, 1381; school, *c.*1430s (PRO, KB27/482, 16 Rex 1; *Calendar of Miscellaneous Inquisitions 1422–85*, 102).

NEWPORT, Isle-of-Wight

School, 1269, possibly 1495 (PRO, SC 6/984/2; PROB 11/10 (26 Vox: will of Simon Englissh)).

NEWPORT PAGNELL, Bucks.

School, 1390; probable grammar school, 1421 (*Inquests and Indictments from Late Fourteenth-Century Bucks.*, ed. L. Boatwright, Buckinghamshire Record Soc., 29 (1994), 193; *BRUO*, i, 29, s.n. 'Thomas Alwyn').

NORHAM, Northumberland

School, by mid 12th century, 1302–48 (Reginald of Durham, 1835, 149–50; Durham, University Library, Dean and Chapter Muniments, Priory Reg. i, part ii, f. 80v; Reg. ii, f. 75r).

NORTHALLERTON, Yorks. N.R.

Reading, song, and grammar school, 1322–1445 (*EYS*, ii, 60–74; Moran, 1985, 264).

NORTHAMPTON, Northants.

Schools, probably of grammar and, until the 13th century, of liberal arts, 1176 → (H. G. Richardson, 1941b; *EEA*, iv, 91–2; PRO, C 1/27/282; *Grace Book Γ*, 176, 189; Salter, 1909, 158; *VCH Northants.*, ii, 234–6; iii, 61).

NORTH ELMHAM, Norfolk

Probable school, 1524–5 (Gurney, 466).

NORTHENDEN, Cheshire

School, *c.*1514–18 (F. J. Furnivall, *Child-Marriages, Divorces, and Ratifications in the Diocese of Chester*, EETS, o.s., 108 (1897), 139).

NORTH WALSHAM, Norfolk

School, *c.*1324 (*CIPM*, viii, 449).

NORWICH, Norfolk

CITY (BISHOP'S) SCHOOL. Grammar school, 1156 → (*EEA*, vi, 195; xxi, 169–70; Saunders, 1932, 85–102; Harries et al., 3–40).

CATHEDRAL. School in the cathedral priory, possibly for the public, 1095×1119 (*Epistolae Herberti de Losinga*, ed. R. Anstruther (Brussels, 1846), no. 55). Almonry grammar school, open to twelve boys from outside, 1424 (Saunders, 1932, 93–100).

NOTTINGHAM, Notts.

School, 1289; grammar school, 1382 → , endowed 1512 (*VCH Notts.*, ii, 216–23; A. W. Thomas, *A History of Nottingham High School, 1513–1953* (Nottingham, 1958), 13–28; Moran, 1985, 264–5).

CARMELITE FRIARY. Endowed reading and grammar school, apparently for children from outside the friary, projected 1492 (PRO, PROB 11/10 (34 Vox, will of Henry, Lord Grey)).

Teaching of writing, *c.*1532 (*VCH Notts.*, ii, 222).

ORSTON, Notts.

School, probably of reading, projected 1522 (Moran, 1985, 265).

OSWESTRY, Shropshire

Endowed grammar school, founded *c.*1423 → (Bulkeley-Owen, 194–5; Oakley, 13–48).

OTTERY ST MARY, Devon

COLLEGIATE CHURCH. Song school for the clerks and choristers, 1338 → ; public grammar school, 1338 → (*EWE*, 165–7; Orme, 1978b, 24).

OXFORD, Oxon.

UNIVERSITY. Higher Studies, 1096×1102 → (*BRUO*, iii, 1754, s.n. 'Theobaldus Stampensis'; Rashdall, iii, 1–273; *VCH Oxon.*, iii, 1–19; Catto; Cobban, 1988; Catto and Evans).

GRAMMAR SCHOOLS. Late 12th century-*c*.1492 (Emden, 1927, 84–6; *VCH Oxon.*, iii, 40–3; R. W. Hunt, 1964, 163–93; Thomson, 1983; Leader, 1983. Statutes, etc., in Gibson, 20–3, 169–74).

BUSINESS STUDIES. 1215–1432 (Salter, Pantin, and Richardson, ii, 329–450).

MERTON COLLEGE. Endowed grammar school for the boys of the college, projected 1270, 1490–1 (Highfield, 69–73, 382; *Registrum Annalium Collegii Mertonensis*, ed. H. E. Salter, Oxford Hist. Soc., 76 (1921), 142).

THE QUEEN'S COLLEGE. Endowed song and grammar school for the boys of the college, projected 1341 (Magrath, i, 45–9, 141–2).

NEW COLLEGE. Song and grammar school for the choristers, *c*.1386 → (New College, Oxford, Bursars' Rolls, 7336–7413; *VCH Oxon.*, iii, 155–7).

MAGDALEN COLLEGE SCHOOL. Song school for the choristers, 1480 → ; endowed grammar school, founded 1480 → (Orme, 1998).

WHITE HALL. School, 1518×1529 (PRO, C 1/589/13).

CARDINAL COLLEGE. Song and grammar school for the choristers, *c*.1525–30 (*Statutes of the Colleges of Oxford*, ii, section 11, 13, 49–50).

KING HENRY VIII COLLEGE. Song and grammar school for the choristers, 1532–45 (ibid., 185, 193–4).

ALL SOULS COLLEGE. Possible grammar school, to 1549 (Frere and Kennedy, ii, 199).

OTHER SCHOOLS. See Orme, 1998, 7–8.

SCHOOLMISTRESS. 1335 (see above, p. 166).

PARTNEY, Lincs.

Grammar school, 1329–34 (*ECD*, 280-3; *VCH Lincs.*, ii, 449–50).

PENRITH, Cumberland

Grammar school, *c*.1341; song and grammar school, 1361 (*Reg. Kirkeby, Carlisle*, ed. R. L. Storey, vol. ii, C&Y, 81 (1995), 47; *Reg. Welton, Carlisle*, ed. R. L. Storey, C&Y, 88 (1999), 73).

PENRYN, Cornwall

GLASNEY COLLEGE. Song school for the choristers, probably *c*.1267 →; public grammar school, 1548, perhaps earlier (*EWE*, 167–8).

PETERBOROUGH, Northants.

School, 1402, *c*.1512–26 (*Peterborough Local Administration*, ed. W. T. Mellors, Northamptonshire Record Soc., 9 (1939), 223; *VCH Northants.*, ii, 202–8; Salter, 1909, 136).

PLESHEY, Essex

Endowed school, possibly founded 1498, 1548 (*CPR 1494–1509*, 173; *VCH Essex*, ii, 516).

PLYMOUTH, Devon

School, 1507 (*EWE*, 103).

PLYMPTON, Devon

School, 1263 (*EWE*, 103).

POCKLINGTON, Yorks. E.R.

Endowed grammar school, founded 1514 → (*LPFD*, i part ii, no. 2964 (70); Leach, 1897; *VCH Yorks.*, i, 463–4; Moran, 1985, 266).

PONTEFRACT, Yorks. W.R.
School, *c*.1139×1140, 1267, 1437–64, 1480 (*EYS*, ii, pp. vii–xiii, 1–15; Moran, 1985, 266).

POTTON, Beds.
School, 1529 (*Bedfordshire Wills, 1484–1533*, ed. P. Bell, Bedfordshire Hist. Record Soc., 76 (1997), 147).

PRESTON, Lancs.
Grammar school, *c*.1327; school, 1358; grammar school, 1400–74 (*Reg. Melton, York*, ed. R. M. T. Hill, vol. i, C&Y, 70 (1977), 34; A. H. Thompson, 1919, 200; *VCH Lancs.*, ii, 569–71; Moran, 1985, 266–7).

RAMSBURY, Wilts.
Endowed grammar school, founded 1459, perhaps in being until dissolved 1539×1547 (*CPR 1452–61*, 502–3; *VCH Wilts.*, xii, 44–5).

READING, Berks.
School, 1133×1139, 1193–8, 1216×1234, 1246; grammar school, *c*.1502–3, probably endowed by 1524 → (*Reading Abbey Cartularies*, ed. B. R. Kemp, vol. i, Royal Hist. Soc., Camden 4th series, 31 (1986), 146, 159, 162; *EEA*, iii, 239–40; xviii, 11–12; J. C. Russell, *Dictionary of Writers of Thirteenth-Century England* (London, Bulletin of Institute of Hist. Research, Supplement, 1936), 67; *Close Rolls 1242–7*, 402; *VCH Berks.*, ii, 245–51).

RICHMOND, Yorks. N.R.
Grammar school, 1393–7, 1486×1487 (A. H. Thompson, 1919; Wenham, 1951 and 1958; Moran, 1985, 267).

RIPON, Yorks. W.R.
MINSTER. Song school for the choristers and public grammar school, early 14th century → (*EYS*, i, pp. lvi–lxiii, 141–56, 236–7; Moran, 1985, 267–8).

ROCK, Worcs.
Endowed grammar school, founded 1513 → (*LPFD*, i part ii, no. 2055 (53); *VCH Worcs.*, iv, 473–4; Orme, 1989a, 37, 46–8).

ROLLESTON, Staffs.
Endowed reading, accounting, and grammar school, founded 1524 → (statutes, etc., in Chichester, West Sussex Record Office, Cap 1/14/1; 1/14/5, ff. 25r-29v).

ROTHERHAM, Yorks. W.R.
Grammar school, *c*.1430 (*EYS*, ii, 110).
COLLEGIATE CHURCH. Endowed writing, song, and grammar school, founded 1483 → (statutes, etc., in ibid., 101–87; Moran, 1985, 268).

ROTHWELL, Northants.
School, 1460×1465 (PRO, C 1/29/347).

ROTHWELL, Yorks. W.R.
School, 1408 (Moran, 1985, 268).

ROYSTON, Yorks. W.R.
Endowed grammar school, founded 1503 → (Page, i, 196; J. Hunter, *South Yorkshire.*, 2 vols (London, 1828–31), ii, 381; Moran, 1985, 269).

RUDHAM, Norfolk
School, 1240 (Saunders, 1908–10, 343; *EEA*, xxi, 169–70).

RUFFORD, Lancs.
Endowed school, founded *c*.1520, 1548 (*ESR*, ii, 123; *VCH Lancs.*, vi, 127–8).

RUSHWORTH (Rushford), Norfolk
COLLEGIATE CHURCH. Song school for the choristers and endowed grammar school for twelve children, founded 1485–90, dissolved 1541 (Bennet).

SAFFRON WALDEN, Essex

School, 1317–45, 1401–40; grammar school by 1423, 1511, endowment projected 1517, endowed 1525 → (Leach, 1913–14, 475–6; *VCH Essex*, ii, 518–22; statutes in Wright, 1852).

ST ALBANS, Herts.

School, 1097×1119, 1183×1195; grammar school by *c*.1286, with partial endowment → (*VCH Herts.*, ii, 47–56; PRO, C 1/584/8; statutes in Riley, 1872–3, ii, 305–15, and *ECD*, 240–53).

ST DAVID'S, Pemb. (Wales)

CATHEDRAL. Song school for the choristers, founded 1363 (W. B. T. Jones and E. A. Freeman, *The History and Antiquities of St David's* (London, 1856), 303, 326).

ST MICHAEL-ON-WYRE, Lancs.

Endowed grammar school, founded 1528 → (*VCH Lancs.*, ii, 603; Jordan, 1962, 39–40; Moran, 1985, 269).

SALISBURY, Wilts.

CATHEDRAL SCHOOLS. Song school for the choristers, 1210 → (*EWE*, 66–78). Grammar school, 1091, 1210–1474 (ibid., 65–76). Grammar school for the cathedral choristers, established 1314–22 (ibid., 70–1). Higher Studies, lectures in theology and canon law, 1220–5, 1240, 1300, 1349–58, 1454 (ibid., 67–8, 73–4).

EMBRYONIC UNIVERSITY. Teachers and students, probably of arts and theology, 1238–79 (ibid., 68–9).

DE VAUX COLLEGE. Endowed college for the study of arts and theology, founded 1262 → (*VCH Wilts.*, iii, 369–85).

ST EDMUND COLLEGE. Founded 1269; attributed with the purpose of supporting the study of theology, but this is doubtful (*EWE*, 68).

SANDWICH, Kent

School, probably of grammar, 1449 (CCA, DCc, U3/11/5/1, p. 67).

SCARBOROUGH, Yorks. N.R.

School, 1407; grammar school 1444–57 (Lawson, 16; *Testamenta Eboracensia*, ii, 209; Moran, 1985, 270).

SEAFORD, Sussex

School, 1320 (*VCH Sussex*, ii, 398).

SEDBERGH, Yorks. W.R.

Endowed grammar school, founded *c*.1525–8 → (statutes, etc., in *EYS*, ii, pp. xli, 287–332; Moran, 1985, 270).

SEVENOAKS, Kent

Endowed grammar school, founded 1432 → (*ECD*, 398–403; Jordan, 1961b, 68–9).

SHAFTESBURY, Dorset

School, 1234 (*EWE*, 103).

SHAPWICK, Somerset

School, 1372×1373 (*VCH Somerset*, viii, 179).

SHERBORNE, Dorset

Grammar school, 1419, 1438, 1524–35 (*EWE*, 103–4; Orme 1980c, 23–6).

SHERBURN-IN-ELMET, Yorks. W.R.

School, before 1321, 1525×1526, 1534 (W. Wheater, *The History of the Parishes of Sherburn and Cawood*, 2nd edn (London, 1882), 34; Moran, 1985, 271).

SHIPDEN, Norfolk

Grammar school, 1455 (Norwich, Norfolk Record Office, Reg/6 Book 11, f. 84r). See also Cromer.

SHOREHAM (NEW), Sussex

School, 1302 (*VCH Sussex*, ii, 398; vi part i, 172).

SHOULDHAM, Norfolk

Grammar school, 1462 (Norwich, Norfolk Record Office, Reg/6 Book 11, f. 131v).

SHREWSBURY, Shropshire

Teaching, 1080–5; school, 1232, 1294; school, probably of grammar, 1530 (Orderic Vitalis, iii, 7–9; *CPR 1225–32*, 506; CCA, DCc, ESRoll/301; *VCH Shropshire*, ii, 154). Unlicensed school, 1294 (CCA, DCc, ESRoll/301).

SIBTHORPE, Notts.

Endowed reading school, founded 1335–43 (A. H. Thompson, 1947, 256, 267; Moran, 1985, 271).

SNAILWELL, Cambs.

School, *c*.1530; reading and grammar school, *c*.1539 (Foxe, vii, 69).

SNETTISHAM, Norfolk

Grammar school, 1477 (Richmond, 135).

SOUTHAMPTON, Hants.

Possible school, 1257 (C. Platt, *Medieval Southampton* (London, 1973), 62).

SOUTH DALTON, Yorks. E.R.

School, 1304–6 (*EYS*, i, 80m-81, 92; Moran, 1985, 245–6).

SOUTHWARK, Surrey

Reading and song school, 1365 (*Select Cases in the Court of King's Bench under Edward III*, ed. G. O. Sayles, vol. vi, Selden Soc., 72 (1965), 141–3).

SOUTHWELL, Notts.

MINSTER. Song and grammar schools, probably by 1238 →; endowed grammar school, projected 1512 (*VCH Notts.*, ii, 183–9; Moran, 1985, 272).

SPARHAM, Norfolk

Grammar school, 1408 (Norwich, Norfolk Record Office, Reg/4 Book 7, f. 102r).

SPRATTON, Northants.

School, 1520 (H. I. Longden, *Northamptonshire and Rutland Clergy from 1500*, 16 vols (London, 1939–52), vi, 189–91).

STAFFORD, Staffs.

Possible school, 1380; school, 1396–7, 1473; endowed grammar school, founded *c*.1500 → (G. Wrottesley, 'Extracts from the Coram Rege Rolls', *William Salt Arch. Soc.*, 14 (1893), 150, 155; *CPR 1377–81*, 547; *VCH Staffs.*, vi, 260).

STAMFORD, Lincs.

School, 1298–1389; endowed grammar school, founded 1532 → (*Select Cases in the Court of King's Bench under Edward I*, ed. G. O. Sayles, iii, Selden Soc., 58 (1939), p. cix; *VCH Lincs.*, ii, 474–5; *BRUO*, iii, 2030–1, s.n. 'William of Wheatley'; Foster and Thompson, 103–4).

HIGHER STUDIES. Secession of scholars from Oxford, 1334–5 (*VCH Lincs.*, ii, 468–74).

STEVENAGE, Herts.

School, 1312 (*VCH Herts.*, ii, 69).

STOCKPORT, Cheshire

Endowed grammar school, founded 1488 → (Varley, 1–54)

STOCKTON, Wilts.

Possible school, 1410 (*VCH Wilts.*, xi, 222).

STOKE-BY-CLARE, Suffolk

COLLEGIATE CHURCH. Endowed reading and song school for the choristers, founded 1422 → ; endowed grammar school, by 1548 (Dugdale, vi part iii, 1419; *VCH Suffolk*, ii, 339–40; *ESR*, part ii, 220; *Reg. Morton, Canterbury*, ed. C. Harper-Bill, vol. iii, C&Y, 89 (2000), 167).

STOKE-BY-NAYLAND, Suffolk

School, 1465, possibly in the household of Sir John Howard but apparently open to others (*Manners and Household Expenses of England*, ed. B. Botfield, Roxburghe Club, 57 (1841), 179, 269).

STONY STRATFORD, Bucks.

Probable school, 1346 (*CPR 1345–8*, 43).

STOW-ON-THE-WOLD, Gloucs.

Probable school, 1381, 16th century (*EWE*, 104, 170–1; Fenwick, i, 264).

STRATFORD-ON-AVON, Warws.

School, 1295, 1402–73; grammar school, 1478; endowed grammar school founded 1482 → (*VCH Warws.*, ii, 329–33; Stratford-upon-Avon, Shakespeare Birthday Trust Records Office, BRT 1/2/420, 1/3/27).

STRUBBY, Lincs.

Grammar school, 1309–44, 1358×1359 (Poos, 19, 184; BL, Harleian Roll AA 31; *VCH Lincs.*, ii, 449).

SUDBURY, Suffolk

Endowed grammar school, founded 1491 → (*VCH Suffolk*, ii, 341).

SUTTON COLDFIELD, Warws.

School, probably of grammar, 1521–3 (*HMC, Report on the MSS of Lord Middleton* (London, 1911), 335–59).

SWAFFHAM, Norfolk

Probable grammar school, 1474, indicated by the bequest of two grammar books to the church by the rector, John Botwright (*BRUC*, 81).

TAMWORTH, Staffs.

Probable school, by 1384 (*VCH Staffs.*, vi, 168).

TATTERSHALL, Lincs.

COLLEGIATE CHURCH. Song school for the choristers and endowed public grammar school, founded *c*.1460 → (*HMC, Report on the MSS of Lord De L'Isle and Dudley*, vol. i (1925), 182).

TAUNTON, Somerset

School, 1286–93; grammar school, 1375, 1523, 1533–45 (*EWE*, 105–6; PRO, E 326/172; CP 40/503, m. 620d).

TAVERHAM, Norfolk

School, 1288 (H. W. Saunders, *An Introduction to the Obedientiary and Manor Rolls of Norwich Cathedral Priory* (Norwich, 1930), 112).

TAVISTOCK, Devon

Possible school, *c*.1530 (*EWE*, 106).

TEMPSFORD, Beds.

Endowed grammar school, projected 1517 (Oxford, Magdalen College, Deeds, Tempsford 96).

TENTERDEN, Kent

School, projected 1525; endowed grammar school, by 1548 (Taylor, 129–31).

THAXTED, Essex

Grammar school, *c*.1460–*c*.1470 (J. Leland, *Commentarii de Scriptoribus Britannicis*, ed. A. Hall, 2 vols (Oxford, 1709), ii, 484–5).

THETFORD, Norfolk

School, 1103×1119; grammar school, 1328–1496 (*EEA*, vi, 22; *VCH Suffolk*, ii, 303–4).

THORNAGE, Norfolk

Grammar school, 1474 (Norwich, Norfolk Record Office, Reg/7 Book 12, f. 40r).

THORNHILL, Yorks. W.R.

School, *c*.1361 (*CIPM*, xiv, 182; Moran, 1985, 274).

TICEHURST, Sussex

School, projected 1489 (*Transcripts of Sussex Wills*, ed. R. G. Rice, vol. iv, Sussex Record Soc., 45 (1940–1), 2–44).

TIDESWELL, Derbs.

School, early 16th century (*BRUO*, iv, 467–8, s.n. 'Robert Pursglove').

TIVERTON, Devon

Possible school, 1390s-1400 (*EWE*, 106).

TONBRIDGE, Kent

School, 1323; endowed grammar school, projected 1525 (*Reg. Hethe, Rochester*, ed. C. Johnson, vol. i, C&Y, 48 (1948), 190–1; *LPFD*, iv part i, nos 1459, 1470–1).

TONG, Shropshire

Endowed reading, song, and grammar school, founded 1411 (Dugdale, vi part iii, 1407).

TOPCLIFFE, Yorks. N.R.

School, *c*.1513–19 (*LPFD*, xiii part i, no. 403 (2); *VCH Yorks.*, i, 415; Moran, 1985, 275).

TOTNES, Devon

Song and grammar school, 1509–26 (PRO, C 1/136/51; *Devon Lay Subsidy Rolls, 1524–7*, ed. T. L. Stoate (Almondsbury, 1979), 195; *EWE*, 107–8).

TOWCESTER, Northants.

Endowed grammar school, founded, probably for this purpose, 1448 → (*CPR 1446–52*, 204; *ESR*, part ii, 146, 151; *VCH Northants.*, ii, 225–8).

TURVEY, Beds.

Endowed grammar school, projected 1504 (*Bedfordshire Wills Proved in the Prerogative Court of Canterbury, 1383–1548*, ed. M. McGregor, Bedfordshire Hist. Record Soc., 58 (1979), 68–9).

VALLE CRUCIS (Llangollen), Denbigh (Wales)

Probable grammar school here or in the vicinity, possibly open to the public, *c*.1480 (Thomson, 1979, 105–13; Thomson, 1982, 76–7).

WAINFLEET, Lincs.

Endowed grammar school, founded *c*.1464 → (Parry-Jones and Wales; Orme, 1998, 72).

WAKEFIELD, Yorks. W.R.

School by 1275, 1296–1317, 1335–8, 1349 (J. W. Walker, *Wakefield, Its History and People*, 2nd edn, 2 vols (Wakefield, 1939), ii, 363–4; Leeds, Yorkshire Arch. Soc., MS MD225, 1348–9, m. 25; Moran, 1985, 275, who argues for a continuation of evidence 1427–1548).

WALLINGFORD, Berks.

COLLEGIATE CHURCH. Song school for the choristers, perhaps by 1444, 1548 (*VCH Berks.*, ii, 104–5).

WALSALL, Staffs.

School, 1377, 1490s, *c*.1503 (*VCH Staffs.*, xvii, 254; *HMC, MSS of the Duke of Rutland*, vol. i (1911), 17).

WALTHAM, Essex

School, *c*.1066–*c*.1177, *c*.1342, 1423 (Watkiss and Chibnall, 28–9, 46–55, 65–7; *VCH Essex*, v, 176; *CPR 1422–9*, 216–17).

WALTHAMSTOW, Essex

Endowed grammar school, founded *c*.1527 → (*VCH Essex*, ii, 527–8).

WARRINGTON, Lancs.

Endowed grammar school, founded 1520–6 → (Chester, Cheshire Archives, DBC 2391/2; *VCH Lancs.*, ii, 601–2, including statutes; Jordan, 1962, 38–9).

WARWICK, Warws.

School, 1113×1123, 1119×1153, 1155; song school, *c.*1315, 1409; grammar school, *c.*1315, 1461–1464×1465, endowed by 1501 → (Fonge), 5–8, 13–14, 21–5, 345; Leach, 1906; *VCH Warws.*, ii, 299–304; Warwick, Warwickshire Record Office, CR 1908/83; *CPR 1494–1509*, 264).

WEEK ST MARY, Cornwall

Endowed grammar school, founded 1506–8 → (*EWE*, 173–82).

WELLINGTON, Somerset

Grammar school, 1371 (*EWE*, 107–8).

WELLS, Somerset

CATHEDRAL SCHOOLS. Song school for the choristers, *c.*1140 → (*EWE*, 78–91; Colchester, 3–25). Grammar school, *c.*1140 → (*EWE*, 78–91; Colchester, 3–25). Possible separate tuition in grammar for the choristers, 1460 → (*EWE*, 80–1; statutes in Watkin, 98–109). Higher Studies, lectures in theology or canon law, 1335–48, early 15th century (*EWE*, 83).

WESTBURY-ON-TRYM, Gloucs.

COLLEGIATE CHURCH. Probable song school for the choristers, *c.*1447 →; endowed public grammar school, founded 1463 →; both dissolved 1544 (*EWE*, 182–4).

WESTMINSTER, Middx.

School, *c.*1443×1460; school, probably of song, 1451, in the chapel of St Mary de Pew (PRO, C 1/17/263; C. L. Kingsford, *English Historical Literature in the Fifteenth Century* (Oxford, 1913), 372).

WESTOW, Yorks. E.R.

Teaching in the church, probably elementary, *c.*1468×1469 (Burton, 336).

WHITCHURCH, Shropshire

Grammar school, 1318 (*Reg. Norbury, Lichfield*, ed. E. Hobhouse, William Salt Arch. Soc., 1 (1880), 154, where ascribed to Oswestry).

WHITKIRK, Yorks. W.R.

Endowed grammar school, founded 1521, probably until 1538 (G. E. Kirk, *A History of the Parish Church of St. Mary, Whitkirk, Leeds* (Leeds, 1935), 244–7).

WICKHAM MARKET, Suffolk

Bequest for a boy to be taught for six years by a priest, John Cade, 1492 (Ipswich, Suffolk Record Office, Wills, vol. iii, ff. 133r, 143r).

WILTON, Wilts.

School 1238; grammar school 1530s (*EWE*, 108).

WIMBORNE MINSTER, Dorset

Grammar school, *c.*1250 (*The Poems of Walter of Wimborne*, ed. A. G. Rigg, Toronto, Pontifical Institute of Medieval Studies, Studies and Texts, 42 (1978), 1–2, 4, 6, 37, 71); endowed grammar school, founded 1497–1511 → (*EWE*, 184–6; Coulstock, 161–89).

WINCHCOMBE, Gloucs.

Endowed grammar school, founded 1521 → (*EWE*, 186–7).

WINCHESTER, Hants.

HIGH (BISHOP'S) SCHOOL. Grammar school, *c.*1154×1159, 1199×1214, 1231–68, 1366, 1373–1488 (*The Letters of John of Salisbury*, ed. W. J. Millor and H. E. Butler, vol. i (London, 1955), 95–6; *EEA*, ix, p. xlii; *VCH Hants.*, ii, 253–7; Keene, part i, 394; part ii, 865).

ST MARY alias WINCHESTER COLLEGE. Song school for the choristers and endowed public grammar school, founded 1373–82 → (Leach, 1899; *VCH Hants.*, ii, 261–308).
ST MARTIN (church or parish). Teaching by the rector, 1410 (Keene, i, 394).
JEWRY STREET. School, 1430 (ibid., 394).

WINDRUSH, Gloucs.
Teaching by the vicar, *c*.1515 × 1521 (Foxe, iv, 237).

WINDSOR, Berks.
COLLEGIATE CHURCH. Song and grammar school for the choristers of St George's chapel, 1352 → (Bowers, 2001, 193–4, 202–8, 214).

WISBECH, Cambs.
Grammar school, 1407, 1446, endowed by 1506 → (Crosby, no. 191 (1901), 75; *VCH Cambs.*, ii, 327).

WITNEY, Oxon.
School, before 1373; possibly *c*.1375 (*CIPM*, xiii, 265; *VCH Oxon.*, xiv, 155).

WOLLATON, Notts.
Grammar school, 1473; school, 1524 (*VCH Notts.*, ii, 217; *HMC, Report on the MSS of Lord Middleton* (London, 1911), 369; Moran, 1985, 277).

WOLVERHAMPTON, Staffs.
Endowed grammar school, founded 1512 → (*LPFD*, i part i, nos 1415 (19), 1804 (25); Mander, 347–50; *VCH Staffs.*, vi, 177).

WOOLAVINGTON, Somerset
Possible school, *c*.1380s (*EWE*, 108–9).

WOOTTON BASSETT, Wilts.
Possible grammar school, *c*.1430 × 1450 (Orme, 1989a, 93).

WORCESTER, Worcs.
CITY (ARCHDEACON'S) SCHOOL. School, 1266–94; grammar school, 1312 → , endowed *c*.1510 × 1532 (Leach, 1913, passim; *VCH Worcs.*, iv, 475–80; Orme, 1989a, 33–4, 42–7). Possible higher studies, 1266 (*EEA*, xiii, 141–3).
CARNARY LIBRARY. Endowed theology lectures, founded 1458–64, dissolved 1539 (Leach, 1913, 29–33; *VCH Worcs.*, iv, 411–12; Orme, 1989a, 36–7).

WOTTON-UNDER-EDGE, Gloucs.
School, 1291 × 1292; endowed grammar school, projected 1349, founded 1384 → (*EWE*, 109, 190–9; Hornsby and Griffin, 1–33; statutes in *ECD*, 330–41).
WRINGTON, Somerset
School, 1507 × 1509 (*EWE*, 109).

WYE, Kent
COLLEGIATE CHURCH. Endowed reading, song, and grammar school, founded 1448 → (Wye College, Statutes, ff. 10v-11v; Hasted, vii, 357–8; *VCH Kent*, ii, 235–6; Jordan, 1961b, 70).

YARM, Yorks. N.R.
Reading school, 1139 × 1140; school, 1383; grammar school, 1520 (Reginald of Durham, 1835, 34; *York Memorandum Book*, ed. J. W. Percy, Surtees Soc., 186 (1973), 13; Little, 1894, 51; Moran, 1985, 278).

YORK, Yorks.
CATHEDRAL SCHOOLS. Song school for the choristers, 12th century → (Moran, 1979, 19–20). Grammar school, as → (*EYS*, 10–29; Moran, 1979, 5–8, 39–40; *EEA*, v, 63; xx, 76–7, 97). Higher Studies, 12th century; lectures in theology, 1293, 1332, 1355, 1369, 1410 × 1429 (*EYS*, i, 17, 18, 24, 26; Little, 1892, 242; Moran, 1979, 25–6).
ST LEONARD'S HOSPITAL. Grammar school, apparently open to the public, 1341–1539 (Moran, 1979, 9–10).

ST MARTIN, CONEY STREET. School, 1408–52; endowed school, projected 1528 (ibid., 12).

ST JOHN'S GUILD. Grammar school, 1531 (ibid., 13).

OTHER SCHOOLS. 1396–1535 (ibid., 11–12, 18–19).

INDEX OF SCHOOLS BY HISTORIC COUNTIES

NOTTINGHAM: Bilborough, Dunham, East Retford, Kinoulton, Kneesall, Newark, Nottingham, Orston, Sibthorpe, Southwell, Wollaton

OXFORD: Banbury, Bicester, Burford, Chipping Norton, Ewelme, Henley-on-Thames, Oxford, Witney

SHROPSHIRE: Battlefield, Bridgnorth, Lilleshall, Ludlow, Much Wenlock, Oswestry, Shrewsbury, Tong, Whitchurch

SOMERSET: Barlinch, Bath, Bridgwater, Bristol, Bruton, Crewkerne, Dunster, Glastonbury, Ilminster, Langport, Mells, Shapwick, Taunton, Wellington, Wells, Woolavington, Wrington

STAFFORD: Burton upon Trent, Cannock, Codsall, Kinver, Lichfield, Rolleston, Stafford, Tamworth, Walsall, Wolverhampton

SUFFOLK: Beccles, Botesdale, Bury St Edmunds, Clare, Covehithe, Dunwich, Eye, Framlingham, Hadleigh, Ipswich, Lavenham, Long Melford, Mettingham, Mildenhall, Newmarket, Stoke-by-Clare, Stoke-by-Nayland, Sudbury, Wickham Market

SURREY: Croydon, Guildford, Kingston-on-Thames, Malden, Southwark

SUSSEX: Arundel, Battle, Billingshurst, Chichester, Cuckfield, Hastings, Lewes, Seaford, Shoreham (New), Ticehurst

WARWICK: Coughton, Coventry, Stratford-on-Avon, Sutton Coldfield, Warwick

WESTMORLAND: Appleby, Brough-under-Stainmore, Kirkby Kendal

WILTSHIRE: Bradford-on-Avon, Chippenham, Coombe Bissett, Devizes, Heytesbury, Malmesbury, Marlborough, Ramsbury, Salisbury, Stockton, Wilton, Wootton Bassett

WORCESTER: Droitwich, Evesham, Rock, Worcester

YORKSHIRE: York

   EAST RIDING: Beverley, Hedon, Hemingbrough, Howden, Hull, Kelk, Kirkham, Pocklington, South Dalton, Westow

   NORTH RIDING: Guisborough, Helmsley, Hovingham, Malton (Old), Middleham, Northallerton, Richmond, Scarborough, Topcliffe, Yarm

   WEST RIDING: Acaster Selby, Barnsley, Crofton, Doncaster, Fairburn, Giggleswick, Halifax, Harewood, Leeds, Long Preston, Pontefract, Ripon, Rotherham, Rothwell, Royston, Sedbergh, Sherburn-in-Elmet, Thornhill, Wakefield, Whitkirk

CHANNEL ISLANDS: Jersey

WALES: Basingwerk (Flint), Brecon (Brecknock), Caernarvon (Caern.), Haverfordwest (Pemb.), Montgomery (Mont.), St David's (Pemb.), Valle Crucis (Denbigh)

IRELAND: For records, see McGrath.

SCOTLAND: For records, see Durkan, Easson, and Grant.

Notes

ABBREVIATIONS

Arch.	Archaeological
BL	London, British Library
Bodleian	Oxford, Bodleian Library
BRUC	A. B. Emden, *A Biographical Register of the University of Cambridge to 1500* (Cambridge, 1963)
BRUO, i–iii	A. B. Emden, *A Biographical Register of the University of Oxford to A.D. 1500*, 3 vols (Oxford, 1957–9)
BRUO, iv	A. B. Emden, *A Biographical Register of the University of Oxford A.D. 1501 to 1540* (Oxford, 1974)
CCA, DCc	Canterbury Cathedral Archives, Dean and Chapter
CCR	*Calendar of Close Rolls, 1272–1509*, 47 vols (London, 1892–1963)
CIPM	*Calendar of Inquisitions Post Mortem, 1216 –* (London, 1904–, in progress)
CPL	*Calendar of Papal Letters, 1198 –* (London and Dublin, 1894–; in progress)
CPR	*Calendar of Patent Rolls, 1216–1509, 1547–* (London, 1891–, in progress)
C&Y	Canterbury and York Society
DNB	*The Oxford Dictionary of National Biography*, 2nd edn, 60 vols, ed. C. Matthew and B. Harrison (Oxford 2004)
ECD	A. F. Leach, *Educational Charters and Documents, 598–1909* (Cambridge, 1911)
EEA	*English Episcopal Acta* (London, British Academy, 1980–, in progress)
EETS	Early English Text Society, o.s. (ordinary series), e.s. (extra series), s.s. (supplementary series)
ESR	A. F. Leach, *English Schools at the Reformation, 1546–8* (Westminster, 1896)
EWE	Nicholas Orme, *Education in the West of England, 1066–1548* (Exeter, 1976)

EYS	A. F. Leach, *Early Yorkshire Schools*, 2 vols, Yorkshire Archaeological Society, 27, 33 (1899–1903)
Hist.	Historical
HMC	*Historical Manuscripts Commission*, printed reports
LPFD	*Calendar of Letters and Papers, Foreign and Domestic, Henry VIII*, ed. J. S. Brewer, J. Gairdner, and R. H. Brodie, 21 vols and addenda (London, 1864–1932)
MED	*Middle English Dictionary*, ed. Hans Kurath and Sherman M. Kuhn (Ann Arbor, Mich., and London, 1956–2002)
MGH	Monumenta Germaniae Historica
MLD	*Dictionary of Medieval Latin from British Sources*, ed. R. E. Latham and D. R. Howlett (London, 1975–, in progress)
n.s.	new series
OED	*The Oxford English Dictionary*, ed. J. A. Simpson and E. S. C. Weiner, 2nd edn, 20 vols (Oxford, 1898)
PRO	London, The National Archives (Public Record Office)
Reg.	*The Register of . . . , Bishop of . . .*
RS	London, Rolls Series
Soc.	Society
STC	A. W. Pollard and G. R. Redgrave, *A Short Title Catalogue of Books Printed in England, Scotland, and Ireland, 1475–1640*, 2nd edn, 3 vols (London, 1976–91)
VCH	*Victoria County History*

The Study of Medieval Schools

1   On this topic, see Orme and Webster, 1–7.
2   Bodleian, MS Wood D 11, ff. 159r–180v.
3   On Wase, see Wallis, 1952, and Wase.
4   Fuller, *The Church History of Britain* (London, 1655), book vi, p. 297.
5   Aubrey, *Brief Lives and Other Writings*, ed. Anthony Powell (London, 1949), 6.
6   For example, R. Furney, 'History of Gloucester' (Bodleian, MS Top. Glouc. c. 4–5); F. Blomefield and C. Parkin, *An Essay Towards a Topographical Description of the County of Norfolk*, 5 vols (King's Lynn, 1739–75), 11 vols (London, 1805–10); and Nicolson and Burn.
7   Carlisle.
8   On Leach's career, see F. Watson's article in the original *Dictionary of National Biography, 1912–1921* (Oxford, 1927), 327–8; Miner 1990, 3–129; and *DNB*.
9   Furnivall, pp. i–lxviii. His many other editions included Caxton's *Book of Curtesye* and *Child-Marriages*, both EETS.
10   Grant.

11   Wylie, 1884–98; Green, 1894.
12   *VCH Worcs.*, iv, 475 note 1.
13   For example, Droitwich (ibid., iii, 76) and Tattershall (*VCH Lincs.*, ii, 237).
14   For some omissions in *English Schools at the Reformation*, see below, p. 395 note 24.
15   On Leach and his contemporaries, see C. H. S. Fifoot, *Frederic William Maitland: A Life* (Cambridge, Mass., 1971), 240–3; A. G. Little's review of *The Schools of Medieval England* in *English Hist. Review*, 30 (1915), 525–9; Wallis, 1963–4; and Miner, 1990, 11–13, 228–46.
16   Bowers, 1999, 210.
17   As Little pointed out in his review. See also above, pp. 214–15.
18   On Hunt's career, see *DNB*.
19   See the articles by Chaplin, 1962–3; Simon, 1954–5, 1955–6, 1963–4; and Wallis, 1963–4.
20   Jordan, 1961a, 22, 151, 301, with a callow remark about 'the ruin of the medieval world'.
21   The largeness of England as a topic must excuse this book's neglect of Ireland, for which see Bliss and McGrath; Scotland, for

which see Durkan, Easson, and Grant; and Wales, for which see Thomson, 1982, and G. Williams, 1976, 1997.

1: From the Romans to 1100

1 B. Cunliffe, *The Extraordinary Voyage of Pytheas the Greek* (London, 2002), 151–69; *DNB*.
2 J. Creighton, *Coins and Power in Late Iron Age Britain* (Princes Risborough, 1996), 146, 170–1; P. Jersey, *Celtic Coinage in Britain* (Princes Risborough, 1996), 27–52.
3 On Roman inscriptions, see R. G. Collingwood, *The Roman Inscriptions of Britain*, 2nd edn, 2 vols (Stroud, 1991–5), and A. R. Burn, *The Romans in Britain: an anthology of inscriptions*, 2nd edn (Oxford, 1969). On particular subjects, see A. A. Barrett, 'Knowledge of the Literary Classics in Roman Britain', *Britannia*, 9 (1978), 307–18; R. Tomlin, *Tabellae Sulis: Roman inscribed tablets of tin and lead from the sacred springs of Bath*, University of Oxford Committee for Archaeology, 16 fasc. 1 (Oxford, 1988); and A. K. Bowman and J. D. Thomas, *The Vindolanda Writing-Tablets* (London, 1994).
4 Tomlin, *Tabellae Sulis*; J. N. Adams, 'British Latin: the text, interpretation and language of the Bath curse tablets', *Britannia*, 23 (1992), 1–26, especially 24–6.
5 On Roman education, see Marrou; Jones, ii, 997–1002; Bonner; and Morgan.
6 Livy, *Ab Urbe Condita*, book iii, section 44.
7 *Theodosiani Liber XVI*, ed. T. Mommsen and P. M. Meyer, 2 vols (Berlin, 1905), i, part ii, 740–5; *The Theodosian Code*, trans. C. Pharr (New York, 1952), 387–90.
8 *Diokletians Preisedikt*, ed. S. Lauffer (Berlin, 1971), 124; *An Economic Survey of Ancient Rome*, ed. T. Frank, 5 vols (Baltimore, 1933–40), v, 345–6.
9 *Theodosiani Liber XVI*, ed. Mommsen and Meyer, i, part ii, 743.
10 Tacitus, *Agricola*, section 21.
11 Bowman and Thomas, *The Vindolanda Writing-Tablets*, 65–7.
12 Lapidge, 1984; *DNB*.
13 On this subject, see C. Thomas, *Christianity in Roman Britain to AD 500* (London, 1981).
14 For references to the names and their interpretation, see R. Sharpe, 'Martyrs and Local Saints in Late Antique Britain', in *Local Saints and Local Churches in the Early Medieval West*, ed. A. Thacker and R. Sharpe (Oxford, 2002), 75–154 at 77; the article is also a valuable survey of late Roman and post-Roman Christianity in Britain.
15 Riché, 1976, 7–11.
16 W. Davis, *Wales in the Early Middle Ages*

(Leicester, 1982), 141–8.
17 Bede, book I.33 (pp. 114–15).
18 The list of early monasteries in Knowles and Hadcock, 463–87, needs revising. On early houses for women, see S. Foot, *Veiled Women*, 2 vols (Aldershot, 2000), i, 49–51.
19 *The Rule of St Benedict*, 90–1, 102–3, 106–8, 120–1, 144–51, 160–3, 176–7.
20 Bede, V.24 (pp. 566–7).
21 Ibid., IV.8 (pp. 358–9).
22 Eddius Stephanus, 4–7.
23 On this subject, see above, p. 32.
24 Bede, III.14 (pp. 256–7), III.20 (pp. 276–9); R. Sharpe, 'The Naming of Bishop Ithamar', *English Hist. Review*, 117 (2002), 889–94.
25 Bede, III.18 (pp. 268–9).
26 Ibid., IV.2 (pp. 332–3); Aldhelm, 1979, 7–8, 163; Brooks, 1984, 94–9; *Archbishop Theodore: commemorative studies on his life and influence*, ed. M. Lapidge (Cambridge, 1995); Lapidge, 1996, 93–121.
27 Bede, III.26 (pp. 308–9).
28 Ibid., pp. xix–xxii, V.24 (pp. 566–7).
29 On Alcuin's career, see Alcuin, 1982, pp. xxxv–xxxix.
30 Ibid., 108–27.
31 Alcuin, 'Epistolae', in *Epistolae Karolini Aevi*, vol. ii, ed. E. Duemmler, MGH, Epistolae, 4 (Berlin, 1895), 166–70; translated in *ECD*, 18–19, and in Alcuin, 1974, 6–10.
32 Aldhelm, 1979, 5–10; Aldhelm, 1985, 5–9.
33 Law, 1982, 77–80; Law, 1997, 106–7.
34 Law, 1982, 64–6; Law, 1997, 105–6.
35 Æthelwulf, 6–7, 10–11, 40–1, 58–9; Lapidge, 1996, 381–98.
36 Bede, III.8 (pp. 236–9).
37 *DNB*.
38 Bede, III.24 (pp. 290–3).
39 Ibid., IV.23 (pp. 408–9).
40 Ibid., III.24 (pp. 290–3); *DNB*.
41 *Die Briefe der heiligen Bonifatius und Lullus*, ed. M. Tangl, MGH, Epistolae Selectae, 1 (Berlin, 1916), 53; Boniface, 59–60.
42 Rudolf of Fulda, *Vita Leobae*, ed. G. Waitz, MGH, Scriptores Rerum Germanicarum, 15 part 1 (Hannover, 1887), 123–5; Talbot, 207–15; *DNB*.
43 Haddan and Stubbs, iii, 314–26; *Venerabilis Bedae Historiam Ecclesiasticam*, ed. C. Plummer, 2 vols (Oxford, 1896), i, 405–23; translated in Whitelock, 735–45.
44 Haddan and Stubbs, iii, 364–5.
45 Bede, V.7 (pp. 468–9).
46 *Vitae Sancti Bonifatii*, ed. W. Levison, MGH, Scriptores Rerum Germanicarum Separatim Editi, 57 (Hannover, 1905), 8–9; loosely translated in Talbot, 29.
47 Bede, II.15 (pp. 190–1), III.18 (pp. 266–9).
48 Ibid., III.3 (pp. 220–1), III.25 (pp. 296–7), where Oswiu is said to have been taught

(*edoctus*) by the Irish.

49 *Two Lives of Saint Cuthbert*, ed. B. Colgrave (Cambridge, 1940), 238–9; Alcuin, 1982, 71.

50 Bede, IV.26 (pp. 430–1), V.12 (pp. 496–7), V.15 (508–9).

51 Aldhelm, 1979, 12, 32; Aldhelm, 1985, 10.

52 Bede, preface (pp. 2–3); *Felix's Life of Saint Guthlac*, ed. B. Colgrave (Cambridge, 1956), 60–3.

53 Ibid., III.5 (pp. 226–7).

54 Ibid., V.6 (pp. 464–7).

55 Eddius Stephanus, 44–5.

56 Orme, 1984, 56–7.

57 Bede, V.13 (pp. 500–1).

58 *Felix's Life of Saint Guthlac*, ed. Colgrave, 78–9; *Beowulf*, lines 2428–31.

59 See above, p. 35.

60 Alcuin, 'Epistolae', ed. Duemmler, 104–6, 107, 146–8; Alcuin, 1974, 48–50, 53–5.

61 On what follows, see Kelly.

62 Bede, II.5 (pp. 150–1); *The Laws of the Earliest English Kings*, ed. F. L. Attenborough (Cambridge, 1922), 4–17.

63 Bede, IV.24 (pp. 418–19), pp. 582–3.

64 See, for example, Donatus, *Ars Grammatica*, in Keil, iv, 367–73.

65 See above, p. 57.

66 *La Vie ancienne de Saint Samson de Dol*, ed. P. Flobert (Paris, 1997), 162–3.

67 Bede, V.2 (pp. 456–9). See also above, p. 56.

68 On the psalter in teaching, see G. H. Brown, 122–38.

69 Bede, II.20 (pp. 206–7).

70 Ibid., IV.2 (pp. 332–3).

71 Ibid., IV.18 (pp. 388–9).

72 Keil, iv, 355.

73 Tatwine, *Omnia Opera*, ed. M. de Marco, Corpus Christianorum, Series Latina, 133 (Turnhout, 1968), 1–141; Boniface, *Ars Grammatica*, ed. G. J. Gebauer and B. Löfstedt, idem, 133B (Turnhout, 1980), 1–99; Law, 1982, 64–7, 77–80; Law, 1997, 105–7, 120–1.

74 Bede, *Opera*, ed. C. W. Jones et al., Corpus Christianorum, Series Latina, 123A (Turnhout, 1975), 1–57.

75 For example, *The Corpus Glossary*, ed. W. M. Lindsay (Cambridge, 1921); *A Late Eighth-Century Latin-Anglo-Saxon Glossary*, ed. J. H. Hessels (Cambridge, 1906); *The Harley Latin-Old English Glossary*, ed. R. T. Oliphant (The Hague and Paris, 1966).

76 Gneuss, passim; Lapidge and Page, 1982, 99–165; Lapidge, 1996, 3–4.

77 Keil, ii; iii, 1–377. On Priscian, see Porter, 9–12.

78 Ibid., iii, 459–515.

79 Aldhelm, 1979, 12, 31; Aldhelm, 1985, 10–11; Bede, *Opera*, ed. C. W. Jones et al., 81–141.

80 Bede, IV.1–2 (pp. 328–33). On Greek at Canterbury, see Lapidge, 1996, 123–39.

81 Ibid., V.8 (pp. 474–5), V.20 (pp. 530–1), V.23 (pp. 556–7).

82 Ibid., V.24 (pp. 568–71).

83 On this subject, see Lapidge, 1993, 105–49.

84 Isidore of Seville, *De Natura Rerum*, ed. G. Becker (Amsterdam, 1967).

85 See above, p. 45.

86 *Codices Latina Antiquiores*, ed. E. A. Lowe, Supplement (Oxford, 1971), 5, no. 1684.

87 Bede, pp. 580–7.

88 Haddan and Stubbs, iii, 178–9, 184.

89 Simeon of Durham, *Omnia Opera*, ed. T. Arnold, vol. ii (RS, 1885), 44.

90 On minsters, see Blair, passim.

91 *King Alfred's West-Saxon Version of Gregory's Pastoral Care*, ed. H. Sweet, part 1, EETS, o.s., 45 (1871), 2–8; translated in Lapidge and Keynes, 123–5.

92 Lapidge, 1996, 409–54.

93 Brooks, 1984, 171–4.

94 Asser, p. 20; Lapidge and Keynes, 75.

95 Asser, pp. 80–1; Lapidge and Keynes, 103.

96 Asser, pp. 58 (where, Prof. B. Yorke points out to me, *nutricum* might refer to governesses rather than nurses), 60, 88–9; Lapidge and Keynes, 90–1, 107; Lapidge, 1993, 12.

97 On this subject, see M. Godden, 'King Alfred's Preface and the Teaching of Latin in Anglo-Saxon England', *English Hist. Review*, 117 (2002), 596–604.

98 Asser, p. 94; Lapidge and Keynes, 91, 110.

99 See, for example, *Select English Hist. Documents of the Ninth and Tenth Centuries*, ed. F. E. Harmer (Cambridge, 1914), nos. 1–11.

100 On the monastic revival, see Knowles, 1963, 31–56, and *Tenth-Century Studies*, ed. D. Parsons (Chichester, 1975).

101 On his career, see Ramsay, Sparks, and Tatton-Brown, especially 1–23, and *DNB*.

102 On his career, see Yorke, especially 89–117; Lapidge, 1993, 183–211, 225–77; and *DNB*.

103 On Oswald, see E. John, 'St Oswald and the Tenth-Century Reformation', *Journal of Ecclesiastical History*, 9 (1958), 159–72, and *DNB*.

104 For a preliminary list of the foundations, see Knowles and Hadcock, 463–87, and for the women's houses, Foot, *Veiled Women*, i, 85–110; ii, passim.

105 On Abbo, see *DNB*.

106 On Ælfric, see above, pp. 42–3.

107 *Regularis Concordia*, 7, 8, 13, 14, 16, 18, 23, 28, 35, 36, 42, 48, 51, 61.

108 Four new ones compensated for those lost in the ninth century (Fig. 10, p. 33).

109 Blair, 355–8.

110 Bertram; Napier.

111 Edwards, 8–9; Blair, 362.

112 Napier, 53–5.

113 Watkiss and Chibnall, 28–9.

114 M. Swanton, *Three Lives of the Last Englishmen* (New York and London, 1984), 7–8.

115 Watkiss and Chibnall, 46–55.

116 Ibid., 65–7.

117 *Councils and Synods I*, i, 97–8.

118 Discussed in detail by Blair, 368–504.

119 *Theodulfi Capitula in England*, ed. H. Sauer (Munich, 1978), 320–5.

120 Ibid., passim; Wilkins, i, 269–70.

121 *Die Hirtenbriefe Ælfrics in Altenglischer und Lateinischer Fassung*, ed. B. Fehr (Hamburg, 1914), 62.

122 *Councils and Synods I*, i, 318, 331.

123 Orme, 2001, 229–30.

124 For example, the priests who taught Orderic at Shrewsbury and John of Salisbury near Old Sarum (Orderic Vitalis, iii, 7–9; John of Salisbury, *Policraticus*, ed. C. C. J. Webb, 2 vols (Oxford, 1909), i, 164). See also above, p. 00.

125 Robinson, 449–50.

126 Ibid., 449; BL, Harley MS 208, ff. 87v-88r.

127 Asser, p. 91; Lapidge and Keynes, 91.

128 BL, Cotton MS Domitian I, f. 56v, illustrated in Leach, 1916, 95, edited and described by Lapidge, 1985, 50–2.

129 On parsing grammars, see Law, 1997, 135–6.

130 Abbo of Fleury, *Quaestiones Grammaticales*, ed. A. Guerreau-Jalabert (Paris, 1982).

131 Byrhtferth, 232–3.

132 Porter, especially 23–39.

133 Byrhtferth, 232–3.

134 Ælfric Bata, 86–7, 112–13, 140–55 (on Cato, see also Ælfric of Eynsham, 1966, 36).

135 Gneuss, nos 151, 252, 493, 497, 534–5, 664, 766, 919; Lapidge, 1985, 33–89, summarised on 82–9; T. Hunt, 1991, i, 66–9.

136 On Avianus, Cato, Statius, and Theodulus, see above, pp. 98–100.

137 Byrhtferth.

138 On Ælfric of Eynsham's life and work, see P. A. M. Clemoes, 'The Chronology of Ælfric's Works', in *The Anglo-Saxons*, ed. P. A. M. Clemoes (London, 1959), 212–47, and *DNB*.

139 For the text, see Ælfric of Eynsham, 1966, and for commentary, T. Hunt, 1991, i, 99–119; Law, 1997, 200–23; Porter, 23–33; and Law, 2002, 193–5.

140 Ælfric of Eynsham, 1966, 23, 225, 231, 260, 262, 273.

141 On the Glossary, see Lendinara, 224–39.

142 Law, 2002, 195.

143 See above, p. 106.

144 On what follows, see Stevenson, 1929; Garmonsway, 1959; Ælfric of Eynsham, 1978; Ælfric Bata; Lendinara, 207–87; and Gwara.

145 Stevenson, 1929, 1; Gwara, 48–9.

146 Ælfric Bata, 2–3, 120–5.

147 See above, pp. 109–18.

148 Ælfric Bata, 140–1.

149 *Memorials of St Dunstan*, ed. W. Stubbs (RS, 1874), 137–8, 140–2, 229–31.

150 *Chronicon Abbatiae Rameseiensis*, ed. W. D. Macray (RS, 1886), 112–14.

151 Ælfric Bata, 138–9.

152 See above, p. 116.

153 Ælfric of Eynsham, 1966, 151.

154 P. Stafford, *Queen Emma and Queen Edith* (Oxford, 1997), 258–9.

155 Ælfric of Eynsham, 1966, 1, 3.

156 M. T. Gibson, *Lanfranc of Bec* (Oxford, 1978), 177, 186–7; above, p. 204.

157 On these changes, see above, p. 87.

158 *EEA*, xxviii, 1–3.

159 *Eye Priory Cartulary and Charters*, ed. V. Brown, 2 vols, Suffolk Records Soc., Suffolk Charters, 12–13 (1992–4), i, 12, 14; ii, 88–9.

160 *EWE*, 57–8. The suspicious proviso is 'all Gloucester', which reflects disputes over the control of the school in the thirteenth and fourteenth centuries.

161 If the Canterbury document had been wholly manufactured in the early thirteenth century, one would have expected the priory of St Gregory (to which it grants the schools of Canterbury) to have claimed control of them after that date. In fact the control of the schools subsequently belonged to the archbishop, suggesting that the charter in favour of St Gregory affirmed an older arrangement.

162 'Villages' translates *viculorum*.

163 On St Oswald's, see C. Heighway and R. Bryant, *The Golden Minster*, Council for British Archaeology, Research Report 117 (York, 1999).

164 For references, see the list of schools, above pp. 346–72.

165 *EWE*, 65.

166 Edwards, 178–84.

167 On towns, see *Anglo-Saxon Towns in Southern England*, ed. J. Haslam (Chichester, 1984).

168 In Colchester the school was associated with the church of St Mary's-at-the-Walls, apparently an Anglo-Saxon foundation and a peculiar jurisdiction of the bishop of London – perhaps the result of ancient minster status (*VCH Essex*, ix, 49, 324).

169 Leach, 1916, 76–9.

170 Leach, 1906, 1–4 and illustration; Fonge, 21–2.

171 See above, pp. 256–7.

172 See above, pp. 106–8, 110–18.

173 See above, p. 165.

174 On cathedral schools in Normandy, see Edwards, 177–8.

2: The Tower of Learning

1 *OED*, s.v. 'school'; *MED*, s.v. 'scole'; *Altfranzösisches Wörterbuch*, ed. A. Tobler and E. Lommatzsch, 11 vols (Berlin, 1915–2002), s.v. 'escole'.

2 M. Aston, *Lollards and Reformers* (London, 1984), 198–9.

3 Chaucer, I (A) 125, 3329.

4 See above, pp. 251–3, 255–87.

5 On the layout and teaching of the alphabet, see, in more detail, Orme, 2001, 246–54.

6 Bowers, 2001, 203–5.

7 Whittick.

8 William Caxton, *Reynard the Fox*, ed. N. F. Blake, EETS, o.s., 263 (1970), 8–9. I am grateful to Jan de Putter for this and the following reference.

9 W. Hornbye, *Hornbyes Hornbook* (London, 1622; *STC* 13814), title page.

10 See above, pp. 27–8, 40.

11 John Rastell, *Three Rastell Plays*, ed. R. Axton (Cambridge, 1979), 55.

12 See above, p. 40.

13 *Age of Chivalry: Art in Plantagenet England 1200–1400*, ed. J. J. G. Alexander and P. Binski (London, 1987), 355.

14 *A Roll of the Household Expenses of Richard de Swinfield, Bishop of Hereford*, ed. J. Webb, 2 vols, Camden Soc., 59, 62 (1854–5), i, 132.

15 *Reg. Grandisson, Exeter*, ii, 1192–3.

16 Nichols and Rimbault, 10.

17 BL, Add. MS 18850; Janet Backhouse, *The Bedford Hours* (London, 1990), 59–61.

18 Orme, 2001, 208–9; La Tour Landry, 16–17.

19 Orme, 2001, 205–9.

20 Chaucer, VII 536 (B² 1726).

21 *The English Register of Godstow Nunnery*, ed. A. Clark, part i, EETS, original series, 129 (1905), 25.

22 On this subject, see Orme, 1984, 103–6, and Orme, 2001, 243.

23 La Tour Landry, pp. xxxvi, 11–13, 192.

24 Elyot, f. 19r (book i, chapter 5).

25 Asser, p. 20; Lapidge and Keynes, 75. On this subject, see also Orme, 2001, 243–4.

26 See above, pp. 74–5.

27 W. W. Skeat, 'Nominale sive Verbale', *Transactions of the Philosophical Soc.* (1903–6), 7.

28 W. Scase, 'St Anne and the Education of the Virgin', in *England in the Fourteenth Century*, ed. N. Rogers (Stamford, 1993), 81–96; P. Sheingorn, 'The Wise Mother: The Image of St Anne Teaching the Virgin Mary', *Gesta*, 32 (1993), 69–80.

29 See above, pp. 39–40.

30 *EYS*, i, 22–3.

31 *VCH Lincs.*, ii, 423–4.

32 *EWE*, 95; reference now Taunton, Somerset Record Office, D\B\bw/115.

33 On medieval English parish clerks, see Orme, 2001, 229–31.

34 See above, pp. 205–7.

35 *VCH Lincs.*, ii, 422–4; Bradshaw and Wordsworth, ii, 157; iii, 299.

36 J. R. Bramble, 'Records of St Nicholas Church, Bristol', *Clifton Antiquarian Club Proceedings*, 1 (1884–8), 148.

37 F. F. Giraud, 'On the Parish Clerks and Sextons of Faversham, 1506–1593', *Archaeologia Cantiana*, 20 (1894), 205.

38 See above, pp. 328–30; F. Clement, *The Petie Schole* (London, 1587; *STC* 5400), 9.

39 See above, p. 48.

40 On cathedral song schools, see Edwards, 166–8.

41 Orme, 2000, 567–8; *VCH Lincs.*, ii, 423–4; *EYS*, i, 22–3.

42 Bateson, 712–13.

43 *VCH Suffolk*, ii, 309–11.

44 Fonge, 5–8, 345; Leach, 1906, 66.

45 *EYS*, ii, 60–2, 84–7.

46 Clanchy, passim.

47 On this subject and what follows, see also above, pp. 282–3.

48 See above, pp. 356, 366.

49 See above, pp. 166–7.

50 Nelson, 13; Orme, 1998, 7.

51 For references, see the list of schools, above, pp. 346–72.

52 Fonge, 5–8; Leach, 1906, 65–6.

53 Lupton, 285.

54 *EWE*, 121.

55 *ECD*, 456–7.

56 *ECD*, 260–7.

57 *Reg. Wykeham, Winchester*, ed. T. F. Kirby, vol. ii, Hampshire Record Soc., 13 (1899), 287.

58 Kirby, 1892, 457; Heywood and Wright, 479.

59 *EWE*, 160–1.

60 *HMC, Ninth Report* (1883), i, 218, section 21.

61 Chichester, West Sussex Record Office, Cap 1/14/5, f. 28r.

62 *VCH Lancs.*, ii, 184.

63 On this subject, see Woolgar, passim.

64 *Testamenta Eboracensia*, i, 296.

65 Thrupp, 159.

66 PRO, C 1/19/491.

67 On the inns of court, see Holdsworth, ii, 315, 493–512; Ives, 1968; A. W. B. Simpson; Ives, 1982; and Orme, 1984, 74–9.

68 Fortescue, 116–19.

69 On this subject, see H. G. Richardson, 1939, 1941a, and Salter, Pantin, and Richardson, ii, 329–450.

70 Salter, Pantin, and Richardson, ii, 407.

71 Ibid., 371–2.

72 Ibid., 372.

73 Ibid., 397, 407.

74 Gibson, 240.

75 Bodleian, MS Lincoln College lat. 129, pp. 46, 61–5.

76 Stow, i, 154.

77 *EYS*, ii, 89–96, 104–85.

78 Nicolson and Burn, i, 573–5; *Valor Ecclesiasticus*, v, 297; *ESR*, part ii, 251–2; Storey, 146–7.

79 Chichester, West Sussex Record Office, Cap 1/14/5, f. 28r.

80 Summerson, i, 365; *VCH Notts.*, ii, 222.

81 Ives, 1968, 152; *LPFD*, ii part i, no. 1368.

Compare *Calendar of Miscellaneous Inquisitions 1422–85*, 102.

82 On the history of French in England from 1066 to 1300, see Lefèvre, Rothwell, Clanchy, and T. Hunt, 1991; on the later middle ages, Suggett; and on the Tudor period, Lambley.

83 Lefèvre, 302, 309; Walter Map, *De Nugis Curialium*, ed. M. R. James et al., 2nd edn (Oxford, 1983), 496–7.

84 Ö. Södergård, 'Le plus ancien traité grammatical français', *Studia Neophilologica*, 27 (1955), 192–4. On these and other grammatical texts, see Dean and Boulton, 157–78.

85 A. Ewert, 'The Glasgow Latin-French Glossary', *Medium Aevum*, 25 (1957), 154–63.

86 M. K. Pope, 'The "Tractatus Orthographiae" of T. H. Parisii Studentis', *Modern Language Review*, 5 (1910), 185–93; Dean and Boulton, no. 288.

87 On Walter's career and treatise, see *DNB*.

88 Walter of Bibbesworth, *Le Tretiz*, 4.

89 The best edition of the treatise is now Walter of Bibbesworth, *Le Tretiz*, 6. See also Dean and Boulton, no. 285.

90 Higden, ii, 158–61. For further analysis of this statement, see above, pp. 105–6.

91 Higden, ii, 158–61.

92 *Rotuli Parliamentorum*, ii, 273; *Statutes of the Realm*, i, 375–6.

93 *Rotuli Parliamentorum*, ii, 275.

94 *Reg. Stapeldon, Exeter*, 309–10; *Statutes of the Colleges of Oxford*, i, Oriel p. 8, Queen's p. 14.

95 Gibson, 171.

96 Jean Froissart, *Chroniques*, ed. Kervyn de Lettenhove, 25 vols (Brussels, 1867–77), ii, 419.

97 Lefèvre, 304.

98 Dean and Boulton, nos 290, 292.

99 Kristol, 3–79, especially 49–50.

100 Translated from ibid., 69–79.

101 *DNB*.

102 Orme, 1984, 127–8.

103 *Dialogues in French and English*, ed. H. Bradley, EETS, e.s., 79 (1900) (*STC* 24865).

104 *STC* 24866–24868, and compare also 1386 and 19166.

105 On the use of French in the sixteenth century, see Lambley.

106 On the Jews in general, see H. G. Richardson, *The English Jewry under Angevin Kings* (London, 1960), and C. Roth, *A History of the Jews in England*, 3rd edn (Oxford, 1964), and on their numbers, Roth, *A History of the Jews*, 276.

107 B. Smalley, *The Study of the Bible in the Middle Ages*, 3rd edn (Oxford, 1982), 78.

108 *The Great Roll of the Pipe . . . 3 and 4 Richard I*, ed. D. M. Stenton, Pipe Roll Soc., n.s., 2 (1926), 32; the term is *magister puerorum*.

109 Clanchy, 155, 201–2.

110 The most general account of higher studies at the cathedrals is by Edwards, 185–205, drawing on R. W. Hunt, 1936, and now supplemented by *EWE*, 52–3, 67–9, 73–4, 83; Courtenay, 88–117; Moran, 1979, 25–6; and Orme, 2000, 565–70.

111 R. W. Hunt, 1936, 21–2; Edwards, 185–6. On William, see *DNB* and above, p. 101.

112 Edwards, 186–7; *EWE*, 2.

113 R. W. Hunt, 1936, 36–7; Orme, 2000, 566.

114 *EWE*, 68–9; *ECD*, 282–9; *VCH Lincs.*, ii, 468–74.

115 On Cambridge and Oxford, see, most recently, Cobban, 1975, 1988, and 1999; Catto; Catto and Evans; and Leader, 1988.

116 Tanner, i, 240.

117 The only secular cathedral about which there is some doubt is Lichfield.

118 On the history of cathedral grammar schools, see above, pp. 167–8, 191–2.

119 Edwards, 197–8; Orme, 2000, 570.

120 *EWE*, 74.

121 *Historical Collections of a Citizen of London*, ed. J. Gairdner, Camden Soc., n.s., 17 (1876), 230–1.

122 Exeter, Devon Record Office, Exeter City Archives, Book 51, ff. 345r, 346v.

123 *EWE*, 74; W. S. Simpson, 413–15.

124 *EWE*, 83; W. S. Simpson, 413–15.

125 *Rotuli Hugonis de Wells*, ed. F. N. Davis, vol. iii, Lincoln Record Soc., 9 (1914), 101–2; *EYS*, i, 17.

126 PRO, C 47/21/2, mm. 2, 6 (kindly supplied by the late Dr J. N. T. Miner).

127 Little, 1940, 624–30.

128 Little, 1892, 242.

129 Bodleian, MS Bodley 859, ff. 261r-290r; *EWE*, 83.

130 *Historical Collections*, ed. Gairdner, 230–1; *DNB*. Notes of Ive's lectures survive in Bodleian, MS Lat. th.e 25, ff. 24r-27r.

131 *EWE*, 74.

132 Ibid., 83.

133 *CPL 1362–1404*, 189–90.

134 W. S. Simpson, 413–15.

135 See above, p. 265.

136 On Carpenter, see *DNB*, and on the history of the Guildhall Library, Brewer; Smith; Borrajo; and *Calendar of Plea and Memoranda Rolls of the City of London 1458–1482*, ed. P. E. Jones (Cambridge, 1961), pp. ix-xiii.

137 Stow, i, 275.

138 T. Hearne, *The History and Antiquities of Glastonbury* (Oxford, 1722), 163–223 at 175–93. On the foundation, see M.-H. Rousseau, 'Chantry Foundations and Chantry Chaplains at St Paul's Cathedral, London, *c*.1200–1548' (University of London, PhD thesis, 2003), 70–1, 81, 115.

139 On what follows, see Orme, 1989a, 206–19.
140 N. P. Tanner, *The Church in Late Medieval Norwich* (Toronto, 1984), 35.
141 John Rous, *Historia Regum Angliae*, ed. T. Hearne (Oxford, 1716), 73. For a contrary view by Edmund Dudley, in 1509–10, see above, pp. 224–5.
142 Exeter, Devon Record Office, Exeter City Archives, Book 51, ff. 345r, 346v; above, note 134; *EWE*, 74.
143 Frere and Kennedy, ii, 133, 216, 311, 377; iii, 31, 42, 49, 115, 145–6, 217, 239, 241–2, 316, 346–7; Orme, 2000, 570.

3: The Teaching of Grammar

1   T. Hunt, 1991, i, 100–18.
2   See above, pp. 106–7.
3   See above, p. 75.
4   Higden, ii, 158–61.
5   T. Hunt, i, 19–53.
6   On this subject, see above, pp. 28–9.
7   T. Hunt, 1991, i, 269.
8   *ECD*, 222–3; above, pp. 67, 153.
9   *MED*, *OED*, s.v. 'donet'.
10 Peter Helias; R. W. Hunt, 1941–3, 1950.
11 Gibson, 26, 33–4, 121, 200, 234.
12 See above, pp. 153–4, 273.
13 On Adam and the writers that follow, see T. Hunt, 1991, i, passim; R. Sharpe, passim; and *DNB*.
14 On Nequam, see R. W. Hunt, 1984, and *DNB*.
15 On his career, see John of Garland, 1927, and *DNB*.
16 On this subject, see Law, 1999.
17 T. Hunt, 1991, i, 88.
18 Alexander of Ville-Dieu, 7–8.
19 T. Hunt, 1991, i, 87–94.
20 Rashdall, i, 443.
21 T. Hunt, 1991, i, 87–94.
22 Evrard of Béthune. On the author, see Grondeux.
23 Evrard of Béthune, 71.
24 Ibid., 19.
25 Ibid., 152.
26 T. Hunt, 1991, i, 92.
27 Ibid., 151–61; John of Garland, 2003; R. W. Hunt, 1964, 163–8.
28 T. Hunt, 1991, i, 165–76; R. Sharpe, 5.
29 T. Hunt, 1991, i, 177–89; R. Sharpe, 52.
30 T. Hunt, 1991, i, 191–203.
31 Ibid., 204–31.
32 Ibid., 125–35.
33 Ibid., 136–143.
34 *STC* 11609, lines 42–5.
35 T. Hunt, 1991, i, 138; *STC* 11607, lines 1–6.
36 T. Hunt, 1991, i, 289–368.
37 On this subject, see Daly.
38 Isidore of Seville.

39 Papias, *Elementarium: Littera A*, ed. V. de Angelis (Milan, 1977). Early printed editions of the whole work are listed in Hain, ii part ii, nos 12378–81.
40 R. W. Hunt, 1958.
41 The work has not been printed. Manuscripts are listed by Marigo.
42 Balbi. Manuscripts of the work are listed by Marigo, and early printed editions in *Gesamtkatalog der Wiegendrucke*, iii, nos 3182–3205.
43 Peter Helias, i, 189–207.
44 For a good outline of the subject, see Law, 2003, 172–9, and also Bursill-Hall, 1971.
45 Martin of Dacia, *Opera*, ed. H. Roos, Corpus Philosophorum Danicorum Medii Aevi, 2 (Copenhagen, 1961), 35–7; Law, 2003, 175–7.
46 T. Hunt, 1991, i, 269–70.
47 Boas; T. Hunt, 1991, i, 59–79.
48 Cato, 1952; translated in Cato, 1922, and in Thomson and Perraud, 58–85.
49 T. Hunt, 1994, 2; C. Brown and R. H. Robbins, *The Index of Middle English Verse* (New York, 1943), nos 169, 247, 820, 854, 3935, 3957.
50 Theodulus, 1902, 1997; Hamilton; translated in Thomson and Perraud, 126–57.
51 Theodulus, 1902, 1997, lines 33–40.
52 T. Hunt, 1991, i, 60–6.
53 Alexander of Ville-Dieu, 7–8.
54 Gibson, 173. *Pamphilus* is edited by S. Pittaluga in *Commedie latine del XII e XIII secolo*, 6 vols (Genoa, 1976–98), iii, 1–137, and translated in Thomson and Perraud, 162–91.
55 Early printed editions are listed in *Gesamtkatalog der Wiegendrucke*, iii, 27–42.
56 Above, pp. 58–9.
57 Meech, 1934, 76–9.
58 Printed in Migne, ccvii, cols. 1153–6.
59 Mackinnon, and *DNB*.
60 Walther, 71; printed in Migne, ccx, cols. 581–94; translated in Thomson and Perraud, 293–325. On the ascription to Alain de Lille, see Alain de Lille, *Textes inédits*, ed. Marie-Thérèse d'Alverny (Paris, 1965), 51–2.
61 Walther, 2521; printed in Migne, clxxxiv, cols. 1307–14.
62 Ibid., col. 1309.
63 On what follows, see Nicholls, passim.
64 Walther, 18581; edited by Gieben; Nicholls, 152–3, 163–5, 167–70.
65 Furnivall, 275–82; Orme, 1989b.
66 Gieben, 57–8.
67 Printed by Morawski; discussed by Nicholls, 145–8. Continental texts of the poem begin *Cum nihil utilius* (Walther, 3692), *Est nihil utilius* being apparently confined to England (Walther, 5777). The name *Facetus* was also given to two other poems, beginning *Doctrine vivum* (Walther, 4683) and *Moribus et vita*

68 Morawski, 5, 6, 7.

69 *STC* 23940.3, sigs. A.v verso–A.vi verso.

70 *ECD*, 300–1.

71 See above, p. 154.

72 *DNB*. The work has not been printed. For surviving manuscripts, see R. Sharpe, 659–60; an early one is Bodleian, MS Auct. F.3.9, pp. 189–340. There were also copies at Cambridge University, the abbeys of Evesham, Leicester, and Syon, and Bridport parish church (*Corpus of British Medieval Library Catalogues*, iv, 139; vi, 300; ix, 17; x, 34; *EWE*, 96).

73 For the Oxford schools, see above, pp. 70–2, and for Sampson, p. 71. A fourth possible Oxford schoolmaster is the elusive Adam Nutzard (T. Hunt, 1991, i, 152).

74 See above, pp. 75–6.

75 See above, p. 76.

76 On Cornwall, alias Brian, see *BRUO*, i, 490, and *DNB*.

77 Higden, ii, 158–61.

78 The unique surviving copy is Bodleian, MS Auct. F.3.9, pp. 1–188. On the work, see R. W. Hunt, 1964, 174–81, and Bland, 88–96.

79 On Pencrich, see *BRUO*, iii, 1456.

80 On Trevisa, see ibid., 1903–4.

81 Thomson, 1984, pp. xiv–xvi.

82 On Leland, see Thomson, 1979, 6–9; R. Sharpe, 274–5; and *DNB*.

83 Orme, 1989a, 92–3 (cf. William Worcester, *The Topography of Medieval Bristol*, ed. F. Neale, Bristol Record Society, 51 (2000), pp. 28–9); Thomson, 1979, 169, 171.

84 For discussion, see Thomson, 1979, 9–12; for early texts, Thomson, 1984; and for later history and texts, Gwosdek, 1991.

85 Thomson, 1984, 82.

86 *Long Parvula*, a later version of *Informacio* (London, Wynkyn de Worde, 1509; STC 23164), sig. Aiv.

87 On Latin to English and English to Latin dictionaries, see *Promptorium Parvulorum*, iii, pp. xiii–lxxi.

88 A copy was bequeathed in York in 1438 (*Testamenta Eboracensia*, ii, 79–80).

89 *STC* 13829–13837.

90 *DNB*, s.n. 'Geoffrey the Grammarian'. Another early tradition calls the author Richard Frauncis (*Promptorium Parvulorum*, i, p. xvi), and a Dominican of this name from Stamford was ordained subdeacon in 1399 (Emden, 1967, 340).

91 *Promptorium Parvulorum*, i, 1–3.

92 *STC* 20434–20439.

93 *Catholicon Anglicum*.

94 T. Hunt, 1991, i, 197.

95 R. W. Hunt, 1964, 175.

96 Bodleian, MS Auct. F.3.9, pp. 10, 70, 91.

97 Thomson, 1979, s.v. 'latinitates', p. 334; E. Wilson; Orme, 1989a, chapters 5–7; Orme, 1995; Orme, 2000, 577.

98 On what follows see, in more detail, Orme, 1989a, 76–9.

99 Ibid., 104.

100 Meech, 1934, 82.

101 Orme, 1989a, 83.

102 Ibid., 103.

103 Orme, 1995, 278.

104 Ibid., 293.

105 Orme, 1989a, 100, 111.

106 Ibid., 106; Orme, 1995, 292–3.

107 Orme, 1989a, 104.

108 Cambridge University Library, MS Additional 2830, f. 101r.

109 E. Wilson, f. 76v.

110 Orme, 1989a, 82.

111 Orme, 1995, 287, 290–1.

112 Orme, 1989a, 108, 110; Cambridge University Library, MS Additional 2830, f. 100r.

113 Ker, i, 180; PRO, C 47/34/13.

114 Orme, 1989a, 109.

115 Cambridge University Library, MS Additional 2830, ff. 99v, 101v.

116 Stanbridge, 64–5.

117 Ibid., 17, 19–20, 22.

118 Horman, ff. 64v-78v.

119 *Memorials of Henry VII*, ed. J. Gairdner (RS, 1858), 14; Orme, 1984, 23–4.

120 Weiss, 1967, 168–70; Weiss, 1937, 349 no. 69, 356. The work is printed in L. Valla, *Opera Omnia*, 2 vols (Basel, 1540, repr. Turin, 1962), i, 3–235.

121 Duff, no. 346; *STC* 19767.7. On Perotti, see W. K. Percival, *Studies in Renaissance Grammar* (Aldershot, 2004), chapters 8–10.

122 *STC* 23425–234277a.7.

123 Orme, 1999, 461–2.

124 On Anwykyll, see Orme, 1998, 4, 15–17, 35–6, and *DNB*.

125 *STC* 695.

126 *STC* 23904; Brodie.

127 On these men and their careers, see *BRUO*, i–iii, now supplemented by *DNB*.

128 See above, pp. 241–2, 293–4.

129 On Stanbridge, see also above, p. 179.

130 *STC* 23139.5–23199.7, including similar treatises not by Stanbridge.

131 For the pre-Stanbridge grammars, see Gwosdek, 1991.

132 *STC* 13809–13812; Horman; on his career, see *DNB*.

133 *STC* 13603.7–13606.5. On Holt, see Orme, 1996b.

134 For example, *Compotus cum Commento* (Rome, A. Fritag, 1493); Petrus Tartaretus, *Expositio super Summulis Petri Hispani* (Paris, J. Bouyer and G. Bouchet, 1496); *Tractatus Musices*

135 *STC* 5542–5543b.9; Allen, 86–7

136 *STC* 15601.3–15604, 15607–15610; Allen, 87–8.

137 On Whittington, see *DNB*.

138 Stanbridge, pp. xxvii–xxxii.

139 *STC* 268–268.7, 315–320.5.

140 *STC* 7013–7017.

141 *STC* 11601–11617.

142 Gibson, 378.

143 Madan, 73–177 passim.

144 Leedham-Green, Rhodes, and Stubbings, 133, 140, 145–6, 158–9, 162.

145 Early school curricula include those of Ipswich, 1528 (*STC* 5542.3, sig. A.iii recto–A.iv verso, reprinted in J. Strype, *Ecclesiastical Memorials*, 3 vols in 6 (Oxford, 1822), i part ii, 139–43); Eton, 1528 (*VCH Sussex*, ii, 417–19); Eton and Winchester, 1530 (*ECD*, 448–51; Wright, 1852); Canterbury, 1541 (*ECD*, 465–9); and St Paul's, London, 1539 (McDonnell, 1959, 76).

146 *STC* 23939.5–23943, 20079–20081.

147 *STC* 252–254.7.

148 *STC* 16110–16128.7.

149 Lupton, 279.

150 Nelson, 96–7, 99; Orme, 1989a, 149–51.

151 *VCH Sussex*, ii, 418; *STC*, ii, 63. There is a facsimile and translation of Sulpizio's work: *Doctrina Mensae*, ed. H. Thomas (Oxford, 1949).

152 Lupton, 272, 280.

153 Ibid., 170; McDonnell, 1909, pp. 45–9.

154 Leach, 1899, 229; Maxwell-Lyte, 100, 106, 145; *ECD*, 458–9.

155 *STC* 315, 23163.13.

156 On what follows, see Orme, 1999, 456–69.

157 *STC* 13829.7, 13833.5.

158 *STC* 18872; Orme, 1988.

159 Breeze and Glomski, 142–3.

160 See above, p. 296.

161 See above, pp. 308–9.

162 Nelson, 19–20.

163 S. Brant, *Narrenschiff*, ed. F. Zarnecke (Hildesheim, 1961), section 27; Alexander Barclay, *The Ship of Fools*, ed. T. Jamieson, 2 vols. (Edinburgh and London, 1874), i, 144.

164 John Skelton, *The Complete English Poems*, ed. J. Scattergood (Harmondsworth, 1983), 235 ('Speke Parott', lines 169–82).

4: The Schoolroom

1 Riley, 1872–3, ii, 310; Gibson, 173.

2 Lupton, 277.

3 The registers are printed by Kirby, 1888, whose edition could be much improved in accuracy and details.

4 Winchester College, A. F. Leach's MS List of Commoners; Sterry, passim.

5 Those of Exeter are listed in Orme, 1979.

6 *EWE*, 84; Orme, 1991, 292–3.

7 Thomson, 1982, 77–9.

8 Orme, 1984, 156–63.

9 See above, pp. 166–7; PRO, CI/290/78.

10 Orme, 2001, 6, 29, 68, 79, 88, 216.

11 Aristotle, *Politics*, book vii, chapter 17.

12 Chaucer, VII 503 (B² 1693).

13 Orderic Vitalis, iii, 6–9.

14 *EWE*, 105.

15 *The Chronicle of John Hardyng*, ed. H. Ellis (London, 1812), pp. i–ii; *CPR 1467–77*, 592; *CCR 1476–85*, 1.

16 Quintilian, *Institutio Oratoria*, book i, chapter 1, sections 15–19; Elyot, book i, chapter 5.

17 Kirby, 1892, 457; Kirby, 1888, 82 etc.; the same was true at Eton (Heywood and Wright, 479).

18 Nelson, 1.

19 Kirby, 1892, 458; the same was true at Eton (Heywood and Wright, 480).

20 Rickert, 1948, 111–12.

21 Leach, 1916, 210.

22 *Reg. Bransford, Worcester*, ed. R. M. Haines, Worcestershire Hist. Soc., n.s., 4 (1966), 186–8, 223, 240. Compare *Reg. Stapeldon, Exeter*, 225–6, 229.

23 *CIPM*, xxiii, 163.

24 *HMC, Report on the MSS of Lord Middleton* (London, 1911), 346, 382–4.

25 Riley, 1872–3, ii, 315.

26 Kirby, 1892, 458; Heywood and Wright, 480.

27 'Extracts from the Proceedings of the Committee', *Norfolk Archaeology*, 4 (1885), 342–4.

28 *Historiae Dunelmensis Scriptores Tres*, ed. J. Raine, Surtees Soc., 9 (1839), 74.

29 BL, Egerton Roll 8776, m. 5; Orme, 1984, 44.

30 On the gentry, see Orme, 1984, 73–4; on townspeople, Thrupp, 155–61, and Orme, 1973, 43, 48; and on yeomen, Hugh Latimer, *Sermons*, ed. G. E. Corrie, Parker Society (1844), 101–2.

31 On this subject, see above, pp. 221–2.

32 Levett, 246.

33 J. E. Thorold Rogers, *A History of Agriculture and Prices in England*, 6 vols (Oxford, 1866–87), ii, 615–16.

34 PRO, E 179/4/1 m. 1; Sterry, passim.

35 Heywood and Wright, 531–2.

36 Highfield, 72, 204.

37 Gibson, 170.

38 Fees of 8d. a quarter are recorded at Nottingham in 1395 (*VCH Notts.*, ii, 216); 8d. at Winchester in 1409–10 (Keene, part i, 394); 12d. at Gloucester in 1410, which had allegedly fallen from 2s. or 3s. 4d., although the claim is made by plaintiffs seeking damages (*EWE*, 63); 12d. at Maldon in 1420

(*VCH Essex*, ii, 516); 4d. for reading and 8d. for grammar at Newland in 1446 (*EWE*, 160–1); 1d. a week at Basingwerk in the late fifteenth century (Thomson, 1982, 77–9); and 10d. (later reduced to 8d.) at Ipswich in 1477 (*VCH Suffolk*, ii, 326). Fees of 3s. 4d. occur at Croydon in 1394 (Rickert, 1926–7, 251–2), and 2d. a week at Beccles in 1403–6 (Leach, 1916, 210).

39 Orme, 1989a, 101; Thomson, 1979, 150.

40 Kirby, 1892, 457.

41 Heywood and Wright; Maxwell-Lyte, 582.

42 McDonnell, 1909, 78–85, 92–4.

43 Highfield, 72, 201; Kirby, 1892, 487.

44 Board of 8d. a week is mentioned at Beverley in 1276 (*EYS*, i, 80m); 10d. at Stevenage in 1312 (*VCH Herts.*, ii, 69); 1s. at Croydon in 1394 (Rickert, 1926–7, 251–4); 1s. 4d. at Lavenham in *c*.1400 (PRO, SC 6/1297/22); 7d. at Beccles in 1403 (Leach, 1916, 210); 1s. 8d. at Ipswich in 1416–17 (this was for Alexander de la Pole, a nobleman's son) (BL, Egerton Roll 8776, m. 5); 8d. at Ewelme in 1464–5 (Bodleian, MS DD Ewelme a.vi/43B, p. 12; Orme, 2004b, 49); 1s. in Norfolk in 1522 (Gurney, 466); and 9d. at Nottingham in 1532 (*VCH Notts.*, ii, 222).

45 *Stonor Letters*, i, 21, translated in Rickert, 1948, 115–16; above, note 29.

46 Richmond, 133; John Hooker, *The Life and Times of Sir Peter Carew, Knight*, ed. J. Maclean (London, 1857), 3–5.

47 *ESR*, part ii, 93.

48 *Close Rolls 1254–6*, 46.

49 Clanchy, 118–19; above, p. 31.

50 T. Hunt, 1991, i, 269.

51 *ECD*, 300–1.

52 Bliss; Whittick.

53 See above, p. 111.

54 Nelson, 22.

55 *HMC, Report on the MSS of Lord Middleton*, 383.

56 Bodleian, MS DD Ewelme a.vi/43B, p.12; Orme, 2004b.

57 See above, note 29; Lupton, 278.

58 Bodleian, MS Selden Supra 38, f. 17v; information kindly supplied by Professor Michael Clanchy.

59 See above, note 29.

60 Hooker, *Sir Peter Carew*, 3–6.

61 Laurence Humfrey, *Joannis Juelli Angli Episcopi Sarisburiensis Vita et Mors* (London, 1573), 17.

62 Riley, 1872–3, ii, 315; *ECD*, 296–7.

63 Heywood and Wright, 479–80.

64 *Reg. Trillek, Hereford*, ed. J. H. Parry, C&Y, 8 (1912), 56.

65 Orme, 1991, 292–3; *EWE*, 84.

66 On benefit of clergy, see Pollock and Maitland, i, 441–57; Holdsworth, iii, 293–302; and L. C. Gabel, *Benefit of Clergy in England in the Later Middle Ages*, Smith College Studies in History, 14 (Northampton, Mass., 1928–9), especially 62–74.

67 *EWE*, 37, 39, 41, 47, 59, 72.

68 PRO, C 115/75, f. 43r; C 115/78, ff. 62r, 108v, 187r; C 115/82, f. 78r; C 115/84, f. 48v; Lobel, i, Hereford, map 3.

69 Lobel, iii, 92, map 2; Keene, part i, 394; ii, 865; *EWE*, 160; W. Parker, *History of Long Melford* (London, 1873), 218.

70 Reginald of Durham, 1847, 59–60; idem, 1835, 149–50.

71 Shinners and Dohar, 106.

72 *Twelfth Night*, III, ii, 72–3.

73 Burton, 338.

74 Darlington, i, 80–1.

75 Jocelin of Brakelond, 41.

76 See above, note 68; Parker, *Long Melford*, 218.

77 Leach, 1906, 86–7.

78 *EWE*, 39, 41.

79 *VCH Oxon.*, i, 461; *VCH Staffs.*, iii, 280–1.

80 Orme, 1989a, 147.

81 *EWE*, 177; Leland, i, 160. I have excluded Higham Ferrers from this discussion; the so-called medieval schoolhouse there was clearly built as a chapel.

82 Leach, 1899, 121–6; Seaborne, 3.

83 *An Inventory of the Historical Monuments in Buckinghamshire*, 2 vols (London, Royal Commission on Historical Monuments (England), 1912–13), i, 150–2.

84 Orme, 1998, 41.

85 Seaborne, 15–16.

86 On manuscripts see, for example, Orme, 1989a, 152. On woodcuts from Italy, see M. Sander, *Le Livre à figures italien depuis 1467 jusqu'à 1530*, 6 vols in 5 (Milan, *c*.1942, repr. Milan 1996), vi, figs. 512–14, 522, 575; from Germany, A. Schramm, *Der Bilderschmuck der Frühdrucke*, 23 vols (Leipzig, 1920–43), vii, figs. 282, 328; viii, figs 484–7; xiii, fig. 83; and from England, Hodnett, figs 75–80, 139–40, 206–7.

87 Also in the school plan of about 1590 preserved at Harrow (Seaborne, 25–6).

88 For example, Stratford-on-Avon, 1427 (*VCH Warws.*, ii, 330), and Wainfleet, 1484 (Oxford, Magdalen College Archives, Candlesby 16, printed in R. Chandler, *The Life of William Waynflete* (London, 1811), 369–70).

89 Seaborne, 25–7, plates 30–1.

90 Ibid., 27.

91 Combe, 'Eton', plate opp. p. 35; 'Harrow', plate opp. p. 16; 'Rugby', plate opp. p. 21; 'St Paul's', plate opp. p. 27.

92 Leach, 1899, 122.

93 For example, Bodleian, MS Canon Misc. 416, f. 1r; *The Flowering of the Middle Ages*, ed. J. Evans (London, 1966), 184–5; Schramm, *Der Bilderschmuck*, ix, fig. 831.

94 Erasmus, 1906–58, iv, 517–18 (translated in Erasmus, 1883, pp. 27–8); Lupton, 277–9.

95 Bodleian, MS Bodley 315, f. 268r, printed by R. H. Robbins, 'Wall Verses at Launceston Priory', *Archiv für Neueren Sprachen und Literaturen*, 200 (1964), 338–43.

96 Combe, 'Harrow', plate opp. p. 16; 'Westminster', plate opp. p. 22.

97 Myers, 1959, 71.

98 Lupton, 278; compare Shakespeare, *The Merry Wives of Windsor*, IV, i, 9.

99 Heywood and Wright, 514; *VCH Suffolk*, ii, 329.

100 *EYS*, ii, 89–91, 109–11.

101 Lupton, 276.

102 Cambridge University Library, MS Additional 2830, f. 98v; above, p. 68.

103 *HMC, Ninth Report* (1883), vol. i, 218.

104 *VCH Notts.*, ii, 217.

105 *EWE*, 198.

106 *ESR*, part ii, under the schools cited.

107 *EYS*, i, 24.

108 *EWE*, 84; Orme, 1991, 292–3.

109 Kirby, 1892, 82, 122–3, 490; Leach, 1899, 187–93.

110 Maxwell-Lyte, 19; *ECD*, 412–15.

111 Nelson, 37.

112 See above, pp. 210, 310.

113 See above, pp. 225–6, 233.

114 Gospel of John, xx, 11.

115 Augustine, *Epistulae*, ed. A. Goldbacher, part i, Corpus Scriptorum Ecclesiasticorum Latinorum, 33 (Vienna, 1895), 205–7 (letter 55, chapter 17).

116 Erasmus, 1906–58, iv, 517–18 (translated in Erasmus, 1883, 27–8); J. Strype, *Ecclesiastical Memorials*, 3 vols in 6 (Oxford, 1822), i part ii, 139; *VCH Sussex*, ii, 417–19; *ECD*, 448–51.

117 One of the earliest pieces of evidence is the statutes of Newland school, 1446 (*EWE*, 161). Other statutes that specify school hours include Chichester (1498), Lancaster (1500), St Paul's (1518), Rolleston (1524), Manchester (1525), Warrington (1526), Cuckfield (1528), Eton (1528–30), Newark (1532), and Winchester College (1550). For references, see the list of schools above, pp. 346–72.

118 *EWE*, 161.

119 Ibid., 41.

120 Hodnett, figs 139–40.

121 *MLD*, s.v. 'ferula'; *OED* s.v. 'ferula', 'ferule'; T. Hunt, 1991, i, 269; Cambridge University Library, MS Additional 2830, f. 100v.

122 Orme, 1998, 47; Maxwell-Lyte, 139–40.

123 *Oxford City Documents, 1268–1665*, ed. J. E. Thorold Rogers, Oxford Hist. Soc., 18 (1891), 161–2.

124 Rickert, 1948, 118.

125 Peacock, appendix, pp. xxx–xxxvii.

126 Langland, A.v.32–3; B.v.34–41; C.vi.137–40.

127 T. Hunt, 1991, i, 269.

128 Orme, 1984, 92.

129 Kirby, 1892, 485; Heywood and Wright, 524–5.

130 Watkin, 103.

131 Vives, 117–20; Woodward, 208–9.

132 Nelson, 39.

133 *Chronicon de Lanercost*, ed. J. Stevenson (Edinburgh, Bannatyne Club, 1839), 38.

134 *Calendar of Miscellaneous Inquisitions 1348–77*, 157.

135 Lupton, 279.

136 *Reg. Grandisson, Exeter*, ii, 1192–3; *ECD*, 314–17; cf. Gibson, 171.

137 Thomson, 1979, 118, above, p. 41.

138 Watkin, 106.

139 *VCH Notts.*, ii, 185.

140 Nelson, 22.

141 R. W. Hunt, 1964, 176.

142 Heywood and Wright, 527.

143 J. C. Robertson, iii, 5–6; Stenton, 27–8.

144 Stow, i, 74.

145 Lupton, 278; Stow, i, 74.

146 BL, Harley MS 1587, ff. 188r–215v.

147 Gibson, 171.

148 R. R. Sharpe, i, 233–4.

149 See above, p. 212.

150 *Paston Letters*, i, 650–1.

151 Alexander of Ville-Dieu, 148 line 2203.

152 Riley, 1872–3, ii, 312; *ECD*, 244–5, 258–9, 294–7.

153 Riley, 1872–3, ii, 312; *ECD*, 244–5.

154 Something like this ceremony is mentioned at Oxford in the 1410s, when money was paid for a boy to give gloves to his schoolmasters 'at the time of versifying' (Magrath, i, 323).

155 On what follows, see Orme, 'Schools and Schoolmasters', forthcoming.

156 *Testamenta Karleolensia*, ed. R. S. Ferguson, Cumberland and Westmorland Antiquarian and Arch. Soc., extra series, 9 (1893), 101; Galbraith, 1941–3, 98.

157 Gunner, 74.

158 *EYS*, i, 28.

159 *BRUO*, i, 239–40; *Corpus of British Medieval Library Catalogues*, ix, 5–7, 10–11, 13–14, 569–70.

160 *ECD*, 220–3, 300–1.

161 *Stonor Letters*, i, 21, translated in Rickert, 1948, 115–16; *The Household Books of John Howard, Duke of Norfolk*, ed. J. P. Collier, 2 vols in 1 (Stroud, 1992), i, 391.

162 Winchester, Hampshire Record Office, W/D1/108 (31). The list reads 'Catonem, Fassetum pedoctrinalem, equivoci regul'.

163 *Testamenta Eboracensia*, ii, 118.

164 Bodleian, MS DD Ewelme a.vi/43B, p. 12; Orme, 2004b, 45–9.

165 Nottingham University Library, Middleton MS, Mi L M 2; *HMC, Report on the MSS of Lord*

Middleton, 212–20.

166 Riley, 1872–3, ii, 314.

167 *EWE*, 107–8.

168 *Testamenta Eboracensia*, ii, 270.

169 Orme, 'Schools and Schoolmasters', forthcoming.

170 See above, p. 273.

171 Leach, 1910, 220–2.

172 Rickert, 1931–2, 257–74.

173 Highfield, 382.

174 Cambridge, Trinity College, MS 0.5.4; Thomson, 1979, 158–68.

175 *EWE*, 161; *LPFD*, iii part i, p. 394.

176 *STC* 315, 695–696, 23163.13.

177 *STC* 16111–16112, 23139.5, 23153.4, 23163.6, 23163.14, 23939.5.

178 *EWE*, 85.

179 Madan, passim; Leedham-Green, passim.

180 Rashdall, i, 219, 489.

181 *ECD*, 131–2. For fifteenth-century examples of the three terms, see Thomson, 1979, 174–5, 301, and Orme, 1989a, 118, 120. At Basingwerk (Wales) the autumn term was dated from 3 October (St Thomas Cantilupe) (Thomson, 1982, 77–9).

182 Bowers, 1999, 197.

183 *CIPM*, iv, 171–2; v, 167; vii, 140, 192; ix, 410; xi, 124; xiv, 182; xxiii, 163.

184 *EWE*, 161, 194.

185 Lupton, 166.

186 BL, Egerton Roll 8776, m. 5; Orme, 1984, 44.

187 Bodleian, MS DD Ewelme a.vi/43B, p. 12; Orme, 2004b.

188 Leach, 1899, 179–81.

189 Maxwell-Lyte, 145–55.

190 Orme, 2001, 188–9.

191 Leach, 1913, 23–6.

192 Kirby, 1892, 90–1.

193 Lupton, 278.

194 J. C. Robertson, iii, 9–10; Stenton, 30.

195 *EWE*, 62.

196 Thomson, 1979, 150, 296.

197 Lupton, 278; *VCH Lancs.*, ii, 584.

198 PRO, C 1/27/343.

199 Orme, 1989a, 139, 145.

200 *Annales Monastici*, ed. H. R. Luard, vol. iii (RS, 1866), 85.

201 *EWE*, 47.

202 *Reg. Melton, York*, ed. R. Brocklesby, vol. iv, C & Y, 85 (1997), 81.

203 Orme, 1989a, 143.

204 Kirby, 1888, passim (not all dates are correct).

205 Ibid., frontispiece, 54 (not 1434, as stated there).

206 Clanchy, 226–30.

207 *Letters and Papers of John Shillingford*, ed. S. A. Moore, Camden Soc., n.s., 2 (1871), 23.

208 Nicholas Orme, 'Wars and Wonders', *Friends of Exeter Cathedral Sixty-Eighth Annual Report*

209 W. Worcester, *Itineraries*, ed. J. H. Harvey (Oxford, 1969), 2–3.

210 *Paston Letters*, i, 631–2.

211 *Floris and Blancheflour*, ed. A. B. Taylor (Oxford, 1927); *Floris and Blancheflour*, ed. E. C. de Vries (Groningen, 1986).

212 Orme, 2001, 154–7.

213 See, for example, Orme, 1989a, 283–6, and J. Dover Wilson, *Life in Shakespeare's England*, 2nd edn (Cambridge, 1913), 49–62.

214 *Self and Society in Medieval France: The Memoirs of Abbot Guibert de Nogent*, ed. J. F. Benton and C. C. Swinton Bland (New York, 1970), book i, chapters 4–6.

215 John of Salisbury, *Policraticus*, ed. C. C. J. Webb, 2 vols (Oxford, 1909), i, 164; translated as *Frivolities of Courtiers*, ed. J. B. Pike (Minneapolis, 1938), 146–7.

216 *Giraldi Cambrensis Opera*, ed. J. S. Brewer, 8 vols (RS, 1861–91), iv, 107; Alexander Neckham, *De Naturis Rerum*, ed. T. Wright (RS, 1863), 503; Jocelin of Brakelond, 44.

217 *The Chronicle of Adam of Usk 1377–1421*, ed. C. Given-Wilson (Oxford, 1997), 12–16.

218 W. Worcester, *The Topography of Medieval Bristol*, ed. Frances Neale, Bristol Record Soc., 51 (2000), 28–9.

219 *EYS*, ii, 110; compare the autobiographical poem of Percival Melsynby, canon of Coverham, which mentions his birthplace and the day on which he was admitted as a canon (Gribbin, 165).

220 Bodleian, MS Ashmole 1137, f. 152v.

221 J. Weever, *Ancient Funeral Monuments* (London, 1631), 834; 2nd edn (London, 1767), 554.

222 *The Autobiography of Thomas Whythorne*, ed. J. M. Osborn (Oxford, 1961), 10–11. For a good tomb inscription, see Orme, 2001, 341.

223 For example, *CIPM*, iv, 171–2; v, 126, 167; vii, 192; viii, 449; xiii, 265; xiv, 182.

224 *EWE*, 109, 198, 213–14; Orme, 1990c, 278.

225 *EWE*, 100.

226 *Calendar of Miscellaneous Inquisitions 1422–85*, 152–3.

5: The Schoolmaster

1 Above, pp. 38, 48, 191.

2 *ECD*, 68–9.

3 There were also cases, at Bedford, Darley near Derby, and possibly Keynsham near Bristol, where the Augustinian house charged with supervising the school occupied a site away from the town itself.

4 William of Malmesbury, *De Gestis Pontificum Anglorum*, ed. N. E. S. A. Hamilton (RS, 1870), 69.

5 Orme, 1984, 56–7; above, p. 252.

6 See above, pp. 81–3.

7 Edwards, 178.

8 *Twelfth-Century Archidiaconal and Vice-Archidiaconal Acta*, ed. B. R. Kemp, C&Y, 92 (2001), 39–40.

9 *EWE*, 72, 82.

10 See above, pp. 237–8.

11 See, for example, Banbury, Kirton-in-Holland, and Wainfleet in Salter, 1909, 3, 68, 271.

12 *EWE*, 38–40.

13 On these terms, see *MLD*, *MED*, and *OED*, s.v.

14 *Ancrene Wisse*, 216–17 (section 422).

15 *Medieval Archives of the University of Oxford*, ed. H. E. Salter, vol. ii, Oxford Hist. Soc., 73 (1919), 207.

16 *VCH Lincs.*, ii, 451; Thrupp, 171; S. Thrupp, 'Aliens in and around London in the Fifteenth Century', in *Studies in London History Presented to P. E. Jones*, ed. A. E. Hollaender and W. Kellaway (London, 1969), 269.

17 *The Bede Roll of the Fraternity of St Nicholas*, ed. N. W. and V. A. James, part i, London Record Soc., 39 (2004), 9.

18 Edwards, 176–84, 205–6.

19 H. G. Richardson, 'The Letters and Charters of Eleanor of Aquitaine', *English Hist. Review*, 74 (1959), 193–4.

20 Most of these masters are mentioned in F. Barlow, *The English Church, 1066–1154* (London and New York, 1979), 217–67 passim. On William of Corbeil, see H. G. Richardson, 'Gervase of Tilbury', *History*, 46 (1961), 103.

21 Orme, 1984, 20–4.

22 Orme, 2000, 568–9; *VCH Lincs.*, ii, 415; Leach, 1910, 217; *EYS*, i, 13.

23 Gibson, 20–5.

24 *VCH Lincs.*, ii, 423.

25 *EYS*, i, 23.

26 Gibson, 170.

27 On degrees in grammar, see R. W. Hunt, 1964, p. 186; Leader, 1983; Thomson, 1983; and Mitchell, i, 239–50. By the early sixteenth century the Oxford graduates were known as bachelors of grammar, presumably to indicate the low status of the degree.

28 *Documents Relating to the University and Colleges of Cambridge*, i, 374.

29 Mitchell, ii, 381.

30 Kirby, 1892, 484–5; Heywood and Wright, 524.

31 *EWE*, passim.

32 For example, Sevenoaks (1432), where the master was to be a BA (*ECD*, 400–1); Wye College (1447), an MGram or other graduate (Wye College, Statutes, ff. 10v–11r); Macclesfield (1502), a graduate (Wilmot, 11); Blisworth (*c*.1505), a graduate of Oxford (*VCH Northants.*, ii, 229); Cromer (*c*.1505), an MA

(Jordan, 1960a, 221–2); Week St Mary (1506), a graduate of grammar or arts (*EWE*, 177); Farnworth (*c*.1507), an MA, BA, or MGram (*VCH Lancs.*, ii, 589); and Malpas (1528), a graduate ('Malpas Grammar School', 199).

33 *EWE*, 161–5, 198–9.

34 Ibid., 61.

35 Crosby, no. 191 (1901), 67 *recte* 75.

36 Mitchell, i, 352–3; ii, 129.

37 *EYS*, i, 28; Leach, 1910, 203.

38 *VCH Yorks.*, i, 420; *VCH Lincs.*, ii, 427; *EWE*, 87.

39 Heywood and Wright, 524–5.

40 *EYS*, ii, 115, 141–2.

41 Orme, 1998, 17.

42 Lupton, 272.

43 *ECD*, 400–1.

44 *VCH Notts.*, ii, 220; *EWE*, 188–90; *VCH Lancs.*, ii, 583.

45 *EYS*, ii, 60–74; *EWE*, 86.

46 *EWE*, 196–7, 199.

47 PRO, C 1/27/371; *VCH Sussex*, ii, 401.

48 *ESR*, part ii, 271–2; PRO, LR 6/115/1–3.

49 *EWE*, 62–3; Mitchell, ii, 129; Orme, 1998, 69.

50 Orme, 1998, 68–9.

51 *BRUO*, i, 29; iii, 1588; Kirby, 1892, 188.

52 Orme, 1998, 18.

53 *EWE*, 73.

54 Ibid., 86.

55 Orme, 1998, 43.

56 *Select Pleas of the Forest*, ed. G. J. Turner, Selden Soc., 13 (1901), 21.

57 Durham, University Library, Dean and Chapter Muniments, Priory Reg. I part ii, f. 80v.

58 E. Powell, *The Rising in East Anglia in 1381* (Cambridge, 1896), 62.

59 Salter, 1932, i, 212, 324.

60 *VCH Warws.*, ii, 319; *EWE*, 48, 61.

61 *EYS*, i, 13, 20; *EWE*, 72.

62 See above, p. 245. The exceptions were Durham, Chichester, Lichfield, St Paul's, and Worcester, where salaries were introduced between 1414 and about 1500.

63 Kirby, 1892, 486, 497, 499, 510.

64 Heywood and Wright, 527, 548, 550, 576; Maxwell-Lyte, 65.

65 Orme, 1998, 5.

66 Lupton, 273–4.

67 *ECD*, 400–1; *ESR* part ii, 5, 12, 19, 34, 37, and passim.

68 *EWE*, 198.

69 A number of schools appear in a royal taxation list for Lincoln diocese in 1526 (Salter, 1909). See also above pp. 298–9.

70 See above pp. 270, 272.

71 Myers, 1959, 137–8.

72 Percy, 44, 47, 51, 97.

73 Elyot, f. 46r.

74 Ascham, 193.

75 Hugh Latimer, *Sermons and Remains*, ed. G. E. Corrie, 2 vols, Parker Soc. (1844–5), i, 101.

76 Elyot, ff. 60v–61r.

77 Starkey, 1989, 135.

78 *BRUO*, iii, 2030–1; *DNB*.

79 *EWE*, 162.

80 *BRUO*, iii, 1727–8; *DNB*.

81 On Waynflete, see Davis, 6–14; Orme, 1998, 1–2.

82 *BRUO*, i, 401–2; *EWE*, 128, 142.

83 Ibid., ii, 953–4; iii, 1555–6, 1705–6; Orme, 1996b, 283–305.

84 Orme, 1998, 54.

85 *Henley Borough Records*, ed. P. M. Briers, Oxfordshire Record Soc., 41 (1960), 28.

86 *EYS*, i, 104.

87 Gray and Potter, 12; *VCH Suffolk*, ii, 327.

88 In fact several during the thirteenth century (J. E. Sayers, *Papal Judges Delegate in the Province of Canterbury, 1198–1254* (London, 1971), 132–3; *EWE*, 85–6).

89 *EWE*, 196 note 5.

90 Ibid., 163.

91 *ECD*, 252–61.

92 Richard of Bury, *Philobiblon*, ed. M. Maclagan (Oxford, 1960), 94–5.

93 BL, Royal MS 13 C XI, f. 254v; G. F. Warner and J. P. Gilson, *Catalogue of Western Manuscripts in the Old Royal and King's Collections, British Museum*, 3 vols. (London, 1921), ii, 106–7.

94 *BRUO*, ii, 675.

95 York, Borthwick Institute, Probate Register 4, f. 85r.

96 *Grace Book A*, 151, 165–6, 168, 191, 203; *Grace Book B*, i, 24, 143. See also John Bracebridge, above, p. 153.

97 *DNB*.

98 *BRUO*, iii, 2030–1; *DNB*.

99 Galbraith, 1941–3; *DNB*.

100 BL, Sloane MS 5, ff. 13r-57r; Orme, 2000, 574.

101 *The Poems of Robert Henryson*, ed. D. Fox (Oxford, 1981), pp. xiii–xxv.

102 Orme, 1989a, 259–65; *DNB*.

103 *The Boke of St Albans*, ed. W. Blades (London, 1905), 7–23; R. Hands, *English Hunting and Hawking in* The Boke of St Albans (London, 1975), pp. xv–xvii.

104 *STC* 9995–10002.

105 *STC* 3308–3315; *The Boke of St Albans*, ed. Blades, 22–3.

106 See above, pp. 105–07.

107 Orme, 1989a, 88, 93; Orme, 1995; Meech, 1934.

108 See above, pp. 120–2.

109 See above, pp. 108–09.

110 Nelson, 1–2.

111 See above, pp. 201–04.

112 Walsingham, 2003, 496–7.

113 Shakespeare, *The Second Part of King Henry VI*, ed. A. S. Cairncross, 3rd edn (London, Arden, 1957), 124 and note.

114 Langland, A.iii.215, B.iii.221, C.iv.278.

115 *Reg. Brantyngham, Exeter*, i, 470.

116 Orme, 1989a, 226.

117 Discussed in Orme, 2001, 154–7.

118 Orme, 1989a, 282, 286–7.

119 See above, pp. 160–2.

120 *CCR 1327–30*, 573.

121 *BRUO*, i, 405; ii, 985.

122 Ibid., iii, 1555–6.

123 *CIPM*, iv, 171–2.

124 Rickert, 1948, 118.

125 PRO, C 1/46/162.

6: Schools from 1100 to 1350

1 Those of Winchester College (1382) and Eton College (1440) are virtually all we possess before the middle of the sixteenth century.

2 The exceptions at present are Chichester, Coventry, Ely, Rochester, and Worcester.

3 See above, p. 48.

4 Le Neve, 1968–, i, 25.

5 See above, pp. 164–5.

6 See above, p. 48.

7 Orme, 1989a, 34.

8 *EEA*, viii, 55.

9 Stenton, 27–8.

10 PRO, SC 8/22/1051.

11 See above, pp. 246–9 and above, pp. 359–60.

12 For these and all subsequent places mentioned, see the list of schools below, pp. 344–70.

13 Reginald of Durham, 1835, 34, 149–50.

14 Rashdall, iii, 33–4, 86–90; *VCH Oxon.*, iii, 2–8.

15 *VCH Surrey*, ii, 155–6.

16 See above, pp. 47–8.

17 *EEA*, vi, 22.

18 *EEA*, iii, 193–6.

19 Canterbury, Carlisle, Durham, Exeter, Lichfield, London, Norwich, and Winchester.

20 *Episcopal Registers of the Diocese of St David's, 1397 to 1518*, ed. R. F. Isaacson, vol. ii, Cymmrodorion Soc., Record Series, 6 part 2 (1917), 524–5.

21 Namely Blofield, Fincham, Harleston, Shipden, Shouldham, Sparham, and Thornage. Some of these places were the centres of rural deaneries, and the distribution of schools in medieval Norfolk suggests that a system of ruridecanal schools may have existed, at least in outline.

22 This was the case at Canterbury, Carlisle, Durham, Ely, Norwich, and Winchester. There is no evidence about Bath or Rochester, and Coventry and Worcester were exceptions.

23 *VCH Suffolk*, ii, 325; *Reg. Romeyn, York*, ed. W.

Brown, vol. ii, Surtees Soc., 128 (1917), 78.

24　*VCH Lincs.*, ii, 422.

25　Edwards, 196–7; *EYS*, i, 22.

26　*VCH Notts.*, ii, 154, 179.

27　*EWE*, 47; CCA, DCc, ESRoll/301; Orme, 1989a, 34, 43.

28　Feltoe and Minns, 202, 289–91.

29　Gibson, 20–3, 169–74. However the archdeacon of Oxford was present in 1306 when statutes were passed by the university regulating its grammar schools.

30　*VCH Herts.*, ii, 52.

31　A. H. Thompson, 1919, 192, 196, 200.

32　*CIPM*, i, 174.

33　*John of Gaunt's Register*, 1372–1376, ed. S. Armitage-Smith, vol. i, Royal Hist. Soc., Camden 3rd series, 20 (1911), 103–4; *ECD*, 372–3.

34　*VCH Suffolk*, ii, 307; Sylvia L. Thrupp, 'The Problem of Replacement Rates in Late Medieval English Population', *Economic History Review*, 2nd series, 18 (1965), 113.

35　On this subject, see above, pp. 48–50.

36　*VCH Beds.*, ii, 152; *The Cartulary of Darley Abbey*, ed. R. R. Darlington, 2 vols (Kendal, 1945), ii, 595–6; *VCH Hunts.*, ii, 107–8; *EWE*, 36, 57–65.

37　See above, pp. 67, 195.

38　Bateson.

39　*EYS*, i, 80m-82, 87–9, 92.

40　*Registrum Brevium*, 4th edn (London, 1687), f. 35r.

41　*EWE*, 57–65.

42　Saunders, 1908–10, 311, 343.

43　See above, pp. 192, 247–9.

44　*Reports del Case en Ley que furent argues en le temps de . . . Henry le IV et Henry le V* (London, 1679), no pagination, sub Hilary term 11 Henry IV; *EWE*, 62–3.

45　*Reports del Case en Ley, sub* Hilary term 11 Henry IV.

46　*Councils and Synods* I, ii, 778.

47　Friedberg, ii, cols 768–70.

48　Tanner, i, 220.

49　*Councils and Synods* I, ii, 1065.

50　See above, p. 176.

51　Tanner, i, 220.

52　Ibid., 240.

53　See above, p. 81.

54　See above, p. 245.

55　For example, *CPL 1396–1404*, v, 300, 542; *CPL 1427–47*, 348–9.

56　*Councils and Synods* II, i, 211.

57　*Reg. Grandisson, Exeter*, ii, 1192–3.

58　*Reg. Brantyngham, Exeter*, i, 61.

59　*ECD*, 422–3; *VCH Suffolk*, ii, 326.

60　See above, p. 222.

61　See above, pp. 220–2.

62　*The Acts of the Parliament of Scotland*, ed. T. Thompson et al., 11 vols (Edinburgh,

1814–75), ii, 238.

63　See above, pp. 327, 330–3.

64　Riley, 1867–9, i, 72–3.

65　Ibid., 196.

66　See above, p. 136.

67　Riley, 1872–3, ii, 314.

68　On the history of holy-water clerks, see *The Clerk's Book of 1549*, ed. J. Wickham Legge, Henry Bradshaw Soc., 25 (1903), and Orme, 2001, 229–31.

69　*Councils and Synods II*, i, 174.

70　Ibid., i, 211, 309, 407, 514, 606, 713; ii, 1026.

71　Dugdale, vi part iii, 1246; *Reg. Bekynton, Wells*, ed. H. C. Maxwell-Lyte, vol. i, Somerset Record Soc., 49 (1934), 82.

72　*Reg. Drokensford, Wells*, ed. E. Hobhouse, Somerset Record Soc., 1 (1887), 13.

73　*Borough Customs*, ed. M. Bateson, vol. ii, Selden Soc., 21 (1906), 212.

74　*Reg. Wykeham, Winchester*, ed. T. F. Kirby, vol. ii, Hampshire Record Soc. (1899), 75–6.

75　*Reg. Waltham, Salisbury*, ed. T. C. B. Timmins, C&Y, 80 (1994), 158.

76　Heywood and Wright, 514.

77　Orme, 1995, 281–2.

78　See above, p. 63.

79　*EYS*, ii, 3–4.

80　*Reg. Drokensford, Wells*, 268; *VCH Hants.*, ii, 255.

81　*ECD*, 252–3.

82　*Reg. Grandisson, Exeter*, ii, 955; above, p. 140.

83　See above, pp. 278–9.

84　C. Rawcliffe, *Medicine for the Soul* (Stroud, 1999), 243–4.

85　*EWE*, 37.

86　Catherine Jamison, *The History of the Royal Hospital of St Katharine by the Tower of London* (London, 1952), 21; *EWE*, 94.

87　*EEA*, xxv, 275–6; *ECD*, 124–7 (the date of c.1190 there suggested for the original benefaction is probably too early).

88　J. Wilson, 297–303; *Taxatio Ecclesiastica* (London, Record Commission, 1802), 318–19; *CCR 1288–96*, 263–4; on Irton, see *DNB*.

89　On Stapledon, see M. Buck, *Politics, Finance and the Church in the Reign of Edward II: Walter Stapeldon, treasurer of England* (Cambridge, 1983), and *DNB*.

90　*EWE*, 48–9; there were eight boys and a tutor in 1354 (Exeter Cathedral Library Archives, D&C 2239), and nine boys in 1535 (*Valor Ecclesiasticus*, ii, 314).

91　*VCH Oxon.*, iii, 108; Cobban, 1988, 183.

92　*VCH Lincs.*, ii, 427–9.

93　On Bredgar, see *VCH Kent*, ii, 230. The three sets of statutes are printed in *Literae Cantuarienses*, ed. J. B. Sheppard, vol. iii (RS, 1889), 15–21, 68–70; Dugdale, vi part iii, 1391–3; and *Reg. Morton, Canterbury*, ed. C. Harper-Bill, vol. i, C&Y, 75 (1987), 109–12.

See also *Reg. Chichele, Canterbury*, ed. E. F. Jacob, 4 vols (Oxford, 1938–47), iv, index, *sub* Bredgar.

94 Jocelin of Brakelond, 95; *VCH Suffolk*, ii, 308, 312.

95 *VCH Herts.*, ii, 49–50.

96 See above, pp. 32, 37–8. On medieval colleges, see now Jeffery.

97 On colleges, see A. H. Thompson, 1947, 132–60.

98 *EYS*, i, 80c–e (Beverley); *VCH Notts.*, ii, 183–4 (Southwell); *EYS*, i, 141 (Ripon).

99 *ECD*, 68–9; *VCH Sussex*, ii, 409–10; *ECD*, 58–9, 86–91, 272–7; *VCH Warws.*, ii, 299.

100 Highfield, 69–73, 382.

101 Cobban, 1969, 50–2; Cobban, 1988, 183; Magrath, i, 45–9, 141–2.

102 *EWE*, 165–6.

103 Tester, 119; J. Thorpe, *Registrum Roffense* (London, 1769), 237. On the college, see also N. Saul, *Death, Art, and Memory in Medieval England* (Oxford, 2001).

7: Schools from 1350 to 1530

1 Orme, 2001, 107.

2 See above, pp. 108–9.

3 See above, p. 185.

4 *VCH Cambs.*, iii, 11.

5 Walsingham, 2003, 444–5.

6 On this subject, see the articles by R. F. Green and S. Crane in *Chaucer's England: Literature in Historical Context*, ed. B. A. Hanawalt (Minneapolis, 1992), and S. Justice, *Writing and Rebellion: England in 1381* (Berkeley and London, 1994), especially 13–66.

7 *The Anonimalle Chronicle 1333 to 1381*, ed. V. H. Galbraith (Manchester, 1970), 146.

8 *Rotuli Parliamentorum*, iii, 294.

9 Langland, C.vi.61–83.

10 *Pierce the Ploughmans Crede*, ed. W. W. Skeat, EETS, o.s., 30 (1867), 28, lines 744–9.

11 *The Paston Letters*, ed. J. Gairdner, 5 vols (London, 1904), i, 28–9. For a similar example, see H. C. Maxwell-Lyte, 'The Hody Family', *Somerset and Dorset Notes and Queries*, 18 (1925), 127–9.

12 *ECD*, 386–7; Leach, 1916, 236.

13 *Rotuli Parliamentorum*, ii, 601–2; *Statutes of the Realm*, ii, 157–8.

14 PRO, SC 2/179/50; Gloucester, Gloucestershire Record Office, D 2700/MA 1/5; H. S. Darbyshire and G. D. Lumb, *The History of Methley*, Thoresby Society, 35 (1934), 182.

15 See editions of the treatise *Modus Tenendi Cur. Baron* listed in *STC*, i, 350, particularly *The Maner of Keping a Courte Baron* (London, 1552; *STC* 7721), sig. Aiii recto.

16 On Lollards and literature, see A. Hudson, *The Premature Reformation: Wycliffite Texts and Lollard History* (Oxford, 1988).

17 M. Aston, *Lollards and Reformers: Images and Literacy in Late Medieval Religion* (London, 1984), 198–9.

18 A. Hudson, *Selections from English Wycliffite Writings* (Cambridge, 1978), 24–9, 150–1; *Fasciculi Zizaniorum*, ed. W. W. Shirley (RS, 1858), 360–9.

19 Wilkins, iii, 317; *ECD*, 394–5.

20 Lyndwood, 282–4.

21 For discussion of his life, see Lloyd, 1–21, and *DNB*.

22 Lloyd, 356–7.

23 On Bingham and his college, see ibid., passim. The statutes of Godshouse and Christ's are printed in Rackham, especially 106–9.

24 *Rotuli Parliamentorum*, v, 137.

25 See above, p. 169.

26 *EYS*, ii, 110; above, p. 72.

27 *Epistolae Academiae Oxoniensis*, ed. H. Anstey, vol. ii, Oxford Hist. Soc., 26 (1989), 381.

28 Edmund Dudley, *The Tree of the Commonwealth*, ed. D. M. Brodie (Cambridge, 1948), 62.

29 See above, pp. 83–5.

30 The standard life of Wykeham is still Moberly; there are good reviews by P. Partner in Custance, 1–36, and *DNB*; a new life is being prepared by Dr Virginia Davis.

31 *Valor Ecclesiasticus*, ii, 4, 262.

32 On the early history of Winchester College, see Kirby, 1892; Leach 1899; and Leach, in *VCH Hants.*, ii, 261–309.

33 The statutes are printed in Kirby, 1892, 455–523.

34 Ibid., 457–8, 490.

35 The earliest register of scholars (1393–1686) is Winchester College Archives, 21490A. This was calendared by Kirby, 1888, but his edition contains errors of names and omissions of evidence. The archives contain a MS list of commoners compiled by A. F. Leach.

36 For biographies of Winchester scholars, see *BRUO*, passim, and G. F. Lytle, '"Wykehamist Culture" in Pre-Reformation England', in Custance, 129–66.

37 See below, p. 306.

38 On King's Hall, see Cobban, 1969.

39 R. B. Dobson, *Durham Priory* (Cambridge, 1973), 170.

40 On the foundress and foundation, see *EWE*, 190–9; Hornsby and Griffin; and *DNB*.

41 The charter and statutes are calendared and partly transcribed in *Reg. Wakefield, Worcester*, ed. W. P. Marett, Worcestershire Hist. Soc., n.s., 8 (1972), 80–9; extracts are translated in *ECD*, 330–41.

42 Despite Leach (above, p. 8). A chantry priest was envisaged teaching in Ireland as early as

1305, but this seems shaped by a different context: providing Anglo-Irish culture in a native Irish environment (*Calendar of the Justiciary Rolls . . . of Ireland, Edward I*, part 2, ed. J. Mills (London, 1914), 141–2). Chantry priests teaching on their own initiative may have included some of the Lincoln and York chaplains mentioned above (pp. 62–3), and there is a fifteenth-century assertion about one doing so in Somerset in the 1380s (*EWE*, 108–9).

43 See above, p. 175.
44 See above, pp. 212–13.
45 Thomson, 1979, 158–68; *VCH Shropshire*, ii, 128–31.
46 *CPR 1408–13*, 280; Dugdale, vi part iii, 1401, 1407.
47 A. H. Thompson, 1918, 270, 272–3.
48 *VCH Northants.*, ii, 223.
49 *CPR 1416–22*, 441; *VCH Northants.*, ii, 217–21.
50 *VCH Durham*, ii, 371–3.
51 On Oswestry school, see Bulkeley-Owen, and Oakley.
52 Dugdale, vi part iii, 1434–5. For the early history of Eton, see Maxwell-Lyte, especially chapters 1–4.
53 *CPR 1436–41*, 521–3.
54 Heywood and Wright, 478.
55 Ibid., 479–80. The known names of the Eton scholars are listed by Sterry.
56 Heywood and Wright, 524.
57 Ibid., 517, 535.
58 *VCH Cambs.*, iii, 376–85.
59 *EWE*, 142–3. For these figures, see *DNB*, where their educational interests, however, receive little attention.
60 *EWE*, 124–7, 133–7.
61 Ibid., 182–4; Orme, 1989a, 36–7, 209–19; Haines; above, pp. 84–5.
62 *CPR 1446–52*, 170. For Alnwick's life, see *BRUC*, 11, and *DNB*.
63 *EWE*, 128–9. For Chedworth's life, see also *BRUO*, i, 401–2, and *DNB*.
64 *EWE*, 80–1; Watkin, 98–109. For Beckington's life, see *BRUO*, i, 157–9, and *DNB*.
65 For Waynflete's life and foundations, see Davis, and *DNB*.
66 *ESR*, part ii, 322–7.
67 Easson, 19; Durkan, 157–9, 164, 167; McGrath, 182; G. Williams, 1997.
68 *CPR 1381–5*, 413–14; *CPR 1441–6*, 388.
69 *ECD*, 398–402; above, p. 173.
70 Lupton, 272; *VCH Notts.*, ii, 220; *EWE*, 122, 188–90; *VCH Lancs.*, ii, 583.
71 See above, pp. 317–22.
72 See above, pp. 176–7.
73 *EWE*, 160–1.
74 *HMC, Ninth Report* (1883), vol. i, 217.
75 Gray and Potter, 7; *VCH Suffolk*, ii, 327.

76 *VCH Lancs.*, ii, 593.
77 See above, p. 134.
78 Above, p. 133.
79 Lupton, 275, 277, 279, 285–6.
80 *EWE*, 178–9.
81 *EWE*, 184–6; Coulstock, 161–89. On her life, see M. K. Jones and M. G. Underwood, *The King's Mother: Lady Margaret Beaufort, countess of Richmond and Derby* (Cambridge, 1992), and *DNB*.
82 Jordan, 1962, 35–6.
83 Ibid., 37–8.
84 Cokayne, ix, 113–15; *LPFD*, iii part ii, no. 2915.
85 *VCH Staffs.*, ii, 280–1; *VCH Oxon.*, i, 461. For Smith's life, see *BRUO*, iii, 1721–2, and *DNB*.
86 *EWE*, 121.
87 *VCH Lincs.*, ii, 479; *VCH Lancs.*, ii, 578–84.
88 See above, pp. 120, 293–4. For Wolsey's life and works, see *BRUO*, iii, 2077–80; Gunn and Lindley; and *DNB*.
89 *LPFD*, iv part i, nos. 1459, 1470–1.
90 On Ipswich school, see *VCH Suffolk*, ii, 142–4, 328–31; Gray and Potter, 16–30; Gunn and Lindley, 113–14, 198–9; and Blatchly, 27–42. Its curriculum is set out in J. Strype, *Ecclesiastical Memorials*, 3 vols in 6 parts (Oxford, 1822), i, 139–43.
91 *EWE*, 154–63; *VCH Lancs.*, ii, 601.
92 *VCH Notts.*, ii, 219; Orme, 1989a, 37.
93 *ECD*, 414–17; Varley, 1–30; *EWE*, 174–7.
94 *VCH Suffolk*, ii, 327; *CPR 1494–1509*, 83.
95 *VCH Northants.*, ii, 225–7; *EWE*, 120, 131–2.
96 A. H. Thompson, 1940–7, iii, 79; *EWE*, 188; Orme, 1989a, 40. See also above, pp. 286–7.
97 *VCH Lincs.*, ii, 426.
98 *The Coventry Leet Book*, ed. M. D. Harris, part i, EETS, o.s., 134 (1907), 101, 118, 190.
99 *ECD*, 422–4; *VCH Suffolk*, ii, 325–6.
100 *ECD*, 439.
101 Leach, 1916, 268–9; Nicolson and Burn, i, 329.
102 *VCH Warws.*, ii, 329–32.
103 *CPR 1446–52*, 402.
104 *VCH Lincs.*, ii, 451; *VCH Cambs.*, ii, 327.
105 *Catalogue of Ancient Deeds*, v, 512; *ESR*, part ii, 235–8; *VCH Warws.*, v, 25.
106 *VCH Notts.*, ii, 220; *EWE*, 138–40.
107 *EWE*, 121, 188; Jordan, 1961b, 72.
108 *VCH Berks*, ii, 275–6; *VCH Yorks.*, i, 463–4, 467. Cf. also Christ's College (Cambridge) at Wimborne (Coulstock, 184–5, 222).
109 *VCH Suffolk*, ii, 340; *EWE*, 163, cf. 130.
110 Langland, A.viii.28–34; B.vii.26–31; C.x.30–5; Dudley, *Tree of the Commonwealth*, 63.
111 *HMC, Report on the MSS of Lord Middleton* (London, 1911), 334, 338, 346, 364, etc.
112 No school has yet been found in Rochester.
113 *VCH Durham*, i, 371–5; *VCH Staffs.*, iii, 280–1; *VCH Sussex*, ii, 402–4; McDonnell, 1909,

13–32; Orme, 1989a, 42–5.

114 Orme, 1996b, 288–9.

115 On the medieval grammar schools of Oxford, see *VCH Oxon.*, iii, 40–3; R. W. Hunt, 1964; Thomson, 1983; and Leader, 1983.

116 A. Wood, i, 638–41.

117 Emden, 1927, 173–7.

118 Gibson, 300.

119 On Magdalen College School, see now Orme, 1998.

120 See above, pp. 198–9; Feltoe and Minns, 202, 289–91; Stokes, 49–57.

121 Gray, 31–3, 61; Gray and Brittain, 30–2.

122 *Calendar of Plea and Memoranda Rolls of London, 1381–1412*, ed. A. H. Thomas (London, 1932), 182.

123 Galbraith, 1941–3, 85–104. On Seward, see also above, p. 181.

124 See below, pp. 359–60.

125 London, Guildhall Library, MS 9531/6 (Reg. Gilbert, London), f. 183r; *CPR 1436–41*, 238.

126 R. R. Sharpe, ii, 508.

127 London, Guildhall Library, MS 9171/5, ff. 270v–271r; *CCR 1476–85*, 28.

128 *ECD*, 416–18; *CPR 1441–6*, 432.

129 *Rotuli Parliamentorum*, v, 137.

130 C. L. Kingsford, 'Two London Chronicles', *Camden Miscellany XII*, Royal Hist. Soc., Camden 3rd series, 18 (1910), 11.

131 Stow, i, 154; above, p. 72.

132 Lupton, passim; McDonnell, 1909, 13–68. For Colet's life, see also *BRUO*, i, 462–4, and *DNB*.

133 See above, pp. 121, 139–40, 142–3, 176.

134 Stow, i, 71–5.

135 Moran, 1985, 237–79.

136 On what follows, see the list of schools below, pp. 344–70.

137 On education in great households, see also Orme, 1984, 44–60.

138 Ibid., 49–51.

139 Cobban, 1969, 60–3.

140 Myers, 1959, 126–7.

141 Hall, 673.

142 See above, p. 122.

143 On Holt, see above, p. 121, and Orme, 1996b.

144 R. Pace, *De Fructu* (Basel, 1517), 28.

145 Cavendish, 18–21, 29–30.

146 PRO, DL 28/1/2, ff. 16r, 26v.

147 *A Collection of Ordinances*, 98–9; Percy, 44.

148 *LPFD*, iii part i, p. 500; *BRUO*, iv, 73.

149 *LPFD*, iv part i, no. 366. On Lovell, see S. Gunn, 'Sir Thomas Lovell', in *The End of the Middle Ages?*, ed. J. Watts (Stroud, 1998), 117–53.

150 See also above, pp. 62–3.

151 PRO, CP 40/440, m. 94.

152 *VCH Notts.*, ii, 221–2.

153 Oxford, Brasenose College, Principal Yate's Book (1668), 97–8. Alkborough was grammar

master at Higham Ferrers in 1526 (Salter, 1909, 131).

154 On this subject, see above, pp. 341–3.

8: The Religious Orders and Education

1 Knowles and Hadcock, 494.

2 See above, pp. 20, 36–7, 45.

3 Knowles and Brooke, 162–4.

4 Orme, 2001, 213–15.

5 Canivez, i, 31, 84.

6 *Historiae Anglicanae Scriptores X*, ed. R. Twysden (London, 1652), col. 1815. Compare Friedberg, ii, cols 571–2.

7 Power, 26–7.

8 *VCH Wilts.*, iii, 247, 249.

9 Power, 26.

10 Ibid.; *VCH London*, i, 518.

11 *Chronicon Abbatiae Rameseiensis*, ed. W. D. Macray (RS, 1886), 268–9.

12 See above, p. 160.

13 J. C. Robertson, i, 213.

14 Humbert of Romans, *Opera*, ed. J. J. Berthier, 2 vols (Rome, 1888–9), ii, 41.

15 Knowles and Hadcock, 212–50, 492–4.

16 Denifle and Ehrle, i, 202; Reichert, iii, 129.

17 Bihl, 39; Carlini, 277, 527.

18 Roth, 1966, 136–7.

19 Moorman, 1952, 107–8; K. Walsh, *A Fourteenth-Century Scholar and Primate: Richard FitzRalph in Oxford, Avignon, and Armagh* (Oxford, 1981), 425.

20 Gibson, 164–5; *Rotuli Parliamentorum*, ii, 290.

21 *Rotuli Parliamentorum*, iii, 502.

22 Moorman, 1952, 106–13; Roth, 1958–61, 266, 385. For a Carmelite instance, see PRO C 1/4/104.

23 On Dominican education, see Mulcahey, especially 59, 75, 83–350.

24 Roger Bacon, *Opera Inedita*, ed. J. S. Brewer (RS, 1859), 426.

25 Reichert, iv, 179.

26 *VCH Yorks.*, iii, 282.

27 *LPFD*, xiii part ii, no. 809.

28 See above, p. 80.

29 Denifle and Ehrle, i, 222.

30 Reichert, iii, 99–100.

31 Ibid., 285.

32 Ibid., 12–13.

33 Ibid., 38.

34 Ibid., iv, 229.

35 Little, 1894, 51–6.

36 For examples of foreign friars in English Dominican houses, see Emden, 1967, 22–7.

37 On what follows, see Little, 1894, 63–7; Little, 1917, 158–73; and most recently Roest, 65–115.

38 Thomas of Eccleston, *De Adventu Fratrum*

Minorum in Angliam, ed. A. G. Little (Manchester, 1951), 50.

39 Ibid., 49–50.

40 *CCR 1241–7*, 447; *CCR 1256–9*, 241.

41 Denifle and Ehrle, vi, 64.

42 Little, 1894, 65.

43 *EWE*, 205.

44 Little, 1894, 68–9.

45 Roest, 79.

46 On what follows, see Roth, 1966, 140–77.

47 *The Friars' Libraries*, ed. K. W. Humphreys, Corpus of British Medieval Library Catalogues, 1 (London, 1990), 116–30.

48 Zimmerman, i, 60.

49 Knowles, 1948–59, ii, 144–5.

50 *CPL 1396–1404*, 1, 19–20.

51 Little, 1917, 168–72.

52 PRO, PROB 11/10 (PCC 34 Vox).

53 Roth, 1966, 177.

54 *Select XVIth Century Causes in Tithe*, ed. J. S. Purvis, Yorkshire Arch. Soc., Record Series, 104 (1947), 108–9.

55 Bodleian, University Archives, Hyp. B2 (not paginated, but about f. 78r).

56 *A C Mery Tales* (STC 23664), f. 10v.

57 *LPFD*, vi, no. 1270.

58 Knowles and Hadcock, 489–90.

59 Harvey, 54–6; Clark, 2004, 43.

60 On Benedictine education in the later middle ages, see Clark, 2002b, and Clark, 2004, 42–78.

61 Harvey, 54–9.

62 S. J. A. Evans, 1940, 24.

63 *Historia et Cartularium Monasterii Gloucestriae*, ed. W. H. Hart, vol. i (RS, 1863), pp. lxxxiv–v.

64 *Literae Cantuarienses*, ed. J. B. Sheppard, vol. i (RS, 1887), 126–7.

65 *The Rule of St Benedict*, 54–5, 124–7.

66 Canivez, ii, 289–90.

67 Pantin, 1931–7, i, 27–8.

68 *The Historical Works of Gervase of Canterbury*, ed. W. Stubbs, vol. ii (RS, 1880), 281.

69 Pantin, 1931–7, i, 75.

70 On Rewley Abbey, see Canivez, iii, 200, 217; *VCH Oxon.*, ii, 82–3; and Dobson, 544–6.

71 Pantin, 1931–7, i, 127.

72 On Gloucester College, see Galbraith, 1924, and Dobson, 546–8.

73 Blakiston, 6–7.

74 Pantin, 1947–85, iv, 9–50.

75 Stokes, 8–12, 87–8; *VCH Cambs.*, ii, 207.

76 *BRUO*, i, 272.

77 M. Robson, 'Franciscan Lectors at Christ Church Cathedral Priory, Canterbury, 1275–1314', *Archaeologia Cantiana*, 92 (1993), 261–81.

78 *BRUO*, i, 277–8, 340–1; iii, 1626; Pantin, 1931–7, i, 181–5.

79 Salter, 1922, 13, 17.

80 Colvin, 320–3; Gribbin, 165–71.

81 For examples, see Gribbin, 166.

82 *CPL 1198–1304*, 516. Golding, 173, suggests that the doctor was intended to operate in Cambridge, but the intention is not clear.

83 Golding, 171–5; *VCH Cambs.*, ii, 254–6.

84 *CPR 1301–7*, 6; *VCH Lincs.*, ii, 469; Golding, 175–7.

85 Friedberg, ii, cols 1166–8.

86 Cocquelines, iii part ii, 203–13 at 210–11; 214–40 at 220–1; 264–86 at 270–2.

87 Canivez, iii, 392–3. For indications of the size of the English Cistercian houses at this time, see Knowles and Hadcock, 110–28.

88 *VCH Cambs.*, ii, 312. At least two Benedictine houses near Cambridge, Bury St Edmunds and Norwich, sent monks to Oxford (*VCH Oxon.*, iii, 303).

89 Stevenson and Salter, 3–110; Dobson, 552–4.

90 E. Evans; Dobson, 554–5.

91 *Customary of the Benedictine Monasteries of Saint Augustine, Canterbury, and Saint Peter, Westminster*, ed. E. M. Thompson, 2 vols, Henry Bradshaw Soc., 23, 28 (1902–4), ii, 157.

92 Fowler, 1903, 84–5.

93 *Customary of the Benedictine Monasteries*, ed. Thompson, i, 402–3; *Historia et Cartularium Monasterii Gloucestriae*, ed. W. H. Hart, 3 vols (RS, 1863–7), i, 53; Clark, 2004, 47.

94 John Amundesham, *Annales Monasterii Sancti Albani*, ed. H. T. Riley, 2 vols (RS, 1870–1), i, 436; Clark, 2004, 48.

95 Gasquet, iii, 224; Aveling and Pantin, p. xiv.

96 *VCH Hants.*, ii, 258–9, where read 'Parkhouse' for 'Porthouse'.

97 PRO, E 315/103, f. 128r-v.

98 C. J. Bates, 'The Border Holds of Northumberland', *Archaeologia Aeliana*, n.s., 14 (1891), 424–5.

99 Jordan, 1961b, 72.

100 A. H. Thompson, 1914–29, iii, 237–8.

101 Orme, 1991, 296; cf. S. J. A. Evans, 1957, 157–8.

102 A. H. Thompson, 1914–29, ii, 171–2.

103 Clark, 2002b.

104 For references, see the *Corpus of British Medieval Library Catalogues*.

105 For example, at the Augustinian houses of Leicester and Waltham (ibid., vol. vi: *The Libraries of the Augustinian Canons*, ed. T. Webber and A. G. Watson (1998), 290–300, 436–42).

106 F. A. Gasquet, *The Old English Bible and Other Essays*, 2nd edn (London, 1908), 225–46 (BL, Harley MS 1587); E. Wilson (BL, Add. MS 60577).

107 *Catalogues of the Libraries of Durham Cathedral*, ed. B. Botfield, Surtees Soc., 7 (1838), 81–2.

108 Fowler, 1903, 97.

109 *Corpus of British Medieval Library Catalogues*, ix, 730, 746, 756.

110 Aveling and Pantin, pp. xiv, xxviii–xxxv, 56–9, 124–7; *DNB*.
111 Fowler, 1903, 97.
112 Orme, 1991, 296–7.
113 W. G. Searle, 182, 184.
114 A. H. Thompson, 1914–29, iii, 373–82.
115 Pantin, 1929; *DNB*.
116 Wilkins, iii, 790–1; above, p. 298.
117 See, for example, A. H. Thompson, 1914–29, iii, 494–5; A. H. Thompson, 1940–7, iii, 282; and Gribbin, 165–6.
118 A.H. Thompson, 1914–29, i, 32; ii, 45; A. H. Thompson, 1940–7, ii, 99.
119 *EWE*, 213; *VCH Hants.*, ii, 258; Pantin, 1931–7, iii, 83; A. H. Thompson, 1914–29, i, 102; *ECD*, 444–5.
120 Watkin, 159–64; Orme, 1991, 296.
121 See above, pp. 294–5.
122 Knowles and Hadcock, 251–89, 494. The modern study of English late medieval nuns rests on Power, supplemented by more recent writers such as Bell, Lee, and Oliva.
123 Power, 244; the nuns of St Mary de Pre (St Albans), however, are said to have been illiterate in the late fourteenth century, a situation reformed by their supervisor, the abbot of St Albans (ibid.).
124 Ibid., 261.
125 A. H. Thompson, 1914–29, ii, 4–6, 9.
126 Power, 247–8.
127 *Reg. Stapeldon, Exeter*, 316.
128 *The Myroure of Oure Lady*, ed. J. H. Blunt, EETS, e.s. 19 (1873), 2–3.
129 *The English Register of Godstow Nunnery*, ed. A. Clark, 3 parts, EETS, o.s., 129–30, 142 (1905–11), i, 25–6.
130 Bell, 66.
131 Ibid., 57–96; Oliva, 64–72; Lee, 136–8, 140–2.
132 Bell, 61–2.
133 Bodleian, MS Rawlinson G 59; Lee, 207–9.
134 C. F. R. Palmer, 'Notes on the Priory of Dartford', *Archaeological Journal*, 39 (1882), 177–9; B. Jarrett, *The English Dominicans* (London, 1921), 11. The attribution of some Latin accounts to a nun of Lacock (Bell, 65) is not supported by the evidence.
135 On almonry boys, see now the excellent survey by Bowers, 1999.
136 *ECD*, 130–1.
137 Ibid., 124–5.
138 Greatrex; Bowers, 1999, 182–7.
139 Cheney, 629, 633.
140 Bowers, 1999, 188.
141 Ibid.
142 S. J. A. Evans, 1940, 38–9.
143 Bowers, 1999, 195, 197.
144 Pantin, 1931–7, i, 70–1, 96; Bowers, 1999, 189.
145 Pantin, 1931–7, i, 258; Bowers, 1999, 192.
146 Bowers, 1999, 190.

147 Pantin, 1931–7, i, 70–1, 96; ii, 32–3; Bowers, 1999, 189–90.
148 Bowers, 1999, 220–2; *EWE*, 205; West, 195.
149 For these and other figures, see Bowers, 1999, 199–200.
150 Fowler, 1903, 91–2.
151 Bowers, 1999, 194.
152 S. J. A. Evans, 1940, 38–9; *ECD*, 296–7.
153 *EWE*, 202, 205, 207.
154 Leach, 1913, 22–3; *ECD*, 298–9; *EWE*, 62.
155 Saunders, 1932, 93–100.
156 Bowers, 1999, 201.
157 *CPL 1427–47*, 348–9.
158 On what follows, see Bowers, 1999, 208–13.
159 See above, pp. 65–6.
160 Fowler, 1903, 62–3.
161 *EWE*, 207; *VCH Hants.*, ii, 259; *EWE*, 203–4. For Tucke, see Woodley and *DNB*.
162 A. H. Thompson, 1914–29, i, 23.
163 Bowers, 1999, 197, 201.
164 W. G. Searle, 106.
165 West, 195; Bowers, 1999, 206
166 Lyndwood, 209.
167 Bowers, 1999, 206–7; Orme, 1991, 294.
168 See above, pp. 3, 5, and on nunneries, Power, 274–5.
169 For references, see the list of schools, below, pp. 344–70.
170 Ibid. Bristol may have been another early case (*EWE*, 36).
171 See above, p. 200.
172 See above, pp. 136, 213.
173 E. Searle, 426; Darlington, i, 80–1; *EWE*, 64–5.
174 See above, pp. 192, 208.
175 Riley, 1867–9, i, 397.
176 C. Reyner, *Apostolatus Benedictorum in Anglia* (Douai, 1626), 224; Orme, 1991, 294.
177 Cheney, 629, 633.
178 *LPFD*, xiii part i, p. 361; *VCH Shropshire*, ii, 77.
179 Pantin, 1947–85, iv, 85–9, 91–100.
180 *LPFD*, xiii part ii, p. 156.
181 On what follows, see Power, 262–84, 568–81.
182 Ibid., 273.
183 Ibid., 568–81.
184 Golding, 171; above, p. 166.
185 Chaucer, I (A) 118–62, 3942–68.
186 *EWE*, 129.
187 Ibid., 121; Jordan, 1961b, 72; *EWE*, 117; Jordan, 1962, 33; *VCH Sussex*, ii, 412–13.
188 Page, 62.
189 A. H. Thompson, 1940–7, iii, 79; *LPFD*, ix, no. 1107
190 *EWE*, 186–9.
191 Orme, 1989a, 40–2; *VCH Staffs.*, vi, 154; see above, p. 242.
192 *STC* 5947, 5947.5; Trowbridge, Wiltshire Record Office, D1/19/1 (Chartularium Redingense), f. 31r; *VCH Berks.*, ii, 70, 250. For Cox's life, see *BRUO*, iv, 145, and *DNB*.

9: The Reign of Henry VIII

1　*Statutes of the Realm*, iii, 2; Orme, 1984, 202–3.
2　On Henry's education, see Orme, 1984, 23–4.
3　J. J. Scarisbrick, *Henry VIII* (London, 1968), 110–13.
4　On Henry VIII College, see *Statutes of the Colleges of Oxford*, ii, section 11, and *VCH Oxon.*, iii, 234–5.
5　Gray and Potter, 31–3.
6　See above, pp. 201–3.
7　See above, pp. 222, 270–1.
8　See above, p. 222.
9　Dickens, 91.
10　See above, p. 126.
11　*VCH Lancs.*, ii, 583.
12　*STC* 5542.3; Flynn, 1943, 95.
13　Wilkins, iii, 722–3, 726.
14　See above, pp. 270–1.
15　G. Williams, 1976, 291–2; *Lincoln Wills, 1532–1534*, ed. D. Hickman, Lincolnshire Record Soc., 89 (2001), 111, 117–18, 125.
16　Frere and Kennedy, ii, 17, 21, 48–9, 56, 63, 85.
17　Wilkins, iii, 722–3. Leach, translating the document in *ECD*, 446–7, gave it a gender bias towards boys; 'children' would be equally acceptable.
18　Hughes and Larkin, i, 231.
19　Claire Cross, 'Oxford and the Tudor State', in McConica, 127–9.
20　Wilkins, iii, 786–91.
21　*Statutes of the Realm*, iii, 493–9.
22　Ibid., 495.
23　*LPFD*, ix, nos. 679, 810, 954; *EWE*, 180.
24　PRO, SP 1/104, 151–4; *LPFD*, x, 461; *EWE*, 180.
25　*Statutes of the Realm*, iv part i, 364.
26　Watkin, 159–64; Frere and Kennedy, ii, 13.
27　On the Dissolution and its chronology, see Knowles, 1948–59, iii, part 3.
28　On the history of the court, see W. C. Richardson.
29　These are now in the PRO: Exchequer, Augmentation Office, Miscellaneous books, E 315. On the surviving records of the court, see *A Guide to the Contents of the Public Record Office*, vol. i (London, 1963), 80–5.
30　Exeter, Devon Record Office, Exeter City Archives, DD 22783; *EWE*, 205.
31　PRO, E 315/103, f. 128r-v.
32　*VCH Berks.*, ii, 251.
33　PRO, SC 6 Henry VIII/4054, f. 7r; E 315/101, f. 36v.
34　*VCH Staffs.*, iii, 298; vi, 154.
35　*VCH Herts.*, ii, 56–7; *VCH Suffolk*, ii, 312–13.
36　*EWE*, 131.
37　Jordan, 1961b, 72; Bodleian, MS DD All Souls c.180, no. 1.
38　*EWE*, 122–3.
39　Ibid., 189–90.
40　Jordan, 1962, 33.
41　*VCH Sussex*, ii, 413–14.
42　On the dissolution of the hospitals, see Orme and Webster, 156–7.
43　Stow, i, 183–5.
44　Watney, 1905, 120–4; Watney, 1906, 132.
45　*EWE*, 147–8.
46　Starkey, 1989, 124; Starkey, 1878, p. lvi.
47　For these and similar requests, see *LPFD*, xiii part ii, nos 306, 866, 1036; xiv part i, no. 183.
48　Wright, 1843, 262–3; *Statutes of the Realm*, iii, 728; *Journals of the House of Lords*, i, 112.
49　Two monastic cathedrals, Bath and Coventry, disappeared in 1539; they were regarded as superfluous because they lay in dioceses that also had secular cathedrals: Wells and Lichfield.
50　Wright, 1843, 263–4.
51　H. Cole, 1–28.
52　*Miscellaneous Writings and Letters of Thomas Cranmer*, ed. J. E. Cox, Parker Soc. (1846), 396–8.
53　H. Cole, 28–74.
54　*LPFD*, xiv part ii, nos 414, 427, 430.
55　A. H. Thompson, 1929, pp. xxxviii–lii, provides a good discussion of the Henrician cathedral foundations, with specimens of the foundation charters and statutes, focussing on Durham. For Canterbury, see also *ECD*, 452–69, and for Ely, Owen and Thurley, 31–43.
56　See, for example, *LPFD*, xx part i, no. 400.
57　*VCH Durham*, i, 374–5.
58　As appears from a survey taken after the removal of the see from Osney (*Hearne's Collections*, ed. H. E. Salter, vol. x, Oxford Hist. Soc., 67 (1915), 29–31).
59　H. L. Thompson, 272–4.
60　*VCH Hants.*, ii, 273–4.
61　Harries, Cattermole, and Mackintosh, 22–7, 45; *CPR 1547–8*, 13–17.
62　Woodruff and Cape, 56; *VCH Durham*, i, 374–5.
63　Bowers, 2001, 213.
64　*VCH Staffs.*, iii, 298; vi, 154.
65　*LPFD*, xvi, no. 1135 (9); xvii, no. 71 (8); xxi part i, no. 321; *ESR*, part ii, 134–5.
66　Ball, 13–14; Cooper, ii, 32. The schoolmaster of Trinity was the ex-master of Burton-on-Trent!
67　*LPFD*, xvi, no. 503 (30); *ESR*, part ii, 316–18. On Barlow's life, see *DNB*.
68　*LPFD*, xx part i, no. 1335 (38–9). On Hales's life, see *DNB*.
69　*EWE*, 139.
70　Frere and Kennedy, ii, 10–11.
71　T. Gascoigne, *Loci e Libro Veritatum*, ed. J. Thorold Rogers (Oxford, 1881), 112. For examples of wills, see *BRUO*, i, 323 (Richard

de Bury); Nicolas, 564, 569; and *Reg. Stafford, Exeter*, ed. F.C. Hingeston-Randolph (London and Exeter, 1886), 395, 402, 406, 408, 413–14.

72   For an example of the obligation being observed in 1548, see *HMC, Reports on Various Collections*, vol. vii (1914), 49.

73   *STC* 15610.5 (1540 old style, i.e. between 25 March 1540 and 24 March 1541). See also Allen.

74   *STC* 15610.6.

75   *STC* 15610.7.

76   Wilkins, iii, 875; *Statutes of the Realm*, iv part i, 111.

77   See above, p. 231; *VCH Northants.*, ii, 223–4.

78   Bennet.

79   *LPFD*, xviii part i, no. 474 (27).

80   Hasted, vii, 357–8; viii, 208, 392; *LPFD*, xx part i, p. 216.

81   *HMC, Report on the MSS of Lord De L'Isle and Dudley*, vol. i (1925), 202.

82   *EWE*, 183–4.

83   *LPFD*, xx part i, no. 846 (41).

84   *EWE*, 167.

85   Ibid., 98–9.

86   Namely Crediton, Evesham, Farnworth, Higham Ferrers, Lewes, St Thomas Acon (London), Ottery, Reading, Tattershall, Warwick, Winchcombe, and Wye.

87   Namely Cirencester, Faversham, and Westbury-on-Trym.

88   Namely Burton-on-Trent, Bury St Edmunds, and St Albans.

10: From Edward VI to Elizabeth I

1   For example, the Crypt School (Gloucester), planned in 1528 (*EWE*, 138–40).

2   See above, pp. 295–6.

3   Kreider, 16, reckoned 2,189 in twenty selected counties out of the English total of thirty-nine.

4   *ESR*, part ii, passim. The four missing counties are Derbyshire, Huntingdonshire, Norfolk, and Surrey.

5   Orme, 1979, 83–4, 88.

6   *EWE*, passim.

7   *Statutes of the Realm*, iii, 988–93; *Journals of the House of Lords*, i, 274–6.

8   Page, i, pp. x–xi.

9   Kreider, 157; cf. Orme, 1979, 80.

10   Abridged from Hall, 864–5.

11   For the commissions and their members, see *LPFD*, xxi part i, no. 302 (30).

12   For the injunctions, see Wilkins, iii, 875–6. The surviving enrolments of the Henrician chantry certificates are in PRO, E 301, and most of the educational entries are extracted in *ESR*, part ii.

13   Orme, 1979, 80, 83–4.

14   Examples of dissolutions under the act of 1546 are given in *ESR*, part i, 64–5; Kreider, 214–15, lists eight.

15   *ECD*, 434–5; *ESR*, part ii, 146; *LPFD*, xxi part ii, no. 648 (39, 52).

16   Frere and Kennedy, ii, 114–29.

17   Ibid., 138–9.

18   Ibid., 145, 148–9, 151.

19   *Statutes of the Realm*, iv part i, 24–33.

20   *Journals of the House of Lords*, i, 306–13; *Journals of the House of Commons*, i, 2–4; *Acts of the Privy Council, 1547–1550*, 193–5.

21   For the commissions and their members, see *CPR 1548–9*, 135–7.

22   W. C. Richardson, 141–2.

23   Orme, 1979, 82.

24   The Edwardian chantry certificates are preserved in PRO, E 301. *ESR*, part ii, prints most of the educational entries, with at least a few omissions of relevant material, e.g. Pleshey (*VCH Essex*, ii, 194), St Briavels (Maclean, 295–6), and Wallingford (*VCH Berks.*, ii, 105).

25   PRO, E 321/37/28.

26   *EWE*, 197.

27   Ibid., 127, 132.

28   *ESR*, part ii, 203–4.

29   Graham, pp. xii–xiv, 51, 54.

30   *Acts of the Privy Council, 1547–1550*, 184–6, 206. On Mildmay, see S. E. Lehmberg, *Walter Mildmay and Tudor Government* (Austin, Texas, 1964), and *DNB*.

31   *ESR*, part ii, pp. vii–1.

32   For examples of the third set, or abstracts, of chantry certificates, see ibid., passim, and for a specimen of a continuance warrant, ibid., 5–7.

33   Ibid., 268–71, 274–6; Orme, 1989a, 38, 46.

34   *ESR*, part ii, 175–6, 273–4; Orme, 1989a, 43–7.

35   *ESR*, part ii, 299–300, 305.

36   BL, Lansdowne MS 897, f. 152r–154r, a reference I owe to the kindness of Professor Claire Cross.

37   Orme, 1976, 111, 130, 150.

38   *CPR 1547–8*, 17, 43–4, 176–7. A chantry worth £4 5s. 6d. per annum was transferred to finance Grimsby school.

39   D. Dymond and C. Paine, *The Spoil of Melford Church* (Ipswich, 1992), 44; *CPR 1548–9*, 79.

40   *CPR 1548–9*, 175–6, 211–12, 339–40.

41   *Journals of the House of Commons*, i, 6–7, 13; *Journals of the House of Lords*, i, 342.

42   Thomas Lever, *A Fruitfull Sermon Made in Poules Church . . . the Seconde Daie of Februari* (London, 1550; *STC* 15543.5), sigs. B.vii verso–B.viii recto. On Lever, see *DNB*.

43   Lever, *A Sermon Preached the Thyrd Sonday in Lent* (London, 1550; *STC* 155447), sigs. E.i recto–E.ii recto. The date was amended to

'Fourth Sunday' in later editions.

44 Lever, *A Sermon Preached at Pauls Crosse the Xiiii. Day of December* (London, 1550; *STC* 15546.3), sigs. E.iii verso-E.iiii verso.

45 For these and other similar examples, see *CPR 1547–53*, passim.

46 *CPR 1548–9*, 211–12; *CPR 1550–3*, 345–6.

47 *EYS*, ii, 248, 364–9. Chantry schools refounded under Edward VI included Chelmsford, East Retford, Giggleswick, Grantham, Louth, Ludlow, Macclesfield, Morpeth, Saffron Walden, Sedbergh, Stafford, Stourbridge, and Stratford-upon-Avon. Maidstone and Wisbech are other possible cases (*CPR 1547–53*, passim).

48 Foundations not apparently connected with the dissolution of chantries and guilds included Abingdon, Bath, Bedford, Birmingham, Bruton, Bury St Edmunds, Grimsby, Guildford, Nuneaton, St Albans, Sherborne, Shrewsbury, and Spilsby (*CPR 1547–53*, passim).

49 *CPR 1553*, 75, 223–4.

50 *VCH Lincs.*, ii, 474–5.

51 *Journals of the House of Commons*, i, 22.

52 *VCH Northants.*, ii, 228.

53 Frere and Kennedy, ii, 93, 97, 144, 150–2.

54 *Catechismus* (London, 1548; *STC* 5993), ff. 150r, 201r.

55 *CPR 1548–9*, 340; cf. *CPR 1549–51*, 192, 437; *CPR 1550–3*, 22, 41, 48, etc.

56 *EWE*, 88.

57 Bray, 340–1.

58 F. E. Brightman, *The English Rite*, 2nd edn, 2 vols (London, 1921, repr. Farnborough, 1970), ii, 796–9.

59 Bray, 346–7.

60 See above, p. 202.

61 Bray, 376–81.

62 Frere and Kennedy, ii, 328.

63 *Statutes of the Realm*, iv part i, 233–4.

64 Ibid., 355–6, 371–2.

65 On Alley, see *DNB*.

66 *Journals of the House of Commons*, i, 38–9.

67 Wilkins, iv, 95–7.

68 *CPR 1553–8*, passim.

69 See, for example, *CPR 1554–5*, 90–1, 323; *CPR 1557–8*, 166, 225–6. One can add to the achievements of Mary's reign the rescue and reopening of the grammar school of Heytesbury, which had been closed by its irresponsible head in 1544 (*EWE*, 147–8).

70 *EWE*, 150, 168; *VCH Northants.*, ii, 227, 230–1.

71 Wilkins, iv, 125–6; T. Meyer, *Reginald Pole: Prince and Prophet* (Cambridge, 2000), 235–40.

72 R. E. G. Cole, passim.

73 *EYS*, i, 42–65, especially 65.

74 *EWE*, 88.

75 Beales, 268–9; *EWE*, 88.

76 *Statutes of the Realm*, iv part i, 397.

77 Frere and Kennedy, iii, 12–13, 21.

78 *CPR 1560–3*, 215; *CPR 1563–6*, 71.

79 *CPR 1563–4*, 509; *CPR 1569–72*, 334–5.

11: Reflections

1 Clanchy.

2 For Jordan's and Moran's works, see the bibliography; Alexander's was published at University Park and London, 1990.

3 Leach, 1916, 244–6.

4 Ibid., 243. For a detailed discussion of laicisation, see Orme, 1989a, 23–31.

5 *The Life and Times of Anthony Wood*, ed. A. Clark, vol. i, Oxford Hist. Soc., 19 (1891), 46.

6 Combe, 'Eton', plate opp. p. 35.

7 *The Great Chronicle of London*, ed. A. H. Thomas and I. D. Thornley (London, 1938), 236.

8 Orme, 1984, 91–4.

Bibliography

LIST OF UNPRINTED SOURCES CITED

Aberystwyth, National Library of Wales
  MS Peniarth 356
Bristol, Archives Office
  Great Orphan Book of Wills
Bury St Edmunds, Suffolk Record Office
  IC 500/2/11/365
Cambridge, Pembroke College
  Framlingham B.I, D.I, F
Cambridge, Trinity College
  MS O.5.4
Cambridge, University Library
  MS Dd.VIII.3; MS Additional 2830; Ely Diocesan Records, G/1/3 (The register of John Fordham); G/1/5 (The register of William Grey)
Canterbury, Cathedral Archives, Dean and Chapter
  BR/Hadleigh/25; CC/B/C/A/13; CC/R/F/11i; ChAnt/M/364/8; ChAnt/M/390; ChAnt/X/4/1, /5; ChChLet/I/18, /II/20; ECIII/53; ESRoll/8, /301; U3/11/5/1; U15/16/8
Chester, Cheshire Archives
  DBC 2391/2; DCH/C/446, /448
Chichester, West Sussex Record Office
  Cap, 1/14/1, /5
Durham, University Library
  Dean and Chapter Muniments, Priory Registers, i, ii
Edinburgh, National Library of Scotland
  MS Advocates A-7–21
Exeter, Cathedral Library and Archives
  D&C 2228, 2239
Exeter, Devon Record Office, Exeter City Archives
  Book 51; DD 22783
Glasgow, Hunterian Museum Library
  MS 472
Gloucester, Gloucestershire Record Office
  D 2700/MA 1/5
Hereford, Herefordshire Record Office
  M 31/8
Ipswich, Suffolk Record Office
  Wills, vol. iii
Leeds, Yorkshire Archaeological Society
  MS MD 225

Lewes, Sussex Record Office
  GLY 996
Lichfield, Record Office
  B/A/1/3 (The register of Roger Northburgh, vol. iii); B/A/1/13 (The register of William Smith)
London, British Library
  Add. MS 10293; Add. MS 18850; Add. MS 47680; Arundel MS 155; Arundel MS 249; Cotton MS Augustus V; Cotton MS Domitian I; Cotton MS Domitian A XVII; Cotton MS Faustina A VI; Cotton MS Vespasian XXV; Egerton Roll 8776; Harleian Roll AA 31; Harley Charter 48 E 46; Harley MS 208; Harley MS 604; Harley MS 642; Harley MS 1527; Harley MS 1587; Harley MS 2904; Harley MS 3860; Harley MS 3954; Lansdowne MS 897; Royal MS 2 A XVI; Royal MS 6 E VI; Royal MS 13 C 11; Royal MS 18 E I; Royal MS 20 B XX; Sloane MS 5; Yates Thompson MS 24
London, Guildhall Library
  MS 9171/4, /5, /9 (Commissary Court of London, Wills); MS 9531/6 (The register of Robert Gilbert)
London, Lambeth Palace Library
  The register of John Stafford; The register of John Morton
London, The National Archives (Public Record Office)
  Chancery: C 1 Early chancery proceedings; C 47 Chancery miscellanea; C 115 Chancery masters' exhibits
  Court of Common Pleas: CP 40 Plea rolls
  Court of King's Bench: KB27 Coram Rege rolls
  Duchy of Lancaster: DL 28 Accounts various
  Exchequer, K.R.: E 101 Accounts various; E 134 Depositions; E 154 Inventories of goods and chattels; E 179 Subsidy rolls
  Exchequer, Augmentation Office: E 301 Chantry certificates; E 315 Miscellaneous books; E 321 Proceedings; E 326 Ancient deeds series B; E 328 Ancient deeds series BB
  Exchequer, Land Revenue: LR 1 Enrolment

books; LR 6 Receivers' accounts, Series 1
Exchequer, T.R.: E 36 Books
Prerogative Court of Canterbury: PROB 11 Registered copy wills
Special Collections: SC 1 Ancient correspondence; SC 2 Court rolls; SC 6 Ministers' accounts; SC 8 Ancient petitions
State Paper Office: SP 1 State papers

New York, Columbia University, Rare Book and Manuscript Library
Plimpton MS 258

New York, Pierpont Morgan Library
MS M. 917

Norwich, Norfolk Record Office
Reg/2/4, Institution Book 4; Reg/4/7, Institution Book 7; Reg/5/9, Institution Book 9; Reg/6/11, Institution Book 11; Reg/7/12, Institution Book 12; DCN 43/79; Norfolk, Consistory Court, Wills

Nottingham, Nottinghamshire Record Office
DDA/10/20; DD/FJ/1/64/40, DD/FJ/1/107/15, DD/FJ/1/292/1, DD/FJ/5/2/2, DD/FJ/10/3/3

Nottingham, University Library
Middleton MS, Mi L M 2

Oxford, Balliol College
MS 354

Oxford, Bodleian Library
MS Ashmole 1137; MS Auct. F.3.9; MS Bodley 13; MS Bodley 191; MS Bodley 264; MS Bodley 286; MS Bodley 315; MS Bodley 577; MS Bodley 581; MS Bodley 859; MS Bodley 965b; MS Bodley Roll 5; MS Canon Class. Lat. 52; MS Canon Misc. 416; MS Charters, Suffolk, a.1;MS DD All Souls c. 180; MS DD Ewelme a.vi; MS Digby 46; MS Douce 8; MS Douce 131; MS Douce 231; MS Douce 245; MS Douce 276; MS Lat. th.e 25; MS Laud Misc. 409; MS Laud Misc.

642; MS Rawlinson C 209; MS Rawlinson G 59; MS Rawlinson Poet. 223; MS Selden Supra 38; MS Top. Glouc. c. 4–5; MS Wood D 11.
University archives: Registers G, H; Hyp. B2
All Souls College: MS DD All Souls
MS Lincoln College lat. 129

Oxford, Brasenose College
Principal Yate's Book

Oxford, Magdalen College
Deeds: Candlesby 16; Tempsford 96

Oxford, Merton College
MS Merton 25

Oxford, New College
Bursars' Rolls, 1336–1413; Warden Chandler's MS

Preston, Lancashire Record Office
DDBK 1

Reading, Berkshire Record Office
D/Q1 Q3

Stratford-upon-Avon, Shakespeare Birthday Trust Records Office
BRT 1/2/420, 1/3/27

Taunton, Somerset Record Office
D\B\bw/115; DD/L P 29/29

Trowbridge, Wiltshire Record Office
D1/19/1; The register of Richard Beauchamp

Warwick, Warwickshire Record Office
CR 1908/83

Winchester College, Archives
21490A

Winchester, Hampshire Record Office
W/D1/108 (31)

Wye College, Kent
Statutes

York, Borthwick Institute of Historical Research
Probate Register, 4

SELECT LIST OF PRINTED SOURCES

The ABC Both in Latyn & Englyshe, ed. E. S. Shuckburgh (London, 1889).

Acts of the Privy Council, new series, 1542–, ed. J .R. Dasent et al. (London, 1890–, in progress).

Ælfric Bata. *Anglo-Saxon Conversations: The Colloquies of Ælfric Bata*, ed. S. Gwara and D. W. Porter (Woodbridge, 1997).

Ælfric of Eynsham. *Ælfrics Grammatik und Glossar*, ed. J. Zupitza and H. Gneuss (Berlin, 1880; reprinted Berlin, Zürich, and Dublin, 1966).

Ælfric of Eynsham. *Ælfric's Colloquy*, ed. G. N. Garmonsway, 2nd edn (Exeter, 1978).

Æthelwulf. *De Abbatibus*, ed. A. Campbell (Oxford, 1967).

Alain de Lille. *Liber Parabolarum*, in *Patrologia Latina*, ed. J. P. Migne, vol. ccx (Paris, 1855), cols 581–94.

Alain de Lille. *Textes inédits*, ed. Marie-Thérèse d'Alverny, Etudes de philosophie mediévale, 52 (Paris, 1965).

Alcuin. *Alcuin of York: his life and letters*, trans. S. Allott (York, 1974).

Alcuin. *The Bishops, Kings, and Saints of York*, ed. P. Godman (Oxford, 1982).

Aldhelm. *The Prose Works*, trans. M. Lapidge and M. Herren (Cambridge, 1979).

Aldhelm. *The Poetic Works*, trans. M. Lapidge and J. L. Rosier (Cambridge, 1985).

Alexander of Ville-Dieu. *Das Doctrinale des Alexander de Villa Dei*, ed. D. Reichling (Berlin, 1893).

Alexandre-Bidon, D. 'La Lettre volée: apprendre à lire à l'enfant au moyen âge', *Annales*, 44 (1989), 953–92.

Alexandre-Bidon, D., and D. Lett, *Les Enfants au Moyen Age: Ve-XVe siècles* (Paris, 1997); translated as *Children in the Middle Ages: fifth-fifteenth centuries* (Notre Dame, Ind., 2000).

Allen, C. G. 'The Sources of "Lily's Latin Grammar", a Review of the facts and some further suggestions', *The Library*, 5th series, 9 (1954), 85–100.

Ancrene Wisse, ed. J. R. R. Tolkien, EETS, o.s., 249 (1962).

[Anwykyll, John.] *Compendium totius Grammatice* (Oxford, 1483).

Armitage-Smith, S. (ed.). *John of Gaunt's Register, 1371–1375*, 2 vols, Royal Hist. Soc., Camden 3rd series, 20–1 (1911).

Ascham, Roger. *English Works*, ed. W. A. Wright (Cambridge, 1904, repr. Cambridge, 1970).

Asser. *Life of King Alfred*, ed. W. H. Stevenson, new edn (Oxford, 1959).

Aveling, H., and W. A. Pantin, (eds). *The Letter Book of Robert Joseph, Monk-Scholar of Evesham and Gloucester College, Oxford, 1530–33*, Oxford Hist. Soc., n.s., 19 (1967).

Aylmer, Gerald, and John Tiller (eds). *Hereford Cathedral: a history* (London, 2000).

Balbi, Giovanni. *Catholicon* (Mainz, 1460, repr. Farnborough, 1971).

Ball, W. W. Rouse. *Cambridge Notes, chiefly concerning Trinity College and the University* (Cambridge, 1921).

Barlow, F. *The English Church, 1000–1066*, 2nd edn (London, 1979).

Bateson, Mary. 'The Huntingdon Song School and the School of St Gregory's, Canterbury', *English Hist. Review*, 18 (1903), 712–13.

Beales, A. C. F. 'A Biographical Catalogue of Catholic Schoolmasters in England, 1558–1603', *Recusant History*, 7 no. 6 (1966), 268–89.

Bede. *Ecclesiastical History of the English People*, ed. B. Colgrave and R. A. B. Mynors (Oxford, 1991).

Bell, D. N. *What Nuns Read: books and libraries in medieval English nunneries* (Kalamazoo, Mich., 1995).

Bennet, E. K. 'The College of S. John Evangelist of Rushworth', *Norfolk Archaeology*, 10 (1884–7), 367–76.

Bennett, H. S. 'A Check-List of Robert Whittinton's Grammars', *The Library*, 5th series, 7 (1952), 1–14.

Bertram, J. *The Chrodegang Rules* (Aldershot, 2005).

Bihl, P. M. 'Statuta Generalia Ordinis Edita', *Archivum Franciscanum Historicum*, 34 (1941), 13–94, 284–358.

Birley, R. 'The History of Eton College Library', *The Library*, 5th series, 11 (1956), 231–61.

Blair, J. *The Church in Anglo-Saxon Society* (Oxford, 2005).

Blakiston, H. E .D. 'Some Durham College Rolls', in *Collectanea III*, ed. M. Burrows, Oxford Hist. Soc., 32 (1896), 1–76.

Bland, Cynthia R. *The Teaching of Grammar in Late Medieval England: an edition, with commentary, of Oxford, Lincoln College MS Lat. 130* (East Lansing, 1991).

Blatchly, J. *A Famous Antient Seed-Plot of Learning: Ipswich School* (Ipswich, 2003).

Bliss, A. J. 'The Inscribed Slates at Smarmore', *Proceedings of the Royal Irish Academy*, 64, section C, no. 2 (1965), 33–60.

Bloxam, J. R. *A Register of the Presidents, Fellows, Demies . . . and other members of St Mary Magdalen College in the University of Oxford*, 8 vols (Oxford, 1853–85).

Boas, M. 'De Librorum Catonianorum Historia atque Compositione', *Mnemosyne*, n.s., 42 (1914), 17–46.

Boase, C. W. (ed.). *Register of the University of Oxford*, vol. i: *1449–63, 1505–71*, Oxford Hist. Soc., 1 (1885).

Bonaventure, Brother: see Miner, J. N. T.

Boniface, St. *The Letters of Saint Boniface*, trans. E. Emerton (New York, 1940).

Bonner, S. F. *Education in Ancient Rome* (London, 1977).

Borrajo, E. M. 'The Guildhall Library', *Library Association Record*, 10 (1908), 380–4.

Bowers, R. 'The Almonry Schools of the English Monasteries *c*.1265–1540', in *Monasteries and Society in Medieval Britain*, ed. B. Thompson (Stamford, 1999), 177–222.

Bowers, R. 'The Music and Musical Establishment of St George's Chapel in the 15th Century', in *St George's Chapel, Windsor, in the Late Middle Ages*, ed. C. Richmond and E. Scarff (Windsor, 2001), 171–214.

Bowker, Margaret. *The Secular Clergy in the Diocese of Lincoln, 1491–1520* (Cambridge, Studies in Medieval Life and Thought, n.s., 13, 1968).

Bradshaw, H., and C. Wordsworth (eds). *Statutes of Lincoln Cathedral*, 3 vols (Cambridge, 1892–7).

Bray, Gerald (ed.). *Tudor Church Reform: The Henrician canons of 1535 and the* Reformatio Legum Ecclesiasticarum, Church of England Record Soc., 8 (2000).

Breeze, Andrew, and J. Glomski. 'An Early Treatise upon Education: Leonard Cox's *De Erudienda Iuventute (1526)*', *Humanistica Louvaniensia*, 40 (1991), 112–67.

Brewer, Thomas. *Memoir of the Life and Times of John Carpenter, Town Clerk of London*, 2nd edn (London, 1856).

Brodie, A. H. 'Anwykyll's *Vulgaria*: A Pre-Erasmian Textbook', *Neuphilologische Mitteilungen*, 75 (1974), 416–27.

Brooks, N. P. (ed.). *Latin and the Vernacular Languages in Early Medieval Britain* (Leicester, 1982).

Brooks, N. P. *The Early History of the Church of Canterbury* (Leicester, 1984).

Brown, Cornelius. *A History of Newark-on-Trent*, 2 vols (Newark, 1904–7).

Brown, G. Hardin. 'The Dynamics of Literacy in Anglo-Saxon England', *Bulletin of the John Rylands University Library of Manchester*, 77 (1995), 109–42.

Bulkeley-Owen, Mrs. 'The Founder and First Trustees of Oswestry Grammar School', *Transactions of the Salop Arch. and Natural History*

Soc., 3rd series, 4 (1904), 185–216.

Bullough, D. A. 'The Educational Tradition in England from Alfred to Ælfric: Teaching *Utriusque Linguae*', *Settimane di studio del centro italiano di studi sull'alto medioevo*, 19 (1972), 453–504.

Bursill-Hall, G. L. *Speculative Grammars of the Middle Ages: the doctrine of* Partes orationis *of the* Modistae (The Hague, 1971).

Bursill-Hall, G. L. *A Census of Medieval Latin Grammatical Manuscripts* (Stuttgart-Bad Cannstatt, 1981).

Burton, J. 'Priory and Parish', in *Monasteries and Society in Medieval Britain*, ed. B. Thompson (Stamford, 1999), 329–47.

Byrhtferth. *Byrhtferth's Manual*, ed. S. J. Crawford, vol. i, EETS, o.s., 177 (1929).

Calendar of Close Rolls, 1272–1509, 47 vols (London, 1892–1963).

Calendar of Inquisitions Post Mortem, 1216– (London, 1904–, in progress).

Calendar of Letters and Papers, Foreign and Domestic, Henry VIII, ed. J. S. Brewer, J. Gairdner, and R. H. Brodie, 21 vols and addenda (London, 1864–1932).

Calendar of Miscellaneous Inquisitions, 8 vols (London, 1916–2003).

Calendar of Papal Letters, 1198– (London and Dublin, 1894–, in progress).

Calendar of Patent Rolls, 1216–1509, 1547– (London, 1891–, in progress).

Calendar of the MSS of the Dean and Chapter of Wells, 2 vols (London, Hist. MSS Commission, 1907–14).

Canivez, J. M. (ed.). *Statuta Capitulorum Generalium Ordinis Cisterciensis, 1116–1786*, 8 vols (Louvain, 1933–41).

Carlini, A. (ed.). 'Constitutiones Generales Ordinis Fratrum Minorum Anno 1316 Assisii Conditae', *Archivum Franciscanum Historicum*, 4 (1911), 269–302, 508–36.

Carlisle, N. *A Concise Description of the Endowed Grammar Schools in England and Wales*, 2 vols (London, 1818, repr. Richmond, 1972).

Catalogue of Ancient Deeds, 6 vols (London, 1890–1915).

Catholicon Anglicum, ed. S. J. Herrtage, EETS, o.s., 75 (1881).

Cato, Dionysius. *The Distichs of Cato*, trans. W. J. Chase, University of Wisconsin Studies in the Social Sciences and Literature, 7 (Madison, 1922).

Cato, Dionysius. *Disticha Catonis*, ed. M. Boas and H. J. Botschuyver (Amsterdam, 1952).

Catto, J. I. (ed.). *The History of the University of Oxford*, vol. i: *The Early Oxford Schools* (Oxford, 1984).

Catto, J. I., and Ralph Evans (eds). *The History of the University of Oxford*, vol. ii: *Late Medieval Oxford* (Oxford, 1992).

Cavendish, George. *The Life and Death of Cardinal Wolsey*, ed. R. S. Sylvester, EETS, o.s., 243 (1959).

Chaplin, W. N. 'A. F. Leach: a reappraisal', *British Journal of Educational Studies*, 11 (1962–3), 99–124.

Chaplin, W. N. 'A. F. Leach: agreement and difference', *British Journal of Educational Studies*, 11 (1962–3), 173–83.

Charlton, Kenneth. *Education in Renaissance England* (London, 1965).

Charlton, Kenneth. *Women, Religion and Education in Early Modern England* (London, 1999).

Chaucer, Geoffrey. *The Riverside Chaucer*, ed. Larry D. Benson, 3rd edn (Oxford, 1988).

Cheney, C. R. 'Letters of William Wickwane, Chancellor of York', *English Hist. Review*, 47 (1932), 626–42.

Chitty, H. F. 'The Second Masters of Winchester College', *The Wykehamist*, no. 551 (April 1916), 2–3.

Churton, R. *The Lives of William Smyth, Bishop of Lincoln, and Sir Richard Sutton, Knight, Founders of Brasen Nose College* (Oxford, 1800).

Clanchy, Michael. *From Memory to Written Record: England 1066–1307*, 2nd edn (Oxford, 1993).

Clark, J. G. (ed.). *The Religious Orders in Pre-Reformation England* (Woodbridge, 2002a).

Clark, J. G. 'Monastic Education in Late Medieval England', in *The Church and Learning in Late Medieval Society*, ed. C. Barron and J. Stratford (Donington, 2002b), 25–40.

Clark, J. G. *A Monastic Renaissance at St Albans: Thomas Walsingham and his circle c.1350–1440* (Oxford, 2004).

Close Rolls, 1227–1272, 14 vols (London, 1902–38).

Cobban, A. B. *The King's Hall within the University of Cambridge in the Later Middle Ages* (Cambridge, Studies in Medieval Life and Thought, 3rd series, 1, 1969).

Cobban, A. B. *The Medieval Universities: their development and organization* (London, 1975).

Cobban, A. B. *The Medieval English Universities: Oxford and Cambridge to c.1500* (Aldershot, 1988).

Cobban, A. B. *English University Life in the Middle Ages* (London, 1999).

Cocquelines, C. (ed.). *Bullarum Privilegiorum ac Diplomatum Romanorum Pontificum Amplissima Collectio*, 14 vols in 28 parts (Rome, 1739–62).

Cokayne, G. E. *The Complete Peerage*, ed. H. A. Doubleday and V. Gibbs, 14 vols in 15 parts (London, 1910–59).

Colchester, L. S. (ed.). *Wells Cathedral School* (Wells, 1985).

Cole, Henry. *King Henry VIII's Scheme of Bishopricks* (London, 1838).

Cole, R. E. G. (ed.). *Chapter Acts of the Cathedral Church of Lincoln, 1520–1559*, 3 vols., Lincoln Record Soc., 12–13, 15 (1915–20).

A Collection of Ordinances and Regulations for the Government of the Royal Household (London, Soc.

of Antiquaries, 1790).

Colvin, H. M. *The White Canons in England* (Oxford, 1951).

Combe, W. *The History of the Colleges of Winchester, Eton and Westminster* (London, 1816).

Cooper, C. H. *Annals of Cambridge*, 5 vols (Cambridge, 1842–53).

Copinger, W. A. *Supplement to Hain's Repertorium Bibliographicum*, 2 vols in 3 parts (London, 1895–1902, repr. Milan, 1950).

Corpus of British Medieval Library Catalogues (London, 1990–, in progress).

Coulstock, Patricia H. *The Collegiate Church of Wimborne Minster* (Woodbridge, 1993).

Councils and Synods I: A.D. 871–1204, ed. Dorothy Whitelock, M. Brett, and C. N. L. Brooke, 2 vols (Oxford, 1981).

Councils and Synods II: 1205–1313, ed. F. M. Powicke and C. R. Cheney, 2 vols (Oxford, 1964).

Courtenay, William J. *Schools and Scholars in Fourteenth-Century England* (Princeton, 1987).

Crosby, J. (ed.). 'Calendar of the Registers of the Bishops of Ely', *Ely Diocesan Remembrancer*, 1–355 (1885–1914).

Cross, M. Claire. *The Free Grammar School of Leicester*, University of Leicester, Department of English Local History, Occasional Papers, 4 (1953).

Custance, Roger (ed.). *Winchester College: sixth-centenary essays* (Oxford, 1982).

Dalton, J. N. *The Collegiate Church of Ottery St Mary* (Cambridge, 1917).

Daly, Ll. W. and B. A. 'Some Techniques in Medieval Latin Lexicography', *Speculum*, 30 (1964), 229–39.

Darlington, R. R. (ed.). *The Cartulary of Darley Abbey*, 2 vols (Kendal, 1945).

Davis, Virginia. *William Waynflete, Bishop and Educationalist* (Woodbridge, 1993).

Dean, R. J., and M. B. M. Boulton. *Anglo-Norman Literature: a guide to texts and manuscripts*, Anglo-Norman Text Soc., occasional publications, 3 (London, 1999).

Denifle, P. H., and F. Ehrle (eds). *Archiv für Litteratur- und Kirchen-Geschichte des Mittelalters*, 7 vols (Berlin and Freiburg im Breisgau, 1885–1900).

Dickens, A. G. *The English Reformation*, 2nd edn (London, 1989).

Dictionary of Medieval Latin from British Sources, ed. R. E. Latham and D. R. Howlett (London, 1975–, in progress).

Dobson, R. B. 'The Religious Orders 1370–1540', in *The History of the University of Oxford*, vol. ii: *Late Medieval Oxford*, ed. J. I. Catto and R. Evans (Oxford, 1992), 539–79.

Documents Relating to the University and Colleges of Cambridge, 3 vols (London, 1852).

Donatus, Aelius. *Ars Minor* and *Ars Grammatica*, in H. Keil, *Grammatici Latini*, vol. iv (Leipzig, 1864,

repr. Hildesheim, 1961), 355–66, 367–402.

Duff, E. Gordon. *Fifteenth-Century English Books*, Bibliographical Soc. Monographs, 18 (London, 1917).

Dugdale, William. *Monasticon Anglicanum, enriched with a large accession of materials*, ed. J. Caley, H. Ellis, and B. Bandinel, 6 vols in 8 parts (London, 1817–30).

Durkan, J. 'Education in the Century of the Reformation', in *Essays on the Scottish Reformation 1513–1625*, ed. D. McRoberts (Glasgow, 1962), 145–68.

Dyboski, R. (ed.). *Songs, Carols and Other Miscellaneous Pieces from the Balliol MS 354, Richard Hill's Commonplace-Book*, EETS, e.s., 101 (1908).

An Early Sixteenth-Century ABC in Latin after the Use of Sarum [ed. W. H. Allnutt (Lanhydrock, Cornwall, 1891)].

Easson, D. E. 'The Medieval Church in Scotland and Education', *Records of the Scottish Church History Soc.*, 6 (1938), 13–26.

Eddius Stephanus. *The Life of Bishop Wilfrid by Eddius Stephanus*, ed. B. Colgrave (Cambridge, 1927).

Edwards, Kathleen. *The English Secular Cathedrals in the Middle Ages*, 2nd edn (Manchester, 1967).

Elyot, Sir Thomas. *The Boke Named the Gouernour* (London, 1531, repr. Menston, Yorks., 1970).

Emden, A. B. *An Oxford Hall in Medieval Times: being the early history of St Edmund Hall* (Oxford, 1927).

Emden, A. B. *A Biographical Register of the University of Oxford to A.D. 1500*, 3 vols (Oxford, 1957–9).

Emden, A. B. *A Biographical Register of the University of Cambridge to 1500* (Cambridge, 1963).

Emden, A. B. *A Survey of Dominicans in England, 1268–1538*, Institutum Historicum FF Praedicatorum Romae ad S. Sabinae, Dissertationes Historicae, fasc. 18 (Rome, Istituto Storico Domenicano, Santa Sabina, 1967).

Emden, A. B. *A Biographical Register of the University of Oxford A.D. 1501 to 1540* (Oxford, 1974).

Erasmus, Desiderius. *The Lives of Jean Vitrier . . . and John Colet*, trans. J. H. Lupton (London, 1883).

Erasmus, Desiderius. *Opus Epistolarum*, ed. P. S. Allen, 12 vols (Oxford, 1906–58).

Evans, Evangeline. 'St Mary's College in Oxford for Austin Canons', *Oxford Arch. Soc. Report*, 76 (1931), 367–91.

Evans, S. J. A. 'Ely Chapter Ordinances and Visitation Records, 1241–1515', in *Camden Miscellany XVII*, Royal Hist. Soc., Camden 3rd series, 64 (1940), i–xx, 1–74.

Evans, S. J. A. 'Ely Almonry Boys and Choristers in the Later Middle Ages', in *Studies Presented to Sir Hilary Jenkinson*, ed. J. Conway Davies (London, 1957), 155–63.

Evrard of Béthune. *Eberhardi Bethuniensis Graecismus*, ed. J. Wrobel (Breslau, 1887).

Fairbrother, E. H. 'The Foundation of Bruton

School, Somerset', *Somerset and Dorset Notes and Queries*, 12 (1911), 49–52.

Feltoe, C. L., and E. H. Minns (eds). *Vetus Liber Archidiaconi Eliensis*, Cambridge Antiquarian Soc. Publications, 48 (1917).

Fenwick, Carolyn C. (ed.). *The Poll Taxes of 1377, 1379 and 1381*, 3 vols, British Academy Records of Social and Economic History, 27, 29, 37 (London 1998–2005).

Flynn, V. J. 'The Grammatical Writings of William Lily, ?1468–?1523', *Papers of the Bibliographical Soc. of America*, 37 (1943), 85–113.

Flynn, V. J. (ed.). *A Shorte Introduction of Grammar* (New York, 1945).

Fonge, C. (ed.). *The Cartulary of St Mary's Collegiate Church, Warwick* (Woodbridge, 2004).

Fortescue, Sir John. *De Laudibus Legum Anglie*, ed. and trans. S. B. Chrimes, Cambridge Studies in English Legal History (1942).

Foster, C. W., and A. Hamilton Thompson. 'The Chantry Certificates for Lincoln and Lincolnshire, Returned in 1548', *Reports and Papers Read at the Meetings of the Architectural Societies of the County of Lincoln*, 36 (1921–2), 183–294; 37 (1923–5), 18–106, 247–75.

Fowler, J. T. (ed.). *Extracts from the Account Rolls of the Abbey of Durham*, 2 vols, Surtees Soc., 99–100 (1898–9).

Fowler, J. T. (ed.). *The Rites of Durham*, Surtees Soc., 107 (1903).

Foxe, J. *Acts and Monuments*, ed. J. Pratt, 4th edn, 8 vols (London, 1877).

Frere, W. H., and W. McN. Kennedy (eds). *Visitation Articles and Injunctions of the Period of the Reformation, 1536–1575*, 3 vols, Alcuin Club Collections, 14–16 (1910).

Friedberg, E. (ed.). *Corpus Juris Canonici*, 2 vols (Leipzig, 1879–81).

Fryde, E. B., D. E. Greenway, S. Porter, and I. Roy, (eds). *Handbook of British Chronology*, 3rd edn (London, 1986).

Furnivall, F. J. (ed.). *Early English Meals and Manners*, EETS, o.s., 32 (1868, reissued 1931).

Gabel, Leona C. *Benefit of Clergy in England in the Later Middle Ages*, Smith College Studies in History, 14 (Northampton, Mass., 1929).

Galbraith, V. H. 'Some New Documents about Gloucester College', in *Snappe's Formulary and Other Records*, ed. H. E. Salter, Oxford Hist. Soc., 80 (1924), 337–86.

Galbraith, V. H. 'John Seward and His Circle', *Medieval and Renaissance Studies*, 1 (1941–3), 85–104; repr. in V. H. Galbraith, *Kings and Chroniclers: essays in English medieval history* (London, 1982).

Gardiner, Dorothy. *English Girlhood at School* (London, 1929).

Gardner, E. J. 'The English Nobility and Monastic Education, *c*.1100–1500', in *The Cloister and the World: Essays in Medieval History in Honour of Barbara Harvey*, ed. J. Blair and B. Golding (Oxford, 1994), 80–94.

Garmonsway, G. N. 'The Development of the Colloquy', in *The Anglo-Saxons*, ed. P. Clemoes (London, 1959), 248–61.

Gasquet, F. A. (ed.). *Collectanea Anglo-Premonstratensia*, 3 vols, Royal Hist. Soc., Camden 3rd series, 6, 10, 12 (1904–6).

Gerald of Wales. *Giraldi Cambrensis Opera*, ed. J. S. Brewer, J. F. Dimock, and G. F. Warner, 8 vols (RS, 1861–91).

Gesamtkatalog der Wiegendrucke, A-Eigenschaften (all completed), 7 vols (Leipzig, 1925–38).

Gibbs, Marion (ed.). *Early Charters of the Cathedral Church of St Paul, London*, Royal Hist. Soc., Camden 3rd series, 58 (1939).

Gibson, Strickland (ed.). *Statuta Antiqua Universitatis Oxoniensis* (Oxford, 1931).

Gieben, S. 'Robert Grosseteste and Medieval Courtesy-Books', *Vivarium*, 5 (1967), 47–74.

Gneuss, H. 'A Preliminary List of Manuscripts Written or Owned in England up to 1100', *Anglo-Saxon England*, 9 (1981), 1–60.

Golding, B. *Gilbert of Sempringham and the Gilbertine Order c.1130–c.1300* (Oxford, 1995).

Goodall, J. A. A. *God's House at Ewelme: life, devotion and architecture in a fifteenth-century almshouse* (Aldershot, 2001).

Grace Book A, Containing the Proctors' Accounts and Other Records of the University of Cambridge, 1454–1488, ed. S. M. Leathes, Luard Memorial Series, 1 (Cambridge, 1897).

Grace Book B. . . 1488–1511, ed. Mary Bateson, 2 vols, Luard Memorial Series, 2 (Cambridge, 1903–5).

Grace Book Γ, Containing the Records of the University of Cambridge 1501–1542, ed. W. G. Searle (Cambridge, 1908).

Grace Book Δ, Containing the Records of the University of Cambridge 1542–1589, ed. J. Venn (Cambridge, 1910).

Graham, Rose (ed.). *The Chantry Certificates for Oxfordshire*, Oxfordshire Record Soc., 1 (1919); Alcuin Club, 23 (1920).

Gransden, A. (ed.). *The Letter-Book of William of Hoo, Sacrist of Bury St Edmunds, 1280–1294*, Suffolk Records Soc., 5 (1963).

Gransden, A. (ed.). *The Customary of the Benedictine Abbey of Bury St Edmunds in Suffolk*, Henry Bradshaw Soc., 99 (1973).

Grant, J. *History of the Burgh and Parish Schools of Scotland* (London, 1876).

Graves, Edgar. *A Bibliography of English History to 1485* (Oxford, 1975).

Gray, A. (ed.). *The Earliest Statutes of Jesus College, Cambridge, issued by James Stanley, Bishop of Ely, 1514–1515* (Cambridge, 1935).

Gray, A., and F. Brittain. *A History of Jesus College, Cambridge* (London, 1960).

Gray, I. E., and W. E. Potter. *Ipswich School,*

1450–1950 (Ipswich, 1950).

Greatrex, Joan. 'The Almonry School of Norwich Cathedral Priory', in *The Church and Childhood*, ed. Diana Wood, Ecclesiastical History Soc., Studies in Church History, 31 (1994), 169–81.

Green, Alice Stopford. *Town Life in the Fifteenth Century*, 2 vols (London, 1894)

Greene, R. L. (ed.). *The Early English Carols*, 2nd edn (Oxford, 1977).

Gribbin, J. A. *The Premonstratensian Order in Late Medieval England* (Woodbridge, 2001).

Grondeux, Anne. *Le Graecismus d'Evrard de Béthune à travers ses gloses* (Turnhout, 2000).

Gunn, S. J., and P. G. Lindley (eds). *Cardinal Wolsey: Church, state, and art* (Cambridge, 1991).

Gunner, W. H. 'Catalogue of Books Belonging to the College of St Mary, Winchester, in the Reign of Henry VI', *Arch. Journal*, 15 (1858), 59–74.

Gurney, D. 'Extracts from the Household and Privy Purse Accounts of the Lestranges of Hunstanton', *Archaeologia*, 25 (1834), 411–569.

Gwara, S. *Education in Wales and Cornwall in the Ninth and Tenth Centuries: understanding* De Raris Fabulis, University of Cambridge, Hughes Hall and Deptment of Anglo-Saxon, Norse, and Celtic, Kathleen Hughes Memorial Lectures, 4 (Cambridge, 2004).

Gwosdek, Hedwig. *Early Printed Editions of the Long Accidence and Short Accidence Grammars* (Heidelberg, 1991).

Gwosdek, Hedwig. *A Checklist of English Grammatical Manuscripts and Early Printed Grammars, c.1400–1540*, Henry Sweet Soc. Studies in the History of Linguistics, 6 (Münster, 2000).

Hackett, M. B. *The Original Statutes of Cambridge University* (Cambridge, 1970).

Haddan, A. W., and W. Stubbs (eds). *Councils and Ecclesiastical Documents Relating to Great Britain and Ireland*, 3 vols (Oxford, 1869–78).

Hain, L. *Repertorium Bibliographicum . . . usque ad annum MD*, 2 vols (Stuttgart and Paris, 1826–31).

Haines, R. M. 'Aspects of the Episcopate of John Carpenter', *Journal of Ecclesiastical History*, 19 (1968), 11–40.

Hall, Edward. *Chronicle Containing the History of England [from] Henry IV to Henry VIII* (London, 1809).

Hamilton, G. L. 'Theodulus: A Medieval Textbook', *Modern Philology*, 7 no. 2 (1909), 1–17.

Hanawalt, Barbara A. *Growing Up in Medieval London* (New York and Oxford, 1993).

Harries, R., P. Cattermole, and P. Mackintosh. *A History of Norwich School* (Norwich, 1991).

Harrison, F. Ll. *Music in Medieval Britain*, 4th edn (Buren, Netherlands, 1980).

Harvey, B. 'A Novice's Life at Westminster Abbey in the Century before the Dissolution', in *The Religious Orders in Pre-Reformation England*, ed. J. G. Clark (Woodbridge, 2002), 51–73.

Hasted, E. *The History and Topographical Survey of the County of Kent*, 12 vols (Canterbury, 1797–1801, repr. East Ardley, 1972).

Hauréau, B. 'Notice sur les oeuvres authentiques ou supposées de Jean de Garlande', *Notices et extraits des mss de la Bibliothèque nationale*, 27 part ii (Paris, 1879), 1–86.

Hauréau, B. 'Additions et corrections [on Guillaume Brito]', *Histoire littéraire de la France*, 29 (Paris, 1885), 583–602.

Heath, Peter. *The English Parish Clergy on the Eve of the Reformation* (London, 1969).

Heywood, J., and Thomas Wright (eds). *The Ancient Laws . . . for King's College Cambridge and . . . Eton College* (London, 1850).

Higden, Ranulf. *Polychronicon Ranulphi Higden Monachi Cestrensis: together with the English translations*, ed. C. Babington and J. R. Lumby, 9 vols (RS, 1865–86).

Highfield, J. R. L. (ed.). *The Early Rolls of Merton College, Oxford*, Oxford Hist. Soc., n.s., 18 (1964).

Historical Manuscript Commission, Reports and Calendars (London, 1874–, in progress).

Hodnett, E. *English Woodcuts, 1480–1535*, 2nd edn (Oxford, 1973).

Holdsworth, Sir W. *A History of English Law*, 3rd edn, 16 vols and index (London, 1922–66).

Horman, William. *Vulgaria* (London, 1519, repr. Amsterdam, 1975).

Hornsby, F. W. D., and P. K. Griffin, *Katharine, Lady Berkeley's School Wotton-under-Edge, Gloucestershire* (Wotton-under-Edge, 1984).

Hughes, P. L., and J. F. Larkin (eds). *Tudor Royal Proclamations*, 3 vols (New Haven and London, 1964–9).

Hunt, R. W. 'English Learning in the Late Twelfth Century', *Transactions of the Royal Hist. Soc.*, 4th series, 19 (1936), 19–42.

Hunt, R. W. 'Studies on Priscian in the Eleventh and Twelfth Centuries', *Medieval and Renaissance Studies*, 1 (1941–3), 194–231.

Hunt, R. W. 'Studies on Priscian in the Twelfth Century, II: The School of Ralph of Beauvais', *Medieval and Renaissance Studies*, 2 (1950), 1–56.

Hunt, R. W. 'Hugutio and Peter Helias', *Medieval and Renaissance Studies*, 2 (1950), 174–8.

Hunt, R. W. 'The "Lost" Preface to the *Liber Derivationum* of Osbern of Gloucester', *Medieval and Renaissance Studies*, 4 (1958), 267–82.

Hunt, R. W. 'Oxford Grammar Masters in the Middle Ages', in *Oxford Studies Presented to Daniel Callus*, Oxford Hist. Soc., n.s., 16 (1964), 163–93.

Hunt, R. W. *The History of Grammar in the Middle Ages: Collected Papers*, ed. G. L. Bursill-Hall (Amsterdam, 1980).

Hunt, R. W. *The School and the Cloister: the life and writings of Alexander Nequam*, ed. M. T. Gibson (Oxford, 1984).

Hunt, Tony. *Teaching and Learning Latin in Thirteenth-Century England*, 3 vols (Cambridge, 1991).

Hunt, Tony. *Le Livre de Catun*, Anglo-Norman Text Soc., Plain Text Series, 11 (1994).

Isidore of Seville. *Isidori Hispalensis Episcopi Etymologiarum sive Originum*, ed. W. M. Lindsay, 2 vols (Oxford, 1911).

Ives, E. W. 'The Common Lawyers in Pre-Reformation England', *Transactions of the Royal Hist. Soc.*, 5th series, 18 (1968), 145–73.

Ives, E. W. 'The Common Lawyers', in *Profession, Vocation and Culture in Later Medieval England*, ed. C. H. Clough (Liverpool, 1982), 181–217.

James, M. R. *The Ancient Libraries of Canterbury and Dover* (Cambridge, 1903).

James, M. R. '[Eton] Chapel Inventories', *Etoniana*, 25–32 (1920–3), especially 28 (1921), 442–4.

Jeffery, P. *The Collegiate Churches of England and Wales* (London, 2004).

Jocelin of Brakelond. *The Chronicle of Jocelin of Brakelond*, ed. H. E. Butler (London, 1949).

John of Garland. *Morale Scolarium of John of Garland*, ed. L. J. Paetow, Memoirs of the University of California, 4 part ii (Berkeley, 1927), 65–273.

John of Garland. *Ars Lectoria Ecclesie*, ed. F. Marguin (Turnhout, 2003).

Jones, A. H. M. *The Later Roman Empire*, 3 vols (Oxford, 1964).

Jordan, W. K. *Philanthropy in England, 1480–1660* (London, 1959).

Jordan, W. K. *The Charities of London, 1480–1660* (London, 1960a).

Jordan, W. K. 'Charitable Institutions of the West of England', *Transactions of the American Philosophical Soc.*, n.s., 50 part 8 (1960b).

Jordan, W. K. *The Charities of Rural England, 1480–1660* (London, 1961a).

Jordan, W. K. *Social Institutions in Kent, 1480–1660*, in *Archaeologia Cantiana*, 75 (1961b).

Jordan, W. K. *The Social Institutions of Lancashire, 1480–1660*, Chetham Soc., 3rd series, 11 (1962).

Journals of the House of Commons, vol. i: 1547–1628 (London, 1803).

Journals of the House of Lords, vol. i: 1509–1577 (London, 1846).

Keene, D. *Survey of Medieval Winchester*, 2 parts, Winchester Studies, 2 (Oxford, 1985).

Keil, H. (ed.). *Grammatici Latini*, 7 vols (Leipzig, 1855–80, repr. Hildesheim, 1961).

Kelly, S. 'Anglo-Saxon Lay Society and the Written Word', in *The Uses of Literacy in Early Medieval Europe*, ed. R. McKitterick (Cambridge, 1990), 36–62.

Ker, N. *Medieval Manuscripts in British Libraries*, 5 vols (Oxford, 1969–2003).

Kingsford, C. L. *Prejudice and Promise in Fifteenth-Century England* (Oxford, 1925).

Kirby, T. F. *Winchester Scholars: a list of the wardens, fellows, and scholars* (London, 1888).

Kirby, T. F. *Annals of Winchester College, from its foundation in the Year 1382* (London, 1892).

Knowles, David. *The Religious Orders in England*, 3 vols (Cambridge, 1948–59).

Knowles, David. *The Monastic Order in England, 940–1216*, 2nd edn (Cambridge, 1963).

Knowles, David, and C. N. L. Brooke (eds). *The Monastic Constitutions of Lanfranc*, 2nd edn (Oxford, 2002).

Knowles, David, and R. N. Hadcock. *Medieval Religious Houses: England and Wales*, 2nd edn (London, 1971).

Kreider, Alan. *English Chantries: the road to dissolution* (Cambridge, Mass., and London, 1979).

Kristol, Andres M. (ed.). *Manières de langage*, Anglo-Norman Text Soc., 53 (1995).

Lambley, Kathleen. *The Teaching and Cultivation of the French Language in England during Tudor and Stuart Times* (London and Manchester, 1920).

Langland, William. *Piers the Plowman*, ed. W. W. Skeat, 2 vols (Oxford, 1886, reissued 1969).

Lapidge, M. 'Gildas's Education and the Latin Culture of Sub-Roman Britain', in *Gildas: New Approaches*, ed. M. Lapidge and D. Dumville (Woodbridge, 1984), 27–50.

Lapidge, M. 'Surviving Booklists from Anglo-Saxon England', in *Literature and Learning from Anglo-Saxon England*, ed. M. Lapidge and H. Gneuss (Cambridge, 1985), 33–89.

Lapidge, M. *Anglo-Latin Literature 900–1066* (London, 1993).

Lapidge, M. *Anglo-Latin Literature 600–899* (London, 1996).

Lapidge, M., and S. Keynes, *Alfred the Great: Asser's Life of King Alfred and Other contemporary sources* (London, 1983).

Lapidge, M., and R. I. Page. 'The Study of Latin Texts in Late Anglo-Saxon England', in *Latin and the Vernacular Languages in Early Medieval Britain*, ed. N. P. Brooks (Leicester, 1982), 99–165.

La Tour Landry, Geoffrey de. *The Book of the Knight of the Tower*, trans. William Caxton, ed. M. Y. Offord, EETS, s.s., 2 (1971).

Law, Vivien. *The Insular Latin Grammarians* (Woodbridge, 1982).

Law, Vivien. *Grammar and Grammarians in the Early Middle Ages* (London and New York, 1997).

Law, Vivien. 'Why Write a Verse Grammar?', *Journal of Medieval Latin*, 9 (1999), 46–76.

Law, Vivien. *The History of Linguistics in Europe from Plato to 1600* (Cambridge, 2003).

Lawson, J. *A Town Grammar School through Six Centuries: a history of Hull Grammar School* (London, 1963).

Leach, A. F. *English Schools at the Reformation, 1546–8*, 2 parts (Westminster, 1896).

Leach, A. F. 'The Foundation and Refoundation of Pocklington Grammar School', *Transactions of the East Riding Antiquarian Soc.*, 5 (1897), 63–114.

Leach, A. F. 'Sherborne School before, under, and after Edward VI', *Arch. Journal*, 54 (2nd series, 5) (1898), 1–83.

Leach, A. F. *A History of Winchester College* (London, 1899).

Leach, A. F. *Early Yorkshire Schools*, 2 vols, Yorkshire Arch. Soc., 27, 33 (1899–1903).

Leach, A. F. *History of Warwick School* (London, 1906).

Leach, A. F. 'St Paul's School before Colet', *Archaeologia*, 62 part 1 (1910), 191–238.

Leach, A. F. *Educational Charters and Documents, 598–1909* (Cambridge, 1911).

Leach, A. F. *Documents Illustrating Early Education in Worcester, 685–1700*, Worcestershire Hist. Soc., 31 (1913).

Leach, A. F. 'Some Results of Research in the History of Education in England: with suggestions for its continuance and extension', *Proceedings of the British Academy*, 6 (1913–14), 433–80.

Leach, A. F. *The Schools of Medieval England*, 2nd edn (London, 1916).

Leader, D. R. 'Grammar in Late-Medieval Oxford and Cambridge', *History of Education*, 12 (1983), 9–14.

Leader, D. R. *A History of the University of Cambridge*, vol. i: *The University to 1546* (Cambridge, 1988).

Lee, P. *Nunneries, Learning and Spirituality in Late Medieval English Society: The Dominican Priory of Dartford* (Woodbridge, 2001).

Leedham-Green, Elizabeth, D. E. Rhodes, and F. H. Stubbings. *Garrett Godfrey's Accounts c.1527–1533*, Cambridge Bibliographical Soc., Monograph 12 (1992).

Lefèvre, Y. 'De l'usage du français en Grande-Bretagne à la fin du XIIe siècle', in *Etudes de langue et de littérature du Moyen Age offertes à Félix Lecoy* (Paris, 1973), 301–5.

Lehmberg. S. E. *The Reformation of Cathedrals* (Princeton, 1988).

Leland, John. *The Itinerary of John Leland*, ed. Lucy Toulmin Smith, 5 vols (London, 1907–10).

Lendinara, P. *Anglo-Saxon Glosses and Glossaries* (Aldershot, 1999).

Le Neve, J. *Fasti Ecclesiae Anglicanae, 1300–1541*, ed. Joyce M. Horn, B. Jones, and H. P. F. King, 12 vols (London, 1962–7).

Le Neve, J. *Fasti Ecclesiae Anglicanae, 1066–1300*, ed. Diane E. Greenway (London, 1968–, in progress).

Levett, A. Elizabeth. *Studies in Manorial History*, ed. Helen M. Cam and others (Oxford, 1938).

Little, A. G. *The Grey Friars in Oxford*, Oxford Hist. Soc., 20 (1892).

Little, A. G. 'Educational Organisation of the Mendicant Friars in England (Dominicans and Franciscans)', *Transactions of the Royal Hist. Soc.*, n.s., 8 (1894), 49–70.

Little, A. G. 'Review of A. F. Leach, *The Schools of Medieval England*', *English Hist. Review*, 30 (1915), 525–9.

Little, A. G. *Studies in English Franciscan History* (Manchester, 1917).

Little, A. G. 'Theological Schools in Medieval England', *English Hist. Review*, 55 (1940), 624–30.

Lloyd, A. H. *The Early History of Christ's College, Cambridge* (Cambridge, 1934).

Lobel, M. D. *Historic Towns* (also *Atlas of Historic Towns*), 3 vols (London and Oxford, 1969–89).

Lupton, J. H. *A Life of John Colet*, 2nd edn (London, 1909).

Lyndwood, William. *Provinciale* (Oxford, 1679, repr. Farnborough, 1968).

McConica, James (ed.). *The History of the University of Oxford*, vol. iii: *The Collegiate University* (Oxford, 1986).

McDonnell, M. F. J. *A History of St Paul's School* (London, 1909).

McDonnell, M. F. J. *The Annals of St Paul's School* (London, 1959).

McFarlane, K. B. *Lancastrian Kings and Lollard Knights* (Oxford, 1972).

McFarlane, K. B. *The Nobility of Later Medieval England* (Oxford, 1973).

McGrath, F. *Education in Ancient and Medieval Ireland* (Dublin, 1979).

Mackinnon, H. 'William de Montibus: a medieval teacher', in *Essays in Medieval History Presented to Bertie Wilkinson*, ed. T. A. Sandquist and M. R. Powicke (Toronto, 1969), 32–45.

Maclean, Sir J. 'Chantry Certificates, Gloucestershire', *Transactions of the Bristol and Gloucestershire Arch. Soc.*, 8 (1883–4), 229–308.

Madan, F. 'The Daily Ledger of John Dorne', in *Collectanea I*, ed. C. R. L. Fletcher, Oxford Hist. Soc., 5 (1885), 71–177.

Magrath, J. R. *The Queen's College, Oxford*, 2 vols (Oxford, 1921).

'Malpas Grammar School', *Transactions of the Historic Soc. of Lancashire and Cheshire*, 65 (n.s., 29) (1914), 194–211.

Mander, G. P. *The History of Wolverhampton Grammar School* (Wolverhampton, 1913).

Mansi, J. D. (ed.). *Sacrorum Conciliorum Nova et Amplissima Collectio*, 31 vols (Florence and Venice, 1759–98, repr., 53 vols in 59 parts, Paris, 1901–7, Graz, 1960–2).

Mantello, F. A. C., and A. G. Rigg (eds). *Medieval Latin: An Introduction and Bibliographical Guide* (Washington, D.C., 1996).

Marigo, A. I. *Codici manoscritti delle 'Derivationes' di Uguccione Pisano* (Rome, 1936).

Marrou, H. I. *A History of Education in Antiquity* (London, 1956).

Mayr-Harting, H. *The Coming of Christianity to Anglo-Saxon England*, 3rd edn (London, 1991).

Maxwell-Lyte, H. C. *History of Eton College, 1440–1910*, 4th edn (London, 1911).

Meech, S. B. 'John Drury and his English Writings', *Speculum*, 9 (1934), 70–83.

Meech, S. B. 'Early Application of Latin Grammar to English', *Proceedings of the Modern Language*

Association of America, 50 (1935a), 1012–32.

Meech, S. B. 'An Early Treatise in English Concerning Latin Grammar', *University of Michigan Publications, Language and Literature*, 13 (1935b), 81–125.

Meyer, P. 'Les Manuscrits français de Cambridge', *Romania*, 32 (1903), 47–58.

Middle English Dictionary, ed. Hans Kurath and Sherman M. Kuhn (Ann Arbor, Mich., and London, 1956–2002).

Migne, J. P. (ed.). *Patrologia Cursus Completus, sive Universalis. Series (Latina) prima*, 106 vols (Paris, 1844–64). *Series (Latina) secunda*, 111 vols (Paris, 1855–64). *Indices*, 4 vols (Paris, 1862–5).

Miner, J. N. T. [alias Br. Bonaventure]. 'The Teaching of Latin in Later Medieval England', *Mediaeval Studies*, 23 (1961), 1–20.

Miner, J. N. T. [alias Br. Bonaventure]. 'Schools and Literacy in Late Medieval England', *British Journal of Educational Studies*, 11 (1962–3), 16–27.

Miner, J. N. T. [alias Br. Bonaventure]. *The Grammar Schools of Medieval England: A. F. Leach in historiographical perspective* (Montreal and Kingston, 1990).

Mitchell, W. T. (ed.). *Register of Congregations 1505–1517*, 2 vols, Oxford Hist. Soc., n.s., 37–8 (1998).

Moberly, G. H. *Life of William of Wykeham*, 2nd edn (Winchester, 1893).

Moorman, J. R. H. *Church Life in England in the Thirteenth Century* (Cambridge, 1945).

Moorman, J. R. H. *The Grey Friars in Cambridge, 1225–1538* (Cambridge, 1952).

Moran, Jo Ann Hoeppner. *Education and Learning in the City of York, 1300–1560*, Borthwick Papers, 55 (York, 1979).

Moran, Jo Ann Hoeppner. *The Growth of English Schooling 1340–1548: learning, literacy, and laicization in pre-Reformation York diocese* (Princeton, 1985).

Morawski, J. (ed.). *Le Facet en françoys* (Poznan, 1923).

Morgan, T. J. *Literate Education in the Hellenistic and Roman Worlds* (Cambridge, 1998).

Mulcahey, M. M. *'First the Bow is Bent in Study': Dominican education before 1350*, Toronto, Pontifical Institute of Mediaeval Studies, Studies and Texts, 132 (1998).

Myers, A. R. *The Household of Edward IV* (Manchester, 1959).

Myers, A. R. 'The Household of Queen Elizabeth Woodville, 1466–7', *Bulletin of the John Rylands Library*, 50 (1967–8), 207–35, 433–81.

Napier, A. S. (ed.). *The Old English Version of the Enlarged Rule of Chrodegang*, EETS, o.s., 150 (1916).

Nelson, W. (ed.). *A Fifteenth-Century School Book* (Oxford, 1956).

Nicholls, J. W. *The Matter of Courtesy* (Woodbridge, 1985).

Nichols, J. G., and E. F. Rimbault, 'Two Sermons Preached by the Boy Bishop', *Camden Miscellany*, Camden Soc., n.s., 14 (1875).

Nicolas, N. H. (ed.). *Testamenta Vetusta, being illustrations from wills of manners, customs, etc.*, 2 vols (London, 1826).

Nicolson, J., and R. Burn. *History and Antiquities of Westmorland and Cumberland*, 2 vols (London, 1777).

Oakley, R. R. *A History of Oswestry School* (London, 1964).

Oliva, M. *The Convent and the Community in Late Medieval England: female monasteries in the diocese of Norwich, 1350–1540* (Woodbridge, 1998).

Oliver, G. *Monasticon Dioecesis Exoniensis* (Exeter and London, 1846).

Orderic Vitalis. *The Ecclesiastical History of Orderic Vitalis*, ed. M. Chibnall, 6 vols (Oxford, 1968–80).

Orme, Nicholas. *English Schools in the Middle Ages* (London and New York, 1973).

Orme, Nicholas. *Education in the West of England, 1066–1548* (Exeter, 1976).

Orme, Nicholas. 'The Early Musicians of Exeter Cathedral', *Music and Letters*, 59 (1978a), 395–410.

Orme, Nicholas. 'Education in the West of England: Additions', *Devon and Cornwall Notes and Queries*, 34 (1978b), 22–5.

Orme, Nicholas. 'The Dissolution of the Chantries in Devon, 1546–8', *Devonshire Association Transactions*, 111 (1979), 75–123.

Orme, Nicholas. *The Minor Clergy of Exeter Cathedral, 1300–1548* (Exeter, 1980a).

Orme, Nicholas. 'The Church in Crediton from St Boniface to the Reformation', in *The Greatest Englishman*, ed. T. A. Reuter (Exeter, 1980b), 97–131.

Orme, Nicholas. 'Two Tudor Schoolmaster-Musicians', *Somerset and Dorset Notes and Queries*, 31 (1980c), 19–26.

Orme, Nicholas. 'The Medieval Clergy of Exeter Cathedral: II, the Secondaries and Choristers', *Devonshire Association Transactions*, 115 (1983), 79–100.

Orme, Nicholas. *From Childhood to Chivalry: the education of the English kings and aristocracy, 1066–1530* (London and New York, 1984).

Orme, Nicholas. 'Hunting and Education in England, 1100–1600', *Proceedings of the XIth HISPA International Congress*, ed. J. A. Mangan (Glasgow, 1987), 74–6.

Orme, Nicholas. 'Martin Coeffin, the First Exeter Publisher', *The Library*, 6th series, 10 (1988), 220–30.

Orme, Nicholas. *Education and Society in Medieval and Renaissance England* (London and Ronceverte, 1989a).

Orme, Nicholas (ed.). *Table Manners for Children: Stans Puer ad Mensam* (Salisbury, 1989b, repr. London, 1990).

Orme, Nicholas. 'The Byconyll Exhibitions at Oxford, 1502–1664', *Oxoniensia*, 55 (1990a), 115–21.

Orme, Nicholas. 'More Pages from a Barlinch School-Book', *Somerset Archaeology and Natural History*, 134 (1990b), 183–5.

Orme, Nicholas. 'Music and Teaching at Tywardreath Priory, 1522–36', *Devon and Cornwall Notes and Queries*, 36 part 7 (1990c), 277–80.

Orme, Nicholas. 'Glastonbury Abbey and Education', in *The Early History and Archaeology of Glastonbury Abbey*, ed. Lesley Abrams and J. P. Carley (Woodbridge, 1991), 285–99.

Orme, Nicholas. 'Education in the Cornish Play *Beunans Meriasek*', Cambridge Medieval Celtic Studies, 25 (1993), 1–13.

Orme, Nicholas. 'An English Grammar School ca. 1450: Latin Exercises from Exeter (Caius College MS 417/447), Folios 16v–24v', *Traditio*, 50 (1995), 261–94.

Orme, Nicholas. 'Lay Literacy in England, 1100–1300', in *England and Germany in the High Middle Ages*, ed. A. Haverkamp and H. Vollrath (London and Oxford, 1996a), 35–56.

Orme, Nicholas. 'John Holt (d. 1504), Tudor Grammarian', *The Library*, 6th series, 18 (1996b), 283–305.

Orme, Nicholas. 'The Medieval Schools of Herefordshire', *Nottingham Medieval Studies*, 40 (1996c), 47–62.

Orme, Nicholas. *Education in Early Tudor England: Magdalen College Oxford and Its School, 1480–1540* (Oxford, 1998, repr. with corrections 2003).

Orme, Nicholas. 'Schools and Schoolbooks, 1400–1550', in *A History of the Book in Britain*, vol. iii: *1400–1557*, ed. J. B. Trapp and Lotte Hellinga (Cambridge, 1999), 449–69.

Orme, Nicholas. 'The Cathedral School before the Reformation', in *Hereford Cathedral: a history*, ed. Gerald Aylmer and John Tiller (London, 2000), 565–78.

Orme, Nicholas. *Medieval Children* (London and New Haven, 2001).

Orme, Nicholas. 'Education in Medieval Bristol and Gloucestershire', *Transactions of the Bristol and Gloucestershire Arch. Soc.*, 112 (2004a), 9–27.

Orme, Nicholas. 'A Boy at Ewelme School, 1464–5', *Oxoniensia*, 69 (2004b), 45–9.

Orme, Nicholas. 'Education and Recreation', in *Gentry Culture in Late-Medieval England*, ed. R. Radulescu and A. Truelove, 63–83 (Manchester, 2005).

Orme, Nicholas. 'Schools and Schoolmasters', in *A History of Libraries in Britain and Ireland*, vol. i, ed. Elizabeth Leedham-Green (Cambridge, forthcoming).

Orme, Nicholas, and Margaret Webster. *The English Hospital: 1070 to 1570* (New Haven and London, 1995).

Owen, A. E. B. (ed.). *The Medieval Lindsey Marsh*, Lincoln Record Soc., 85 (1996).

Owen, Dorothy M., and Dorothea Thurley (eds). *The King's School Ely*, Cambridge Antiquarian Records Soc., 5 (1982).

The Oxford Dictionary of National Biography, 2nd edn, 60 vols, ed. C. Matthew and B. Harrison (Oxford, 2004).

The Oxford English Dictionary, ed. J. A. Simpson and E. S. C. Weiner, 2nd edn, 20 vols (Oxford, 1989)

Pafort, Edith. 'A Group of Early Tudor School Books', *The Library*, 4th series, 26 no. 4 (1946), 227–61.

Page, W. (ed.). *The Certificates of the Commissioners Appointed to Survey the Chantries, etc., in the County of York*, 2 vols, Surtees Soc., 91–2 (1894–5).

Pantin, W. A. 'Abbot Kidderminster and Monastic Studies', *Downside Review*, 47 (1929), 199–211.

Pantin, W. A. (ed.). *Chapters of the English Black Monks, 1215–1540*, 3 vols, Royal Hist. Soc., Camden 3rd series, 45, 47, 54 (1931–7).

Pantin, W. A. *Canterbury College Oxford*, 4 vols, Oxford Hist. Soc., n.s., 6–8, 30 (1947–85).

Pantin, W. A. *Oxford Life in Oxford Archives* (Oxford, 1972).

Pantin, W. A., and W. T. Mitchell (eds). *The Register of Congregation 1448–1463*, Oxford Hist. Soc., n.s., 22 (1972).

Parry-Jones, Brenda, and Derrick Wales. *Five Hundred Years of Magdalen College School Wainfleet 1484–1984* (Wainfleet, 1984).

Paston Letters and Papers of the Fifteenth Century, ed. Norman Davis, 2 vols (Oxford, 1971–6).

Peacock, G. *Observations on the Statutes of the University of Cambridge* (London, 1841).

Percy, T. (ed.). *The Regulations and Establishment of the Household of Henry Algernon Percy, Fifth Earl of Northumberland* (London, 1770, repr. 1905).

Peter Helias. *Summa super Priscianum*, ed. L. Reilly, 2 vols, Toronto, Pontifical Institute of Mediaeval Studies, Studies and Texts, 113 (1993).

Plimpton, George A. *The Education of Chaucer* (London and New York, 1935).

The Plumpton Letters and Papers, ed. Joan Kirby, Royal Hist. Soc., Camden 5th series, 8 (1996).

Pollard, A. W., and G. R. Redgrave. *A Short Title Catalogue of Books Printed in England, Scotland, and Ireland, 1475–1640*, 2nd edn, 3 vols (London, 1976–91).

Pollock, F., and F. W. Maitland. *The History of English Law before the Time of Edward I*, 2nd edn, 2 vols (Cambridge, 1968).

Poos, L. R. (ed.). *Lower Ecclesiastical Jurisdiction in Late-Medieval England*, British Academy Records of Social and Economic History, n.s., 32 (London, 2001).

Porter, D. W. (ed.). *Excerptiones de Prisciano* (Woodbridge, 2002).

Power, Eileen. *Medieval English Nunneries, c.1275 to 1535* (Cambridge, 1922).

Prescott, J. E. 'The Grammar School of Carlisle', *Transactions of the Cumberland and Westmorland Antiquarian and Arch. Soc.*, n.s., 16 (1916), 1–28.

Priscian. *Ars Grammatica*, in *Grammatici Latini*, ed. H. Keil, vol. ii; vol. iii, 1–377 (Leipzig, 1855–8, repr. Hildesheim, 1961). See also Porter, D. W.

Promptorium Parvulorum sive Clericorum Lexicon Anglo-Latinum, c.1440, ed. A. Way, 3 vols, Camden Soc., 25, 54, 89 (1843–65).

Rackham, Harris (ed.). *The Early Statutes of Christ's College, Cambridge, with the Statutes of the Prior Foundation of God's House* (Cambridge, 1927).

Ramsay, N., M. Sparks, and T. Tatton-Brown (eds). *St Dunstan: his life, times and cult* (Woodbridge, 1992).

Rashdall, Hastings. *The Universities of Europe in the Middle Ages*, ed. F. M. Powicke and A. B. Emden, 3 vols (Oxford, 1936).

Read, Conyers. *Bibliography of British History: Tudor Period, 1485–1603*, 2nd edn (Oxford, 1959).

Regesta Regum Anglo-Normannorum, 1066–1154, ed. H. W. C. Davis et al., 5 vols (Oxford, 1913–69); vol. i, 2nd edn, ed. D. Bates (Oxford, 1998).

Reginald of Durham. *Reginaldi Monachi Dunelmensis Libellus*, ed. J. Raine, Surtees Soc., 1 (1835).

Reginald of Durham. *Libellus de Vita et Miraculis S. Godrici*, ed. J. Stevenson, Surtees Soc., 20 (1847).

The Register of John de Grandisson, Bishop of Exeter, ed. F. C. Hingeston-Randolph, 3 vols (London and Exeter, 1894–7).

The Register of Thomas de Brantyngham, Bishop of Exeter, ed. F. C. Hingeston-Randolph, 2 vols (London and Exeter, 1901–6).

The Register of Walter de Stapeldon, Bishop of Exeter, ed. F. C. Hingeston-Randolph (London and Exeter, 1892).

Regularis Concordia, ed. T. Symons (London, 1953).

Reichert, B. M. (ed.). *Monumenta Ordinis Fratrum Praedicatorum Historica*, 14 vols (Rome and Stuttgart, 1897–1904).

Richardson, H. G. *An Oxford Teacher of the Fifteenth Century* (Manchester[?], 1939); repr. with corrections from *Bulletin of the John Rylands Library*, 23 (1939) 436–57.

Richardson, H. G. 'Business Training in Medieval Oxford', *American Hist. Review*, 46 (1941a), 259–80.

Richardson, H. G. 'The Schools of Northampton in the Twelfth Century', *English Hist. Review*, 56 (1941b), 595–605.

Richardson, W. C. *History of the Court of Augmentations, 1536–1554* (Baton Rouge, 1961).

Riché, P. *Education and Culture in the Barbarian West, Sixth through Eighth Centuries* (Columbia, S.C., 1976).

Riché, P. *Les Ecoles et l'enseignement dans l'Occident chrétien de la fin du Ve siècle au milieu du XIe siècle* (Paris, 1979).

Riché, P., and D. Alexandre-Bidon. *L'Enfance au Moyen Age* (Paris, 1994).

Richmond, C. *John Hopton: a Fifteenth-Century Suffolk Gentleman* (Cambridge, 1981).

Rickert, Edith. 'Extracts from a Fourteenth-Century Account Book', *Modern Philology*, 24 (1926–7), 111–19, 249–56.

Rickert, Edith. 'Chaucer at School', *Modern Philology*, 29 (1931–2), 258–74.

Rickert, Edith. *Chaucer's World* (London, 1948).

Riley, H. T. (ed.). *Gesta Abbatum Monasterii Sancti Albani*, 3 vols (RS, 1867–9).

Riley, H. T. (ed.). *Registrum Johannis Whethamstede*, 2 vols (RS, 1872–3).

Robbins, R. H. *Secular Lyrics of the Fourteenth and Fifteenth Centuries*, 2nd edn (Oxford, 1955).

Robertson, Dora H. 'Notes on some Buildings in the City and Close of Salisbury', *Wiltshire Arch. and Natural History Magazine*, 48 (1937–9), 1–30.

Robertson, Dora H. *Sarum Close: a picture of domestic life . . . and the history of the choristers*, 2nd edn (Bath, 1970).

Robertson, J. C. (ed.). *Materials for the History of Thomas Becket*, 7 vols (RS, 1875–85).

Robinson, F. C. 'Syntactical Glosses in Latin Manuscripts of Anglo-Saxon Provenance', *Speculum*, 48 (1973), 443–75.

Roest, Bert. *A History of Franciscan Education (c.1210–1517)* (Leiden and Boston, 2000).

Roth, F. *Sources for a History of the English Austin Friars*, reprinted from *Augustiniana*, 8–11 (Louvain, 1958–61).

Roth, F. *The English Austin Friars, 1249–1538* (New York, 1966).

Rothwell, W. 'The Role of French in Thirteenth-Century England', *Bulletin of the John Rylands Library*, 58 (1975–6), 445–66.

Rotuli Parliamentorum, ed. J. Strachey, 6 vols (London, 1767–77). *Index to the Rolls of Parliament*, ed. J. Strachey et al. (London, 1832).

The Rule of St Benedict, edn O. Hunter Blair, 5th edn (Fort Augustus, 1948).

Salter, H. E. (ed.). *A Subsidy Collected in the Diocese of Lincoln in 1526*, Oxford Hist. Soc., 63 (1909).

Salter, H. E. (ed.). *Chapters of the English Augustinian Canons*, Oxford Hist. Soc., 74 (1922).

Salter, H. E. (ed.). *Registrum Cancellarii Oxoniensis, 1434–1469*, 2 vols, Oxford Hist. Soc., 93–4 (1932).

Salter, H. E., W. A. Pantin, and H. G. Richardson (eds). *Formularies Which Bear on the History of Oxford, c. 1204–1420*, 2 vols, Oxford Hist. Soc., n.s., 4–5 (1942).

Saunders, H. W. 'A History of Coxford Priory', *Norfolk Archaeology*, 17 (1908–10), 284–370.

Saunders, H. W. *A History of the Norwich Grammar School* (Norwich, 1932).

Seaborne, M. V. J. *The English School, its Architecture and Organization, 1370–1970* (London, 1971).

Searle, E. *Lordship and Community: Battle Abbey and its banlieu 1066–1538* (Toronto, 1974).

Searle, W. G. *Christ Church, Canterbury*, Cambridge

Antiquarian Soc. Publications, 34 (1902).

Sharpe, R. *A Handlist of the Latin Writers of Great Britain and Ireland before 1540* (Brussels, 1997).

Sharpe, R. R. (ed.). *Calendar of Wills Proved and Enrolled in the Court of Husting, London, 1258–1688*, 2 vols (London, 1889–90).

Sheppard, J. Brigstocke (ed.). *Literae Cantuarienses, the letter books of the monastery of Christ Church, Canterbury*, 3 vols (RS, 1887–9).

Shinners, J., and W. J. Dohar (eds). *Pastors and the Care of Souls in Medieval England* (Notre Dame, Ind., 1998).

Simon, Joan. 'A. F. Leach on the Reformation', *British Journal of Educational Studies*, 3 (1954–5), 128–43; 4 (1955–6), 32–48.

Simon, Joan. 'The Reformation and English Education', *Past and Present*, 11 (1957) 48–65.

Simon, Joan. 'A. F. Leach: A Reply', *British Journal of Educational Studies*, 12 (1963–4), 41–50.

Simon, Joan. *Education and Society in Tudor England* (Cambridge, 1966).

Simpson, A. W. B. 'The Early Constitution of the Inns of Court', *Cambridge Law Journal*, 28 part 2 (1970), 241–56.

Simpson, W. S. (ed.). *Registrum Statutorum et Consuetudinum Ecclesiae Cathedralis Sancti Pauli Londiniensis* (London, 1873).

Smith, R. 'The Library at Guildhall in the Fifteenth and Sixteenth Centuries', *Guildhall Miscellany*, 1 (1952), 3–9; 6 (1956), 2–6.

Sneyd, Charlotte Augusta (ed.). *A Relation . . . of the Island of England*, Camden Soc., 37 (1847).

Stanbridge, John. *The Vulgaria of John Stanbridge and Robert Whittinton*, ed. Beatrice White, EETS, o.s., 187 (1932).

Starkey, Thomas. *England in the Reign of King Henry VIII: Part I, Starkey's Life and Letters*, ed. S. J. Herrtage, EETS, e.s., 32 (1878).

Starkey, Thomas. *A Dialogue between Pole and Lupset*, ed. T. F. Mayer, Royal Hist. Soc., Camden 4th series, 37 (1989).

Statutes of the Colleges of Oxford, 3 vols (London and Oxford, 1853).

The Statutes of the Realm, from Magna Carta to the end of the reign of Queen Anne, 10 vols (London, Record Commission, 1810–24).

Stenton, F. M. *Norman London, with a Translation of William FitzStephen's Description by H. E. Butler*, London, Hist. Association Leaflets, 93–4 (London, 1934).

Sterry, Sir Wasey. *The Eton College Register, 1441–1698* (Eton, 1943).

Stevenson, W. H. 'The Introduction of English as the Vehicle of Instruction in English Schools', in *An English Miscellany Presented to F. J. Furnivall* (Oxford, 1901), 421–9.

Stevenson, W. H. (ed.). *Early Scholastic Colloquies*, Anecdota Oxoniensia, Medieval and Modern Series, 15 (Oxford, 1929).

Stevenson, W. H., and H. E. Salter. *The Early History of St John's College, Oxford*, Oxford Hist. Soc., n.s., 1 (1939).

Stocks, G. A. *The Records of Blackburn Grammar School*, 3 vols, Chetham Soc., n.s., 66–8 (1909).

Stokes, H. P. *The Medieval Hostels of the University of Cambridge*, Cambridge Antiquarian Soc. Publications, 49 (1924).

The Stonor Letters and Papers, 1290–1483, ed. C. L. Kingsford, 2 vols, Royal Hist. Soc., Camden 3rd series, 29–30 (1919).

Storey, R. L. 'The Chantries of Cumberland and Westmorland, Part II', *Transactions of the Cumberland and Westmorland Antiquarian and Arch. Soc.*, n.s., 62 (1962), 145–70.

Stow, John. *A Survey of London*, ed. C. L. Kingsford, 2 vols (Oxford, 1908).

Suggett, Helen. 'The Use of French in the Later Middle Ages', *Transactions of the Royal Hist. Soc.*, 4th series, 28 (1946), 61–83.

Sulpizio, G. *Doctrina Mensae, table manners for boys*, ed. H. Thomas (Oxford, 1949).

Summerson, H. *Medieval Carlisle*, 2 vols, Cumberland and Westmorland Antiquarian and Arch. Soc., e.s., 25 (1993).

Talbot, C. H. *The Anglo-Saxon Missionaries in Germany* (London, 1954).

Tanner, Norman P. (ed.). *Decrees of the Ecumenical Councils*, 2 vols (London and Washington, 1990).

Tate, W. E. *A. F. Leach as a Historian of Yorkshire Education: with an index of the Yorkshire schools, c.730 to c.1770, referred to in his works*, York, St Anthony's Hall Publications, 23 (1963).

Taylor, A. H. 'The Grammar Free School at Tenterden', *Archaeologia Cantiana*, 44 (1932), 129–46.

Testamenta Eboracensia, ed. J. Raine, 6 vols, Surtees Soc., 4, 30, 45, 53, 79, 106 (1836–1902).

Tester, P. J. 'Notes on the Medieval Chantry College at Cobham', *Archaeologia Cantiana*, 79 (1964), 109–20.

Theodulus. *Theoduli Eclogam*, ed. J. Osternacher (Linz, 1902).

Theodulus. *Ecloga*, ed. F. M. Casaretto (Florence, 1997).

Thomas, Keith. *Rule and Misrule in the Schools of Early Modern England* (Reading, 1976).

Thompson, A. Hamilton (ed.). *Visitations of Religious Houses in the Diocese of Lincoln, 1420–1449*, 3 vols, C&Y, 17, 24, 33 (1915–27); Lincoln Record Soc., 7, 14, 21 (1914–29).

Thompson, A. Hamilton. 'The Statutes of the College of St. Mary and All Saints, Fotheringhay', *Arch. Journal*, 75 (2nd series, 25) (1918), 241–309.

Thompson, A. Hamilton. 'The Registers of the Archdeaconry of Richmond, 1361–1442', *Yorkshire Arch. Journal*, 25 (1919), 129–268.

Thompson, A. Hamilton (ed.). *The Statutes of the Cathedral Church of Durham*, Surtees Soc., 143 (1929).

Thompson, A. Hamilton (ed.). *Visitations in the*

Diocese of Lincoln, 1517–1531, 3 vols, Lincoln Record Soc., 33, 35, 37 (1940–7).

Thompson, A. Hamilton. *Song Schools in the Middle Ages*, Church Music Soc. Occasional Papers, 14 (1942).

Thompson, A. Hamilton. *The English Clergy and Their Organization in the Later Middle Ages* (Oxford, 1947).

Thompson, H. L. *Christ Church*, University of Oxford College Histories (London, 1900).

Thompson, J. W. *The Literacy of the Laity in the Middle Ages*, University of California Publications in Education, 9 (Berkeley, Calif., 1939).

Thomson, David. *A Descriptive Catalogue of Middle English Grammatical Texts* (New York and London, 1979).

Thomson, David. 'Cistercians and Schools in Late Medieval Wales', *Cambridge* [later *Cambrian*] *Medieval Celtic Studies*, 3 (1982), 76–80.

Thomson, David. 'The Oxford Grammar Masters Revisited', *Mediaeval Studies*, 45 (1983), 298–310.

Thomson, David. *An Edition of the Middle English Grammatical Texts* (New York and London, 1984).

Thomson, I., and L. Perraud. *Ten Latin Schoolbooks of the Later Middle Ages* (Lewiston, N.Y., 1990).

Thrupp, Sylvia L. *The Merchant Class of Medieval London* (Chicago, 1948).

Thurot, Charles. 'Notices et extraits de divers manuscrits latins pour servir à l'histoire des doctrines grammaticales au moyen âge', *Notices et extraits des manuscrits de la Bibliothèque impériale*, 22 part 2 (Paris, 1868), 1–592.

Ullman, W. (ed.). *Liber Regie Capelle*, Henry Bradshaw Soc., 92 (1961).

Valor Ecclesiasticus tempore Henrici VIII auctoritate regis institutus, ed. J. Caley, 6 vols (London, Record Commission, 1810–24).

Varley, B. *History of Stockport Grammar School*, 2nd edn (Manchester, 1957).

Vickerstaff, J. J. 'A Gazetteer of Durham County Schools', *Durham County Local History Soc. Bulletin*, 41 (December 1988), 3–14.

Victoria History of the Counties of England: articles on medieval schools:
    Bedfordshire, vol. ii (1908), 149–86, by A. F. Leach.
    Berkshire, vol. ii (1907), 245–84, by A. F. Leach.
    Buckinghamshire, vol. ii (1908), 145–222, by A. F. Leach.
    Cambridgeshire, vol. ii (1948), 319–56, by E. M. Hampson.
    Cheshire, vol. iii (1980), 223–54, by A. T. Thacker.
    Derbyshire, vol. ii (1907), 207–82, by A. F. Leach.
    Durham, vol. i (1905), 365–413, by A. F. Leach.
    Essex, vol. ii (1907), 501–64, by C. Fell-Smith and A. F. Leach.
    Gloucestershire, vol. ii (1907), 313–448, by A. F. Leach.
    Hampshire, vol. ii (1903), 150–408, by A. F. Leach.
    Hertfordshire, vol. ii (1908), 47–102, by A. F. Leach.
    Huntingdonshire, vol. ii (1932), 107–19, by C. G. Parsloe.
    Lancashire, vol. ii (1908), 561–624, by H. J. Chaytor and A. F. Leach.
    Lincolnshire, vol. ii (1906), 421–92, by A. F. Leach.
    Middlesex, vol. i (1969), 290–314, by J. D. Mellor and H. P. F. King.
    Northamptonshire, vol. ii (1906), 201–88, by A. F. Leach.
    Nottinghamshire, vol. ii (1910), 179–264, by A. F. Leach and F. Fletcher.
    Oxfordshire, vol. i (1939), 457–90, vol. iii (1954), 40–3, by M. D. Lobel and M. Midgley.
    Rutland, vol. i (1908), 259–300, by F. Fletcher.
    Shropshire, vol. ii (1973), 141–64, by D. T. W. Price and A. T. Gaydon.
    Somerset, vol. ii (1911), 435–66, by T. Scott Holmes and A. F. Leach.
    Staffordshire, vol. vi (1979), 149–81, by D. A. Johnson, C. R. J. Currie, and M. W. Greenslade.
    Suffolk, vol. ii (1907), 301–55, by A. F. Leach and E. P. Steele-Hutton.
    Surrey, vol. ii (1905), 155–242, by A. F. Leach.
    Sussex, vol. ii (1907), 397–440, by A. F. Leach.
    Warwickshire, vol. ii (1908), 197–373, by A. F. Leach.
    Wiltshire, vol. v (1957), 348–68, by E. E. Butcher.
    Worcestershire, vol. iv (1914–24), 473–540, by A. F. Leach.
    Yorkshire, vol. i (1907), 415–500, by A. F. Leach.

Vives, J. L. *Vives on Education*, trans. Foster Watson (Cambridge, 1913).

Wadley, T. P. (ed.). *Notes or Abstracts of the Wills in the Great Orphan Book and Book of Wills, Bristol* (Bristol, Bristol and Gloucestershire Arch. Soc., 1886).

Wallis, P. J. 'The Wase School Collection: a neglected source in educational history', *Bodleian Library Record*, 4 (1952), 78–104.

Wallis, P. J. 'Leach – Past, Present, and Future', *British Journal of Educational Studies*, 12 (1963–4), 78–194.

Wallis, P. J. *Histories of Old Schools: a revised list for England and Wales* (Newcastle-upon-Tyne, 1966).

Wallis, P. J., and W. E. Tate. *A Register of Old Yorkshire Grammar Schools*, Leeds University Institute of Education, Researches and Studies, 13 (1956), 64–104, and reprinted.

Walsingham, T. *Chronicon Maiora*, ed. J. Taylor, W. R. Childs, and L. Watkiss (Oxford, 2003).

Walter of Bibbesworth. *Le Tretiz*, ed. W. Rothwell, Anglo-Norman Text Soc., Plain Texts Series, 6 (1990).

Walther, H. *Carmina Medii Aevi Posterioris Latina*, vol. i: *Initia Carminum ac Versuum* (Göttingen, 1969).

Warton, Thomas. *History of English Poetry from the Twelfth to the Close of the Sixteenth Century*, ed. W. Carew Hazlitt, 4 vols (London, 1871).

Wase, Christopher. *Considerations Concerning Free Schools as Settled in England* (Oxford, 1678).

Watkin, A. (ed.). *Dean Cosyn and Wells Cathedral Miscellanea*, Somerset Record Soc., 56 (1941).

Watkiss, L., and M. Chibnall (eds). *The Waltham Chronicle* (Oxford, 1994).

Watney, J. 'Mercers' School', *London and Middlesex Arch. Transactions*, n.s., 1 (1905), 115–50.

Watney, J. *Some Account of the Hospital of St. Thomas of Acon*, 2nd edn (London, 1906).

Watson, Foster. *The English Grammar Schools to 1660: their curriculum and practice* (Cambridge, 1908).

Weaver, F. W. 'Foundation Deed of Bruton School', *Somerset and Dorset Notes and Queries*, 3 (1892–3), 241–8.

Weiss, Roberto. 'The Earliest Catalogues of the Library of Lincoln College', *Bodleian Library Quarterly Record*, 8 no. 94 (1937), 343–59.

Weiss, Roberto. *Humanism in England during the Fifteenth Century*, 3rd edn, *Medium Aevum*, Monographs, 4 (Oxford, 1967).

Wenham, L. P. 'Two Notes on the History of Richmond School, Yorkshire', *Yorkshire Arch. Journal*, 37 (1951), 369–73.

Wenham, L. P. *The History of Richmond School* (Arbroath, 1958).

West, Thomas. *The Antiquities of Furness*, 3rd edn (Ulverston, 1822).

Whitelock, D. (ed.). *English Historical Documents c.500–1042*, 2nd edn (London, 1996).

Whittick, C. 'A Didactic Slate', *Sussex Arch. Collections*, 131 (1993), 106–9.

Whittington, Robert: see Stanbridge, John.

Wilkins, D. (ed.). *Concilia Magnae Britanniae et Hiberniae, 446–1717*, 4 vols (London, 1737).

Williams, B. H. Garnons. *A History of Berkhamsted School 1541–1972* (Berkhamsted, 1980).

Williams, G. *The Welsh Church from Conquest to Reformation*, 2nd edn (Cardiff, 1976).

Williams, G. *Wales and the Reformation* (Cardiff, 1997).

Wilmot, D. *A Short History of the Grammar School of Macclesfield, 1503–1910* (Macclesfield, 1910).

Wilson, E. *The Winchester Anthology: A Facsimile of British Library Additional Manuscript 60577* (Cambridge, 1981).

Wilson, J. 'Peculiar Ordination of a Cumberland Benefice', *Scottish Hist. Review*, 5 (1907–8), 297–303.

Wood, Anthony. *Survey of the Antiquities of the City of Oxford*, ed. A. Clark, 3 vols, Oxford Hist. Soc., 15, 17, 37 (1889–99).

Wood, Diana (ed.). *The Church and Childhood*, Ecclesiastical History Soc., Studies in Church History, 31 (1994).

Wood, N. *The Reformation and English Education* (London, 1931).

Woodley, R. *John Tucke: a case study in early Tudor music theory* (Oxford, 1993).

Woodruff, C. E., and H. J. Cape. *Schola Regia Cantuariensis: A History of Canterbury School* (London, 1908).

Woodward, W. H. *Erasmus Concerning the Aim and Method of Education* (Cambridge, 1904).

Woolgar, C. M. *The Great Household in Late Medieval England* (New Haven and London, 1999).

Wormald, C. P. 'The Uses of Literacy in Anglo-Saxon England and Its Neighbours', *Transactions of the Royal Hist. Soc.*, 5th series, 27 (1977), 95–114.

Wright, Thomas (ed.). *Letters Relating to the Suppression of Monasteries*, Camden Soc., 26 (1843).

Wright, Thomas. 'Rules of the Free School at Saffron Walden in Essex in the Reign of Henry VIII', *Archaeologia*, 34 (1852), 37–41.

Wright, Thomas (ed.). *Anglo-Saxon and Old English Vocabularies*, ed. R. P. Wülcker, 2 vols (London, 1884).

Wylie, J. H. *History of England under Henry the Fourth*, 4 vols (London, 1884–98).

Yorke, B. (ed.). *Bishop Æthelwold: his career and influence* (Woodbridge, 1988).

Zimmerman, B. (ed.). *Monumenta Historica Carmelitana*, vol. i (Lingen, 1905–7).

Index

Forenames precede surnames before 1200, and follow them afterwards.